HOLY
SIEGE

HOLY SIEGE

THE YEAR THAT SHOOK CATHOLIC AMERICA

KENNETH A. BRIGGS

HarperSanFrancisco
A Division of HarperCollinsPublishers

FIRST EDITION

Library of Congress Cataloging-in-Publication Data
Briggs, Kenneth A.
    Holy Siege : the year that shook Catholic America / Kenneth A. Briggs. — 1st ed.
        p.
    Includes bibliographical references and index.
    ISBN 0–06–061058–1 (alk. paper)
    1. Catholic Church—United States—History—20th century.
    2. United States—Church history—20th century.   I. Title.
    BX1406.2.B75   1992
    282'.73'09048—dc20   91–58156
                                                                                           CIP

92 93 94 95 96 ❖ RRD(H) 10 9 8 7 6 5 4 3 2 1

This edition is printed on acid-free paper that meets the American National Standards Institute Z39.48 Standard.

Contents

Chronology

— ⟶

· 1986 ·

AUGUST 18. The Reverend Charles E. Curran is notified that the Vatican has stripped him of his right to teach as a Catholic theologian.

AUGUST 18. A memo from Bishop Joseph T. O'Keefe orders pastors in the New York archdiocese to ban public officials who disagree with church teaching from speaking in their parishes.

SEPTEMBER 4. Archbishop Raymond G. Hunthausen of Seattle announces that the Vatican has stripped him of five areas of responsibility in the archdiocese and given them to Auxiliary Bishop Donald Wuerl.

SEPTEMBER 4. Governor Mario Cuomo assails New York archdiocesan speaker ban.

OCTOBER 5. The Vatican releases evaluation of thirty-eight freestanding seminaries in the United States.

OCTOBER 10–12. Women in the church conference takes place in Washington, D.C.

OCTOBER 16. Father Curran debates dissent with Archbishop Roger M. Mahony of Los Angeles at the University of Southern California.

OCTOBER 16. Archbishop Edmund C. Szoka orders his Detroit priests to cease using general absolution. Protest by priests follows.

OCTOBER 30. The Vatican puts forth a document on the pastoral care of homosexuals that prompts heated reactions.

NOVEMBER 10. The Vatican analysis of U.S. religious communities is made public.

NOVEMBER 10–13. American bishops hold their annual meeting in Washington to address the Hunthausen crisis and complete their landmark pastoral letter on the economy.

DECEMBER 7. Groups supporting Archbishop Hunthausen hold prayer vigils across the country.

DECEMBER 19. In a letter, Archbishop James A. Hickey of Washington, D.C., forbids Father Curran to teach at Catholic University during the upcoming semester.

DECEMBER 29. A report on Renew is released.

· 1987 ·

JANUARY 6. Epiphany Plowshares activists trespass at Willow Grove Naval Air Station to protest the arms race.

JANUARY 12. Father Curran declares his intention to teach at Catholic University despite Archbishop Hickey's demand that he not do so.

JANUARY 13. Archbishop Hickey repeats his demand in a letter to Father Curran, threatening to deter him by invoking canon 812 of the Code of Canon Law.

JANUARY 15. The academic senate at Catholic University appoints a seven-member committee to investigate the Curran case.

JANUARY 19–21. A conference on tensions between theologians and bishops is held at the University of Notre Dame.

JANUARY 28. The Reverend John J. McNeill is dismissed from the Jesuit order for speaking out against the church's teachings on homosexuality.

JANUARY 28. Archbishop Szoka announces that the pope will add Detroit as the eighth stop on his tour of the United States in September.

FEBRUARY 7. Archbishop John R. Quinn of San Francisco defends the Vatican's latest statement on homosexuality in the February 7 issue of *America*.

FEBRUARY 9. The Vatican appoints a three-member *ad hoc* commission to explore the crisis swirling around Archbishop Hunthausen in Seattle.

FEBRUARY 26. Italian officials issue arrest warrants for Archbishop Paul C. Marcinkus, president of the Vatican Bank, in connection with the collapse of Banco Ambrosiano.

FEBRUARY 27. The Vatican defies the arrest order and pledges full support for Archbishop Marcinkus.

MARCH 2. Father Curran files a civil suit to allow him to teach nonecclesiastical courses at Catholic University.

MARCH 6–7. *Ad hoc* commission holds hearings in Menlo Park, California, on the Seattle situation.

MARCH 10. An instruction on biomedical methods of reproduction is released by the Vatican and evokes sharp criticism.

MARCH 13–15. In San Antonio, a third regional lay consultation is held in connection with the upcoming Synod on the Laity.

MARCH 16–21. Bishops hosting the pope on his U.S. tour hold talks with him, briefing him on sources of disaffection among Catholic Americans.

APRIL 6. The trial of Epiphany Plowshares ends in a hung jury.

APRIL 8. Archbishop Hunthausen meets Cardinal Joseph Bernardin, head of the *ad hoc* commission, in Chicago.

APRIL 8. California's twenty-eight bishops vow to care for AIDS sufferers and to fight the disease.

APRIL 15. Father Curran announces that he will spend the next academic year as a visiting professor at Cornell University.

APRIL 19. The *National Catholic Register* reports that the Vatican intends to force Archbishop Hunthausen out of Seattle as part of its solution to the problem.

MAY 5. The federal amnesty program for illegal aliens takes effect.

MAY 7. Archbishop John L. May, president of the bishops' conference, calls on President Reagan to grant special status to those family members of illegal aliens who didn't qualify for amnesty.

MAY 7. Archbishop Hunthausen agrees to a settlement.

MAY 16. At the University of Notre Dame graduation ceremonies, the Reverend Theodore Hesburgh, C.S.C., retires.

MAY 21–24. The National Black Catholic Congress is held at Catholic University.

MAY 18–22. The second Epiphany Plowshares trial ends in another hung jury.

MAY 27. Archbishop Hunthausen and his new coadjutor, Archbishop Thomas J. Murphy, hold a news conference to announce the settlement.

JUNE 7–9. The culminating session on what concerns laypeople is held for bishop-delegates to the Synod on the Laity at Saint Mary's College.

JUNE 10–13. The annual meeting of the Catholic Theological Society of America discusses academic freedom and Father Curran.

JUNE 19. Twelve major Jewish groups protest the pope's plan to greet President Kurt Waldheim of Austria at the Vatican.

JUNE 25. Pope receives President Waldheim.

JULY 9. Cardinal Agostino Casaroli, on a visit to the United States, meets with four Jewish leaders in an effort to calm the tempest.

JULY 15. The third trial of two of the four Epiphany Plowshares defendants ends in mistrial.

JULY 17. The Italian supreme court quashes arrest warrants against Archbishop Marcinkus.

JULY 31. Archbishop Hunthausen delivers the keynote speech to a gathering of the Catholic peace group Pax Christi.

AUGUST 14. Archbishop Mahony of Los Angeles issues a pastoral letter on women.

AUGUST 31–SEPTEMBER 1. Nine top Jewish officials meet with the pope in efforts to heal the breach over Waldheim.

SEPTEMBER 10. Pope John Paul II arrives in Miami.

SEPTEMBER 11. The pope meets with Jews in Florida, and later with ecumenical leaders in Columbia, South Carolina.

SEPTEMBER 12. In New Orleans, the pope addresses audiences of black Catholics, young people, and presidents of Catholic colleges and universities.

SEPTEMBER 13. In San Antonio, the pope speaks to Catholic Charities workers and focuses on Hispanics.

SEPTEMBER 14. The pope's stops in Phoenix include gatherings of health care workers and of Native Americans.

SEPTEMBER 15. In Los Angeles, the pope addresses young people with the aid of a tri-city telecommunications setup and talks to a crowd of media moguls.

SEPTEMBER 16. On day two in Los Angeles, John Paul hears four bishops examine the special character of American Catholicism and lectures them firmly against dissent.

SEPTEMBER 17. In Monterey for a brief stop, the pope presides at a mass at Laguna Seca Raceway.

SEPTEMBER 17. At Mission Dolores in San Francisco, the pope greets AIDS sufferers.

SEPTEMBER 18. Still in San Francisco, the pope hears eloquent appeals for understanding by lay representatives and responds in traditional terms.

SEPTEMBER 19. In Detroit, the pope greets Polish Americans, speaks on social justice, and celebrates mass at the Pontiac Silverdome before leaving the country.

OCTOBER 1–30. The Synod on the Laity is held at the Vatican.

HOLY SIEGE

Introduction

— ▲ ◄ —

T O THE OUTSIDER, THE CATHOLIC CHURCH IN AMERICA CAN sometimes look like a ballet without a choreographer, a stage bustling with vibrant motion, dotted with epicenters of loosely related activity.

I say that as a loving outsider, a non-Catholic Christian who has spent several years watching this ballet from the vantage point of a journalist, first with *Newsday*, then the *New York Times*. Never have I been less than fascinated by the spectacle. An ancient religious tradition has been in the throes of a process Alvin Toffler called "future shock," change coming so swiftly that brief interludes of tranquility perpetually collapse into confusion and even chaos.

Until the Second Vatican Council (1962–65), the Roman Catholic church attempted to shield its centuries-old dance troupe from the disruptive forces of modernity. The Council itself then sanctioned an effort to come to terms with the modern age by welcoming much of what it had to offer. Before that sweeping turn, the church looked very much like a classical ballet company, with a choreographer-conductor very much in command. But in calling the Second Vatican Council, Pope John XXIII, in effect, partly relinquished his commanding role. At the behest of their own muses, the various elements of the church have been performing at an increasingly brisk pace, all claiming the same stage but dancing, more or less, to their own choreography. The current pope, John Paul II, would like to reclaim mastery, but the odds against him appear to be very long.

As a reporter, it has been my good fortune to witness a remarkable chapter of church history. My time as a religion writer in the daily press began under the papacy of Paul VI in the aftermath of Vatican II. Later I stood vigil in St. Peter's Square awaiting the elections of John Paul I and John Paul II. I have on four occasions roamed the austere Vatican press office during an International Synod of

1

Bishops. As the implications of Vatican II unfolded, I listened to both the defenders of traditional church teaching and the dissenters from it, watched the liturgy take on more of the trappings of local cultures, and heard debate around issues of theology, morality, ministry, and justice. Along the way, countless priests and laypeople have graced my path. I have gained immensely from their insights, patience, and kindness. Their gifts have added immeasurably to my understanding of what it means to be a Christian in these times.

Inevitably, a Protestant looking though a magnifying glass at the Catholic church invites both curiosity and suspicion. Many Catholics, unaware of my religious identity, asked about it, perhaps to set their minds at ease before getting on with any serious business. A degree of wariness makes sense among people whose forebears were once badly treated and their faith terribly distorted by American nativists. This memory lingers almost three decades after John F. Kennedy's election to the White House quelled many residual fears of anti-Catholic bigotry. In that still somewhat guarded climate, then, some Catholics wanted to pin down my religious label, though I cannot recall any instance when my reply, usually a polite demurrer or the minimal admission that I was "not Catholic," threw any substantial roadblocks in my way.

My aim is to look at the Catholic church for what it is, not what I might want it to be, but I would never claim anywhere near pure objectivity. Because I care deeply about the welfare of Christianity, my own views of the church and its mission inevitably creep into my reporting. My hope is that my perspective, always in flux, is never obtrusive or blinding but is clear enough to permit honest disagreement.

At the same time, research for this book has shored up one conviction in particular, and I state it forthrightly. Perhaps it will seem self-evident, even paradoxical, but here it is: The Catholic church, in my opinion, is an essential point of reference for all other branches of Christianity unlike any other church, not because it is rooted in a divine or infallible blueprint, but because it is, rather, the trunk line bearing the whole legacy, good and bad, from which the rest take their points of departure. At the risk of heresy within my own Methodist tradition, I must say that, with respect to that premise, Protestantism is uniquely contingent on Catholicism.

The background I bring to this book, then, includes the disinterest of a journalist and the interest of a Christian. Many outstanding writers have engaged in the more scholarly task of sizing up Catholicism in the longer view, especially the seismic impact of Vatican II, and I am indebted to them. My scope is much more modest. I propose to look at a thin slice of that history, a year or so, for its own sake and for the larger themes embodied within it. As the biologist examining tissue finds the imprint of the larger organism, so I hope that this probe of a sample will be valuable in its own right while yielding evidence about the shape of things to come.

No year is ordinary; most provide ample opportunity to find hypothetical "turning points" and "watersheds," so claims about the lasting significance of a sampling of the recent past are by their very nature subject to considerable correction. The time span under review, therefore, may eventually be seen as far less important than I will suggest. But I think not. I am inclined to believe that its importance will increase in the trailing streams of hindsight.

The year under scrutiny—more like fourteen months—covers the period between the summer of 1986 and the fall of 1987. The approach is reportorial, which is to say that it relies heavily on intuition and hopscotching habits and only secondarily on the surveys of social science, valuable as they often are. Because of inevitable limitations, I do not presume to have been comprehensive. Certain groups, such as Hispanics and young people, could have received greater attention. The attempt has been to see the broad brush strokes that most defined that year, with apologies in advance to those who feel unjustly ignored or under-represented.

My goal, then, has been to portray the church as a kind of Joseph's coat of many colors and to examine three main strands.

One strand is the "public" church, the scene of the action for church officials and important policy bodies, including the Vatican, the National Conference of Catholic Bishops, and various interest groups, such as theologians defending academic freedom.

A second strand is made up of the thinking that Catholic America was doing in books, journals, and speeches. The cerebral function, as would be expected, was exercised for the most part on the issues of the moment, among them homosexuality and the nature of church authority.

The third strand relates to the lives and concerns of people in the trenches. A small group of Catholics was interviewed intermittently throughout the year—to hear about their experiences and their responses to major church issues—and their testimony is interspersed through the book. People are heard and seen in a variety of other settings as well, from retreat centers to places of work.

In preparing this account, I spoke with hundreds of Catholics—laypeople, priests, bishops, and church officials in various church roles—and benefited greatly from their perceptions, experiences, and knowledge. Naturally their personal gifts, quirks, passions, virtues, and vices went right along with them into the parish sanctuary, the rectory, and the chancery. They talked about the church, often eloquently and from many points of view, some immersed in it, others distant. Inevitably, perhaps, it had left a mark on them, and, sometimes explicitly but more often implicitly, their lives bore that imprint quite conspicuously.

A few agreed to be interviewed over the span of all or most of the year. They were invited to reflect on their lives and the church's effect on them. Conversations were usually free flowing. In the interest of safeguarding their privacy and welfare (some were in special need of this safeguard), the names of everyone comprising this special "gang of ten" have been changed, as have many of their circumstances and descriptions.

Now to introduce them.

Maureen lived in the suburbs in a Middle Atlantic state and was employed as an administrative assistant at a large university. Nearing the end of her forties, she was married and had three children at various stages of adolescence.

Paul was a senior at a Catholic college in the Midwest, not far from where his parents lived. He hoped to become a lawyer. Though close to the church, he was rethinking many of its precepts.

Sister Ruth was the senior citizen of the group. At eighty-one years of age, she maintained a vigorous schedule as a minister to hospital patients, retreat leader, and foreign tour guide, to mention just some of her activities. In all that, she continued to be an unrelenting gadfly.

Hannah hailed from a small farm town on the northern tier of the Great Plains. There she taught in the public school and served her parish as organist and lector and in several other leadership roles. She had been married for twenty-five years and was the mother of three; her youngest, a son, had just left for college.

Father Caron occupied the president's chair at a Catholic college in California. A youthful man of slight build, hearty laugh, and piercing eyes, he was leading a drive to revitalize the college and to preserve academic freedom. It was a challenge he relished.

Craig earned his wings as a Marine fighter pilot during the year. He was a tall, strapping young man with fitting self-assurance and poise. Craig was the youngest of six children raised by a devout Catholic couple now living in Kentucky.

Bishop Sawicki was a model of what it meant to be a bishop in the spirit of Vatican II, according to his many admirers in his Rust Belt diocese and beyond. He was a cheerful, personable man who revered the church but saw serious failings within it.

Anthony, a genial soul with strong emotions and a big heart, had spent most of his adult life in the headquarters of a multinational corporation in the upper Midwest. Now in his fifties, he had risen from his origins in a run-down section of a large city—which he still called home—to the pinnacle of a successful career. He and his wife had three grown children and were looking ahead to retirement.

Gilbert was an accomplished university professor with a self-appointed mission to discredit liberal Catholicism. He was a charming, tough-minded, loquacious man of modest stature but commanding presence, a dashing, outspoken foe of much of what Catholic America has come to represent.

Caleb and Cindy were a young married couple from a small community on the East Coast whose baby, their second child, was baptized in the fall of 1986. Caleb had been raised Catholic by parents who had immigrated from Poland. He thought of himself as a very traditional Catholic. Cindy's parents were devoted United Methodists, and she retained a strong commitment to that church.

Further access to the thoughts and feelings of Catholic Americans was provided by visits to three parishes in widely scattered locations across the country. I spent several days at each during the regular routines of parish life. Thanks to the kindness and generosity of the pastors, I stayed at the rectory in two of the three parishes (the third apologized for having no room for guests). The value of these experiences was inestimable both personally and professionally. Both priests and laypeople made themselves available for long talks in which they often revealed their innermost thoughts and feelings. I was welcomed into homes and a diversity of parish settings for meetings, celebrations, funerals, weddings, and, of course, many, many liturgies. These encounters were never less than gracious.

As in the case of the "gang of ten," the identities of the parishes and their people have been changed to protect their privacy.

One parish, Saint Benedict's, was on the fringe of a moderate-sized city on the East Coast where historical roots tend to be reflected in an affinity for traditional ways of doing things.

Incarnation parish was located in the heart of the Midwest, where Catholicism was distinctly less formal and mirrored a more populist outlook. This parish was resolutely suburban, in look and busyness, and was burgeoning.

On the West Coast, the Church of the Holy Apostles reflected a radically different environment. It stood in a neighborhood once thick with middle-class Catholics; few of its current residents, poor and black, were Catholics. Faced with possible extinction, Holy Apostles, under the guidance of a visionary pastor, refashioned its identity in response to changed circumstances, becoming an advocate of the poor and a provider of food, clothing, medical care, legal aid, and other services.

A word about format: This is a book of snapshots arranged in monthly albums. Each set of pictures is a collage, a series of self-contained journal entries. Some pictures will relate to previous ones, but they often stand alone as single snapshots. The intent is to offer samplings indicative of life in Catholic America as it unfolded month by month, much as the photographer imparts a sense of place and time by selecting a series of photographs that are related but in no discernible "order" or sequence.

This impressionistic form permits shuffling back and forth from the "big" pictures to the small ones, the news-making events to the passing glimpses of everyday life. I hope that this collection of albums, containing loosely related episodes, fragments, reflections, and anecdotes, will yield underlying themes, reflect key sentiments, and generally suggest the direction that Catholic America was taking during this short time. If the small pieces are found to have value in and of themselves, that is fine. If the pieces mirror the whole, so much the better.

To help identify pseudonyms, instead of full names I have used a first name (e.g., Craig) or an ecclesiastical title with a first or last name (e.g., Father Bob or Bishop Sawicki).

September
1·9·8·6

—▬ ▬—

I N EARLY SEPTEMBER OF 1986, RUMBLINGS FROM ROME CULMI-
nated in thunderclaps over Catholic America. The tempest set
currents in motion that riled the psychic and spiritual Catholic
mainstream. U.S. Catholics were moving farther from their Roman
wellsprings than ever before, perhaps irreversibly.

Trouble was no stranger to relations between the Vatican and the church in
America. The "Americanist" movement in the last century, which had sought
with congenital American optimism to marinate Old World Catholicism in the
brine of the modern world, had been unceremoniously crushed by Pope Leo XIII
way back in 1899. Intermittent squabbles had erupted during the ensuing
decades, the most prominent being reaction to the Second Vatican Council
(1962–65) and the 1968 papal encyclical outlawing artificial birth control. The latest drive against Catholic immersion in New World habits had the blessing of Pope
John Paul II. But American Catholics seemed to be paying less and less attention.
The mental distance between Saint Peter's and St. Paul, Minnesota, and the perceived irrelevance of so many of the particular points of contention meant that
for most Catholics the problem stirred little more than vague discontent.

Something was needed to crystallize this uneasiness into a more conscious
disposition for or against the rulings of the magisterium, the bishops and the pope,
who, together, constituted the church's highest teaching authority. The actions by
Rome at the onset of September provided such an occasion. During a political
campaign, at some point certain pivotal events, many of them inadvertent, shake
voters out of their lethargy and indecisiveness, swaying decisive numbers of them
finally to choose one candidate over another. In a similar way, the series of initiatives from Rome precipitated a climactic change in basic opinion that would leave
a deep imprint on Catholic America.

In two celebrated cases Catholic Americans found their loyalty to Rome set against their commitment to American constitutional values. The result was a testing of the relative strength of those allegiances. The Vatican, wittingly or not, took a considerable gamble and, from all appearances, lost big—at least temporarily.

The test cases were (1) the deposing of the Reverend Charles E. Curran as a Catholic theologian for allegedly taking too many liberties with official church teachings and (2) the usurping of the powers of Archbishop Raymond G. Hunthausen of Seattle on grounds that he had failed to keep proper church order.

Both actions touched upon the American penchant for pragmatism and due process and, at a theological level, pitted the "classical" Vatican outlook, which emphasized the church as eternal and immutable, against the modern "historical" view, widely held among Catholic Americans, which stressed an evolutionary view, arguing that dogma and church structure had developed over time and continued to change by God's design. One side saw fixed, unquestioned principles and rules with certain allowances for exceptions; the other regarded working principles as subject to expanding insights from the ongoing experience of the faithful. The tension that surfaced between Rome and America over who was in charge was intimately bound up with the question, What is to be believed? For many Catholic Americans, the debate was framed by an additional pair of criteria endemic to their native land: Was the church fair? and Would its teachings find acceptance?

The Curran case went to the heart of two quintessential American issues related to church-state separation and personal rights: the legitimate place of open inquiry and free speech within the Roman Catholic church and the question of how much control religious authorities may rightly exercise over faculty at a private Catholic university. The Hunthausen travail centered on principles impinging on church tradition and American democracy, respectively: the age-old practice of autonomy by a bishop within his diocese and the carryover "representative" duty of a leader to respond to the needs of a constituency.

Now a look at each case in greater detail.

▬ ▬

On AUGUST 18, FATHER CURRAN, WHO HAD BECOME TO SOME CHURCH OFFICIALS the enfant terrible of moral theology, was handed a fateful letter from the Congregation for the Doctrine of the Faith. The bearer of the letter was Archbishop James A. Hickey, head of the Archdiocese of Washington, D.C., and chancellor of Catholic University, where Father Curran was a professor. "The purpose of this letter," wrote Cardinal Joseph Ratzinger, head of the congregation, "is to inform you that the Congregation has confirmed its position that one who dissents from the Magisterium as you do is not suitable or eligible to teach Catholic Theology." There it was. After almost two decades of sparring with Rome, Father Curran had been told that he was neither suitable nor eligible to ply his trade with the Vatican's blessing.

The man so judged was known among his colleagues as modest and reserved, with immense conviction and fortitude. Most of his peers considered his moral theology more or less a reflection of their own and well within the Catholic mainstream. He was highly regarded, even among critics of his views, foremost as a priest of simplicity and piety. His bishop, Matthew Clark of Rochester, had described him in a statement released March 12, 1986, as "a priest whose personal life could well be called exemplary." A statement of support from nine past presidents of the Catholic Theological Society and the College Theological Society and signed by 750 other theologians said Father Curran "enjoys the complete respect of his colleagues," adding, "We can think of no Catholic theologian in this country who is more well-liked and personally admired." Hardly the picture of a callous renegade that some opponents made him out to be.

But behind this mild demeanor was a tough, provocative moral theologian who challenged the "classical" position of an unchanging set of moral precepts. Father Curran taught that in some areas of sexuality the church's rules—its prohibitions—did not always apply and should be changed. His laundry list of reforms included openness to artificial contraception, divorce, sterilization, premarital sex, homosexuality, masturbation, and abortion. The church banned all of these absolutely, but Father Curran argued either for outright change (so as to permit divorce, for example) or for greater elasticity, such as approving homosexual acts under certain conditions.

Father Curran's conclusions on sexuality were shared in whole or in part by many other Catholic moral theologians. So why had he become the target? The answer stemmed from at least three factors: his important position at the flagship Catholic University, the impact of his writings, and his stubborn refusal to knuckle under to what he believed to be unjust exercise of authority. The interplay of these factors made him particularly visible and influential. Accordingly, guardians of orthodoxy saw him as a formidable threat to the integrity of Catholic teaching. Not surprisingly, then, he became the focal point of an effort by Rome and its American allies to rid the U.S. church of what they saw as a spreading cancer on the body of moral theology. By making an example of Father Curran, Rome had sent a message to the larger company of like-minded moral theologians.

Even as the smoke cleared, the implications of lifting Father Curran's license were not entirely clear. Certainly it seemed the intent of declaring Father Curran unfit to teach as a Catholic theologian was to remove him from Catholic University's "ecclesiastical faculty," the special department deputized by Rome to award pontifical degrees (especially important credentials for getting ahead in church careers). Catholic University, where he was a tenured faculty member, was the only Catholic-related university in the nation to have such a department directly under the thumb of Rome. By declaring him "not suitable or eligible," Cardinal Ratzinger had taken a crucial step toward stripping Father Curran of his "canonical license," issued through the resident bishop, Archbishop Hickey, as a prerequisite for teaching in such a specialized department. By itself, however, the cardinal's letter did not actually remove Father Curran's license. Though it provided a pretext for such action by the archbishop, the effort would involve archbishop, priest, and university in a lengthier process. Archbishop Hickey, in responding to the Vatican's action, declared that he would immediately set the process in motion. A lot of the implications remained fuzzy. If Father Curran were deprived of his license, might he still qualify to teach theology in another department? Apart from the issue of a license from Rome, what guarantees did he have as a tenured professor with a valid contract the Vatican could not overturn?

The news of how Rome had lowered the boom on Father Curran was greeted by howls of protest from those who believed the Vatican had violated the canons of free speech and wrongly meddled in the affairs of an American university, thereby undermining its academic integrity. "The decision was not surprising," *Commonweal* said in an editorial (September 12). "That does not make it any less shocking." Many warned that Father Curran could be the first victim of a wider purge. Church officials generally stood by the Vatican and counseled calm. They attributed the action to the unique arrangement between Rome and Catholic University. Lightning could never strike theologians on nonecclesiastical faculties, they insisted. In other words, what happened to Father Curran could not be construed as a real threat to other theologians or teachers of religion.

But there was the little matter of canon 812 of the newly revised Code of Canon Law, which appeared to pose the very same problem for any teacher of Catholic theology: "Those who teach theological subjects in any institute of higher studies must have a mandate from the competent ecclesiastical authority." Presumably, if the canon were carried out to the letter, everyone instructing theology in Catholic higher education, from Stonehill to Santa Clara, would need some sort of formal approval from a religious superior, ordinarily a bishop, regardless of the person's standing as a scholar within the institution itself. Such a procedure, critics said, would amount to outside influence on the hiring, promotion, and firing of certain faculty members, functions that were generally regarded as the sole prerogatives of the university. Many Catholics saw this as a breach of church-state agreements that could easily be used as a pretext for cutting off public funds to Catholic colleges.

Adding to the anxiety was the latest draft of Vatican guidelines on higher education that had made the rounds earlier in the year. Aimed at making the "Catholic character" of church institutions "more evident and powerful," the draft document saw the need for greater centralized control. It urged the involvement of bishops in university life and spoke of their right to take action against both faculty members and universities deemed to lack sufficient "Catholic identity." Professors should be measured not only on the basis of "academic and pedagogic ability," the document said, but also "by doctrinal integrity and uprightness of life."

Presidents of 110 of the 235 U.S. Catholic colleges and universities, including its largest and most prestigious, jointly assailed the proposed guidelines in a statement sent to the Vatican on February 11. "The crux of the document is perceived by many to be the assertion of a power on the part of the bishop to control theologians and to assure 'orthodoxy' in their teaching," the presidents said. They continued, "What is proposed here is contrary to the American values of both academic freedom and due process, both of which are written into most university statutes and protected by civil and constitutional law." The university "is the home of the theologian, not the bishop, and the bishop must respect that fact. The same freedom must be given to theologians as to the faculty in all other disciplines."

The verdict against Father Curran, though stemming from special circumstances, stood as a warning of what could happen if the hierarchy took a stronger hand in university affairs. If Archbishop Hickey succeeded in removing the priest's permit to teach, he would soon be out of a job on the ecclesiastical faculty of Catholic University.

After the blow had been struck, Father Curran held a news conference to respond to three points in Cardinal Ratzinger's order.

First, on the issue of dissent itself, the cardinal's letter, he said, "gives the impression that on the specific moral issues involved in the dispute the official teachings are opposed to such actions and I am in favor of them. That is not the case. I have always developed my moral theology in the light of accepted Catholic principles. My positions on the particular issues involved are always carefully nuanced and often in fundamental agreement with the existing hierarchical teaching. Yes, occasionally I have dissented from the official teaching on some aspects of specific issues, but this is within a more general and prevailing context of assent."

Second, Father Curran claimed once more that he had restricted his dissent to teachings that are "noninfallible," a category that included the issues of sexual ethics he had explored. The cardinal declared that "the teaching of the Second Vatican Council . . . does not confine the infallible Magisterium (the body of infallible teachings) purely to matters of faith nor to solemn definitions." Father Curran argued that he was within his rights under the norms for dissent included in the U.S. bishops' pastoral letter "Human Life in Our Day." "My disagreements are on the level of complex, specific actions which involve many conflicting circumstances and solutions," he said. "By their very nature these specific concrete questions are far removed from the core of faith."

Third, he raised the issue of due process. Cardinal Ratzinger tried to assure Father Curran that he had been accorded every right he was entitled to under church provisions. Father Curran complained that whereas "most legal systems in the contemporary world recognize that the defendant has a right to the record of the trial including the right to know who are the accusers," he had received "no such record."

Father Curran said he would appeal the decision through the university. Meanwhile, Archbishop Hickey, Cardinal Ratzinger's dutiful courier, deprived Father Curran of one of his leading pillars of defense by suddenly and single-handedly nullifying the 1968 statement by the U.S. bishops that spelled out norms for responsible dissent. The bishops had said in part, "There exists in the church a lawful freedom of thought and also general norms of licit dissent. This is particularly true in the area of legitimate theological speculation and research. When conclusions reached by such professional theological work prompt a scholar to dissent from noninfallible received teaching, the norms of licit dissent come into play." Father Curran claimed to have stayed within those rules.

Archbishop Hickey of Washington, D.C., whose staunch ally, Archbishop Pio Laghi, the Vatican's ambassador to the United States, was pitching him to the pope as a worthy candidate for a cardinal's red hat, flatly dismissed the norms. "I think we have seen that these norms, as applied to public dissent, are simply unworkable," the archbishop said in a statement released August 19. "Indeed, the Holy See has gone on to clarify that for us and to say there is no right to public dissent." No significant challenge arose from his fellow bishops. The norms were rescinded just like that, with no further explanation—end of discussion.

The judgment on Father Curran evoked further outcries from his sizable number of vocal backers, while a smaller bloc of noted Catholics applauded the Vatican's action. Many of his critics were members of the Fellowship of Catholic Scholars, a conservative group founded largely by theologians who had broken away from the alleged liberalism of the Catholic Theological Society of America after the society issued its controversial statement on sexual ethics in 1976. The statement had challenged many of the church's offical teachings.

Conservatives welcomed the curb on Father Curran as a necessary means of trying to halt a slide into moral relativity and disarray. They propounded a theological version of the old domino theory. For the church to relent on certain issues was to imperil the whole foundation upon which moral theology rested, the revealed word of God that allowed no substantive revision. One of Father Curran's colleagues, William May, a professor of theology, said at a September 4 press conference in support of the Vatican's finding, that it was time for other Catholic universities to follow CU's example, to "fish or cut bait" on tolerance of dissent. He urged enforcement of standards such as those used against Father Curran in all the church's learning institutions.

Those in agreement with Rome generally understood the theologian as a faithful transmitter of the unvarnished truth, subordinate in every key respect to the bishops. Speculation, exploration, and personal opinion had little or no place in the transmission process. Disagreements, where they existed, were to be hashed out far from public view, in keeping with the practice of earlier times, and not "test marketed" through publication, lest they create confusion and scandal.

Father Curran had come to personify a different perception of the theologian that had taken hold firmly among many American Catholic scholars. From this vantage point, the theologian had a more independent role, using the tools of scholarship and intellect to rigorously examine the tradition for its strengths and weaknesses. To the opposing camp, this approach led to the kind of individualism that eventually destroyed church unity. By contrast, Father Curran and many others believed that free inquiry helped the church apprehend truth by confronting the insights of a rapidly changing universe of knowledge, enabling it to better carry on its mission to that world.

Some Catholics found themselves caught in the middle of the dispute, generally sympathetic with Father Curran's right to teach but less than enthusiastic about either his theology or his strategy. Not a few viewed the issue as largely moot for theological practitioners themselves. One scholar, for example, pointed ironically to the fact that, because students were arriving at Catholic colleges so poorly educated about their faith, in reality most instructors in theology were doing nothing like the kind of "frontier scholarship" that Father Curran pursued; instead, they were teaching what amounted to catechetical courses. No wonder the Vatican was so concerned that these untutored students get the church's straight teachings, he said. And to this scholar, the Curran case revealed once more the gap between American and Roman assumptions.

"Americans fail to properly distinguish between logical thinking and Roman authority," the scholar said. "We're accustomed to thinking that conclusions should reflect the best arguments. For better or worse, people at the Vatican believe the Holy Spirit guides the church. So it's not enough to say there is no good theological argument against ordaining women, for example. So long as the pope says women can't be ordained, that is a theological argument." He also had advice on how to handle disputes with Rome: "You don't disagree out front, in the teeth of Roman authority. You can say, 'I think we need more study of this or that'—or, 'Might we not examine this matter further?'—but don't say, 'The Vatican is wrong.' That disqualifies you from the discussion."

In his book *Faithful Dissent,* Father Curran indicated that he had weighed the options and decided in favor of a frontal attack. Admitting that his positions might someday be shown to be wrong, he nonetheless thought the church would someday allow for the kind of flexibility he espoused. "I remain convinced that in the end the hierarchical magisterium will definitely recognize the possibility of legitimate pluralism in these areas and ultimately will modify its teachings. I am aware of the temptation to both bitterness and arrogance, and I pray that I might avoid such responses. I want to remain a believing Catholic" (p. 96).

While the furor was still in its initial stages, Father Curran left CU to teach at the invitation of Cornell's new institute on Catholic thought. He would be the institute's first visiting professor.

ON SEPTEMBER 4, ARCHBISHOP RAYMOND G. HUNTHAUSEN GRIMLY DISCLOSED that his ecclesiastical wings had been severely clipped, telling reporters that five major areas of responsibility had been taken from him and handed over to Auxiliary Bishop Donald Wuerl. A letter from Cardinal Bernardin Gantin, head of the Congregation for Bishops, had made it official.

The bad news for Archbishop Hunthausen followed months of an intense guessing game. Rumors to the effect that Bishop Wuerl had been deputized with "extraordinary powers" had been bruited about since his arrival in Seattle the previous January.

The purpose of the Seattle action was clear. Rome was convinced that the archbishop had let the church in Seattle get out of control. The response was to make Donald Wuerl a bishop and send him to Seattle to clear up the mess.

Catholic historians could not recall similar punishment ever before meted out to a U.S. bishop. It was an odd move for the tradition-bound Vatican to make, wedded as it was to an outward appearance of hierarchical harmony. From the start, the Seattle offensive looked awkward and amateurish for an institution usually so sophisticatedly covert.

It also flew in the face of a precept that was sacrosanct among hierarchs. By tradition, a bishop was invested with monarchical power over his own diocese, free to exercise wide-ranging prerogatives according to almost sacred custom. Depriving Archbishop Hunthausen of his near-autonomous functions was therefore tantamount to an attack on the bishop's presumed rights.

At the very least, it was a not-too-subtle threat against any American bishop who stepped out of line. And by dealing directly with Archbishop Hunthausen, Rome conspicuously bypassed the bishops' own intermediary fraternity, the National Conference of Catholic Bishops, which had become the sounding board for a growing number of in-house and wider social issues and problems.

Dozens of bishops, then, could identify with Archbishop Hunthausen's plight. The same conditions that had led Rome to tie one hand behind his back existed in their dioceses too, likely as not. The archbishop was to his fellow bishops what

Father Curran was to his fellow theologians. Both were representative rather than radical exceptions; both were held in high esteem; both exemplified the "new" church in conflict with the "old." Whatever was "wrong" with them was "wrong" with a big chunk of Catholic America.

Bishop Wuerl, a Pittsburgh native whose many years within the inner circles in Rome had prepared him to become a Vatican troubleshooter of sorts, had arrived in Seattle with the stated goal of simply helping the archbishop better do his job. There was no mention of taking over anything. Bishop Wuerl's first public statement January 31 resounded with assurances of harmony. "We are in complete agreement," he said. "We are on the same wavelength."

But the two bishops were soon drawn into serious disagreement over the exact meaning of Bishop Wuerl's marching orders.

The difference of opinion focused on terms agreed to by Archbishop Hunthausen in a December 2, 1985, letter to the papal pro-nuncio, the Vatican ambassador to the United States, which cleared the way for Bishop Wuerl's assignment in Seattle. The agreement noted five "problem areas" identified by a two-year papal investigation as sources of alleged abuse and poor management. The areas cited were the marriage tribunal, the office of liturgy, the role of men who had left the priesthood, ministry to homosexuals and the ethics of health care, and the training of seminarians. It was understood that the new auxiliary bishop would assume special responsibility in these areas.

Archbishop Hunthausen later said he interpreted the terms to mean that he would give Bishop Wuerl oversight of the five areas but always under his ultimate authority. Bishop Wuerl, by contrast, claimed that his own word in those areas was final. Soon a test case brought those differences to a head. In March 1986, a proposed ordinance upholding job rights for minority groups, including homosexuals, was before a local county board. The two bishops discussed what stance the archdiocese would take. Archbishop Hunthausen said the archdiocese would support it; Bishop Wuerl said that on his authority the archdiocese would oppose it. The resulting stalemate prodded Archbishop Hunthausen to seek a ruling. In June, Archbishop Laghi, the papal delegate, told him that Bishop Wuerl had it right. The rest was anticlimax. The archbishop later received the official decision from Rome. He would be required to relinquish total authority in the key areas outlined.

The news conference at which Archbishop Hunthausen somberly made public the Vatican's remedy marked the start of an intense campaign by the archbishop and his supporters to bring the case to the attention of Catholic America through the media. The archbishop's character and reputation lent powerful strength to the public relations effort. He was a teddy bear of a bishop who enjoyed more love and affection than probably any bishop in the country. He was known as a "people's bishop" who eschewed the perks and privileges of high church office and forsook the more typical exercise of hierarchical authority. He preferred to consult his priests, religious, and laity rather than instruct them, to hear their advice rather than proclaim his answers, to cooperate and collaborate rather than direct. His interfaith relations were believed second to none.

But he was at the same time a consummate loyalist capable of the most heartfelt tributes to the pope and saturated with dedication to the church. Some saw him as a man of such spiritual conscience and political innocence that he was genuinely puzzled by all the fuss he generated. Others saw him as a somewhat shrewder figure with a more astute sense of what he needed to do. But he was hailed almost universally as a churchman through and through, blessed with an abundance of a very biblical faith and an open-ended benevolence.

Behind the kindly and humble teddy bear image was also a will of iron ready to put his social convictions on the line. He had won his spurs among justice and peace activists many years before. On a regular basis he joined rallies against the Trident nuclear submarines at their base in nearby Bangor, Washington, once decrying the presence of the subs as the "Auschwitz of Puget Sound." Since 1982, he had refused to pay half his federal income taxes as a protest. The Vatican's repeated denials that the archbishop's peace activities had anything to do with his troubles with the Vatican failed to convince many Catholics, who believed the Reagan White House had been instrumental in working revenge against a thorn in its side. He stood up for the rights of homosexuals, blacks, Hispanics, and women.

All in all, many Catholics saw him as the incarnation of what a Vatican II bishop was supposed to be: a "pastor" who listened and heeded his people, who displayed mercy and forgiveness, who showed a courageous "prophetic" stand against injustice, who sometimes stood aside to let conscience overrule the exact demands of law. That was his problem, said critics. They saw him as a bishop who let his heart override the dictates of church teachings. Supporters said his only crime was in being "too compassionate" and trusting his people too much. Detractors didn't generally question the archbishop's sincerity or his character but faulted him for losing his grip on the archdiocese and fostering disorder. Something had to be done, they argued, in order to safeguard the church's patrimony.

A low-key inquiry into reports of certain questionable goings-on in the archdiocese began in 1978. In 1983, Archbishop Hickey was sent on a fact-finding mission to look into the "criticisms" from anonymous accusers. Archbishop Hickey took testimony from seventy priests, nuns, and laypeople. He interviewed the archbishop himself for thirteen hours. As he left Seattle, Archbishop Hickey said he was "overjoyed" at progress made in the church there and that he would be "very, very surprised" if the Vatican saw fit to force Archbishop Hunthausen to change his ways. But the Seattle archbishop would never be allowed to see the

Hickey report to the Vatican. The most direct outcome was the appointment of Donald Wuerl, announced December 3, 1985, by the papal pro-nuncio.

Archbishop Laghi informed Archbishop Hunthausen about a list of "concerns" the Hickey investigation had uncovered. The laundry list of alleged violations of church discipline included widespread use of general absolution, a rite of communal forgiveness that often substitutes for the normal practice of individual confession; assignment of resigned priests (who had been granted lay status by the Vatican) to parish responsibilities; allowing non-Catholics to take communion with Catholics; letting the Seattle chapter of Dignity, a national organization of gay Catholics, use the cathedral for a special mass; underemphasizing the authority of hierarchical teachings; and laxity in selection of candidates for the archdiocesan seminary.

News of the archbishop's dressing-down by Rome unleashed a torrent of protest by the most active elements in the Seattle church, who were solidly behind their archbishop. The core of the church's leadership mobilized with startling quickness and force. Within a day, 150 of the archdiocese's most prominent figures denounced the Vatican's intervention in a sharply worded statement. Within a week a group called Concerned Catholics launched a petition demanding a reversal of the decision. Chancery officials said the staff overwhelmingly and wholeheartedly disapproved of what Rome had done.

Seattle leapt into visibility as the symbol of the struggle by "progressive" Catholic America against the "repression" of Rome. In the process, most theological distinctions were reduced to political language. The most potent and effective voice of this cause became the *National Catholic Reporter* (NCR), the stalwart evangelist of the Catholic left, brimming with exuberance for a "people of God" church flavored by American values and brimming with indignation about injustices inside and outside the church. Based in Kansas City, Missouri, the independent weekly became a major journalistic player in the tense drama.

Letters from NCR readers typified the outrage among its far-flung constituency. They largely embraced some common themes: the collegial spirit of the Vatican Council had been violated, an injustice committed, and a good man attacked.

The exasperation growing out of the actions against Hunthausen and Curran threw NCR editors into the doldrums, asking rhetorically and apocalyptically in a September 19 editorial, "Why bother remaining an active, dedicated Catholic?" Given the paper's whole rationale for existence, the editors were, of course, only begging the question. Served up with familiar helpings of self-seriousness, grit, and defiance, it did nonetheless express the ultimate dilemma among many Catholic Americans. "Why stay? For the same reason St. Francis stayed. For the same reason we never leave our families—even if we walk away. For the same reason we respect a reasoned faith and the spiritual insights of those generations of Christians who came before us. For the same reason we're still here. The pope and Roman Curia are not the final arbiters."

At his September 3 news conference, Archbishop Hunthausen was the model of compliance. He was contrite. He said he had not originally understood the extent of Bishop Wuerl's role. "I don't know where the blame is," he added, but it had "caused a great deal of suffering for both of us." He had handed over the five departments to Bishop Wuerl's complete control after getting clarification.

On September 19, Bishop Wuerl addressed the hornet's nest of priests in a pastoral letter. He said he had been asked repeatedly to denounce the investigation as "unjust." "This," he wrote, "I cannot do." The final report had "pointed out issues to be addressed," he declared, and the Vatican had "empowered me to assist him in a unique and special way." The sooner the problems were cleaned up, he said, the sooner the crisis would be over.

But for large numbers of Seattle's Catholics, Bishop Wuerl's presence was itself the crisis.

MAUREEN OPENED A REAR DOOR OF HER RED PEUGEOT AND NESTLED HER SON'S viola case safely on the seat cushions. It was a Thursday ritual. Sean, the youngest of her three children, came in to the university for his weekly music lesson, and his mother shuttled the viola back home for another round of practice sessions. Closing the door, she strolled the few steps through the entrance of the gray administration building and down the musty hallway to her desk within the office of the academic dean. Her day was done, and the office was empty, save for an assistant dean whose muffled voice, holding up one end of a telephone call, could be heard through a closed door. She tidied up a batch of items for the next day's agenda then gave the pile a little pat as a gesture that these things could wait their turn. Maureen was finished directing the flow of memos, letters, speeches, and various other attempts at communication during the hectic first days of the new semester.

Having put aside her work, she settled back in her chair, eager to talk. Like all interview subjects, she had been asked initially to reflect on her life and the effect of Catholicism upon it.

Maureen looked somewhat worn but seemed full of mental energy. She was medium height, trim, and smartly dressed, with the spark of intelligence in her brown eyes. In her manner, she was high-strung and a touch coy; in mood, often rueful; in conversation, curious and engaging. She had been raised by her mother in New York City under conditions of hardship. Her early bond with the church had been, in large part, based on its promise of sanctuary from her troubles. She had retained that bond despite feelings of rejection from the church after going through a divorce. She was as dogged toward the church as she was in other areas of her life.

She had had a flood of thoughts, she said, and had taken notes to help recall them.

Though the major public events of the church seemed far removed from many of those I interviewed at length, the news had a direct affect on Maureen. The Vatican's actions against Father Curran and Archbishop Hunthausen had troubled her deeply, she said, because she felt the two clerics were "victims" whose treatment by the church reflected her fate. "These events have brought many things into focus for me," she said firmly.

She began to fill in the blanks, and, as she did so, her smile buckled under the strain. Though she was generally spirited, dark inner shadows sometimes transformed her features. Now forty-nine, for the past sixteen years she had been married to a man who, before they met, had resigned properly as a diocesan priest. Before that, she had been married to another Catholic man with whom she had a daughter. She made no apologies for her first marriage, describing it as a good one that failed rather than one that had never been right to begin with. She therefore had seen no need to ask the church to annul it. By church law, she had been excommunicated since her remarriage, but she had managed to achieve reasonable peace with her situation.

Recently, however, her husband had begun urging her to reconsider. He wanted her to apply to have her first marriage annulled, that is, declared invalid on one of several grounds now permitted by the church's marriage tribunals, which review the applications (psychological impairment has become the most often used criterion). The pressure to do so had reopened old wounds and brought back sharp reminders of the church's exclusionary codes. Pope John Paul II's frequent reminders about the sanctity of Catholic teachings on marriage had also contributed to a reawakening of unease over the church's standards. It provoked in her a conflict that became a recurrent theme in our discussions: the contrast she saw between the mercy Jesus preached and what appeared to her to be the church's system of rewards and punishments.

"The Catholic church is constantly saying we should follow Christ. Christ was never punitive. He always gave people a chance to rebuild their lives. Jesus always gave a person a chance to take a new direction. I really wonder how the Catholic church cannot offer divorced people a chance to rebuild their lives. Jesus was the person with alternatives, but the Catholic church seeks no alternatives. How, then, can we say we're following Christ?

"Being a divorced Catholic has become an extremely painful thing for me. I know lots of Catholic women who feel rejection from the church because of it. It has just done them in. I've lived in a gray area a long time. The Catholic church feels very strongly about people like me. They say we either have to go to church and not take the sacrament or try an annulment. I feel an annulment would be a denial of my daughter. We got divorced, but we worked together to raise her. We didn't divorce our daughter.

"If you want to be a practicing Catholic, you either have to stay away from the sacraments, which the church says are more important than practically anything, or you make it a matter of conscience and go ahead and participate. I take the sacrament—hoping my way is acceptable and that I'm really not a sinner.

"But this punishment thing has started bothering me this fall. I really had been patiently waiting for the church to move toward modern society, but it's not happening. There aren't even gray areas any more. It seems to be all black and white."

Maureen's mother, of German descent, had been married first to an alcoholic, who died, leaving her with a son. Her second husband became Maureen's father. He was a man of Slavic roots who worked on a city garbage truck. "My mother prayed for a girl," she said. "She says I am the gift of Saint Theresa."

Her early life was lonely, she recalled, and the church helped fill many gaps.

"My mother and I went to mass and to novenas. I grew to love the mass. I went every morning before walking twenty-four blocks to school. Prayer developed into a sense that if God could see us it was important how we conducted our lives. When we failed to turn around, to rebuild we could use prayer as a way to do the right thing."

Maureen was sixteen when her father died. For financial reasons, she gave up her study of the performing arts, taking a part-time job at a radio station to help pay the bills while she finished high school. In those difficult days, she said, the church was a mainstay. Though she was now in tension with her church, she said she could never leave it. "I don't see any point in changing. A long time ago I said I didn't see anything better. The Catholic church has that liturgy with all that beauty and symbolism."

It was perhaps the power of conviction learned in childhood that contributed to her tenacious hold on the beliefs she had reached as an adult, among them the conclusion that seeking an annulment from her first husband would be wrong. When her daughter had been married two years before, she had stood beside her first husband at the altar in the Catholic church with the young couple. She remembered the scene acutely: "I danced with him. We knew our work together was over. It was a very soulful moment. When the dance was over, we both headed for the restrooms to cry."

NEARLY THREE HUNDRED LAY CATHOLICS MET IN CHICAGO FROM SEPTEMBER 12 to 14 to mull over what it meant to have a religious calling in the workaday world. The conference was sponsored by the National Center for the Laity (NCL), a

Chicago-based organization with a pointed agenda. Few questioned that the laity were becoming more prominent in the church, but there was much debate over how far laypeople should go and in what direction. Many lay programs stressed training the unordained for the greater variety of functions open to the laity within the church. But the NCL, along with others, had different ideas. Its intention was to develop a body of thought and action directed at Catholics at work and home. In its estimation, too much attention had gone toward molding Catholics for in-house duties under the aegis of the clergy and far too little attention paid the Catholic pursuing a vocation in the midst of the hurly-burly.

The Chicago gathering—The National Consultation on the Vocation of the Laity, and the second of its kind—tested that proposition and supplied evidence to bolster the NCL's cause. The invited participants included many who had little to do with church activities but were heavily immersed in the world. Among them were corporate executives, entrepreneurs, lawyers, union leaders, and doctors. Most were affluent and at least tangentially Catholic.

John McDermott, the spunky, bespectacled, bow-tied head of the organization, set down the group's no-nonsense platform in an opening address. "We are no longer the huddled masses or the sons and daughters of the huddled masses from Europe's teeming shores," he said. "We are no longer poor and weak. . . . We have arrived in America. We have prospered and are part of the American society. We are helping to manage and lead this society. . . . We say plainly that the central importance and intrinsic value of the lay vocation in the world must receive more attention, nurture, support and honor." He continued: "Indeed, we say boldly that the institutional church must come to see itself largely as a support system for its frontline troops, lay Catholic Christians in the world."

Testimony from many participants portrayed the church as having little impact on how these Catholics went about their influential business. Religion seemed separate from the rest of life, and the church was not seen as engaged in trying to redress the imbalance. A law professor spoke of the "divorce of professional behavior from personal morality" as the "essential characteristic," as standard in his profession. "I and my friends in the law need a theory of work, a spirituality of work," he said. "Without such a spirituality, we will never be able to integrate our faith with our practice in comprehensive and consistent terms." Another diagnosed the sweeping changes within the family, adding, "It is a sad reality that the church absents itself from this struggle to explore and explain this upheaval."

Joseph Sullivan, the chairman and chief executive officer of a Chicago fertilizer and chemical company, Sullivan and Proops, offered a telling example of the gap by laying out the problems he experienced, as a Catholic, trying to run a corporation. Sullivan's firm employed 1,500 people and had done $350 million in business the year before. In his talk, Sullivan invoked a standard capitalist rationale for his business operations, devoting considerable attention to how the application of ethical values facilitated smooth and effective functioning of his firm.

"Our objectives in managing this company are to produce a profit and create a positive environment for the individuals who work for the company and for the long-term health and survivability of the company itself," Sullivan said. The corporation's supreme goal was growth, he pointed out, and to that end Sullivan and Proops demanded high performance for the good of the workers and the company. "We keep reminding ourselves that we, as a company, do not invest people with human dignity," Sullivan said. "They have it before, during and after employment with us. As managers, what we can do is to provide an environment that can enhance that dignity. A key way to do this is to demand and reward high performance." He added that the company offered help to those who were not pulling their weight, as well as other kinds of training, development, and community involvement for employees.

"You will notice that my frame of reference as a businessman is growth, the survivability of a firm, market shares, and improving products and service. What does this have to do with Christian values? How does one find God in that kind of world? Our religious language fits easily into the work of the Mother Teresas of this world. But have we a religious language that fits the kind of work I do?"

He had drawn some general conclusions on his own about links between the two. One was that business training was superb preparation for providing leadership to volunteer projects. Another stemmed from the logic of growth. Among its usual salutary effects, Sullivan said, were the raising of morale and incentive and the creation of jobs. "Dedication to the concept of growth rests on the moral and Christian issues that business, in the last analysis, is carried on for the sake of the common good." A third area for Christian concern was, "How do we streamline our business for survival in a responsible, moral way?" to wit, how can the company protect itself and the welfare of some workers by firing others as humanely as possible?

Had the church helped Sullivan with these concerns? Not from the pulpit, apparently. In thirty years of attending church, he said he had heard only one homily that "had anything really relevant to say concerning the issues a manager faced." Otherwise, "Catholic teaching has seldom seemed to address the moral and ethical issues that I was faced with as a manager." A happy exception, he said, was the forthcoming pastoral letter by the American bishops on the U.S. economy.

Sullivan's audience followed with rapt attention as he put forth his personal credo. "I think of business as a vocation. It serves an obvious public function: it creates employment, and it offers needed products and services to sustain and enhance life. Business has been a major source of technological advancement. Yet rarely have I heard business described as a vocation, either by the clergy or by the laity. We as Catholics tend to apply the same highly individualistic rhetoric that American culture generally does. . . . In sum, for a long period being Catholic and a manager in the marketplace was made a more solitary, often lonely, endeavor because of little enrichment from the church. Fortunately, this situation is changing and for the better."

The signs of improvement Sullivan cited included the bishops' letter and an increased number of seminars and discussion groups on ethics and business. But he saw the need for a much bigger and bolder effort to close the gap. "Church professionals, with the help of the laity, must approach this task with the same enthusiasm and commitment as those who ministered to the union movement in years past. In today's world owners and managers need the kind of committed, informed ministry that the church provided to the working class fifty years ago."

It was an intriguing idea. If the laborer typified Catholic America during the European immigrant phase, then the corporate executive came closer to symbolizing the Catholic of today. Otherwise their situations relative to the church were sharply different. Whereas the church had served as a sort of chaplain to organized labor, whose principles had been embraced since Pope Leo XIII, the relationship between the church and capitalism had been complicated by solid criticisms from various popes of the excesses that free enterprise tended to produce. If Catholic owners and managers wanted a simple baptism of their capitalist beliefs and practices from the church, they were unlikely to get it. Though many Catholic leaders were eager to bless the free enterprise system, rejoicing that Catholics had come to profit so much from it, a growing body of thought and teachings pointed to inherent conflicts between capitalism and Christianity. It was becoming less possible for Catholic business executives to expect within the church only approval and justification for purely entrepreneurial goals. Nor would it do to confine "Christian duty" in the corporation to ethics with regard to daily conduct toward employees. The bishops' critique, among others, was broadening the discussion to address the very premises of the system. Sullivan's appeal was for comfort for those afflicted by reverses in business; the bishops were more concerned with afflicting those like Sullivan who were comfortable.

THE COUNTDOWN BEGAN. TWELVE MONTHS FROM NOW, IN MID-SEPTEMBER 1987, the pope was scheduled to tour America as the nation marked the two-hundredth birthday of the Constitution's completion. No document, except perhaps the *Communist Manifesto,* had thrown a more formidable roadblock in the path of traditional Catholicism than the venerable blueprint for American democracy. No figure represented a sterner challenge to the extremes to which democratic pluralism strayed than the pope. Elaborate preparations were under way for both events.

Miami, the city of glamor cops, mammoth drug busts, and cultural clashes, was the first planned stop on the pope's tour. For the head of the archdiocese, Archbishop Edward McCarthy, the papal visit became a rallying cry for an end to strife in church and city and a summons to the lost sheep to return to the fold. On September 8, a year and two days before the pope was to arrive, Archbishop McCarthy issued a stirring pastoral letter, "Blessed Too the Peacemakers," in which he proposed that Catholics spend the next year healing the wounds that divided them within themselves, from each other, and from God. In calling for "reconciliation," the archbishop was asking, in effect, for a good spiritual housecleaning and a closing of ranks before the family patriarch rang the doorbell.

In the letter, the archbishop decried both the "disease of alienation" that is "destroying human society and family life" and the "'dog-eat-dog' strategy" that is the "cynic's secret of survival." He encouraged inactive Catholics to come back to church, reminding the faithful that "we need to assure them that we miss them, that we are concerned for them and that we are anxious to welcome them and to assist them in coming home again in the church." There were plenty of candidates for recruitment. The archbishop cited startling facts from the church's own survey. Of the 1.1 million Catholics in the archdiocese, 62 percent of whom were Hispanic, only 528,000 were registered in parishes and 218,700 attended mass weekly.

In a dramatic move aimed at smoothing the reentry for some Catholics, Archbishop McCarthy granted priests special authority to absolve those who confessed either to having committed the mortal sin of abortion or to having assisted in the procedure. He spoke of the need for penance, the "sacrament of reconciliation," for all in the church, reminding his flock that sins "can be against groups as well as individuals" and lamenting that the penance rite "is not fully appreciated" as it has become widely ignored. No finer preparation would be appropriate for the "pope of peace" than following the way of peace and humility. "Faithfulness to the spirit of reconciliation," the archbishop said, "suggests that we are willing to do penance, to make amends, to manifest our sorrow to those we have hurt, to apologize, to make restitution, to symbolize our desire for reconciliation, as well as to confess to the Lord. In our self-indulgent and undisciplined day, there is a need to rediscover the practice of penance."

A poll of Miami Catholics conducted for the archdiocese by a University of Miami researcher earlier in the year indicated that there were plenty of fences to mend. Miami's Catholic population was atypical in that it was 62 percent Hispanic (mostly Cuban in origin), but for that very reason instructive. Various estimates said that by the turn of the century as many as half of all Catholic Americans would be Hispanic. The patterns in the Miami archdiocese, therefore, had a certain predictive value.

In terms of personal faith, 96 percent of those surveyed believed in the Trinitarian God, the divinity and resurrection of Christ, and the reality of sin. Nine in ten thought religion was "very" or "fairly" important. Eighty-seven percent had been confirmed. But measured by religious behavior, Miami Catholics reflected the sizable degree of indifference by Hispanics toward the practices of the institutional church. Religion among Spanish-speaking Catholics was often described as oriented more around home and festival than around the parish.

Only two-thirds of Catholics (65 percent) had been married in the church (54 percent of those under age thirty-five). Fifty-two percent of non-Hispanic families were registered in parishes, compared to 41 percent of Hispanics. A third of Hispanics went to church two or fewer times a year. Nearly half (46 percent) never received communion, and 59 percent never went to confession (51 percent of women, 67 percent of men). Fifty-four percent of the adults had attended Catholic elementary schools; 18 percent of children did so at the time of the survey. Fifty-one percent of Miami's Hispanic Catholic children received no religious education. About three-fourths (74 percent) said that, contrary to church law, divorce and remarriage were "generally acceptable" (a divorced Catholic lived in a fifth of the households polled); 69 percent condoned the use of artificial contraception, and a fourth (25 percent) rejected abortion under all conditions, while another 64 percent found it objectionable under most circumstances.

Given the overall picture, church leaders faced huge challenges. In his pastoral letter, Archbishop McCarthy spoke with keen awareness of the distance between many Catholics and the church: "Please God, may the visit of His Holiness be a great homecoming for those who have been alienated from the Lord and inactive in the life of the church." The "jubilee year of preparation," he said, "will be a unique opportunity for the faithful of the church of Miami to whom God has given the 'ministry of reconciliation . . . ambassadors for Christ, God as it were appealing through us.'"

SISTER RUTH HAD AN IRONIC CHUCKLE THAT CONVEYED BOTH VITALITY AND IMPishness. She was eighty-one years old when the first interview took place, and from all appearances, she was no less a maverick than ever. If anything, the reformer's fires had flared even more intensely over the years. Her life in the church—as witness and participant—had paralleled great upheavals and innovations. She had been a pioneer, a leader, and a gadfly. She remained so, busily rushing about teaching seminars, comforting the sick in hospital wards, leading tours to foreign shrines, guiding retreats, and giving counsel to a great variety of seekers after her wisdom.

Over her six decades as a nun, she had been an explorer and a boundary tester, recognized widely for her leadership and creativity. Her life *was* the church, yet like Thomas Merton, she had had experiences outside the church in her youth that had disposed her to put the church in a larger cultural framework. She had entered the convent of missionary nurses in 1930 at age twenty-two, after having already completed a degree in biology at a secular college. Her father, a convert, had encouraged her to think for herself ("His concept of the church," she recalled, "was what was best for us"). As the only novice in her group never to have attended a Catholic school, she was required to undergo basic training in Catholicism. At a time when novices were stereotypically innocent, scrubbed adolescents, she was, to say the least, an unusual candidate.

After religious and nursing instruction, Sister Ruth worked in public health and was later placed in charge of formation for new members of the community. In an effort to better equip herself for the task, she studied theology, Scripture, and psychology. She welcomed the encouragement that had recently been given to nuns by Pope Pius XII to pursue such studies. During the Second Vatican Council, Sister Ruth heard firsthand from theologians who had attended its sessions. Her exposure to "the thinking patterns" of Vatican II, she said, made her feel hopeful and uplifted. As the Council came to a close in 1965, she was chosen as president of her congregation. Meanwhile, changing patterns of health care, shaped by such programs as Medicare and Medicaid, brought about a need for corresponding shifts in the delivery of service by the nuns. Sister Ruth was at the center of that redesign, then decided "to do something about the spiritual dimensions of public health." Out of that concern grew a program of pastoral care.

In her many years of attending to sick and dying people, she said she had heard one refrain again and again: "People of every age would say, 'I wish you were a priest.' People were ready for it, but, of course, the church was not." This and other factors entered into her decision to become a founding member of the Women's Ordination Conference in 1976, but those countless hours at hospital bedsides had an awful lot to do with it. "These days," she said simply and directly, "those in pastoral care should be given the opportunity to be totally pastoral people." She kept pressing the cause of women's ordination, though some Catholic feminists had abandoned that goal. "I don't want to give up the term or the idea of ordination," she said cheerfully. "People really can't ignore it."

Sister Ruth had the optimism that so often seems to accompany the gifts of competence and gratitude. She had adapted to big transitions and advised others to keep their chins up and work for better days in the church. "I don't get discouraged very easily," she said. "I work with many young people who do get discouraged. My role is to give them hope. There is great mystery in the church, a lot to be hopeful about."

SHOPPING FOR A PARISH WAS ONCE ALMOST EXCLUSIVELY A PROTESTANT THING to do. Catholics were supposed to attend the parish within whose boundaries they lived, whereas Protestants looked around for the church that best suited their

tastes, often hiking a fair distance to make the right match. But now growing numbers of Catholic Americans were indulging in the same behavior, spurred by such
factors as the higher value placed on personal choice within the church, the variety of liturgical practices inspired by Vatican II, easy mobility, and the tendency
of highly assimilated Catholics to act like Protestants. A corollary of this migra-
tory pattern was that more parishes specialized in one way or another and appealed, therefore, to like-minded people. Parishes had usually reflected their social
and economic settings, but parish shopping introduced the new element of self-
selectivity. Catholics hankering for the same things—certain ways of doing liturgy
or preaching, involvement of laypeople, a particular pastor—sought parishes
that satisfied their preferences. Some parishes, then, showed increasing homo-
geneity, organized unofficially around "interest group" Catholicism.

Bishops had known about parish hopping for some time but understandably
hesitated to condone deviation from the geographical parish system that had
served the church well for centuries. But the handwriting had been on the wall for
some time. Admonitions could not halt a practice among Catholics who were, in
other areas of their lives, habituated to studying the "best bets" recommendations
from their newspapers in selecting VCRs, Mexican restaurants, colleges for their
children, and a host of other things. Comparison shopping became a way of life
that applied to churches as well as to microwave ovens. Some bishops worried
for good reason that popular priests were drawing people away from unpopular
parishes and were therefore reluctant to give the green light to open market competition for parishioners. But many bishops, feeling either unwilling or unable to
stamp out parish switching, surrendered to popular will by looking the other
way or, in one case, openly trying to accept and regulate under conditions he set
down a practice he felt he could not control.

Bishop Joseph Ferrario of the Diocese of Honolulu thereby took the lead on
parish hopping. During the summer, the bishop issued a "decree on proper
parishes" that approved switches under certain conditions. While restating that the
choice of one's parish "is normally determined by one's domicile or quasi-domicile,
where one actually lives," Bishop Ferrario said there were justifiable exceptions for
"crossover" parishioners.

"To ensure the pastoral care of the people and to ensure their acceptance of responsibility of being a 'parishioner,'" the bishop said, "it would be best to officially allow such choices but to expect that they be official choices, i.e., the person
and/or family must register in the parish of their choice, and they would be expected to be active in the life of the parish with an honest investment of their time,
talent and treasure."

The rules of passage were intended to keep close tabs on this commuting and
to bar interlopers: "Pastors are to be vigilant to screen properly the people seeking

membership in a parish. Since there will be attempts to circumvent proper church authority and proper church law and values, actual registration and participation would be and must be required as preconditions for people to be considered 'crossover parishioners' of a particular parish." The former pastor was to be informed forthwith.

In closing, Bishop Ferrario acknowledged that the decree only made reality official. "The main thrust of this statute," the bishop said, is to codify a practice that is already in existence and to ensure proper care and proper responsibility on the part of all."

WITH THE RESUMPTION OF THE BUSY FALL ROUTINES IN 1986, ABOUT 10 PERcent of the parishes in Catholic America were without resident priests, due to the worsening clergy shortage, and the percentage was expected to triple by the year 2000. A quarter of the nineteen thousand parishes had two priests, and more than half had just one. Many of these Lone Ranger priests, living alone in rectories built to house a clergy team the size of a basketball squad, had felt the burdens grow heavier even with the influx of lay help.

On a crisp September morning, one of those pastors sat disconsolately behind a cluttered desk in his rectory office sorting out his day's duties. Dark circles lined his eyes, making him look much older than his forty-three years. He said he had been at this parish, which was regarded as a plum in the diocese, for five years. During that time, he said he'd enjoyed the people and loved performing priestly functions. But he felt run-down, unable to slow down. Two years before he'd undergone open heart surgery. "I'm responsible for three thousand families," he said. "There's one of me. I'm running from the altar to the funeral home to meetings at the chancery and back to a pile of phone messages and requests for everything from prayers at the kickoff game for Holy Spirit High School to lending a hand at the Legion of Mary retreat. I'll tell you, it's sometimes hard to be religious. Like right now I have all these bills in front of me. It's difficult being spiritual when you've just opened up an envelope with a seven-thousand-dollar invoice from an insurance company."

PAUL, TWENTY YEARS OLD AND FROM CHICAGO, HAD SETTLED IN FOR HIS FINAL year of college with the relaxed exuberance of a runner who knew he could glide to the finish line. He'd signed up for a full academic load, but most courses were, truth to tell, the sort of comfortable electives that leave lots of time for other things. He had worked hard to complete the course requirements for a major in political science and was geared up to do some studying but not as much as he had done during three previous years. Besides, he had been elected to an office in the student government, and that would take big chunks of time. He had returned to the campus of the sprawling midwestern Catholic university with enthusiasm, ready to create some final memories of his college days before being catapulted, he hoped, into a decent law school.

He liked knowing his way around and being known. There were perks of seniority that made this last lap around the track all the more enjoyable. He spoke of his last year in assured, easygoing tones, confident but not cocky, as if he were prepared to step up his pace on his way to graduation.

But Paul was never quite as nonchalant as he appeared. He had a contemplative side that deterred him from imagining that any pink cloud would last forever. An abundance of common sense kept his head out of the clouds most of the time anyway. Nature and adversity had imbued him with an awareness of tragedy that counseled realism.

Paul was a slightly built young man with curly black hair, a round dark face wired for whimsy, and a sincere, trusting manner. He was born in Maryland during the summer of 1966 into a faithful, mass-going family. His father filled a middle management slot in a pharmaceutical company, and his mother was a housewife. He had one sibling, a sister two years older than he. His family went to mass regularly at the nearby Catholic parish, and Paul attended Catholic schools through the eighth grade. Then his father was transferred, and the family moved to the Midwest. Though his father wanted him to enroll in a Catholic high school, the nearest possibility was too far away, so he went to a public high school. He described himself during those years as an academic underachiever who excelled in soccer and swimming. In his senior year, he had his pick of athletic scholarships.

But then misfortune struck. Eye problems were plaguing him. Doctors diagnosed the malady as a chronic condition that threatened permanent loss of vision. Major surgery was the only remedy. Two delicate operations and recoveries later, Paul's eyesight had been restored, but he could no longer compete in sports. It was a painful experience both physically and emotionally. He decided to attend Saint Augustine's because it was near his family. Later he said he "couldn't have been happier" with his choice. He has made friends, found challenging ideas, gained some practical political experience, and thrived in the generally upbeat climate of the school. By working hard he had earned a respectable class rank and looked forward to someday practicing labor law.

Though he felt good about being at a major Catholic university, he said that it sometimes bothered him that most students came from similar cultural and religious backgrounds. "It reeks of Catholicism," he said puckishly. "Sometimes I think I'd learn more about my faith if I were at a school where I'd have to defend it. Lots of people here don't put much thought into it; they believe because they've always been surrounded by Catholics. In my freshman seminar, I remember a discussion of premarital sex. Everyone spoke against it in class, even some guys and girls who were doing it. They just really hadn't thought about the contradiction."

Paul, like many of his cohorts, grew up in a Catholic ethos, but one shorn of many features that had marked the piety of Catholic life in the past. His family never said the rosary, for example, or engaged in any devotions together. Prayer was reserved for holidays. "My father was shocked that I didn't know the words to the prayers in church," he said. The family rarely went to confession. Paul thought he had gone perhaps five times in his life. "I never came to grips with penance as a sacrament," he said. "I just never saw my parents going. Before my first communion in the second grade, we were told that if we went to confession and told the truth about 100 things and withheld just one thing, we'd be telling 101 lies. I find it hard to believe that if I'm alone in bed saying I'm sorry for my sins I won't be forgiven."

The family went to church every week, and for many years Paul's father held the important elected post of president of the parish council. "Everyone in town knew who he was," Paul said. Yet Paul never remembered having had a conversation with his father about religion. For Paul's family, religion was largely a private matter. Paul loved and admired his father's character and integrity: "He shows you can be a good man and do all right in a corporation. He doesn't play stupid political games." When it came to his religion, Paul explained, his dad just preferred action: setting up chairs for bingo, standing up publicly for the parish's best interests, leading meetings.

Paul recalled an incident that had marked a turning point in his parents' religious consciousness. After the birth of her two children, his mother had wanted to start taking birth control pills but held back because of church teachings against it. She sought out a priest in a neighboring parish who had a reputation for being sympathetic. "He said, 'If that's all you're worried about, go on the pill. There's nothing wrong with it,' " Paul recalled. "She wonders if all priests gave the same advice. She was twenty-one at the time." She still used birth control, and so would he, without hesitation, he said. As he spoke, it was clear that the lingering memory of that incident indicated that for Paul's mother, as for so many other Catholics, a decision in and around birth control had indeed made a lasting difference in how they saw the church.

Paul, robust and energetic, eager for the first football game of the new season, was attending mass every Sunday and glad to be Catholic. He said he worried about the many people his age who did not go near the parish anymore. "These days, almost all the thoughts I have about the church concern its role with young people. I'm worried that the church is losing its appeal. When I go home, I don't see a lot of young people at mass unless they're with their parents. Most of my friends say they don't go to church anymore. A lot of older people say it's nothing but laziness and the young people always come back, so don't worry about it. But I don't see how it will all work out that well. I don't see anything drawing young people to the church."

IN EARLY SEPTEMBER, A SIMMERING DISPUTE ERUPTED AGAIN BETWEEN MARIO Cuomo, governor of New York and often mentioned as a possible nominee for president, and the Archdiocese of New York. Since Cuomo's highly publicized speech on religion and politics during the heat of the 1984 presidential campaign, he had become the titular lay spokesman for free-thinking Catholics and, by the same token, an irritant to many church authorities, who insisted that Catholic public figures must submit to the teachings of the church in the conduct of their offices.

At Notre Dame, Governor Cuomo vigorously crossed swords with those bishops who appeared to oppose the Democratic vice presidential candidate, Geraldine Ferraro, because of her position on abortion. Ferraro said she was against abortion personally but supported a woman's legal choice to have one. Cuomo, operating from a similar position, took up the cudgels on her behalf. In his speech, he argued that his duty as a public figure was to uphold the law, whatever his personal convictions. Catholics would do well to work for a change in the consensus that fostered the law and to improve conditions of poverty and desperation that gave rise to abortion.

Conservatives declared that efforts to draw a line between private and public stances were as morally bankrupt as opposing slavery personally but making no attempt to abolish statutes that upheld it. They repeated the contention by many right-to-life advocates that the key issue was the fundamental right of a fetus, as a human being, to equal protection under the law rather than the civil right of a woman to retain control over her own body.

The conference of bishops had moved in to try to erase the impression that it condoned "single issue" partisanship in the 1984 campaign by disavowing claims that Ferraro or other candidates were being judged solely on their stands on abortion, but the damage had been done. And the debate over the relation between a politician's private beliefs and public morality continued to hang in the air. Each side was implacable. But significantly, the proponents of free conscience had found a champion whose stature and authority rivaled, or even exceeded, that of any bishop. Mario Cuomo was indeed a powerful, attractive symbol of a new independence among Catholic Americans. He suddenly represented a formidable lay assault on hierarchical authority. Not surprisingly, some bishops and conservative lay Catholics saw Cuomo's challenge as the tip of the iceberg, indicative of an enormous threat.

Mario Cuomo was, to say the least, no ordinary Catholic layman. Unlike a magnetic John F. Kennedy, whom much of the church liked to claim despite his loose connection with it, Cuomo claimed the church, took it seriously, actually read its theology, and brooded over it. He was dangerous because he knew what the church said. He told the *New York Times Magazine* (September 14) that church teachings directly influenced his choice of work. The Second Vatican Council had given legitimacy, he said, to pursuing "the concerns of this world, rather than feeling that you had failed because you had not gone into the monastery to weave baskets to fill the uncomfortable interval between birth and eternity." He read Augustine and Thomas More.

The frictions sparked by the 1984 political tussle had only gone into temporary remission two years later when a memo from the chancery of the New York archdiocese set things off again. Among the items from the then vicar general, Bishop Joseph T. O'Keefe, administrative head of the archdiocese, was one that said, "Great care and prudence must be exercised in extending invitations to speak at parish-sponsored events, e.g., Communion breakfasts, graduations and meetings of parish societies, etc. It is not only inappropriate, it is unacceptable and inconsistent with diocesan policy to invite the individuals to speak at such events whose public position is contrary to and in opposition to the clear, unambiguous teachings of the church. This policy applies as well to all Archdiocesan owned and sponsored institutions and organizations."

The memo had been sent August 18 but came to the attention of the New York press in early September. The fur began to fly. One side saw it as a Curran-like test of the right within the church to speak freely. The other side saw it as a question of upholding church integrity. Political antennae activated immediately. Was it aimed at Cuomo? Monsignor Peter Finn, the archdiocesan spokesman, insisted it was not. Bishop O'Keefe said the directive had been produced after the Ancient Order of Hibernians (Irish Americans) asked for guidance in selection of speakers. Cuomo had spoken to a national convention of Hibernians in Buffalo in July. In fact, the more immediate target was John Dearie, a Democratic assemblyman from the Bronx, who had been barred that summer from speaking at his own parish (St. Raymond, the Bronx) because he favored the use of Medicaid funds to pay for abortions. But the governor took it personally. Interviewed on the same day he publicly defended a woman's right to abortion, he confronted the New York hierarchy.

"We laypeople have a right to be heard," a defiant Cuomo said. "The church has the right to make rules for itself; there's no doubt about that. The church has the right to make rules. It can say, 'If you want to belong, these are the rules.' But depending on what the rule was, one can say whether it was wise or whether it was unwise."

Taking direct aim at the chancery, the governor said, "The Catholic church is not the cardinals, the bishops, the priests, and the nuns. The Catholic church by definition in canon law is the hierarchy, the religious, and lay members. We are the church, all of us together." He added, "The laypeople are part of the church. We have a right in some cases to be heard on the rules."

He later raised questions about how the church could ever enforce such a rule. Cuomo had been a staunch opponent of the use of the death penalty, siding with the church on that issue. Did the church's teaching on capital punishment automatically disqualify everyone who argued for it, including President Reagan and many Catholic legislators, such as New York Senator Alphonse D'Amato? (In a bizarre sidelight, Monsignor John Kowsky, the chaplain of the New York City Police Benevolent Association, ended his benediction at the organization's annual convention by asking, "For our governor, just one little thing he's got to do, Lord: learn to turn the switch." The crowd cheered.) And during the 1984 race for the White House, Cuomo quipped, Reagan "was surrounded by priests and cardinals."

Cardinal John O'Connor, who knew a thing or two about institutional loyalty, jumped to the defense of his vicar general. In his weekly column in the archdiocesan newspaper (September 11), he rejected as "nonsense" charges that the archdiocese was imposing "thought control" by denying free speech and praised Bishop O'Keefe for using common sense. Referring to the directive and those it was intended to exclude, Cardinal O'Connor said, "Common sense dictates that you try to keep the fox out of the chicken coop." In remarks to a reporter, the cardinal linked the directive more directly to abortion. "The church's support or seeming support, perceived support, of a speaker who was explicitly supporting abortion—that would be a scandal, I think. It wouldn't matter who it would be— a political figure or anyone else."

DRIVERS BREEZING ALONG THE MAJOR INTERSTATES TOWARD DOWNTOWN Cleveland caught sight of a 236-foot stainless steel Gothic spire that stood like an abandoned orphan, set off starkly against alien surroundings in the old East Twenty-third Street and Woodland neighborhood. Once Saint Joseph commanded that very environment teeming with immigrant single- and multifamily dwellings, but the Cleveland diocese had decided earlier in the year to close its doors. Only a stay of execution resulting from pressure by a group called Friends of Saint Joseph kept the wrecking ball from destroying one of the remaining symbols of a once-flourishing urban ethnic Catholicism. A September 3 letter from the diocese to the parish gave the group four months to come up with a workable salvage plan.

The parish had been founded by German-speaking people 131 years ago. In 1861 it was taken over by Franciscans. Though five other parishes once stood within a few blocks, the graceful facade of Saint Joseph was the crown jewel. Things were fine until urban renewal tore through the neighborhood in 1958–59. During the 1960s the area was totally devastated to make way for the major highways that now afford such striking views of the parish. Before-and-after pictures show an area flattened like a city hit by aerial bombings. Families by the hundreds were displaced. Saint Joseph's, like the neighboring parishes, was doomed. In the early 1970s, eight hundred families still kept their membership there. By 1986, barely two hundred names were on the rolls, twenty-five from the immediate neighborhood, and the diocese estimated $1 million would be needed to restore the structure, $250,000 for immediate repairs. There seemed no way around the dilemma. The diocese neither had the subsidy nor could justify that kind of expenditure, given the other demands on the budget, and the loyalists at Saint Joseph were left to figure out how to save a beautiful landmark. Saint Joseph aroused passions in people who had long since moved to the suburbs. But would their passion be enough to come up with a plan to rescue the parish? Their campaign at least won the parish a short-term reprieve.

On September 14, more than a thousand mourners packed Saint Joseph for a final liturgy presided over by Bishop Anthony M. Pilla. Marsha Basel, seventy-eight years old, took her place at the organ where she had played for forty-four years. A flood of tears washed down the cheeks of worshipers. Mass over, the doors were locked for good.

Saint Joseph's fate told the story of Catholic America. The immigrants had prospered and moved to the suburbs. Only remnants of vitality remained behind to fight for the parish's survival in one form or other.

THE WALL STREET JOURNAL HAD LAID OUT THE SHOCKING DIMENSIONS OF THE problem in May. Thousands of nuns who had labored long and hard for the church were destitute in old age. Retirement programs were either woefully inadequate or totally lacking. Consultants from Arthur D. Little estimated that it would take the whopping sum of $3 billion to fill the gap.

There were 114,000 nuns and 57,000 priests in religious orders. The women were, for the most part, hit the hardest by the lack of retirement resources. The median age of nuns was sixty-two. A third were over seventy. Their crisis had remained largely out of view. Many Catholics just assumed that the needs of the nuns, the most visible parish work force most of them had ever encountered, had been systematically taken care of by the church. They were, therefore, scandalized and embarrassed by the news. For some bishops, the revelations were a new complication in what was already a difficult situation. Because relations between bishops and women's orders tended to be tense and distant, a problem often became something of an ecclesiastical football. It was unclear in many cases how to sort out who or what was responsible for the current delinquency—the hierarchy, religious orders themselves, or some combination of factors.

The disclosures prompted reactions of amazement, concern, guilt, denial, and offers of help. A group of lay Catholics from Washington took the lead in September by kicking off a campaign called Save Our Aging Religious.

THE MONTH BEGAN WITH A CHORUS OF AFFIRMATION FOR CATHOLIC AMERICA'S best-known dissenter, Father Curran, but ended on a note of dissent against dissent.

The Fellowship of Catholic Scholars, a conservative group that sprang into existence as the result of a rupture within the Catholic Theological Society of America over its controversial 1976 sexuality statement, which argued for liberalization of the church's views, met in New York from September 26 to 28. The president of the fellowship, Monsignor George Kelly, a theologian from Saint John's University in New York, reported that membership had shot up by more than a hundred, to seven hundred, during the previous months because of the group's backing of the Vatican's action against Father Curran. He said the members included theologians, philosophers, scholars from other fields, doctors, lawyers, and other professionals.

The attitude of the fellowship toward those who openly diverged from church doctrine was made clear at a closing panel for the benefit of the press. Public rejection of church teaching caused confusion, distortion, and fragmentation, said the panelists from Marquette, Catholic University, and Notre Dame. Far more important than the personal views of individual theologians, they suggested, was the preservation of truth.

At the opening session, many of the 225 participants were heartened by a message from Auxiliary Bishop Edward Egan of New York. Bishop Egan, who had returned to serve under Cardinal John O'Connor after a thirteen-year assignment in Rome, declared that he saw a new day dawning. Coming back after a long break had afforded him a fresh look, he said, and the trends were promising. Catholics in America were tired of trendiness in the church and yearned instead for the safety and reliability of hallowed tradition.

He offered three signs of hope. First, that Catholics were rejecting attempts to merge religion with psychology and sociology in favor of good, sound philosophical and theological nourishment. They now preferred as their seers Thomas Aquinas and Teresa of Avila over Carl Rogers and John Kenneth Galbraith. "Catholics who are concerned about things spiritual are now demanding something solid, something tried and above all something true," Bishop Egan assured the gathering. "They want the object of their faith to be articulated correctly, clearly, and fully; and for this reason they are focusing in on serious philosophy, serious theology, and historical accuracy as well."

Second, the bishop saw Catholics "looking for their roots" in their spiritual practices. Gone was the tendency to shun the church's spiritual masters. There was a return to disciplines of the past. "And where do I see signs of this trend?" he asked. "Frankly, everywhere. Retreat masters now suggest Thomas à Kempis, Thérèse of Lisieux, and even Jean-Pierre de Caussade without apology. Parish missioners commonly advise daily mass, holy hours, and family prayer in parishes that are thriving or coming alive. In faculties of religious education, courses such as 'Patristic Prayer' and 'The Spirituality of Francis de Sales' are supplanting 'What Jung Has to Say to Christians' and 'Radical Creeds of the 1960s,' at least in the number of students in attendance."

And, third, contrary to rumors that had reached him at the Vatican, he saw few indications that Americans were inclined to think their situation entitled them to special exemptions within the universal church or that they wanted to set up an "American church" apart from Rome. From his perspective, American Catholics were increasingly reaching out to touch base with the rest of the Catholic world rather than withdrawing from it.

To sum up, Bishop Egan listed the major trends as "away from the merely psychological and sociological and toward the clearly philosophical and the theological," "away from embracing every religious novelty that comes upon the scene and toward reconsidering and recapturing what is truly authentic from our Catholic past," and "away from looking in on ourselves as American Catholics and toward broadening our horizon to include the entire Catholic world."

The turbulence and experimentation that followed the Second Vatican Council were largely over, Bishop Egan forecast optimistically. If he proved right, the dissenters were running against the tide. If he had it wrong, Catholic America would continue to struggle in the throes of modern, shaping forces.

October
1·9·8·6

—⌐

S TARING OUT FROM AN AD IN NEWSWEEK'S SPECIAL CAMPUS edition (September 22), a man with the hint of rakish intent in his deadpan expression sat in a cozy restaurant twirling spaghetti. He wore the garb of an Italian padre, complete with broad-brimmed fedora, and his face conveyed the confidence of one who had found a way to make the system work for him. The "model," actor Don Novello, was known to "Saturday Night Live" audiences as Father Guido Sarducci, the parody priest, and the ad was intended to woo young men to the priesthood by suggesting that the job had some enticing, earthy side benefits.

"Eat Free at Italian Restaurants" read the big black type above the picture. The Missionary Oblates of Mary Immaculate, an order based in Chicago, had sponsored the lighthearted, whimsical effort to meet a crisis. Increasingly, dioceses and orders were resorting to media campaigns in an attempt to fill their depleted ranks. It was a partnership between an institution that had been marketing its wares for twenty centuries and the modern commercial missionaries of Madison Avenue.

The tongue-in-cheek come-on from Father Sarducci read, "You think they're gonna let the check slide if you're a doctor or lawyer? Don't hold your breath. But when you're a priest it's on the house! One of what I call the padre perks. Other padre perks are sleeping late, getting the first crack at parish rummage sales and helping your fellow man. Could be these perks are right up your alleyway. Which makes you priest material. To find out more . . ." (there was a number to call).

On October 5 the Vatican handed down a report, the State of U.S. Freestanding Seminaries, on the quality of training for those men who had been successfully recruited in the past. The Vatican Congregation on Education had studied thirty-eight seminaries defined as "freestanding" because they were self-contained, supplying all components of instruction for those candidates who had already finished college.

The investigation had had its inception in the U.S. bishops' somewhat reluctant bow to necessity back in 1981. First, the pope made it known that he wanted U.S. seminaries inspected. The idea was greeted with suspicion and hostility by Catholics who feared that it was the start of a Vatican campaign to purge seminaries of free thought and such innovations as opening their faculties to women. But clearly, Rome wanted it, and the U.S. bishops, whatever their personal reservations, accepted the inevitable and went through the motions of pretending the idea was their own. Following church protocol, the bishops extended an "invitation" to Rome to do the study. The Vatican then announced acceptance of their request. Bishop John Marshall of Vermont was appointed to head the investigation team. The probe had turned out to be far less ominous than some had predicted.

The seminary was becoming an empty institution for a vanishing species. Over two decades, from 1964 to 1984, the number of students pursuing the priesthood plummeted from 47,500 to 12,000, and it was continuing to drop. The Center for Applied Research in the Apostolate, an arm of the bishops' conference, estimated that the total had shrunk to 10,372 by the start of the 1986 academic year, a dip of 439 from the previous year. The drop meant that by 1988 only about three hundred men would be ordained for the whole nation, according to one reliable estimate. The reduced need for training facilities meant that seventy-six seminaries either shut down entirely or merged between 1962 and 1987.

Despite this drastic decline, the Vatican's report hinted at nothing so catastrophic. Issued in the name of the congregation's prefect, Cardinal William Baum, the former archbishop of Washington, it spoke in assured tones of the need to conduct business as usual, with a few suggestions for tightening up here and there and, in some particular circumstances, buckling down harder to conform to the hierarchy. If Cardinal Baum worried that the shape and content of seminary training—to say nothing of celibacy—might be hampering recruitment, there were no qualms voiced here. By remaining strictly within its own mandate, it provided a sterling example of compartmentalized thinking within the Vatican bureaucracy.

In the report, Cardinal Baum allayed some fears that wholesale indictments might be on the way by passing out bouquets. "The picture that emerges so far," the report said, "is that the theologates [seminaries] of the United States are generally satisfactory. Some, in fact, are excellent, a few have one or more serious deficiencies and the majority are serving the church well in preparing candidates for the priesthood" (Origins, October 16, vol. 16, no. 18, p. 315).

The specific problems that in some cases needed fixing had to do with priorities that Rome considered inviolate: making sure the priesthood was sharply distinguished from the laity, expunging theological dissent, and getting back to basics wherever they were neglected or compromised by outside influences.

Distinctiveness—the belief that priests were set apart by ordination—was the watchword in sizing up the priesthood, a counterbalance to the trend toward erasing differences that had been given impetus by the Second Vatican Council. Among the themes in portions of the Vatican II documents was the concept that all Catholics derive a ministry from baptism. This perspective played down the division between lay and clerical status and served as a rationale for new ventures in pastoral services. But many, including the pope, felt that the pendulum had swung too far toward a sort of "uni-ministry." Though the clergy and laity both have their legitimate place, the pope said, their separate purposes should not be confused.

Thus the seminary report, like many documents addressed to clergy, bore the traditional stamp of "separate but equal." In the United States, many laypeople had taught seminary courses or enrolled in them. Cardinal Baum urged caution, perhaps even cutbacks, in such lay contact, lest the special mission of the seminary be harmed. Likewise, seminaries that had become involved too much in "adult education" programs outside the conventional bounds of the seminary might have to curtail such activity. "Some seminaries," the report said, "have come under much pressure to develop into schools of all kinds of ministerial formation in such ways that neither correspond to nor cohere with the 'agenda' given to the church by Vatican Council II, which both emphasized the importance of the laity and yet retained a policy of promoting seminaries as distinct institutions for the formation of future priests" (p. 315).

What was prescribed for seminaries was modified quarantine. They were not to be as hermetically sealed away as in pre–Vatican II days, but definitely set apart. Limited contact with lay teachers and students could be good, the report said, but too much could prevent the future priest from drawing a clear enough line between his vocation and the ministry of the laity.

Cardinal Baum noted that the average age of entering seminarians has risen in the past decade. Though they were on the whole not as well educated in church lore as their predecessors had been, the cardinal said, they nonetheless showed "a strong consciousness of God." (p. 318). In their desire to welcome new recruits, seminaries should thoroughly screen certain types of candidates. The motives and "special circumstances" of older men seeking admission, for example, should be carefully examined. Recent converts and bereaved widowers had sometimes "been too hastily accepted into seminaries" (p. 318). Others might not be ready to study, display too little "flexibility of character," or have a "background of chemical dependency" (p. 318). Special caution should be exercised with regard to men whose marriages had been annulled. Acceptance of such applicants, the cardinal said, should be "very rare" (p. 319).

Before the investigating teams made their rounds, the report said, a number of seminaries had permitted the spiritual direction of seminarians to be "entrusted to people who were not themselves ordained to the priesthood." That practice, which had included the use of women as spiritual directors, must be halted. Regarding celibacy, Cardinal Baum had found cause to rejoice: "We were very heartened to note the explicit and constructive ways [in which] the freestanding theologates are preparing their students for lifelong priestly celibacy." Only sketchy details were provided. If an effective method had been found to stanch the flow of defections due to the celibacy requirement, the rest of the Catholic world had been kept in the dark about it. Priests in significant numbers continued to leave in order to get married (p. 321).

Though celibacy training was given a passing grade, the academic side of seminary life got a mixed review. Some seminaries had embraced contemporary topics to the neglect of "subject matter of more foundational or central importance for the priesthood," the cardinal wrote. "In a few seminaries a number of important courses are missing altogether: God, grace, creation, eschatology, Mariology, being the most glaring examples" (p. 321).

If allegiance to church authority was the rule, the report stated, there were nettlesome exceptions, particularly in the area of moral views. Dissent was "not a major characteristic" of seminary life, Cardinal Baum allowed, but "confusion about it" was common. "There would seem to be a number of seminarians who, at the end of their moral theology courses, are either not sure of what the church teaches in a particular matter or who think that the church's teaching is only one theological opinion among a number of other equally valid theological opinions," the cardinal wrote, "in which case it is mistakenly denied its magisterial authority" (p. 322).

Alluding indirectly to Father Curran and those who took a similar dissenting tack, Cardinal Baum said that "the present errors and debate" over what could not be questioned (infallible) and what could be (fallible) should "not be permitted to confuse" the seminarian into thinking that what was fallible was "somehow non-binding." He went on, "To weaken the presumption of truth that rests with the church's teaching is to do a great disservice not only to the candidate for the priesthood, but to those who will in the future turn to hear the church's words of life and salvation" (p. 322). He who would perplex the innocent seminarian would have to bear the sins of apostasy for generations to come.

The Father Curran case had heightened awareness that teaching moral theology in a hierarchically controlled school meant walking through a field of land mines.

Cardinal Baum gave no clue as to the impact of that wariness when he touched on the subject with no evident irony. "Frequently enough theologates experience difficulty in recruiting good professors of moral theology," he wrote. "It seems that some prospectively good professors are shy of taking it on" (p. 323).

Two aspects of the cardinal's report related to the orientation found among students. First, in the area of social justice, the cardinal said "there is still much to be achieved, particularly with regard to the poor and to ethnic minorities. Sometimes we have the impression that social justice is perceived as mere politics." Efforts must be made to encourage future priests to "forgo the natural attractions of functioning only among those of his own class and his own culture . . . [to make it possible for him] to spend his life at the service of God's people regardless of class or color, income or comfort, race or language, especially the Spanish language" (p. 324).

The second comment put a damper on the upscale vision of the priesthood to which TV's Father Guido Sarducci beckoned. Asceticism was, indeed, out of fashion, a finding that displeased Cardinal Baum. Lamentably, he said, only two seminaries emphasized "self-denial in matters of food and drink and luxury" and the "need to be self-critical of comparative wealth and possessions, and to be selfless in generosity in serving others regardless of social preference and personal inconvenience. We would hope that these emphases be found in other theologates, but they did not strike the members of the visitation teams so strongly that they commented on them elsewhere" (p. 324).

CRAIG WAS DUE TO BEGIN THE THIRD PHASE OF MARINE CORPS FLIGHT TRAINING in another week. He had spent months learning the ins and outs of basic flight, first at the controls of a propeller-driven plane, then in a simple jet aircraft. He had passed the exacting tests of mental and physical acuity with flying colors. There remained the final drive to master the complex skills needed by the Marine fighter pilot.

Craig had the "right stuff" they look for in candidates. He was a tall, strapping young man of twenty-four who took to the high-pressure instruction with enthusiasm, retaining his calm composure under the most intense fire. Though thriving under pressure, he had no acute craving for competition. He was bright, college educated, and confident, eager to press his own limits. His look was straight and honest, and he spoke with care and deliberateness. The strength and toughness emblematic of the Marine Corps were there, all right, but there were other sides to him equally striking, such as warmth, humor, and sensitivity.

He was, by his own description, an unlikely Marine. "I've never quite fit in anywhere, including the Marines," he confided. "I'm not totally gung ho or willing to go strictly by the book. I've never shot anything in my life. I've never been hunting. I don't like the policies of the National Rifle Association." Young men with weak egos could too easily be molded by the Marine Corps mentality, he thought. But he loved adventure, and he loved to fly, and he jumped at the chance to prove he could do it.

The blend of devotion and detachment stemmed from his family background. He was the youngest of five sons in a household that was ardently Catholic. His father's influence on him had been especially profound.

He described his father, a professor of humanities, as a "deeply religious man" who was well versed in the historical and intellectual dimensions of the church. "You could get into great conversations with him about popes or the Crusades or whatever," the son said admiringly. "But you really didn't discuss faith with him in personal terms." His saw his father as something of a spiritual loner, even within the family, who at the same time agonized about the suffering of others. He was not only a fairly traditional Catholic; he also helped start chapters of Amnesty International. Craig wondered if his father had harbored yearnings for the priesthood or even for becoming a monk. As a boy, Craig remembered going with his father to the Trappist monastery in Kentucky where Thomas Merton had once lived. "We went on the tour and attended mass with the monks," he recalled. "I never remember when my father seemed to be more at peace."

The son mirrored the qualities one would have expected to find in the father: a man with his own inner gyroscope who could not easily be co-opted by popular conventions or slick slogans, a man whose conscience was shaped by the spirit within rather than the pressure of public opinion without.

Despite the taxing routine, designed to weed out the unfit, Craig was immensely enjoying the vicissitudes of flight school. Lots had already washed out, and, though not happy to see the hopes of others dashed, he was pleased to be a survivor. He felt he had never really applied himself to anything else before. At the large Midwestern university he attended, he majored in history, took an interest in writing, competed in sports, and generally had a good time. But looking back, he thinks he mostly did just enough to get by. He was looking for a way to test his own mettle. One summer at Marine Reserve Officer Training School convinced him the challenge was there if he wanted it. He nearly turned it down, then decided to see what would happen if, for once in his life, he gave it his best shot.

Craig wasn't sure just how religious he considered himself. The church was a big part of his upbringing, and during college he had gone to mass regularly at the university Newman Center, but since flight training had begun, he had slacked off. He was a believer, he said, but felt a need to think about just what he did believe. Some of the church's statements on sexuality bothered him and made him wonder about other things the church was saying. But his demanding routine had allowed him little time for anything but a round of study and takeoffs and landings.

One factor in his life was making a difference in his religious outlook, however. He had recently become engaged to a young artist whose father happened to be a Methodist minister in the South. When that reality hit, he said, he conjured stereotypes of hard-core fundamentalists who took a dim view of Catholics. He could now laugh at how badly misinformed he had been. The family had welcomed him, immediately quelling his fears of rejection. The father, moreover, proved to be an intelligent, well-educated man with interests like his own.

And how did the prospect of a daughter-in-law from a minister's family strike his own parents? His answer spoke volumes about the modern family in Catholic America. "Great," he said. "They just love her. Besides, they're happy I'm marrying a Christian. I'll be the only one. Three of my brothers married Jews and one a Buddhist."

FEMINISM POSED A QUANDARY FOR A GROWING NUMBER OF CATHOLIC WOMEN. According to one analyst, the reason some women stayed in the church while others left came down to "whether or not they believe in the church, not whether they like the church."

The same point could have been made about Catholics torn by the competing claims of the church and modern life along other lines. But among many women for whom the insights of feminism had been liberating, even salvific, in their own right, the decision about whether to remain and, if so, how, was especially troublesome. If the analyst was correct, the response rested on a prior question of whether or not women "believe in the church" no matter what its imperfections are. Those whose faith inclined them to believe that the church was the mediator of the truth about existence—a divine vehicle though badly flawed—would be more likely to remain within it, no matter what their complaints, than those who completely wrote the church off as hopelessly tainted by patriarchal theology.

Some three thousand women at various points along the spectrum between those extremes took part in a Washington, D.C., conference, Women in the Church, October 10–12. The turnout was surprisingly high, reflecting rising interest in women's issues among Catholics. Trends in the larger society generally took something like a decade to gain momentum in the church, and feminism was no exception (though, of course, a stalwart vanguard had been pressing the issues for years). Though the women's movement was facing tough sledding overall, it was picking up among Catholics. The conference marked new heights in that surge and, in the view of some of its leaders, moved women's issues from the fringe to the mainstream of the church.

Large numbers of nuns mingled at the conference with many laywomen and a few men. Many were well versed in feminist thinking; others were getting their first real introduction. The tenor of the meeting was, on the whole, moderate; sessions were mostly scholarly and cerebral rather than evangelical and practical. The atmosphere resembled more a teach-in than a political rally. A growing body of research and intellectual effort made such a pedagogical program possible. Women theologians, Bible scholars, and social scientists had been reexamining the sources of Christian belief and practice. Their findings, sometimes grossly downplayed by the church's leadership, raised havoc with basic assumptions about the origins and history of the church. Though publicity about church feminism centered largely on political concepts such as rights, justice, and power, feminist scholars had been working in the realm of ideas, making possible a protracted theological critique of attitudes close to the very heart of church identity.

Groups of activists at the conference complained that its agenda was too tame and safe. As participants entered a special mass, some activists released balloons and staged a silent protest to raise the issue of women's ordination and to promote a conference the following year that was expected to include more radical viewpoints. But the conference stayed its moderate course and offered to the gathering the staples of feminist religious thought. Collectively, the group of speakers provided a rich sampling of the lines of thinking that had been generated by the movement among women in the church.

At the root of the discussion was the underlying debate over what exactly the church was. Either God had dictated the blueprint for an unchangeable church, including an all-male clause in the leadership section, or the church was forever on the path of new discoveries—revelations—in constant need of additional insights and self-correction. It was either fixed for all time, as some argued, or subject to revision in light of developing understanding. If the church was thought to be evolving, then the further question was, How much was fixed, and how much could be negotiated? Did issues of concern to women belong to both categories? Either? Neither?

The conference was obviously built on the assumption of malleability, which maintained, in effect, that the men who formulated church tradition at the behest of the Holy Spirit nonetheless wrote it their way, borrowing heavily from patterns of male control that had come down to them, thus ignoring the gospel's implicit call for inclusiveness. Speakers examined how, in their view, the male bias had generated false notions with regard to Scripture, concepts of God, how revelation works, and the style of church leadership. One speaker specifically explored the problem of anger among women who felt alienated from the church.

In the keynote address, Sister Joan Chittister, prioress of the Benedictine Sisters of Erie, Pennsylvania, testified about the increasing feminist search into the

Scriptures. The title of her talk, "Sexism in the Church," got the conference down to business in a hurry, touching almost immediately on the barrier against women entering the priesthood. The church baptized, confirmed, and blessed women, she said. It performed their marriages and preached to them the same as it did to men, "that in their lives God gives them graces, too." She continued, "Yet, sadly, it is always said that women may not be carriers of grace, or dispense it, or preach it or use it in the church in any official way. God's grace, it seems, goes sour when it gets to women."

She lifted several examples from the Bible—Ruth and Naomi, the mother of Moses and the daughter of Pharaoh, the Samaritan woman, Esther, Mary of Bethany, Mary Magdalene, Eve, and the Virgin Mary—all of whom, she said, illustrated aspects of sexism. Their hardships are often overlooked, she said, and the lessons to be drawn from their lives have been largely blunted. "They witness to the need for affirmation of the feminine, full inclusion in ministry, and recognition of the basic moral equality and fullness of female personhood," she said.

Urging her listeners to "write and research and question the limited status of women's lives until the questions are heard and the answers make both good sense and good church," Sister Chittister added, "We must give the lie to lies. We must press for a resolution of the tension between the definition of church and the practice of clericalism."

It remained for another Benedictine, Sister Mary Collins, to deliver some stout hammer blows against the male monopoly of the clergy. Sister Collins, codirector of the Center for Benedictine Studies in Atchison, Kansas, and a university professor, echoed other feminists by tracing the church's male exclusivity to the influences of outside forces on early Christianity. In the earliest times of the church, she said, "clerics did not exist as a separate class with a separate viewpoint." Then came the influence of Hellenism, which injected a liking for hierarchical arrangements and a propensity for dualism, which, relegating existence into "good" and "bad" spheres, fueled hostility toward women by setting them off against the alleged superiority of masculinity. The church bought both concepts, Sister Collins said. By becoming the official religion of the Roman Empire, she continued, the church simply took over the apparatus left by the outlawed pagan priesthood.

"Imperial Rome did not require a celibate priesthood," Sister Collins told her highly attentive audience. "However, the Roman sense of imperial order did require that only males would hold public offices in the clerical or any other social order. Imperial Rome also bequeathed some of the organizational language left over from the pagan priesthood. The bishop of Rome became the new Supreme Pontiff, presiding now as did his pagan predecessor, over a 'college' of official collaborators. The church even adopted the imperial Latin tag *ius divinium,* by divine right or divine law, as the formula for stabilizing and protecting the Roman regulation of public cult everywhere in the empire." For women, the upshot was, "The Roman church, presided over by a Supreme Pontiff and a male, celibate hierarchically ordered clerical class since the fourth century, has deliberately, even if unconsciously, denied itself access to the experience of women's spiritual gifts."

Those claims, and others like them, would get an argument from those who defended the legitimacy of the church's ordained leadership. They could agree on the bulk of the historical facts, but they parted company on interpretation of them. Defenders of church tradition saw a divine design in early Christianity's seeming appropriation of certain aspects of Hellenistic and Roman culture. What struck feminists as a series of human actions intended to bolster the power and status of male clerics impressed the defenders of tradition as God's plan. At the core of the debate was the most critical issue: whether Jesus had ever intended to institute an all-male priesthood in the first place. Feminists were contending that the circle of authentic ministers extended beyond the dozen disciples to women; their opponents argued that the priesthood belonged properly only to those first apostles.

Feminists had put Scripture, revelation, history, and theology to the test. The Women in the Church conference signified the scope of the challenge.

THE BROOKLYN DIOCESE MADE GOOD ON ITS SPEAKING INVITATION TO MARIO Cuomo, thereby showing no inclination to join the New York Archdiocese in a ban against offering church platforms to Catholic public officials who, like Cuomo, refused to press antiabortion legislation.

Cuomo appeared as scheduled on October 2 at the Saint James Pavilion, across from the cathedral, and repeated the theme from his 1984 Notre Dame speech that had sparked the rhubarb with Cardinal O'Connor, among others, and been a precipitating factor behind the notorious ban in the archdiocese. Cuomo said that the 1984 controversy had made it clearer "that a Catholic official could agree with Catholic teaching at the same time that he or she 'disagreed' over whether or how it should be translated into law that would apply equally to believers— who didn't need it—and to those who, because of differing beliefs, rejected it."

Dissent should be valued rather than attacked, the governor said, adding, "How, after all, has the church changed and developed through the centuries, except through discussion and argument?" He went on: "We have dissent and argument enough to occupy us. But there is no dissent and argument on the obligations to feed the hungry, shelter the homeless, care for the ill, and educate the young."

Cuomo reminisced about his own difficulties in his early years as he moved beyond the habits and customs of his boyhood to a wider world. It was a parable that implied that differences, far from being dangerous, were the natural stuff of life and potential sources of growth. He had left his Italian ethnic roots to pursue the opportunity America afforded. He recalled his father's fear that this seeking after success meant rejection of the old ways. "Only gradually," Cuomo said, "did my father come to understand this, to know that his son in a suit and tie, with the big desk and the office, the son who seemed so at home in another language and in another world, was bound to him and my mother in ways that could never be broken." The church was likewise a family, he said: "After all the headache and the heartache of the moment's contentions, that will prove to be the greater truth."

ARCHBISHOP REMBERT WEAKLAND OF MILWAUKEE UPDATED THE STATE OF UNREST between bishops and people in the October 18 issue of *America*. He took up the question pressed thirty years before by the renowned Jesuit, John Courtney Murray, namely, how the Catholic church could adapt to a pluralistic society, and a companion issue, how bishops might relate constructively to a church vexed by rising discord. The article, "Tensions Between Laity and Clergy," urged the American hierarchy to shun strategies from the past that have attempted top-down control of both the faithful and the social order. He also argued for greater cooperation between clergy and laity in tackling tough ethical issues and concluded that the church must be prepared to compromise with the nation's various interest groups in molding public policy.

The archbishop had already become the spokesman for boldness in a field of hierarchical timidity. His relative outspokenness and resistance to some of Rome's tactics had cost him considerable favor at the Vatican. Ammunition came from the Catholic right in America, which regularly attacked him in articles and letters that were dispatched to sympathetic officials at the Vatican. For those reasons, he was widely rumored to be on Rome's short list of targets for investigation, à la Hunthausen, but many believed the Vatican was hesitant to tangle with someone of Archbishop Weakland's stature.

Since Pope Paul VI appointed him to Milwaukee in 1977, Weakland, a Benedictine monk, had acquired a reputation for being something of a Renaissance man. Among the bishops, he was considered exceptionally bright, thoughtful, cultured, and multitalented. His background set him apart. Unlike most of his colleagues, who had followed a straight career path, Rembert Weakland had, after finishing seminary, attended the esteemed Juilliard School to study piano and Columbia University graduate school. He took his artistic and intellectual interests instead to the monastery, rising eventually to the head of the world Benedictine Order. Pope Paul, himself a cultured man who admired such traits, named him to the hierarchy.

Most church observers doubted that Pope John Paul II, who took over in 1979, would have given Archbishop Weakland a promotion to the hierarchy or to such a prominent archdiocese. For all of Archbishop Weakland's obvious commitment to the church, there was about him an air of detachment more typical, it seemed, of bishops who came out of religious orders than out of the diocesan system, and that disposition had led him to some independent thinking of the kind John Paul often seemed to consider thorny. The same talents that lent force to some of Archbishop Weakland's more pronounced liberal positions on church policy made him all the more a danger to conservatives. His increased visibility as the chairman of the bishops' committee in charge of the pastoral letter on the economy only heightened his status as a force to be reckoned with. A month before, he had sounded a pointed warning about the dangers of Vatican repression. Writing his weekly column, entitled "The Price of Orthodoxy," in the archdiocesan newspaper (September 18) of Milwaukee, the archbishop expressed alarm at moves by Rome to stifle dissent.

In his *America* piece, Archbishop Weakland declared that the church had entered a "new and critical phase" along two fronts: first, "how its clergy—and especially its bishops—will relate as teachers to its highly intelligent and trained laity"; second, "how the church as a whole will enter into the debate in American society on political, social, and economic issues" (p. 201). The laity, on the whole, was poorly informed about what the church had already said about social issues, the archbishop said; on the other hand, the hierarchy had failed to "find a way of addressing political and social issues in an enlightened manner that respects the knowledge, competency and conscience of the individual Catholics who comprise it" (p. 202).

So by what means could the church educate the laity, take their views seriously, and become a key player in the forming of national consensus on social issues?

The archbishop rejected two existing alternatives. One was "integralism," which emerged from the medieval idea that the rest of society was subordinate to the Catholic church. "Those Catholics who sought a complete or integral Catholicism in the political realm demanded the perfect coalescence of Christian morality with the legal realm of the state and, thus, the suppression of all error. No concept of separation of church and state was considered orthodox. Error had no rights, they said; and, since the Catholic church was considered the source of all truth, its doctrine alone should dominate in political affairs." Though this notion had largely vanished, he said, "it still colors much Catholic thought in our time" (p. 203).

The other unacceptable solution, he said, was the two-tiered "Catholic Action" approach commonly used in Europe. "In this new model," he wrote, "the role of the clergy, especially of the bishops, is one of teaching. The clergy are the teachers of tradition and of social justice. That teaching remains on a theoretical level and does not descend to concrete situations and cases. These are left to the laity whose task it is to put the theory into practice" (p. 204). Laypeople carried out their job either as individuals or in Catholic "movements" such as political parties or labor unions.

Among the faults the archbishop found with the European concept were that the "laity can appear like the puppets of the clergy" and the assumption that the bishops acting alone are capable of providing adequate theory in response to the proliferation of modern problems. On the practical level, laity were likely to be misled if they thought "that the choice of the morally most acceptable solution will be easy and self-evident, even if the theory is clear" (p. 205). That, of course, is what Mario Cuomo had been saying: principle and application are two different things.

Having advised against the clergy-centered concepts, Archbishop Weakland then appealed for "another process" that would go beyond mere lay consultation toward a mode that would "permit both clergy and laity to be active and involved in reflection on specific contemporary issues that face the church in our society." Not exactly "democracy" but closer to it than the current system of a closed hierarchical shop. In a single sentence, the archbishop cast his lot against the top-down versions that had flourished under Pope John Paul II. "The search for orthodoxy," the archbishop wrote, "is not a clerical prerogative." The teaching of the church, he added, must profit from "the knowledge and expertise of lay and clerical members alike" (p. 205).

Modern conditions demanded a new lay-clerical cooperative approach, the archbishop said. Such a system would allow a fuller response to the immense complexities of contemporary dilemmas by opening the discussion. "I am sure," he said sardonically, "bishops would be relieved to know they do not have all the answers all the time" (p. 215).

Under real conditions, the ideal could never be achieved, of course, and compromise was a "solution inevitable in a pluralistic society," the archbishop said. Referring vaguely to the Cuomo situation, the archbishop said that "laity are church as fully as the clergy. The laity do not have a different kind of conscience from the clergy's that permits them to make more compromises in a pluralistic society" (p. 215). But where to compromise? Abortion? Divorce? Birth control? What happens if most Catholics disagree with a "no compromise" position by bishops? If the church cannot convince society of its stand, what should Catholic officeholders be expected to do? The archbishop supplied only the questions. These perplexities only underscored the need for a new method of cooperation between clergy and laity. He did not specify what form it should take. Meanwhile, he counseled the church to "move very carefully in declaring any position to be one

that allows for no compromise (unless the individual conscience so declares it) as
we work toward a consensus on any issue and before we have obtained such consensus in the wider political arena" (p. 216).

DURING THE RUSH HOURS AT SAINT BENEDICT'S, THOUSANDS OF PARISHIONERS
streamed in and out of the wood frame church, choosing among seven masses, five
in the upstairs sanctuary and two in a downstairs hall. Three parish priests divided
up the duties. As the throngs poured back out the doors, they became a noisy,
swollen stream of Catholic humanity, exchanging quick greetings and collecting
brief messages, many of them appeals for help.

The first Sunday liturgy had begun promptly at 6:30 A.M. and the final mass
of the morning at 12:15 P.M. Two other masses were also available for fulfilling the
weekly obligation, Saturday at 7:00 P.M. and Sunday evening at 6:00. Monsignor
Bosco, the energetic pastor, calculated that on average, about 5,000 of the 9,300
people who were registered with the parish attended regularly, somewhere near 55
percent. Good, he said, but nowhere near good enough.

Measured by vital signs, Monsignor Bosco's parish was among the strongest in
the proud old East Coast urban diocese. It had once been a Slavic ethnic parish but
more recently had become the hub of a thriving neighborhood of police officers,
fire fighters, and other civil employees whose jobs required them to live in the city.
This far edge of the city had grown most rapidly during the period of "white flight"
from areas closer to downtown. The area was 75 percent Catholic and 100 percent
white. Nearly all parents sent their children to the bulging parish school. The
area was an urban-suburban vestige of earlier parish life, compactly Catholic and
reminiscently ethnic, far better educated and much more affluent than the Catholic ghettos of old and, of course, far more mobile.

Monsignor Bosco, now in his mid-fifties, had been pastor for nearly five years.
He had two assistants, one fresh from seminary, the other in his forties, a veteran
of several other parishes. They lived in a cramped rectory with the retired pastor
and took their meals in a dusky room decorated only with a reproduction of the
Last Supper. Food was served on a large oak table by subdued, attentive women
from the kitchen who took turns being on call. The parish office, complete with
mimeograph machine, was in the basement, brightened somewhat surprisingly by
a wall-size blowup of the spectacular "Spaceship Earth" picture shot by the astro-
nauts from the moon.

Saint Benedict's was in many ways a throwback to an earlier era when religious duty supervised by priests was the norm and concepts such as individual
conscience, ministry of the laity, and dissent were foreign. Monsignor Bosco's
concept of the church largely typified the old school of thought that prevailed in

the diocese. It was a view that saw the sacraments as the source of grace neces-sary for the salvation of the soul. Nothing could be more important than regular reception of forgiveness and communion. Church was where you found the spir-itually right stuff by enacting ritual. Exposition and adoration of the Blessed Sacrament, a once-common practice of displaying the consecrated communion host that had declined sharply after Vatican II, was still promoted at Saint Benedict's.

At the same time, things like "inclusive" worship, intellectual discussion, and folk masses, which absorbed the attention of many contemporary Catholics, counted for little at Saint Benedict's. For that reason, numbers counted. Life flowed from the sacraments, and a priest's job was largely to lead people to them. The church was not primarily intended as a social or emotional self-help institution. It was the fount of grace flowing from the sacraments, and nothing could ever come before that.

The same basic theology was expounded across the whole church, of course, but at Saint Benedict's the emphasis was more matter-of-fact and less intent on pleas-ing the constituents than it was in many places. The parish belonged to an eastern establishment, clergy-centered style of Catholicism that, by and large, treated the church's beliefs and practices as objective and beyond debate. The church was a demonstration, not an experiment. If—to borrow the categories of the corpora-tion—some parishes did research and development while others leaned toward marketing or personnel, clearly Saint Benedict's field was accounting.

The pastor, in effect, ran the parish, as had his predecessor, and that system fit with the tradition of the diocese. Relations among the three priests were cool and distant. They had separate responsibilities and tended to those, but rarely if ever did they meet to consult, plan, or just schmooze. "I'd rather do everything myself," Monsignor Bosco conceded, "though I know it's not the right way to do it." (It was ironic. Here was one of the declining number of pastors who actually had assis-tants, probably the envy of many other priests forced to work alone, and he wished he were by himself.) A finance committee existed, but had never advised the pastor on budgetary policy. Its sole function was to serve as a kind of collec-tion agency in cases where parents sending their children to the parochial school had failed to make their expected weekly contribution to the church of eight to twelve dollars (all year round and tax deductible, said the pamphlet explaining the rule to new parents).

Saint Benedict's finances were as solid as granite, and the pastor tenaciously held on to its assets. Its record of sending children to Catholic schools was, from a diocesan standpoint, exemplary. But Monsignor Bosco worried about slippage. Though 70 percent of the parish was considered "practicing," he had seen more Catholics staying away over the years, and that troubled him.

Unlike many parishes in the area, Saint Benedict's did have a parish council, an innovation from Vatican II intended to introduce a degree of collaboration. It met every other month and handled many small housekeeping matters but never considered major church issues (even Monsignor Bosco thought the council was overtimid: he said he'd gone to his first meeting "waiting to be attacked, but they were almost too docile"). No council elections had been held in seven years, during which time the ranks had shrunk to eleven members from the mandated total of fifteen. No one, it appeared, was even interested in being appointed to the council. The school board, on the other hand, generated plenty of interest and enthusiasm. The parish school enrolled 950 students, kindergarten through eighth grade. Apart from the expected contribution to the parish, the school charged no separate tuition. Lots of parents wanted some influence over their children's education, so the three remaining nuns and the lay board had considerable say in running the school.

Except for the school, however, which had always been the turf of the nuns, the parish was almost totally in the hands of the pastor, and, overall, parishioners were highly pleased with that arrangement. They felt "involved," crediting much of that to the previous pastor, who was widely hailed for challenging them to practice their religion and stimulating their thoughts about what it meant to be a Catholic. They were proud of their parish and what it had accomplished. It had a good reputation for keeping the faith and staying fiscally sound.

During October, the parish was in the midst of its semiannual "pastoral visitation and canvass." For six weeks or so, the priests fanned out across the width and breadth of the parish, knocking on the doors of fifteen homes a day to gather information. The procedure helped keep parishioners on their toes and, the priests hoped, reminded them of their obligations.

Half of the 2,500 families would be visited in the fall, the other half in the spring. Each family had received a questionnaire to fill out and give to the visiting priest. The priest gave the family a copy of *In the Presence of God,* the religious book chosen for distribution that year. The purpose was to make personal contact, collect facts, and gently nudge backsliders. "I'm concerned about people not going to church and to the sacraments," Monsignor Bosco said in reference to the survey. "I can see it in their faces if they're not practicing." His voice lacked judgment or scolding; in his understanding, a little coaxing could save souls. In that spirit, the priests, the chief accountants of the parish, did their audit.

From the canvass and other records, a profile of the parish from the previous year was available. All sorts of data appeared in the report. On the parish rolls were twenty-eight Hispanics, no blacks. Seventy-two weddings had taken place, seventeen of them between a Catholic and a non-Catholic. Communion had been served 182,000 times, 145 marriages were considered invalid by church standards

(40 of which, it was estimated, could be "fixed" by the church courts), and on an average Sunday those attending church placed $14,000 in the collection baskets. The parish took in almost $1 million from all sources and dispensed almost $800,000.

Underscoring the family orientation of the parish was the fact that only 295 members of the 9,500 lived alone. There had been 18 converts and 149 confirmations. Only 152 children from the parish attended public schools: 80 elementary, 40 junior high, and 32 high school. The rest went to Catholic schools. The parish paid $240 tuition for every child attending one of the city's Catholic high schools.

Listed as "very active" were the choir, the financial council, the parish council, the lectors, the Altar Society, the Legion of Mary, the school board, senior citizens, and the Boy Scouts and Girl Scouts. Under "somewhat active" were included the Catholic Youth Organization and the liturgy committee. The Holy Name Society and Sodality had become defunct.

Monsignor Bosco felt he was still becoming familiar with his relatively new assignment. A somber, slightly distracted man of medium build with soft features and receding jet-black hair, he said he'd wanted to be a priest from the time he was ten years old. "I never seriously thought of anything else," he recalled. "And being a priest has far exceeded what I thought it would be. I never realized how much good you could do, leading people back to God, leading a Christian life." He believed his vocation was to pass on doctrine rather than question it. "I'm right down the line on the church's teachings," he said during a rectory dinner of pot roast, carrots, and potatoes. "I haven't done enough to implement the Vatican Council. But I have no problem with anything that the church has decreed."

He also recognized himself not chiefly as an enforcer of rules but a pastor to persons who, inevitably, invited exceptions. He told of a woman who had come to register herself and her child in the parish. In the course of conversation, the woman said she had conceived her child through artificial insemination and did not know the donor, a practice in violation of church moral codes. His reaction? "All I could think of," he remembered, "is that she's the most beautiful child in the world." They were duly registered.

Over the years, he said, pastoral experience had also tempered his views toward other moral problems. Without denying the church's teachings, he felt certain situations strained their applicability. Masturbation, condemned by the church, could be a harmless "part of the growing up process" so long as it did not become an ingrained habit. Sympathy and understanding petitioned unstinting loyalty. A homosexual had come to him: "My heart went out to him. He said how much he and his partner had grown to love each other and liked being together. The thought of separating was painful. I had to tell him that the church teaches they can just be friends but not get into sexual action. It must be hard. I guess it's easier said than done if you're attracted to somebody."

Birth control was even tougher. "I know I can suggest natural family planning," Monsignor Bosco said softly. "But in cases where the woman can't get pregnant again for health reasons, what can you do?"

For reasons owing to conviction and disposition, he could not stand publicly with Father Curran against the church's doctrine. He seemed a most unlikely ally: a nondissenter who saw his role as carrying out the policies of his superiors rather than questioning them. Yet he, too, felt the dilemmas and saw the nuances that seemed to present extenuating circumstances. The important thing, he said, was to keep matters in perspective. Homosexuals and couples engaging in premarital sex or birth control were "not evil or malicious," he said. Then he got to the nub of it, the belief that God's saving acts in the sacraments mattered more than these other things when all was said and done: "Habitually missing mass is much more serious than birth control or any other sexual sin. Faith can become so weak."

By late Wednesday of the same week, a dozen or so groups, including Alcoholics Anonymous and three troops of Brownies, had already held their regular meetings in the parish school, two funerals had been conducted in the sanctuary, the adult volleyball enthusiasts had worked up their Tuesday night sweat in the gym, four couples had undergone wedding preparation in the rectory, and the pastor had received word during dinner that a teenage student from the parish had tried to hang himself. The suicide attempt was unsuccessful. The young man, considered a model parochial-school citizen, was said to have become despondent after being rebuffed by a girlfriend.

Evening mass would begin as usual at 7:00. The Fairlawn section was quieting down by then, schoolchildren having walked home or arrived by bus, most of their parents having made the return trip from downtown jobs by car. The area was crowded with neat, freshly painted one- and two-story homes. Despite many of the trappings of suburbia, the area had distinct earmarks of city tradition. There were streets full of modified row houses; neighbors converged on sidewalks, and children played street games. Unlike suburbia, with its cultivated privacy, Fairlawn maintained a modest degree of public life.

About 150 people arrived for mass, clad informally, stopping to dip their fingers in the holy water and crossing themselves before entering, genuflecting toward the crucifix behind the altar before taking seats in the pews, keeping silent. They ranged widely in age. Several were alone. A burly man wearing a Teamsters jacket came with his diminutive, sandy-haired wife and seven children.

Monsignor Bosco, aided by a chunky adult altar server in white, wasted no time. He rolled through the ritual briskly but carefully while the worshipers followed reflexively and quietly. In a brief homily, Monsignor Bosco noted the chilling darkness that fell over souls such as Judas', a desolation that found solace only in "the light of Christ." Communion wafers were, in the custom of that parish, placed on the tongue rather than in the hand, an option approved by the bishops a few years before. They sang together an antiphon, "Keep in mind, that Jesus Christ had died for us, and has risen from the dead. He is our Saving Lord; he is joy for all ages." They were dismissed. Twenty-five minutes had elapsed from start to finish.

Some parishioners stayed to talk about the ways their Catholicism affected their lives. Florence, a petite woman with a caring, dignified mien, had moved into the parish with her husband, a retired surgeon, in 1958. Fred, a man with pleasant features and an eagerness to discuss his faith, had converted to Catholicism five years earlier. Jim, a blonde, rangy engineer, was new to the parish, having moved to the area from the Midwest with his wife. Karen, an inquisitive, gregarious teacher, was a fifteen-year veteran of Saint Benedict's.

Florence had spent a few memorable months on the road with a Broadway theater company before meeting her future husband and settling down to raise five children. All sixteen years of her formal education, from grade school to college, were spent in Catholic institutions. Her words were simple and sure: "Catholicism means everything to me. It permeates everything I do. I wouldn't want to face life without it. I ask the Lord for help each day, confident that he'll give it to me. My life's been a fairy-tale existence in many ways. Yet there are crosses. My faith sustains me. One thing I'm grateful for is that my husband said when I met him that he wanted to marry someone with whom he could kneel down and say the rosary. We still do."

Fred, a draftsman by occupation, was raised an Episcopalian and married a Catholic. He hovered at the margins of Saint Benedict's, even serving on its school association, for almost twenty-five years before signing on. Far from caving into pressure, he said, his conversion had been an act of faith. A major factor, he said, was that Vatican II had moved the church "from a stringent-type Catholicism to a more open type," and that change helped dispel many of his objections to the church. "No one tried to saddle me, argue with me, or convince me, including my wife." But the mood and spirit of Saint Benedict's began to get to him.

"To me this parish is a family, a large one in which the Lord works to show his presence to someone on the outside. I always sensed God's love here, though I didn't always recognize it. I could feel it in church, in the gym, in school meetings and masses in homes. I could feel that touch. More and more I could feel God's love flowing through this place. As a Protestant I always thought the Lord was around me, but I never felt I knew him. Now I feel at the Eucharist I take him into my body."

Recently he had been laid off from his job. "After the realization set in, I asked God to sustain me. He gave me peace. I didn't worry where I was going. I found peace in the Eucharist. If something happened to me, I'm more confident that he'll take care of things. Not that I won't trip and fall on my face, but I'd have a quicker recovery." While exuberant in his faith, he thought the church still needed to root out many "wrongs." Allowing women into the priesthood might be a good place to start, he suggested with a sly smile.

Jim and his wife felt their faith severely crushed three years before when their child was born dead. "Martha and I went to the hospital and held our five-inch baby—it really hurt me. I was numb and lost, wondering who God was and how good he was." But the people from the young couple's Toledo parish, including those with whom they worked in the music program, came forward. "Those loving people were ministering to us. Everyday people. Musicians, singers, altar boys. It touched me."

Shifting gears from the more lay-oriented Midwest to Saint Benedict's had entailed some getting used to. The couple had worked in a parish where the liturgy committee carefully planned the music. He played guitar and sang; his wife sang. At Saint Benedict's there was no liturgy committee. "We meet Sunday morning and only then try to figure out what we're going to sing."

Karen, a pert woman in her late thirties, taught theology in a Catholic high school. It was her second career, following several years as a nurse during which she had risen to the position of supervisor. During that time, she felt "touched in my own way by the Lord," an experience that sent her back to school to earn a master's degree in religion. The career switch had left some family members and hospital colleagues baffled. "I had been a nurse for thirteen years, but I felt a real sense of vocation," she explained. "Even my family didn't understand it. At the farewell reception for me at the hospital, people asked what I was going to do, and I said, 'Teach.' They said, 'Teach nursing?' I said, 'No, religion.' They laughed uproariously."

At Saint Benedict's, where awareness of the wider disputes in the church was generally very dim, Karen was a notable exception. She had a sharply honed social conscience and was known as an unsparing critic of the church. Her days as a dissenter had begun in the 1960s, and she had continued to focus on areas where she saw injustice. "As Catholic Christians," she said fervently, "we should be on the cutting edge of justice in our culture and others. I hope for one thing that someday the voices of priests and people will be heard—to allow the universal church to really speak."

Karen had dropped out of church for a few years and said she still felt disappointed by failures she saw in it. The students she taught, she said, were no more amenable to rigid doctrine than she had been. "But I won't go anywhere else.

There's nowhere else for me to go. Right now as a teacher the issue of academic freedom and the threat to Father Curran really concern me. But I'll fight. The Vatican Council basically had the right idea. The church isn't supposed to be divided into ministers and people ministered to. We're all in it."

Despite some misgivings, Karen remained at Saint Benedict's because she felt at least tolerated. She believed the diocese suffered from "inbreeding" and lacked sufficient awareness of the international dimensions of the church, but she and her family had become anchored there, and she would remain a house "radical." When women had first become eligible to become lay readers of Scripture at mass, she was asked by the pastor to participate. "The first time I did it," she recalled, "all I could think of as I stood there in front of all those people was 'I'm a woman.' I'd volunteered because nobody else had." After mass, a male parishioner grumbled to a priest, "There was a blonde up there reading. I'm leaving the church." The priest said, "Good-bye."

Everyday life commanded the supreme attention at Saint Benedict's, as it did everywhere. Parishioners saw their church in a positive light. Their children and, increasingly, their grandchildren, saw the area as desirable for buying homes, raising children, and becoming part of parish life. They worried that young people were getting away from the church, but expected them to drift back someday. They worked hard, worshiped earnestly, and felt something solid under their feet.

They were reminded again and again by Monsignor Bosco and his associates that everything good began with the sacramental reception of grace. "Sometimes I hear people say, 'I don't get anything out of mass,'" Monsignor Bosco said the following Sunday in his homily. "Well, you won't if it's just an obligation. When we come looking for the Lord to inspire us, we will hear the Word. At the celebration of Eucharist we have to pray for an ever stronger faith. When faith is strong, it can change us and transform us."

ON OCTOBER 16, FATHER CURRAN SQUARED OFF AGAINST THE ARCHBISHOP OF Los Angeles, Roger Mahony, in a setting that seemed almost comically unlikely, the University of Southern California. At least it was neutral ground. Though the school's roots were in Methodism, that tie had been long since dissolved, and the prevailing image of the institution was, fairly or not, one of bronzed bodies indifferent to the pleadings of venerable philosophical or moral traditions.

But there they were, the two debaters poised to seize the subject of authority and dissent before a packed auditorium of 1,700 people. They were two men from the same generation, both respected, decent churchmen in their fifties whose unusual skills had led them to prominence at distant points on the Catholic compass, two Irish-American Catholics on different sides of the church fence.

Archbishop Mahony, appointed to Los Angeles the year before, was regarded as a key player in the Vatican's desire to restore order in the American church: talented, forceful, and loyal. He fit the mold that the Vatican seemed partial to: liberal on issues of social justice and conservative on doctrine criteria. His stout support for Mexican Americans in general and the farm workers organized by Cesar Chavez in particular was well known and widely applauded. At the same time, he was a law-and-order man on doctrine.

The archbishop's willingness to leave the safe confines of the chancery to face off against Father Curran—an admittedly difficult task that immediately cast him in the role of the "heavy" against the popular nonconformist—won him a large measure of esteem among those in the crowd. Though the archbishop would insist on limits to dissent, the debate itself was a magnificent demonstration of the free exchange that typified America. Only a climate in which all sides agreed beforehand that free expression was a virtue could host such a give-and-take. All Catholics, whatever their theological position, were conditioned by that climate.

The exchange was amiable in manner but pointed in substance. Neither man backed down. Each went to the heart of the matter in an opening statement supposed to last twenty minutes (in fact, the *National Catholic Reporter* noted, Mahony took thirty-seven; Curran twenty-two).

Archbishop Mahony argued his case with allusions to the fathers of the early church, the revised canon law, and modern American society. The hierarchy must preserve and teach the truth, he said, and sometimes rule out "some theological opinion" as "incompatible with the Christian message. Such a ruling has to come from the pope or the bishops" (*NCR*, October 24, p. 20). Theologians have a right to probe but must stop short of usurping the bishops' role as the one and only source of genuine teaching authority.

In the custom of those who plead causes well, the archbishop adroitly anticipated objections to his position and tried either to parry them or parlay them into support for his case. It was true that Americans craved freedom, but the church through the bishops desired to "liberate its members from domination by passions or worldly forces that would blind their minds or chain their wills." Therefore, "If the church sometimes seems to be stern in its discipline, this is only for the sake of leading its members to that true freedom which Christ has purchased for us all." A bishop was an "authentic teacher of the faith" and not "merely an 'ecclesiastical policeman,'" he said (*NCR*, p. 20).

So could a theologian disagree with church dogma? Archbishop Mahony: "This question admits of no simple yes or no answer." The church library was stacked high with pronouncements, some more important than others. So it depended somewhat on the object of dissent. An infallible dogma by the pope was one thing. An off-the-cuff remark by a bishop was something else altogether. What was perhaps more important was how that dissent was made. If the theologian kept it to himself and a few friends, all right. "Private dissent of this kind is readily tolerated in the church." On the other hand, if certain people tried to organize a "party or pressure group" aimed at changing church thinking, that was disallowed (*NCR,* p. 20). Neither must teachers of church doctrine, preachers, or seminary professors openly disagree with the church as they perform their official duties, lest the faithful get confused. Though he never mentioned Father Curran by name, it was clear that the priest's only real mistake was that he had gone public.

Theologians do have a valued function, the archbishop said, even one that may involve dissent regarding noninfallible church teaching and conceivably even infallible dogma. Scholars must play "a critical and creative role in grappling with new and unsettled questions." The church "needs a research arm in which difficult questions are raised and new ideas are debated." But the job required some difficult balancing. Theologians must nowhere appear "to put their own judgment above that of the hierarchy magisterium and in so doing inevitably discredit the latter" nor show less than "reverence due to ecclesiastical authority." The church that "opened its pulpits and theological chairs to persons of every opinion would lose all credibility" (*NCR,* p. 20).

The burden of proof lay heavily on dissenters, the archbishop contended, but even if dissent arose, "it does not replace authentic Catholic teaching but remains dissent from it. . . . Confronted with a dissenting opinion, authentic Catholic teaching remains what it is: authentic teaching." That said, he concluded by repeating his hope that the bishops and the theologians would continue to work together for the good of the church (*NCR,* p. 20).

Father Curran, whose thin, raspy voice belied his stocky build, began by applauding Archbishop Mahony's efforts in behalf of social justice and defined himself as "a Roman Catholic doing Roman Catholic theology within the Catholic faith commitment" (*NCR,* p. 20). The basic issue, he said, was whether theologians could question the noninfallible teachings of the church, and, of course, he had been proceeding for more than two decades on the assumption that they could. On this evening, he would not attempt to outline his points of dissent on the several areas of sexuality he had studied. He would confine himself to the overall principle.

The magisterium had been wrong many times in the past, he asserted, and recounted some specifics. Among other things, the church had discarded its fierce opposition to usury and its solid support for slavery. Moreover, he said, he wasn't attacking central beliefs of the church, without which, he stated, there would be no church. Though the hierarchy's special teaching role must be honored, Father Curran said, "the primary teacher in the church is the Holy Spirit. The Spirit dwells in the hearts of all people of goodwill and speaks in many different ways.

Thus there will always be some tension in the church precisely because no one in the church—pope or theologian—has a monopoly on the Spirit, who is the primary teacher" (*NCR*, p. 20).

The issue had been joined. Archbishop Mahony had proposed a flow of truth from the Spirit through the bishops to the rest of the church in vertical fashion. Father Curran's version was full of democratic spirit. The Holy Spirit, to borrow the biblical phrase, "blows where it will." So the truth might emerge from many places.

Father Curran continued, firmly but without rancor, uncorking a final jab to the hierarchical jaw. Authority must itself submit to truth, he said, and theologians should be primary explorers. "Theology by its very nature should be on the cutting edge—probing, pushing, expanding the horizons. Theology and theologians will make mistakes. The hierarchical teaching office must encourage the creative fidelity of theologians, but the hierarchical teaching office by definition will tend to lag behind the theological enterprise. History reminds us of the truth and the tensions of this reality" (*NCR*, p. 20).

AT ITS ANNUAL MEETING IN JUNE, THE NATION'S MOST PROMINENT GROUP OF Catholic theologians had stood by Father Curran. In a succinct resolution approved by 92 percent of the members present and voting, the Catholic Theological Society of America (CTSA) declared, "For the good of Roman Catholic theology, Catholic higher education, and the Catholic Church in North America, we strongly urge that no action be taken against Charles Curran that would prohibit him from teaching on the theological faculty at the Catholic University of America."

Now that Rome had taken away Father Curran's license, a special panel had been appointed at Catholic University to decide whether, in its view, the Vatican's action was sufficient reason to deprive him of his teaching post. Inasmuch as the panel was charged with conducting a broad inquiry, it was open to various sorts of testimony and witnesses in writing and in person at formal hearings. Seizing the opportunity, the CTSA board of directors, at its October meeting, drew up a strong statement of support for Father Curran to be submitted to the panel.

The five-page statement was full of praise for Father Curran and his contributions to theology. His thinking, reflected in his writing, "is rooted in the Catholic tradition," the board said, and "in all matters essential to the faith he is in overwhelming assent with the hierarchical teachings office of the church." Moreover, in those few areas where he disagreed with the church, he had "done so in a responsible manner." Vouching for his competence and his moderation in dissent, the board concluded, "Removing him from his teaching post is incomprehensible on professional grounds, unjust in the singling out of this one scholar from many of his peers with similar opinions, and indefensible in light of traditional understanding of what a theologian rightfully does."

Defending the right of theologians to examine church teaching critically, the board rejected efforts to force compliance on those teachings that were not infallible. One of the "most disturbing" aspects of Cardinal Ratzinger's letter announcing Rome's disciplining of Father Curran, the board said, was that it blurred "the distinction between infallible and non-infallible teaching. . . . All teaching seems to be gathered into one general category which the faithful must accept seemingly without question. Such an idea is a dangerous novelty, difficult to support from any theological, doctrinal, legal, or historical basis. If it were widely accepted, theology's contribution to faith's seeking understanding would dry up altogether."

In the board's judgment, tradition allowed for dissent on noninfallible teachings, and Father Curran had dissented in good conscience. "It is a measure of [Father Curran's] integrity as a scholar and a believer," the board said, "that he stayed with the truth as he had glimpsed it within the context of faith, despite the cost." The U.S. bishops had themselves recognized the right of responsible dissent in their 1968 pastoral letter "Human Life in Our Day," setting forth criteria for acceptable conduct of scholarly inquiry. Father Curran had passed with flying colors, the board said.

The final section of the statement warned that assaults on academic freedom by the Vatican could be understood as a serious breach of church-state separation and thereby risked suspension of government aid to Catholic schools.

In closing, the board forwarded the testimony to the university panel in hopes that "an equitable and just outcome may yet be arrived at in the case of Charles Curran."

HANNAH'S ROUND BROWN EYES LIT UP WITH IRONIC GLEE WHEN SHE RECALLED the time that something as mundane as being put on a committee had "rescued me." She supposed that most folks thought of committees as she had—pretty dull, more stifling than rejuvenating. But two decades back, the unexciting prospect of joining a church committee had lifted her out of despondency.

It happened after Hannah and her husband had moved far down the road from her small hometown to his, Olny, a dot on the Great Plains, population three hundred. There she had suffered the severest loneliness of her young life: none of her family to visit, no friends to call on, almost no Catholics to cluster with. The nearest parish, which she attended every Sunday, was thirty miles away.

But soon her parish priest, attentive to the needs and abilities of the newcomer, arranged for her to be named to the justice and peace committee of the tiny diocese. It was that event she now regarded with some amusement as "an act of God." Within that group she got well acquainted with some other church people, rekindled her social conscience, and once again plugged into the larger world of Catholicism. "I found people who sustained me," she said.

She spoke during a break at a diocesan workshop she had driven a couple of hundred miles to attend. Since that start, Hannah had raised three children in Olny, where her husband had taken over his father's small farm-machinery business. At her parish, she had become a mainstay at the organ and in the choir and served the church in a variety of other capacities as she was needed. All the while, she had practiced her profession as a teacher in Olny's public school.

Hannah had been raised by parents who respected the church and attended services but kept their involvement minimal. Her father died when she was nine. During college, she met a professor, a nun, whose sagacity and example left a deep impression. The nun-professor had dazzled the wide-eyed student with her learning (she had earned a Ph.D. while still a novice), her strength of character, and her faith. Among other things she engendered in Hannah was an acute awareness of injustice. "It was my first mature conversion experience," she recalled. "I saw her as a real model. Here was an adult, very intelligent woman unafraid to talk about the hard issues. I felt God's love for me through her."

Hannah said that her exposure to the nun-professor had prompted within her a "radical commitment" to some kind of service to the poor as an expression of her own deepened faith. The time was the 1960s, and along with the religious tug she felt the pull of the decade's idealism. She had not heeded her inner urges to set off for distant parts. Instead, she married a young fellow student with whom she had fallen in love ("If I hadn't," she half-joked, "I think I'd have gone to the Haight-Ashbury") and settled down.

Their wedding had been twenty-five years ago. The couple's last child, Mike, had left for college just the month before. In Hannah's eyes, the nest suddenly seemed not just empty but cavernous.

Though she never trekked off to join the caravan of the sixties, Hannah had remained an emotional and spiritual adventurer, though little in her outward appearance would hint of the untamed impulses inside. In her middle years, she was the picture of middle-American stolidity and domesticity. Her auburn hair was worn straight, her complexion was pink, and her ongoing debate with herself over her roundish figure had never seemed to become a serious quarrel. She had no interest in standing out.

Internally, though, her years had been marked by a continuing series of quantum leaps of insight. She had, years before, for example, literally awakened one morning to the realization that she was capable of loving other people without taking away from her love for her family. "I'd discovered that it's possible for me to really love more than one person," she said. "That didn't make me unclean, or an aberration." Her orientation had changed: "My faith moved away from being based on rules and regulations. Now I ask if something opens me up to the life and love of God. Does it bear good fruit for me? Or does it make me more closed and manipulative?"

She and her husband had agreed that the two of them, alone in the house now, needed to get to know each other. As they began, twenty-five years' worth of unfinished business lined up for attention. "Communication is a high priority for both of us," Hannah said. "It's not too deep at this time. There are certain topics we just haven't been able to talk about. Unfortunately, they're some of the ones closest to my heart."

Hannah had continued to find her sustenance in the church. From her remote outpost, she continued reaching out across the diocese, sitting on important boards, committees, and evaluation teams. It was in those circles that she had been exposed to the hopes and struggles of the larger church and the wider world. She had also seen something of the inner workings of the diocese, particularly how church officials could "do a lot of good by freeing things to happen" or "a lot of harm by blocking things." She saw a greater necessity for a meeting of minds. Neither dictatorship nor majority rule struck her as the answer; rather, "consensus, because that requires the hard work asked of us by God, to hash out our differences."

AT USC, ARCHBISHOP MAHONY HAD MADE A STRONG CASE THAT BISHOPS HAD the final word and that even the noninfallible laws of the church were binding. Father Curran's brief said, in effect, noninfallible teachings must be respected but are, otherwise, fair game to those who find justifiable fault with one or the other of them.

Reflecting on a theme that underlay the Mahony-Curran debate a year later, the Reverend Raymond E. Brown, S.S., the most celebrated Catholic New Testament scholar in the country, posed disturbing questions about the biblical legitimacy of certain aspects of church tradition in an article in *America* on October 31, 1987.

To what extent could the Catholic church's doctrine be traced to the New Testament? How could doctrine that emerged after the New Testament was written be linked somehow to concepts in the New Testament? The urgency of Father Brown's questions arose in part from the circumstances in which Catholic Americans found themselves. America was still, relatively speaking, a nation of biblical faith. Father Brown himself had said that any Christian group must be grounded in Scripture if it is to make headway in evangelism. The Catholic church had taught that the church was a composite of God's unique revelation told in the Bible

and subsequent "truths" that illuminated that revelation. But how was it possible
to tell what was reliable either in the Bible or in the church's postbiblical doctrine?

Advanced Scripture scholarship had made some things clear, Father Brown
said. There was "growing understanding of the limitation of human perception of
divine truth" (p. 287). As a case in point, the writer of Genesis, lacking a scientific view, had borrowed the legends of the time to tell the story. Revelation was not
pure, as scholars understood it; it was mediated through human beings. (That
assumption meant all of the Bible was, to one degree or another, conditioned and
fallible.) Another discovery was that the New Testament does not yield evidence to
support some of the dogma that claim to be rooted in Scripture. Nowhere in the
New Testament, for example, do bishops appear as successors to the apostles,
though the church made that claim in the name of Jesus. The actual tradition
whereby bishops were defined that way appears to have emerged long after Jesus'
ministry.

The problem applied to certain infallible teachings as well, Father Brown wrote.
What about the claim that Jesus did not have a human father? Father Brown asked.
The biblical evidence was scant and probably inconclusive. The church nonetheless, in Father Brown's assessment, correctly teaches that it was so. As with many
postbiblical debates over doctrine, different sides might grasp threads of documentation from Scripture to support their arguments. "The debated point, then, is
not so much the New Testament evidence," Father Brown wrote, "but the validity
of church developments related to the New Testament" (p. 289).

Both Protestants, in rejecting some of the traditional accretions of Catholicism,
and right-wing Catholics tended to want to root central beliefs in the Scripture,
Father Brown noted. For the mainstream Catholic church, he continued, "How
to decide what is truly doctrinal and truly an infallible insight into God's revelation
in the area of post–New Testament lines of development, as distinct from what is
passing or even development into a blind alley, is now a major problem in theology" (p. 289).

⎯ ◄ ►⎯

AS THE GRAVITY OF THE AIDS EPIDEMIC WAS GAINING THE ATTENTION OF THE
public, the Vatican issued a set of instructions to bishops governing their treatment
of those most at risk for the disease, homosexuals. Cardinal Ratzinger's
Congregation for the Doctrine of the Faith (CDF) released the instructions on
October 30. Its conclusions were tougher than many Catholic officials had expected or wanted, while others rejoiced in the congregation's forthright judgments.

A landmark statement from the CDF in 1975 had drawn a crucial distinction
between simply being homosexually inclined, which the congregation took to be

acceptable, and committing homosexual acts, which were regarded as immoral and "intrinsically disordered." But the Vatican believed that this limited nod of approval to homosexual tendencies had created a loophole wrongly used to justify homosexual behavior.

One paragraph in particular caused a sensation. It said, "In the discussion which followed the publication of the [1975] declaration . . . an overly benign interpretation was given to the homosexual condition itself, some going so far as to call it neutral or even good. Although the particular inclination of the homosexual person is not a sin, it is a more or less strong tendency ordered toward an intrinsic moral evil and thus the inclination itself must be seen as an objective disorder" (Origins, November 13, p. 379).

The revisionists had attempted to close the loophole: Now the tendency as well as the behavior had the taint of sinfulness, because the tendency led to the act. The congregation briefly summarized its biblical and theological case against homosexual behavior as an affront to "the Creator's sexual design." It continued, "This does not mean that homosexual persons are not often generous and giving of themselves; but when they engage in homosexuality they confirm within themselves a disordered sexual inclination which is essentially self-indulgent."

The main target of the instructions was the organized movement of Catholic homosexuals, the most prominent part of which, called Dignity, had established chapters in dozens of dioceses, often with the support of church officials. Dignity was founded in the mid-1970s as a ministry to homosexuals and advocated acceptance of homosexual behavior in stable relationships. The Vatican saw the movement as a guerrilla operation under its own roof trying to erase the stigma from homosexual acts. A large chunk of the instructions told bishops to resist pressures that urged them to treat "the homosexual condition as if it were not disordered and to condone homosexual activity" (p. 380).

Without ever mentioning Dignity by name, the congregation demanded that "all support should be withdrawn from any organizations which seek to undermine the teaching of the church, which are ambiguous about it or which neglect it entirely" (p. 382). Bishops were especially warned against allowing such groups to use church property for meetings or religious services (one of the accusations against Hunthausen was that he had allowed Dignity to worship in the cathedral). Any program for homosexuals should declare the church's law in no uncertain terms, encouraging "programs where these dangers are avoided. But we wish to make it clear that departure from the church's teaching or silence about it, in an effort to provide pastoral care, is neither caring nor pastoral" (p. 382).

Violence against homosexuals was condemned by the congregation, but, in a sentiment reminiscent of rationales used by the authorities against civil rights advocates, it was pointed out that rabble-rousers do stir up resentment, unfortunate as that may be. It might be better just to stay home. The congregation noted that "the proper reaction to crimes committed against homosexual persons should not be to claim that the homosexual condition is not disordered" (p. 381). When people campaign for homosexual rights and laws, the congregation said, "neither the church nor society at large should be surprised when other distorted notions and practices gain ground, and irrational and violent reactions increase" (p. 381). Too bad, but understandable.

Some homosexual activists don't quit even in the face of the AIDS scare, the congregation said in a passage that came closest to blaming homosexuality itself for the epidemic. "Even when the practice of homosexuality may seriously threaten the lives and well-being of a large number of people, its advocates remain undeterred and refuse to consider the magnitude of the risks involved" (p. 380).

There was an alternative, of course: the "chaste life." Homosexuals were urged to join their "sufferings and difficulties" to the "sacrifice of the Lord's cross" (p. 381) in good Catholic tradition. After dwelling on the evils of homosexuality, the CDF urged bishops to provide legitimate pastoral programs to aid its victims spiritually (encouragement of confession was explicitly mentioned), psychologically, and sociologically, so long as this assistance was "in full accord with the teaching of the church" (p. 382).

Advocates of greater acceptance by the church of homosexual behavior were immediately shocked and outraged by what they regarded as the congregation's hammer blow against efforts for better treatment of homosexuals. Other Catholics welcomed what they saw as a clarification of the church's policy that could stop the advance of creeping permissiveness toward a life-style they considered especially dangerous.

The congregation had again placed the church squarely against homosexual eroticism of any kind. Those on the other side, many of whom had argued all along that an attempt to draw a line between "tendency" and "act" was unrealistic to begin with, now felt even more strongly that Christianity allowed for same-sex partnerships that met the same ethical standards required of heterosexual couples. To be created a homosexual by God, they insisted, meant fulfilling that purpose. Their adversaries had, in the new document, a firm response. Even the tendency was "disordered," a twisting of God's plan.

— ‑ ‑

RELAXING ON THE PATIO OF HIS SPACIOUS HOME IN A COMFORTABLE SECTION of a large midwestern city, Anthony personified the realized dream of millions of Catholic Americans. His family was healthy and growing, he had reached the upper echelons of his corporation, and he was looking forward to a fruitful retirement in a few short years.

But the difficulties of his past hung over him still—he had scars. Anthony had grown up on the far side of the city, the youngest of ten children. From scraps of evidence he had put together, his mother had suffered a severe mental breakdown at the time of his birth. On the basis of what he knew, she had believed he was a twin and that the other baby had been taken from her. When he was three, she was committed to a mental institution, where she underwent a frontal lobotomy. She remained confined there until she died at eighty-eight.

His parents had emigrated from Italy, drifting to several places around the country before settling in Anthony's home city. His father unloaded boxcars in the market district. English was not spoken at home. After their mother was taken away, the children were left to mostly fend for themselves.

Anthony became the only one of his siblings to earn a college degree, a fact he credited to the enormous boost given him by Catholic schools. He was full of gratitude for that gift and for his good fortune.

Seated in a lawn chair, he was the picture of a man of leisure and muted good cheer. He had a round face of rubbery features, warm green eyes, and receding curly gray hair. In the midst of his general content, one of the most disturbing decisions of his life knocked about in his mind: whether or not to leave the parish into which he had poured his time, money, and devotion.

If he went through with the defection, the direction he was leaning toward, it would be by his reckoning the most defiant act of his life. But he was upset enough to think he could actually carry it out.

His troubles were like those that churn the stomachs of parishioners from time to time all over the Catholic realm. Anthony was close to the previous pastor, an older man who ran things his own way and who was slow to embrace the Second Vatican Council. That suited Anthony fine, but other parishioners preferred something more up-to-date. Anthony had been a mover and shaker on the parish school board and helped out the old pastor where he could. Then came the test issue. The school board, taking a cue from the pastor, decided to fire the school principal. A group of parents supported the principal, and the two sides fought all the way through the summer. The bishop finally upheld the wishes of the school board, and the principal left, but by then relations between the pastor and a large number of parishioners had become so tense that the bishop appointed a new pastor. The new priest purged several key backers of the old pastor from top spots in the parish command and introduced Vatican II innovations, like congregational singing and using lots of laypeople at the altar, that Anthony balked at.

Anthony felt his sensibilities were being trampled upon. He was bitter, like so many caught on the losing end of a major, seemingly arbitrary, shift in parish personnel, caught in the backlash. Beneath his goodwill was a remnant layer of defensive pride. He just might pick up his marbles and go elsewhere, though the thought of being less than obedient to the church—even in a relatively secondary matter—pained him.

"I miss the old days. I really do," he said.

In other respects, he was no reactionary by any stretch of the imagination. He thought there should be some way to allow married priests to serve the church and believed Father Curran had been poorly treated. People were quite capable of listening to all sides and making up their own minds, he said, adding, "There has to be room for Curran. If you don't, you don't have a legitimate debate. Ideas have to be kicked around. You can't have an organization telling people what they have to think. They make Curran out to be an egotist trying to overthrow the church. I think he ought to be part of the thought process. Let people decide for themselves."

November
1·9·8·6

—◂ ▸—

L EADING CATHOLIC JOURNALS WERE INCREASINGLY BECOMING
sounding boards for a defense of Catholic America against the
challenges from Rome. Many writers and academics offered
stout arguments for freedom of thought, often served up with an
overtone of defiance in the wake of the Curran-Hunthausen crackdown. In their articles, a variety of authors directly and indirectly addressed many of the conceptual and theological issues that were at
the root of the growing discord.

The bluntest of these responses was by William Shea, then professor of theology at the University of South Florida and past president of the Catholic Theological Society of America, in the November 7 issue of *Commonweal*. In "The Pope,
Our Brother," Professor Shea, comparing recent Catholic quarrels to strife among
loving family members, depicted John Paul II as an intransigent father-figure
pontiff whose unbending attitudes were bringing him "perilously close to losing
his claim on our trust, obedience and loyalty" (p. 587).

"This pope is an extraordinary man," Shea wrote. "He is intelligent, serious, energetic, charismatic, a talented manipulator of the media, a moving linguist and
homilist. He may even be holy enough to clear a future Vatican committee on
canonization. He is also proving himself dangerous. Precisely because he is so
unusually gifted, he is doing great harm to himself, to the church, to his office.
He is a strong-willed man who seems no longer able to distinguish what he wants
from the will of God for the church. He is deeply convinced of the primacy of his
office in the church. He could use a spot of detachment from it. He has made his
own authority the center of our attention, and I fear that he and the church will
suffer the consequences of that mistake" (p. 588).

The pope should pay as much attention to abuses of personal freedom and dignity within the church as he does to justice in the world, Shea insisted. Instead, he continued, John Paul had countenanced "suspicion of inquiry, intolerance of difference and suppression of dissent" and had "decided to crush those he cannot cow" (p. 589). Among the remedies Shea proposed to the pope was "a good belt of hesitation and doubt" (p. 588).

America, meanwhile, devoted its November 1 issue to "New Perspectives" in the church. Much of its contents were generally related to the theme of rights within the church. Among the subjects discussed were the laity, Catholic higher education, women, and conscience. In contrast to the highly publicized clashes over church figures, *America*'s editor, the Reverend George W. Hunt, S.J., assured readers that "none of these essays sidesteps conflict, but each addresses disputed questions in a reasonable tone" (p. 236).

Three entries offer a sample of the directions taken among the authors.

The Reverend Avery Dulles, S.J., a noted middle-of-the-road theologian at Catholic University, reviewed the tradition of *sensus fidelium,* or "sense of the faithful," according to which the truth of the church inhered within the overall mind of Catholic believers. A proposition (a doctrine in the making, perhaps) that goes against the grain of common agreement may still be right because popular opinion itself can become distorted, Father Dulles said, but nonetheless the mind of the masses must be taken seriously into account. Consensus can and had overturned opposing belief and played a key role in winning approval for many ideas. Among those that had, over time, won the Vatican seal of approval: the real presence of Christ in the Eucharist, which was accepted in the ninth century, and the definition of the Immaculate Conception of the Blessed Virgin that won the church's blessing a thousand years later.

The "sense of the faithful" was more than "a mere head count," Father Dulles cautioned (p. 242). It was tricky. "In some cases, no doubt, the vast majority of Christians will easily recognize where the truth lies, but in other cases the authentic teaching may be upheld only by a faithful minority. . . . Unlike public opinion, the supernatural sense of the faith must be ascertained, in the last analysis, through responsible discernment" (p. 241).

Still, there was a kind of pocket veto at the disposal of the faithful. Push as it might, there was no way the church could make the flock swallow what it found unpalatable. Father Dulles, ever the trustee of a balanced, nuanced theological approach, advanced cautious endorsement of the concept, credited to that coveted friend of all sides of a theological quarrel, Cardinal John Henry Newman, that "infallibility does not belong either to the hierarchy alone or to the believing people alone" but rather, borrowing Newman's phrase, to the "remarkable harmony of the Catholic bishops and the faithful" (p. 242).

Attempts to put something past the common view of the Catholic masses had failed in the past, Father Dulles said, underlining the claim among many Catholic Americans that the church could not legislate belief or morality that failed to make "sense." "Church history affords several instances in which the 'non-reception' of devout believers or church authorities has been a factor in overturning the teaching of popes and councils," Father Dulles wrote (p. 263).

The most glaring example of "non-reception" was, of course, the church's 1968 ruling against artificial birth control; more than three-fourths of American Catholics rejected the teaching. Father Dulles never mentioned that controversy but, inadvertently perhaps, supplied opponents of the ban with encouragement. "Generally speaking," he wrote, "the sense of the faithful will be most reliable in matters that are close to the experience and behavior of the average Christian. The laity should have a lot to say about the order of worship, for example, or matters of personal and family morality" (p. 242).

Large numbers of Catholic Americans had been saying for years that the birth control ruling was, in effect, an unenforceable law. Father Dulles seemed in a limited way to be lending substance indirectly to that conviction. Moreover, the gentlemanly, sagacious Father Dulles had added credence to the assumption that doctrine could evolve with the gradual advice and consent of the faithful.

In her article, "Conscience Reconsidered," Sidney Callahan, a psychology professor and author, complained that the church had sent mixed signals. While professing respect for individual conscience, she wrote, Rome had undercut that integrity by demanding conformity. The contrasting message was a re-creation of the "classic double bind," she said, whereby a Catholic was told to be "a mature Christian"—one who took "responsibility by one's own free acts of conscience"— and, at the same time, "to submit and be obedient to the external authority of the church" (p. 251).

Professor Callahan agreed that the church's collective wisdom should be honored. But in the end, she argued, Catholics were obliged to "finally accept personal responsibility. Simply put, can I envision meeting the Lord with the excuse that I knew something was wrong but the church told me it was all right, or that I knew something was the right thing to do, but the Pope told me it was wrong?" (p. 252). Disobedience, she said, "can only consist in not relying upon one's conscience" (p. 253).

No amount of browbeating and forced assent (or "psychological versions of the rack," as she described the methods employed by the Vatican in recent conflicts with dissenters) could compel inner compliance, she said. "One cannot 'decide' by an act of the disassociated will to override one's rational perception of what is, or is not, really the case. . . . Psychologically, it is impossible to believe that what I believe to be so is not so. . . . After a humble self-scrutiny and an all-out effort to seek the truth, I can only believe what I believe" (p. 252–53).

At the core of the church's skepticism toward conscience, Callahan concluded, was "deep fear" and "excessive distrust of human nature" that inhibit the exercise of a God-given ability to make free decisions (p. 253).

A third article, "Women in the Church Since Vatican II," was by Sister Mary Luke Tobin, S.L., director of the Thomas Merton Center for Creative Exchange in Denver, Colorado, and a past president of the Conference of Major Superiors of Women. It was a succinct, polite declaration that the cause of women's equality in the church would not go away. The grievances women bore, Sister Tobin insisted, were chronic, and solutions would be difficult to come by.

She spoke of Vatican II as "just a tiny crack in the door to a recognition of the vast indifference toward women and the ignoring of their potential within the whole body of the church" (p. 244). The feminist movement, the reform of religious women's orders and the increasing number of women scholars in religious studies had, among other things, contributed to the growing awareness of the problems, Sister Tobin wrote.

In the mid-1970s, the movement cohered around the issue of women's ordination, but that drive lost momentum because of heightened consciousness of "a rigidity and oppressiveness in the clerical state and the inflexibility of patriarchal structures and spirit" (p. 244). Fewer women, in short, wanted to be part of a clerical structure they regarded as corrupted by sexist attitudes. In place of the highly visible campaign for ordination, Sister Tobin said, women had banded together to "develop more collegial ways of worship on their own," a stage of separateness some envisioned as an interim state before reinclusion in a reformed "whole church" and others saw as a point of no return (p. 244).

Before the problems could be confronted, Sister Tobin said, some hard realities had to be faced. She reminded readers that in 1985 the Leadership Conference of Women Religious, the superiors of religious orders, had advised the bishops to refrain from going ahead with their proposed pastoral letter on women, or at least to postpone it many years. The sources of women's alienation from the church were manifold, she said. Among them were the exclusion of women from key roles in worship and authority and the lack of church support for the equal rights amendment and for day care. Before any reconciliation could take place, Sister Tobin wrote, women must gain dignity in the church and men must examine their own thoughts and feelings for evidence of sexism. In any event, there was no turning back. "The truth of women's minimal role in the church," she wrote, "is becoming daily more visible" (p. 246).

Sister Tobin underscored the continuing importance of ordination among Catholic women. "Even though many women may not choose to be ordained," she said, "such a message would encourage them because it would convey some recognition of the inequality they have experienced through the years" (p. 246).

For more than a decade, the Reverend John J. McNeill, S.J., had obeyed a gag order from the church, neither speaking publicly nor writing about homosexuality. He had been muzzled in 1975 after writing a book, *The Church and the Homosexual,* that argued for a change in church thinking. He was also a cofounder of Dignity, an organization that served Catholic homosexuals. Despite the restriction placed on him, he had remained perhaps the most prominent church spokesman for greater acceptance of homosexuality.

At a 1985 meeting of Dignity, Father McNeill, who described himself as a homosexual, skirted the line by speaking on freedom of conscience. The Vatican believed he had crossed it. As a result, Father McNeill was warned again in October and told further to cease his ministry to homosexuals. Two weeks later the Vatican released its letter to bishops regarding treatment of homosexuals.

Father McNeill, unable to restrain himself in the face of the letter, issued a scathing rejoinder at a news conference on November 2, thereby defying the silencing order and sealing his fate as a Jesuit. By week's end, the superior general of the order, the Reverend Peter-Hans Kolvenbach, had tripped the mechanism to expel him. For many of Father McNeill's supporters, it was a kind of martyrdom they had come to expect. To the sixty-one-year-old Father McNeill, a psychotherapist and teacher who had served under General George C. Patton in World War II and spent half a year as a Nazi prisoner of war, the expulsion was an unavoidable penalty for the exercise of his own conscience.

In his last hurrah on November 2, Father McNeill, in a statement, called parts of the Vatican's document on homosexuality an incitement to "fag-bashing" and zeroed in on its judgment that a homosexual inclination was by itself an "objective disorder." He said, in part

When they assert that homosexual orientation is an "objective disorder" without taking into account all the scientific evidence that calls that judgment into question, when they accuse all of us who have sought civil justice for gay people as being "callous" to the risk of the lives of our gay brothers and sisters because of the AIDS crisis, and, finally, when they lay blame for the "irrational and violent reactions" of homophobes on the victims of that violence because they have had the effrontery to speak for justice and their civil rights, the Vatican betrays a mean and cruel spirit that is in conflict with both the spirit and letter of the Gospels. I cannot continue to be silent in the face of this evil.

Homosexual rights advocates predictably responded with similar outrage, calling it harsh, even cruel. "We find it absolutely appalling, un-Christian, un-Catholic, unloving and totally unacceptable," protested Elinor Crocker, national vice president of Dignity, to the National Catholic News Service (November 7). The Reverend Dan Berrigan, who devoted time to counseling AIDS patients, told the *National Catholic Reporter* (November 14), "It's a horrible statement. Can you imagine being a Catholic dying of AIDS and hearing something like this?" Writing in the *Washington Post* (November 8), Coleman McCarthy, a Catholic columnist, asked, "in a world all but paralyzed with wars, starvation, economic chaos, underdevelopment and overpopulation, why is this global institution frittering away its moral force with homophobic rantings?"

Catholics for whom the issue seemed a remote, distant reality and those who held fast to the church's moral tradition read the document as a sensible restatement of church teachings and wondered at all the fuss. A few ministers to homosexuals saw the statement as a plus. Among them was the Reverend John F. Harvey, founder of Courage, a small Catholic support group for homosexuals that preached chastity and strict adherence to church teaching. Father Harvey predicted that the statement would boost organizations such as his. In a comment to the National Catholic News Service (November 7), Father Harvey, a priest of the Oblates of Saint Francis de Sales, said the letter "is not against homosexual persons. It's saying that the action [erotic acts] is wrong." The priest said he agreed that "the inclination itself is a disorder" but added that "to say something is a disorder is not to say that it's demeaning."

LAYING ASIDE THE LECTURE NOTES HE WOULD BE USING LATER THAT MORNING, Gilbert glanced through the window of his office to the manicured, chilled campus below, took a sip of coffee, and said calmly, "I may be the most untroubled Catholic you could meet. I've never had any doubts about the faith. I've had no complications with it, no difficulties."

Gilbert's style and elegance more than matched his perspicacity and daunting intelligence. He was of medium height and a model of meticulousness. His raven black hair was combed precisely from his temples back over his ears, the pleats of his gray herringbone suit were pressed razor sharp, and his black shoes were polished to a mirror gloss. He was fifty-one years old.

In fact, his difficulties were with those who had difficulties, those Catholics, especially teachers like himself, whose minds had become riddled with the doubts and questions endemic to the modern age.

For more than two decades, he had been a professor of religious thought in a Catholic university. It was a position to which he had felt powerfully drawn as a young man. Teaching on a Catholic faculty was the fulfillment of a calling, an opportunity to instill the great truths of Catholicism in generations of students. To those students, he had been a superb conduit of age-old religious genius, inculcating through didactic force and sardonic wit the lessons from the pillars of Catholic tradition as he understood them. He was an outstanding teacher, a magnet for those looking for a guide to no-nonsense orthodox Catholicism, and a prolific writer whose works included academic tomes and fictional accounts of people who, in his words, "come to see their lives as significant despite their seeming insignificance."

Gilbert felt teaching was a high calling indeed and was stimulated by it. But he was discouraged about the setting in which he taught. He believed that his university and others like it were losing their Catholic anchorage, drifting from certainty and affirmation to relativism and doubt, even in the field of theology. The trouble, as he saw it, was that the tendency toward radical questioning, the hallmark of empiricism, had been allowed to permeate every aspect of the curriculum.

Gilbert's declaration that he held a sure, uncomplicated faith in a sea of growing turmoil and skepticism was more a statement about the contemporary Catholic church than a claim to personal piety. He looked around him and saw clouds of agnosticism rolling in over the plains of sturdy, trusting faith, obscuring the divine sunlight. His depiction of himself as a simple soul in the midst of worldly snares was, of course, hugely deceptive. Almost nothing was simple or without some conscious design. Clothed in the knightly armor of unquestioned Catholic dogma, he aimed at nothing less than jousting against what he conceived as the destructive forces of the age: disbelief and permissiveness.

The Curran dispute had revived in Gilbert the meaning of the struggle against those forces. Father Curran represented to Gilbert the danger of individuals taking church teaching into their own hands. It permitted a free-for-all, abandonment of the church's special revelation, eventual anarchy. "He foresees a future where the church will agree with him," he said testily, "where everything is up for grabs. He has bought into skepticism as a means of inquiry. And I think he's right about most theologians agreeing with his views. They're skeptical intellectuals." Far from demonstrating the "heavy hand of the Vatican," Gilbert said the Curran case had signaled that "there are limits of Catholic discussion; when people push against those limits with their own ideas, they find reminders that they have gone too far."

Moral theologians like Father Curran "mislead lots of people" by creating "the wrong impression of what being Catholic is," Gilbert said. "They are endorsing everything wrong in this society. By making sexuality an absolute value, they can't bring themselves to say that certain acts are wrong simply because of the kind of acts they are. They are adjusting rules to the believers rather than helping believers accept the rules. If there are moral absolutes—as I believe there are—they are means by which people reach fulfillment. But if you say there are no moral absolutes—such as that which forbids homosexuality—then you can't rule out anything as wrong."

Gilbert said that many people who scoffed at the concept of absolutes when applied to the church's sexual morality were quite willing to espouse other kinds of absolutes without hesitation. His favorite example was the feminist movement, which, he said, taught the equality of women and men as an absolute conviction.

His outlook, against the prevailing tide, had led to a degree of isolation that he had not felt in his early years at the university. He remembered moving, just a year out of graduate school, into a closely knit "family" bound by a common faith and a code of mutual aid. The school provided funds for new faculty members to make down payments on homes and rallied around families in time of crisis. Gilbert's oldest child died during those early years. The kindness of university people at that time had left an indelible memory.

Looking back, Gilbert saw the university as having given him a marvelous opportunity to exercise the purposes entrusted to him. It was for him a distinctly Catholic incubator where he felt at home. But the base had eroded, he believed. Hotshot yuppie administrators, loaded with the latest management catchphrases like "dead in the water" and "bottom line" had taken the place of the priests who once ran the place. In earlier times, almost all administrators had come from the faculty, but the new breed came from MBA programs and, in Gilbert's estimation, "looked condescendingly on faculty" and cared little for the values of old.

Moreover, he said, the faculty now reflected so much pluralism that the Catholic foundation had been seriously undermined. The department of philosophy had changed so much, Gilbert said, that "if you asked them what impact Catholicism had on their work there would be total silence."

Perhaps the greatest loss, he said, rising from his swivel chair and grasping his lecture notes for his upcoming class, was the "sense that there was an advantage being a believer as an intellectual. Most of the thinkers I know are believers. If truth is one, believing in truth ought to be an advantage. But in an age of skepticism it is thought to be a detriment. Some Catholic thinkers are even embarrassed about their faith."

He bade good-bye quickly but with characteristic graciousness. He bounded down the hall alone, convinced as ever he was doing what he was called to do, lonelier, perhaps, but no less determined to impart the tradition to waiting minds.

BITTERSWEET NUN NOSTALGIA HAD BECOME THE STUFF OF TELEVISION, STAGE, and movie screens. The "Flying Nun" was television's candied version of popular fantasy; Broadway portraits included the procrustean *Sister Mary Ignatius* and the more lighthearted *Nunsense,* both evocations of the nun-staffed Catholic school that was becoming extinct; Hollywood went for the jugular in a macabre adaptation of the play *Agnes of God,* a tale about a novice seized by what audiences were led to believe was a form of Catholic madness.

This boomlet focused almost entirely on nun stereotypes of yesteryear. Many Catholics in the audiences sought a glimpse of their own past that, no matter how ambivalent their feelings about it, they could never offer their children. Future generations would not be imbued with the same tales of nun-run parochial schools. The in-jokes, the code words and routines of that particular Catholic culture, were fast disappearing. Those over age thirty knew that world; those younger only heard the exaggerated tales, if that.

Vatican II opened the doors of convents and largely swept away those past images of figures in flowing habits who oversaw every aspect of the parish school. No area of the church went through more upheaval than communities of religious sisters. For reasons that would be counted both positive and negative by nuns and former nuns, droves of women left, about seventy thousand between the mid-1960s and the mid-1980s. Conditions for most of those who stayed were drastically altered. Habits were discarded, communities collaborated on new constitutions that allowed greater personal autonomy, and sisters entered a wider variety of occupational fields.

Much of the reform effectively removed many sisters further from male control. As the women asserted a measure of freedom, many church officials became nervous. But the sisters had some trump cards. They had been the church's greatest source of cheap labor. With their selfless dedication, nuns had been the backbone of schools, hospitals, and service centers and remained vital to many of those institutional systems. As their numbers had diminished in Catholic schools, their lay replacements, though low-paid, came at great extra cost to the church. The hierarchy, therefore, had much to lose by reacting against the nuns' newfound freedom and running the risk of still greater losses. That gave many of the sisters a strong bargaining position. Accordingly, many adopted a discreet "Don't Tread on Me" attitude when they felt threatened.

Understandably, then, the pope's instigation of an examination of U.S. religious communities in 1984 had evoked an angry and defensive response from many nuns (some men's communities came under similar scrutiny, but the focus of greater concern was women religious). Moreover, the pope's order came in the midst of a bitter dispute between the Vatican and a group of twenty-four nuns and four men religious who had signed a *New York Times* ad that claimed their right to dissent from the church's official stand on abortion. To the Vatican, the move represented the height of disloyalty; thus proceedings to dismiss the nuns from their orders were begun immediately. The handling of the incident, apart from the nuns' actions, angered many nuns and generated resentment even among some religious communities whose members disagreed with the ad signers. The pope's announcement, therefore, raised fears of further retaliation.

In his letter to the American bishops, the pope directed them to render a "pastoral service" by studying religious communities and to look specifically for reasons why so few young people enter religious life.

The report from the bishops' committee in charge of the study, headed by the deft archbishop of San Francisco, John R. Quinn, was made public November 10. It was a model of conciseness and, within the diplomatic strictures of church politics, candor. Many sisters said the assessment was fair and better than they had expected at the outset. They said success was due in large measure to Archbishop Quinn, whose sensitivity and acumen eased tensions and engendered trust (and who was later lavishly praised for adroitly intervening on behalf of most of the signers of the New York Times ad to prevent their expulsion and forestall further publicity over the incident). Many nuns felt that their testimony had been reflected well by the committee in its statement.

In their report to the bishops, "Religious Life and the Decline of Vocations," the bishops conceded that the pope's initiative "was greeted with anxiety among many religious" but felt that in their extensive talks with nuns "both bishops and religious came to understand each other better." The sessions had yielded information about both positive and negative aspects of religious life. Among the positive: "a new understanding of and provision for the uniqueness of the individual in religious life," a "growing appreciation of the feminine," deeper spirituality, and "greater solidarity with the church." On the negative side: "a loss of identity" in some communities, "a decline in respect for the Pope and the magisterium of the church," loss of members, and financial troubles (Origins, December 4, vol. 16, no. 25, p. 467).

Several factors were cited as reasons for the dropping numbers. They included "new attitudes toward freedom, authority and obedience," shifting views toward sexuality, "new attitudes toward the role of women," and the "difficulties of permanent commitment." Vatican II, with its emphasis on the laity, was said to have fostered the notion that a faithful Catholic did not have to enter religious life "in order to pursue the call to holiness" (p. 468). The Council had opened the way to other options for service. As Catholics became more assimilated into the American mainstream, the choice of a vocation had become even more anomalous. And as opportunities for women had expanded in society, vocations had naturally declined.

Pope Pius XII had encouraged religious women to become more professional, the report pointed out. As greater numbers of sisters obtained advanced degrees, their concept of service had broadened, abetted by their activism within the civil rights movement. As a result, the bishops said, "they came to see the religious vocation no longer exclusively confined to maintaining church institutions, but also in terms of service to the world and particularly in the promotion of justice and human rights" (p. 469). The link between their grievances and their wider concern for human rights was inextricable.

Contributing to the shortage of vocations was that young people had fewer role models of religious, that standards were higher, and that entry was permanent and required celibacy. All things considered, the bishops said, "it is likely that we are not going to see a notable increase of religious vocations in the foreseeable future" (p. 469).

The bishops reserved their most salient comments for their summary. They noted that recent popes, starting with John XXIII, had appealed for just treatment of women in the secular world. No less must be expected of the church, the bishops said. It was natural that the same principles "be applied by women not simply to their life in society but also to their life in the church. This movement for the promotion of women must be seen in its positive dimensions insofar as it reflects the biblical revelation of the basic equality of men and women even though it may have some negative features which are not compatible with the teaching of the church which must be clearly acknowledged" (p. 469).

This movement would only increase, the bishops insisted. Women would continue to be disturbed by certain church practices. "For instance," they said, "there is considerable and spreading concern over the limited scope for participation by women in policy and decision-making roles in the church. In view of this, some potential candidates find other modes of service and hesitate to enter religious life." Though religious life was generally "in good condition," the bishops said, there were "certain tensions which exist between some religious and the Holy See" (p. 469).

The bishops' admonitions were, not surprisingly, somewhat understated, but the fact that they were expressed at all was out of the ordinary for such documents. The phrase "ordination of women" never appeared, of course, but in voicing women's displeasure with their decision-making roles the bishops were, between the lines, appealing for major change in church attitudes and governance. The most powerful exhortation for change in attitudes and roles regarding women took the form of an innocuous-looking concluding quotation from Gregory the Great, a sixth-century pope. By invoking one of the church's most renowned authorities, the bishops were subtly bolstering the argument for reform.

The quotation read in part:

Since the dawn is changed gradually from darkness into light, the church is fittingly styled daybreak or dawn.

While she is being led from the night of infidelity to the light of faith, she is opened gradually to the splendor of heavenly brightness, just as dawn yields to the day after darkness. . . .

The dawn intimates that the night is over; it does not yet proclaim the fullness of day. While it dispels the darkness and welcomes the light, it holds both of them, the one mixed with the other. . . . Are not all of us who follow the truth in this life daybreak and dawn? While we do some things which already belong to the light, we are not free from the remnants of darkness.

It will be fully day for the church of the elect when she is no longer darkened by the shadow of sin. It will be fully day for her when she shines with the perfect brilliance of interior light.

THE BUILD-UP OF INTEREST IN THE REGULAR FALL MEETING OF THE U.S. HIERARCHY was more intense than for any session in the recent history of the National Conference of Catholic Bishops. Most such meetings had been carefully stage-managed and quite predictable. But this one had suspense.

The wound in Seattle was festering. Archbishop Hunthausen would appear to plead his case in closed session. Bishops were divided over what, if any, show of support they should give their fellow bishop, ever aware that sympathy could be interpreted as disloyalty by the same Vatican top command responsible for taking Archbishop Hunthausen to the woodshed. To do nothing would look like sheer cowardice. To do too much would invite retaliation. For a change, no one seemed to know what would happen. It was a meeting impossible to script.

The other major item on the agenda was final action on the bishops' ambitious pastoral letter on the economy. Without the Hunthausen affair, the long-awaited economics pastoral would have easily taken center stage. It had been in the works for six years, carefully shepherded by Archbishop Weakland; approval of the twice-revised document was expected easily. But no such unanimity toward it existed across Catholic America. Many regarded it as sounding an unwelcome sour note in the rhapsody of the "Reagan recovery." Indeed, it was disquieting, taking the nation to task for neglecting the poor, inflaming greed, and sandbagging the third world, among other things. A group of Catholic laity, spearheaded by two of the Catholic superrich, J. Peter Grace and William E. Simon, issued a disgruntled rejoinder before the first draft was even officially released.

The bishops had nipped at the heels of capitalism, a cow more sacred to many Catholic Americans than the church itself, and had heard protests from the Catholic captains of free enterprise well in advance of their meeting. Because it struck so many nerves, the document had the potential for firing more debate than the bishops' earlier letter on nuclear war. But at the meeting, its impact was overshadowed and blunted somewhat. For the moment, at least, the economics pastoral, which had gained a strong consensus among the bishops, would take a backseat to the more volatile crisis within the bishops' ranks.

As they assembled in their traditional setting, the ballroom of the Capitol Hilton in Washington, D.C., the bishops were aware of a somewhat more obscure issue that could eventually determine the fate of the conference itself. Cardinal Ratzinger, in widely publicized remarks, had raised the question of whether such groups had any competence to teach on their own. The cardinal presumably spoke for others at the Vatican, perhaps the pope himself, who felt that bishops' conferences, created by Vatican II, had arrogated to themselves power they were not entitled to exercise. At the 1985 extraordinary synod of bishops in Rome, the issue had surfaced again, and the synod had proposed a study of the question. There it was left.

The issue was the nature and extent of initiative that the regional and national groupings of bishops could properly take. This much was sure: Vatican II had made a commitment to help adapt the church to its local surroundings—to help it become more effectively "indigenous"—a task in which those conferences were expected to take the lead.

On one level, it was generally agreed that the conference was there to assist Rome in implementing church teachings to the U.S. church. Beyond that, however, remained the question of whether a conference had any legitimate right to formulate teaching on its own. If so, then the conference system could be seen as a move toward decentralization of authority. In effect, a layer of church government appeared to have been inserted between the Vatican and the local bishop.

Some of the more powerful cardinals and archbishops, who had previously enjoyed conducting their business directly with Rome, objected to having to clear so many of their proposals through an intermediary, consultative body such as the bishops' conference. Other bishops welcomed the change as a more democratic method of making policy and as an effective means of shrinking the gap between the handful of kingmaker prelates, who had wielded great influence, and the majority of bishops, whose voices carried far less weight.

The U.S. bishops, not known for their assertiveness, had on the whole responded with enthusiasm to the conference arrangement and had inched down the road toward boldness in recent years, especially in writing their letter on nuclear arms, which at one time flirted with going further than the pope in condemning the strategy of nuclear deterrence. The letter was a sign of the growing vitality among bishops' conferences that, in some respects, alarmed the Vatican.

Cardinal Ratzinger, in particular, was upset by any trend that would diminish Rome's prerogatives. His remarks had touched off a backlash against any move by the bishops' conferences to claim teaching authority of their own. Nearly a year after the extraordinary synod made its study proposal, the issue remained very much unsettled. Many bishops, noting John Paul II's preference for centralized leadership, felt that the outcome would be an effort to clip the fledgling wings of the bishops' conferences. The Vatican had allies disposed to support such a reaction. Most often mentioned in the grouping of Vaticanists were Cardinal Bernard

Law of Boston, Cardinal John J. O'Connor of New York, Archbishop Theodore E.
McCarrick of Newark, Bishop J. Francis Stafford of Denver and Archbishop Roger
M. Mahony of Los Angeles. If the National Conference of Catholic Bishops was
to be weakened, it was widely believed that this coterie of bishops would be instrumental in mounting the attack.

The suggestion that the U.S. bishops might be trying to take too many matters
into their own hands was disturbing to most of these men who had made their
way in the church through exemplary obedience. They did not want to rile the
Vatican. Yet they were in a jam. Their people were becoming more disaffected with
Rome (a November 2 Gallup Poll showed that nearly six in ten wanted the church
to amend its views on sexual ethics). And one of their own archbishops had been
treated in a manner most considered shoddy no matter what they thought about
the reasons behind it. The fall meeting was nothing if not auspicious.

SUCH WAS THE SUSPENSE AND ANTICIPATION WHEN THE BISHOPS' MEETING CON-
vened on the morning of November 10. The main event of the morning was the
valedictory address by Bishop James W. Malone of Youngstown, Ohio, who was
finishing his three-year term as president of the conference. It was an astute,
often eloquent assessment of the state of the church from one of its most respected
leaders.

Bishop Malone paid tribute to the strength of the Catholic church in America,
calling it "not perfect but sound." He also praised the growth of collegiality among
the bishops, citing their work together on the major pastoral letters and on the
studies of religious communities and seminaries. In effect, Bishop Malone said,
American Catholics have nothing to apologize for.

Having described the church in the United States as strong and dedicated,
Bishop Malone turned to the troubled relationship between Catholic America
and Rome. He did so with candor, touching on the primary sources of friction.
Roman Catholicism was not a "federation of local churches," he said, rather a *communio* in which all parts are bound to one another by the Spirit and through the
pope's authority.

"But no one who reads the newspapers of the past three years can be ignorant
of a growing and dangerous dissatisfaction [the word was *disaffection* in the official written version] of elements of the church in the United States from the Holy
See," Bishop Malone said. "Some people feel that the local church needs more freedom. Others believe that more control is in order. Some feel that appeals to authority are being exercised too readily. Others applaud what they perceive to be a
return to needed central control. Wherever you stand, this division presents the
church in the United States with a very serious question: How will we move to address this developing estrangement, to strengthen the cognitive and affective

bonds between the church here and the Holy See? We do not exist alone. We cannot exist alone. We are a 'communio.'"

With regard to the Hunthausen dispute, Bishop Malone said the bishops' conference had no legitimate right to review the Vatican's disciplinary action and would limit itself to offering "fraternal support to Archbishop Hunthausen and Bishop Wuerl in their future efforts to minister to the church in Seattle." His position left the door open. Though the bishops' were stymied in terms of canon law, the "fraternal support" open to them could mean any number of possible responses. The bishops were left to decide for themselves how to define their reaction without directly challenging the procedures the Vatican had used or the judgment it had reached—not the easiest of tasks, at least as Bishop Malone had reckoned it.

The retiring president, his white hair glowing in the full glare of television lights, pointed to three other problem areas: women, the priest shortage, and theological dissent.

Though the church has declared the essential equality of the baptized, Bishop Malone said, women remained unequal. "The years given to us to recognize this inequality and to remedy it are not limitless," he cautioned. In a statement fraught with ambiguity, he asserted that the bishops "do not and cannot stand with those who argue that the only response to this inequality is ordination of women to the priesthood. The teaching of the church is clear on this point. To pretend it is not clear is unjust and not helpful to our legitimate inquiry into this issue. At the same time we must recognize the need to continue our efforts to promote the legitimate roles women can assume in society and in the church."

The bishop had said that ordination was not the only response, but he had left open the possibility that it was, perhaps, one among many, all deserving attention. And he stated the church's clear teaching without indicating whether the teaching itself was right. Efforts to "promote the legitimate roles women can assume" need not leave out reexamination of women's ordination, if Bishop Malone's statement was interpreted in the most liberal way.

Regarding the priest shortage, Bishop Malone noted its most worrisome impact, the decline in availability of the Eucharist. Intensified efforts to recruit priests were only part of the answer, he said. More effective placement of existing priests and consolidation of parishes were other possible strategies. He raised again the growing nature of the crisis and let the matter rest with a question: "What are we doing as local bishops and as a conference of bishops to address this issue?" In the past, he had voiced support for a married priesthood under special conditions, but he stopped short of that proposal here.

The Ohio bishop approached theological dissent with the same blending of deference toward the Vatican and recognition of American interests. The bishops' role as teachers of "authentic doctrine with and under our chief pastor, the Pope" must not be immune from "scholarly questioning or all forms of open, honest discussion," and the distinctions must be clarified, Bishop Malone said. Then, again adopting the honored church tradition of making a point by asking a question (as opposed to proclaiming categorical imperatives), he asked, "How can the church insure the stability of its teaching while at the same time encouraging that freedom of conversation which, even in theological terms, makes for its testing and development?" (It was just such diplomacy that some bishops felt Father Curran practiced too little in favor of frontal assaults.)

He then added an exhortation for which his stature gave him license: "If bishops fail to recognize the questions that the whole world knows we have, the plausibility of the church becomes lessened and its life becomes paralyzed."

Looking ahead to the papal visit to the United States, Bishop Malone had an optimistic prognosis. "Given current tensions and controversies," he said, "we all know that there are some persons who question its timeliness and utility. But they are mistaken." Shrewdly, he portrayed a favorable scenario whereby Catholic Americans could "affirm our unity with him" and at the same time take the opportunity to better acquaint the pope with the church in the United States. It could result in "a graced occasion for the Holy Father to confirm the church in the United States" and for dialogue and healing to take place within the ranks. Bishop Malone was among those bishops who believed that the Vatican had been misled about the church in America by the right-wing Catholic press, which depicted it as a hotbed of rebellion and apostasy. The visit was seen by these bishops as a chance to set the record straight.

Bishop Malone finished. He had laid down a program for the bishops and for the wider church. He received a standing ovation from grateful colleagues. The bishops would now get on with the business.

The other noteworthy item on the morning schedule was the customary appearance of the apostolic pro-nuncio, Archbishop Pio Laghi. Under the Reagan administration, and over the objections of some church-state separationists, the United States had resumed formal diplomatic relations with the Vatican. So in addition to remaining the pope's liaison to the church in America, Archbishop Laghi's position had been upgraded to the rank of ambassador.

As Rome's point man in this country, Archbishop Laghi was responsible for gathering intelligence on the U.S. church and for submitting names for promotion to bishop. In the space of a few years, a pro-nuncio could shape the character of the nation's hierarchy by filling vacancies with candidates of a particular stripe.

Archbishop Laghi, an admirer of Cardinal Ratzinger, had previously been posted by the Vatican to Nicaragua, India, Pakistan, and Argentina (where critics assailed him for being too chummy with the country's ruling elite). His looks and manner belied his reputation as the Vatican "heavy" who was in the thick of the

Curran and Hunthausen disputes and was the pope's bishopmaker. He was a trim, slightly stooped man with gray, wispy hair combed back, an aquiline nose, bushy eyebrows, and sparkling blue eyes. His quick, warm smile flashed a playful hint of the sly, even mildly irreverent humor he could display in private. In public, he was never less than courtly and painstakingly courteous. An accomplished, veteran diplomat, he was frequently mentioned as a leading candidate to replace Cardinal Agostino Casaroli as the next Vatican secretary of state. But that might depend on how well he resolved the current discord in the U.S. church. He was particularly worried whether Rome might hold him responsible for the mess in Seattle, for having read the situation wrongly and backed an inappropriate response.

His speech to the bishops was brief, but one paragraph stood out. As a rule, pro-nuncios, including Archbishop Laghi, played down their influence in picking bishops. But on this occasion, the pro-nuncio mentioned it as a point of unabashed pride. "As I look out over this assembly," he said, "permit me to express satisfaction at the presence of so many who have been appointed to the hierarchy during my tenure as Papal Representative. We have not yet reached the 'magic number' of one hundred, but we are not very far from it."

Whatever the archbishop might have primarily intended to say, the remark had a surprisingly political overtone. Laghi appointments now comprised nearly one-third of the bishops' conference and, by implication, would soon be half. That meant the pope's forces were closing in on majority rule and that the moderate-liberal days of the conference appeared to be drawing to a close. Archbishop Laghi could point to his key conservative promotions—Law in Boston, O'Connor in New York, Mahony in Los Angeles, Szoka in Detroit, and others—with the assurance that even in the midst of his current crisis he was doing his job.

The political reality of his observation was starkly illustrated during the bishops' meeting as the conservative tally hovered around the "magic number" on several test votes. The clearest barometer of rising conservative strength was the showing of Cardinal Law, a chief conservative standard-bearer. The cardinal lost all eight races in which his name appeared on the ballot: for conference president, vice president, and election of six delegates to the next synod of bishops. His support repeatedly peaked around one hundred votes. Liberals were relieved but saw the handwriting on the wall. Though defeated, the law-and-order church seemed to be the wave of the future.

Speeches over with, the bishops plunged into their thick stack of unfinished business through Monday afternoon and Tuesday morning. The election of officers assured moderates of control for the time being. Archbishop John May of St. Louis, a stocky, circumspect prelate with a distaste for controversy, was chosen to replace Bishop Malone as president, and Archbishop Daniel E. Pilarczyk of Cincinnati, another moderate, beat out Law for the vice presidency 159 to 116.

THOUGH BUSY WITH HOUSEKEEPING MATTERS, THE BISHOPS WERE PREOCCUPIED by the impending session on the Hunthausen case. Archbishop Hunthausen looked drawn and tense, and many bishops reflected the pervasive strain. By noon on Tuesday, the waiting was over. The doors were closed, and the executive session began.

Three weeks before Bishop Malone called the bishops to order, maneuvering for the strategic advantage in the showdown had already begun. The Vatican sought the high ground by coercing the bishops' conference into releasing a "chronology" of the events that had culminated in the action against the Seattle archbishop. The account was sent to all the U.S. bishops with a covering letter from Bishop Malone that neither endorsed nor rejected its veracity.

As would have been expected, the chronology fully justified the Vatican's decision. Rome had responded to a "high volume of complaints" that church regulation had been abused. The archbishop had conceded that there were infractions that required "corrective action." The archbishop took care of some of them, the chronology said, but "substantiated complaints" continued to pile up. In the end, the investigation had been triggered by some unspecified annoyance with Archbishop Hunthausen's method of answering these charges. The chronology put it this way: "the decision to inquire further was primarily provoked by documented responses of the Archbishop himself."

Though the session was closed to the press and public, details became readily available from a variety of sources. Copies of Archbishop Hunthausen's own addresses to the body were even distributed to the press in advance.

From the outset, strong emotions threatened to derail efforts by the conference leadership to steer the bishops in a safe, pragmatic direction. Before the bishops lay three documents: Bishop Malone's draft of a proposed public statement by the bishops on the Seattle situation, Archbishop Hunthausen's response to the Vatican, and a speech the archbishop would deliver at the behest of Bishop Malone. These texts, together with a chronology of the case that was submitted by the pro-nuncio, framed the debate.

Bishop Malone's draft statement was a diplomatic attempt to limit the scope of inquiry and discussion. In it, the president of the conference pledged unswerving loyalty to the pope on behalf of all the bishops, declared that the dispute was outside their area of jurisdiction, and proclaimed total confidence in the propriety of the Vatican's actions. The operative sentence read, "While we are not authorized to judge the facts of the case, it is clear that the process employed by the Holy See was in accord with the law of the church and was just and reasonable."

Bishop Malone then offered the accused any help the conference could give. In other words, the bishops would abstain on technical grounds from commenting on the justice of the case but would make themselves available for damage control and helping attain a better solution. If they accepted these terms of discussion, the bishops would alternately plead helplessness and vow helpfulness.

The statement had the backing of the powerful fifty-member administrative board. It had been written before Hunthausen's statements in his own defense were available. Many of Hunthausen's most ardent backers saw the Malone statement as a hands-off whitewash of Rome's heavy-handed moves. They would protest especially against use of the word *just* in describing the procedures. But Hunthausen's detractors resisted anything less than full support for Rome. They felt that the "permissiveness" by which the archbishop had spoiled Seattle was spilling over into other dioceses and must be stopped for the good of the church. The bishops must offer nothing less than full approval of the discipline, though it had regrettably caused anguish.

The deliberations got under way. Archbishop Hunthausen was the first to speak. Described by one report as "visibly tense," he read an impassioned twenty-one-page speech that, in certain areas, overlapped the contents of a reply he had already delivered to the pro-nuncio's chronology but exuded far more of the affective humanity for which he was so well known in Seattle.

Archbishop Hunthausen had a short, compact build with the look of the Northwest outdoorsman that he was by birth and habit. His hair was receding in the pattern of a flock of geese flying toward the front of his head. His face was broad and expressive; his manner was gently gregarious. Lack of pretension and a prayerful, simple piety had gained him enormous personal respect and esteem even among many bishops who questioned his effectiveness as a bishop in keeping the church's sails trimmed. Now in his sixty-fifth year, his twenty-fourth as a bishop, his eleventh as head of the Seattle archdiocese, he had been projected into the limelight as the exemplar of a style of leadership known as "pastoral."

The style of pastoral leadership that flowed from Vatican II was hospitable to pluralism and democracy and was, therefore, on the wane under the papacy of John Paul II. No area of the Catholic world had originally welcomed the shift to the pastoral style more than the United States. And no American bishop exemplified it more strikingly than Raymond G. Hunthausen. An attack on him, therefore, was seen by his allies as an attack on American Catholicism itself.

With respect to basic Catholic belief, Archbishop Hunthausen was a paragon of orthodoxy. He had never publicly questioned the church's doctrines. His stand as a pacifist was upheld by Catholic tradition, its legitimacy having been underscored with the Vatican's tacit approval in the U.S. bishops' pastoral letter on nuclear war. But as a "pastoral" bishop he was also known to interpret the law less literally and legalistically than his more conservative colleagues. Though he had no history of flouting church rules, neither was he inclined to relish enforcing them or utilizing them as instruments of discipline.

In contrast to the Vatican's portrayal of him as lacking "sufficient firmness," he was known in his home city as a man of resolve who had refused to exercise his authority in certain obtrusive ways. His ardent and persistent opposition to the Trident nuclear submarines based near Seattle testified to his persistence in the minds of many Washingtonians. Not a few believed that the whole attack had been cooked up by the Pentagon in retaliation but lacked direct evidence of a conspiracy. The Vatican chronology explicitly denied any connection between its action and the archbishop's social stands. At the same time, aides to the archbishop gladly acknowledged that the promptings of his heart often outweighed the directive programmed in his head, regardless of cost.

Looking out over the bishops in Washington, the archbishop drew himself up and began by suggesting that the crisis, far from being "some sort of battle of wits between a maverick archbishop and the Holy See," threatened them all, constituting "an ecclesial matter with serious theological implications which touch very directly and profoundly on our individual role as bishops and on our corporate responsibilities as members of the college of bishops." Translation: the Vatican could lower the boom on any bishop just as easily and arbitrarily unless the bishops' conference could somehow either stop such attacks or blunt them.

He assailed the rules and methods by which the Vatican had carried out its investigation of him. He had two specific complaints: (1) that he had neither been consulted about the need for such a probe nor presented with a list of charges against him; and (2) that he had never been allowed to see the "formal visitation report, including the testimony against me and the appraisal made by Archbishop Hickey."

Both points placed the Vatican at odds with basic elements of American constitutional rights, including the protection afforded by writs of habeas corpus, the right to confront accusers, and the presumption that defendants are entitled to full knowledge of proceedings and judgments against them. Some church officials repeatedly scoffed at such analogies on grounds that the church was unlike any other society and therefore had its own way of doing things. But on a popular level, appeals to the standards of American justice in defense against attacks by church leaders drew a sharp and emotional response even among many bishops.

Archbishop Hunthausen said he had insisted on going public with the investigation, against the wishes of the Vatican, because secrecy "does not work" and "should not work." Secrecy had already inflicted damage, he said. There had been "a total absence of dialogue with me as to whether a visitation was needed in the first place, and if so, why and according to what specific ground rules." Instead, he said, he was "presented with a fait accompli," at which point he decided to disclose the news to the press. Instead of a "bill of particulars," he said he had been grilled by Archbishop Hickey about several issues involving alleged irregularities. Some alleged infractions, he maintained, "were clearly based on simple misunderstandings or miscommunications of facts"; others had been "dealt with in what I had been led to believe was a satisfactory manner"; and "one or two . . . admittedly needed further attention on my part."

Despite repeated requests, the archbishop said, he had never been allowed to see the Hickey report to the Vatican, which he assumed to be the official summary of "allegations, findings, judgments and conclusions." He said it was understandable that the pledge of secrecy made by the Hickey team and the dozens of witnesses must be kept, but added, "Such unwitnessed, private questionings with no opportunity for the subject of the hearings to face his accusers, to have or to be informed of their allegations, or to defend himself are not a just manner of proceeding. This kind of approach seriously wounds the community of faith and trust in the church."

The entire process, which he called "extraordinarily inadequate," was a proceeding that violated the spirit of Vatican II. Moreover, though he said he had been assured from the outset that the investigation had no "punitive design" but was, rather, a "fraternal" visit whose purpose was to enhance understanding, "the action taken as a result of the visitation could hardly be interpreted as anything other than punitive." The implication once again was that if it could happen to him it could happen to anyone.

He turned to the Vatican's laundry list against him, the areas in which he had been found wanting and forced to surrender to the command of Bishop Wuerl. There had been problems, of course, but they involved "pastoral judgments" every bishop faced with the possibility of making mistakes. There was no telling how many bishops at that moment were recalling how often in their own experience they had been unsure how to handle sticky pastoral situations. How many were thinking they could as easily have been in Hunthausen's shoes for taking certain liberties with church regulations or, on occasion, looking the other way, decisions that might have as easily earned them a Vatican indictment?

Perhaps because he knew that so many of them could relate to his difficulties with regard to homosexuality, the archbishop spent more time on that topic than any other on the Vatican's list of offenses. Though the church's teachings are "abundantly clear on the matter of specific immorality of homosexual acts" and he had "always made it plain that I stand in full accord with that teaching," the question of "the best way to minister to these members of our community is nowhere as clear and, I suppose, it never will be."

A sore point with his critics, perhaps the sorest in the litany of accusations, was his decision in 1983 to allow the Catholic homosexual advocacy group Dignity to hold a mass in the cathedral. Here was the crunch point for many in his audience.

He said, "My public statement at the time reaffirmed church teaching and described my decision as a pastoral judgment. I have subsequently been informed it was an ill-conceived judgment. Perhaps it was. I am willing to stand corrected. But my decision does not differ in kind from the decision made by many bishops to allow local Dignity groups to celebrate Mass in one or another church on a regular basis." He had apparently exerted an effort to act like a responsible John Paul II–type "pastoral" leader by rehearsing again the church's position. But that had not been enough. Now, according to the new Vatican document, the church was supposed to withhold aid and comfort from groups such as Dignity that supported the concept of valid homosexual relationships. But, pleaded the archbishop, how could he be held responsible for a policy that had only surfaced a month ago?

The archbishop alluded briefly to the other allegations against him, ending with an effort to assure the bishops "that when abuses have been brought to my attention I have promptly and appropriately dealt with them, as the records will show."

What was at the heart of this imbroglio? The cause was neither dissent on his part nor "personal obduracy or obstinacy," the archbishop declared. But the challenge "given to us" to be "good pastors" required both fidelity to truth and the practice of love. Again the reminder: they would have to hang together or hang separately. He held up the example of Jesus: "Never did he compromise the truth he had come to reveal, but neither did he fail to extend to all he encountered the warm and compassionate embrace of a loving God. That's the challenge I face day after day in my ministry in Seattle, and I know it is the struggle of each of us in this room."

The charge against the archbishop was, his supporters insisted, that he showed too much compassion. By relating his dilemma to that felt by the Lord himself, Archbishop Hunthausen said, with a touch of defiance, "My understanding of the virtue of obedience has never allowed me simply to acquiesce. It has, rather, prompted me to engage in a process of dialogue, one which, to the best of my ability, I have always carried out in a respectful, docile and faith-filled manner."

Then, in an apparent effort intended, on the one hand, to refute insinuations that he had been a publicity monger and, on the other, to bolster his case against secrecy, the archbishop said Catholics had "come of age" and "deserve to be treated as adults" by being informed about certain crucial facts about operations of their church.

His situation, he said, had again revived the age-old, unresolvable question of how much freedom the church had actually granted a local bishop to carry out his mission under the overall supervision of Rome. Some rights were well established in canon law; others were either implied or relatively undefined. The ambiguous status of the bishops' conference as a mediating structure added to the imprecision.

The archbishop threw an implicit challenge at the feet of the bishops' conference. The procedure against him "ought to have been carried out in close collaboration between the Holy See and this conference. I am further of the mind that this conference should have been the very agency for carrying out the visitation."

He continued: "I believe, too, that it is the proper role of a conference such as this to address the issue of the legitimacy as well as the limits of local adaptation which are truly reflective of a particular church, its history, traditions, and lifestyle, not to mention its special characteristics and problems." He was appealing to the conference, in effect, to assert its collective manhood, to stand up to those in Rome and their allies who would minimize or reduce the competence of the conference. It was a modified Monroe Doctrine: American bishops should take responsibility for these matters within their own sphere of interest. He obviously wanted the help of the body in repelling Rome's incursion, but, given the habits of hierarchical deference, he could not say so very directly.

He made his appeal by calling on the bishops to employ the same values of justice in the church as they preached to society in their pastoral letters. Then he asked for their help in repairing a situation that he described, in starkest terms, as "being all but impossible, even to the point of being unworkable."

The bishops could assist him to erase the marks against him and to rid the Seattle archdiocese of "the unworkable situation as far as Bishop Wuerl's special faculties are concerned." The bottom line "for the good of the church in Seattle and beyond," he said, was that the "governance of the church of Seattle needs to be returned to normal as soon as humanly possible. I would even say at once." The special faculties had to go, and the bishops could be the instrument for removing the cancer. He rested his case, urging the conference to come to his assistance, voicing in understated language the bishops would understand the desperation and frustration behind the speech.

He ended with another reference to higher motives. "My friends, we need not look upon this as a win/lose situation. I do not feel the need to win so that others will have to lose. Winning or losing is not what this is all about. The good of the church is what is at stake here. Nothing less."

As he sat down, emotionally spent, resounding, sustained applause thundered through the meeting hall. It was a visceral, robust show of confidence, the truest measure of support he would receive from his fellow bishops. What would emerge from their heads would be, by comparison, timid and restrained.

Despite its underlying tone of passion, its flourishes of exasperation and its moments of implied judgment against Rome, the contents of the speech were, on the whole, only moderately contentious. By comparison, the archbishop's written response to the pro-nuncio's chronology, which the bishops received beforehand, was a harsher, more specific rebuttal.

In it, Archbishop Hunthausen took exception to several assertions in the Vatican's version. Acting in the interests of the Vatican, he said, he had warned Archbishop Laghi that to release the Vatican document would be folly because it "would raise more questions than it could possibly hope to answer" and "ultimately reflect unfavorably on the Holy See, the very thing both Archbishop Laghi and I had striven to avoid all during this time." But, of course, the pro-nuncio had ignored this generous bit of advice and gone ahead anyway.

If the Vatican had received "substantial complaints," as the chronology indicated, then he "was never told who made them or who substantiated them and on what basis." Nor had he been privy to "what some of those complaints were" until the decision to initiate the investigation had already been made.

As for Rome's assertion that the decision to investigate "was provoked by the documented responses of the archbishop himself" to some of the complaints, Archbishop Hunthausen replied that "if certain responses I made to inquiries made by the Holy See—some of them as far back as 1978—were viewed as unsatisfactory, then I must ask why I was never informed of this fact at the time I made those responses. Why, instead, was I politely and routinely thanked for the information I provided, only to hear nothing further at all until the major decision was made to undertake the extraordinary step of an apostolic visitation?"

Further, the chronology had made it sound as if the archbishop, in turning the five areas of diocesan responsibility over to Bishop Wuerl, had indicated that he was finally getting around to implementing an order that he had received the previous December. That impression was wrong, the archbishop said. The "agreement" had, in his mind, been only recently struck as the result of an apparent misunderstanding.

According to the Vatican's version, it was plain from the start of Bishop Wuerl's tenure that the archbishop would totally divest himself of the five areas of pastoral responsibility to the new auxiliary. Bishop Wuerl would receive these "special faculties" giving him complete authority over these areas from the archbishop rather than from Rome, the chronology stated, as a face-saving gesture to the archbishop (giving the move a less heavy-handed appearance). But the archbishop had dragged his feet until pressure from the Vatican caused him to carry out the original order.

Archbishop Hunthausen smarted at the implication that he had knowingly delayed or resisted an order. He expressed dismay at the "intimation" that "in dealing with Bishop Wuerl and, specifically with regard to his special faculties, I did not carry out my promises, that I exhibited a certain intransigence or even that I acted in bad faith. This is simply not true." He sought to assure the bishops that he "would never carry out a public charade by pretending to be something I was not" (i.e., a bishop totally in charge), nor had it anything to do "with any need I had to hold on to power." It was, rather, a case of getting his wires crossed with the Vatican.

"In a crucial letter dated December 2, 1985, which I wrote to Archbishop Laghi," Archbishop Hunthausen wrote, "I agreed to give substantive authority without, however, relinquishing my ultimate authority." By his reckoning, he still retained final control over the areas to be administered by Bishop Wuerl. The Vatican settled the matter months later when he sought clarification. Nowhere did he indicate how or when he became aware of the misunderstanding. The gap prompted continued speculation that he had indeed held out against Rome until forced to do otherwise.

Previous suggestions that he had "acted in bad faith" had troubled him, he said, adding, "I did not." He said he had fought the idea of such an infringement on his authority, "preferring the course of resignation to what would amount to pretending to be what, in fact, I was not" (an archbishop without the full authority of an archbishop) but had agreed to the deal, on the advice of trusted bishops and close aides, only out of selfless regard "for the ultimate good of the church in the Archdiocese of Seattle."

Each bishop who wished to speak was allotted three minutes and was asked to focus his remarks on Bishop Malone's draft statement. Altogether, twenty-seven bishops took the floor. Despite a number of insurgents who scornfully dismissed the proposed statement as sheer artifice, the forces of discretion easily won out. The conference leadership successfully framed the debate and held protests in check.

Those who gave solid backing to the Malone statement included Cardinal Joseph Bernardin of Chicago, the reputed leader of the "moderate" camp, and two key conservatives, Cardinal John Krol of Philadelphia and Cardinal John J. O'Connor of New York.

Some were critical. Archbishop William Borders of Baltimore, noting a widespread impression among Catholics that Archbishop Hunthausen had been treated unfairly, urged a review of the church's investigatory procedures. Bishop Joseph Sullivan, an auxiliary from Brooklyn, called on the bishops to appeal to the Vatican to review the Hunthausen case. Archbishop John Roach of Minneapolis–St. Paul declared that the Hunthausen testimony made a mockery of the Malone statement, which should be rewritten to incorporate the broader views within the conference. Archbishop Weakland made essentially the same argument.

Several speakers poured out highly personal tributes to Archbishop Hunthausen. Among them was a bishop who said his mother had reacted to the Vatican discipline with chagrin, asking him how the church could treat a bishop in such fashion.

The bishops were, as a body, plenty perplexed themselves. In its coverage of the meeting (November 21), the *National Catholic Reporter* paraphrased a bishop's description of the dilemma as "the need to address a perceived injustice without ending up pointing a finger at Rome."

That meant the usual nuances and dancing around hard realities. But the bishops were wizards at it, having been molded in the ways of indirection and calculated obfuscation. They adjourned Tuesday afternoon, and, by the time they resumed the discussion the next morning, the Malone statement had undergone strategic surgery. Most significantly, the statement no longer described the Vatican's action as "just," but substituted for a more noncommittal assurance that "the process employed by the Holy See was in accord with general principles of church law and procedures" (leaving aside, of course, the question of whether those principles were themselves just). It continued, "As such, it deserves our respect and confidence."

There was no call to rally to Hunthausen's side. The statement reiterated the contention in the earlier draft that the bishops were not "authorized to judge the facts of the case" and, at the same time, vowed to "offer any assistance judged helpful and appropriate by the parties involved." The conference should, furthermore, also act like a family by taking steps to prevent "a painful situation from happening again."

The revised version was adopted overwhelmingly; that was not to say enthusiastically. They had vacillated their way to a noncommittal conclusion.

In a show of good sportsmanship and team play, Archbishop Hunthausen said he supported the bishops' statement. What could he show for his efforts? Some of his closest allies looked in vain for positive signs. One said, "I was asked before our meeting whether we would leave Hunthausen out to dry. I laughed and said, 'Of course not.' But that's exactly what we did." Other bishops made much of the fact that the conference had gone as far in airing the crisis as it did, affording the archbishop a chance to speak his piece so visibly. That in itself sent Rome a message, they said. There were still other bishops who thought Hunthausen had been given too prominent a day in court and thereby garnered undeserved backing against Rome.

The refrain heard again and again by church officials and observers after the confrontation was that the bishops had done the best they could under the strictures they were bound by. In fact, there was no precedent for this kind of thing. Had the bishops done more, they would have, in effect, created church law where none existed. Archbishop Hunthausen had hoped for more, but the bishops who felt for him, probably a clear majority, had to try to satisfy themselves that they had gone as far as they could under the conditions.

WHEN THE DOORS OPENED AGAIN FOR THE RESUMPTION OF THE REGULAR MEETing, a thick layer of despondency lay over the rows of cloth-covered tables where the bishops sat quietly. I had never experienced a heavier, more sullen mood among them. They were almost motionless, as if in a state of shock. But the paralysis would soon lift. Pent-up anger and frustration was about to be displaced onto the next item of business, a resolution on the relatively obscure topic of general absolution.

The issue up for consideration was a technical proposal to restrict the limited conditions under which a bishop might allow a priest to administer the rite of penance to large groups rather than insist on the traditional one-to-one form of confession. A minor matter in dioceses that were still pretty well stocked with priests, it was a growing concern in areas where the shortage of clerics was becoming acute. The proposed regulation would, at the behest of the Vatican, tighten up the already tough set of guidelines for permitting the practice. As such, it had the capacity to arouse tensions between the liberal wing, which resisted certain of Rome's moves as unjustly intrusive, and the conservative wing, which applauded efforts to bring the church under firmer control as steps toward strengthening orthodoxy.

Moreover, the proposal on general absolution was prompted by reports of too many "abuses," the same set of causes that were behind the Hunthausen disciplining. Only this issue directly touched many bishops instead of one. Loaded with similar sources of friction and positioned as it was on the schedule, right after the Hunthausen debate, the rather arcane topic of general absolution became the flash point for unresolved tensions.

The debate raged around the subject at hand, only skirting the underlying causes, and became intense. The barely cooped-up emotions were being vented. In the end, the bishops by a vote of 128 to 121 sent the resolution back to committee. The freedom-from-control forces, protecting local autonomy, had skirmished briefly with the freedom-is-control forces, believers in a strong role for the Vatican. Both revealing and, perhaps, cathartic, it proved to be the sharpest clash of the meeting. After the vote, one bishop grumbled to another in the nearby men's room about what he considered the resolution's regressive intent: "Well, I suppose the situation will change when there are fifty thousand Catholics for every priest."

Having equivocated on Hunthausen and punted on general absolution, the bishops moved on to a familiar item that they were prepared to ratify with firmness and dispatch.

The pastoral letter on the economy had been in the pipeline for nearly six years. Two previous drafts had been rigorously examined and extensively amended. The third was before them now, reworked beyond any conceivable serious objection.

Like the bishops' previous letter on nuclear arms, the pastoral on economics was distinguished as much by the process that produced it as by its contents. It, too, was the result of an extensive round of deliberations, consultations, hearings, and floor debates. As never before in their recent history, the bishops were taking a page from American democratic practice. Their procedures had, to a remarkable extent, taken on the mechanisms of civil legislature. It was a dramatic and, by their own admission, an invigorating shift. Only a dozen or so years ago, bishops' meetings were completely sealed from public scrutiny. Now they were submitting to open discussion complex "bills" such as their letter on the economy.

In the course of garnering theories, opinions, and facts for the economics letter, the bishops' committee, headed by Archbishop Weakland, heard testimony from 150 witnesses. They included economists, theologians, labor leaders, business executives, poor people, government officials, and citizens of the third world. In response to the committee's first draft alone, the bishops filed ten thousand pages of comments and recommendations.

The writing of the letter came during a particularly auspicious time in the nation's economic history. A wave of capitalistic fervor was on the rise in reaction against the "stagflation" doldrums, marked by a celebration of individualistic, entrepreneurial drive. Symbols of business and finance took over much of the popular imagination. Investment bankers and venture capitalists became hot. Radio and television began featuring financial reports and business shows. The making of money had been raised to a new level of visibility, attended by a host of gurus and prognosticators who had hitherto plied their esoteric trades out of the public spotlight.

So the bishops were venturing into shark-infested waters, equipped with some arcane papal encyclicals, the preachments of Scripture, and the church's largely favorable experience with American free enterprise.

But they felt constrained to go ahead anyhow, convinced that many crucial issues should be addressed. And there before them was the document in its penultimate form, all one hundred pages of it, for what was expected to be a final series of pokes, jabs, splices, trims, and minor embellishments before a decisive vote made it official. The sailing was smooth, under the captaincy of the extraordinarily capable admiral, Archbishop Weakland. Finally, 225 bishops voted in favor of adoption and only 9 against. Archbishop Weakland was tendered a standing ovation.

What had the bishops wrought?

The letter was above all an appeal to conscience. It asked Catholics to examine their attitudes and measure their economic views by the criteria they distilled from church tradition. But it was also a self-conscious effort by the bishops to join the public discussion of economic priorities.

At least two distinct voices emerged within the letter: one appealing for corporal works of mercy toward the poor and helpless, the other, echoing an immigrant past, exhorting the nation to make good on its promises of justice and fairness.

The document was the handiwork, by and large, of bishops who had personally experienced economic hardship on a large scale. Many of them remembered the Depression era, often painfully. They recalled a time when most immigrant Catholic Americans were hard-pressed. Archbishop Weakland's own family had been on welfare. Many of his brother bishops were raised by fathers who relied upon the labor movement for survival. For many of them, the New Deal became an enduring symbol of the need for mutual aid and solidarity. Support for the weak and the downtrodden was an article of faith that had never gone away.

It was a theme that had reverberated with growing force in the church as well. Beginning with Leo XIII's 1891 encyclical *Rerum novarum,* popes urged the church to promote social and economic justice. In the words of Paul VI in his 1971 encyclical *Populo progressio,* social justice was "a constituent element" in preaching the gospel. The same pope had drawn on the gospel and tradition to emphasize the church's "preferential option for the poor." The older bishops thus had found their early instincts and predilections reinforced many times over. These were the bishops largely responsible for a pastoral letter on the economy, addressed as it was to an increasingly affluent Catholic America. They were the bishops who could replay scenes of bread lines, bank holidays, union halls, and neighbor helping neighbor. Those lessons were elemental. The ranks of the hierarchy would soon be dominated by bishops born during the post–World War II Catholic renaissance. They would no doubt inject somewhat different perspectives. But for now, the New Deal bishops still held sway. In retrospect, the economics pastoral might be seen as the lasting monument to their generation of bishops.

In their letter, they laid down principles of economic justice and made concrete recommendations with regard to unemployment, poverty, agriculture, and relations with the third world. They stated emphatically that they endorsed no economic system in particular. ("The pastoral letter is not a blueprint for the American economy. It does not embrace any particular theory on how the economy works nor does it attempt to resolve the dispute among schools of economic thought.") Rather, economic policy was to be judged by its consequences, "whether it protects or undermines the dignity of the human person" (Origins, November 27, vol. 16, no. 24, p. 411).

Building on the concept of corporate responsibility, the bishops asserted that all people were entitled to take part in the economic life of a society, adding, "All members of society have a special obligation to the poor and vulnerable" (p. 411).

Economic rights such as shelter, clothing, basic education, work, rest, and health care were as fundamental as political rights, the bishops said. Society had a moral obligation to tailor its economy so that these rights were safeguarded and so that the standards of decency and dignity were fulfilled. But selfishness, avarice, and idolatry threatened to thwart the attainment of those goals.

The conviction that the poor had a special claim on our economic interests took several directions. The bishops invoked a picture of a hoped-for biblical society in which people acted as one another's keepers but also pointed to the clear and present dangers that stood in the way of that end. Concentrations of wealth and power undermined the possibility of making essential goods available to all people, the bishops said. Greed, materialism, and the stockpiling of land and resources at the expense of the downtrodden were also decried.

Looking at America, they were thankful for the progress and freedom brought about by the country's political and economic climate, but lamented some grievous shortcomings in economic performance. They saw a nation where the disparity in income and assets was much too wide, where far too many people were unemployed, where too much job discrimination still existed, where a dangerous and disproportionate chunk of the federal budget went to defense while social programs suffered, where there was union busting and where too few efforts were being made to improve the lot of a bulging underclass.

Their severest reprimand accompanied the observation that "harsh poverty" is "increasing in the United States, not decreasing." Some 33 million Americans were poor and another 20–30 million needy, they reported, citing government statistics. "That so many people are poor in a nation as rich as ours is a social and moral scandal that we cannot ignore" (p. 414).

In setting forth binding principles, the bishops had attempted to evoke the church's traditional precepts of economic morality, mutual responsibility, human dignity, and justice through participation of all people. They then laid down a number of specific proposals. Implicit in their view was that the federal government should and must help realize the goals of a fair and just economy by doing what private initiative and local jurisdictions could not or would not do.

Thus, the bishops called for full employment, urging the federal government to help create jobs and expand job training. They advocated a rise in the minimum wage, reform of welfare programs, and a narrowing of the income gap between rich and poor. Pointing out that the gap had been increasing and was one of the widest among nations in the industrial world, the bishops said that Catholic social teaching did not require "absolute equity in the distribution of income and wealth." Some inequality was acceptable as a source of economic incentive. But the "norms" of that teaching also suggested that "extreme inequalities are detrimental to the development of social solidarity and community. In view of these norms we find the disparities of income and wealth in the United States to be unacceptable" (p. 430).

The bishops also spoke about farms and foreign relations. They bewailed the decline of the family farm as a detriment to the "diversity and richness in American society" (p. 433) and as a loss of meaningful work. Government should help increase productivity on smaller farms, and farmers should enhance their prospects by cooperating in such matters as the purchase of heavy machinery. They added, "Farmers must also end their opposition to farm-worker unionization" (p. 435).

Acknowledging that economic relations between the United States and third world countries involved highly complex issues, the bishops nonetheless cut through the thicket with some clear imperatives, the foremost being the demand that policies and practices be governed by the "preferential option for the poor" (p. 437). Business and trade must be conducted with a view toward avoiding exploitation and fostering sound economic growth in the third world. The bishops encouraged constructive investment abroad but warned that it could "create or perpetuate dependency, harming especially those at the bottom of the economic ladder. . . . Foreign investors, attracted by low wage rates in less-developed countries, should consider both the potential loss of jobs in the home country and the potential exploitation of workers in the host country" (p. 439).

The bishops took the United States to task for failing to provide adequate foreign assistance. "We are dismayed that the United States, once the pioneer in foreign aid, is almost last among the 17 industrial nations in the Organization for Economic Cooperation and Development in percentage of gross national product devoted to aid." American grants to the third world were, in the bishops' estimation, too geared to military competition with the Soviets. Weapons comprised far too much of the aid budget. In 1985, they noted, "the United States alone budgeted more than 20 times as much for defense as for foreign assistance, and nearly two-thirds of the latter took the form of military assistance (including subsidized arms sales) or went to countries because of their perceived strategic value to the United States" (p. 440). The arms race was condemned as a menace that must be reversed.

As a general strategy for attacking these ills, the bishops proposed a "New American Experiment: Partnership for the Public Good." The concept involved cooperative economic planning between industry and labor, among local and regional organizations, and on the national and international level.

In its final section, the bishops exhorted Catholic Americans to take up the challenges posed by their pastoral instruction and to put its concepts to work in their lives. Catholics were urged to renounce materialism and self-centeredness and to practice those principles and values outlined in the letter. Their personal economic choices at home and on the job should be made in light of those teachings. "In the workplace the laity are often called to make tough decisions with little information about the consequences that such decisions have on the economic lives of others. Such times call for collaborative dialogue, together with prayerful reflection on Scripture and ethical norms" (pp. 444–45).

The church likewise must be called to account for its own economic policies. "All the moral principles that govern the just operation of any economic endeavor apply to the church and its agencies and institutions; indeed the church should be exemplary" (p. 446). Among other things, the church must pay fair wages, honor the right of its employees to organize, be ready to divest stock in ethically unacceptable situations, and make generous use of its substantial property.

Subjecting the church to these standards opened their flanks to some stinging criticism. The underlying issue, justice in the church, had all sorts of ramifications, particularly among women, many of them teachers in Catholic schools and employees in church organizations.

Having finished their second major pastoral letter in three years, the bishops faced the even more formidable task of bringing it to the attention of Catholic Americans and convincing them of its pertinence. Toward that end, they approved an implementation budget of $525,000. The campaign to educate the public had already begun. On November 9, public television aired an hour-long documentary, "God and Money," that highlighted church projects that exemplified the letter's concern for the poor.

A HIGHLY VISIBLE COTERIE OF OPPONENTS HAD ALREADY TAKEN AIM AT THE DOCument. Most were well-known, well-heeled, die-hard apologists for capitalism who seemed to take particular umbrage at the bishops' intrusion into territory they considered sacred unto themselves.

The most prominent center of resistance was the Lay Commission on Catholic Social Teaching and the U.S. Economy, a group of twenty-nine conservatives headed by Michael Novak of the American Enterprise Institute and William Simon, the multimillionaire former treasury secretary. Two years before, as the bishops were to take up the first draft of the pastoral letter, the commission had gone public with a lengthy criticism of the letter's analysis. That revised rebuttal surfaced again in the wake of the pastoral's passage.

Though professing sincere respect for the bishops' work, Novak, Simon, and company perhaps inevitably sounded patronizing, assuming for themselves a knowledge of worldly affairs that was presumably out of the reach of clerics. Better if well-meaning bishops had stayed out of matters they cannot hope to comprehend, the commission report seemed to say, but since they had gone ahead and done it anyway, it is our duty as Catholic gentlemen to courteously reprove them.

Significantly, the commission found grounds for claiming that the third draft was improved enough over its predecessors to qualify it "clearly as a procapitalist document," thus absolving it of the lay commission's darkest suspicions. But there was still plenty to grouse about.

Though it was "admirable" for the bishops to seek the betterment of the poor, the commission said, the letter's proposals were more likely to "hurt those it intends to help." The bishops were seen as barking up the wrong trees. Their document was faulted for assigning too large an economic role to government, showing an "inadequate grasp" of how wealth is created and of profits and market dynamics, and for displaying an "inadequate exposition of liberty." The discussion of "poverty, welfare, unemployment and taxation" were interpreted as "significantly one-sided" in favor of government initiatives and sacrifices by the rich.

The lay commission also used the bishops' pledge to practice economic justice within the church as an opportunity to prod them to "remove the scandal" of retired nuns living in poverty. They said the church's word was contingent on rescuing the nuns: "economic justice for all must be preceded by economic justice for nuns."

On a sun-dappled campus at the other end of the continent from Washington, D.C., the news of Hunthausen and the economics pastoral caused nary a ripple.

From his modestly appointed president's office, Father Caron monitored the campus rhythms as reflexively as a meteorologist tracked the seasonal fluctuations of the weather. Like his counterparts at other Catholic colleges, he belonged to two spheres, the church and the academy. There was the liturgical year and the calendar of the semesters. Each had its own cycle and tempo, sometimes overlapping, as when Thanksgiving unfolded into Advent, sometimes thematically similar, as in the late spring, when the joys of commencement and Pentecost distantly echoed each another.

As he sat behind his uncluttered desk of polished teak, his lanky frame filling the generous contours of the black leather chair emblazoned with the maroon-and-white school insignia, Father Caron mused about the various hats he wore.

As a priest, he was part of a small religious community that knelt together at the Eucharist, took meals together, and accepted direction under the order's overall ministry. That was his generic bond, he said. But it was more complicated than that, for some of the brethren with whom he shared equality in community were also faculty members whose destinies were, to an extent, in his hands, requiring from him a degree of awkward detachment. Furthermore, when he entered the classroom to teach ethics, he became a theologian subject to the pressures to stay within church doctrine. He had pushed the limits, which made him potentially susceptible to the discipline of the local bishop, a staunch conservative. In the midst of all those competing loyalties, Father Caron sometimes felt as if he existed in no-man's-land.

Despite the perplexities and necessary adjustments, he said with a self-deprecating grin, the rewards had been more than bountiful.

This was his seventh year at the helm of Saint Ambrose and the forty-third of his life. He was a child of the East Coast, where the American church was the most hidebound. All of his formal schooling, through his Ph.D. at an Ivy League university, had taken place east of the Mississippi. The West Coast had taken some getting used to. Church regulations and observances meant even less among the 60 percent of Saint Ambrose's Catholic students than they had among those in the eastern schools where he had taught. Ecumenism, on the other hand, meant more—perhaps, he felt, because of the widespread indifference to the church.

The relative complacency toward religion both kept him on his toes as a spokesman for the faith and added to his solitude. He recognized the situation for what it was—a Catholic priest who was something of a stranger even in his own land—without appearing to use it as an excuse for feeling sorry for himself.

On the contrary, he was glad to have the job and still surprised to have been picked for it. He had been teaching at a Catholic college in the Northeast, prepared to stay a long time. Someone had placed him in nomination, the list was whittled down in short order, and, next thing he knew, the offer was his.

Several personal attributes had commended him. Among them were an impressive record as student and teacher, administrative competence, an outgoing manner, youthful enthusiasm, dedication to his priestly vocation, and the ability to mend fences. Those talents had been stoutly tested. Saint Ambrose was creaking along when he arrived, badly in need of new blood. The last president, though immensely respected, had postponed many necessary changes in his final years. Like many small Catholic colleges, Saint Ambrose was struggling for survival with integrity. It had been time for boldness.

With his innate confidence and a healthy supply of optimism, he had plunged in, making the rounds of alumni dinners, befriending potential donors, reshaping the curriculum, hiring new faculty, attempting to salve old frictions among professors, hearing student complaints, teaching courses of his own, seeking to improve the college's applicant pool, and much else. Steadily, morale improved, the endowment climbed, and Father Caron got a better feel for the lay of the land.

He was pleased with the changes and quick to describe the results as a team effort, crediting faculty, members of the board, and administrators for providing the crucial ingredients. A large dose of humility was not primarily a diplomatic gesture, he said. It was an acknowledgment of reality.

Though the college's vital signs had improved, Father Caron was anxious about the recent actions by the Vatican against Archbishop Hunthausen and Father Curran. They were ominous signs, he thought, and potentially very mischievous for one trying to keep a Catholic college on an even keel. He was especially adamant about maintaining free and open inquiry on Catholic campuses. If the church tried to put clamps on the intellect, he predicted big trouble. Like Father Curran, he was a moral theologian. The ax had cut close. He was preparing a speech for delivery at the college soon; in it he would argue that it was not only possible but necessary to retain both Catholic values and academic freedom. The church had no reason to be afraid of dissent. He would condemn attempts at indoctrination, contending instead that "the university must be a place where intellectual debate and scholarly inquiry flourish."

His own vocational choice had been the outgrowth of much self-inquiry. He was raised in New Jersey, the elder of two sons born to a dentist with French-Canadian roots and a housewife from an Irish-Italian background. The family was devout. The four said the rosary together before dinner and faithfully attended mass. As a boy, he was diligent, studious, well-behaved, and an avid tennis player; he completed his homework assignments on time and tried his best to please his parents. The choice of a Catholic college seemed natural. He went off to pursue mathematics, play on the tennis team, and quite possibly realize his father's hopes by settling on a career in medicine.

By his sophomore year, however, he had switched his major to philosophy. Moreover, his interest in the work of residence halls priests of the order was inclining him toward the seminary. When the choice became definite in his senior year, his father's initial response was disappointment, but that eventually gave way to acceptance. His enthusiastic mother, on the other hand, hastened his enrollment in the group of novices set to enter seminary the summer after his graduation. He awaited induction as a lifeguard at a hometown pool.

The year's novitiate, he recalled, was sheer hell. He depicted the novice master as a martinet who was especially fond of harassing and ragging those who had already been to college. He credited his absorption in a stack of books he'd brought along with enabling him to survive the ordeal. Many didn't. A class of forty-eight began the training; seventeen finished.

Though his theological studies took place during the upheavals of the 1960s, the social revolution, by his own admission, pretty much passed him by. His most memorable service during that time was counseling adolescent boys who were locked up for committing federal offenses. Finishing seminary studies, he received ordination and began teaching college students in a religious studies program. That experience deepened his conviction that he belonged in higher education. Graduate school was next, accompanied by more teaching and a taste of administration. Along the way he developed a parallel interest in the religious needs of homosexuals. He became chaplain to a local group of Catholic homosexuals and took a leading role in creating a new ministry to gays.

Just as he had gravitated toward the priesthood, then the academic life, so too he had found himself easing into a college presidency. He hadn't felt quite prepared, but it seemed right. There was an inner logic to it that impressed itself on him as a stage in a vocation with its own godly reasons and its own source of validation. From his president's chair, he said with a hearty laugh that he felt that, for now at least, he was just where he ought to be.

December

1·9·8·6

——

ADVENT 1986, THE FIRST SUNDAY OF DECEMBER. TWO OF THE four purple candles, arranged in a wreathlike circle and lit in succession on the Sabbaths leading to Christmas, glowed softly near the altar of Annunciation parish.

Caleb and Cindy had brought their infant daughter, Paula, to be baptized on that day. They and the godparents, Caleb's friend Bob and Cindy's sister, Karen, had gathered at the front of the sanctuary between two other baptismal parties. Two babies slept; the third was being cradled in the arms of his mother. The grownups, decked out in their finery, shuffled nervously while Father Reilly, straight from celebrating the final mass of the morning, readjusted his liturgical bearings from the sacrament just completed to the one coming up. He looked tired.

Caleb, a lanky man of thirty-three with dark, angular features, struck a dapper pose in his three-piece gray suit, blue shirt, and red tie. Cindy, twenty-nine, blonde and fair, looked striking in a white skirt and turquoise blouse. Paula's frilly christening dress was a family heirloom: it had been worn by her mother, her grandmother, a great aunt, and an aunt. It was, as the godfather joked, a weighty tradition for a three-month-old to carry.

Otherwise, tradition was being tailored. Caleb was a lifelong Catholic of Polish origins; Cindy was ancestrally a Methodist. Paula was being baptized Catholic, as her older sister, Susan, had been, by negotiated agreement rather than by default. The couple had been married for five years, but their religious lives could not be said to be smoothly intertwined. That set them apart from the mainstream of intermarried couples. About 45 percent of Catholics married non-Catholics these days. Each intermarried couple took that reality with a different degree of seriousness, and for each it created a different degree of complexity in their lives.

For many, religion counted for so little that the differences meant nothing. Some couples sidestepped the issue entirely in an effort (sometimes dreadfully unsuccessful) to keep peace; others attempted to resolve real and potential difficulties by jointly adopting the religious identity of one or the other (in the 1950s, 75 percent of the conversions were to Catholicism; now the Catholic church was losing more to other faiths than it was gaining). Caleb and Cindy were unusual. They were deeply devoted to separate churches and determined to acknowledge and honor those distinct loyalties, with respect, in their home.

It had not been easy, for both cared. Cindy had signed the papers promising not to stand in the way of her children's receiving a Catholic upbringing, but with some qualms. For Caleb, reared in the old school of Catholicism, the requirement made perfect sense. They both approached baptism, however, as a solemn duty and celebration.

The Catholic concept of baptism itself had undergone some transformation as a result of the Second Vatican Council. No longer was it seen as a hedge for victims of infant death against consignment to limbo—traditionally, a place at the edge of heaven whose inhabitants were spared punishment but denied full access to God's glory. Limbo had lost credibility in official Catholic theology. Otherwise, baptism had lost none of its powerful significance. Its purpose had only shifted farther away from "protection" to "inclusion" into the family of the church.

But in the popular mind, of course, entrenched folkways died hard. As a boy, Caleb had imbibed the strange, exotic, mildly chilling tales of limbo, which smacked of superstition and therefore couldn't be entirely sloughed off. To cover all bases, he had baptized both his children in the maternity ward of the hospital right after they were born, acting under a special provision that allowed nonclerics to perform the rite under certain conditions. But that was just insurance until it could be done officially in church.

Caleb's parents, Polish immigrants, sat in the small gathering of celebrants, as did Cindy's, a couple with many generations of American forebears. The families had greeted one another beforehand and would meet later at Caleb and Cindy's home. Cindy had popped a ham in the oven before leaving for church. The two sets of relatives, still strangers to one another religiously and culturally, would rejoice over the common meal.

Father Reilly raised his head, made a summoning scan with his eyes, and began the rite. After asking each couple to speak the name they had chosen for their child, he asked them, "You have asked to have your children baptized. In doing so you are accepting the responsibility of training them in the practice of the faith. It will be your duty to bring them up to keep God's commandments as Christ taught us, by loving God and our neighbor. Do you clearly understand what you are undertaking?"

They answered together: "We do."

There followed a Gospel reading, intercessions, the "prayer of exorcism," anointing, and the "renunciation of sin and profession of faith" that asked them to reject Satan. Finally came the baptism. Paula was second. As her mother tilted her backward on a bracing arm and her father gently laid his hand over her heart, the priest poured the first stream of baptismal water "in the name of the Father" over Paula's forehead toward the crown of her head. He repeated the ritual, once "in the name of the Son" then "in the name of the Holy Spirit."

Each child was then silently anointed on the head with chrism oil to symbolize entrance into Christ's ministry of priest, prophet, and king; clothed in a white garment as a sign of Christian dignity; and given a candle as a reminder that they "are to walk always as children of the light." Father Reilly touched the mouth and ears of each child as he prayed that Jesus would "soon touch your ears to receive his word, and your mouth to proclaim his faith . . ."

Together they recited the "Our Father," Caleb and Cindy, their parents, and friends uniting in the ancient prayer of Christ that predated the fracturing of Christianity into separate churches. Father Reilly blessed them and dismissed them. Paula and her fellow pink-cheeked initiates, David and Kathleen, sweetly unaware of the larger purposes behind the ministrations bestowed on them, were ushered into the expansive household of God.

Later, at their split-level home among rolling hills and scattered subdivisions, Caleb and Cindy reminisced about the steps they had taken to accommodate each other's backgrounds. Over coffee and oven-fresh gingerbread, they recalled their first meeting—a blind date—when he was finishing his training in optometry and she was teaching elementary school. It was instant attraction for both. They were married two years later, but not after encountering some resistance on religious grounds. Caleb's godmother objected strenuously to his choice of a Protestant partner and had not spoken to him since. The pastor of his home parish refused to take part in the wedding; a monsignor friend agreed to fill in. The ceremony took place in Cindy's Presbyterian church with the minister and the monsignor presiding.

They had thought about having children and where they would go to church. "Neither of us wanted to convert," Cindy said, "and we didn't expect either one to change. But I had to sign the paper that I would not stop my children from being Catholic. It gave me a strange feeling—What right did the Catholic church have to say that?—but I loved Caleb, so I went along with it."

The arrival of their first child, Susan, two years later, led to discussions about where she should be baptized. "I finally said, 'Fine, we'll have her baptized in the Catholic church,'" Cindy said, "and I was taking her to church with me out of convenience. Caleb was going to his church by himself. It didn't bother me so much because I had her with me. Along came Paula, and we had more discussions. We were going through a rough time, off to our own churches alone. I guess I wanted his church to be more broad-minded, not to think it's the only church there is, and if that's the way it was, I didn't want Paula baptized in it. I didn't know what to do. It was a sore subject. So I talked to my minister, and he suggested a compromise. He said that if we baptized the baby in the Catholic church Caleb could come to my church every other Sunday or so. We agreed. He goes to his church every week and to mine every two weeks or so."

The children would go "back and forth" between churches, Cindy said, so as to "grow up with a look at the good points and bad points of both religions." One other provision in their common accord: The children would not attend Catholic schools. "That I couldn't handle," Cindy said.

Would either care if the children eventually embraced the church of the other?

Caleb: "I wouldn't let them silently escape me. If I thought in my mind that I'd done my best to give them a good example and they'd seen the beautiful things of my faith—then I'd probably not be disturbed. But if I'd been slack and didn't make it enjoyable to go to mass, then I'd be disappointed."

Cindy: "No, I wouldn't be disappointed, because I'm facing it now. I'm the one giving them up by baptizing them in the Catholic church. I supposed it wouldn't bother me, but I don't know. We just have to accept each step as we go along. We'll just have to see."

THE CATHOLIC CONFERENCE OF MARYLAND SOUGHT TO APPLY SALIENT FEATURES of the recent U.S. bishops' pastoral letter on the economy to conditions close to home. A statement of analysis and specific proposals regarding taxes, joblessness, poverty, hunger, and housing was issued in the name of the conference leadership, which included the bishops of Baltimore (birthplace of the American hierarchy in 1789), Washington, D.C., and Wilmington, Delaware. The statement was replete with hard facts and blunt advice. Echoing the central appeal of the national pastoral approved in November, the December 6 statement by the Maryland conference declared that policies must be judged by their effect on the poor. It called for revision of the state tax codes to ease burdens on the lowest income groups and criticized the Maryland tax system as "regressive" and unfair. Noting that one hundred thousand Marylanders wanted work but could not find it, the bishops urged a "full-employment consensus" that would spur job creation through private and public initiatives and training in adequate employment skills. One in ten residents of the state lacked "sufficient material resources required for a decent life," the statement said, altogether about seventy thousand families. Maryland ranked sixth nationally in per capita income and twenty-sixth in the aid it provided families with dependent children. More than seven hundred thousand citizens went hungry at some point each month. Proposed remedies included a boost in welfare assistance and augmented food and nutrition programs. The homeless were "a very diverse group" who did not "fit the stereotype of the drifter or the Skid-Row bum," the statement said. Emergency government help was necessary, the bishops said. "But we cannot pretend that soup kitchens and shelters are more than Band-Aid responses to the critically serious problems of poverty and homelessness." They added: "We therefore believe that major new efforts are needed to assist people in obtaining decent places to live at prices that are affordable. We especially need creative efforts to produce affordable new housing and to preserve existing housing for low-income families."

ON THE HEELS OF COMPLAINTS THAT NON-CATHOLICS WERE VIOLATING CHURCH rules by receiving communion—one of the charges Rome lodged against Archbishop Hunthausen—the U.S. bishops' December newsletter on liturgy announced that henceforth all missalettes—booklets used by parishioners to follow the mass—would be required to carry a written caveat aimed at separating sheep from goats. The bishops' liturgy committee had waged an intense internal battle over the issue, some favoring it as necessary to stop non-Catholics' slipping through the net and to discourage priests from looking the other way, others warning that such a move carried an undesirably negative connotation (some of the latter were described as "irate" about the outcome). There was little doubt that heightened ecumenical harmony had lowered the barriers. In the clarification notice place in the missalette, Catholics were reminded that "persons conscious of grave sin must first be reconciled with God and the Church through the sacrament of Penance" (this group included, of course, Catholics in "irregular marriages" who had divorced and remarried without securing an annulment) before qualifying to take the sacrament. For "those Christians who are not fully united with us," the notice continued, "it is a consequence of the sad divisions in Christianity that we cannot extend to them a general invitation to receive communion." It continued: "Reception of the Eucharist by Christians not fully united with us would imply a oneness which does not exist, and for which we must pray." It would be there in black and white.

NOW THAT THE COMPLETED VERSION OF THE BISHOPS' PASTORAL LETTER "Economic Justice for All" was signed, sealed, and delivered, what would become of it? The question went to the heart of the rationale for devoting the enormous time and energy required to promulgate such statements. Would it gather dust or spark discussion?

Some timely, pertinent thoughts on the subject were contained in a perceptive article, "After the Pastoral," in the December 5 issue of *Commonweal,* by two Georgetown scholars, R. Bruce Douglas, chairman of the government department, and William J. Gould, Jr., a doctoral candidate in the same department.

The letter had made few waves so far, the authors said, either in the public realm, where it was intended as a prod to debate over economic policy, or among academicians. Among the reasons was that the public, buoyed by the current round of prosperity, showed "a strong disposition to turn a deaf ear to the challenge the bishops are seeking to mount." The mood was unreceptive "to considerations of justice, much less charity." Another cause for inattention, they said, was that the economics pastoral had simply been overshadowed by issues such as abortion and the Hunthausen-Curran disputes. They added that at times, it seemed, even among the bishops "economic justice may be something less of a priority than the letter makes it out to be" (p. 651). The patrons' poor appetites were, in other words, more than matched by the desultory behavior of uninspired cooks.

Moreover, the bishops' economic analysis ran into two major roadblocks. The American public assumed, number one, that the economy ran best when left alone by outside influences and, number two, that without restraints the economy would produce pretty much what the bishops desired. Nothing seriously was wrong with things the way they were, in the public mind. By contrast, "What the authors of the letter assume to be problematic, therefore, the average American is not inclined to see as problematic at all. Indeed, what the bishops think is problematic the average American is probably even inclined to see as perfectly natural, if not exemplary" (p. 652).

Catholic Americans were largely unaware that their own religious tradition stood in sharp tension with many of their unquestioned assumptions about the economy, the authors contended. The church had failed to do its teaching job. "With respect to economics far more than, say, sexuality, American Catholics appear to be ignorant of their own tradition" (p. 652).

The pastoral letter could be the centerpiece for an ambitious educational effort, the scholars argued, as long as it was seen as "a point of departure" (p. 653) rather than the final word. Success, in their view, was contingent on overcoming certain of the document's built-in flaws and limitations.

Foremost among the problems, in their estimation, was that the document was far too fixated on the goal of justice. "Even the theology of the letter is essentially a theology of justice," they wrote, "and the notion that there are other aspects of modern economic life with theological significance is barely acknowledged." There was an urgent need to develop a discussion about the "'purposes' to be pursued in economic life." "For all of the thousands of words which the authors have written, they do not really convey a clear, coherent vision of the place that economic activity should play in our lives" (p. 653).

Among the themes said to deserve attention were "the moral and spiritual significance of work, the uses of leisure, the role of consumption in human well-being, the social consequences of economic behavior, and, above all, its significance" (p. 653).

The two writers shared the view, widespread among Catholic conservatives, that the economics pastoral bore a decidedly liberal stamp. They concluded that "the logic of the concepts involved is still unmistakably liberal, and the impression is thus created that the concerns which the church has in this realm can be appropriately defined in liberal terms."

Assuming that to be the case, the letter presented a golden opportunity to explore the question of if and how Catholic teaching could be reconciled with liberalism, both political and economic. The American economic stress on individualism, for example, presented problems for traditional Catholic concepts of community. A tough-minded assessment of such issues was difficult, but the pastoral letter was a good place from which to start.

Douglass and Gould most ardently desired that the statement touch off wider discussions within the academy. "For all of the obvious significance which economic forces have in our lives," they exclaimed, "economic life simply has not attracted anything like the sustained philosophical attention devoted to other topics of comparable practical import." If time could be made for concerns such as nuclear arms and medical ethics, "it is time to insist that room be made for economics as well" (p. 654).

PROTESTANT CHURCHES HAD, BY DEFAULT, HELD A NEAR MONOPOLY ON THE TERM *minister* until the Second Vatican Council revived the concept within Catholicism. The council fathers dusted off the age-old idea that every Catholic became a minister of the church by virtue of baptism, thereby personally summoned to employ his or her talents in furthering God's mission on earth. In many respects, Catholicism was belatedly embracing Martin Luther's restatement of the theme of Christian vocation—that each person was "called" to a special work by God—a cornerstone of the Reformation four centuries earlier.

Several designated "ministries" were opened up to the laity as a consequence of the council's formulation, including the liturgical functions of lector and eucharistic minister in which many people had been enlisted since Vatican II. As the idea of ministry continued to evolve into practice, however, some traditional-minded Catholics, among them John Paul II, worried that the results were eroding the difference between priests and laity. If everyone was a minister, the argument went, how could the priesthood preserve its distinctive, set-apart character? Why be a priest, in effect, if you could be just as much a minister and remain a member of the laity? The answer had implications for the critical area of seminary recruitment. The pope believed strongly in the special nature of the priesthood and warned against diluting its meaning. The word *minister,* therefore, had been pretty well expunged from the Vatican's vocabulary during his tenure. But there still remained the mandate from Vatican II to take the concept of ministry seriously, to which the Pope pledged himself at least in theory, so the church had gone ahead in fits and starts.

Catholic Americans, imbued with the value of the individual and the worth of common people, were especially receptive to broadened concepts of ministry, albeit with many misgivings in the face of the limited definition most had grown up with in the pre–Vatican II church. The council's call for revision raised many nettlesome theological and practical questions about structure and implementation, but the challenge prompted energetic and thoughtful discussion. The following were three contributions to this ongoing colloquy from very different perspectives during the days of Advent.

The pastoral council of the Cincinnati archdiocese, made up of laypeople, religious, and priests, had pondered the topic at length and now released its final report, "An Expanded View of Ministry." Despite expected resistance, the report said, "It is obvious that the need for an expanded view of ministry is an idea whose time had come." As defined by Vatican II, the Cincinnati council said, "ministry" referred to "any action of Christian persons which reveals and furthers God's presence in the world on behalf of the church and at the service of those in need" (Origins, January 15, 1987, vol. 16, no. 31, pp. 553–55).

Two notions of ministry actually existed within the church, their report said. "The more restricted view holds that ministry is restricted to officially designated ecclesial ministry," that is, the ordained. "The broader view," the one obviously favored by the pastoral council, held that "there are three focal points of ministry: ecclesial ministry [priests, lector, acolyte, director of religious education, and all others related to the parochial setting], ministry in the market place [Catholic laity at work] and family ministry" (p. 556).

The council asserted that it was no longer appropriate to confine images of ministry to rectory and altar. It suggested five characteristics to differentiate the "many forms of ministry": "ecclesial recognition" such as ordination; the "amount of time spent in ministry" (full time or part time); the "type and scope of activities" from generalists such as priests to specialists in areas like religious education; the amount of preparation needed to engage in a particular ministry; and the "setting in which the ministry or service is performed, ranging from a cathedral to a classroom, from the family to a downtown street corner." No form of ministry should "diminish the importance or acceptance of another," the council added, underscoring the new note of equality that underlay much of the wider discussion (p. 555).

This expanded version of the ministry had sparked "tensions" in the church that must be addressed and overcome, the council said. Four specific groups were identified as sources of opposition. They were "passive Catholics who see their participation as requiring only mass attendance (possibly at whatever church is convenient)"; everyone, "ordained and lay, who believe that ministry 'belongs' only to the ordained"; those who think whatever they do should be blessed as a valid ministry "without sufficient regard for quality, acceptability and the needs of the community"; and "those who are threatened by the working of the Spirit through contemporary prophets," presumably prophets such as antinuclear protesters who consider their actions done as a ministry of the church (p. 557).

From Cincinnati, the message was clear: The need to continue broadening the scope of church ministries was urgent, though many of the problems encountered on the way did not yield to easy solutions. By giving careful attention to an issue of growing importance, the pastoral council had taken an unusual and creative step. Few such bodies had shown similar initiative.

The new thinking about ministry had its greatest immediate bearing on employees of the church. Many teachers, administrators, hospital workers, and others began seeing their roles in a different light, less as auxiliaries in a system run by the ordained and more as partners with the clergy with a valid ministry of their own. That analysis is too reductive and simplistic, to be sure; few made such a clear or bold transition. But the wheels did begin to turn. How was an accountant for the church different from an accountant at a downtown firm? The development of a ministry of the laity that would pertain to the downtown accountant was a more difficult problem because the church had done so little to address it in the past. For the moment, attention on ministry would focus more intently on those who held jobs within the church.

Margaret O'Brien Steinfels, the thoughtful editor of *Church,* a publication of the National Pastoral Life Center, adroitly examined the dilemmas of the church employee in a December 7 address to clergy, religious, and lay graduates of Immaculate Conception Seminary on Long Island. In her vespers talk "Working for the Church: Ambiguities of an Enlarged Understanding," Steinfels recognized the increasing strain on church workers in the throes of change. What made the situation of herself and fellow church employees unique, she said, was that "our paycheck is tied to our cosmology, our work to our deepest beliefs."

Everyone on the inside of church institutions was caught up in a degree of disorientation, she said, adding, "This altered sense of the church requires new job descriptions as well as new understanding of how people work together."

Laypeople were not the only ones perplexed. "Priests and women religious too have had to rethink, reconsider, the nature of their work. Everyone has more questions than answers, more problems than solutions."

Success or failure depended on the outcome of several factors, said Steinfels, a short, energetic woman with dark hair and round, wire-framed glasses. One was how well the church's hierarchical command structure could be reconciled with the more democratic orientation stemming from Vatican II. Obviously, the trend toward lay workers placed more emphasis on nonhierarchical methods of collaboration and mutual responsibility. The evolving situation also required adequate standards of competence. In the past, priests and nuns were believed to be the consummate generalists. As specialization made inroads in the church, she said, special care was needed to avoid either a return to naïveté or an overdose of worldly professionalism. "Just as zeal and sacrifice are not enough to run a high school religious education program," Steinfels said, "an M.Div. degree from Harvard is not sufficient unto itself either."

The "gender" factor was particularly intractable, Steinfels told her audience. "There are tensions every day, everywhere about appropriate roles for men and women. The church is not unique in this, but its history and practices present unique problems. The most obvious is the congruence of ordination with office and power, a congruence that makes us a male-focused church." Specifically, laypeople were exposed daily to "the awkwardness of many clergy and some women religious in dealing with the opposite sex." Perhaps the discomfort would pass with the generations, she said, but meanwhile, whenever "a priest seems to have moved me to the periphery of his vision and is looking somewhere over my left shoulder, I remind myself that he is probably just disoriented by my efforts to look him straight in the eye."

Complicating the problem, she said, was the gap created by vastly different processes of "socialization" between laypeople, on the one hand, and clergy and religious, on the other. Laypeople, as a result, tended to exhibit "directness about self-interest, authority and responsibility," whereas clergy and religious were inclined to "manifest a degree of obliqueness, deference and self-effacement that reflects an ideal of obedient service to the community." In real-world settings, where the groups interact, she indicated, "These two sets of behavioral expectations and norms are hard to mesh, especially if they are overlaid by gender questions. Lay women working with priests; lay men working with women religious. The behavior that flows from one set of norms can seem unreal, even duplicitous, and certainly unpleasant and rude to someone operating under the other set of norms." These were sobering thoughts for graduates set to pursue their church vocations.

— —

Less than a week after these words were spoken at the seminary, Christina Silvestro resigned as religious education director of a large parish in a prosperous section of a bustling Midwestern city. It had been her second job on a parish staff. She had entered the field as a self-conscious effort to fulfill a ministry. She was now leaving for good, she said, out of utter frustration.

Christina was a twenty-nine-year-old woman of medium height and meticulous appearance. Her full auburn hair flowed to her shoulders, and her alert brown eyes, together with her round soft features, conveyed both intelligence and attentiveness. Her demeanor was intense and serious, as if the most urgent matters lay unresolved within her, but once her wit was activated that mood collapsed suddenly into laughter. She was now single, a brief, traumatic marriage having ended in divorce. Because she had not remarried, she remained in good standing with the church.

Christina was raised in Illinois by religiously observant Catholic parents and attended church schools from kindergarten through college. After receiving her B.A., she became a third-grade teacher in a Catholic school. She enjoyed it, but felt drawn toward the broader parish responsibilities increasingly available to the laity. To equip herself, she had gone back to school and earned a theological degree. This qualified her superbly for one of the growing number of openings for lay professionals. She was snapped up quickly by a pastor-monsignor looking for a lay pastoral associate.

"The pastor was an older man," Christina said. "He was a champion of collaborative ministry. He had no hangups about having talented, qualified people around. He was what I call a 'Vatican III' type of priest. He really treated me as an associate. He presented me as a complete, total colleague. When people asked where they should go with questions about the parish, he'd say, 'Speak to Christina or me.'"

Among her specified duties were convert instruction, organizing CCD (Confraternity of Christian Doctrine) classes for public school students, supervising youth groups and adult education, and doing parish planning. She also spent many hours on her own, counseling individuals and families and making house calls to deal with particular problems. It was a full-time job and more at a salary of twenty thousand dollars a year. Because the pastor gave her unqualified backing, she enjoyed influence and visibility as a full-fledged member of the parish team. But frictions arose. Some within the parish's inner circle, including the assistant pastor, increasingly saw her as a threat to their access to the pastor, an intruder in what she referred to sardonically as the ongoing game of "Who's closer to Father?" The aging monsignor, having found in Christina a kindred spirit, seemed to her unaware of the rivalry.

Though the pastor welcomed the presence of someone he regarded as a true colleague in an uphill battle to instill the reforms of Vatican II in a stiffly conservative parish, the experience was, for Christina, both a blessing and a curse. She could see progress in her work. But she also felt acutely the growing animosity toward her expressed on a daily basis by the parish secretaries and, most of all, by the assistant pastor.

"The more the pastor treated me as an associate, the more the assistant pastor hated me," she said. "One day I remember pulling into the parking lot just as he was getting into his car with the secretaries, who sided with him. I got out quickly to speak to them, but they slammed their doors and burned rubber as fast as they could going to lunch.

"To the group of vocal critics I was never a member of a team but a woman who was just a little too forward, the overpaid golden child of the pastor. Once the pastor asked me to dinner at the rectory. I thought the housekeeper would have a stroke—me having dinner with a priest. She never referred to me by name that evening. She'd say, 'Does that one want dessert?'

"My opponents didn't even know me, but they started ripping me apart: everything from my makeup to why I had an office upstairs in the rectory. They resented the fact that the pastor was calling me a minister. They refused to accept me in a ministerial role. Then came the rumors about my sexual behavior, and that really hurt. It was totally untrue, but what could I do? It came to the point where one Sunday both priests—even the assistant pastor felt the need—gave sermons about the danger of lies, malicious gossip, and jealousies. After that, it just got worse.

"They started saying I was ambitious, using this job to build a big career for myself. The funny thing is, I couldn't imagine what career that might be. What big careers are there for laywomen in the church? And the clincher was when they said, 'Is it right to call someone a minister who's divorced?'

"I had become the subject of controversy, even scandal, and it was horrible. One day at a staff meeting I learned that a group of women critics was planning to place the 'Christina Silvestro issue' on the agenda of the next parish council meeting. I said, 'That's it, I'll never allow myself to go through this.' I told the pastor without hysteria or fanfare that that was the last straw. I said I hoped we could still be friends. His reaction? He said it had been hell and that he felt guilty for what had happened. In the past he'd tried to talk me out of quitting but not this time. He told me that I had suffered the cost of discipleship and that he saw me as a lamb among wolves. Then I cleaned out my desk and quietly left."

Though defeated and dispirited, Christina was not inclined to give up her ministerial hopes because of a bad experience in one parish. She wanted to give it another try. Not long after, she was hired as director of religious education by another parish.

The new setting was bigger and even more affluent than the last, with 1,800 mostly upper middle-class families as members and a satellite dish in the front yard. The well-equipped, high-quality school was a source of great pride to the pastor, whom she described as "aloof and uneasy with anyone except other priests and still part of the old Catholic ghetto in his thinking." She was actually hired by the assistant pastor. "The pastor didn't really know what a director of religious education was," Christina said. "He never saw me as a colleague or a team member. My duties were never defined to the parish. People didn't really know what I did and of course didn't understand what I was trying to do."

Her salary dropped to sixteen thousand dollars, but her hours increased. Instead of working an average of fifty hours a week, she now put in about sixty, six days a week. "The job was totally open-ended. It snowballed and grew. The assistant pastor, who was agreeable and considerate, told me after I got there that he didn't get along with kids so I would be in charge of the youth ministry in addition to the other things I was supposed to do. That was fine up to a point. We started out with zero, and within a year we had two hundred kids and a real active program. But I was coming in at ten or eleven in the morning, and I'd usually lock up the building late at night. Nobody knew the hours I worked. But I really liked the work itself."

Then the assistant was transferred and a new one brought in. "During the week before the new one got there, the pastor came by to talk to me. He said he thought it would be a good idea during this interim to keep busy by ordering candles and keeping the pamphlet racks full. He was worried that I might be getting away with something if there was no one to look over me. At that point I had nearly three theological degrees.

"My fortunes hung on the whim of the assistant pastor. The first one personally liked me, so it was okay. The second one turned out to be a prince charming, an obnoxious person who told me he was uncomfortable with people crying. When he first got there he came into my office without knocking and announced that he'd been working with youth in his last parish and was 'very talented' at it. 'I do the kids,' he said. It was clear after that that it wouldn't work."

She had to give up much of what she had started and enjoyed. Her role became more restricted. Relations with the day school staff declined as she attempted to improve the after-school program for public school students who used the same facilities. The ground had shifted, and she felt unable to achieve much. "There was lack of support in general," she said, "plus all the criticism that happens anyway when people don't grasp what you're trying to do."

After a few months of struggling with the new situation, Christina resigned. In the immediate aftermath, she sounded relieved and said she would never again seek a position on a parish staff. She intended to complete studies for a Ph.D. with the hope of teaching theology on the college level.

She admitted to feeling a little "naive" about the parish ministry. Now she could understand, she said, why lay professionals last only about four years on the average. The most difficult part for her, she said, was the feeling of helplessness. "I never had any kind of job security. I never even had a contract. It was all up to whatever the priests decided.

"I could be defined out of existence as quickly as I was defined into existence."

HIS STATUS WAS BISHOP, BUT HIS JOB WAS TRANSLATOR. BISHOP PLACIDO Rodriguez had migrated to the United States from Mexico with his parents and thirteen brothers and sisters when he was a boy of twelve. He spent the next years translating Spanish thoughts into English. Then as a Claretian priest and, later, auxiliary bishop of Chicago, he had been attempting to translate Hispanic Catholicism to the church in America. That demanding task was at the heart of his vocation.

A man of youthful good looks and quiet charm, Bishop Rodriguez was one of sixteen Hispanic bishops in Catholic America. His Mexican-American compatriots comprised about 60 percent of the approximately 19 million Hispanics from nineteen Latin American countries, Spain, and Puerto Rico estimated by the Census Bureau to live in the United States, and they were the fastest growing subgroup, up 22 percent to 11.8 million since 1980 (in 1910 the census total had been just 382,002).

Most Hispanics were at least nominally Catholics, but their defection to Protestant churches was believed to be growing much faster than many church officials acknowledged. Though church leaders tended to minimize such losses, some sociologists calculated that more than two in ten Hispanics now belonged to a Protestant church and that the proportion was climbing. By any measure, however, the Hispanic proportion of Catholic America had risen to at least a quarter and was perhaps closer to a third. Moreover, even those who professed optimism about Hispanic defections were agreed that an evangelism campaign aimed at keeping or reclaiming Hispanics was an urgent priority. On the front lines of the effort were two thousand Hispanic priests, 3 percent of the U.S. total, along with Bishop Rodriguez and his hierarchical colleagues.

An immediate concern was the impending implementation of the new federal immigration law that would qualify aliens who had been in the United States since January 1, 1982, for legal resident status. May 5, 1987, was the effective date of the new law, but the church was gearing up. The United States Catholic Conference announced this month that 160 of the 183 dioceses had assigned a director to coordinate parish activities to help process applications. The broad-based initiative was seen by church leaders as both humanitarian and evangelistic, a display of compassion for the plight of illegal aliens that could, as a by-product, bear dividends for the church.

Though Hispanics were gaining in numbers and influence, they were still largely unseen strangers within Catholic America. It fell principally to Bishop Rodriguez and his compadres in the forefront of the church's Hispanic leadership to change that by interpreting the religious culture of Spanish-speaking Catholics into a language that their Anglo coreligionists could understand.

The personable bishop carried on this endeavor in the pages of this month's *U.S. Catholic* magazine. In an interview with the magazine's editors, Bishop Rodriguez assumed a familiar role as liaison, as it were, from one neighbor to another.

Asked whether Hispanics consider mass-going important, the bishop said, first, that "they do not feel welcome in many United States parishes, therefore many of them stay at home or switch to Protestant churches." Attending church may be the prevailing standard in the United States, he said, but Hispanics "have a different cultural and religious perspective—one more rooted in the very structure of society, faith, and life." Moreover, they were more inclined than Anglos to "celebrate the strong moments of grace in their lives with God and their community: birth, death, marriage, Confirmation, feast days, and festivals. Understood this way, this can be a profoundly spiritual commitment" (p. 36).

Mass wasn't unimportant to Hispanics, Bishop Rodriguez explained, but their sense of devotion was broader than liturgy, blending "faith, culture, and language." And the people were less likely to attend the vast majority of liturgies, which use English rather than Spanish. Those who did attend were overwhelmingly women and children. "We're not entirely sure of the reasons," the bishop said. "Maybe we're projecting too much of a feminine church. . . . Perhaps the men see the church only between the altar and the sacristy and not alive in the world they live in" (p. 36).

Bilingual masses were only part of the answer, he said. Hispanics had a more flexible concept of time, which could create misunderstandings. For example, "Unless it's been explained to them, 95 percent of the Hispanics who come to the rectory for services arrive without an appointment. And if the pastor says he won't see them without an appointment, they'll take it personally. They'll think: 'The pastor doesn't want me; he doesn't like me. I'm not going there any more. He's just so cold.' Meanwhile the pastor is probably thinking, 'Why won't they respect me? I can't be available every minute of the day.'" While Hispanics needed to learn more discipline from Anglos, he said, Anglos could benefit from Hispanic elasticity so as to "refuse to make time commitments more important than people's needs" (p. 37).

At times of celebration, Hispanics joined closely together in jubilation. Bishop Rodriguez praised Hispanic "warmth," which, he said, enlivened worship, fiestas, and Marian devotions. "Specifically, our tradition, much of what we can contribute to the U.S. Catholic church," he said, "can be summed up in two words: popular religiosity—the strong sacred connection between life and faith" (p. 37).

Slowly the Hispanic community was overcoming prejudice and shedding "a spiritually destructive attitude about its heritage," Bishop Rodriguez said. Hispanic traditions such as wedding celebrations had been retained and cherished. Instead of following the Anglo customs, he said, "we have our own way," which included a cluster of couples, the wedding party, and "padrinos, or sponsors," walking down the aisle with the bride and bridegroom. The padrinos each supplied something: "One pays for the kneeler the nuptial couple kneels on; another sponsors the music and hires the musicians; still another couple brings up the rosary and the Bible" (p. 38).

As a Hispanic bishop, he said, he believed he was helping Catholics from other backgrounds "to develop a greater acceptance, not only of Hispanics, but of themselves." He was open about his own origins, he said. "I don't hide it. I'm not ashamed of it. I was raised on the poor side of Chicago, and I used to shine shoes—this is part of who I am" (p. 39).

In order to attract Hispanics, Bishop Rodriguez said, the church "must develop a sense of credibility, a sense of openness and freedom for dissent" while remaining true to its convictions. It must also evangelize Hispanics by welcoming them and their cultural ways. "You know, when Hispanics come to this country," he said, "they feel completely uprooted. But all of a sudden they realize they can turn to the Catholic church; it is their one hope. And so the moment is right for us to welcome them with open arms" (p. 39).

MORE THAN THREE MONTHS HAD ELAPSED SINCE THE ARCHDIOCESE OF NEW York had forbidden anyone who openly disagreed with church teaching from speaking at official church events. Two prominent Catholics, Governor Mario Cuomo and state Assemblyman John Dearie, were singled out as subjects of the boycott because of their stands on implementation of legalized abortion. Both rejected abortion personally, but Governor Cuomo had vowed to uphold the law granting free choice and Assemblyman Dearie had voted once to provide Medicaid funding for abortions.

The initial disclosure of the ban fired an intense dispute between those who affirmed the church's right to deny the platform to dissenters and those who decried it as a more restricted tactic aimed at pressuring only certain public figures to take a more forceful stance toward abortion. Weeks after the first angry exchanges between church leaders and critics, the debate continued to simmer.

One of the archdiocese's most astute political observers, the Reverend Monsignor Harry J. Byrne, reignited the cross fire in a December 6 article in *America* acerbically titled "Thou Shalt Not Speak." Monsignor Byrne, a former chancellor of the archdiocese and pastor of Epiphany parish, took issue with the promoters of the new rule, Bishop Joseph T. O'Keefe, the vicar general of the archdiocese, and Cardinal O'Connor.

Recalling the American tradition of church-state separation, Monsignor Byrne upheld the right of the church to instruct its members as it saw fit so long as church officials avoided partisan politics. In his view, the speaker prohibition stepped over the line by targeting some politicians. "Does the archdiocesan directive pose the danger of imposing church authority on participants in the democratic process?" he asked. "To ban a speaker who dissents on one issue from talking on any issue, such as local housing, at his parish Communion breakfast carries serious political fallout if he is running for office. Is this simply an exercise in the teaching mission of the church?" (p. 357).

Did it apply to non-Catholics as well? If a rabbi spoke to a parish liturgy committee about the Jewish Passover, Monsignor Byrne asked, would that "weaken his audience's acceptance of the divinity of Christ? Or would a Unitarian minister invited to address a parish social action committee on local housing problems somehow infect its members' belief in the Trinity? To ask the questions is to provide an answer?" (p. 357).

Assemblyman Dearie, a University of Notre Dame graduate, as Monsignor Byrne pointed out, had consistently supported legislation to aid Catholic schools and otherwise backed the church's social concerns—except the one vote on Medicaid funding for abortions. "Is abortion the single issue that bans a specific candidate?" Monsignor Byrne asked. "The single issue that triggers penalties? Is it applicable only to Catholic candidates?" (p. 358).

Moreover, he implied, the policy flew in the face of the U.S. Catholic bishops' warning against the church's taking sides in political races. Both Governor Cuomo and Assemblyman Dearie were being subjected to an "underlying rationale," Monsignor Byrne said. "Since they are Catholic, they are expected to enunciate and vote the Catholic position" (p. 358).

The Second Vatican Council had proclaimed the principle of religious freedom, he said, and John F. Kennedy had interpreted its meaning for the Catholic politician in America, asserting that "conscience" was the middle ground between the church and the secular order. "The 'conscience' view of John F. Kennedy has been accepted by many, Catholics and non-Catholics alike, who think that a religious body has every right to instruct its members but does not have the right in a pluralistic democracy to bind directly a public official" (p. 359).

Further, to go beyond instruction in an effort to "coerce a particular political position of an official who voted 'the wrong way' by banning him or her from speaking on any topic at a church affair is fraught with enormous risk" (p. 359). The church could easily protect its teaching by requiring speakers to address subjects other than those on which they disagree with the church. As it was, he said, "The totality of the ban, with its obvious political consequences, carries the unmistakable aura of punishment and penalty" (p. 362).

The ban had emerged in an atmosphere laden with "a new authoritarianism," Monsignor Byrne said (p. 356). The unfortunate result, he said, was "the potential of violating a candidate's conscience, of improperly intruding on the political process, and of disqualifying Catholics from public office in the minds of significant portions of the electorate" (p. 362). If those dangers weren't enough to dissuade his church superiors, Monsignor added a final objection, claiming that overt tactics would backfire. "It is a fact of life," he said, "that American voters will never elect someone whom they view as politically subservient to a religious body" (p. 362).

—◆ ◆—

AMBER LIGHT OF LATE DAY GAVE THE INTERIOR OF SAINT JAMES CATHEDRAL A muted, comforting radiance. The basilica, seat of the Brooklyn diocese, was a small, unpretentious gem, a cathedral of unique distinction among all its peers of varying shapes and sizes.

From the outside, Saint James looked undistinguished, largely obscured by the sprouting high-rise offices and condominiums of downtown Brooklyn. But inside was a splendorous beige Romanesque enclosure, a cozy space that enfolded those who entered in a hen-gathering embrace. Compared to the regal, dwarfing quality of Saint Patrick's across the East River in Manhattan, Saint James bespoke an unimposing, human scale. Its modest elegance surprised newcomers and invited them to make it their own, prayerfully.

Fifty or so people had gathered in the basilica on the afternoon of December 7: the second Sunday of Advent, the forty-fifth anniversary of the attack on Pearl Harbor, twenty-one years to the day since the close of Vatican II, and the vigil for the next day's 510th official observance of the feast of the Immaculate Conception. This group, the Concerned Catholics of Brooklyn and Queens, had still another purpose in mind, a prayer service for Archbishop Raymond Hunthausen. Groups in the state of Washington and elsewhere were holding similar observances.

Women outnumbered men. Most were middle-aged or older; apparel varied from dressy to casual. Halfway back sat a single nun in a blue habit. As they awaited the start of the program, they conversed jovially and welcomed one another with smiles, handshakes, pats on the back, and embraces.

The leadership of Concerned Catholics consisted of a handful of priests, nuns, and laypeople. Their purpose this day was to protest the plight of Archbishop Hunthausen, whom they revered as an oppressed prophet, and to do so as indirectly and unobtrusively as possible. They had originally asked Bishop Francis J.

Mugavero for permission to conduct a "dialogue"—by which they meant a kind of teach-in—on the subject of Archbishop Hunthausen for an hour preceding the four o'clock vesper service. The bishop said no, on the grounds that this was not the time or place to inflame feelings on the subject, but allowed them to hold a more innocuous-sounding prayer and penance service.

Heeding the bishop's ruling, the planners organized a service of hymns, quiet times, prayers, and reading selections aimed at highlighting issues related to the case of Archbishop Hunthausen and others deemed to be victims of the abuse of church authority. Of the four readings, two were taken from documents of Vatican II, "On the Laity" and "Decree on the Bishop's Pastoral Office in the Church"; one was by a non-Catholic theologian, Langdon Gilkey ("Catholicism Confronts Modernity"); and the fourth by Archbishop Rembert Weakland, "The Price of Orthodoxy," which cautioned against construing Catholic theology too narrowly. The readings were delivered by a nun, a layman, and two laywomen. They did not comment, but the inferences were clear. The thinking of the church often clashes with its behavior, resulting in abuse. The church did not always live up to its own words or its own best interests.

The most piercing and graphic comment on the fate of Archbishop Hunthausen was the thinly veiled reference by Sister Mary in the opening prayer, likening him to a "torn ligament." "Like our human bodies," she said, "we need the uniqueness of each one for the well-being of all. Yet we hear conformity being equated with loyalty. How can a body with even one torn ligament function very smoothly? How can the gifts of one member crush the gifts of another? Oh God of people, teach us reverence for each individual so that through rich diversity we may come to wholeness."

Nothing, it seemed, inspired creative subterfuge like a measure of restraint from a bishop. The service was sprinkled with the language and imagery of coded outcry against the perceived sources of injustice. Bitterness mingled with mournfulness, faith, and resolve. At the conclusion of the prayer service, they stood with lighted candles under the smooth dome of the darkened basilica and prayed the collect from the second Sunday in Advent: "God in heaven, the day draws near when the glory of your Son will make radiant the night of the waiting world. May the lure of greed not impede us from the joy which moves the hearts of those who seek him. May the darkness not blind us to the vision of the wisdom which fills the minds of those who find him."

Vespers began. The choir in gray robes filed into the nave, the cross-bearer leading the way to the altar, followed by the procession of two candles and the purple-robed cathedral rector. Psalm prayers and choral works were sung and intercessions spoken, and Sister Camille D'Arienzo, R.S.M., spoke. She taught at Brooklyn College and was associate editor of the diocesan newspaper, the *Tablet*.

She was also in the vanguard of Catholics Concerned, an outspoken nun who had often stepped forward to address church issues. She had a round face with sparkling eyes and graying hair and wore a dark skirt, a plaid vest, and a white blouse. She would extend the spirit of the prayer meeting by speaking on the text from Isaiah, "Let justice descend, O heavens, like dew from above; like gentle rain let the sky drop justice down."

She pictured John the Baptist in the desert longing for Jesus. "In the desert, there's equality," she said, meaning, among other things "divestiture of property." She intoned the names of other symbolic desert-dwellers, among them Curran and Hunthausen.

Justice, Sister Camille said, "is sorting out what belongs to whom and returning it to them."

When she finished, and the rector had brought the vespers to a close, the gathering broke up and left quietly. As they exited, they were offered form letters to register their displeasure over the Hunthausen situation with Cardinal Ratzinger, head of the Vatican Holy Office; Archbishop Laghi, the papal delegate; and Archbishop John May, president of the American bishops' conference. The letter expressed dismay, outrage, and grief and asked for the complete restoration of Archbishop Hunthausen's powers. They were snapped up quickly. The Concerned Catholics of Brooklyn hoped that their small splash would contribute to big ripples.

— ◂ ▸ —

THREE DAYS AFTER THE PROTEST RALLIES, ARCHBISHOP HUNTHAUSEN ENTERED Providence Medical Center, where, on the sixteenth, he underwent surgery to remove his cancerous prostate gland. Microscopic traces of malignancy were also taken from the adjoining lymph nodes.

A routine medical examination had alerted the archbishop to the possibility of serious trouble before he left for the bishops' meeting in November. Tests conducted the day after he returned from that momentous session to a tumultuous welcome from Seattle Catholics identified the exact nature of the disease. He was informed of the cancerous tumor on November 25, whereupon, according to the *National Catholic Reporter,* he went hiking with family members in the Montana mountains, keeping the distressing medical news to himself.

Following the surgery, the archbishop was described as being "in excellent condition" (*NCR,* December 26, p. 1) by the doctor who performed the operation. No chemotherapy was anticipated, the doctor said, but some radiation might be advisable. The patient was expected to remain in the hospital another two or three weeks and to convalesce another two or three months. During his recuperation, his duties would be divided between Bishop Wuerl and the Reverend Michael G. Ryan, the vicar general and chancellor of the archdiocese.

Father Ryan held considerable power in the archdiocese. His role was even broader than his official titles might imply. He was, in fact, the archbishop's aide-de-camp, his confidant and chief strategist, the ghost writer mainly responsible for the dramatic interventions at the bishops' meeting. Father Ryan was known not only as the archbishop's right hand but as the hard-liner in his small circle of advisers, among the least inclined to accept compromise with the Vatican. Even his temporary assignment as the archbishop's surrogate was enough to make some church officials nervous. Ironically, he and Bishop Wuerl had been seminary classmates in Rome. Both had been considered bright prospects for promotion to bishop, but Father Ryan's advocacy on behalf of Archbishop Hunthausen, added to his liberal views in general, had all but eliminated him as a candidate.

Archbishop Hunthausen's cancer was defined as type C bordering on the more serious type D, which indicated an invasion of the lymphatic system. The news of his life-threatening disease loosed a nationwide torrent of concern for the archbishop, and, among his admirers, his future was cast into hitherto unknown and incomparable depths of gloom. To the supporters, fighting the good fight now meant something entirely new.

FOR ALL THE CONTROVERSY ABOUT HOMOSEXUALITY IN AND AROUND THE church, there was very little open, two-way discussion about it. Most of what passed for debate consisted of attacks and defenses hurled by one side at the other across a broad divide. Typically, homosexual groups exhorted the church to relent, and church officials stood their ground by restating Catholic teaching. Only rarely did the two sides engage each other directly.

The Vatican's statement on homosexuality in October had only widened the gulf by redefining the church's moral stand. Previously, the Vatican had attempted to maintain a clear distinction between homosexual orientation, judged morally acceptable, and homosexual erotic acts, condemned as sinful. In the latest document, however, the line had been all but erased. Under the revised terms, culpability was identified with the inclination itself.

Given the worsening polarization and mutual isolation between gay rights activists and church officials in the wake of the Vatican document, the willingness of Cardinal Joseph Bernardin to respond in *Commonweal* (December 26) to an "open letter" from one of his charges, a homosexual member of a religious community in Chicago, was most unusual and significant.

Cardinal Bernardin had a reputation for being cautious to a fault, ever watchful for how any move he made affected his image. Many liberals thought that, underneath this political guise, he came as close as anyone in the top ranks of the American hierarchy to seeing things their way, though it was difficult to find solid evidence to prove it. He was at least mildly progressive, sometimes politically manipulative, seen by many inside and outside the hierarchy as the main bulwark of moderation against a strenuous rightward push from the Vatican. His conduct on public issues appeared to support such a temporizing role. In order to advance a bit to the left, he tried to shore up his support on the right without appearing too far out on any wing. His leanings might be liberal, but his instinct for retaining protective cover was at least as great.

The writer of the "open letter" took the pseudonym Steven Elred. He described himself as a "member of a religious community" who taught religion in a Chicago Catholic high school. He said he had lived an openly gay life before entering the order and "continued to celebrate my gay identity within religious life," adding that he had never "been promiscuous" and had been "totally serious about the vow of celibacy" since entering the community. Had he used his real name he felt certain the cardinal "would be pressured to take action against me, and I don't think I owe anything to the lynch-mobs which are currently wreaking havoc in the church" (p. 680).

Elred went to the heart of the cardinal's objection to the gay rights legislation defeated by the Chicago city council: that it would license homosexual behavior that the church considered immoral. For wholly different reasons, Elred came to a conclusion similar to that found in the recent Vatican document, to wit, distinctions should not be drawn between inclination and the sexual behavior that expresses it. "Simply put," he wrote, "I do not accept the church's attempt to distinguish (nay, sunder) homosexual orientation from homosexual activity" (p. 680).

"I reject your distinction between orientation and activity not because it affects what I 'do,' but because it attacks what I am," he wrote. "After years of suffering, doubt, study, and prayer, I am convinced that the desires of my heart and loins are 'of God'; they are not morally neutral, they are morally good, equal in dignity to those of my heterosexual brothers and sisters" (p. 680).

Elred was appealing for the church to accept homosexuality on the same terms as heterosexuality, within the same conditions of mutual fidelity. Anything less than recognition of homosexuals as whole persons, gifts of God, sexuality and all, denied human dignity. Under current conditions, the church laid down an ultimatum, he said, "In other words: work to constructively integrate your sexuality, and we will cut you off at the knees; admit you are 'sick,' and 'mercy' will be yours. This is not pastoral compassion; it is functional condescension" (p. 681).

He attempted to respond to some of the more common fears and objections regarding homosexual behavior. Homosexuality did not include procreation, as the church required at least potentially in married life, but neither did "marriage between the infertile, and those beyond childbearing age." Church teaching had always been opposed to homosexuality, but a new theology was needed "in which gay people can live." Societal norms and good common sense would be enough to hold exhibitionism in check among homosexuals as well as heterosexuals in the event that broader gay civil rights laws were enacted. Parents need not worry that their children would be recruited into homosexuality (p. 681).

Cardinal Bernardin's response was gracious and sympathetic and understandably measured. He began by thanking his anonymous correspondent for his "thoughtful and respectful" letter and, with notable charity, suggested the common bonds that drew them together in the church's larger mission. The cardinal acknowledged that, he, too, struggled "to live the Gospel faithfully and without compromise" and bestowed his "respect" on "the integrity with which you seem to have claimed your homosexual identity and embraced your celibate religious life" (p. 682).

Widespread ignorance of homosexuality had spawned much "bias or bigotry" and a "certain exclusion" of homosexuals from mainstream society, the cardinal wrote.

"Sometimes, the bias of our culture is reflected among some members of the church. At times, our attempts to teach our theology of sexuality have been 'heard'—though not intended—as speaking of condemnation and rejection. The result has been alienation of many homosexuals from the church. Our teaching on sexuality stands. I believe in it, and I shall continue to proclaim it. But while remaining faithful to our beliefs and values, we must also work aggressively to eliminate the sense of alienation experienced by homosexuals and to ensure that all of God's daughters and sons feel at home in his house" (p. 683).

Focusing directly on the church's teachings, the cardinal said that the sexuality of the homosexual should not only be affirmed but incorporated into an appropriate spirituality. The teaching, he said, remained crystal clear: "To say it simply, our Roman Catholic tradition holds that heterosexual marital intimacy is the only proper context for the genital expression of human love-making and life-making. The genital expression of a homosexual is precluded (p. 683).

"I realize that these can be heard as 'hard' words and that, for many, they may appear unreasonable. To such persons the church's teaching is not persuasive. We must work to make it such" (p. 683).

Gay rights bills such as that which came before the Chicago city council failed to serve a positive end, he said, because in his view they encouraged acceptance of homosexuality on a par with heterosexuality. "As a teacher of morality and a citizen," he wrote, "I want to protect the rights of all citizens, but I cannot support public protection or sanctioning of sexual activity or a way of life which compromises the normativeness of heterosexual marital intimacy" (p. 684).

The cardinal ended on a note of sorrow that sounded somewhat apologetic. He regretted angering both homosexuals who thought his dichotomy—orientation yes, but activity no—"partitions the human person" and others who resented his willingness to give homosexuals "any rights." He had been "troubled by the discord" surrounding the gay rights bill and vowed to "assist efforts to resolve this conflict in any appropriate way." He assured Stephen Elred of his prayers.

Beyond this civil, courteous exchange, a frightening scenario was unfolding. Priests were dying of AIDS. Accounts of deaths were slowly and gradually surfacing against the pressures to keep them secret. Within dioceses and religious communities, fear of the treacherous disease was rising.

RENEW HAD INDEED PROVEN TO BE AN IDEA WHOSE TIME HAD COME. THE ORIGinal idea had sprung out of a desire by Archbishop Peter L. Gerety of Newark to help his parishes grasp the spirit of Vatican II. From that start, in 1976, the program began to spread to dioceses all over the country, becoming a means by which Catholics in parishes of every size and description received a vital shot in the arm. Among other things, it had become an antidote to religious individualism and fragmentation.

Of the 183 U.S. dioceses, 86, or nearly half, had adopted Renew and more than ten thousand parishes had enlisted in the three-year course in spiritual rejuvenation. That meant that about 2 million parishioners, or 4 percent of Catholic America, had undergone the regimen. Church leaders considered the growth phenomenal and saw Renew as an impressive success story, though some, mostly on the right wing, complained loudly that its overall emphasis was too soft on orthodoxy. Detractors saw it as too much psychology and sociology and too little inculcation of revealed truth, too much socializing and emotionalism and too little solid doctrine. The critics also questioned whether the program had attained anywhere near the results its supporters claimed.

As conceived by its founders, Renew was intended to draw people into friendly, open groups where they could talk about their faith and, among other things, read and discuss Scripture, focus on issues of justice, ponder the meaning of the church in their lives, and take part in the liturgy.

Defined as a "spiritual renewal process," Renew in its guidelines said its aim was to help Catholics to "develop a closer relationship with Christ, to make an adult commitment to Jesus as central in their lives and to open them[selves] to the power of the Holy Spirit so they become more authentic witnesses" (Origins, January 8, 1987, vol. 16, no. 30, p. 547).

The accent was personal and spiritual, affording Catholics an opportunity to explore their beliefs and experiences honestly and openly with other Catholics, something that many had never done before. Likewise, most had never examined the Scriptures together. Small group testimony had been pretty much a hallmark of "prayer meeting" and "Bible study" Protestantism. Renew was in some respects a sign of further absorption of Catholics into that mainstream evangelicalism.

When Renew came to a parish, people signed up for five six-week sessions, alternating between fall and Lent. It was hoped that the faith of participants would be recharged such that their personal lives were renewed and their commitment to social justice sharpened. It was a tasteful call to revival: to the lost sheep, to the tired sheep, to the prize sheep.

On its tenth anniversary, Renew received a report card from the hierarchy. A bishops' review committee in December 1986 weighed in with its assessment of the program's pros and cons. The jury of three bishops was tilted toward law-and-order conservatism. Two, Bishop William J. Levada, then auxiliary of Los Angeles, and Bishop Wuerl of Seattle, were former Vatican hands. The third, Bishop Elden F. Curtiss of Helena, Montana, was a moderate.

Given Renew's considerable popularity, the bishops were under some pressure to be as positive about it as possible despite whatever reservations they might hold. Accordingly, their report noted that the program had "touched the lives of a significant number of people," affirmed its "overall value," and commended several of its specific achievements, such as identifying spiritual needs and training laypeople (p. 549). The praise was sincere but hardly effusive. In somewhat patronizing fashion, Renew was patted on the head for "potential" and "promise" rather than performance. The bishops devoted the far greater share of the report to their analysis of the program's shortcomings.

Their criticisms were mostly reducible to the conclusion that Renew was not Roman Catholic enough. Thus, the bishops found a "tendency toward generic Christianity," which meant that "basic Christian themes are presented without sufficiently relating them to their specific form as experienced in Roman Catholic tradition and practice. The [Renew] literature does not identify, to the extent we think it should, what is distinctly Catholic in our faith process" (p. 548).

The bishops also saw an imbalance toward the human dimensions of faith—in emphases such as "community" and "immanence"—to the exclusion of the church's teachings on hierarchy and transcendence.

Among the things they found missing were "a clearer presentation of the distinctive nature of the Catholic church, not merely as a community of faith but as a structured, hierarchical, visible, sacramental community bound together in a tradition that includes Scripture as a font of faith but also the authoritative development and interpretation of the doctrines of faith by the magisterium of the church; a more balanced presentation of the models of the church which broadens considerably the sole emphasis on community; the insistence that God's revelation, and not just personal experience, is the norm for deeper understanding and appreciation of authentic faith" (p. 548). Though the ministry of the laity received justifiable attention, the bishops said, the unique ministry of the priesthood was neglected.

Likewise, the bishops said they applauded Renew's focus on the emotional and personal sides of the believer but saw a need for greater stress on "the cognitive, intellectual aspect of faith," adding, "We are concerned that the emphasis of Renew on personal and shared 'experience as the locus of revelation' can lead to fundamentalism and the privatization of religious truth. Our people must always be made aware of the objective content of revelation as the basis for our faith in Jesus Christ" (p. 549).

It was at least as plausible to regard Renew as a symptom of the great extent to which faith had already become private and subjective in Catholic America. Renew was not so much a potential cause as a demonstrated effect. The bishops, understandably uneasy about this trend toward defining spirituality in personal terms, gamely argued for a return to "objective truth" of revelation even as the preconditions for it were being steadily eroded by the scientific assumptions of modernity. Renew recognized that, to a large extent, spirituality had become little more than subjectivity.

The bishops' call for more Catholic content in Renew could be read as a much broader appeal for a return to those foundations of the faith that science and relativity had eroded. As the "truths" of the theological past—the bedrock, objective claims of the dogmaticians—were shaken by modern consciousness, the longing for restoration and retrieval grew all the more acute.

The leaders of Renew took the bishops' critique in stride, playing up its general endorsement of the program and accepting the suggestions for improvement with equanimity. Monsignor Thomas Kleissler, executive director of Renew's national office, thought the report had a basically positive and encouraging tone. In preceding months and years, he had fended off many charges from the far right to the effect that Renew was a thinly veiled version of the human potential movement, so, by comparison, he found the words of the bishops reassuring. The review by the bishops had been done at the behest of Renew, and the results, Monsignor Kleissler said, meant that the program could continue expanding at a fast clip, with some midcourse corrections. He described the bishops' suggestions as sensible and expected them to be incorporated soon. On the whole, he said, the report was complimentary and "didn't find any evidence of heresy," a finding that would help him in his constant sparring with conservative critics.

Though the bishops' report dwelled mostly on matters of church doctrine and authority, Monsignor Kleissler was eager to dispel any notion that Renew's primary purpose had ever been to teach or indoctrinate. It was, he maintained steadfastly, a program for awakening and strengthening personal relationships with Christ. "Renew is about sharing of faith, not ecclesiological arguing," he said. "Faith has to come before content in our secular society. We are helping people talk about their faith in Jesus. For mainline Christians to do that more comfortably is a great step forward. You have to come to the point where you ask, 'Do I trust? Do I believe?' We're helping people do that. People are hungry for God, and we're trying to give a solid spiritual message. Without those underpinnings of faith and trust, it's hard to lay a lot of doctrine and morality on people."

The need for inner conversion as the cornerstone of Renew had deep personal roots for Monsignor Kleissler: "For me, it was trusting in Jesus when I was young that became the turning point of my life."

BISHOP SAWICKI WOULD BE LEAVING LATER IN THE AFTERNOON FOR A HOLIDAY gathering of priests and nuns at a diocesan retreat house, but until then he was enjoying a rare day at home.

He was a man of average height and build, with subtle round features and smiling eyes. His manner was exceedingly receptive and forgiving, and he spoke with calmness and humor. Now in his mid-sixties, he saw himself as having grown more circumspect and tolerant with the passing years. If he had become more willing to take life on its own terms, he said, it was because the pain, hardship, and strife that he had witnessed over the four decades of his priesthood had vividly impressed upon him the gift of each day.

Bishop Sawicki's diocese was bent low under the sorrows of the Rust Belt. Chronic high unemployment wreaked havoc on families, drove up the number of drug addicts, and tore apart the social fabric. Buildings decayed, and merchants boarded up haberdasheries and hardware stores. On the church map, the diocese could hardly be considered a plum assignment, but Bishop Sawicki loved it and had made it clear to higher-ups that he wanted to live out his ministry there. Though most of the diocese felt the effect of plant closings and economic decline, pockets of comparative affluence kept the bishop apprised, as well, of the joys and agonies of upscale, mainstream Catholic America. The diocese in all its diversity was very much his home; its plight his plight; its Catholicism his Catholicism.

The parishes and people of his diocese were his first concern, but as a member of the national hierarchy Bishop Sawicki was also immersed in the headline-making agenda of the wider church. He was acutely aware of those issues, well informed about their complexities, and ready to lend a hand in their solution. His own approach, by instinct and outlook, was probably best described as progressive. That is, he felt that the answers of the past were not always suitable or sufficient to current circumstances. He was more willing than many of his colleagues to see value in change and like Pope John XXIII, whom he admired greatly, to allow that the world had something to say to the church.

In keeping with that view, he saw a constructive, though limited, place for American values within the church. Though his reverence for the See of Rome was deep and durable, he had come to believe that the future of Catholic America was ill served by a heavy-handed Vatican over-intent upon stamping out American influences. As a diocesan bishop, he professed to know something about the need for balance among levels of church authority, and as an American bishop he felt he knew something about the special gifts offered by the church in this country. Among the reasons he sought resolution to problems beyond his diocese was his awareness that, in an open society such as this, the impact of big issues quickly reverberated in the neighborhood parish.

The actions taken at the bishops' meeting scarcely a month before were still very much on Bishop Sawicki's mind. Looking back on that scene, he characteristically chose his words carefully, for he was judicious and guarded regarding Rome's judgments on sensitive matters.

The outcome of the Hunthausen challenge had left him uneasy. He spoke about the case with some ambivalence, framing it in terms of the political realities and the exigencies of the everyday life of bishops.

"Some people thought it would be us taking sides: Hunthausen or the pope," he said, "but that kind of formulation was nonsense to begin with. It's not set up that way. Our responsibility was to be fraternal in our response to Hunthausen and collegial in our relationship to the Holy Father. I think we did that. Some said we should have drawn the line, affirmed Hunthausen, said he was right and the pope wrong. Those categories are so gross; they don't represent reality. We can't paint the picture with a white knight and a black knight."

His voice carried both sympathy and irritation. Though he lamented the fate of a beloved colleague, he was annoyed at the Seattle archbishop's refusal to side-step the crisis the way other bishops had. Truth was, Bishop Sawicki said, abuses such as those charged against Archbishop Hunthausen were common. "All bishops resonated with the problem," Bishop Sawicki said, "because they have the same ones themselves." Many were culpable, wittingly or not, of skirting church rules in much the same way.

The difference, as Bishop Sawicki saw it, was that most bishops behaved differently in the face of such accusations. Most averted a crisis by smooth-talking the Vatican, showering Rome with investigative reports from an astonished bishop who all but effusively thanked his superiors for bringing these aberrations to his attention, thick with assurances that the difficulties had been rectified and would, God forbid, never happen again. Law and order had been restored, with the Vatican's invaluable assistance.

But Archbishop Hunthausen had dug in his heels, Bishop Sawicki said, stoutly refusing to respond diplomatically to initial complaints of abuses from conservative

Catholics in Seattle. In the great Northwest, where brush fires soon get out of control, Archbishop Hunthausen's early reluctance to defend himself fanned the flames, Bishop Sawicki believed, and led to the all-out conflagration. It wasn't for nothing that Archbishop Hunthausen's nickname was "Dutch," his friend of many years said. He was stubborn, and it cost him, much to the chagrin of his allies in the hierarchy who believed that a little conciliation would have gone a long way.

In Bishop Sawicki's opinion the Holy See had actually showed sensitivity in its judgment. In an effort to save face for the archbishop, he explained, Rome had technically allowed Hunthausen to give Wuerl power rather than imposing it directly from Rome. "Now I know there are many interpretations of what happened, and it's not clear," Bishop Sawicki said. "It looks, I suppose, like a classic shoot-out at the old corral that lends itself to all sorts of speculation." Yes indeed.

He was delighted by the pastoral letter on the economy and had voted for it with enthusiasm. He recalled that the pope, knowing his interest in it, had cautioned that the economics pastoral would be difficult to write and to teach because Americans, as a generally affluent people, would have a hard time understanding poverty and the need for addressing it. The letter had been greeted as a breath of hope by most of those in his economically hard-pressed diocese who knew something about its message. Though the area was deep in depression, the letter had put forth an agenda from which reconstruction could start. That pleased him, though he was grimly realistic about how much could be built in the short run. Bishop Sawicki was proud of the bishops' record on social issues. The bishops had made their views known on a range of issues from sex to nuclear war. The toughest involved sex, he said, "because there church teachings touch believers where they live and require them to face up to personal choices." By contrast, other issues didn't confront believers "with as much stress."

On the political tussling between the conservatives backing Cardinal Law and moderates supporting various candidates, including Archbishop May, the winner of the conference presidential crown, Bishop Sawicki was equally coy. The Law bloc had consisted of ninety or so bishops and, because of the pope's pattern of appointing conservatives, was reaching majority, but as Cardinal Law's repeated losses on ballots for various offices showed, it was not yet in command. There was room, said Bishop Sawicki—an astute conference politician himself who sided with the moderates and progressives—for a variety of voices among the bishops. "There is no reason the conference ought to be satisfied surviving on some kind of gruel," was how he put it, "when it can thrive on a diet of a stew piquant."

Like many bishops, Bishop Sawicki was perturbed and disheartened by the apparent upsurge in influence of the Catholic right. He held to the notion common among bishops that a few extreme conservative groups raised havoc way out of proportion to their small numbers by flooding Rome with tattletale accounts of church law-breaking. Those bishops who yelled foul most loudly, including Bishop Sawicki, argued that the church in the United States was being misrepresented, though it was not always clear whether they were objecting to the content of these end-run indictments or, in the tradition of American majority rule, sought to disqualify them solely on grounds that they represented only an insignificant minority.

Bishop Sawicki had heard the drumbeat from the right, echoing the tub-thump from the American political right, and was worried about its ability to stir reaction. The right measured "orthodoxy" by a rigidly defined set of issues of its own choosing. The investigation of Renew, long a target of the right, was conducted in part because of that pressure. Among the right's accusations was that Renew was too lay-centered, lacked leaders qualified to teach Scripture, and de-emphasized the hierarchy. "The obvious response," Bishop Sawicki said sardonically, "is that the program was introduced by the bishops and we keep an active interest in it. It's doing good things here—and I know elsewhere too."

What greatly bothered Bishop Sawicki was what he called an "ahistorical" perspective on the right, which "knows history and how things have changed but refuses to acknowledge it," preferring to think that things have always been the same, eternally fixed and absolute. It was a mentality that illegitimately abstracted the church from its human and historical setting.

Was Father Curran a heretic? He posed the question himself, rhetorically and playfully. Far be it from him to draw the line between fallible and infallible teaching, he said, so he could not say for sure what was fair game for dissent or how it could be properly expressed. He offered his unmistakable approbation, however: "In my opinion Curran is a prayerful, gifted, reflective, caring, ecclesiastical academic who is trying to do what he feels theologically called to do. He enjoys a right as a responsible theologian to speculate and offer insights and opinions as a Catholic theologian." In bishop talk, that sounded like an endorsement, though Bishop Sawicki was quick to add some reservations. Under the best circumstances, he said, theologians should bandy about their dissenting views among themselves and out of public view. Like possible cures for AIDS, he said, investigations should be explored and tried out with great care and discretion. And he didn't agree with some of Father Curran's ideas, such as those regarding contraception and abortion, which the bishop considered too extreme. It was a vote of confidence in Father Curran, albeit a highly conditioned one.

Bishops and theologians hadn't quite figured out how to get along, the bishop said, looking off through the window into the distance, but they needed each other. That point was sometimes missed, he said. "We should not look for an ideal solution," he said. "If we don't have bishops conserving teaching, we're in trouble. If we don't have theologians exploring these teachings, we're equally in trouble."

Bishop Sawicki saw some areas in the church needing special, perhaps emergency, attention. Something must be done to enhance the "gifts and talents of women," in part to counteract the negative fallout from the fact "that we won't ordain them." Efforts must be made to bring Hispanics into the church. The agenda of the economics pastoral must be pursued. Two other trends were subtle but potentially powerful. One involved "Catholic identity." Whereas once "there were identifying ways people knew we were Catholic, those externals are disappearing, and as they do, we need some new ways to define ourselves." The other ominous sign was the drifting away of youth. "I see a graying of congregations and worship. I ask myself, 'Where are the young people at worship?'"

It was time for him to go. He stood up and stretched. For most of the afternoon, he had given his nimble, receptive mind to close, sometimes tough analysis of the church he had served for close to fifty years. Now he would go forth to celebrate it around a bowl of Christmas grog.

January
1·9·8·7

W ITH MOVES WORTHY OF A MASON DEFTLY WIELDING A trowel, Maureen extracted slices of pizza from two large, flopped-open boxes and placed them neatly on adjoining serving plates, one laden with the most exotic variety of toppings, the other a no-frills cheese-and-tomato standard issue. She had picked up the piping hot pies on her way home from the university, having stopped first to retrieve her son, Kevin, from his high school.

Her husband usually remained at his accounting office until well into the evening, and her other two children were living away from home, so she and her son were regular dinner companions. She welcomed the chance to spend the time with Kevin, a fifteen-year-old with round, kind eyes, dark hair, a short solid build, and a soft voice with a quality of sureness to it. A sophomore at a private school, Kevin was pretty much "all everything"—superb student, outstanding baseball player and skier, accomplished violist, a model high school citizen.

Maureen was tired but relaxed. As she asked Kevin about his day, she munched on a slice of pizza and picked at the tossed salad she had made before leaving for work.

Later in the evening mother and son planned to watch another part of *Shoah,* a film about the Holocaust. In addition to supplying them information about the incalculable horrors of that slaughter, the graphic film and narrative account had led them to think about their Jewish friends. "It's difficult to watch, but important to watch," Maureen said earnestly. "It's important not to forget it." Neighbor friends, Jack and Naomi, had once had that most perverse symbol of hatred—the swastika—painted on their front door. At the time, the couple's child had been the only Jewish student in the local school.

137

Maureen and Kevin saw in this filmed account of suffering an urgent appeal for understanding and acceptance of differences among religious, racial, and ethnic groups. Maureen had looked more closely at her appreciation for Judaism. "I've come to know something about Jewish tradition," she said. "Naomi and I are both traditionalists in our own way. She invited us over to their Passover seder, and I've been known to have Jewish friends over at Christmas. I think my husband and I have gotten the point across with our children that we don't ordinarily refer to 'our black friends' or 'our Protestant friends' or 'our Jewish friends.' Our kids don't care who's Protestant or Jewish. That's a change from my day, when people would reinforce prejudice all the time without even knowing it."

Kevin had valued his many Jewish friends. "Like a lot of teenagers, we tend to question things about religion," he said. "Everyone does. Nobody should try to play better than anyone else." His sense of religious egalitarianism had received a jolt one Sunday at mass. "I remember one day when a priest visiting in our parish said that the Catholic faith was the only truth. It made me very angry."

After being raised in a densely Catholic city neighborhood, Maureen increasingly had felt the influence of interreligious crosswinds. She had recently gone to a Presbyterian church with a friend, the first time she had ever attended a Protestant service, and had come away spiritually renewed. Another friend, a Jewish man, had told her he had started taking his children to the synagogue because of her example. Maureen recalled the man saying, "'I owe that to you. I looked at your faith and was inspired by it, and thought I should do something for my own children.' It's interesting how people see you. I certainly never imagine myself being an example."

Kevin himself had come to be a somewhat wary beneficiary of his parents' concept of religious responsibility toward their children. The household exercised that rule of Christian domesticity, not invoked much these days, whereby offspring were expected to haul themselves to church while they lived under the parental roof. Kevin, in the flower of Holden Caulfield skepticism, did his duty but professed little interest in church. He had been an altar boy but "never really got into it." In Catholic grade school he recalled a "crucifix in every room, and we went to church a lot and had religion class every day. The one class I remember most was in eighth grade—the history of the church. I did well in that class and read the Bible a lot because I liked the stories."

His liking of Scripture and his proficiency as a reader sparked his interest in becoming a lector in his parish. He had put in his request to the nun in charge of the program but never got a response. The nun eventually explained to his mother that someone thought he would be too busy with school to take on another activity. But nobody ever called him. Maureen, noting that a lector's task was less time-consuming than an altar boy's, believed Kevin was deemed unfit because he was the son of a woman who had once been divorced. She marked the beginning of his lack of interest in church as stemming in large part from the rebuff he had felt from that experience.

The lector episode had also reopened her inner wounds of rejection. The pangs she felt as an outsider in her own church—a woman divorced and remarried in contravention of church laws, hence excommunicated—aroused her nurturing and protective instincts toward those Catholics who, like herself, fell short of church standards, and they extended to the world's misfits and outcasts in general. Her vocation was caretaker. Two of her four children (one from her previous marriage) were adopted. She had taken in several foster children. A steady stream of stray dogs and cats had crossed her threshold, most of whom she had met while on duty as a volunteer for the ASPCA.

Her struggle had confirmed her conviction that Christianity, at heart, is an appeal of compassion toward those who suffered or found themselves beyond the pale. Her theology had become, more than ever, centered on the image of Christ as the comforter of lost and forsaken souls. "If we have a lot of people sitting out there in church and we're only ministering to the virtuous, that's not enough," Maureen said. "Jesus didn't just minister to the virtuous. Jesus was very nurturing. He was always allowing the person to come back into the fold without shame. I don't think the church allows for that. Jesus made it mandatory for the shepherd to go for the lost sheep. The church doesn't do that."

As for herself and her troubles with church law, she said she had come to terms with her status. "The issue of indissolubility really has nothing to do with me anymore, except that I would have liked for the children to feel more comfortable while they were growing up. Like many of her friends, she said, she had "worked out problems like divorce and birth control" in therapy.

Her Catholicism made her far less receptive to another theme she associated with the therapeutic movement, the emphasis on self-assertiveness. "Therapeutic values say you have to be good to yourself first. That's not my thinking, and I don't want to change it, because it's part of my Catholic thinking. I have a problem with people who always look out for number one. I don't object to people taking personal time for themselves, but if a member of the family needs something, that comes first.

"It's that old Catholic thinking—being a selfless person. What is the purpose of life? What am I doing? Where is my contributing act? Jesus helped people in his path. That's our obligation. You can't always have a calling as a nun or to lead a religious life. But I can pray for the strength to do what I'm called to do.

"Last year I took a couple of courses, and the children were disturbed because I wasn't home to make dinner. I said, 'Well, it's my turn now, and asked them for their help. I've learned that it makes a difference if you ask for support than if you just say you're going to do something because you want to."

Maureen had not allowed her differences with the church to stand in her way of seeking spiritual sustenance each Sunday at her parish. "I see the mass as my bond with the teachings of Jesus," she said. "I like to pray rather privately, alone in the corner. I'm there for the prayers and the consecration. I listen to the homily." She took communion.

Though she savored solitude at mass, she took similar comfort in seeing herself as part of a church at the fringe, the swelling ranks of Catholics who were pressing for change. She counted herself among the company of protest and appeal. "Catholics are going to have to get on the picket line, and they will," she predicted. Disputes involving sexual ethics as well as those centering on personalities such as Father Curran and Archbishop Hunthausen might have a salutary effect.

"It may be God's natural way toward bringing the church rejuvenation," she said. "Catholics, I think, have become rather horrified at the situation that has come about after Vatican II. But another John XXIII will come along. In the meantime, I remember a black gospel song I heard at a service for Martin Luther King, Jr.: 'Faith Itself Is a Victory.'

"I don't see myself having a crisis of faith because there's dissension in myself or in the church," Maureen said with firmness. She had been reading the novel *The Name of the Rose,* by Umberto Eco. She had been struck by the obsessive bickering of the medieval monks depicted in the novel over the question of whether Jesus had ever smiled. "I guess church scholars will always spend time over such things," she said. "But Catholics have to put shoes on their kids' feet. We should all be more concerned with the mundane things."

ON JANUARY 6, THE CELEBRATION OF EPIPHANY THAT SYMBOLICALLY MARKED the revelation of Christ's lordship over all humanity through the recounting of the wise men's visit to the infant Jesus, two lay Catholics and two priests carried out a surprise visit of their own to a U.S. military base to protest the nation's policy on nuclear arms.

The foursome, calling themselves the Epiphany Plowshares, stole undetected into the Willow Grove Naval Air Station north of Philadelphia and vented their antinuclear frustrations on some remote tokens of America's huge fighting force. It was an exercise in mischief aimed at attracting attention to moral issues of war and peace. Brandishing masons' hammers, they smashed instrument panels and severed wires on three aircraft, a P-3 Orion prop jet and two helicopters (a Marine Sea Stallion and an Army "Huey"). They finished their mission by pouring a container of their own blood on the damaged goods and leaving behind a statement.

In their statement, the four described their invasion as an attempt "responsibly to say 'no' to our nation's nuclear and interventionary war-making policies.

These policies are, at present, killing innocent people and seriously endangering the existence of all life on our planet." Another purpose, they said, was to "tear down the idol" of militarism.

The "Plowshares" tag was a conscious effort to link themselves to a line of peace activists dating back to 1980, when a group of eight Catholic laypeople and clerics, among them Philip Berrigan and his brother, the Reverend Daniel Berrigan, banded together as the Plowshares Eight and stood trial for injuring some nuclear missile nose cones at a General Electric plant in King of Prussia, Pennsylvania. The Plowshares movement, which saw itself as following the biblical injunction to turn "swords into plowshares," counted this as the sixteenth act of protest act by the group, each designed as a dramatic, seemingly absurd assault by the weak against the mighty.

Carrying out this foray at Willow Grove were Lin Romano, thirty, a member of the Community for Creative Non-violence in Washington, D.C.; Greg Boertje, thirty-one, a former Army officer and member of an alternative community, Jonah House, in Baltimore; and two priests from the Archdiocese of Philadelphia, the Reverend Thomas McGann, thirty-six, and the Reverend Dexter Lanctot, thirty-seven.

Authorities promptly arrested the four on charges of conspiracy, destruction of national defense material, destruction of government property, and trespass. They were placed in the Northeast Detention Center in Philadelphia. The government estimated the extent of damage to their aircraft at more than three hundred thousand dollars, but members of the Epiphany Plowshares claimed that figure was inflated.

Six days later, Father McGann received a letter from the archdiocese informing him that, under the terms of canon 1399, Cardinal John Krol had suspended him from the priesthood. Father Lanctot received the same notice on January 19. The priests could be restored according to the "prudent, pastoral judgment of the archbishop."

TWO DAYS AFTER THE INCIDENT AT WILLOW GROVE NAVAL AIR STATION, FRANK Shakespeare, a former president of CBS Television, and a prominent Catholic layman, officially began his duties as U.S. ambassador to the Vatican by meeting with Pope John Paul II for thirty minutes to present his diplomatic credentials. His became the second appointment to that post since formal relations were reestablished in 1983 after a hiatus of more than a century. In 1983, Congress had repealed an 1868 law forbidding full recognition of the Vatican. While that law was on the books, several presidents had dispatched personal envoys to Rome. The first full-fledged ambassador to be appointed to the Vatican by President Reagan was a longtime friend, the wealthy Catholic businessman William Wilson.

His successor, the sixty-one-year-old Shakespeare, had held several positions in government and private industry since stepping down from CBS in 1969. When nominated to fill the Vatican post the previous September, he was serving as ambassador to Portugal. He also had been director of the U.S. Information Agency during Richard Nixon's first term and before accepting the ambassadorial appointment to Portugal in 1985 had been chairman of the board of International Broadcasting.

Within the church, the new ambassador's most visible contribution had been as a member of the Lay Commission on Catholic Social Teaching and the U.S. Economy which responded critically to the U.S. bishops' pastoral letter on economics. As part of the commission's effort to correct what it saw as serious flaws in the letter, Shakespeare had identified himself with a outlook that was ardently free enterprise and wary of government programs to alleviate poverty. The commission's decidedly procapitalist posture represented deeply held convictions about the relationship between Catholic faith and social responsibility. Shakespeare and the other commission members took this interpretive understanding seriously enough as Catholic laymen to oppose openly their own bishops. They saw their task of correlating capitalism and Catholicism as a mission sufficiently important to run the risks of dissension and tension.

INTEREST IN THE BISHOPS' PASTORAL LETTER ON THE ECONOMY, WHICH SOARED right after its passage in November, tailed off considerably as Christmas approached, but rose briskly again in January. While analysts pored over its contents, strategists were plunging ahead with plans for getting its message to the grass roots of Catholic America.

Even before the first draft of the pastoral appeared, business leaders and the publications that served them in many cases sneered at what they considered ecclesiastical interlopers uttering nonsense, which they branded socialism. *Forbes* staff writer Michael Cieply, in an opinion piece (April 25, 1983), sniffed, "From sermonizing prelates, making up in presumption what they lack in knowledge of economic affairs, O Lord, deliver us. Intelligent businesspeople are right to be annoyed at much of the current preaching about profits and business." *Fortune,* in its December 26, 1983, issue, with more than a touch of condescension, accused the bishops of espousing socialism to give themselves "a role to play, while capitalism—reliance on impersonal market forces—leaves them in the cold."

The bishops, at least those entrusted with writing and distributing the pastoral letter, refused to be hooted down. The chest-thumping and shouts of "no trespassing" from the business and financial worlds failed to dissuade them from insisting that they could suggest remedies for the immense human suffering of those left in the wake of the boom. The bishops' focus was on the swelling ranks of those for whom the trickle-down theory from supply-siders was a cruel hoax. While wealth had ballooned at the top, the poor—the subjects of the prelates' preferential attention—were worse off, at the wrong end of a widening gap. No hoopla and celebration of the bonanzas among the most affluent investors could dispel the harsh realities the bishops had identified and addressed in their pastoral letter. They held firm despite the attacks from the business and financial fronts, including that hurled from within by the Lay Commission on Catholic Social Teaching and the U.S. Economy.

The tension between the bishops' letter and the commission's response was creating an impression of a clergy-lay split that worked to the detriment of the hierarchy. The implication, accented by the flurry of criticism, was that fuzzy-headed, idealistic clergymen were out of their depth, whereas their lay critics reflected expertise and hardheaded, real-world logic. Some Catholics suggested that the bishops should have released the letter with the endorsement of prominent business and civic leaders in order to blunt any suggestion that in any sense the Lay Commission represented "the laity" against "the clergy." The lack of that kind of united front had lent strength to that assumption; the bishops were stuck trying to establish their credibility at the same time they endeavored to persuade others of the merits of their arguments.

Among the most trenchant analyses of the pastoral letter to appear during the month was written by James Gaffney, a professor of ethics at Loyola University in New Orleans. Writing in the January 24 issue of *America,* Professor Gaffney forcefully defended the bishops against charges that they lacked competence to tackle economic questions.

"The attempt to discredit bishops on the ground that they are not experts resurrects a familiar fallacy based on the absurd suggestion that talking intelligently about the economy means talking as a qualified economist or at least an experienced businessman," Gaffney wrote. "We remember the same sophistry from earlier pretensions that talking significantly about war means talking as a military strategist or tactician. It is like pretending only gynecologists could talk meaningfully about women, or pediatricians about children—or, for that matter, theologians about religion. Economics is, at least arguably, a science, but the economy involves immensely more than the subject matter, however generously defined, of that science. And an important part of what it additionally involves is morality. If the bishops' intervention did no more than remind us of that fact, it would serve an admirable purpose" (p. 45).

The commandment to love one's neighbor and its corollary, belief in the equal dignity of all human beings, served as the guiding principles by which the bishops evaluated economic activity, Gaffney said. But their job was rendered especially difficult by the absence of precedent and the complexity of the task. Whereas the church had "a venerable doctrine, compactly formulated and much analyzed and criticized, concerning morality in war, there is no comparable tradition respecting economic morality." Notwithstanding that problem, he continued, "the U.S. bishops, having heard cries of pain, have taken a serious practical interest, whereas a great many of their critics quite plainly have not . . . they call for moral indignation and moral resolve. Poverty in any society is bad. But poverty in a rich society is wrong" (p. 47).

Having asserted that the bishops' effort was legitimate, Gaffney chose to differ with some of their emphases and to lament others he felt were unwisely excluded. Overall, he argued, the bishops would have come out ahead if they had made poverty "the central subject matter of their pastoral, taking account of its wide ramifications, instead of the economy in general." Likewise, he questioned the placement of unemployment ahead of poverty as an issue in need of urgent attention (p. 47).

The nature of work itself—specifically types of choices people had in the kinds of work they could do—had itself been slighted in Gaffney's view. "The ethical significance of those choices remains, in my opinion, one of Catholicism's worst moral blind spots, perhaps as a result of Catholicism's traditionally narrow conception of *vocation* as a topic of religious and moral significance," he wrote. "In any case, it would seem plain enough that a great many employments that provide adequate pay and quite decent working conditions remain, for much more intrinsic reasons, morally despicable" (p. 48).

Gaffney applauded the bishops' proposal for "a new American experiment" in cooperation and planning among government and private participants in the economy as a strike against "rampant individualism." And he noted with irony that despite the bishops' clearly stated opposition to highly centralized state planning, critics twisted their appeal into advocacy of socialism. "Actually," he wrote, "and although I personally take no satisfaction in the fact, the bishops' letter contains no genuinely socialist recommendations whatever" (p. 48).

Gaffney found other deficiencies in the letter: too little discussion of the effect of budget deficits, silence with regard to environmental threats and the population explosion. Finally, in response to his own question, "To whom, really and effectively, are the bishops talking?" he concluded that their aims depend on their own example.

"I do not know if the bishops can, or if they will even try to generate a strong Catholic movement for the kinds of economic reform they have advocated," Gaffney said. "If they do, I think their success will depend on more than what is usually meant by preaching." He continued, "It is one thing for bishops to talk about warfare, in which they do not participate, but quite another for them to

talk about the economy, in which their participation is extensive, as owners, producers, employers and managers—sometimes on quite a grand scale. If indeed,
what they call a 'preferential option for the poor' is at the heart of their message,
they have, as every Catholic knows, abundant opportunities to demonstrate that
in their personal and institutional economic behavior" (p. 49).

Barring that, nothing will happen, Gaffney said, adding that the "typical response I am hearing from even rather devoted Catholics to the bishops' pastoral,
while not hostile, is decidedly cautious. They are not saying, 'No, nothing doing!'
They are saying, 'Maybe, but you go first'" (p. 49).

Meanwhile, the taint of socialism ascribed to the pastoral letter by its detractors
was alone enough to commend it to Dale Vree, the editor of the *New Oxford Review*,
a low-budget journal that encouraged both theological orthodoxy and leftist economics. *NOR*, offbeat and unconventional, had become a refreshing alternative
to the more established and familiar Catholic periodicals. Underwritten by the
Pallotine Fathers, the magazine had assembled a heterodox stable of writers who
did not fit the standard religious molds. Among them were Robert N. Bellah,
Christopher Lasch, John C. Cort, and Robert Coles, a Harvard psychiatrist who
contributed a regular column of his reflections.

Dale Vree, in the January-February issue, read the public trashings of the pastoral letter by partisans of big business as sure signs that the bishops had struck a
vital nerve. Dismissing the widespread assumption that "conservative theology
and conservative politics always went hand-in-hand," Vree, obviously identifying
himself among those who defied the stereotype, applied that thought to the bishops' document. "And so, it is shocking—perhaps scandalous—that out of an antique and conservative church such as this we are presented by its bishops in
America with a pastoral letter on the economy that is strikingly progressive and
has earned the wrath of America's political conservatives, not least those who hold
power in Washington, D.C. If it is shocking it is because the pastoral is nothing
much more than a restatement of traditional Catholic social teaching, which in
America is one of the Church's best kept secrets. And if it is scandalous, it may
have something to do with the gospel" (p. 14).

Vree praised the bishops for urging the government to do more to fight the
problems of poverty and joblessness and the widening gulf between rich and poor.
He also lauded them for warning against the destructive excesses of economic
competition and individualism and for backing greater worker ownership and
management of enterprises. "Of course, the bishops don't invoke the word 'socialism' in their pastoral—and they'd be crazy if they did," Vree wrote. "Socialism
is a dirty word in America. Moreover, it is not the vocation of the Church to baptize particular 'isms' or prescribe economic panaceas. But if the critics of the pastoral accuse it of socialism, it might be salutary to accept the charge and see in it

further evidence of the scandal of Catholicism. For indeed, the Church, like the gospel, has 'bite'—in the area of economics as well as in the area of sex" (p. 18).

The church was a scandal, he argued, because it challenged precious notions of both political right and left. "No, Christianity is not just a junior partner in the conservative project," he declared. "It has a life and mind of its own. It is not a captive of conservative personalities, ideologies, or interests. It is able and willing to challenge the reigning ideologies and vested interests—whether of the Right or of the Left." The church's message was an indictment of the "proclivities for self-indulgence" of those on both ends of the political spectrum in terms of their particular cravings and vices, he said (p. 18). "What Catholicism offers," he concluded, "is a consistent vision of Love, which is sacrifice, while the world offers dreams of money, power and fast pleasure. In the eyes of the world, the Church is foolish. Let's hope she always remains so—foolish, that is, for the Lord and Savior who gave her birth" (p. 19).

As the reactions continued rolling in, the machinery for putting the pastoral letter into action was cranking up. From January 22 to 24, the United States Catholic Conference hosted more than four hundred social action coordinators from dioceses across the country at a Washington, D.C., session designed to better inform them about the letter's contents and to begin developing methods for bringing it to the attention of both the church and the public. The letter was available in paperback, along with implementation guides for diocesan leaders, and television and radio promotions were on hand to sample. In a dispatch from the session, the National Catholic Reporter said that the pastoral impinged in a very practical way on the choice of the site for the meeting. Leaders abandoned plans to use the Crystal City Sheraton, which operated without a union, and moved to the unionized Mayflower Hotel out of deference to the prolabor stance of the letter.

Bishop Anthony M. Pilla of Cleveland, head of the bishops' follow-up team, spelled out his guidelines for implementation in the January 31 issue of America. The bishop outlined a five-point initiative. He called for a "substantive commitment" on grounds that "none of us—bishops or laity—can afford to be silent on the questions of economic justice" (p. 76) and emphasized that "everyday economic choices cannot be separated from our religious and moral convictions." Second, he urged integration of the letter into all church life in such a way that it "enriches, not displaces, other activities and programs" (p. 77). Third, the bishop stressed the importance of teaching the moral principles at the foundation of the letter. Fourth, he called for continued debate on the best ways to put these principles into practice to achieve justice. And, fifth, Bishop Pilla exhorted the church to be an "agent of reform" within itself by examining its own economic behavior and using its resources to "speak and act against injustice in the marketplace" (p. 78).

The marathon gun had been fired, and the economics pastoral was just off the starting blocks.

PAUL'S DREAM OF GLIDING EASILY THROUGH HIS SENIOR YEAR AT SAINT AUGUS-
tine's had been shattered one day before the end of the semester when a professor accused him of using material for a term paper without giving proper credit.
Put starkly and coldly, it was a charge of plagiarism. To compound the matter,
the accusation had been publicized campus-wide, undermining Paul's integrity
as a student government officer in addition to covering him with personal embarrassment.

In his defense, Paul said he had been sloppy rather than larcenous in his use
of another's words and ideas. He conceded that his understanding of proper foot-
noting standards had been too foggy, but he insisted that he had not purposely
acted deceptively or in violation of the rules. He felt more stupid than guilty. As for
the unusual publicity accorded the case, Paul attributed it generally to his visibility as a student official and specifically to a campus political rival whom he suspected of planting the story to discredit him for personal gain.

A university committee had certified the professor's complaint. The penalty
deemed fitting for an infraction of this magnitude was for the student to rewrite
the term paper to a standard acceptable to the professor. It would be averaged in
among course requirements as a failing grade nonetheless. Paul had promptly set
to work on it.

The crisis had occurred just before the Christmas break and had predictably
placed him at the center of a personal and social storm. Though freely acknowledging that the problem could be traced to carelessness, he was dismayed at the
scandal that had ensued. He had always considered himself ethical; his choice of
a Catholic university in his own mind signified that concern. For the first time in
his life, he felt himself exposed to unfair public humiliation. This was not supposed to happen at a Catholic school, he had thought. But there he was in the
midst of a trauma that would test his personal and Christian character.

His first move after the bad news arrived had been to call his parents. He recalled the conversation: "My mother's first reaction was, 'Well, there goes law
school.' They jumped on me—they usually don't do that. Twenty minutes later
they called back. My mother said she was upset at what she had said. They told me
they loved me and were behind me. I talked to them every day for two weeks after.
My family plays such a big role in my life. I have a sense that wherever I am they're
always a rock to lean on."

Friends, including his eight housemates and his close student government allies, stuck by him, he reported with gratitude, but university officials, he said, were
silent. "No priest ever got in touch with me, though I'm not particularly close to
any of them. And I didn't discuss with any administrators what I was going

through." He felt unspoken censure from some other students, but little overt pressure to step down from his elected post. It was "eerie," he recalled, trying to carry on as usual with controversy swirling around his head.

Speaking of the incident only a month later, Paul showed neither self-pity nor bitterness. He was in characteristic good humor, seated in a shopworn leather chair in his neatly kept room, sun streaming in through the western exposure. The second semester had not yet started, so he was enjoying the pregnant lull. A faded school sweatshirt and brown chinos adorned his trim, muscular frame, and all around four years of college were on display—banners, mugs, buttons, posters, the usual artifacts of student life.

What had the harrowing experience taught him? "I learned that I could hold myself together through a crisis," he said somberly. "I also learned to trust people around me a bit more. I'm the kind of a person other people tell problems to. I learned that I need people to fall back on myself. I've found out who my best friends really are.

"I feel a lot different than I did a year ago. I'm more self-confident now, though it's funny, my parents always thought I was overconfident because I act that way sometimes. If I'm having a shitty day, I'll say it's great. If I say it often enough, it'll turn out that way. It's a kind of faith that I suppose has been building up in me my whole life and is now getting expressed in some new ways."

Paul had survived his first political scrape with some apparent success. It had been no small victory for someone who aspired to public office someday. The turmoil had led him to size himself up more intently as he stood on the threshold of graduation and envisioned a role for himself as an adult. From his self-appraisal, he had drawn certain conclusions.

He was expansive and composed as he began the analysis. He saw himself first as a builder of coalitions ("I'm the kind of person who seems able to bridge gaps between people"), an admirable prerequisite for politics; a "people pleaser" especially toward "people who don't know me," a trait he found both a plus and a minus ("basically I don't like anybody to be unhappy"); trusting ("mostly, especially now, I reserve judgment when I hear something bad about someone"); resolute ("when I'm in the public eye, I don't mind someone not liking me so long as I know where I'm coming from"); and balanced ("I'm not the kind of student who'll knock himself out to get above a 3.2 grade point average, but, on the other hand, I think I have a better than average social life").

Paul felt the need to be a "good person" no matter where a career took him. He drew inspiration from his father. "He lives a corporate life and has for a long time," Paul said. "But he has integrity. He has always tried to stay away from the political and ethical games that go on there. He shows me that it can be done." Though most people thought he took after his father, he said, "Actually, emotionally, my mother and I are much more similar. It's hard to know what my father thinks, but my mother and I seem to send messages back and forth by intuition all the time. He must sense there's some kind of understanding between me and my mother that he's not in on."

He strove to emulate his father's detachment from the seamier side of corporate life. His entry into campus politics had been, after all, as a candidate on a slate of mavericks who were running as outsiders protesting the cozy relationship between previous student leaders and the administration. "The example of the last few student officers was that it was a chance to get in tight with the administration, to get into their good graces, the sort of cronyism that involves having three-hour lunches. Our approach is that we could do more good by trying to represent student interests and by not wasting our time ass-kissing during three-hour lunches.

"It may seem that you get something from stroking people like that and playing that game," he ventured, "but I don't think so. I think administrators see right through it too. I think they respect you more if you stick to business."

Paul's grasp of right and wrong had been fortified by his church and his family. He expected to practice it wherever he went and to choose a profession that would allow him to express those values. A moral code had formed at the core of his character. He believed that the going would sometimes get tough, but his father had, in his own way, shown him the direction in which to go.

The first stop was law school, a possibility that, despite his mother's initial fears, had in no way been precluded by his difficulties. He had taken the law boards, attaining a high-average grade, and gone about the laborious task of applying to five law schools. He could do nothing more than sit back and await the verdicts.

What kind of law would he see himself practicing? "I don't see myself in divorce court," he said with gusto, "more like a labor negotiator."

— ◂ ▸ —

SINCE AUGUST, WHEN THE VATICAN, WITH THE POPE'S APPROVAL, HAD PUBLICLY judged Father Curran neither "suitable nor eligible" to teach as a Catholic theologian because of his dissenting views on aspects of sexual morality, his standing as a faculty member at Catholic University had been seriously undermined.

In announcing the Vatican's verdict, Archbishop Hickey, chancellor of Catholic University by virtue of his position as leader of the Washington archdiocese, declared that he would take immediate steps to remove Father Curran's "canonical mission," the official church approval required to teach in the three "pontifical faculties" of the university directly under Rome's control (theology, canon law, and philosophy). The official permission needed by Father Curran to retain his membership in the theology department was now, therefore, in jeopardy.

The full implications of Archbishop Hickey's intentions remained unclear and untested through the fall semester while Father Curran completed a year-long sabbatical. He had, however, signified that he would resist any attempt to deprive him of the professorship he had occupied for twenty-two years. The day after the archbishop's announcement, Father Curran vowed he would continue teaching moral theology at CU. He had also availed himself of his church right to a hearing of his case before a committee of his peers. The committee would decide whether or not, under the university's statutes, the Vatican's ruling constituted a "most serious reason" for removing Father Curran's canonical mission.

Through his difficulties, he had, moreover, retained the support of key allies—the dean of religious studies, the Reverend William Cenkner, and the head of the theology department, the Reverend David N. Power—in addition to official backing from the College Theological Society and the Catholic Theological Society of America. The American Association of University Professors had also come to his aid.

Not all had rallied to his cause, of course. Siding against him and calling for his ouster had been one prominent member of his department, the Reverend William May, who circulated a letter to that effect that was signed by thirty-three Catholic academics, most of them members of the Fellowship of Catholic Scholars.

The question of whether Father Curran would be allowed to teach outside the areas of the curriculum run by the Vatican remained, meanwhile, in abeyance. Under the university's bylaws, the theology department was actually split between courses required of students pursuing Vatican-related degrees in canon law, philosophy, and theology and "nonecclesiastical" electives that did not fall under Rome's jurisdiction. Father Curran's courses for the spring term were nonecclesiastical, therefore, he argued, out of harm's way.

But the issue was left hanging until the second week of December, when Archbishop Hickey, in a letter to the theologian, implied that a full suspension was in order until the matter was settled. It was a cease-and-desist order. Dated December 19, the letter meant that Father Curran would be prevented from teaching his courses Christian Social and Political Ethics, Moral Theology and Practice, and Bible and Moral Theology. Archbishop Hickey noted that the seventeen bishops on the forty-two-member Catholic University board agreed with his decision.

In his January 9 response, the fifty-two-year-old priest reminded Archbishop Hickey that his canonical mission remained in effect. He further insisted that he could legitimately offer his scheduled courses without the need for a canonical mission and indicated he would go ahead with plans to teach them. Citing the ecclesiastical statutes governing the Vatican-related portion of the theology department, Father Curran said the statutes "explicitly state that there is a 'nonecclesiastical' portion" of the theology department where those statutes do not apply and under which he felt "ready, willing and, I believe, lawfully entitled, to teach. . . . If there was no problem with my teaching those courses in the past—and no one, not even Cardinal Ratzinger, has said that there was, there can be no objection to my teaching the same courses again, especially since the courses do not directly deal with the matters in dispute between Rome and myself."

Father Curran stood defiant. Dismissing the suspension as improper, he pledged at a news conference January 12 to ignore the archbishop's instructions by showing up for classes. He also hinted that he might challenge the suspension in the civil courts as a violation of his rights as a tenured professor.

Faced with the prospect of open rebellion—the start of the spring term only two days away—the archbishop reacted decisively. On January 13, he again wrote to Father Curran, this time in a blunter, perhaps-I-did-not-make-myself-clear manner. The letter parried Father Curran's arguments: though "there are non-ecclesiastical programs in the Department of Theology," Archbishop Hickey wrote, "there are no non-ecclesiastical teachers. . . . I do not believe that such a situation was ever intended, and I reject any interpretation of the Canonical Statutes that would permit it.

"Let me emphasize that I regard it as untenable for you to teach your proposed theology courses this spring in view of the Holy See's judgment." He then dropped a trump card never before used by a bishop against a theologian—the threat to invoke canon 812. The statute, inserted into the revised code of canon law promulgated in 1983, made it necessary for *anyone* teaching Catholic theology to have "a mandate from a competent ecclesiastical authority."

Father Curran was to consider himself suspended with full pay pending completion of the hearings.

The threat suddenly and dramatically raised the stakes. Until then, the issue had been narrowly confined. It involved the requirement that those teaching in certain areas of Catholic University—the only church university in the nation with any direct supervision by the Vatican—hold a canonical mission. No teacher at any other Catholic college or university need worry about securing a canonical mission. Canon 812, on the other hand, could be used by any "competent ecclesiastical authority"—normally a bishop—to revoke any Catholic's right to teach theology on any campus. So Archbishop Hickey's threat held wide repercussions.

It was one thing for Rome to intrude into the affairs of the one university over which it arguably held legitimate, though limited, authority. It was another to invoke a canonical prerogative that could, in other academic settings, challenge the traditional American principle of academic freedom whereby religious authorities were enjoined from interfering in the autonomous right of a university to determine its own standards for teaching and learning. Many Catholics involved in higher education feared that canon 812 represented the pretext for violating that principle and, by giving the hierarchy power over internal university affairs, breaching the wall of separation of church and state that allowed state funds to flow to Catholic universities in substantial amounts.

At the same time that Archbishop Hickey leveled his threat, he made sure that Father Curran would have no classes to teach. Having failed to persuade the theologian to back off, the archbishop went directly to university officials and ordered them to cancel the three courses in question. The theology department posted the announcement on the afternoon of January 14. Father Cenkner and Father Power, both of whom had tried to dissuade the archbishop from issuing the suspension, told the campus newspaper, the *Tower* (January 23, 1987), that they had complied with the order because of the archbishop's threat to invoke canon 812 against Father Curran. Father Cenkner, in his comments to the newspaper, warned that such an incident could have a severe effect not only on this university, but on "all of Catholic higher education" (p. 3).

His courses erased from the schedule, Father Curran relented. In a news conference Thursday in the classroom where his first class would have been held, he said he had abandoned his effort to overturn the suspension out of concern for his students and to avoid the first use of canon 812.

Voicing determination to carry on his struggle for full reinstatement, Father Curran said the application of canon 812 would result in "a great catastrophe" whereby "decisions about the hiring, promotion, tenuring and dismissing of faculty members would be made by church authorities who are external to the academic community. This denial of academic freedom would have serious consequences for academic accreditation, government funding and a host of other issues important to Catholic higher education in the United States."

Explaining his stand to Archbishop Hickey in a letter dated January 14, Father Curran asked the prelate to reveal whether he intended to invoke canon 812 no matter what a committee of peers might decide about the case, thereby rendering due process superficial and inauthentic. He also said he was backing down for the sake of his students' welfare: "In the past I have never used my classroom to involve my students in any way in my difficulties with authorities in the church or at the university. Neither will I at the present time make my students hostages in this ongoing controversy, or risk injustice to them even as I struggle to attain justice for myself."

The same week, the academic senate of the university appointed a seven-member committee to pass judgment on the merits of the case. In the meantime, Father Curran had been banished. By decree of Rome and the acquiescence of American bishops, he had become a Socrates, declared persona non grata on grounds that his views were corrupting the moral theology of Catholic youth. But he had refused to drink the hemlock.

A͟T A RANDOM CALL AT SAINT BRIDGET'S PARISH, A STOCKY BRICK STRUCTURE within hailing distance of Pittsburgh, the housekeeper answered the bell. She was a short, pleasant woman with dark hair tied back in a bun and a skittishly cautious manner that volunteered very little. The pastor was not in, she explained. An assistant, perhaps? Well, not exactly, she said, struggling to square facts with her ingrained disposition toward the whole truth. He was there, but it was his day off, and he should only respond to something urgent. Was it urgent? It was agreed that the assistant should himself decide. The request, for a short visit with a book-writing stranger, sounded whimsical enough, he said later, to give a try. He had appeared at the door and offered welcome.

Philip was twenty-nine years old, a thin layer of priestly mannerism grafted onto a solid trunk of character that was part monk and part yuppie. The forehead of his square, friendly face was still damp from his six-mile run. Though the byways outside were thick with the hard-packed snow of January, Philip had fulfilled his thrice-weekly obligation to himself. He carried some bulk on his large frame, but two years ago had carried much more, sixty-eight pounds to be exact. He thanked the roadwork for most of the trimming.

He wore jeans, a short-sleeved shirt, and running shoes. His dark features were highlighted by black-framed designer glasses. His voice was a rich baritone, and he spoke quietly, staccato fashion, choosing words carefully so as to be sure of himself.

He led the way to his cramped office and draped himself in a lounge chair snug by the twenty-four-inch color television set. The capsule introduction continued. He was still something of a "priestling," he said with a sly smile. Fresh from seminary three years ago, he had been assigned to a city parish, then nearly two years ago to Saint Bridget's. It was a growing parish in a burgeoning suburb with an "on-the-go" group of people rushing to get everywhere in a hurry, "even sometimes to heaven, I think." The suburb, as he described it, was a "whites only" enclave. Blacks were shut out of the real estate market. "There is quite a lot of animosity toward them," he said. It was hardly surprising that Martin Luther King's birthday had passed scarcely without notice that week, a grim sign of racial attitudes in the township, he assumed, and a reminder of the bias he still felt lodged within himself.

Philip himself was still sort of settling into the priesthood, if what he was doing could even be described quite that precisely. He was the only assistant in the parish, under the thumb of a pastor who left no detail unsupervised and who was the same age as his own father. He liked the variety, the routines, and the mingling with people.

Under the pastor's watchful eye, Philip taught confraternity classes (religious education), initiated the youngsters into the mysteries of the sacraments, and filled in wherever needed. Just beyond the watchful eye, he did what he enjoyed most, joining Catholic charismatics in their exuberant praise of God in prayer and song. Charismatics celebrated the "gifts of the Spirit" spontaneously and rambunctiously. Philip attended rallies, raised his hands in the air with them, cried aloud his shouts of joy, and helped newcomers feel welcome. The pastor had never given an opinion about these goings-on, but Philip thought he looked a bit askance at it. Perhaps it was a generational thing, Philip said; the pastor, the product of a more subdued time, may have found the charismatic style disagreeably bouncy.

Saint Bridget's generally resembled countless other suburban Catholic parishes across the land. Philip, on the other hand, stood out immediately as a young man not quite at home in his setting. As we sat in his office, drinking coffee, then trudging around the parish neighborhood, he took up the invitation to tell just how he came to be there.

Toward the end of high school, little more than a decade ago, Philip had his future firmly drawn. Included were a bachelor's degree in accounting, a master's at the Wharton School, a career in investment and real estate, a wife, kids, a suburban house—the whole shooting match. As the first step, he gained early acceptance to college. He was working at a restaurant to earn money. He liked nice things and intended, within tasteful limits, to sample his share of them. Everything was going according to plan.

Along the way to the starting line, he wrecked his car and found himself walking to his destinations, engulfed in unexpected solitude. "That's how my spiritual awakening began," he recalled. "Suddenly I had quiet time to be with God." His family had not, by his reckoning, "been exactly pillars of the church." His parents were on their way to a divorce. But he had gone to mass fairly regularly, and now he found himself suffused by the belief that God "had created me for a reason and that he would show me what to do." He had remembered a quote from Saint Augustine: "'God knows us better than we know ourselves.' If we follow him we will be happier." Most people thought that sounded pretty saccharine, he said, but "it involved a real struggle that I never thought would happen, trying to understand what I was supposed to do."

An uncle was a priest and an aunt a sister, but Philip felt that their examples had had little influence on his course. At the suggestion of a parish priest, he had sought vocational guidance from Trappist monks, and soon after he had been swept up by a charismatic revival meeting near home. "I learned I had something," he said, "a sense of prayerfulness others had looked for all their lives."

During his time with the charismatics, he'd undergone a bone-rattling, ecstatic conversion, the "baptism of the Holy Spirit" hallmark of the movement. It was a powerful experience that, by his account, both drew him to the church and imbued him with a freer spirit than could be easily contained within the confines of the conventional priesthood. Touched by the Spirit that, scripturally speaking, blows "where it will," his would be no ordinary route to a life of service.

His first taste of seminary, a three-day exploratory visit, was, as he looked back, "everything I thought it would be, and I didn't like it. It was very academic, a think tank. I didn't find the depth of prayer life there. I was being very judgmental. Besides, I asked myself, why would I want to get on a sinking ship? People were abandoning seminaries. It was 1976. The Vatican had just issued strict guidelines on sex ethics and said no to the ordination of women. I didn't agree with much of it, and I was very open to marriage. But this thing kept nagging me. Almost in spite of myself I realized I was meant to be there."

Within a month, he had been admitted to the seminary, scuttling his ideas of college and the house with the backyard swimming pool. Almost. Distant as that aspiration now seemed, at the same time it bubbled through his conversation as an ever-accessible pipe dream. Philip spoke as a man who still straddled a line, having made an "either/or" choice but wondering why it could not be "both/and."

He had become a priest, however, and when discussing his vocation there was no room for idle speculation about what might have been. He was all business in the role of the traditional cleric who never looked back. "I went into seminary with a very liberal mind," he said resolutely, "but I left with a very orthodox, dogmatic mind-set. I'm comfortable with that." As he spoke, his fingers ran over the tops of his sizable record collection made up mostly of rock and modern jazz. Before him on a magazine table lay two books he was reading: *Les Miserables* (he hoped to see the Broadway show) and that mainstay of psychopietistic bravado *The Road Less Traveled.*

As a once-budding broker and a now-ordained priest, Philip had a healthy respect for authority. He had little sympathy for Archbishop Hunthausen's tussle with the Vatican and took a dim view of Father Curran's deviation from official moral teachings. But he also favored maximizing career opportunities. He would have no objection to opening the priesthood to women and/or married men.

Beyond the routines of parish life, which were much to his liking, his outlet was the subculture of the charismatic. He felt it as an exercise of freedom—emotionally, personally, spiritually—opening people up to their own gifts and their fullest selves. Was it therapy? "Not exactly," he said, "but maybe it's the kind of healing and wholeness Club Med should be." The night before he had helped introduce a hundred people into the ways of Pentecostalism, teaching them to "pray spontaneously, a most un-Catholic thing to do."

"The world is acting more hostile to the church," he added. "Jim and Tammy Bakker appear on television, and people think that's religion. As that kind of thing deteriorates, people need a real spiritual emphasis even more."

The informality of the charismatics tended to break down barriers between clergy and people, Philip said, and that came as a relief. With no thought of crossing, he felt close to that other side and welcomed the narrowing of differences.

Philip was one of eight ordained in his class. "Some say, 'you're a priest, you've made it,' but that's ridiculous." There was the "constant struggle" of celibacy, among other things. "The Lord creates us as sexual people inclined to procreate, to be in union with others. You never conquer it.

"Now I'm enamored of little children. I'd love to be a father—the whole idea of establishing roots with a woman. I talk about it a lot with friends. Do I ever think of what it would have been like with a family and a career in finance? Yes, very much so."

Whatever there was of a divided mind was once again overruled. "I think growth in celibacy will be developmental," Philip-the-priest said. Then, firmly and with assurance, "God gives us the grace to live out our vocation. Can I give it up? Yes. It's a fragile gift. But I had the freedom to accept my invitation to be ordained. I wasn't coerced into being a priest. He wouldn't give me something I couldn't handle."

ONE WEEK AFTER FATHER CURRAN'S SUSPENSION, AN UNUSUAL GATHERING OF thirty-eight bishops, theologians, and educators sat down at the University of Notre Dame to explore a common defense against threats from Rome. The two-day unofficial parley, from January 19 to 21, had been planned long in advance of the latest twist in the Curran case, but that development lent acute urgency to the agenda. The issues included academic freedom, the threat from new Vatican regulations on Catholic higher education, and the need to prevent similar conflicts between theologians and Rome.

The Reverend David Burrell, C.S.C., a Notre Dame theologian and former head of the department, convened the invitation-only group with the blessing of the university's outgoing president, the Reverend Theodore M. Hesburgh, C.S.C. Thirty-eight invitees accepted: eleven bishops, thirteen theologians, and fourteen academic administrators. Among them were Bishop Raymond A. Lucker of New Ulm; the Reverend William Byron, S.J., president of Catholic University; and Dr. Monica Hellwig, professor of theology at Georgetown University and president of the Catholic Theological Society of America.

As conceived by Father Burrell, the sessions provided opportunities to thrash out mutual problems and to test the feasibility of building a united front against assaults on intellectual integrity. The Vatican's proposed schema on higher education contained a provision (fortifying canon 812) that gave bishops veto power over theological appointments. Many theologians were nervous about that, of course, and were, in addition, dispirited both by the apparent unwillingness of the bishops to fight harder for Father Curran or take a tougher stand on academic freedom. And administrators, the most likely to be caught in the middle, were especially eager to forestall quarrels between bishops and theologians, both as a practical matter of keeping harmony and to prevent the loss of further academic credibility (many felt the Curran case had already cost them some). Many had also become increasingly vocal about the possible suspension of government aid if Vatican intrusion was ruled in violation of church-state separation.

In his opening remarks, Father Burrell served the first volley by declaring that "two buzz-words which have marked recent exchanges" between bishops and theologians, namely "dissent and academic freedom," were "not only misleading but can easily provoke hostility in different groups." Dissent implied false opposition between a clearly unquestionable set of truths expounded by the hierarchy and clearly rebellious opinions by theologians. In fact, Father Burrell suggested, Vatican II had collapsed that dualism by placing all parties to the discussion in a kind of interdependent relationship. Likewise, he said, the freedom of Catholic scholars was conditioned inasmuch as their work was rooted "in the community of the faithful."

Those themes echoed through the meeting. Behind closed doors in the Center for Continuing Education, the participants engaged in a free and open discussion of their hopes and worries. Father Curran's name was invoked several times, as was that of the venerable and ever quotable Cardinal Newman. Other reports from the sessions alluded to the presence of a powerful backing for the right of theologians to teach and do research free of harassment. "We felt theologians just have to be free of the kind of suspicion and fear that has pervaded the academy in the past few years," said one participant, summing up the discussion.

Less settled was the question of what "model" of academic freedom fit church institutions that presupposed a faith commitment by its teachers of theology but did not want to compromise their scholarship. The church had a right to expect something of those teaching in its name that would not ordinarily be required in nonchurch settings, most agreed. But what form should this limitation take? How far should it go? The question was very much alive.

There was also broad consensus on the need for what some called the "American genius" for closer collaboration in problem solving. The achievements in Catholic higher education in America were hailed as unequalled in the world, and a cooperative effort was needed to safeguard this treasure. With regard to conflict-resolution between bishops and theologians, a proposal was making the rounds that would implement a set of step-by-step guidelines through the Conference of Bishops. It was being steered through a series of sensitive discussions on its way to a final draft. Options for settling disputes in other ways were also given a hearing.

By the concluding session, many of those who took part said they were most grateful for the chance to get acquainted with people with whom they shared so many interests but had seldom or ever encountered face-to-face. "What we achieved was mutual education," Father Burrell said. "There is no forum for talking about these things. A lot of people are just learning. It tends to be a lonely world for administrators and bishops and theologians. It's important for them to talk with one another. If we look at each other just through political glasses we all look like pawns on a chess board. Father Hesburgh said it: We should know we're all we've got and better listen to one another. And we really did explore together some tough issues."

— —

WENDING THEIR WAY THROUGH THE STREETS OF WASHINGTON, D.C., IN A DRIV-ing snowstorm, an estimated five thousand pro-life marchers on January 22 protested the Supreme Court's decision legalizing abortion on the fourteenth anniversary of the ruling.

As in past demonstrations, a mood of determination and defiance pervaded the crowd representing fifty states. Many hoisted umbrellas to blunt the sheets of snow, which had accumulated to a depth of six inches before the march had ended, and held hand-painted signs of resistance. "Don't Buy the Big Lie of Abortion" read one. Another said, "It May Be Cold Here, But It'll Be Hot Where Baby-Killers Go." The marchers chanted slogans and cheered as speakers, including President Reagan, denounced the continued practice of abortion and vowed to end it.

The president's remarks, broadcast by way of telephone hookup to the crowd gathered at the Ellipse, echoed his message to similar gatherings in previous years. Calling the practice a "national tragedy," he said, "Our commitment to the dignity of all human life must begin with respect for the most basic civil right of all, the right to life."

The storm reduced the protest crowd, organized by the National Right to Life Committee, to a tenth or less of its usual size. Leaders were optimistic about chances for a reversal of the landmark *Roe* v. *Wade* decision because of the rising strength of the antiabortion sentiment on the Supreme Court resulting from Reagan's conservative appointments. The original 1973 decision was by a 7 to 2 margin. In 1986, following two Reagan appointments, the Court reaffirmed *Roe* v. *Wade* by the slimmest 5 to 4 majority.

Some Catholic Right to Life lobbyists were quietly conceding that a total prohibition of abortion stood no real chance of national acceptance. Though still insisting publicly that they would brook no compromises, they acknowledged privately that sufficient support was lacking for an absolute ban and were prepared to make some concessions, as few as possible and only in extreme situations. The Catholic bishops had themselves once debated endorsing the Hatch Amendment, which would have opened the door to multiple standards by returning the issue to the states. The general expectation was that the courts would settle the matter in their favor and that legislative remedies were becoming more difficult to enact. A handful of proposals had lost in the previous fall's elections.

The marchers reflected the rising optimism of the movement and its dogged persistence. The crowd was largely white and middle class, but they raised their banners, they said, on behalf of a cause that was universal and unending.

THE REVEREND AVERY DULLES, S.J., DELIVERED AN ADDRESS ON JANUARY 23 AT the Rockford Institute Center on Religion and Society, a neoconservative organization based in New York City, his theme that the nation's bishops had endangered their spiritual roles by focusing their attention on social issues.

By virtue of his reputation as a scholar and an irenic spirit, Father Dulles had attained a stature rare among theologians. That is to say, his words won a respectful hearing even among many Catholics who were not inclined to follow theological debate. A spare skyscraper of a man, Father Dulles had attracted widespread praise and recognition for his books on ecclesiology, most notably his fertile work *Models of the Church*. He was near retirement, about to become an elder statesman.

Father Dulles had been known as a careful, fair-minded scholar during his many years at Catholic University (the week before, he had been named to the special university committee investigating Father Curran's appeal), enthusiastic about the renewal of the Second Vatican Council but at the same time a loving conservator of church tradition. In recent years, he had taken a more partisan direction, theologically and politically, allying himself with the Christian neoconservative movement reacting to perceived liberal excesses in the churches. His was a voice that helped give the movement legitimacy. Though conservative, he steered clear of the extremism of the Catholic right, the antimodernist forces of reaction that continued to regard him as a dangerous moderate. Given his stature and his ability to deliver lucid, tightly reasoned analyses fit for a broad audience, his speech was destined to reverberate widely.

Although Father Dulles recognized the bishops' right to reiterate abiding moral principles, he questioned whether the bishops "ought to give detailed answers, in controverted areas such as nuclear policy, taxation, welfare programs and the like." Clearly he did not.

Though the bishops drew much public attention with their specific recommendations, Father Dulles said there were "reasons for restraint." Their time might be better spent on business closer to home. Instead, "The impression is given that the bishops are more at ease in criticizing the performance of governments than in shouldering their own responsibilities in the church."

He followed with his most cutting remarks, the meat of his attack: "Few of the American bishops today enjoy a great reputation for their mastery of theology, liturgy or spiritual direction, yet many of them are known for their views on politics and the economy.

"When the bishops devote so much attention to worldly affairs they can unwittingly give the impression that what is truly important in their eyes is not the faith or holiness that leads to everlasting life, but rather the structuring of human society to make the world more habitable. The church has in the past managed to convey the conviction that poverty and worldly suffering are only relative evils because the wretched of the earth, if they are pure in heart, are loved by God and destined for eternal blessedness. Conversely it has conveyed to the rich and prosperous the warning that if they become proud and use their riches selfishly they must fear divine retribution. Such, as we have seen, was the message of Jesus. The appeal to sociopolitical analysis in recent episcopal teaching, coupled with an almost total lack of eschatological reference, gives the impression that the church's pastors have little confidence in its spiritual patrimony. It is scarcely surprising if a church that gives such high priority to politics and economics suffers a decline in priestly and religious vocations.

"While there is no doubt that an individual bishop may be well-versed in questions of military strategy or economics, the publication of elaborate and highly technical conference statements on nuclear weapons and the economy arouses suspicions that the bishops are exceeding their competence."

The greatest price of the bishops' misguided strategy, Father Dulles said, was their very credibility. "By speaking out on issues of a secular character bishops undermine their authority in areas that clearly fall within the scope of their mission."

Father Dulles appealed for a traditional division of labor: the assignment of secular work to the laity. It was an argument that had been used variously by conservatives to cut both ecclesiastically and politically. In the former sense, it was a call for an older, hierarchical flow of authority. Politically, it was often used by lay conservatives to justify keeping liberal-minded bishops from shaping policy with regard to "secular" issues.

"When concrete instructions are issued by the hierarchy on issues of a social and political character," Father Dulles said, "the question arises whether the laity are being deprived of their distinctive responsibility. Vatican II asserted that the renewal of the temporal order is the special responsibility of the laity and that the clergy should not be expected to offer concrete solutions to complex secular questions. . . . I agree that it is generally best for the concrete applications of Christian social teaching to be made by lay people who are regularly involved in secular affairs, especially those who are specialists in the pertinent disciplines."

There were three situations when bishops should be specific, he concluded, lest they always confine themselves to "speaking in airy generalities": first, when it seemed instructive to indicate how moral principles might, hypothetically, "work out in practice"; second, when certain applications were so obvious that "no room is left for reasonable disagreement"; third, in "urgent situations in which it is imperative for Catholics to act in unison in order to prevent an opportunity from being lost."

IN NOVEMBER, THE REVEREND JOHN MCNEILL HAD BROKEN A CHURCH-IMPOSED silence to blast the Vatican's latest pronouncement on homosexuality. Since then he had awaited word of his certain ouster from the Society of Jesus. The cold reality struck on January 28 in a letter delivered to him from the Vatican Congregation for Religious and Secular Institutes, signed by its prefect, Cardinal J. Jerome Hamer, O.P. The congregation notified Father McNeill that it had approved a dismissal request from the superior general of the Jesuits. He was thereby "expelled from the religious house according to Canon 703 of the Code of Canon Law."

Much of the letter sounded gothic, even apocalyptic. Father McNeill's advocacy of a more accepting attitude by the church toward gays, in the form of public statements deploring the Vatican's latest denunciation of homosexuality, had caused "widespread, grave, external scandal" which was, in turn, "injurious to the magisterium of the Holy See." His "pertinacious disobedience" toward his superiors, consisting of "spreading of doctrines condemned by the magisterium of the Catholic Church," had constituted "grave, external, imputable and juridically proven" conduct. Though he had been given "sufficient warnings," he had responded with "incorrigibility," and his defense was judged to be "entirely insufficient."

Dismissal was necessary, the congregation said, so as to prevent no less than "very grave imminent harm to the salvation of souls and to the good of the Society of Jesus."

Father McNeill was given ten days to appeal. He did, more from honor than from any hope of reprieve. In his appeal, he was unapologetic and steadfast. "I have publicly challenged the teaching and practice of the magisterium concerning homosexual persons," he acknowledged, but he disputed the interpretation placed upon that conduct by his superiors. He saw his actions and his ministry to homosexuals as obedience "to the will of God insofar as I see that will."

The sixty-year-old priest noted that he had kept silent for nine years before his outburst against the most recent Vatican document, which was becoming known among many gay-rights supporters as the "Halloween Statement." His effort to change church views was based, he said, "on my perception that its present teaching and pastoral practice have caused enormous amounts of unjust suffering among gay people."

To the charge that his ministry endangered souls, he said, "I am aware of hundreds, even thousands, of gay men and lesbian women who as a result of my writings and ministry have returned to their faith and the church, developed a new sacramental and prayer life, and many have entered religious life and the priesthood."

— —

PARISH PASTORS WERE GETTING SOME MUCH NEEDED ATTENTION. THOUGH THE pastor was the impresario of the parish, he had curiously been virtually ignored by post–Vatican II revisionists. He had remained the odd man out, the foreman caught between the demands of management and labor, the often overlooked middleman in the spiritual commerce of the church.

Efforts to atone for that neglect had begun. The U.S. bishops were finishing a major document on the role of the pastor, and several prominent study groups were focusing greater attention on priests-in-charge. An important step in giving the subject wider exposure had been the decision by FADICA (Foundations and Donors Interested in Catholic Activities, Inc.), a Washington-based philanthropic association, to make them the topic of a national symposium.

The symposium, titled The Role of Pastor, Changes and Challenges, brought together a selected number of influential lay Catholics, bishops, and priests, both pastors of churches and assistants. In a day-long gathering January 30 at a hotel in West Palm Beach, Florida, they looked at a largely obscured world from the view of those inside it.

Over four sessions marked by striking candor, participants heard pastors tell about the drastic shift in what was expected of them since the Second Vatican Council, listened to their struggles to balance the pressures from higher-ups with the aspirations of a more active laity, heard predictions about a radically revamped pastorate in the future, and were presented a summary of what the bishops would include in their forthcoming document on pastors.

By day's end, some of the lay onlookers were jarred and disturbed by the nature and severity of critical concerns that had been delivered so calmly and dispassionately. Taken collectively, the forgotten men were loyal priests but unhappy laborers in the vineyard. They felt beset by serious frustrations, caught too often between colliding forces and left to fend for themselves in the confusing, even disorienting terrain of the modern parish. The sharp decline in the numbers of priests had, not surprisingly, been demoralizing. Colleagues and seminary classmates they had known had left the priesthood. Not only was there a loss of camaraderie; the work load had mounted accordingly.

Speakers at the symposium appealed less for sympathy than for support and for clarity in recognizing and addressing the problems. Though they were unusually blunt in going semipublic with those complaints, they did so as men with a deep love of and commitment to the church. Theirs was a genteel call for help.

Troubled though the pastor might be, the evidence suggested that his importance as the prime mover of the parish was undiminished. The Reverend Philip Murnion, director of the Parish Project for the National Conference of Catholic Bishops, summed up recent studies that had underscored that critical function. Noting that becoming a pastor inevitably means "being beleaguered," Father Murnion said the role entailed being "at the juncture of the different dynamics in parish life. He is at the center of the spiritual life of the parish and its organizational life, trying to hold the two together."

Father Murnion continued, "To a large extent one can predict the vitality of a parish, or the lack of vitality of a parish, by the quality of the leadership of the pastor. Not that there needs to be the same style of pastoring in all instances, but the pastor's leadership is key to whether or not a parish feels itself to be a real community of believers or just a community of faithful trying to worship and act together."

The pastor's job in the course of the day was likened to such functions as juggler, magician, and orchestra leader. Bishop Thomas Larkin, chairman of the bishops' committee preparing the document on pastors, emphasized that far too little attention had been given to the duties and needs of the church's most visible representatives. "The reason for the document is that in the literature of the post–Vatican II Church, there is a great deal about parish life, religious education, sacramental ministry and even priesthood," Bishop Larkin said in his synopsis of the committee's findings, "but there is very little about the role of pastor, who is a key person in the parish." It was as if McDonald's had prepared a manual for every employee in the chain except the franchise manager.

During his pre–Vatican II years as a pastor, Bishop Larkin said, there was "no parish council, no school board, no Cursillo [weekend retreat], no marriage encounter, no charismatic renewal, and none of the parish renewal programs we have today." These and many other new duties had left many pastors feeling "unhappy and lonely and uncertain about the future," Bishop Larkin said. The pastor had found himself faced simultaneously with the demand for sweeping liturgical renewal, an "increasingly well-educated" laity that wanted more parish responsibility, growing spiritual yearning of people "in a secularized society," and "changing parish and neighborhood conditions." Said another participant, "The pastor feels torn apart."

These pressures had, in turn, required new patterns of relationship among pastors, parish staff, and parishioners, Bishop Larkin said. An emphasis on "collaboration" implied an end to the older style of the pastor who spoke with authority on everything. Pastors were required to learn mutuality, and many, especially in the beginning, did not like it. "When expressions such as 'shared authority' and 'participating in decision-making' came into practice, the post–Vatican II pastors could not help but feel a sense of resentment," Bishop Larkin said. "Finally, they were in a position of power, and now everything could be questioned and everything was questionable." No longer did "Father" necessarily know best in the eyes of the laity.

Pastors had become more involved in preparing teachers rather than teaching themselves, the bishop said. Rather than serve as remote performers of impersonal rites, they were expected to relate sacraments to people's lives. "Before Vatican II, for example," he recalled, "pastors would go over to church on Sunday afternoon and baptize maybe twelve to fifteen infants, perhaps never having seen the parents before, took all the information right there on the spot and probably didn't see the parents very often afterward. But now we have the beautiful preparation ceremony for baptism which makes it so much more meaningful for our people."

Though the church's formal structure was no less hierarchical than before, its working style was perhaps more congregational, involving more laypeople. The term increasingly used to describe the concept behind the network of ordained and lay ministries within the parish was "ministerial church." The pastor, often unsure of his place, was required to train lay ministers for a variety of tasks with which he was even less familiar. "No longer is he simply the person who says Mass, hears confessions and visits the sick," said Monsignor Alexander Sigur, pastor of Our Lady of Fatima in Lafayette, Louisiana. "He must be the spiritual leader, efficient business manager, and role model to his people. The challenge is that pastors cannot accomplish this alone; they must invite lay participation [collaborative ministry] and provide training in Church doctrine and practice."

Among the dangers Monsignor Sigur warned about was that of "a developing new laicism" that "we are ill-prepared to accommodate." The rise of new cadres of full-time lay ministers on parish staffs meant, in the estimation of one priest, that "much more ministry [was] going on" than ever these days, even with fewer clergy. At the same time, the influx of lay ministers posed several problems, he added, including the need for adequate salaries and benefits and safeguards against incompetence.

The extent to which a parish could evolve its own relative congregational autonomy was illustrated by an account from another pastor, the Reverend Thomas Caroluzza of Holy Spirit Church in Virginia Beach, Virginia. He had been assigned to the parish only a few months before. The previous pastor had left three weeks before his replacement arrived. "He simply turned the parish on 'automatic pilot,'" Father Caroluzza said. "Nothing was canceled; everything went on as usual: parish council, liturgical committee, finance council, ministry to the sick and needy, religious education. Checks were signed; everything happened on time with no priests present. The community even gathered on weekdays to pray and receive communion, even though there was no priest present for three weeks."

On arrival, he had been called by a man named Al, the "coordinator of Mass coordinators, who informed me that he was there to train me on how to say mass in Holy Spirit parish. At first as I walked through this, I felt like an altar server! But, as Al said, 'Some priests come in here and confuse all the other liturgical ministers, so I always train them first, so they don't mess this parish up.' So I was grateful for his ministry to me and for the way he helped me avoid confusion."

It was generally agreed that such equanimity on the pastor's part took considerable maturity and personal security, more than many pastors possessed. Father Caroluzza saw the future of lay ministry extending far beyond that. Pastors must learn to help equip laypeople for their ministries in the world. "The energy will shift," he said, "as it is already shifting, from parish center to the marketplace, the work place, the play place and, mostly, the home . . . when you study Vatican II's documents on the laity we have not even begun to deal with what it says about the laity. We have turned them all into church ministers. We have neglected to address the missionary vocation of the laity."

Training the spotlight on pastors revealed a vocation in rapid transition. A Portland, Oregon, pastor took his opportunity during the symposium to look backward and forward to the most futuristic vision offered during the symposium.

The Reverend Bertram F. Griffin, pastor of Saint Pius X Church, looked back somewhat wistfully to the period after he was ordained in 1957, when he did "the youth ministry . . . all of the catechetical work, all the marriages, all the baptisms. I am seeing that aspect of the priestly ministry being done now by laypeople. I enjoy my pastorate. I am still dealing with my own Irish guilt about not doing many of the parish visitations, the pastoral things I did when I was younger. I am still trying to leave room for a collaborative church and to allow the lay ministers on my staff and the volunteers to do many of the things that I did as a young priest."

Father Griffin saw an enormous transition taking place. "When I was ordained a priest, I was ordained a priest-minister. Now I am more and more a priest and less and less a minister. All the 'fun' things in my parish are being done by the pastoral ministers that I am hiring. More and more, I see my job, unfortunately, as being a bishop, an administrator in a large congregation with nonordained ministers."

The pastor as "bishop," as Father Griffin envisioned the role, entailed preaching and teaching and "celebrating the sacraments in a cumulative sense, that is, lay

catechists will prepare the RCIA [Rite of Christian Initiation of Adults], will run
the catechumenate, and bring them to the pastor for confirmation. The Eucharist
will be composed of many, many eucharistic ministers and many experiences of
Sunday liturgy culminating in the Eucharist when the priest is able to come.
Confession will be the culmination of many types of reconciling ministries in the
congregation, finally celebrated by the priest with the laying on of hands. I think
we are moving in a direction in which the priest is more and more a bishop than
a deacon. The priest role is going to involve sharing in diocesan government and
providing those relations of legitimization, facilitation, and empowerment on the
parish level. That is a big change."

Seminaries were still not training priests for this overhaul of vocational self-
image, Father Griffin said. He foresaw, with some trepidation, the emergence of
"a two-tiered kind of ministry: priesthood and a tremendously well-educated
and ordered pastoral ministry whose purpose is to prepare the church itself to conduct its apostolate." The priest of the future would be called to be "the religious
symbol, certainly; the celibate, the representative of an otherworldliness."

As the new pastor came into being, the old order died hard, he said with a
hint of foreboding: "There is an institutional 'death and dying'; the old camaraderie
of the clergy is dying. And we are denying that; we're bargaining with it; we're
getting angry about it. It is really a very normal and healthy process. Grief takes
about a year when it is an individual and it may take a generation when it is a
church. It is a change that we just have to accept."

—◄ ►—

FOR MANY OF DETROIT'S CATHOLICS, THE PROUDEST DAY IN THE CITY'S RECENT
history had been October 14, 1984, when their stalwart Tigers clinched their
final World Series victory over the San Diego Padres. Now suddenly there loomed
a church event to top even that public excitement: the pope was coming to the
Motor City.

A gleeful Archbishop Edmund C. Szoka made the surprise announcement at a
January 28 news conference that John Paul II would add Detroit to his September
itinerary. The schedule for the papal tour had been announced the month before,
but Archbishop Szoka had lobbied successfully to become the eighth stop on the
ten-day visit.

"Even though the pope travels all over the world," the archbishop said, "it is a
relatively small number of bishops who are able to welcome him."

In campaigning hard for the honor, Archbishop Szoka negotiated from
strength. He shared Polish ancestry and a long friendship with the pope. While
still the archbishop of Krakow, the pope had paid two visits to the largest Polish
theological school in the United States, Saints Cyril and Methodius Seminary,

located within the archdiocese. Detroit's Polish-American community of six hundred thousand was second in size only to Chicago's. It had all the elements of a rousing, homey conclusion to a papal journey that was expected to run into some flack from dissenters along the way.

Detroit also had something of a prior claim. The pope's first trip to the United States in 1979 in effect skipped over Motown, the only city in the Northeast with a cardinal to be passed over. Some believed the omission to have been a deliberate insult to Detroit's then archbishop, Cardinal John Dearden, whose progressive views were out of favor in Rome. But the cardinal had retired, and the pope's hand-picked replacement, Archbishop Szoka, could effectively cash in a rain check.

Archbishop Szoka had understandably appealed to these natural advantages in landing the big prize, but many Detroit Catholics felt he had taken no chances, displaying his conservative loyalties in such a way that no one at the Vatican could possibly mistake him for his predecessor, however slight that risk might have been. The issue around which the archbishop dug in his heels was one familiar to all Catholics—confession.

Increasingly a bishop's stance regarding "general absolution" had become a litmus test of his compatibility with the papacy of John Paul II. As was well known, the practice of individual confession had nosedived across Catholic America, though the old-fashioned wooden confessional remained perhaps the most graphic symbol of the Catholicism of yesteryear. In 1986, the Gallup Poll found that about a quarter (23 percent) of the Catholics surveyed said they had been to confession during the past thirty days, still a respectable figure but only about a third of what it had been before Vatican II. The rate for Catholics aged eighteen to thirty was 14 percent.

Under the revised 1973 Rite of Penance, three forms were allowed. As an alternative to the traditional individual confession, Catholics could attend a communal service followed by individual confession, a form intended to be more hospitable. The third form—and the murkiest—was general absolution. Under certain emergency conditions, a priest could absolve an entire group of penitents. As spelled out in the Rite, situations in which this exception might be allowed included "danger of death," as in the case of impending disaster from war or other calamity, and "where in view of the number of penitents, sufficient confessors are not available to hear individual confessions properly within a suitable period of time, so that penitents would, through no fault of their own, have to go without sacramental grace or holy communion for a long time."

It was up to the local bishops to decide whether conditions in their dioceses warranted the use of general confession. Many had discreetly given permission either through direct word or by granting pastors latitude to decide for themselves. Two factors in particular supported greater use: fewer priests to hear confessions and widespread popularity of general confession among the laity. In the last years of Paul VI, the trend was toward greater flexibility.

But with the change of popes the growing choice of general confession became a token of what the Vatican saw as the permissive extremes to which the post–Vatican II church too often had strayed. Rome viewed the spread of the new rite with alarm, as the kind of abuse that had to be corrected in pursuit of the wider goal of bringing Catholics back to personal confession.

Archbishop Szoka had enthusiastically stood with the Vatican's drive to close what was seen as an unintended loophole. Though none of his doing, Detroit was rife with the frowned-upon alternative. Under Cardinal Dearden, general absolution had become a regular practice in many Detroit parishes, especially during Advent and Lent, when demand for individual confession was at its highest level. It was reportedly much in favor among both priests and laypeople. The new archbishop, installed in 1981, had waited a respectful period of time before acting on a situation he found distressing.

Early in 1986, the archbishop had issued general guidelines on penance. Then, in an October 16 letter, he bypassed the diocesan planning committee by ordering his priests to halt the practice of general absolution. The prohibition sparked loud protest from both priests and laypeople, who felt suddenly stripped of a valuable resource. Vociferous objections were voiced by the clergy at an all-day hearing on November 19 presided over by the archbishop and a Vatican official, Archbishop Lajos Kada of the Congregation for the Sacraments and Divine Worship. Seventy priests signed a letter against the order. Some spoke of a return to the authoritarian rule of the past.

Meanwhile, the U.S. bishops had been presented at their turbulent fall meeting with a Vatican-inspired proposal that would have virtually ended general absolution in all the nation's dioceses. Opponents barely staved off its passage by a slim seven-vote margin, 128–121, thereby referring it back to committee. Many bishops with huge territorial dioceses and few priests were particularly disturbed by the effort to effectively eliminate the communal penance.

The dispute in Detroit intensified and grew more acrimonious. Proponents of general absolution contended that it was a legitimate means of drawing people into the sacrament who would otherwise stay away from one-to-one confession with a priest; from their perspective the third form of the rite was a supplement, not a replacement. People had responded well to the practice, the priests said, and to deprive them of it meant limiting their access to the sacraments. The archbishop's backers insisted that the Vatican II fathers had never intended a liberal interpretation of general absolution and that the efficacy of the sacrament of reconciliation depended on its proper observance. Communal penance was intended for extreme emergencies only and should be reserved for those rare situations.

The archbishop stood fast; a group of priests, about a quarter of the archdiocesan total, formed a group, Friends of the Sacrament of Penance, to press their protest against the decision, airing their views during a January seminar.

Underlying the debate was the question of how decisions about matters that go to the heart of parish life were reached and implemented. An informal experiment had been running for several years with much perceived success by parishioners and their priests. Their "lived experience" had gained an authority of its own. Habits and views about something as personal and *Catholic* as penance changed. The archbishop made his judgment on other criteria, in conformity with the highest constituted church authority. "I have to do what's right," Archbishop Szoka told Jacki Lyden of National Public Radio. "Doing what's right is not always popular. . . . It doesn't always engender great love for you."

The two varieties of authority had clashed. The archbishop had done his duty as he understood it, as a shepherd concerned with the best interests of his church. His opponents were certain that they had come to a new understanding of old truths and that their findings had been ignored. The fallout from the clash was expected to continue in and around penance and other issues.

ADVOCATES OF A GREATER ROLE FOR WOMEN IN THE CHURCH COULD FIND SIGNS that their cause was both "in" and "out." Monsignor George Higgins, longtime church gadfly, ally of organized labor, and friend of common sense, argued in the January 3 *America* that the women's movement represented an appeal that the church had best heed sooner than later. In urging "an open-ended approach to the complex issues being raised by the feminist movement," he was not without criticism of the cause. Nor was he sanguine about the church's response. He said it would be

> a serious mistake for the church in the United States or for the Holy See to underestimate the importance of the feminist movement or to try to defuse it with superficial and token changes in the field of canon law and pastoral practice. If history is any guide, I am afraid that the church at every level may be tempted to do precisely that. There is reason to fear that church officials, identifying too much with the rigid cultural patterns of another era that is gone forever, may be tempted to think that the movement is a passing fad that does not have to be taken seriously. If the church succumbs to this temptation, she may have to pay the same price she paid 100 years ago for underestimating the demand of the European proletariat for justice and equality. That is to say, she will run the risk of losing the allegiance of women just as she lost the allegiance of a large segment of the working class over a period of several generations in 19th century Europe (p. 4).

While Monsignor Higgins was urging the church to keep doors open, a loose network of traditionalists was demanding that Rome slam one door shut once and for all by imposing a ban against altar girls. The practice of using female altar servers was widespread in the United States, but the new Code of Canon Law had left the matter ambiguous. The code specifically permitted women to engage in the more significant roles of lector and eucharistic minister, but somehow the issue of altar servers had been skipped over. Meanwhile, those fighting the practice, including prominent members of such right-wing Catholic groups as the Wanderer Forum and Catholics United for the Faith, protested to Rome on the basis of a 1980 directive from the Congregation for the Sacraments and Divine Worship that had less authority than the code but spoke to the subject. It said, "In conformity with norms traditional in the Church, women (single, married, religious) whether in churches, homes, convents, schools, or institutions for women, are barred from serving the priest at the altar." But the head of the congregation himself said that he did not think that statement precluded altar girls. The pope had announced that a commission would make a final ruling.

The protesters fought change on grounds that using altar girls would be yet another camel's nose under the tent of an exclusively male clergy. It would, in their view, only encourage females to think they could be priests.

CRAIG BREEZED THROUGH TWENTY WEEKS OF PRIMARY FLIGHT INSTRUCTION AND entered the intermediary level, which involved squeezing into the cockpit of a jet trainer for the first time. He was enthralled and excited enough to burst the gold buttons on his crisp black Marine Corps tunic.

"I'm absorbed unlike any other time in my life," he exclaimed. "I don't mind the long days, because I can't think of anything that I'd rather do. It's a combination of thought and skill, and we're a tight-knit community. I just can't help thinking when I'm up there flying that this is so much fun—and so challenging—it makes it easy to get up every day." He paused and fumbled for a metaphor to contain it all. "It draws you into it the way an alcoholic is drawn to drinking."

The working day began at sunrise and lasted far into the evening. The five months of stage two included instrument work, aircraft familiarization, flight acrobatics, handling emergencies in landing patterns, ten "touch and go" landings (descend, skim runway for twenty feet, take off again), air-to-air gunnery practice, formation flying, night flying, and, the finale, the first aircraft carrier landings. In addition to the constant physical tests, there was a steady diet of book learning. Exactness was everything. The risk of washing out only heightened the thrill of making it.

He could feel his desire to excel grow more acute. "I didn't really know if I had what it takes," he said briskly. "But I'm doing fine, even though I realize other guys may have better eye-hand coordination or a better engineering background. Having lost a gallon of sweat on a training mission—and that's kind of average—you realize your limitations. They don't give any opportunities to slack off at all."

It could be sobering ("I get great grades and show people what I can do and then realize my buddy can do it better"), but everybody was measured by exactly the same standard: the ability to jockey a sleek bundle of wires and gears in a winged metal sheath from a dead stop to subsonic speeds. The standard was despotic. "You can be a super nice guy, but if you can't fly worth a darn, nobody's going to take you seriously. The idea is that flying is all that matters. I don't know if that's a good way to go about it, but I like the competition.

"A lot of our instructors served in Vietnam. For them, flying well was not a thing just about pride or ego. It was a matter of life and death." Craig found himself endlessly comparing his performance to that of others. He caught himself noting when other students did poorly, thinking that his response "was not a good way to regard people." He saw in himself a critical streak like his mother's, a prideful edge Catholic schools had failed to wear away.

"Certainly my education said I should be more humble and throw off aspirations of being powerful," he said. "My Christian background said I shouldn't put all my stock in such things. This community of marines runs counter to that." Karen, now his fiancée, helped keep him from becoming "too wrapped up in this thing. She reminds me it's not necessarily the most important thing in the world."

Not necessarily, but probably for now. Craig's world was the obsession of the fighter pilot portrayed, for better or worse, in the hit movie *Top Gun*. "Many guys here have it on video," Craig said. "A lot of it is garbage, but a lot of it captures things pretty well. There's that incredible high-pitched whining of a jet engine, the sound of a jet that just brings goose bumps. It's not exactly mysticism, maybe, but it's a certain feeling you get, even most guys who think they're super-cool. I don't know about touching the face of God, but I know this; it's a gigantic release."

And it made him feel better about himself. There had been times in college when he had been stricken with aimlessness and futility, but pilot training had purged him of that doubt and distress. He saw his reflection in his mind's eye as a *competent* person with solid ground to stand upon. "I'm happy and proud of what I'm doing," he said with firmness, "but I'm not a flag-waving marine."

On Christmas, he had accompanied Karen to a small Episcopal church of one hundred people or so where she sang in the choir. Admiringly, he heard her perform a solo. After church, the rector had invited them to dinner. It had been, he recalled, a pleasant, comfortable time, a contrast to his experiences in the local Catholic parish, which he found "colder than any church I'd ever been to." During the Christmas liturgy he had wondered, "How, being of Irish Catholic heritage, could I ever consider worshiping on a more permanent basis in an Episcopal church?" But wondering he was.

Craig had always preferred a sort of muscular Catholicism. "All the weirdos got involved in the church youth groups," he said, "I wanted to be on the jock side. I wasn't the kind of person who took an active role at the parish, being an acolyte every day. But I did a lot of reading." With his parents, he had attended mass every week, but only one parish had impressed him. It was situated near a college, he recalled, and the team of priests offered folk masses and "excellent sermons that seemed meaningful. I don't know if it was just intellectual snobbery, but I really liked what I heard. One priest cited things from literature; another could really speak." Other parishes had been big and, by Craig's account, impersonal. It made sense, then, that the warmth of the little Episcopal church near the base was a powerful drawing card.

He still had difficulty thinking of himself as anything but Catholic in the larger sense, though on plenty of specific issues, particularly regarding church teachings on sex, he felt distant and detached. His Catholic sensibilities played back and forth. Only a few days previously, he had been upset by the highly publicized case of a child in a neighboring city with a heart disorder who had become the subject of masses, music programs, rosaries, and other prayer services. He sympathized, but he questioned. "I couldn't help thinking that somewhere buried on the back pages were stories of children who died of terrible diseases because their parents couldn't pay for medical attention," Craig said. "I felt something bad about the Catholic church because of that week-long focus on one child when so many other children were born in far worse situations."

Probably no church was any better, he reasoned, so he couldn't expect exemplary behavior by going elsewhere. Anyway, the greatest obstacle to switching, aside from his own qualms, was his mother. She had been raised Protestant and converted to Catholicism after a difficult childbirth during which a caring parish had rushed to her aid by donating life-saving pints of blood. She would be crushed if he crossed over in the other direction, he thought. Of her five boys, Craig, the youngest, was the only remaining Catholic churchgoer.

Craig's father, quiet and cerebral, was busy teaching his college classes and cranking out letters and appeals through Amnesty International in behalf of political prisoners. Among his special causes was an effort to free aging Catholic priests in China. Amnesty was also in the forefront of a drive to end the death penalty.

Though pilots in training were full of swagger and cockiness and gusto and macho, they danced on a gravestone. Death—the unmentionable—underlay the entire enterprise. Craig was learning to inflict death, during emergencies, and he felt at ease with it up to a point. "I was never a violent kid," he said, "and I never liked to fight. When I made the decision to go into the military, I didn't anticipate actually getting involved in conflict. I would have a difficult time taking the initiative, being a commando type sneaking around. Somebody would have to be shooting at me first."

Pure Christianity was an impossible goal, Craig thought; therefore societies had to defend themselves. That meant to him that sometimes the death penalty by civilian authorities was justified, for "the few crimes heinous enough to deserve it." Likewise, nations could not sit by nonjudgmentally when wrongdoers sought to inflict pain and sufferings on others. "Why not go back to Jesus who said, 'Your own slate isn't clean, how can you judge others' sins?'" he said. "If you keep going that way, you get a breakdown of the system that protects people from one another. Some things are so bad you can't wait for God to sort them out."

February

1·9·8·7

E ARLY ON THE MORNING OF FEBRUARY 2, PUNXSUTAWNEY PHIL dutifully stuck his head outside his Pennsylvania burrow, saw his shadow, and retreated, thereby rendering his forecast of six more weeks of winter in the finest tradition of groundhog mete- orology. According to experts, it was only the ninth time in ninety- nine years that had happened.

By sundown on this annual *fete de woodchuck,* the question was how long the wintry discontent among Catholic Americans would go on. Fissures were running deep between conservatives and liberals; men and women; clergy and laity; Hispanics, blacks, and whites; gays and straights; America and Rome. The vision of "one holy Catholic church" was cracking under the strain. Individual cases, notably those regarding Hunthausen and Curran, and issues such as the eco- nomics pastoral and the homosexual policy statement had become flash points for some of these tensions. Other ongoing conflicts simmered just beneath the sur- face. Partisans of heated causes found civil discussion among themselves increas- ingly difficult, if not totally impossible. The unthinkable possibility of schism had become more thinkable.

Concern for prompting tolerant discourse across some of those friction zones provided the rationale for the meeting that began several hours after Punxsutawney Phil had retired to his den. Ninety-two Catholics from various theological and ideological camps convened at Xavier Center of Saint Elizabeth's College in Convent Station, New Jersey. The prime mover and sponsor of the three-day conference was a new organization, the Pallotine Institute for Lay Leadership and Apostolate Research, or PILLAR, based at Seton Hall University in South Orange, New Jersey.

PILLAR had somewhat mysteriously sprung into existence only eight months before with the avowed purpose, according to the executive director, Joe Holland, of becoming a "brokerage house" for differing points of view in hopes of reducing the "present danger of wounding the structural unity of American Catholicism." Besides Holland, the staff of PILLAR included a nun, Pat Pressler, S.S.J.; two laywomen, Anne N. Barsanti and Harriet Heaney; and a member of the Pallotine order, the Reverend Flavian Bonifazi, S.A.C.

PILLAR saw itself as a neutral meeting ground for warring factions and, beyond that, as an incubator for a synthesis that would allow Catholic America to surmount conceptual and cultural assumptions that blocked progress toward harmony. While pledging to offer a forum where voices could be lowered and understanding heightened, PILLAR also vaguely identified itself with a point of view that politely rejected the various camps of conventional thinking as inadequate to the challenge and welcomed futuristic efforts to go beyond it. The effort was very much in the groping stages of vagueness and confusion. Barsanti perhaps best summed up this aborning state in a later interview. "We want to build on an idea," she said, "but we can't exactly get a fix on it."

Holland, longtime head of the American Lay Catholic Network and key figure in the liberal activist Center of Concern in Washington, was a bearded, intense intellectual in his forties with an ardent commitment to keeping the church afloat by airing its conflicts and building something new. He dreamed of that synthesis for which he, too, had difficulty finding precise terms but that might well include, he said, the transcendence of Western Christianity, the immanence of tribal cultures, and the interiority of modern individualism. Beyond that were the many riddles, puzzles, and enigmas, which marked the spiritual explorer. "We must be more traditional than the traditionalists," he said, "and more progressive than the progressives." It must be holistic and creative and able to recapture the meaning of sexuality, community, and symbol. The church's renewal was contingent on a respectful reading of nature. And so on. To one wag, PILLAR came across as the exemplar of "Spaceship Church."

For the purpose of the conference, PILLAR's first public attempt to call attention to its mission, Holland set forth three themes he saw as representing major models of thought and action across Catholic America. All three were seen as responses to the central question of how faith should relate to culture, specifically the Roman Catholic faith to American culture. The goal was to explore these alternatives, Holland explained, with an eye on their relative strengths and weaknesses and a commitment to listening across boundaries.

One, he said, was the emphasis on *"Restoration:* a desire to protect the Catholic heritage from the past by restoring certain pre-modern classical European values seen as undermined by modern American culture." The second was *"Integration:*

a desire to energize American Catholics for responsible participation in American society by further integrating American Catholicism within modern American culture." The third was *"Regeneration:* a desire to help American Catholics to assist in the birth of a post-modern American culture, drawing especially on the deep ecology movement."

Evening sessions were given over to each of these themes. They were addressed to an attentive audience made up of Catholics of divergent positions on theology, economics, and politics. It was a solid, modest mix, devoid of the extremes but richly heterogeneous.

The first evening belonged to Michael Schwartz, director of the Free Congress Research and Education Foundation, a new right organization founded by Paul Weyrich, an adherent of the Melkite Eastern Rite, Christians belonging to the ancient patriarchates of Antioch, Alexandria, and Jerusalem. Schwartz set forth the "restorationist" claim, the most conservative of the three major theses. His talk, "Restoring Traditional Faith: The Crisis of Modern American Secularization," upbraided Catholic America for capitulating to worldly ways.

Whereas the church before Vatican II had wrongly isolated itself from culture, Schwartz said, it had in the aftermath of the Council sold out to culture. Only the leavening influence of the right-to-life movement had spared the church from total surrender to Americanism. Recalling how the challenge posed by legalized abortion had halted this profligacy, he said, "We desperately wanted to be accepted. But we were still Catholics, not barbarians. We draw the line at murdering the young." The pro-life movement had the potential to convert America "to a culture infused with Catholicism" that would "be ready to listen to everything else the Church teaches about social justice" (The *Advocate,* February 11, p. 8). Otherwise, the nation would continue "outside the pale of Christendom" (*National Catholic Reporter,* February 20, p. 6).

Catholicism free of culture contamination offered an answer to the national malaise, said Schwartz, who was once in charge of public relations for the Catholic League for Religious and Civil Rights, but only if Catholics remembered that "there is only one truth that saves and that the keys to that truth are held by Peter." But secular temptations obscured that conviction. "Contemporary America offers us a glimpse of a nation in search of its soul, in search of a reason to live and a body of beliefs that will give meaning," Schwartz said. "But at the very time this opportunity presents itself, Catholicism in America suffers an identity crisis of its own" (The *Advocate,* p. 8). It was time to bring back the Catholicism of old.

Evening two featured Ed Marciniak, president of the Institute of Urban Life and professor of urban studies at Loyola University in Chicago, whose topic, "Integrating the Faith with Secular Life: Catholics Entering the Modern American Mainstream," proposed the "integrationalist" alternative. Marciniak had sparked a drive to give substance to the concept of lay vocation. Toward that end, he had founded the National Center for the Laity, which had, under his direction, organized the two national consultations on the Vocation of the Laity in the World.

The buoyant Marciniak had been for many years devoted to the cause of enabling Catholics to think of their earthly pursuits as holy callings (for which he was sometimes criticized for providing Catholics a rationale for sanctifying unexamined, perhaps unholy, pursuits). For too long the church had encouraged a two-tiered spirituality that placed priestly and religious work on a higher level than that of laypeople in their day-to-day occupations. Such theology was misguided, he insisted. Properly understood, every act of work, clerical or lay, inside the church or in the marketplace, could become a reflection of the Incarnation. Vatican II had released an abundance of lay energies, he agreed, but unfortunately most of the focus had been placed on laypeople taking roles as assistants to clergy within the parish church. He saw the need for much greater attention to the subject of lay ministry on the job and in the home.

Marciniak sounded these themes pungently. The church had backed too far from the world and must find more and better ways to *integrate* believers into it, he asserted. The vocations problem for the church was not so much a shortage of priests and nuns as a paucity of Catholics who grasped their Christian calling in their daily lives. This "work ethic" must come from the laity themselves rather than from ordained clergy. "God encounters each man and woman individually to seek a personal response," he said (The *Advocate,* February 11, p. 9). Laypeople must seize the initiative rather than depending on clerics or theologians to instruct them.

Integration, as Marciniak saw it, was a declaration of freedom from being defined by the "church above," laypeople determining the nature of their own vocations. In that respect it was bold and assertive, and it refrained from exhorting the laity to question the church's store of doctrinal beliefs, hierarchically determined. Marciniak recognized that his vision was far from realization. "Faith and work are disconnected," he said, "so is Sunday worship and weekly activity. There is little understanding that the Church gathered on Sunday is the Church scattered on Monday" (The *Advocate,* p. 9).

He had few illusions about the persistence of a wide gap: "When someone is described as an active Catholic, it means, usually, that he or she goes to church on Sunday, is a lay minister, serves on the parish council, acts as an usher, etc. It does not signify usually that one can be actively Catholic or Christian in the family, neighborhood, work place, concert hall or political arena." It was time, therefore, to integrate (The *Advocate,* p. 9).

It remained for Charlene Spretnak of Berkeley, California, a writer and cofounder of the U.S. branch of the "Greens," to bring the concluding and—some may have hoped—quasisynthetic appeal from the more radical regenerationists. The title of her address was suggestive and enigmatic: "Regenerating the Co-creativity of Life: The Birth of Post-Modern American Consciousness."

Her package included key elements of the Greens approach—warnings about dehumanizing technology, calls for building compassionate communities informed by lessons drawn from ancient wisdom, adherence to natural life cycles, nonviolence, reverence for "creation mystics" such as Saint Francis and Julian of Norwich, aspects of pagan religions, recovery and equality of the feminine, grass-roots-based economics, personal integrity with a commitment to social justice, and a fusing of the ecological with the spiritual.

Spretnak sketched a manner of thinking and living that fundamentally questioned modern suppositions and presumed to move beyond the mess that those assumptions had created. Western religion had failed, according to this view, by alienating human beings from their own world. Restoration lay in willingness to be transformed or converted by a way of looking at the world that was, like any somewhat esoteric faith, difficult to translate into conventional terms. Its effect was to overcome the deadly dualisms that had been planted in Western consciousness: male/female, heaven/earth, spirit/flesh. It aimed at transforming this awakening into a restructuring of human community. It was both audacious and tantalizing, utopian and concrete, universal and, in adapted form, Catholic.

The restorationists, integrationists, and regenerationalists having spoken their pieces—and hours of discussion and debate having followed in small groups—the conference ended with a general note of relief and applause. The laboratory experiment was, overall, considered a success, judging by the favorable notices from some of those who attended. One of them, Sister Joan Bland of Trinity College in Washington, D.C., was quoted by the *National Catholic Reporter* (February 20, p. 6) as saying the meeting was the most diverse of its kind she had attended since Vatican II "that did not end in mayhem and disaster."

Writing in the February 22 *National Catholic Register,* another participant, Dale Vree, editor of the *New Oxford Review,* hailed it as "rare" and "valuable," an event during which "more harmonious notes than dissonant ones were heard." PILLAR, he said, had scrupulously avoided taking sides, thereby justifying its claim to be "an honest broker." Efforts such as this, creating an umbrella under which Catholics of different leanings could reason together, were, Vree said, most welcome as means of getting conservatives and liberals to stop condemning each other.

◄ ►

BOTH JERZY AND TERENCE HAD LONG, BUSY DAYS AHEAD OF THEM. BUT THEY HAD made time to talk about their beliefs and their work over breakfast on an unseasonably warm February morning at a Bob Jones restaurant near their suburban

Indiana homes. They had been picked as likely candidates for such a discussion by the pastor of their thriving parish and had left home earlier then usual to fit it into their schedules.

Jerzy, a compactly built man in his early forties, was president of a chemical laboratory business. Terence, a financial planner, was a few years older. His pastor described him as a self-effacing man who helped out in a hundred ways around the parish. The two men knew each other as fellow parishioners but not well. Each described himself as a weekly communicant, but they rarely attended the same mass in the large parish. Their upbringings were in many ways similar, though Terence had suffered the death of his mother when he was four. Jerzy's rearing was tinged with Polish customs, whereas Terence was a product of Irish ways, but both had been shaped by nightly family rosaries, Catholic schooling, fasting, holy days, and countless hours on their knees at church. Jerzy still tried to recite the rosary in his car each day. For Terence, prayer was part of daily life. Both had wives and children. They were men of worldly achievement whose bonds to the church were powerful.

Over eggs, bacon, sausage, toast, and coffee, they fielded questions about their lives as Catholics.

They had passing acquaintance with the U.S. Catholic bishops' 1983 pastoral letter on nuclear weapons that, among other things, condemned nuclear war and judged the use of "first strike" nuclear strategy immoral. Terence had little to say about it, but Jerzy had been weighing its general conclusions. The CCD class that he taught had grappled with it, though he suspected that no more than 10 percent of their parents were familiar with its contents.

Whereas Jerzy commended the bishops for their arduous effort to address a gigantic threat, their results sounded a little too naive to suit him. "The thing that separates this issue from Christ's saying about turning the other cheek," he said, "is that we're dealing here with *nuclear* weapons." Jerzy feared the spread of nuclear arms to other nations and felt it necessary to maintain ours to defend ourselves if need be. Like the bishops, he was against an offensive nuclear arsenal.

They were only generally aware of the bishops' more recent pastoral letter on the U.S. economy but shared a strong impression that the bishops were too eager to rely on government to relieve poverty. "By throwing it back into social programs, they get further from what I'd call a charitable point of view that left it up to private people or groups," Terence said. "If it's handled right, you can get a lot of charity out of people." Jerzy saw some need for social programs but not if people really didn't need them.

Both men found their parish a place where their moral and spiritual values were fortified. "It is wonderful for my relations with God, with family, and with community," Jerzy said. "The parish makes me feel good as a person. People know me and don't dwell on my weaknesses." Almost as an afterthought, he added, "If only we could do that in business, we'd be getting somewhere." Terence worried that the blessings of parish life outlined by Jerzy might disappear if the supply of priests kept dwindling so rapidly. No vocations had come from their parish in recent memory. Career pressures in the suburbs steered young people from even considering a vocation, he said. Parents wanted their children in the professions. (Of this situation their popular, earnest pastor had once said, with evident pain, "For all the nice things they say about me, no one follows in my footsteps.")

Terence would be glad to have his son go into the priesthood, he said, though the teenager had shown no interest in it. Jerzy thought it was important "to get a commitment early in life" because the lures of the outside world ("athletes making a million dollars a year and so on") close in pretty quickly. Both men favored the right of priests to marry and thought the option would help fill the ranks.

They agreed that the pope and his aides should hearken to the voice of the laity before fixing policies such as celibacy or birth control. Jerzy and Terence spoke as American businessmen who valued teamwork and cooperation. The pope had a tough job, Jerzy allowed, and he deserved great respect. But at the same time, Jerzy said, "One man can't make the decisions. He's got to listen more to cardinals and bishops, first of all, then [he's] got to continue the flow all the way down. The Catholic church was having a one-way discussion for years, even in our prayers. We're starting to do it differently now, to include more people, but the process is far from perfected yet."

Discord between Catholic Americans and official teachings could lead to the tragedy of "two Catholicisms: one here, one in Rome," Jerzy continued. Perhaps the pope's forthcoming trip to the United States could heal the rift, he said, but only if John Paul understood the reality of the disaffection. "The crowds will and should show respect," Jerzy said, "but the pope will misunderstand if he thinks the respect means that people agree with him."

Closer to home, each man's work involved particular moral questions. As a financial planner, Terence advised clients on where to invest their money. He felt it his duty to point advisees toward reliable market choices and stood by to warn against pitfalls they might fall into. And occasionally, he said, "somebody wants to avoid investing in something like nuclear power, so we do."

But ordinarily he saw himself as giving guidance and expediting whatever choices clients then made. Decisions were, to all intents and purposes, fiscal. "I don't normally get involved in the types of investments—whether they are good or bad for other reasons," Terence said. His aim was to be as honest a broker as he could be in order to realize the best return possible for people who trusted him with their hard-earned income. That was for Terence a high moral responsibility.

"The Lord has been good to me," he said. "I get a feel for where people are, where they are coming from, and help determine where they will go."

Jerzy's chemical laboratory performed tests to identify certain diseases. Some were conducted to identify ailments or deformities in unborn fetuses, among them, cerebral palsy and spina bifida. The laboratory's role was simply and impartially to dispense the results, but Jerzy had grown increasingly troubled by the fact that such information was often the prelude to abortion. "Unless we had a program that offered women an alternative to abortion, so the woman could accept the child, I wonder if we should continue doing the test," he said. "I know some women choose to abort the child."

In his business, moral implications of testing were taboo subjects, he said, and he had trouble discussing it with friends at church. Spina bifida, he said, presented the most agonizing quandary. It meant that the child would be born with a backbone that was detached and floating. "All we say is yes or no," Jerzy said, "but what bothers me is that we're out of the discussion from then on. We don't usually talk to the doctor. If the doctor is pro-abortion, the fetus will probably be terminated. I wouldn't agree that every single one of those abortions is not warranted, but it's very difficult for me, because I don't believe in abortion. But if the person has understood the consequences—and has talked it all out—from what I see, at least, I don't say every abortion shouldn't be done."

Terence, quickly offering support, said many situations in real life had ambiguous consequences. "There are variations of everything," he said quietly, "and we can't always get the answers beforehand."

They finished their coffee, said their cordial good-byes, and headed off to the day's occupations.

— —

THE YEARLY GET-TOGETHER OF THE ASSOCIATION OF CATHOLIC COLLEGES AND Universities (ACCU) fell during the first week of February. It took place at a Washington, D.C., hotel in an atmosphere of rising anxiety and combative alert.

Almost exactly a year before—February 11, 1986—presidents of half of the 235 U.S. Catholic degree-granting institutions had blasted the Vatican's proposed statement of policy, or *schema,* on higher education. In a stinging critique, the normally cautious, diplomatic Catholic presidents had taken off the gloves to repel what they saw as potential incursions on the sacred American principles of academic freedom and university autonomy.

Among other things, in its current form, the schema required theologians to be certified by their local bishops or equivalent church authority, a provision the presidents considered an illegitimate intrusion into university affairs. Other aspects stirred dismay and further convinced them that the Congregation for

Catholic Education either misunderstood American academic tradition or was deliberately challenging it.

In taking up the issues, the presidents found themselves in political clover, able to wax passionately and righteously against Rome with firm assurance that they enjoyed the solid backing of their constituents. Cheering them on were their lay boards of trustees, eager to protect the institution's state charter from church meddling, and aroused faculties intent on guarding the code of scholarly independence. But though some observers saw the presidents' attack primarily as a no-lose, low-risk endeavor, others commended them for rising to the occasion nonetheless, pointing out that crucial principles were involved and that such concerted action by the presidents could never be taken for granted.

The presidents' response to the Vatican draft statement, drawn from their answers to a questionnaire, had been coordinated, written, and forwarded to Rome by Sister Alice Gallin, the resourceful executive director of the Association of Catholic Colleges and Universities. It was worded so as to get the desired attention.

The draft schema stated that professors should be hired, promoted, and fired on the basis of "academic and pedagogic ability as well as by doctrinal integrity and uprightness of life." The presidents warned that adoption of such a policy could bring about "distrust and suspicion." They continued, "There is no way within the statutes of our universities that teachers or administrators who lack something as vague as 'doctrinal integrity and uprightness of life' could be dismissed.

"The real crux of the document is perceived by many to be the assertion of power on the part of Rome to control theologians and to assure 'orthodoxy' in their teaching. What is proposed here is contrary to the American values of both academic freedom and due process, both of which are written into most university statutes and protected by civil and constitutional law." Underscoring their view that the rights of theologians must accord with the standards applied to all American academics, the presidents said bluntly, "The university is the home of the theologian, not the bishop, and the bishop must respect that fact. The same freedom must be given to theologians as to the faculty in all other disciplines."

Apart from Rome's juridical notions and threats to academic freedom, however, the schema also urged church-affiliated colleges and universities to deepen their "Catholic character." That was widely conceded to be a valid issue. It had intensified debate on both ends and means. Many of the distinctive traits of Catholic higher education had been played down or even erased since Vatican II. In keeping with the Council's opening toward the world, Catholic colleges had moved closer to the nation's nonsectarian educational standards. The substantial drop in the percentage of priests and nuns from faculties and administrative posts removed much of the distinct Catholic facing. More non-Catholics were being enrolled, the religious factor in hiring faculty and staff was increasingly overlooked, and religious requirements for students often eliminated.

Though the appeal to elevate "Catholic character" evoked a generally sympathetic response among many of the educators attending the ACCU conference, they were less sure what such a promotion would mean concretely to their institutions. It made sense to try to slow the tide of secular influence, but how? They were well aware that some of the nation's prominent universities had long ago lost any meaningful connection with their religious origins. Hardly anyone recalled that Brown was established by Baptists or Northwestern by Methodists or Penn by Quakers. Was the same in store for Fordham, Marquette, and Georgetown? On the one hand, that struck them as a valid question; on the other, they knew of no sure-fire strategy for blunting secular inroads, short of semicloistered isolation, an unthinkable alternative for all but a handful of small, tightly controlled schools intent on doctrinal conformity.

For some, a partial answer lay in a reassertion of explicitly "Catholic" attributes such as greater emphasis on religion in the curriculum and more Catholic faculty. But others regarded these aims as misguided nostalgia for an imagined past, either patently unworkable or at odds with the search for high-quality teaching and scholarship. Besides, there was a considerable body of opinion that said the worst fears of a secular takeover were overblown. Catholic symbols and worship remained in place, according to this view, and these elements of tradition were fully compatible with the spirit of open inquiry and human diversity, traits that were of the essence of a true Catholic outlook. The sloughing off of some Catholic habits and customs should not therefore necessarily be construed as a loss of Catholic character. This was precisely the handshake between Catholicism and modernity that the Catholic right found so dangerous to the integrity of the church.

What remained between the relatively laissez-faire position of the left and the fortress mentality of the right was the bulky middle, which took seriously questions of character and tone while putting issues of academic substance to one side, at least for the time being. There was a widespread feeling that in terms of tone and style the moment was ripe for new directions. Interviewed before the ACCU meeting, Sister Gallin reflected on the shift in mood among many Catholic educators. "During the sixties and seventies we were trying to move into the mainstream of American higher education," she said. "In the process we lost our destination and our distinct mission. Now many are taking another look." Though certain needs once moved schools in a more secular direction, the exposure to the "real world" had "impressed upon us the need for church-related colleges to make a contribution to the commonweal that the state university doesn't make." She did not specify what that might mean, but, like many others, suggested that the difference had to do with imparting Catholic values that students, in turn, might translate into their adult lives.

But few Catholic educators would presume to know the process by which a set of Catholic values could be transmitted, short of unacceptable forms of indoctrination. In the past, Catholic values went with the territory, inculcated by a preponderance of nuns and priests, participation in common rituals, and dormitory life regulated by strict routines. Now most of that was gone, and little had replaced it. Barely 10 percent of Catholic young people attended Catholic colleges, according to Dr. Dean R. Hoge of Catholic University, so there was incentive to make the most of the experience for those few who did attend. But how?

Many Catholic colleges and universities were basking in financial prosperity and academic respect as never before. But as their secular standing rose, the question of "Catholic character" became the more acute: were the gains signs of continuity or discontinuity? A statement from one religious community involved in higher education had pinpointed the problem: "At a time when our universities have undeniably met with success and prestige, we must move swiftly and decisively to survive that success."

Pressures to succumb to nonreligious values came from one direction and pressures to conform more closely to Vatican prescriptions from the other. Particularly worrisome for some educators were efforts by the church hierarchy to step into the realm of higher education. Apart from the Vatican's action against Father Curran, two incidents had raised concern. Both involved Archbishop Roger M. Mahony of Los Angeles, a bishop with strong Vatican loyalties.

In one instance, Archbishop Mahony had initiated an inquiry into Fordham University, looking for information about curriculum and about former priests on the faculty. No specific reason was given for the investigation. Fordham officials refused to cooperate with the broad-gauged inquiry but indicated it might be possible to respond to particular questions. The same archbishop had also made a preemptive move against the three Catholic schools that belonged to the ecumenical Graduate Theological Union (GTU) in Berkeley, California. Archbishop Mahony wrote to the resident prelate, Bishop John S. Cummins of Oakland, suggesting that the bishop sever ties between the schools and GTU. Incensed at the suggestion, Bishop Cummins and his colleague across the bay, Archbishop John R. Quinn of San Francisco, put an immediate stop to it by flying to Los Angeles to confront Archbishop Mahony with their steadfast opposition.

Such accounts had a disquieting effect, not surprisingly, and helped galvanize a group conscience. The educators may not have known exactly what Catholic character was, but they pretty well knew what it wasn't.

The American Civil Liberties Union had heard nothing since its brief was filed, but the ongoing disputes gave the membership plenty to think about. The conference provided a platform for venting some of the collective restiveness and irritation. Among the appeals was this punchy defense of academic freedom from Professor William Shea. "If the pope can embrace Arafat and Jaruzelski," he told the group, "we and our students can afford to hear respectfully Mario Cuomo and even Eleanor Smeal (and maybe even a Republican or two). I think of the health of society and a church in which reasonable disagreements and searching criticism ought to replace repression and acrimony."

IN THE MIDST OF THE CONFUSION AND FEAR OVER ACADEMIC RIGHTS THAT WAS chilling the climate of openness on many Catholic college campuses, the University of Notre Dame carried out a calculated display of free speech. On the night of February 9, the theology department sponsored a debate on abortion.

Both the subject and the choice of one of the participants, Dr. Daniel Maguire, a former priest, now Marquette ethics professor, whose dissent from church teachings had made him a pariah on some Catholic campuses, signaled the university's refusal to be cowed. The symbolic importance of the event outweighed the value of its content.

Within the official church, abortion was perhaps the least negotiable moral teaching and Professor Maguire regarded by some Catholics as among the least qualified to question it. As a board member of Catholics for a Free Choice, Professor Maguire had been a principal sponsor of the paid statement in the October 7, 1984, *New York Times* that argued that Catholics held more than one legitimate position on abortion. The ad had created a furor and led to Vatican disciplinary action against more than two dozen nuns and male religious who signed it.

Dr. Maguire attracted unusual notoriety because of his considerable standing among his colleagues. He had been president of the Society for Christian Ethics and had lectured widely on abortion and other subjects. He had once occupied the John A. O'Brien visiting professorship of theology at Notre Dame. But when the storm broke over the *New York Times* ad, doors closed. Speaking dates had been canceled at Boston College, Villanova, Saint Martin's, and Saint Scholastica, he reported. Notre Dame had gone ahead with its plans in the face of this trend, for which Professor Maguire was grateful. In a December 9 press release announcing the event, he was quoted as saying he applauded Notre Dame for "behaving like a genuine university in allowing the multiple Catholic views on abortion to be heard and debated." He thereby restated the multiple-view premise that opponents, including his partner in debate, found so objectionable.

His opponent in debate was the Reverend James Burtchaell, C.S.C., Notre Dame theologian and one-time provost of the school. Father Burtchaell's book, *Rachel Weeping and Other Essays on Abortion,* forcefully made the case against abortion. He had spoken widely on the subject, upholding church teaching as a cornerstone of Catholic moral theology. He also had delivered his opening shot in the December press release. Affirming the right of students to hear "opposing views expressed by those who actually hold them," he noted that the university had in the past invited such controversial figures as former Alabama Governor George Wallace to speak. Drawing a direct comparison, Father Burtchaell said, "As was true of Wallace's views on the subject of race relations, Dr. Maguire's views on the subject of abortion are influential, widespread and, in my view, profoundly wrong. I welcome the opportunity to debate about them."

The six-hundred-seat auditorium was filled to capacity, the *National Catholic Reporter* (NCR) said in its account of the debate. The build-up among some on-lookers had caused others to expect some kind of titanic clash that, of course, was not in the cards. From all indications, Professor Maguire's views would face tough sledding among Notre Dame students, but he would be welcomed, by and large, as a worthy opponent.

The latest survey of college freshmen conducted by UCLA for the American Council on Education indicated something about campus opinion. It had found, for example, first-year enrollees at Notre Dame considerably less favorable to-ward abortion than their peers nationwide. Though 60 percent of the national sample advocated legal abortion, only 29 percent of Notre Dame freshmen took that stand. The Notre Dame freshmen were also more likely to describe themselves as conservative (34 percent compared to 27 percent nationally) and more likely to back the death penalty (35 percent, 28 percent).

That being the case, it was all the more significant that a nonconformist posi-tion on abortion was simply being given a fair hearing. It signified that, contrary to the trend toward suppression of dissent, Catholics could hear the arguments and weigh their strengths and weaknesses.

According to the agreed-upon format, each man spoke for a half hour, then both fielded questions and concluded with separate five-minute summaries. Professor Maguire, in what was described as a winsome, breezy style, defended free choice on abortion on grounds that a sound ethical position must take ac-count of many factors, among them the reasoning of non-Catholics and a variety of social, psychological, and economic forces that impinge on the person faced with the decision. He also criticized what he defined as jumping too quickly from ideals of human sacredness "to the practical conclusion that binds all people. . . . I see in a position such as this the seeds of fanaticism."

Father Burtchaell, in a manner reported as more somber and formal, relied heavily on the response of the early Christians to abortion to bolster his support for official church condemnation of all abortion. From earliest times, he said, Christians regarded protection of the unborn as an "essential moral duty" that harmed those who violated it even more than their victims.

Tom Fox, the pro-life editor of NCR, wrote of the outcome, "Both men seemed pleased with their presentations, and both received loud applause after their concluding remarks, with an edge probably going to Burtchaell, the local theologian. Several brief interviews after the debate found no pro-choice or antiabortion believer who admitted to having changed his or her mind as a result of the exchange. At least a few said Notre Dame and academic freedom came out the clear winners" (*NCR*, February 20, p. 25).

Sister ruth's nearly eight full decades on earth had only whetted her appetite for discovery. Since our last talk in the fall, she had made many new forays. The latest was a seminar the county had asked her to conduct for 150 public health nurses on the spiritual dimensions of their work.

The classes had been invigorating, she said, consisting of two lively sessions, two hours apiece, a week apart. Because of the government sponsorship and the religiously mixed composition of the group ("I didn't even know their backgrounds," she said), the presentations had to be nondenominational. The word *spirituality* had come to serve such purposes superbly. It was a perfect nonsectarian catchall term for a host of soul-stirring phenomena. Whereas *religion* tended to refer to specific traditions, *spiritual* was usually taken to mean something more universal.

"I tried to indicate how God language related to spirituality," she said. "Since their responses to this were so encouraging, I tried to distinguish between faith and religion. Faith is more important because that is where we really act on a personal basis." She had worked intermittently on the seminar for a month and was gratified with the results, particularly the energetic, probing discussions among the women.

Three weeks before, in mid-January, she had led a day of prayer and reflection for the faculty of a Catholic academy on one of her favorite liberation themes, women of the Old Testament who had served as agents of freedom. Examples included the "women preparing for the Exodus," among them Moses' mother and sister and Pharaoh's daughter and maid, "who crossed racial, religious, and national boundaries" to render aid. Another was Abigail "who taught David values.

"People said they never knew the Bible was so interesting," Sister Ruth said buoyantly. She especially delighted in shining the spotlight on biblical women who had been so often ignored. The slighting of women in Scripture," she liked to point out, "reflected a long history of neglect. Men wrote the Bible, translated it, interpreted it, and taught it until very recently," Sister Ruth said. "Now we have to recapture things that are there that have never been highlighted."

A concern for women both in the church and in society had long churned within her, partly as a consequence, she felt, of her father's encouragement and interest in seeing her pursue her own talents. Her concern was both intellectual and personal and intersected most every area of her life and thought. She was a long-distance, temperate, keen-minded crusader for the cause of women's welfare. It was in her bones to such an extent that it came naturally and without obvious self-conscious forethought.

When asked to discuss her life, Sister Ruth inevitably talked about her activities, for, to a remarkable extent, she seemed to have erased the usual dichotomy between public and private selves. Her personal feelings and beliefs shone though her work. And her feminist commitments ran deep.

She could turn her acerbic wit on alleged offenders of feminist sensibilities. For the past few months, she said, an auxiliary bishop of the diocese had moved into the facility that housed her religious community. "He lives here with us," she quipped, "and has been trying hard to educate us."

With the beginning of Lent still more than three weeks away, Sister Ruth had, for some reason, she said, been more than usually preoccupied with its emphases on penance and service. She had been dwelling on the meaning of Holy Thursday in particular, the day identified with the birth of the priesthood. As a steadfast member of the Women's Ordination Conference, she found herself searching the records for origins. The Holy Thursday observance was rooted in Jesus' last supper with the disciples, his celebration of the Passover meal as recorded in the New Testament.

Sister Ruth had been musing over the scriptural sources. Catholic tradition held that Jesus commissioned his disciples at that meal in a manner tantamount to ordination; hence the start of apostolic succession and an all-male clergy. But Sister Ruth wondered. Perhaps a broader understanding of that event was justified and gave support to a more inclusive priesthood.

"We don't even know who was at the Last Supper," she said. "My feeling is that lots of people were there. Nothing in the Gospels tells us precisely." The act of breaking bread was customarily performed among Jews by the head of the household. Jesus accordingly assumed that role with his disciples. Though men most often carried out the ritual, Sister Ruth reasoned, some women headed households, especially among Greek-speaking Jews, and would have carried out the proto-priestly function of breaking bread in those settings. "In the book of Acts," she continued, "Peter goes to the home of Mary, obviously the head of her household. The emphasis in John's Gospel is service—it doesn't have a Eucharist, just the foot-washing."

Moreover, her self-styled argument followed, the New Testament offers "no indication who were ordained priests. The only place the priesthood is clearly connected with Jesus is in the letter to the Hebrews where Jesus is described as the High Priest." It was more plausible, she contended, that the early Christians saw "the whole body of people as a priesthood."

She believed that formal notions of priesthood and hierarchy were imposed upon this original Christian concept. "Peter sure didn't know he was the pope," she said, "and my feeling is that the disciples didn't know they were priests."

Sister Ruth neither assumed her cause would prevail nor wallowed in self-pity. She simply carried on, applying her mind to the task at hand, combing the Scriptures for fuller pictures, and embodying her thought in practice. She was getting ready to lead laypeople at a renewal center through a series of weekly sessions on understanding of the Pascal mystery. While doing that, she kept up her regular hospital visits and maintained a brisk schedule of consultations.

All together, she said, it seemed a fitting preparation for the soul-searching of Lent.

It was an apt setting for a beehive of social activism: the top floor of a three-story walk-up amid a large cluster of identical drab brick apartment buildings inhabited largely by lower-income racial and ethnic minorities. The complex was just over the Washington, D.C, line in Mount Rainier, Maryland. From here the Quixote Center, named for none other than Cervantes's impossible dreamer, carried on its mission as Catholic gadfly and lobbying agency. Its vigorous pursuit of justice and peace causes—some within the church, others in the body politic—attracted fierce loyalists, staunch opponents, and grudging admirers, including some church officials who dared not whisper their support publicly.

On the strength of exceptional leadership, the center had devised deft strategies including timely surveys, crisply written newsletters, effective mail appeals, well-placed newspaper ads, and public protests to attract attention to their concerns. Accordingly, the Quixote Center had gained influence disproportionate to its bare-bones staff and shoestring resources.

For the staff and many close associates, the Quixote Center was much more than a staging area for political and ecclesiastical causes; it was also a spiritual community where every Wednesday evening they joined together for a liturgy.

The three apartments on the top floor had been converted into an open warren of makeshift offices, meeting rooms, and living quarters for some of the staff. Within a reception area to the left at the top of the stairs were found the staples of any activist campaign: telephone, typewriter, computer terminal, and printer. Opposite, a small sitting area was furnished with secondhand odds and ends and a tattered rug. But another feature of the room imparted luster to the threadbare surroundings. It was a cross from the Andes attached to the wall facing the entrance. Painted by an Indian artist in vivid orange, red, green, and yellow, it portrayed llamas, mountains, flowers, and Indian people at the foot of the cross bearing Christ, a bronzed image like their own. The cross conveyed awesome majesty, humility, and warmth. It took the room up into its vision and gave it back, bathed in its light.

At mid-morning on a blustery February day, wind whistling around the brick walls outside, this and other rooms at the Quixote Center were bustling with activity. The staff had recently tripled in size to one part-time and sixteen full-time workers because of the center's Nicaragua project.

The majority of workers were in their early to mid-twenties, several fresh from college, and together they evoked much of the movement spirit of the 1960s, highly motivated and idealistic, though perhaps less rebellious. They went about their task—rustling up donations for the Nicaraguan "Quest," moving incoming loads into the warehouse for repacking, and a variety of other routine jobs—with the energy and resolve of Peace Corps volunteers.

Quest for Peace, the focus of most of their efforts, was the biggest project the center had ever tackled, a drive to send $100 million of relief supplies to Nicaragua to match the U.S. government's aid package to the anti-Sandinista Contras. They had met their last goal of $27 million in supplies in response to the previous congressional allotment of an equal amount to equip Contras and were passionately devoted to reaching their new target. The total so far was $22 million. Their deadline was September 30, the date at which congressional funding ended.

The Quixote Center owed its origins and character to two unusually daring and stalwart activist ministers, Dolly Pomerleau and Bill Callahan, who presided over all its activities, she with a light touch, he with a heavier hand.

Dolly was an indomitable spirit of French-Canadian roots from northern Maine with single-minded dedication to the cause and a sparkling sense of humor. Her spare build and a pale complexion gave her an appearance of frailty, but that was more than offset by a wellspring of inner strength that was manifested in determination, hard, perceptive analysis, fearless, whimsical eyes, a broad smile, and a hearty laugh. She had once been a teacher and a member of a religious community. She continued to teach and motivate and encourage the stitching together of the tapestry of this community. She was admired as a superb organizer who kept the wheels turning.

Bill was of obvious Irish stock, a Jesuit from Massachusetts. He was a bearded, good-natured bear of a man who might have been leading Outward Bound forays into the Amazon jungles. He was bright, with a Ph.D. in physics from Johns Hopkins to his credit (to which he called no attention), resourceful, confident, and blessed with immense powers of persuasion and a talent for human relations, a radical who was capable of befriending the local head of the Veterans of Foreign Wars. The Jesuits had silenced him on the subject of women's ordination and otherwise weren't quite sure how to handle him, but had allowed him to remain in the fold. He had once taught physics; now he was consumed by two passions: injustice in Central America and the demands of his vegetable garden.

The Quixote Center had marked its tenth year of existence in 1986, much to the bemused amazement of its founders, who had barely scraped by in the early years. From small beginnings it had steadily gained something of a foothold, taking on a growing number of issues to the point where it was now busier and more committed than ever before.

Quest was by this time consuming 95 percent of Quixote's resources and the bulk of its energies. By comparison, the two other major programs of the center took but small slivers of the budgetary pie. One, Catholics Speak Out, a campaign to protest the recent Vatican clampdown on dissidents, was allotted $50,000–60,000. Its organizers took out an ad with 3,500 signatures in support of Archbishop Hunthausen in the January 9 *National Catholic Reporter.*

The other project, Let Live, the group's long-standing campaign against capital punishment, would receive no more than $15,000. Though more modest in size, however, these and other programs were by no means neglected. They were vigorous features of the bold, multifaceted Quixote character.

SINCE THE U.S. BISHOPS HAD MET IN NOVEMBER, THE DISTRESS IN SEATTLE OVER the plight of Archbishop Hunthausen had only deepened. The broad clamor for the archbishop's full reinstatement had grown angrier; likewise the resentment against Bishop Wuerl's role as the Vatican's unwanted troubleshooter. Rome had been silent and had made no public moves to settle the conflict, but it was obvious to most informed observers that something had to be done.

A signal came on February 9 when the United States Catholic Conference announced that the Vatican had appointed three powerful bishops to an *ad hoc* commission to "assess the current situation in Seattle." The troika—moving East to West—consisted of Cardinal John O'Connor of New York, Cardinal Joseph Bernardin of Chicago, and Archbishop John Quinn of San Francisco. The statement said that Archbishop Hunthausen had "expressed his concurrence" and nothing more.

The move was seen by some Hunthausen backers as an indication that Rome was retreating in the face of the outcry and as evidence that the U.S. bishops at their fall meeting had made the right moves by exercising restraint, avoiding confrontation with Rome, and offering to mediate the dispute. On the whole, Hunthausen supporters thought the composition of the team augured well. Presumably O'Connor's conservatism would be outweighed by the moderate views of Bernardin and Quinn, both of whom had served as presidents of the National Conference of Catholic Bishops. Moreover, Cardinal Bernardin had built a reputation as a master negotiator and compromiser and could therefore be counted upon to steer a safe course through Rome's rapids.

Such instant analyses came from the most optimistic of Hunthausen partisans. Others were much more cautious, preferring to wait to see how the commission would actually conduct itself and whether it would be free to do a fair investigation. They warned that the Vatican's record did not bode well. And they believed the bishops had shown timidity rather than firm discretion in their handling of the case. But even to the more pessimistic, the Vatican move was a break in the impasse, an indication of movement of some kind.

Within a day of the announcement, the newly baptized commission was huddling with Archbishop Hunthausen and Bishop Wuerl at Archbishop Laghi's behest during a bishops' seminar on bioethics in Dallas. Together, they discussed the ground rules, emerging from their closed-door talks with what many eyewitnesses took to be a note of modest optimism that the problem could be solved agreeably.

Until a concrete result either fulfilled or dashed that hope, the airwaves over Seattle and much of Catholic America were expected to be full of static. As one well-traveled church official put it, "There's a certain nastiness in the church right now."

The naming of the commission, for example, took place against the backdrop of a sharpening of political lines among the bishops that had been graphically demonstrated in voting patterns at the November meeting. Liberals and moderates still held a majority, but, as some of the votes had shown, the nearly one hundred John Paul II appointees, generally known as favoring strict adherence to doctrine and strong hierarchical authority, were asserting themselves. If the pope continued on this course, the balance of power would tip in the direction of the pope's forces in anywhere between five and ten years, with all that implied.

The January PILLAR conference had confined itself largely to an exchange of theological motifs that underlay the divisions among Catholic Americans. The jawboning and emotional plea bargaining among the bishops during the tense hours of their Hunthausen trial spoke much more graphically of the political realities that caused those fractures. The entire church in the United States was somehow convulsed in a polemical battle. Only a fraction of its members took an active part, but all felt it in one way or another, whether they were aware of it or not.

The battle had been joined because a small but vigorous movement on the Catholic right staged a counterattack against the massive cultural and religious drift of Catholic Americans toward the doctrinal left. With a kindred spirit on the chair of Saint Peter's, the right sensed that the time had come to strike. They had thrown the complacent leaders of moderation and cultural adaptation into a tizzy. Angry liberals denounced the right as a ruthless guerrilla force that took no prisoners. Catholic Middle America, far removed from the actual skirmishes, was nonetheless stung by some of the right's strategies. The campaign against Archbishop Hunthausen had been the most devastating by far.

A column in the February *U.S. Catholic* magazine reflected the state of agitation across much of the church. Robert E. Burns, writing in his usual space inside the front cover, proclaimed Archbishop Hunthausen a "victim" of a "vendetta" spearheaded by "those ultra-reactionary Catholics who have appointed themselves guardians of Catholic orthodoxy in the United States" (p. 2). Not content to state their own views, they had gone on the warpath to punish their alleged foes.

Continuing, Burns estimated that no more than 5 to 10 percent of Catholic America belonged either to the liberal or conservative wings. The huge majority, he said, 80 to 90 percent, were in the middle. Here he recited the litany of special virtue that more and more church leaders were invoking to defend the integrity of Catholic America against Rome. The Americans, when all was said and done, were among the most loyal Catholics in the world, Burns repeated, and Rome had better keep that in mind when tempted to tread on American sensibilities. It was a veiled threat that had been getting greater circulation as tensions had risen.

"It seems to me that Roman recognition of the generosity of American Catholics and especially their faithfulness to the pope and the teachings of the church is long overdue," Burns wrote. "I only wish that the American bishops would stand up more forthrightly for the good people they know *are* faithful" (p. 2).

So it was that people at various places in the church spoke worriedly of polarization, of a "nastiness," of an "us" versus "them" among bishops and theologians, of a need to redress "bad" propaganda about the U.S. church in Rome, of an urgency to "cleanse" the church of those who defiled it from within, of a great demand to "straighten things out."

Almost by default, Father Curran's cause had been all but totally abandoned by church leaders. Cardinal Bernardin had made some typically quiet moves to avert the mess at Catholic University, but after that had failed, there were no substantial rescue attempts. By the time of the Notre Dame conference of theologians, administrators, and bishops, it was clear that Father Curran was, to all intents and purposes, alone. Some of his would-be defenders said they were powerless to intervene or demurred on grounds that the case lacked sufficient stature to warrant a full-blown fight ("He is not John Courtney Murray"—the renowned American Jesuit—said one, drawing the invidious comparison). That argument was seen by others as disingenuous, a purging of guilt for inaction by blaming the victim.

Archbishop Hunthausen, having been cut adrift similarly by the bishops, or at least so it had seemed to many, appeared to have had his case reopened. But it was too early to tell what that meant.

IF THE DESIRE FOR GREATER DOMESTIC TRANQUILLITY WITHIN THE U.S. CHURCH were not motivation enough to spur Catholic leaders to look for ways to lessen tensions, there was in addition the upcoming inspection tour by the pope to jolt them into action. As the *Miami Herald* noted in a February 22 front-page story, the pope's plane was due to touch down at the city's international airport on September 10 for the start of the trip in just 201 days. The tempo in Miami, the paper said, was already frenzied, with South Floridians "already sweating over every detail of his historic visit."

Excitement was running high. Saint Mary's Cathedral, John Paul II's first church stop, was getting spruced up from stem to stern, including its first coat of paint in thirty years and a two-story altar with a hundred-foot cross designed by a Miami architect. Planners were predicting the largest crowds in the city's history, the equivalent of four Super Bowls, according to one source quoted by the *Herald*. Special phone lines buzzed daily with inquiries from faraway pilgrims wanting to make travel plans.

The scope of the logistics was staggering. Looking ahead to the outdoor mass at the end of the pope's Miami stay, a priest-planner ticked off "some" of the checklist items for the *Herald* reporter: "Sound. Signage. Fencing. Clean-up. Landscape. Survey and planning. Utilities. . . . Communications. Lighting. Scaffolding. Temporary roads. VIP seating. Emergency vehicles. Standing generators. Toilets. Press. Barricades. Uniforms. Large-screen TV. Handicap areas. Design. Security. Traffic. Buses. Insurance. Water trucks. Helicopters." Estimated price tag, excluding government supplied security: $2 million.

Similar tornadoes of preparation were swirling in the other eight cities on the pope's itinerary. As the visit came closer to reality, interest in it was rising accordingly. Many Catholics in or near the stops on the pastoral visit were astir with jubilation. Among those who closely followed church politics, there was growing speculation as to what line the pope might take, approving or disapproving, toward the U.S. church.

The question rested on a prior issue, that of the mind-set that the Vatican—and to a large extent also the pope, who was a creature of those influences—brought to these shores. Rome traded in a different variety of Catholicism than did its American cohort. The Vatican easily played upon its prestige and its patrician European legacy to induce a sense of inferiority in the Americans and thereby gain mastery over them.

Rome still dealt mainly within the framework of Latin jurisprudence, which set forth ideal principles while granting many exceptions or dispensations. It was a system ready-made for favoritism, patronage, and cronyism. Exceptions were worked out through personal deals. Anglo-Saxon law, by contrast, set great store by particular statutes. The stress here was on the letter of the law rather than the exceptions. America prided itself on being a nation of laws that applied equally and fairly to everyone.

Catholic Americans were therefore particularly susceptible to lectures on strict obedience to church law even as large numbers disobeyed and either left active participation in the church or lived uneasily in it. They kept thinking that the means to change was through legislating by the will of the people because that's what they learned in their democracy, but they were constantly told by Rome that the church did not work that way, so they were stuck with what amounted to "bad law" in some instances that they were bound to heed. It would be easy for the pope to push the moral buttons of Catholics in America, even those of the disaffected, because in all sorts of ways even the estranged Catholic had a tendency to feel accountable.

The topics most often heard discussed in reference to the pope's tour were money and diplomacy.

Though no official estimates of the bill for the pope's trip had been released by the United States Catholic Conference, the figure being bandied about by those in charge of the arrangements was between $25 million and $30 million. Catholics reacted to that outlay according to their enthusiasm for the trip and their ranking of priorities. Some thought it a small price to pay for such a blessing. The pope's ability to inspire and challenge could give the church a much-needed lift, shine the spotlight on Catholicism in a favorable way, and provide impetus for evangelization.

Those who expected the pope to spend most of his trip scolding Americans, by contrast, believed the venture was not worth the price and might even further alienate Catholics from their church. The vast majority took a ho-hum, wait-and-see attitude.

A squabble had already broken out around one tactic to defray costs. The Diocese of Monterey, which expected to incur $2 million in expenses, had taken the entrepreneurial step of offering to the highest bidder television rights to coverage of the pope's stop in the diocese. The notion of hawking access to the pope during his planned five-hour visit appalled many Catholics and evoked gasps of astonishment from network executives, who professed shock at such monetary motives and vowed in the name of the loftiest journalistic principles never to "buy news."

But officials in Monterey argued that the smallest diocese on the papal tour had to do something to fill its meagerly endowed coffers. They compared it to selling rights to the Statue of Liberty the previous year. Ted Elisee, the diocesan director of communications, declaring that the Monterey church had "no choice," because "we are a poor diocese," invited sixty area broadcast outlets to submit their bids for coverage of the mass at the Laguna Seca motor raceway. But a groundswell of opposition from the bishops' conference seemed likely to squelch the idea. And several key broadcasters had already refused to participate in the competition. Another piece of the strategy was to charge parishes in the diocese fifteen dollars per ticket of admission to the papal mass.

One bulwark of papal support, the 1.4-million-member Knights of Columbus, was the first major benefactor to announce a substantial contribution to the national fund-raising effort. Virgil C. Dechant, the supreme knight of the organization, won approval from his board to make $250,000 available to the National Conference of Catholic Bishops.

The issue of diplomacy was a continuation of the debate over who spoke for the American church. Nothing counted for more among liberals and moderates than the success of efforts to counteract what they considered hideous distortions of the U.S. church by the Catholic right. According to this view, the right had conspired to capture the near undivided attention of the Vatican with their tales of American apostasy and infidelity. The church must be represented fairly, moderates countered, if the pope was to speak authoritatively about conditions as they actually existed here during his trip. His performance in 1979, the moderates said, seemed based on a misreading of the situation here supplied by the likes of the Wanderer Forum and Catholics United for the Faith. The balance must be redressed, they argued, if the coming trip was to avoid becoming a sorry repeat of the past. If the pope knew the church in America accurately, they reasoned, he would celebrate its glories rather than decrying imagined deficiencies.

Gallup Polls showed that the pope's popularity had slipped rather precipitously. From 1983 to 1984, 82 percent of American Catholics rated the pope highly favorably. In 1986, amid the strains between the U.S. church and the Vatican, that rating had dropped to 65 percent. The tone and approach he took on the upcoming visit could have a further dramatic effect.

By now it was well known in church circles that a meeting of bishops and archbishops who would be hosting the pope during his visit would be held in March. That would presumably be the time for the bishops to put their best feet forward in behalf of their flocks in an effort to undercut the presumed hegemony of the right by setting the record straight. It was widely assumed that the effectiveness of that confab would greatly determine the pope's attitude during his journey. If the bishops presented a convincing, upbeat picture of Catholic America, then the Americans might anticipate a well-disposed pope. If not, well, he could arrive in a much more somber mood. Both scenarios were contingent to a considerable degree on what was done about the epidemic of anger in Seattle. It was contagious and constituted an emergency.

Meanwhile, nine dioceses where the pope would set foot—Miami, Charleston, New Orleans, San Antonio, Phoenix, Los Angeles, Monterey, San Francisco, and Detroit—were scrambling to put together the pieces of the greatest reception they had ever held. A special set of catechetical materials was being distributed this month in conjunction with the pope's planned visit, to be used during Lent. The purpose of the teaching materials, the introduction said, was "to invite all Catholics to prepare for the pastoral visit of John Paul II through prayer and study," so as to unite "in the work of service for the building up of the Body of Christ." It was a goal that was ardently desired but still seemed far off.

CATHOLIC AMERICA HAD BEEN FAR LESS RESEARCHED THAN MOST OTHER SEGments of the religious population, but sociologists and pollsters had begun lately to make up for lost time.

Among the best-known examiners was Dr. Dean Hoge, a Presbyterian sociologist at Catholic University. Recently, Hoge had been advancing a thesis that the Catholic populace had been rapidly assimilating to the broad set of social influences within American society. As a result, Catholicism had suffered losses in institutional strength similar to those experienced among the Protestants whose behavior Catholics were imitating. Melding into the American middle class by both Protestants and Catholics seemed to bear bad results for the churches.

Among young people, he said, assimilation understandably occurred at a faster rate. Therefore prospects for lower church participation in the years ahead by the succeeding generations of young people was a distinct possibility. Catholics could follow the examples of Lutherans and Episcopalians by growing less distinctly denominational and more absorbed in the culture. Indeed, he claimed, German Catholics and German Lutherans in certain areas of the Midwest were already virtually indistinguishable.

Some trends seemed irreversible, Hoge said, reaching into his sociologist's grab bag, among them, that only about 10 percent of Catholic young people were going to church-related colleges and that 40–45 percent of Catholic young people were marrying non-Catholics. He believed that the social forces were greater than church officials could possibly control.

He had addressed these issues in a lecture published the previous year in the *Review of Religious Research* (June 1986, vol. 27, no 4). In it, he asked three questions: Was the assimilation trend over with? Could church leaders alter its course? And did other groups offer Catholics lessons in what might happen?

To the first, he answered that though certainty was impossible, "we cannot say that assimilation has run its course." With respect to the second, he again demurred somewhat before asserting that assimilation "cannot be slowed down by church pronouncements or attempts to enforce moral strictures which the people don't fully agree with. But some limited impact could be gotten through Catholic schools, Catholic universities, and revitalized parish life" (p. 295).

Regarding the third, whether the example of other church groups had anything to teach Catholicism about cultural captivity, Dr. Hoge was decidedly unsure. "Probably the situation in the Catholic future," he wrote, "will resemble that in Protestantism today—the more affluent and educated the group, the less success in transmitting church commitment to the young" (p. 296).

He had predicted growing tension between the values imbibed by Catholic Americans within their culture and those taught in their church. "Assimilation will not stop. American Catholics will not stop believing in citizens' participation and democratic processes. And the pope appears to be unbending. He will be less welcome when he visits the United States in 1987 than he was when he came in 1979" (pp. 297–98).

Opinion samplings of Catholics offered an assortment of statistical glimpses. Among those finding their way into print were these items from a survey of Catholic teens, aged fifteen to seventeen, sponsored by the Catholic Press Association: asked how many of the New Testament Gospels they could name, 37 percent identified all four, but 56 percent couldn't recall a single one; 76 percent knew why Christians celebrate Easter.

If many bishops were defensive about polls, it was usually because the results were used to fortify critics in their claims that there was widespread dissent from church teachings and rulings. In the hands of reformers, the statistical profiles were, in other words, ammunition.

There were exceptions, however, and a new book by George Gallup, Jr., and James Castelli, *The American Catholic People: Their Beliefs, Practices, and Values,* was an example. The volume was chock-full of data about Catholics collected over recent years, and, to the extent there was a tilt to the authors' interpretation, it was a rebuttal to the purveyors of bad news about Catholic America.

Among other things, concluded Gallup and Castelli, the survey destroyed various negative claims. Contrary to common assumption, they said, attendance at mass remained high (53 percent weekly, 78 percent within the last month); college graduates were more, not less, inclined than less-educated Catholics to go to church; Catholic women were not rebelling in any dramatic way against the church; and Catholics had stayed relatively liberal despite a rush to the Republican ranks. The overall portrait was greeted as a positive assessment by some; others noted important gaps in the information (women's response to the church broken down by age group—to cite just one) and posed questions about the validity of some key aspects of analysis.

The Gallup-Castelli book seemed likely to become documentation in the wider liberal-conservative struggle to amass favorable evidence for its side. The sides would square off, armed with polls and their own version of the "spin doctors."

ON THE EVENING OF FEBRUARY 14, ANTHONY AND HIS WIFE, LYNN, HAD VISITED the home of a colleague for a quiet dinner to mark Anthony's thirty-first anniversary as an employee of Celestron Corp.

The two men had met soon after Anthony's arrival at the company, fresh from college with a degree in English, and they had become fast friends. Werner had been in the marketing department for four years already when Anthony came aboard.

Anthony said of Werner, "If you can go through life with one good friend like him, you're fortunate." Werner had been raised a Lutheran but married a Catholic and converted at that point to her church. Anthony admired that because Werner had given up a lot. "He went through hell just sacrificing his Luther League activities," he said of his friend. "But he became a very good Catholic. He raised seven kids."

So the couples had spent a leisurely evening rummaging through the stockpile of memories: kids, work, outings, and the parish.

The next day Anthony offered a bittersweet retrospective. At fifty-six years of age, he figured he had another five to eight decent years to go before he slowed down and took his leave. He spoke of the remaining years as treading water as best he could until the current carried him to the finish line.

"It's been a satisfying career," he started, then abruptly switched gears. "But I'd liked to have achieved more, gone a bit higher on those rungs, so I could have made those decisions that people on those rungs couldn't or didn't have the guts to make."

He had received his last promotion two years before, a modest one within the international division. It came after a health scare. On Easter morning, Anthony woke up with the cold sweats and was rushed to the hospital. It was diagnosed as "a stress attack," he recalled, noting with a touch of pride, "like Mickey Mantle once had." A vice president presented him with the new job offer days later. The flaw in that otherwise positive development, as far as he was concerned, was the new boss who came as part of the package. Anthony could remember only two people in all his years at Celestron with whom he did not hit it off. That boss had been one of them.

The relationship put a damper on everything. Work had ceased to be as engrossing as it had been. He no longer looked forward with the same zeal to getting to his desk at 7:00 A.M., an hour before the company routines began. He had, in spite of all the accumulated years of good reports, begun feeling that gnawing sense of being unappreciated and taken for granted.

Worst, he took the conflict as a very personal defeat. Getting along with people had been his calling card, he said, the key to his achievements. "It goes back to fifth grade or so with the nuns and priests, maybe even before that," he said. "I don't know if God gave me many brains, but he gave me the capacity to be liked. And people like me. I never try to abuse that. I try to give people back what they say they like about me. I talk the same way to the individual who cleans my office as I do my boss. I've always thought that how I relate to people is more important than what I've got to say."

But there were those occasional stumbling blocks like that boss—and the new pastor at his parish. Not only had the priest replaced the aging longtime pastor whom Anthony revered but had, in addition, insisted that the parish make all sorts of Vatican II changes that the old pastor had never approved of. The young pastor had riled Anthony and some other pillars of the parish simply by making sure the parish was in conformity with standard church practice. Anthony was still smarting, too, over the firing of the former parish school principal. Though he had backed the firing at the behest of the old pastor, the fight between the opponents and supporters had torn apart the parish. In the end, the principal had been forced out, but Anthony's role as a key supporter of the old pastor in the fight had set him at odds with the new pastor. Relations between them had been cool, at best, and Anthony took it hard. He had not yet decided whether to leave the parish.

Those setbacks aside, he counted his gains. He had learned at a very early age in an ethnically diverse neighborhood that the world was indeed a polyglot, and that, he said, had allowed him to surmount differences among people. Making an issue out of religious creeds and traditions struck him as especially ludicrous. He worked with some Catholics, of course, but most were Protestants of one stripe or another. "The church made such a thing when I was a kid telling us not to go into Protestant churches," he sighed. "Well, it was totally wasted energy so far as I'm concerned. They'd be far better off trying to foster common Christian relations than emphasizing differences.

"We were also told we weren't supposed to read the Bible while I was growing up. I guess they didn't think we were smart enough to interpret it. That was wrong too. They didn't give us enough credit. I'm glad that's changed now."

He poked his head into the Bible from time to time these days, usually the dog-eared Douay Version he and his wife had received when they were married. A few years ago he had attended a weekly Bible study group at his parish. From fifty to seventy-five people had gathered each week. The leadership rotated among several laypeople.

Anthony thought of the church in terms of personal bonds, primarily between priest and laity. He thought most Catholics "want the same thing from their parish: a relationship with the priest at the altar." Certainly he did. That is why his inability to connect with the new pastor was such an egregious sore spot in his life.

He belonged to the last generation of Catholic men for whom the challenge of entering the priesthood was a common struggle. Many wrestled long with the choice, attended seminary for a while, and decided reluctantly against it. But for many of them, the attraction had never really left. The worsening priest shortage often rekindled the inner debate, sometimes laying bare long-buried guilt. They worried a lot about where vocations would come from.

Anthony was fairly typical. He had thought about it in high school. Then as an Air Force recruit, he had served as a chaplain's assistant in Northern California, where, he said with an enduring sense of achievement, he had "got lots of guys in the habit of going to mass in the day room."

"I often wonder what it would have been like to be a priest," he allowed. "But of course I have a beautiful wife and great kids."

THE RANCOR ERUPTING FROM THE VATICAN'S OCTOBER STATEMENT ON HOMO-sexuality had prompted Cardinal Bernardin to an unusual attempt at reconciliation in *Commonweal* two months earlier: an exchange of views with an anonymous homosexual who belonged to a religious order and described himself as sexually inactive. The cardinal had found himself in a delicate position inasmuch as he had opposed the most recent version of a gay rights proposal before the Chicago city council.

Meanwhile, the Vatican statement had remained a source of festering resentment among gay activists and of embarrassment to many bishops who regarded it as a setback. By labeling homosexual orientation itself "an objective" disorder and implying that violence against homosexuals could be blamed on gay activism, the document had, in the view of the concerned bishops, retreated on positions taken in earlier church statements, including one issued by the U.S. bishops' conference in 1976.

Archbishop John R. Quinn found himself in perhaps the most sensitive situation among his episcopal colleagues. As archbishop of San Francisco, he had been confronted with the appeals and demands of a large and resourceful gay community. All about his downtown chancery office, the AIDS scourge raged with a fury unparalleled in the nation. Little wonder, then, that a bishop with Archbishop Quinn's exceptional intelligence and reputation for deep compassion toward AIDS patients should find himself in a profound quandary, attempting to uphold church teachings in a setting rife with anger and anguish.

But being the conscientious and obedient son of the church that he was, the archbishop did not shrink from what appeared to be a no-win situation. In the February 7 issue of *America* he strode forth through the thicket in an article titled "Toward an Understanding of the Letter on the Pastoral Care of Homosexual Persons."

Whereas Cardinal Bernardin's contribution had focused on the fractured state of human relations between the church and gays, Archbishop Quinn characteristically took a more scholarly approach by concentrating on the causes of tension within the actual Vatican statement.

The archbishop started by asserting that the statement was written for bishops rather than the general public and that its language, therefore, was technical, "not likely to be understood correctly by those who are not familiar with it." Likewise, he wrote, the document must be seen for what it is, an "authentic teaching of the Holy See" whose contents mingle fixed doctrine with nondoctrinal "social commentary," such as its linking of gay activism with violence. As a hybrid of binding and nonbinding statements, the document "is not a dogmatic definition," the archbishop wrote, though where it proclaims teachings that are "doctrinal in character" it does lay particular claim to "internal and respectful assent" (p. 92).

At the center of the document, the archbishop wrote, was the church's unalterable conviction that sexual relations outside marriage, including homosexual acts, were immoral. He quoted what he called the statement's "central moral affirmation": "It is only in the marital relationship that the use of the sexual faculty can be morally good. A person engaging in homosexual behavior therefore acts immorally" (pp. 92–93).

Regarding homosexual behavior, Archbishop Quinn said flatly that the Bible had explicitly condemned it. To think the church would ever change its mind, he added, was "soaring into the realms of fantasy." Though there was "more to be learned at the empirical level" about homosexuality, that moral judgment would, in the archbishop's view, remain constant (p. 93).

He then cited a list of "positive aspects" of the Vatican statement, most having to do with its affirmation of the dignity and sanctity of the homosexual person. He noted that the statement allowed that homosexual orientation "may not be 'the result of deliberate choice.'" Though the homosexual inclination itself was understood as "an objective disorder," he said, it had also pointed out, in the tradition of Catholic moral theology, that the person with that inclination is not inherently sinful. The inclination was a inner disposition that, left to its own devices, inclined a person toward sin. Therefore, by the church's thinking, it was a defective instinct rather than a moral offense (p. 93).

"Consequently," the archbishop wrote, "the document affirms the spiritual and human dignity of the homosexual *person* while placing a negative moral judgment on homosexual *acts* and a negative philosophical judgment on the homosexual *inclination* or orientation, which it clearly states is not a sin or moral evil" (p. 94).

Growing acceptance of homosexuality and the "threat to family life" by "certain militant elements" had been among the factors that had prompted the Vatican to issue the document, the archbishop said. But nothing in it should deter the church from offering its full pastoral care to homosexuals (p. 94).

Of the "many lengthy responses" to the archbishop's article, *America* reported receiving, two were chosen for publication in its March 21 issue.

The longer one, by Monsignor William H. Shannon of Rochester, New York, sharply criticized the archbishop's analysis and examined his motives. "The purpose of your article, as I read it, was to say all the positive things that could be said about the C.D.F. [Congregation for the Doctrine of the Faith] letter," Monsignor Shannon wrote. But in the end, he continued, "The sense I get is not that you are welcoming a document that might be helpful in the church's effort to minister to homosexual persons, but attempting to justify one that might well be harmful to ministries that already exist. Forgive me if I am misinterpreting your words, but what I seem to hear—perhaps subliminally and perhaps because this is what I choose to hear—is a plea for understanding: The letter is not really as bad as it sounds. It says some worthwhile things. It's not going to hurt as much as you think" (p. 238).

Though the archbishop had said in his article that "for the first time in a magisterial document, the letter admits the possibility that the homosexual orientation may not be 'the result of deliberate choice,'" Monsignor Shannon pointed out that Archbishop Quinn had a few paragraphs later quoted from "a magisterial statement of the American bishops" ("To Live in Jesus Christ") ten years earlier that had said the same thing—which begged the question of what relationship there was between Vatican statements and those issued by local conferences of bishops. Were they listening over there? Why did the congregation seek no advice from those who had dealt with the issue?

"One is forced to ask the question: Why was such consultation of the bishops omitted?" Monsignor Shannon wrote. "Did the C.D.F. feel that the bishops had nothing to contribute on this issue? Did they feel no need to learn about the pastoral practices already going on in the many local churches? Did they believe they possessed *a priori* all the truth necessary to address the topic of the letter? Do we not have to face the fact that many Catholics of good faith are going to ask the question: How much credibility can be given to a document that ignores the ongoing experience of many local churches?" (p. 240).

The monsignor also challenged the archbishop's assumption that passages from the Bible adequately summed up the case against homosexuality. There was much to suggest that the writers of Scripture had a limited understanding of homosexuality, associating it with certain aberrations, such as male temple prostitution or gang-rape. "They certainly would have had no notion of homosexuality as a way of relating humanly to another person in the context of love, fidelity and mutuality," the monsignor wrote. Making a moral evaluation of such a possibility should, at the very least, be based "on our particular understanding of sexuality, not on a hermeneutic [interpretation] that would ask biblical writers to condemn something they could never even have thought of" (p. 241).

Monsignor Shannon likewise disputed the archbishop's claim that the document's key moral affirmation was its reiteration of the church's condemnation of sex outside marriage. Though that declaration "is certainly central to official Roman Catholic teaching on sexuality," he wrote, "the affirmation that is at the heart of this letter—the affirmation homosexual persons find most painful—is the declaration that the homosexual orientation is itself 'an objective disorder.'" The document gave ample evidence, the monsignor said, that the congregation's intent was to correct its own 1975 statement that judged homosexual acts "intrinsically disordered" but drew no such conclusion about the orientation. The latest document had changed that (p. 241).

The shift had inflicted much suffering, Monsignor Shannon asserted. "Whether one agrees with the position or does not," he wrote, "it is not difficult to see the psychological damage that could be done to a person by telling him/her that his/her very person was ordered toward intrinsic moral evil. It would be like telling someone that he/she is carrying a moral time bomb around with him/her. It would be to say that such persons are a constant proximate occasion of sin to themselves" (p. 242).

Michael W. Hovey of Somerville, Massachusetts, wrote a briefer response. He, too, detected a desire by the archbishop to "mitigate the anguish and pain" caused by the Vatican document but concluded that despite the archbishop's effort "to put a positive 'spin' on some of the more appalling statements of the letter, one is still left with a pervasive sense of sorrow and a measure of indignation." Given the archbishop's caution regarding the statement's technical language, Hovey wondered sardonically if the archbishop thought "the letter might have been less offensive had it been written in 'popular, everyday' language?" (p. 243).

Though, as the archbishop indicated, the congregation document did indeed deplore attacks against homosexuals, Hovey wrote, "its next paragraph comes dangerously close to justifying the 'irrational and violent reactions' of those who

adamantly refuse to extend them the 'respect, friendship and justice' to which
the U.S. bishops declared all human beings . . . are entitled" (pp. 243–44).

Hovey acknowledged the archbishop's observation that moral maturation was a
slow and uneven process; so, too, he said, was the church's growth in understanding
and care toward homosexuals. "Without intending to do so," he wrote, "it would
seem that the authors of the letter 'On the Pastoral Care of Homosexual Persons' have
stimulated rather than ended discussion of a truly complex and sensitive issue. This,
in my opinion, is perhaps its only potentially positive contribution" (p. 244).

Piercing all the discussion of the Vatican document was awareness of the
lengthening shadow of AIDS among gays and a small but growing number of
heterosexuals. Stopping its spread was becoming a major national concern. In
the face of this campaign, the church had come under pressure to at least tolerate
the use of condoms as a crucial means of prevention. Proponents argued that the
benefits derived from condoms as life-saving devices far outweighed whatever
harm might be done to the church's ban on contraception. They also contended
that, technically speaking, gays did not use condoms as contraceptives anyway.

In December, Archbishop Mahony had refused to allow an AIDS education program that contained information on condoms to use a church site in Los Angeles.
Meanwhile, a debate was raging on how the bishops' conference should respond
to the issue of condom education and advertising. On February 11, the general
secretary of the conference issued a limited statement, firmly rejecting the proposal
to sell condoms on television.

Monsignor Daniel F. Hoye, the general secretary, called the proposal "a short-
sighted, self-defeating, and ultimately false solution to a serious moral problem."
Such advertising would foster "the implicit encouragement of permissive and immoral behavior," and "promotion of the illusion of freedom from disease will do
more harm than good," Monsignor Hoye said. "Ultimately we must be interested in
teaching young people to be good, not to be 'safe.' The solution must be found in
changing attitudes through moral education, and not in the sale of contraceptives."

At the end of the month, the California bishops gave limited endorsement to a
public school AIDS education bill in the state legislature. The bishops said that
pertinent information mandated by the bill, which includes facts about condoms,
was "necessary and legitimate," though they insisted that condom use be declared morally wrong.

➤ ➤

THEY BUMPED INTO EACH OTHER ON A DOWNTOWN SIDEWALK DURING PRES-
ident's Weekend. She was back in town visiting her parents. He was running his
usual weekend errands. He was in his mid-thirties; she a shade younger. For several
years they had worked together: she as a high school English teacher; he as her

supervising assistant principal. But she had taken a position in a distant community and moved away the previous summer. They had not seen or heard from each other since. There was much catching up to do, so they decided to duck into the nearby coffee shop to have some lunch.

During the years of working together, they had gladly recognized each other as members of the same religious clan. Both were raised in Catholic homes where the church was cherished. Each had emerged from adolescence and secular college with faith intact. Neither had undergone an acute bout of unbelief, though their approach to the faith was conditioned by distinct needs and personal traits. Her commitment was more solid and less questioning. His was more analytical and searching. They had liked being members of the same clan, though they had seldom spoken about it. On Sundays, they were typically found at mass in their respective settings, hers an Italian national parish, his the standard territorial variety.

The topic arose when he suddenly blurted out that he was no longer a Catholic. She was shocked and wanted to know more. Things were building up, he said. He had felt "out of sync" with the church because of its "doctrinal rigidity, its lack of intellectual ferment, and its treatment of women" but had overlooked those complaints because of his admiration for the pastor at his parish. He had been writing a commemorative book for the parish anniversary. Then out of the blue the pastor had been transferred. Not only had the priest refused to talk to him about the reasons behind the unpopular and abrupt move, he said, but had staunchly defended the church's action and treated anyone who questioned it with contempt.

After that bitter experience, he told her, he no longer felt the parish was "a home." Perhaps, he thought, he would have left another parish long ago, but the pastor had made this seem special. He was lost, heartbroken. In his despondency, the church now seemed more "intellectually repressive" than it had. He said he had wandered around in a daze, a man without spiritual bearings. The crisis had peaked one Sunday morning when he asked his wife if she wanted to go to church. No, she had replied. He didn't either. She had said, "When are we going to do something about this?" He had been using her as an excuse not to leave, contending it would upset her too much. Now *she* wanted to move.

They had gone to an Episcopal church he had been eyeing for some time. They never looked back. Of the eight couples in the new member group, six were Catholic by background. It had been a momentous change, he said. His wife's family had not accepted it. But both he and his wife felt right about it.

She listened intently, saying little. It was a scenario she could not imagine unfolding in her own life. She did not appear so much upset as incredulous. She responded by reflecting on the roots of her own unshakable loyalty. She had grown up in the church. From her teen years, she had sung in the choir. She came back to her old parish as often as possible. The church had provided her the most irreplaceable security. Though she could find much to criticize in the world, she felt enormous trust in the guidance of the church. It was her bulwark. She said simply and sincerely that she "could not imagine a circumstance that would cause me to leave Catholicism." It was a testimony rather than a rebuke.

They finished lunch, reminisced about people and events, wished each other well, vowed to keep in touch, and said their good-byes.

—   —

ON FEBRUARY 18 THE VATICAN PRO-NUNCIO ARCHBISHOP PIO LAGHI SET FORTH his views on Father Curran and Catholic higher education with uncommon public candor in a talk at Seton Hall University in South Orange, New Jersey. Asked about the proposed Vatican schema that would assert greater church control over Catholic colleges and universities, Archbishop Laghi said that those institutions must uphold their Catholic character even if it meant transgressing the American understanding of church-state separation and losing public funding. "We have to stick to principles," Archbishop Laghi said, "we have to pay a price to keep Catholicity." If church institutions were deemed to have lost their autonomy under such a schema, thus becoming ineligible for funding, the archbishop was confident that Catholics would chip in to make up the difference (federal and state contributions amounted to $500 million annually). He also insisted that the church was pledged to seek "the whole truth" and to that end fostered "freedom of research, freedom of teaching and freedom of the spread of ideas." The question was still whether what the church regarded as "error" was included in that freedom or, as in the traditional formulation, had "no rights." Asked about the case against Father Curran, Archbishop Laghi said the priest was free to speak for himself but not as a teacher of authentic church doctrine. As quoted in the *National Catholic Reporter,* the archbishop said, "Faith has to say to a Catholic theologian who goes out of line, 'Hey, wait a minute, you have to get back in line.' The church has to say, 'This is white and this is black'" (February 27, p. 6).

The surge of controversial issues and personalities recast some alliances and strained or scrambled others. Father Curran, for example, won the support of many conservative Catholics whose interests were primarily economic—Reaganite capitalists—because their free market mentality strongly endorsed the unimpeded flow of ideas. But many conservatives who identified primarily with preserving the church's legacy of authority and doctrine—the traditionalists and participants in the American new religious right, whose agenda was heavily moral—sided against him. Archbishop Hunthausen, too, attracted a variety of admirers, some of whom felt uneasy with other backers, whose commitments they questioned. The archbishop was generally classified as a "progressive," but his stated theology could pass any test of orthodoxy. So even though he was the target of ultraconservative groups who believed he ran too loose a ship, he drew votes from many right-of-center Catholics who thought he had been unjustly accused. So were loose, uneasy coalitions created.

WINTER ON THE PLAINS HAD TREATED ITS INHABITANTS MERCIFULLY THIS YEAR and was inexorably drawing to a close. Hannah both welcomed and resisted the signs of nature's reawakening. On the previous Sunday, she had immensely enjoyed a drive with her husband, with whom she was strangely alone in the house after twenty-five years of marriage and children, along thirty miles of dry riverbed in the magnificent countryside.

So she looked forward to the growing warmth and hospitality of the outdoors, but it would require emerging from her comfortable shell. For in the shadowy chill of winter she had been making headway on what she called her mid-life review.

Without intending to, Hannah had fallen into the grips of a rigorous inventory that yielded sore regrets about her past and evidence of newfound convictions. She was trying hard to resolve the two. "One of the things I've been thinking about is that what is most important to me is my spiritual life," she said. "I'm also reassessing the relationships I've had so that I won't continue making the same mistakes. I'm not sure how to be honest and open in a spiritual sense without betraying and hurting other people."

It was also the time of year when the renewal of her teaching contract from the Olny school board arrived in the mail and awaited her disposition. She would sign it, but with reservations. She had taught elementary school in various capacities for nearly twenty years. Now she instructed third and fourth graders in reading and language arts. She liked her work but had become restless. "For many years now, I've felt it might be time for a career change," she said. "If I'm going to get out of the classroom, I want to do it while I'm still a good teacher. I love being with my kids, but I'm exploring other opportunities."

Whenever she pictured herself elsewhere, however, her fondness for the classroom stopped her short. She had never considered teaching a "ministry" as such, and there often was "not a lot of affirmation," she said, but there were those kids. "When someone I've had a couple of years ago gives me a big hug and tells me what's going on, I know exactly what it means to feel real dedication in trying to do a good job. I don't know how many times I've sat at my kitchen table in the

early morning, coffee in one hand, intent on being open to God in prayer. Sometimes I'm afraid it will be a tough day in a classroom with sixty children. But out
of that experience an ordinary day becomes something pretty special."

When she did think of doing something else, it was usually some kind of full-
time work for the church. But she wondered if the price would be the loss of the
autonomy she enjoyed as a church volunteer. "You're generally not as free when
you're drawing a paycheck from an institution," she said. "I remember an old
maxim: 'The more you have to protect, the less free you are.' When someone has
our paycheck, we tend to lose our principles."

That ambivalence toward working for the church had deepened as the result
of serving on a special task force for evaluating overall diocesan structures as a prelude to recommending reforms. All ten members of the committee were professionals, and she felt honored to be among them. The experience had proven to
be both an inspiration and a spur to her aspirations for a church career and a
source of dismay and disillusion with the actual workings of the institution.

Through the intense round of committee proceedings, Hannah had discovered a need to set aside some of her idealism. It had meant giving up her ingrained
trust that the hierarchical establishment could be relied upon for superior wisdom.
And it meant overcoming her aversion to conflict. As a member of an important
decision-making group, she felt called upon to inject herself into the sometimes
abrasive give-and-take and to question diocesan officials. At first she had shrunk
from the challenge, she said, but eventually she shed her illusions and learned to
mix it up with other Catholics. It was all part of maturing as a Christian, she
thought.

"It is forcing me to be less childlike," she said. "There comes a time, I guess,
when you have to become a grown-up in the faith, not a child. And that sometimes
involves conflict and confrontation with the hierarchy. I've begun to see some of
the conflicts members of the hierarchy have to live with and am coming to grips
with the fact that they are just human beings. I'd given them the status of 'answer
men.' I see that that's not the case always. They as much as we have to be guided
by God."

Conquering her fear of open disagreement was to Hannah a crucial step in her
religious growth. During the lively committee sessions, she had at first acted
timidly and agreeably, she said, but soon wanted to go beyond that. "Though I like
being accepted and approved of, I realized that if that's the primary consideration
it's not good," she said. "It was scary for me to begin to say what I thought. If I
can accept the fact that I sometimes have to stand alone and not pout about getting hurt, then I've found an important part of what being a Christian is all about."

She had come to see that committee members could have differences and still
share a common love for the church. Conformity for its own sake was to her no

longer a virtue. She had taken chances and spoken her own piece without having "any assurance that it was okay," she said. Issues were not always resolved, and no authority could come to the rescue with a grand, infallible solution. She had sensed the loneliness and the courage of standing alone, bereft of the childlike fantasies about guardians of the faith somehow answering all the questions and making it all right. Hannah felt the burden.

At her intimate home parish, she received uplift for her teaching and her ventures into the wider church. A couple of weeks before, she had been asked by the pastor and the sister to plan for the funeral of a member of a farm family. She and the priest played guitar at the simple mass. "The next day so many people said that the spirit of celebration had permeated the whole service," she said. "I couldn't help think that's the way it should be."

She was also sponsoring Steve, a thirty-year-old farmer who would enter the Catholic church on Palm Sunday. They had met when he joined a Bread for the World chapter she had started. He was married to a woman of Hispanic descent whom he got to know while they were attending the same college. They had two preschool children. His wife was Catholic, but he had no church upbringing. Hannah helped prepare him for the Rite of Christian Initiation of Adults. "It meant a lot to me that he asked me to be his sponsor," she said. "I feel honored to be a part of their lives."

She looked forward to the day Steve would be received into the church. It was the kind of thing she was trying harder to appreciate. Recently, in the midst of her mid-life self-scrutiny, she had taken the Myers-Briggs psychological profile, and the results showed, among other things, that she was strongly intuitive. The way she interpreted it, "I have to stop being quite so abstract and start being more concrete in order to get more balance in my life. I'm trying not to worry about things I can't do anything about. I'm focusing on the here and now. That has brought me a lot of joy."

March
1·9·8·7

T HE GROUP WAS SEATED IN THE CUSHIONED DEN OF AN ELE-
gantly modified ranch house in a midwestern suburb. They
were there to explore their personal faith, volunteering to
delve into themselves and speak of matters they might normally
think too private even for fellow Catholics to hear. They had been invited by the parish program Renew to be honest and open about
their lives as Christians.

On that evening of March 1, they would be among dozens of such groups
huddled in homes within the boundaries of Incarnation parish. Altogether, eighty
clusters involving more than eight hundred parishioners would, during the ensuing week, inaugurate their second year of the national program that had aroused
so much attention as an ambitious effort to awaken and deepen personal faith in
God and the church's mission. At Incarnation, the first six-week phase of the
program had been conducted during Lent of the previous year and had been
generally well received. On this the dawn of the new Lenten season, it was time
to resume with reconstituted groups and many new leaders. Understandably, then,
there was nervousness about the prospect of getting acquainted in an exercise
that expected some soul-baring. The practice of personal testimony seemed more
natural to Protestants, especially among evangelicals who expressed feelings
openly, than to Catholics more accustomed to restraint. Witnessing, telling one's
story, did not seem like a particularly normal Catholic thing to do.

Included in this group were business executives, nurses, a carpenter, house-
wives, a member of the staff of a home for retarded persons, and a pharmacist,
six couples whose paths had crossed fleetingly at mass and at parish functions.
Significantly, the topic specified in the Renew guidelines for Week 1 was risk.
Taking chances involved the possibility of failure but, more importantly, the

213

"opportunity for a fuller life," the materials said. The session outline included meditations on the subject, reflections on how Jesus exemplified the theme in his life, readings from the gospel, and such discussion-starter questions as

> Have you recently resisted or given in to the temptation to stay back, not to risk the call to be yourself? Give examples.

> Do you sometimes hedge in making decisions about Christian values in your home, job, life? How?

The response was slow and awkward. Willingness to speak was offset by self-conscious caution. But in fits and starts the conversation began.

All acknowledged that they had held back at various times in their lives. All said they had hesitated to apply Christian values. "Parents get lots of pressure to hedge," said one man. "This week I did my taxes. That's an area where I'm also sorely tempted." A nurse confided that she recently had demurred from speaking out against abortion after being goaded by pro-choice colleagues. One corporate executive thought the bishops could have helped him by making him "aware of how morals bear on business." Another offered a terse summary of the common struggle: "Putting on the gospel," he said, "can be very painful."

Following a closing prayer and consideration of a possible "action response" by the group—aiding a fatherless teenage boy—the attentive hosts served coffee and fresh-baked cherry cobbler. Skittishness had long since dissipated. Chords had been struck. Conversations continued on their own.

In many respects, Renew seemed tailor-made for Incarnation. It was a parish that defined itself as a friendly place that encouraged people to take initiative and get involved. At the helm was the Reverend Karl Weitzel, pastor for the last six years. During his tenure, the roll call of family units had skyrocketed from three hundred fifty to one thousand, in part because the community in which the parish was located had been suddenly engulfed by urban sprawl and in part owing to Father Weitzel's extraordinary qualities as a leader.

Parishioners recited a remarkably common litany of Incarnation's selling points: its hospitality, friendliness, informality, breadth of activity, youth programs, high-quality school (K–6), and Father Weitzel's inimitable homilies. It had benefited from parish-shopping in the area. Among the new-member sketches in a recent parish newsletter was that of a couple who said they had picked Incarnation after trying "three or four other parishes." Some drove thirty miles or more to attend.

The membership was largely made up of affluent families (the *average* income was $43,000) in which the husband held a position in middle or upper corporate management and the wife stayed at home with the children. Half had moved in from other states. There were loads of children, eight hundred alone in the after-school religious education program for public school students and two hundred fifty in the parish school. The huge majority of parishioners had been to college, and their interests ran toward the practical and entrepreneurial rather than the cultural or intellectual. Their time was consumed mostly by work and family. They were accustomed to running things and thinking for themselves on most matters. On church issues, the most conservative among them, according to Father Weitzel, were middle managers in the thirty-five to forty-five age range.

On average, 70 percent, or about 2,200 of Incarnation's members, were in church each weekend, a considerably higher figure than that registered nationally by the Catholic church. Their yearly donations for general expenses reached $700,000, with another $800,000 contributed to the building of a new church. Among those at mass were a large but uncounted number of people who had been divorced and remarried without securing a church annulment. Father Weitzel let them and others like them know they were more than welcome.

Father Weitzel was by common agreement a remarkable pastor. Among the qualities for which he was highly esteemed were a keen mind, a seemingly inexhaustible source of good cheer and compassion, a gentle, a playful sense of humor, a gift for preaching, and an indefatigable supply of energy for conducting the endless list of parish duties. Raised on a farm as one of ten children, he had grown accustomed to hard work in his early years. He worked the parish as if he were doing the chores on the farm, with gladness and proficiency, seven days a week. A few years before, he had undergone cancer surgery, but had recovered well and professed good health. He loved being a priest and could never remember wanting to be anything else. Though he was candid about where he thought official Catholic teachings were inadequate, he was bountiful in his expressed love for the church.

With one priest in a bustling parish with a ton of duties to be done, lay leadership counted for much. An active parish council met monthly (its actions limited by the standard veto power granted to parish pastors); an energetic liturgy committee helped promote congregational involvement in worship; two religious education coordinators oversaw 130 lay teachers in CCD for children from grades one to twelve; a bundle of special programs and projects from a singles group to an effort to feed the hungry relied mostly on the enthusiasm and drive of dozens of men and women in far-flung corners of the parish.

In keeping with the "democratic" flavor of Midwestern Catholicism, Father Weitzel visualized a parish primarily as a horizontal rather than a vertical organism. "I consider myself a parishioner who happens to be ordained," he said. "I like consensus, though by nature I'm dictatorial. The point is that this is not my parish; it's ours. I try to avoid this we/they thing." In his ministry, relationships counted for more than laws. When faced with many personal problems involving the church, he tended to overlook the fine points of canon law in favor of compassion and forgiveness. "We're in the mercy business, not the judgment business," he liked to say.

His emphasis on inclusiveness, cooperation, and Christian egalitarianism had been embraced to a considerable degree during his years at Incarnation. An almost Protestant ethos of congregationalism had gripped members of Incarnation. When the new sanctuary was ready, many said they saw no need to bow to convention by having it dedicated by the bishop as representative of the extended, universal church. They preferred that their own pastor do the honors. Incarnation *was* the church, so far as many of them were concerned.

They treasured their own traditions. They sang at the top of their lungs at mass, an *un-Catholic* thing to do. Until the bishop put a stop to it, those who served Communion had taken the elements together with Father Weitzel at the altar. Despite static in Seattle and elsewhere over general absolution, Incarnation planned to hold two such rites during Lent. If the past was an indication, six hundred parishioners could be expected at each celebration of the rite. Parish leaders were still debating whether to install kneelers in the new building. While they were worshiping in temporary quarters in the school pending completion of the new $2.4-million facility, they had gotten along fine without kneelers, and many were reluctant to bring them back.

Moreover, they were accustomed to hearing their pastor in his homilies express his honest differences with the highest authorities of the church. Among other things, he had respectfully suggested that the church had it wrong in its teaching about birth control. He liked to distinguish between "God's law and church law," intimating that the church's version sometimes missed the mark. "It doesn't mean I'm smarter than the pope," he said. "I just see things differently."

Despite the pastor's candor and the parish's swings into unconventionality, Incarnation was no hotbed of radicalism. They welcomed their pastor's dissent over birth control because it mirrored a view commonplace among the laity. They rallied around a congregational concept of their parish as a special place and otherwise liked alternatives to tradition that appealed to their common sense or convenience, but they were hardly a band of church rebels with an ecclesiology to rival that of the Vatican. They were dissenters to the extent that their American loyalty to democracy and self-determination had shaped their idea of how a parish should operate, within some constitutional limits. But even that influence was probably mostly unconscious.

And for all their participation in the parish itself, many leaders thought there was too little progress in relating the faith to everyday life, whether the home or business. Incarnation's language and style were personal rather than legal, communal rather than hierarchical, and pastoral rather than doctrinal, but the impact of that faith community on the outside world had yet to be explored. Two recent events pointed up the parish's orientation. A talk on suicide—a matter of great personal concern—had drawn 450. A talk soon after on the bishops' economics pastoral, however, brought out a scant 120. That low turnout seemed telling in a parish loaded with corporate bigwigs whose vital economic interests the bishops' had directly tried to address. Was it indifference? Opposition? Coincidence?

Incarnation was a busy parish for the people and largely by them, one that touched only marginally on issues of the outside world. It was not a "people's church" as that term was understood by many Latin American Catholics to describe centers where, through Scripture and liturgy, views toward economic and political conditions were reshaped.

Early Monday morning, the parish week began with the daily 6:45 mass attended by a small group of regulars. Shortly thereafter the schoolchildren filed out of their classrooms to the parking lot, a span of sectioned black asphalt the size of a small airstrip. The occasion was the annual burning of palm branches from the previous year's Palm Sunday, the residue from which would be used to smudge the foreheads of parishioners two days hence on Ash Wednesday.

The ashes having been safely ensconced in the church, attention shifted to the monthly staff meeting. Seven women who held key positions in the parish joined Father Weitzel around a table in a room adjacent to the school office. Near the table's center a lighted Renew candle promoted thematic continuity. It was time to review the stack of upcoming events, to call attention to details, and to offer comments and suggestions. The staff included Alice, principal of the parish school; Margaret and Portia, the religious education coordinators; Linda, the principal liturgist and music director; Roseann, the coordinator of Renew; Mary, the keeper of records; and Gwen, the secretary for religious education.

In front of each lay an open scheduling calendar crammed with notations of meetings and programs and sundry reminders. By turns, each woman brought up those items that fell especially to her. Collectively, they displayed an unassuming sense of efficiency and competence and a deep affection for Incarnation. Many of their reports reflected the parish's heavy accent on young people.

March, the bulk of the Lenten season, was brimming with notable events. A special stations of the cross would be conducted for schoolchildren. A general advisory: the stations' narration should be pitched higher than a third-grade level so as not to insult the junior high kids. The intergenerational retreat for ninth graders and their parents was set for a Sunday afternoon later in the month. The seventy-three confirmation candidates would be presented at the 11:00 mass on the fifteenth and would trek to the cathedral two weeks later to be greeted by the bishop. A class for parents with children to baptize was also in the offing. Such sacramental occasions were seen as prime opportunities to engage adults in explorations of their own faith.

The approaching fashion show stirred much interest, and the date of the regular bloodmobile stop was noted. The evening of the twenty-seventh was set aside for adult stations of the cross, and the first communal penance rite would be conducted on the evening of the fifteenth. The parish-produced passion play was reported to be in the works, and emphasis was given to the scheduled visit of an evangelist and spiritual healer who would conduct a sort of revival meeting in the parish in the near future. The review of programs went on.

Many details needed tending to ensure smooth sailing. At least three people were needed to proofread wedding programs, said Father Weitzel, so to avoid situations in which "names get murdered." The increased volume of calls to the parish required additional help monitoring the phones, perhaps even a new system. Six to eight men must be recruited to set up for the worship following the fashion show. The singles' group could begin using the gym, on condition that they do the necessary janitorial work. And there was need for volunteers to clean the worship area once a week, straightening up, snagging hidden coffee cups, and replenishing depleted pamphlet racks. "Perhaps some of the older ladies would do it," the pastor suggested. "Let's put a notice on the bulletin board and see who shows up."

Alice prefaced her report on the recent principals' convention by passing along a maxim she had come across: "You make a living from what you get; you make a life from what you give." Gwen told the group that the Great Books program was going "okay" and echoed the general feeling that an emphasis on adult education was sorely needed. Should notice of the new mass schedule be posted outside the church? No reason to bother, it was decided, because the regulars would know anyway, while many irregulars, the "Christmas and Easter Catholics," probably wouldn't read it anyway and could be counted upon to appear at the wrong time no matter what.

Those and other matters came before the staff. Their nuts-and-bolts know-how, their common sense, and their dedication were largely responsible for keeping Incarnation functioning as well as it did. To them fell many of the thankless mundane tasks on which the character of the parish stood as well as the decisions requiring wisdom and maturity. After the meeting, some lingered to talk about their parish and their concerns.

Of the issues that came before them, none raised more difficult challenges than the effort to pass the Catholic faith on to young people. They had been raised in a day when the church taught with unquestioned authority. Now it seemed up to every Catholic to come to personal conclusions. "The church used to be black-and-white," said Roseann. "It used to say, 'This is it.' Now you have to decide for yourself. The old way would be easier—but I really wouldn't want to go back."

Neither did the others, but the trouble was that there was no substitute that had the same apparent clout with the kids. At the same time the heavy-handed approach had faded, so had home devotions like the rosary. It was getting more difficult—even embarrassing—to bring up religious subjects with their own children, they said. They didn't trust their own knowledge and didn't feel comfortable broaching the topic. "I can do it with a room full of children," Alice said. "Where I find myself most tongue-tied is with my own children."

Many parents, like their counterparts everywhere in America, simply had little or no idea what was going on in the minds of their teenage offspring, religiously or otherwise. They expended enormous material and emotional care on them and lodged great hopes in their potential, but the circumstances of suburban life had a way of accelerating the spin of the two generations into completely separate orbits. The promise of the church was that it could provide a desperately needed meeting ground. For some, it became that; for many others, it did not. Those not well synchronized enacted a scene replicated all over the nation: somber, silent teens trooping to church behind their elders, looking awkward and uncomfortable in their dress-up finery, with blank looks and distant expressions that suggested they were aliens unacquainted with such customs, unable to understand the language or the behavior.

On Ash Wednesday, many of those families joined the steady stream of parishioners who entered Incarnation to receive ashes. The wearing of the black mark was one of the few visible signs of Christian identity remaining in the modern age. It was a badge of distinctiveness in a time in which the prevailing rule was to blur religious distinctions for the sake of inoffensive pluralism. But a sizable number came to the parish that day, not nearly as great a percentage as in the past, but a pretty fair turnout nonetheless. Each was invited to complete a pledge printed on a small piece of purple paper that read, "As a special gift to Jesus during Lent, I will . . ." The stack of returns was sealed away at day's end.

Among the four masses of the day was one designed for the school students at eleven o'clock in the morning. Seated by grades, they wore standard Catholic classroom garb: boys in dark trousers, white shirts, and ties; girls in green, yellow, and red plaid skirts and vests with white blouses. As the mass began, two boys dressed like monks carried a large brown cross down the center aisle. On both sides, behind the students, mothers and other relatives sat, many holding babies. Over the sound system boomed a taped bagpipe rendition of the hymn "Amazing Grace."

One of the boys led the congregation in the penitential rite. "Today on Ash Wednesday," he said, "we receive ashes on our head as a sign of our human weakness and our desire to be more like Jesus." Among the misdeeds for which he asked the Lord's mercy were for "the times we didn't share with classmates or in the playground," the incidents when "we may have obeyed our parents but we didn't do it cheerfully," and those occasions "when we didn't use our time well at school."

Father Weitzel's homily featured two props, a peach-and-white colored poster with the word *sin* inside a circle with a line through it, signifying the urgency of "saying no to sin" (including drugs, drinking, and strangers). A similar sign with the word *joy* was encircled to indicate that happiness goes with holiness. From his smiles and affectionate quips, it was clear that the pastor immensely enjoyed the youngsters. He served up his message playfully and held most of his squirm-prone audience in thrall.

The children, teachers, and all others joined hands and recited the Lord's Prayer. Those who had already undergone first communion then approached the altar to receive the Eucharist.

They remained in their places for the monthly awards ceremony during which honors were bestowed for the following achievements, among others: multiplication, "super attitude toward scholarship," "neat work," "super job reading maps," "always following directions," artist of the month, "always willing to help someone," "kindness and dependability," and "good worker." The winners went forward to receive their certificates amid rounds of applause.

At the close they sang together "Blessed Be the Lord" and returned to their classrooms.

That evening one of the many groups was settling down to its first meeting of the Renew season. Though the same course outline was used with every group, the tone, content, and outcome varied greatly, of course, according to the makeup of the group and the skills and disposition of the leader. The Wednesday night group, for example, was more expansive than that visited three nights before, partly because the leader was more able to stimulate discussion.

On the theme of how they had experienced "risk" in their lives, the following were some of the responses:

"For me it was saying the prayer at the company's department Christmas party. I took the risk. I did it. Now they expect me to do it, and I do every year."

"I like the Bible study in Renew. We never studied the Bible before. For me risk means changing at work. So far nothing has improved my attitude. I'm very impatient toward other people. I expect too much."

"In my bridge group there's a woman who brought a magazine with a condom ad. I said I thought it was encouraging kids to be promiscuous. Others chimed in. But most were against me."

"With me, it involves setting a curfew for my kids when they come home from college. They complain about it a lot, give me a hard time. I tell them that as soon as they can make the house payments they can set their own hours."

"It's tough for me seeing homeless people. I almost shy away. I have trouble being humble. I was raised with the idea that you can be exactly what you want to be and that much of their problem is retardation or something. You call them bums, derelicts. But I guess many of them can't go further. They're so scarred by life experiences they can't make it."

Many of Incarnation's leaders invested Renew with great potential for opening up the mind, heart, and soul of the parish. A largely unspoken worry was that the parish had become too ingrown, too self-satisfied, too indifferent to the wider world, perhaps even superficial. But Renew offered hope of breaking out of this supposed confinement. People had begun to talk about their faith, and that was something new on that scale. Increased devotion to Scripture and prayer was likely in the view of some leaders to lead to heightened sensitivity to wider social problems, including those in their midst. "For all we do," said one prominent member, "I'm not sure how well we even deal with our own single parents."

By week's end, it was time for the vast fleets of late-model cars to fill and empty the parking lot in accord with the rhythm of the Sabbath mass schedule. Saturday evening at 5:00, Sunday morning at 8:00, 9:30, and 11:00. It was during this weekly ingathering that Incarnation most fully displayed what its members called a community. People stopped and visited, sang and prayed together, consumed gallons of coffee and dozens of doughnuts between masses. It *was* a place of warmth and friendliness.

Father Weitzel resonated with vigor and ebullience through the taxing schedule. He was in constant, easy motion among the people, laughing and joking, listening, advising, and directing with striking calm and humility. On the go, he reflected on himself and the parish as community. "My dignity doesn't come from ordination," he said, "it comes from baptism." And: "I know of fifty of our laymen I could present for ordination who could carry on the work of this parish, but I don't know if there are fifty priests."

The homily focused on worry. It was a blight that took a heavy toll in anxiety and illness, Father Weitzel told the packed pews of suburbanites accustomed to fretting over careers, families, and bills, among other things. Worst of all, the pastor suggested, was the anxiety over materialism, a subject near and dear to his parishioners' hearts. He held up a large yellow cardboard key with *Jesus* printed on it in red. The key was trust in Jesus, Father Weitzel said. And in words that seemed unwittingly to beg the question for Incarnation at this moment, he continued, "That's what unlocks us if we're all locked up."

━ ━

SPIRALING BUDGET DEFICITS AND FINANCIAL MARKET SCANDALS IN THE UNITED States were paralleled in scaled-down fashion at the Vatican. The most urgent item concerned the news that Italian officials had ordered the arrest of Archbishop Paul C. Marcinkus, the American head of the Vatican Bank, for his alleged role in a

$1.3-billion banking collapse. The February 26 announcement sent shock waves throughout Catholic America, further damaging faltering confidence in the Vatican's ability to handle its finances.

The action against Archbishop Marcinkus was the latest development in a long-simmering crisis. The bank over which he presided, officially named the Institute for Religious Works (*Instituto per le Opera di Religione,* or IOR in its Italian abbreviation), had been implicated as a conspirator in fraudulent actions that preceded the 1982 demise of Banco Ambrosiano based in Milan. Officials of the court investigating the collapse had issued arrest warrants for Archbishop Marcinkus and two of his aides after otherwise failing to gain the bank's cooperation in the probe. The magistrates said they had issued the warrants in an effort to extradite the bank officials and in order to compel their testimony.

Archbishop Marcinkus, the son of a Lithuanian butcher from Chicago, had been the subject of allegations that he had enabled his good friend Roberto Calvi, the then president of Banco Ambrosiano, to maintain a fraudulent cover to prop up his failing institution. The Vatican Bank at the time owned 1.5 percent of Banco Ambrosiano as well as several dummy companies that had received large loans from the Milan bank. Documents showed that the Vatican Bank supplied certain "letters of comfort" to Calvi (who was found hanged in London in 1982) to assure nervous creditors that banking operations involving Banco Ambrosiano were sound when, in fact, the bank was on the verge of collapse. The Vatican officials were therefore accused of knowingly perpetrating a fraud. Somewhat puzzlingly, however, the bank voluntarily paid $240 million to Ambrosiano creditors in 1984, explaining it as a "voluntary contribution" made in the "spirit of conciliation and collaboration."

A day after the arrest warrants were issued, the Vatican declared its full support for Archbishop Marcinkus and indicated that under no circumstances would he be turned over to Italian authorities for such questioning. Church officials reasserted their claim that under treaties between Italy and the Vatican state, the Italian government had no authority over the officers of the Vatican Bank. Archbishop Marcinkus, a husky, gregarious six-footer, had denied any wrongdoing from the first. The pope, known to count the archbishop among his most trusted aides, had expressed unswerving confidence in him.

Word of the archbishop's new troubles dealt a severe blow to efforts to increase U.S. Catholic aid to the Vatican. Archbishop Marcinkus was widely known in Catholic America. In 1979, he had been at the pope's side as bodyguard and adviser on his first trip to the United States. Amid rising jitters about the possible cloud that the latest publicity about the archbishop could cast over the ambitious fund-raising plans, the president of the U.S. bishops' conference, Archbishop John L. May, issued a subdued vote of confidence in his American colleague on March 6.

Extending his "personal and fraternal support," Archbishop May acknowledged that he lacked all the facts but hailed his fellow archbishop as "a man of integrity and honesty" and of "high moral character."

Meanwhile, the central government of the church was set to announce a deficit of $67 million on the eve of a special council of ten cardinals named by the pope to solve the Vatican's fiscal crisis.

Any bailout plan depended on the largesse of the church in the United States. For all the disdain shown by curial officials for Catholic America's alleged materialism and religious apostasy, sneering turned to reverence when the subject turned to money. Catholics in the United States were quite logically expected to be the Daddy Warbucks of the church universal. Their faith might be zany, but their money was good, and the Vatican was rapidly digging itself into a deep fiscal hole that was eating up its reserves.

America had been contributing almost half the annual Peter's Pence collection for the pope. U.S. receipts from the last collection the previous June were about $12 million of a world total of $32 million. The annual U.S. figure had reached only $3–5 million until Archbishop Edward T. O'Meara took charge in 1981 and instigated a more vigorous promotional campaign. But after climbing to the $12–13-million zone, it had leveled off, and some feared a downturn as a backlash by those upset with the Vatican's recent hard line against the U.S. church.

The stated purpose of Peter's Pence was to fund the pope's charities, but in fact the money was going directly to defray current operating expenses of the curia. For public relations purposes, the church obviously preferred the fund's image as a fount of papal charity. For as one church fund-raiser put it, "People don't give to a deficit."

This bit of flimflam was a sample of what many Catholics in the United States saw as the Vatican's fiscal folly. When it came to fiduciary matters, the church bore a distinctly pre–Vatican II stamp. Business was conducted by those at the top behind closed doors. It was a paternalistic system on the old hierarchical model of secrecy and patronage. As budget shortfalls worsened, Rome was, in effect, driven to make at least a minimum of concessions and began providing certain morsels of information in an effort to ease tension and dramatize the crisis. The current Vatican budget was announced: $113 million. With a $67 million deficit, the picture was gloomy. There was even talk of turning the papal palace into a museum to help raise money. And, of course, the perennial proposal to sell off valuable pieces of art made the rounds.

For all the mystery and intrigue surrounding Vatican finances, it seemed more like a seat-of-the-pants mom-and-pop operation than a slick, sophisticated multinational conglomerate. According to a top Vatican financial officer, Cardinal Giuseppe Caprio, the value of the church's holdings totaled $570 million, $275 million of which was invested, the rest being largely artworks and real estate. But it had no pension fund for retired Vatican employees, for example, which made it necessary to pay that ongoing expense out of the budget for operating expenses. And there seemed to be no coherent accounting system keeping this scattered portfolio together.

Because America was the key to righting a listing ship, the church in the United States presumably had certain trump cards to play. Not only did Rome hope for greater returns from Peter's Pence; there were also plans afoot to raise substantial sums from wealthy U.S. Catholics to endow the Vatican. The figure of $100 million was being tossed about. In addition to that was the $25-million bill for the coming papal visit to America. With demands such as these in the works, the Americans were, at least theoretically, in an excellent position to lay down some conditions of their own.

U.S. Catholic business and finance leaders who were drawn into the discussion insisted on fundamental changes in the way the Vatican conducted its financial affairs. If Americans were to respond to the legitimate needs of the central church, then its operations would have to be brought into line with American standards of accountability. That meant balance sheets and statements of income and expenses that could be easily grasped and digested as well as an international commission of experts to monitor the church's ledgers. Secrecy as the primary *modus operandi* must be ended, in the view of the Americans, in order to clear the air and generate confidence.

Late in the month, the council of ten cardinals dropped a minor bombshell on their brothers in the hierarchy. Following their urgent meeting to review Vatican finances, the cardinals sent a letter to the world's bishops, dated March 25, declaring that if the Peter's Pence collection failed to raise sufficient funds, each diocese would, in effect, be expected to make a generous contribution to help cover the difference.

ON MARCH 10, THE CONGREGATION FOR THE DOCTRINE OF THE FAITH RELEASED a forty-page instruction designed to cover a broad spectrum of biomedical questions related to reproduction. It was a sweeping document that judged the morality of many techniques, even calling on governments to curb some of them. The document captured bold headlines in the nation's newspapers and touched off widespread discussion.

The pronouncements in the statement hardly came as a surprise to those familiar with the forces of consistency with the principle that life was sacred and so was sex within the existing rules. But for the Vatican to so boldly declare its intention to enter the worldwide policy debate over the uses and limits of the new technology was significant indeed.

From the outset, the instruction made clear its purpose: to examine biomedical methods in light of church teachings. Criteria were laid down according to the church's long-held line of moral reasoning. The "natural" design of God's creation meant that conditions under which new life began were reducible to the loving sexual act of marital union alone. Unity and procreation *were* the purposes of sex within marriage; the sexual, therefore, must never be separated from the reproductive. Moreover, the instruction repeated the church's conviction that a human being existed from the moment of conception. Those beliefs set the parameters for a strict-constructionist interpretation.

A series of moral conclusions followed. One category had to do with conception itself. Artificial insemination, including that between spouses, was ruled out on grounds that it separated reproduction from the marital sex act. All forms of in vitro fertilization were forbidden. Likewise disallowed was the impregnation of unmarried women or widows, even with sperm from a deceased husband that had been kept in a sperm bank. Surrogate motherhood was condemned as a violation of the nature of the family and of divinely ordained parenthood.

Procreation within the marital act remained the sole source of conception. There was one procedure, however, in which technology could play a legitimate role for married couples who experienced difficulty conceiving normally. After natural sexual intercourse, the husband's sperm could be collected by a syringe and aspirated toward the egg. Church officials let it be known that a particular method was approvable for expediting this procedure: use of a perforated condom that would allow some sperm to escape, in keeping with the requirements of the "natural" act, while retaining by far the greater measure. Use of a normal condom would, of course, break the church's law against artificial contraception.

The other major set of judgments concerned treatment of the embryo. Prenatal screening for the purpose of possibly aborting embryos with serious defects or deformities was declared immoral. Experiments on embryos, their destruction or mutilation, was proscribed, along with their creation and/or freezing for laboratory use. Among the objections to in vitro fertilization was that the technique often led to the elimination of unwanted fertilized eggs. Thus, "life and death are subjected to the decision of man, who thus sets himself up as the giver of life and death by decree."

Though intervention for the purpose of eliminating an unwanted embryo was rejected, the instruction endorsed prenatal testing and therapeutic treatments—including possible chromosome repairs—that offered healing and improved health, on condition that the parents gave their free consent and the risks were not "disproportionate." In no case, it continued, should a prenatal screening result "that shows the existence of malformation or a hereditary illness . . . be the equivalent of a death sentence." Development of fertility drugs was also encouraged.

The Vatican used the document to press for tight government controls on scientific involvement in reproduction. It specifically called on nations to prohibit surrogate motherhood and experimentation on living embryos. In entering the political debate, church officials said they hoped to seize an opportunity to influence policies in an area that was thus far virtually unregulated.

Within the church, the response to the instruction was sharp and often heated. Many commentators credited the Vatican with underlining important issues and for forcefully restating the church's concerns for the dignity and integrity of human life. But they also raised strong criticisms about the method used to produce the document and some of its conclusions. Among the most common complaints were the following:

- The document was too ambitious and comprehensive. It had attempted to lump together too many disparate issues. The issue of technical assistance for infertile couples, for example, simply didn't belong in the same discussion as surrogate parenting.

- Despite the document's claim that it was the "result of wide consultation," leading Catholic ethicists in America said they knew nothing of any such efforts to seek counsel or insight either from experts in the field or from couples experiencing difficulty. Some saw the statement as another attempt by celibate male clerics to define reproductive rights of women without hearing from women themselves.

- The instruction was entirely too hostile to science, hence defensive. Rather than viewing technology, with all its problems, as an important ally in a common effort to enhance life, the document unfortunately portrayed science as an alien threat, stampeding the human race toward a science fiction nightmare. Such an attitude sadly exhibited the old antipathy by the church toward its perceived enemy.

By far the most furor was kicked up by the document's response to the plight of childless couples. In denying them the right to in vitro fertilization or ordinary artificial insemination, the instruction struck a sensitive nerve and sparked some protest. Paradoxically, the cause of infertile couples ardently longing for children stood out more poignantly against a cultural backdrop of lower birthrates, diminishing fertility, and delayed parenthood. In an age of contraception, therefore, the desire to conceive seemed more momentous, more chosen. The Catholics among them were likely to have had that desire further whetted by the great emphasis the church placed on parenthood and family. They were offered little by the instruction.

Initial indications were that couples seeking a child and institutions offering reproductive services would be undeterred by the instruction's thinking, though many might go through it with a heavier heart. A Catholic patient at a San Francisco fertility clinic told the *New York Times:* "The church says practicing birth control is a sin. But we've been trying every way we know to have a child for five years, and we can't. We're desperate. How can it be a sin if my husband's sperm is to be used to fertilize an egg from me, and I give birth from my womb? I think God wants us to have children. How can that be a sin?" (March 12, B11).

THE CHURNING CLOUDS SHONE WITH A FLUORESCENT GLARE AND THE AIR WAS heavy and sticky as travelers made their way, singly and in small groups, to Casa San Jose retreat house on the outskirts of San Antonio, Texas. They had been invited there to deliver personal testimony about their lives as Catholic laypeople, a subject that had been largely ignored in the post–Vatican II church.

They hailed from thirty-one dioceses, having been picked by their bishops to take part in this the third of four such weekend sessions organized by the bishops' laity committee of the United States Catholic Conference. It was part of a larger plan by the committee to canvass laypeople in advance of October's Synod on the Laity. By collecting and collating results from questionnaires and meetings with laypeople at various levels of the church, the committee hoped to send some clear messages about the minds of laypeople to the four bishops representing the U.S. church at the Rome synod.

From the first announcement of the synod, the concept had encountered some resistance. For one thing, some laypeople scoffed at the very notion of a conclave on the *laity* being run by *bishops*. It was a contradiction in terms, they said. There was also the problem of agenda. What was *thinkable* by laity was not necessarily *do-able* at the synod. Laypeople wanted things from the church that the bishops could not necessarily deliver on their behalf. Since Pope Paul VI had resumed synods after Vatican II, they had served mostly as forums for working out the implications of existing church laws and policies rather than laboratories for breaking new ground.

By default, certain issues, such as the ordination or women or amendments to the church's sex ethics, were outside the realm of discussion, as was *any* serious critique of church teachings or principles. But it was feasible to press the meaning of certain teachings concerning the laity and to urge the church to fulfill the potential outlined in Vatican II documents.

Topics considered useful and practical included the meaning of the lay vocation, adult education, spiritual formation, the role of the rising number of lay ministers, the experience of service on parish and pastoral councils, lay spirituality, the
legitimate role of women in church and society, the ministry to youth, the link
between spirituality and service to the world, lay-oriented programs such as
Renew or Cursillo, and evaluation of diocesan synods.

The survey form distributed to laypeople across the country stuck closely to
those categories, encouraging both positive and negative reactions. Over fifteen
thousand questionnaires had been returned already, and many thousands more
were expected. The official in charge of the survey, the Reverend Robert Kinast of
the Washington Theological Union, described the bulk of respondents as well
educated, working adult men and women with children who were active in their
parishes. Among those in short supply were young people, young adults, and
alienated Catholics.

Apart from the relatively controlled instrument of the survey, however, there
were the give-and-take discussions where content was less manageable, in which
broader, more free-wheeling exchanges could take place. The regional consultations, heavily stocked with those who were uncommonly committed to the church
and highly articulate about their faith, had been notably lively. There to listen
and respond were bishops who were either synod delegates or alternates or members of the bishops' lay committee.

So far the road show had appeared in Burlingame, California, and Belleville,
Illinois. After San Antonio, there remained one more like it in Holyoke,
Massachusetts, and an additional gathering, similar in format but different in composition, in Belleville in late March. It would comprise representatives from fifty-
six national Catholic lay organizations.

The assembly at Casa San Jose fit the general profile of the other consultation
groups: mostly middle-aged, middle class, and devoted to the church. Of the one
hundred participants, thirty-six were employed full-time by the church, eight
worked for the church in a voluntary or part-time capacity, and the majority,
fifty-six, had no occupational ties with the institution. Joining them were four clerics, including two priest delegates and Bishop Stanley J. Ott of Baton Rouge, a delegate to the synod, and Bishop Bernard J. Gantner of Beaumont, Texas, a member
of the bishops' lay committee, and a nun.

Among those employed outside the church were a tile-setter, a retired aero-
space engineer, a mechanical engineer, an electrical engineer, a Montessori teacher,
a Navy lawyer, an official of the United Farm Workers of America, a physician who,
with his wife, codirected the diocesan family life office, an owner of a commercial
furnishings company, public school teachers, a college president, a county supervisor of the Farmers' Home Administration, a bank vice president, social workers,

an architect, a real estate broker, office managers, an insurance company manager, the founder of an electrical supply company, and a probation officer.

Church employees included parish administrators, directors of diocesan development, family life coordinators, diocesan directors of lay ministry, youth ministers, a diocesan director of Hispanic affairs, a diocesan director of black ministries, editors and writers for church publications, religious educators, a Christian counselor, diocesan right-to-life directors, and a parish maintenance supervisor.

Nobody better grasped the suspicions that hung in the air about the worth of the consultations than Dolores Leckey, the highly capable executive director of the bishop's lay committee, who had in her years of service become acutely tuned to the politics of the church. She wasted no time getting to the point at Friday evening's opening session. "Does what we do make any difference?" she asked. "I hope to show that it does." She offered assurance that an inexorable movement toward increased lay involvement and responsibility was well under way and that weekends such as these would further the cause no matter what its precise impact on the synod. The laity *would* prevail, she seemed to say, but that would require much patience. "There's a new style of ministry emerging, but it's never been done this way before," she said. "Nobody knows how to do it."

At the very least, she suggested, the synod had become an occasion for laypeople to meet and swap notes. That was certain to give the movement a boost. She was cautiously, respectfully upbeat. "Consultation does affect the national agenda," she said, "but it does take a little time."

Bishop Gantner held open the door. "I hope we have the opportunity to have an honest dialogue about your experience of the church," he said. "I hope you'll feel free to say whatever you came to say."

The person responsible for eliciting those thoughts and feelings was the Reverend George Wilson, S.J., a consultant on church organization for Management Design Corporation in Cincinnati. In seeking his goal, Father Wilson used the techniques of small group process and large group interaction. The method's rationale was basically democratic: encouraging people to become involved in the flow as much as possible. One goal was to discover the will of the group rather than impose one on it. Another was to make participants feel equally important. It was a self-conscious alternative to the top-down model by which the Catholic church had taught and exercised authority. As such, many found it refreshing, if awkward.

With Father Wilson's guidance, the people broke into small groups and reported back on "What's it like being a layperson in the church in the USA?" The brainstorming produced eighty-six cryptic observations that Father Wilson hastily scribbled on sheets of dull white newsprint.

Certain basic themes stood out, most related in some way to feelings of pow-
erlessness and distrust: anger among laypeople who felt unjustly treated as adolescents and second-class citizens by the church; insistence that laypeople claim
what is rightfully theirs without waiting for permission from the clergy or hierarchy; protest against the church's denial of full participation to women; ambivalence toward priests (on the one hand, gratitude for their service and empathy
toward them as bearers of unrealistic expectations, including mandatory celibacy,
on the other hand, dismay toward those seen as authoritarian); uncertainty and
feelings of nonsupport among lay ministers; desire for more spiritual life than most
parishes provide; enthusiasm for the Vatican II emphasis that everyone—clergy
and laity—derives ministry from the same source, baptism, but impatience at how
slowly this idea had caught on.

Specific comments from the group feedback included these:

"We're like adolescents waiting to grow up."

"We're like adult children whose parents won't let go—who still have dominating, controlling parents."

"The fact that we've been raised in a democratic culture puts us in conflict
with a hierarchical church."

"Everyone tolerates lay ministers for a while, then they demand Father."

"Unless the bishops at the synod do something this time about the inequality
of women, some of the most intelligent women in the church will go away."

Responses from the small groups were placed within the larger framework of
opinions registered on the national survey conducted by Father Kinast for the bishops' committee. Most of the returns analyzed by Father Kinast, a rangy, convivial
priest and scholar, closely paralleled their attitudes and concerns in one way or
another. From the fifteen thousand surveys completed so far, Father Kinast had
drawn several tentative conclusions that he proceeded to summarize for the group.

The respondents, above average in church involvement, were sold on the
Vatican Council's assertion that baptism itself confers equality in the church
and is, in Father Kinast's analysis, "the basis for the vocation of the laity, in
some ways prior to and more important than ordination, religious vows, or marital vows."

Laypeople increasingly tended to reject distinctions between clergy and laity,
church and world, lay spirituality and clerical spirituality, women and men.
Accordingly, questions were being raised about the nature of ordination and how
it was, if it was, different from baptism. The concept of democracy through baptism

also prompted Catholics to ask whether that did not imply equality of all baptized Christians, Catholics or not.

The survey showed that laypeople had a deep spiritual yearning that, Father Kinast said, came from "already experiencing God in their lives. It doesn't come out of spiritual emptiness; we're not talking about spiritual orphans." That is, they had their own legitimate spiritual lives independent of what clergy might have contributed. When they went to church, they wanted inspirational sermons, "not necessarily doctrinal." They wanted priests to be spiritual leaders facilitating prayer life. Where the church had been least effective was in relating spirituality to work and family life.

The surveyed laity believed strongly that all Catholics were called upon to use their talents and energies for the sake of the church and the world. But defining ministries under the mandate of Vatican II had resulted in rising frictions between priests and laypeople exercising ministries. The priest was the key to these emerging forms of ministry, but many priests were perceived as threatened by lay involvement and determined to be in control.

From the evidence, it looked to Father Kinast as if tensions between clergy and laity over collaboration posed the greatest threat to parish serenity. The synod could render a great service by exploring this sensitive area of the church's mission and ministry, he said.

Laypeople were sure that the church's ministry should involve the secular world but had little idea what that meant. Usually this mission was defined as charity work or helping the homeless, almost never as striving for "structural or policy changes" in society, for example, "how to use your position in the bank to bring about greater justice. They're not clear in what sense ordinary people represent the church. They have a high regard for the bishops' recent letter on the economy, for instance, but are uncertain how to put it into practice."

Discrimination against women was both identified and strongly opposed by women and men. A majority of respondents favored the ordination of women. Qualities generally described as "feminine" rated high compared to those considered "masculine." Still, women reported overwhelmingly that in the church "their advice was not valued as highly as that of men" and complained about the limits imposed on women as leaders and about the perpetuation of sexually exclusive language and sexist stereotypes used by the church in public.

Despite their many misgivings about its teachings and policies, Catholics were optimistic about their church. "These faithful are not really dependent on what happens at the synod," Father Kinast said. "Their investment of themselves in the church is not seen as a waste. If the bishops listen to them and will take steps to improve their situation as laity, praise God; but if not, these faithful indicate they will continue right on with what they're doing."

After Saturday lunch and time to stroll the pathways of the spacious Casa San
Jose retreat grounds, the small groups reassembled. Their assignment was to pick
a topic from the list compiled from the earlier session and go to work on it.

Group 6 took some liberties with its task. Sexuality had been largely ignored,
so why not look at that as well as the murky issue of how sexuality could relate
to spirituality? The subject was too little talked about in the church. The group
agreed and decided to go ahead.

The discussion ranged freely and spontaneously from one person to another
around the circle of eight chairs. There was a mixture of appreciation for the
church's sexual morality and dismay that those who wrote the rules seemed ill
informed about the realities of what they were prescribing. Some believed the
church had sent an ambivalent message: sanctifying sex within marriage but subtly ranking the chaste life above it. Gratitude for the guidance of the church mingled with frustration over its purported inability to listen. There was considerable
sentiment for greater acceptance by the church of separated and divorced people
and, to a lesser extent, of homosexuals.

The most common focus of their remarks was the subject of birth control.
One group member doubted that a majority of priests endorsed the church's lone
option, natural family planning, as a sufficient method. Birth control had been "a
source of tremendous agitation in my life for fifteen years," she said.

"The church doesn't speak our language; it's not in touch with us," said Charles
Balsam, a diocesan director of family life from Beaumont, Texas. He himself was
"comfortable with the church's birth control teaching," he said, but he was "willing to sit down with people who don't accept it to find out their experience," implying that the church should show the same openness.

John Jensen, a financial planner from Conyers, Georgia, had with his wife
raised nine children. "Every time my wife said she was pregnant, it was a traumatic
experience. Looking back, I guess I'm glad for the church's teachings, because I
wouldn't want to give any of them back."

"One of the satisfactions of the church is the value it puts on family life and
the affirmation of sexual expression within a committed relationship," said Vee
Marshall, a religious educator from Phoenix, Arizona. "But the church doesn't listen to the experience of the laity. It dictates regulations but doesn't offer day-to-day
support. Too often sexuality is used to reinforce male dominating power."

A digest of their thoughts was reported along with those of the other small
groups at a plenary session later that afternoon. Again, the findings were inscribed
with magic marker on newsprint. Enough had been flushed out to begin to formulate some points that the entire body could approve. The process was working;
the raw materials of discussion were being channeled into conclusions that Bishop
Ott was expected to respond to on Sunday morning.

By afternoon's end, the group was tired and somber, depleted by the day's exercise in criticism—a draining experience no matter how constructive—feeling the weight of negativity that invariably resulted from hard, sometimes painful diagnosis of the church, for the stinging critiques were, after all, aimed at the church they loved.

It was time to go to church and affirm the unity that brought them there. In Meditation Chapel, with its black-and-brown marble floor and a dominating gold cross bearing the black figure of Jesus, the two bishops led the liturgy. "Your table is prepared. Please come and gather for the celebration," the bishops proclaimed. They came forward from the pews, and, circling the altar with hands joined, they intoned the Lord's Prayer together. They then received the wafer and, as they filed back toward the pews, drank the wine from one of four glass cups held by two men and two women. They sang, and they embraced.

The evening was given over to festivity and restoration: a reception with drinks and snacks, a banquet of Mexican food, and a mélange of music, tales, and talk. The heaviness of the day dissolved into the mystery of Catholic peoplehood.

Bishop Ott had sat quietly taking notes through the previous sessions, but now on a bright Sunday morning it was his turn to review their advice to himself and the other delegates to the synod. He could not promise them any results from the synod, he explained, but vowed he would take what they had said and "try to absorb it, digest it, and get the flow, to get a feel for what is uppermost on your minds."

As he warmed to his task, he digressed into an appeal that seemed to arise from an intense inner dialogue. "I want to assure you that regarding the sense of pain and discouragement some people feel, the concerns some people feel—we are listening," he said. "Remember, we must be realistic. We are in solidarity with you. We are on your side in this. We try very much to affirm the laity. Christ needs you. The Church needs you . . . bishops really have a desire to serve . . . it's very good to be open and frank. Bishops listen to critics—constructive criticism, what's going to be good to build up the church."

The rest of his comments were marked by a similar ambivalence between wanting to please and holding the line. He would address the concerns voiced by the small groups. Two groups apiece had discussed "mission and ministry," "leadership," and "spiritual yearning/lay spirituality." One each had selected "the Catholic family," "baptismal consciousness," "human sexuality," "lay Catholic witness in the world," "workplace," and "youth." It was a pretty safe batch of issues—not that the recommendations that grew out of them were necessarily tame.

As Bishop Ott prepared to take up those suggestions, he counseled patience, forgiveness, and sensitivity. His leadership style was positive and affirming, and he intended to exercise that to the fullest.

On "mission and ministry" he noted the importance of prayer and Scripture to prepare for service. Only 13 percent of parishioners took an active part in the parish, he said, underscoring the "need for more hands to carry on the important work." Regarding "leadership," he emphasized that church leaders were venturing out among the people a good deal more and conceded that they could "do a much better job" in communicating with people. Likewise, the church should do better responding to "spiritual yearnings" by, among other things, encouraging priests to present good homilies. On the stated need for lay theology, he asked, "Who will do it? Hopefully yourselves."

The bishop was optimistic about the proposals on "family life" and "baptismal consciousness," seeing progress on both fronts as a result of programs such as Renew and the Rite of Christian Initiation of Adults. And he wholeheartedly agreed that "human sexuality" was too often shunted aside. "There's a lack of discussion and dialogue," he said. The pope had supplied a "rich mine" of talks to aid that process of inculcating the church's teachings. "We're going to get a lot of flak and bruises [for teaching the church's doctrines], but we must say what must be said. It is extremely serious trying to bridge the right and the left. There are no easy solutions. But it's not being done by the church."

On the issue of "lay Catholics in the world," Bishop Ott commended the bishops' pastoral letters on nuclear arms and the economy as "masterpieces" that could provide proper guidance in two major worldly areas. The pope had by happy coincidence supplied an encyclical on work that should help answer needs expressed in that group.

Lastly, there were the topics of "youth" and "women." The church admittedly "was not doing a good job with youth," he said. "We indeed must find ways to give them Christ with love and joy." With reference to women, the bishop said many of the concerns expressed there—"your frustration and impatience"—had been taken up in a 1980 church publication on the laity, "Called and Gifted." "We're trying to move along with you," he said. "We see the need for increased ministry for women within the roles that are possible. We have made mistakes."

He finished a survey that was both conciliatory and cursory. Throughout, he had conceded the validity of many points without endorsing the specific proposals put forth as remedies. He had adroitly encouraged his listeners, even appeared to embrace their advice without doing so. He had perhaps leaned as far as a bishop could in accommodating people he seemed genuinely to like and respect without casting aside his role as a bishop.

The small groups got their chance to respond to the bishop's reading of their aspirations before he closed with final comments. Some groups were full of praise for Bishop Ott as a careful listener who had, indeed, absorbed their concerns for the synod. "We feel we've been heard, and we're full of hope," said one group's leader. "We represent the 13 percent actively involved in the church. The majority—87 percent—haven't really been addressed." Said another, "We felt peace because we feel our concerns will be heard. Our emphasis would be on the need for education to bring Christ to life in our world."

Other groups faulted him for toning down their proposals. Group 6, which had focused on sexuality, was among the complainants. "We didn't feel entirely heard," its leader said. "Our messages were filtered, softened, and modified. We want the intensity of faith that underlies this to be heard also. We don't need responses in terms of more theological action. We want affirmative action and real collaboration, not only more documents. We expect and deserve major policy and process change at every level. We don't need more processes designed from the top." Another group thought "he has heard us well" but claimed that there had been "a certain amount of glossing over major items—sexuality, women's issues, and youth." Group 8 had winced when the bishop pledged to strive for the inclusion of women in the church "to the extent possible," quoting from "Called and Gifted." "It looked to us like it was closing a door," the group leader groused.

Group 2 mentioned no criticism but felt it necessary to restate its main appeals for "affirmation in the vocations of marriage, family sexuality, and youth ministry" and for progress in "incorporating masculine and feminine qualities in the church." Its leader added that the group wanted the bishops in Rome to know their commitment to applying the "preferential option for the poor" to all their church decisions.

Bishop Ott had described the procedure at the synod that gave each delegate eight minutes to speak. Group 9 suggested he seize the moment to give a dress rehearsal.

That idea was the cleverest attempt to answer the central question of the consultations—how much would their advice actually count at the synod? A practice run by Bishop Ott might provide some clues. Other groups were blunter and more straightforward. Said one, "At every level, what can we expect as the outcome of this process? How will this information and our input be received at the national level? How will that change how that level deals with us in the future and how we deal with them?" At this, loud applause broke out across the room.

The outburst signified clearly that the uneasiness over the process had, if anything, grown in the wake of Bishop Ott's response. "What can we realistically expect?" asked another group leader. Someone else put it more specifically: "After the synod, what vehicle of accountability and feedback exists for dialogue between the bishops who are synod delegates and the U.S. pre-synod representatives?" They pressed for answers. They wanted action on their bill of particulars.

Bishop Ott rose again to reply. He was a man on the spot attempting to assure them that he was doing his best. Once more he tried to lower expectations. "We don't have all the answers today," he said with candor, "and we don't have all the solutions. We'll probably have to await the next world for that."

He declined the invitation to perform a dry run of his synod speech, giving as his reason that "at the moment I don't know what I'd say." He added, "Frank, open, and candid exchanges of views are healthy. They're very good. We realize we are together. Everyone has expressed satisfaction and joy being here. That's a big plus. We're not going to solve all the problems."

The greater portion of his remarks were addressed to the discontent over the status of women and the demands that the synod take steps to remedy the perceived injustices. The issue epitomized the conflict between the irresistible force of rising appeals for change and the unmovable obstacle of church law. Bishop Ott didn't think his quote from "Called and Gifted" should be taken as closing doors. The bishops were preparing a pastoral letter on women and, in the process, had heard women "expressing themselves intensively, loudly and clearly.

"We've [the bishops] tried to listen and tried to respond. Women's ordination is not part of the synod. We can only go so far at a time. I think there'll be more progress on that in the future."

He was presenting himself as a sort of noncommittal advocate.

"I hope we can be courageous and forthright with one another about how we really feel about women's rightful place in the church. I hope we can make progress and move the church on in that area.

"To me it's been a great joy to experience this weekend with you. I assure you we are all the church. We want you and need you to play your rightful role."

— ⸺

THE QUESTION OF THE "RIGHTFUL ROLE" OF LAYPEOPLE HAD BEEN THE SUBJECT of a pungent critique, "The American Laity—Memory, Meaning, and Mission," in the March 7 issue of *America,* by David O'Brien, the noted Catholic historian at Holy Cross College. The article was based on an address he had delivered at the previous fall's conference of the National Center for the Laity (NCL) in Chicago.

Whereas the consultations focused on lay participation in the church, O'Brien's point echoed the emphasis by the NCL on developing a theology of lay life beyond the parish.

He argued that the Catholic church in America had effectively isolated religion from the world and had reduced religious activity to that which went on in church. During the early decades of the American republic, the church had functioned more along democratic lines, he wrote, but with the huge influx of immigrants in the nineteenth century this openness to lay influence had diminished.

Faced with the challenge of imbuing the newcomers with a strong Catholic identity, the church had folded in on itself, becoming a subculture largely apart from the American mainstream. "By the 1950s, American Catholicism had become one of the world's great success stories," O'Brien wrote. Making use of the available opportunities, Catholic America had ridden the wave of upward mobility. But along the way the church had become myopic, depriving "that dramatic story [of lay success] of religious significance" (p. 191).

"Lay success did not enrich Catholic culture, and church teaching had little impact on the lay lives of the laity," he said. "Church leaders had confined the church to church, they had defined religion in terms of sacramental practice, organizational unity and group loyalty and settled for a subculture in which the highest responsibilities of church members were to attend Mass, to support the parish and school and to denounce the church's enemies" (p. 191).

The neglect of worldly involvement meant that the church was ill equipped to tackle the social problems that arose in the 1960s. Laity were accustomed to thinking of their lives apart from the parish per se as taking place in a separate domain where, in the absence of church guidance, they were pretty much on their own. Not surprisingly, the values they were likely to adopt toward work and social issues came from the surrounding secular culture rather than the church. This, O'Brien contended, had contributed to a widening of the gap between the inner church and the outer world of lay Catholics.

No wonder the hierarchy had found it difficult to reach the laity with their recent pastorals on nuclear arms and the economy. The laity had not been conditioned to think of their political and economic lives as areas where their Catholicism had meaning and implications.

Bishops had become increasingly disturbed by what they saw as the drift by Americans into secularization and paganism, O'Brien said, but had failed to notice "that Catholic separatism had made its contribution to the much lamented segmentation of modern culture" (p. 192).

"Acceptance of such descriptions would seem to deny Catholic responsibility for what the nation has become," O'Brien wrote, "and center their attention exclusively on the community of disciples" (p. 192).

— —

CHARLES M. (CHUCK) WILSON HAD REACHED SOME QUITE DIFFERENT CONCLUsions about the state of the church. He had observed the San Antonio consultation from the sidelines as a registered member of the press. What he saw and heard only confirmed his belief that the participants pushing for greater lay authority were on the wrong track.

Wilson was on the job as executive director of the Saint Joseph Foundation, an activist organization that sought justice for Catholics who believed they had been deprived of their rights under canon law. In its brief seventeen-month existence, the foundation had filed more than a dozen complaints to church authorities on behalf of Catholics, mostly arch-conservatives, who claimed that they had been denied such things as authentic church teaching and worship. Priests were charged with improperly altering the liturgy; other cases involved such matters as protests against sex education in parish schools. More often than not, the allegations erupted from long-simmering, highly emotional conflicts. The foundation, based in San Antonio, subsisted on donations; its services were free.

Chuck Wilson was in his forties, a stocky man of medium height with large round eyes and a slightly drooping mouth that lent him an occasional bulldog look. He spoke deliberately, with a deep voice, in a twang that traced his upbringing to the upper Midwest. Des Moines, Iowa, to be exact. The sound was gruff, but the bark was much bigger than the bite. He was serious about himself and his mission, but hardly grim. Burdened though he seemed by his weighty duty, and dejected as he was over much waywardness he perceived in the church, he came across not only as bright, modest, amiable, and considerate but as a man with an ample measure of irony and whimsy.

As executive director, the foundation's only full-time investigator, Wilson handled the painstaking tasks of deciding whether the often tangled clot of strained feelings and heated allegations actually constituted a genuine offense and processing the mounds of paperwork necessary to file the appeals under church law. But he appeared undaunted by the details and the wrangles and the procedural delays in dealing with Rome. The same zeal that had led him to start the foundation spurred him on. On the one hand, he was a defender of the Catholic right's ideal of an undefiled church; on the other, he was a son of the American frontier ideal of righting wrongs.

After college, he had signed on as a manufacturer's representative in the printing business. Over the years, work assignments had stationed him in Houston, New York, California, and, finally, San Antonio. In 1966—twenty-one years ago— he had made a momentous decision, leaving the Episcopal church to become a Roman Catholic. He was taken into the church three months after the closing of Vatican II. "My wife was a lifelong Catholic, but when we married I didn't contemplate becoming Catholic," he recalled. "But then I took instructions in the church, and it appealed to me. It made sense." He retained "great affection" for his former church, he allowed, as bearer of "a lot of the truth."

What convinced him that the Catholic church was "a more complete version of religious truth" was its teaching that the bread and wine of communion become the actual body and blood of Christ and the primacy of the pope. "Did Christ mean to establish a particular person to be his representative on earth? As an

Episcopalian I never thought of it. But either he did or he didn't. Peter had a special role. Was it as successor? It sounded reasonable to me that he would provide a continuity to that office: a person who was Christ's vicar who has the responsibility of safeguarding the sacred deposit of faith when the need comes to proclaim what the truth is."

Having assented to that conviction, he was prepared to defend that view of the papacy against all comers. He stood among the classicists who held that church doctrine was defined from on high, once and for all, and was guaranteed for the sake of the church by the vicar of Christ. It was therefore incumbent on the laity to affirm that truth and to refrain from trying to amend what God had proclaimed for all eternity.

It followed that all the talk about the need to incorporate "lived experience" of the laity into church teachings sounded good but was based on a false premise. Human experience, no matter how profound, could not amend the essence of doctrine that was divinely revealed through the pope acting in special concert with his fellow bishops. "Catholic truth determined by 'lived experience' is a product of the Enlightenment," Wilson said. "It is highly personal. But there is a body of revealed truth whatever people's experiences tell them."

Truth was also inseparable from the earthly vessels in which it was meant to be conveyed, meaning that worship had been prescribed in certain forms that must be kept inviolate. A priest who tampered with those forms was denying Catholics full access to the benefits of right worship.

Keeping order was among Wilson's paramount concerns. That implied respect toward the traditional lines of authority. "Although, as Catholic laity, we do have the right to true worship and true teaching," he wrote in response to the lay collaboration he had witnessed, "we do not have a comparable right to participate in the governance of the church . . . efforts to increase the scope of lay authority in the visible hierarchic structure of the Church are, for the most part, misdirected."

The qualifying words "for the most part" pointed to an important loophole. Though in general the laity must avoid grabbing for clerical power, Catholics could seek redress against authorities who did not keep to the letter of the law. In that sense, he, too, advocated lay power, but of a different kind. Many of the complaints were directed by parishioners against priests for, in effect, dereliction of duty. At a time when many laypeople were calling on the clergy to act less clerical, Chuck Wilson was among those demanding that clerics exercise their prerogatives to the fullest in the interests of preserving an orderly, hierarchical church.

For several years, he had been an inconspicuous parishioner largely undisturbed by the wider church. But then he began hearing some loose talk from some Catholic pulpits to the effect that morality was more or less a matter of personal opinion. "I also noticed a lot of liturgical changes that didn't particularly bother me," he recalled, "but I saw the pain they were causing other people, and my sense of justice was offended." Soon he was seeking out others who felt a similar need to defend moral doctrine and liturgical purity against prevailing forces of relativism and secularity. That led him to involvement with Catholics United for the Faith and the Wanderer Forum, two staunch upholders of classicist principles.

All the while, he was hearing of alleged violations of church practice from a variety of aggrieved Catholics asking for his help. Through a scholar at Catholic University, he became convinced that "laity can vindicate their rights before church courts." Soon the idea of forming a sort of canon law practice to plead the causes of distressed Catholics had firmly planted itself in his mind.

Practically speaking, the decision to go ahead with the idea was an abrupt career switch that posed a formidable test of his acumen and endurance. He was not a man of independent means, and he knew relatively little about canon law, the one prerequisite generally considered essential to the head of such a Catholic rights league. For a time, on-the-job training would have to suffice. He plunged into the work and, at the same time, enrolled in a master's degree program in canon law at Oblate College. He entered the field at a propitious moment. The huge revised code of canon law had been promulgated just the year before, in 1983, so specialists around the country and the world were busy acquainting themselves with its provisions. To the budding canonist from suburban San Antonio, it was a good time to get in on the ground floor of the inquiry, inasmuch as, in his words, "even good canon lawyers can't figure out the new code."

He had made much progress in a short time. Meanwhile, the fledgling foundation began attracting cases. Competent screening quickly became essential. Did the circumstances constitute a valid complaint? Often, it turned out that the facts, separated from emotions, did not constitute an actual violation. "The majority of cases don't go beyond me," he said. "Most people don't differentiate between what they don't like and what's wrong. For example, communion in the hand is not illegal," he pointed out, "but if they don't permit you to receive it on the tongue, that's wrong." Together with his consultants, he analyzed situations and tried to provide dispassionate advice. "We don't lead them by the hand," he said. "We tell them, 'This is what we think you ought to do.'"

There was another consideration to be factored in: the possibility that a formal complaint might bring unacceptable scandal and harm to the church. "We might have a case that involves both the rightness of a person's position and the good of the church," he explained carefully. "The position might be right, but pursuing it might not necessarily be for the good of the church.

"If it's an extremely controversial case, we'll probably go to the bishop and say, 'This is a delicate situation. If it's causing problems we'll back off.' We're not trying to bash bishops."

Any Catholic was eligible to file a claim, he insisted. Even Father Curran. "We don't limit ourselves to orthodox Catholics," he said. "With a couple of exceptions, we're dealing simply with a lack of pastoral care. People sometimes contact us to say we should do something about Father Curran. The answer has been that we will help him if he comes to us. We'd consider his case, though I don't sympathize with his position and think he was treated fairly by the church." In fact, Father Curran's ouster had shown him that the church still asserts a right to determine what it means to be a Catholic university.

Despite Chuck Wilson's rejection of a "democratic" church, he was in many ways an illustration of how deeply American democratic values had influenced Catholics at all points on the theological spectrum. Here was a man deeply committed to a hierarchical, classicist church who, at the same time, devoted himself to combating the misuse of power by church officials, who took up the cudgels for the little people against the highest officials, who espoused a kind of populism that insisted that the letter of the church constitution be obeyed for the good of the people. All this he did more or less in the name of traditionalist Catholicism that warned against equating the church with such egalitarian-sounding concepts as "the people of God."

With cases piling up, he found himself with more work than one person and an administrative assistant could handle. If the organization were better funded, he could easily occupy three or four more members of the staff. But for now, expansion seemed unlikely.

The Saint Joseph Foundation had set a 1987 budget goal of $130,000. Receipts from the previous year reached only about $80,000, so meeting the new target would take some doing. Wilson also served as the foundation's president. The Reverend Christopher G. Phillips, a fellow convert to Catholicism from Episcopalianism, was chairman of the board. Father Phillips was something of a rarity, one of the few married Episcopal priests admitted to the Catholic priesthood after the Episcopal church voted to ordain women. As a husband and the father of two children, he now served as pastor of Our Lady of Atonement parish in San Antonio. Among his activities were television spots promoting the priesthood, admonishing priests to honor their vow of celibacy.

Christifidelis, a newsletter whose stated purpose was "to defend Catholic truth and uphold Catholic rights," was the foundation's chief means of communicating with its constituents. The mailing list was up to 3,600 names. In addition to bringing readers up-to-date on the foundation's progress, the newsletter served as a salty reminder of what it stood for. A "Straws in the Wind" section noted practices that foundation leaders regarded as abuses of church law or watering down of its teachings.

Various articles defined the foundation's positions on a handful of key issues. Among the targets of opposition: widely used programs of sex education, alleged liturgical abuses, universities judged no longer "Catholic," and the movement to allow girls and women to be altar servers.

Chuck Wilson belonged to that interlocking network of traditionalist activists struggling to hold the line. He belonged to the board of Catholics United for the Faith. Several of his board members played prominent roles in that and other conservative groups. One, Father Joseph Fessio, was editor of Ignatius Press, the major publishing vehicle of the movement.

Though the head of the Saint Joseph foundation was unflagging in his efforts, he said he sometimes felt that he was fighting a rearguard action. As he spoke of defeat, he showed no bitterness. He exuded dignity and reasonableness, a decent man out to contribute to justice as he saw it. Sometimes it seemed that he had much more in common with the lay activists at the consultation than he might have imagined.

He wasn't at all certain where the church was headed, but felt part of a remnant. "I feel we've lost," he said of those who shared his viewpoint. "If you liken the church in the U.S. to a revolution, we've lost."

— ▪ —

AT THE REAR OF SAN FERNANDO CATHEDRAL, TO THE LEFT OF THOSE WHO ENtered, stood a marble tomb, accompanied by a plaque on the wall behind it that read, "Here lies the remains of Travis, Crockett, Bowie, and Other Alamo Heroes."

At the opposite end, near the foot of the altar, a tidy woman approached a microphone and looked out over the rows of wooden pews. In one hand she held a blue prayer book; in the other, a set of pearly white rosary beads. Wearing a red print blouse, a red skirt, and a white sleeveless sweater, her jet-black hair arranged in a bun, she began reciting the rosary in lyrical Spanish cadences. A knot of women in flowing mantillas, fingering rosaries of their own, knelt in front pews and responded in kind.

The tomb and the Spanish rosary signified the dual legacies hovering about the cathedral and the entire Southwest region of Catholic America. The heritage of Latin America lived side by side with that of North America, separate and, for the most part, unequal. The church that entombed the dust of the posthumous victors had become a spiritual home to the children of the vanquished. Within the church that claimed the title as the "oldest cathedral sanctuary in the country," from whose turret the Alamo was warned of the impending attack of Santa Anna's army, the struggle for reconciliation was still seeking resolution.

Soon the pope would witness for himself this magnificent landmark and sample its confluence of influences. Shortly before 6:00 P.M. on September 13, John Paul II, touring the United States, was scheduled to enter the chalky white interior of the cathedral and there, in its musty coolness, address seminarians and those preparing for religious orders.

The pope's decision to spend a day in San Antonio further underscored the city's importance to the church both regionally and nationally.

San Antonio, three-fourths of whose citizens were Spanish-speaking, had become the hub of Hispanic vitality in the Southwest. Nowhere in the nation did the Catholic church more clearly bear the imprint of Hispanic character or more forcefully serve its interests. The personable, gracious head of the archdiocese, Archbishop Patrick Flores, the son of Mexican migrant farm workers, was the first from his ethnic background to be elevated to such a position. With his blessing, the church helped establish a parallel political base, Communities Organized for Public Service (COPS), within thirty parishes. COPS had enhanced both the church's credibility and its visibility. Among other things, it had assisted Henry Cisneros in his successful bid to become the city's first Hispanic mayor.

Two other assets promoted San Antonio's reputation as a center of Hispanic influence and creativity.

One was the rector of the cathedral, the Reverend Virgilio Elizondo, an exceptionally dynamic and articulate priest who had become well known and respected across the country as an interpreter of Hispanic affairs. Gifted with a perceptive, scholarly mind and a common touch, the fifty-one-year-old Father Elizondo had adapted themes from liberation theology and applied them with striking effectiveness to the cause of justice for Hispanics.

The other was the Mexican American Cultural Center, an outgrowth largely of Father Elizondo's emphases and energies. The center drew clergy and laypeople from far and wide to provocative programs and courses in various aspects of Hispanic life. The underlying agenda was the call for both religious and social change. Begun in 1973, the center was both a laboratory for learning practical skills and a think tank for analyzing and improving the economic and political conditions in which Hispanics found themselves.

San Antonio, then, as the region's capital of Hispanic religious and political activity, would afford the pope his most thorough immersion into Spanish-speaking America during his ten-day trip. His San Antonio stay would be a uniquely *Hispanic* event.

In anticipation, the city and the archdiocese were getting into high gear working out the details. A pair of area developers had solved one problem by donating a 144-acre parcel for the elaborate outdoor papal mass, 80 percent of which would be in Spanish. The site, in nearby Westover Hills, contained a natural amphitheater. Hotels were busy booking reservations for those coming to the city to see the pope. The better hotels, sensing a sellers' market, were demanding a three-night minimum stay. Memento merchants were hawking their wares well in advance. Among the items most available throughout the city was a five-inch bust of John Paul II by a Mexican-born artist, "finished in bisque texture like porcelain," for $9.45.

The archdiocese, meanwhile, was campaigning to raise funds to offset the high cost of their honored guest's brief stay. The church in San Antonio was far from affluent, and, even with so many public services provided free for the occasion, the price tag was steep. Various money-making ideas had been put forward, some of them deemed more ingenious than prudent. Among those rejected was a proposal by one vendor to sell a medallion bearing the pope's visage for four dollars, with three dollars promised to the archbishop.

The archbishop himself had arrived in Rome on March 15 with the other host bishops for meetings with the pope to talk over the trip and the state of the American church. San Antonio media were outdoing themselves in covering Archbishop Flores' every move at the Vatican. One newspaper had hired a former priest to report from Rome and to stay glued to the story of the papal stop in San Antonio. In his first bylined story, he promised boldly that the Rome visit would "contribute immensely" to change within Catholic America.

For all the chasing about in Rome, it seemed quite likely that little actual news would emerge. The bishops had pledged to keep quiet about their discussions with the pope.

There had been much speculation that the meetings could mark a major turning point in efforts to ease tensions between the Vatican and Catholic America. Just how that might happen was anybody's guess. The least likely possibility was that the bishops would openly confront the problems. A better bet in the view of many observers was that the bishops would emphasize positive aspects of the U.S. church in hopes of indirectly displacing some of the Vatican's negative perceptions. Of the forecasters, the minimalists most felt that history was on their side.

A litmus test of improved relations, in any case, would be the nature and content of the speeches that the pope would deliver to his American audiences. In them, he would indicate how he sized up the American church and whether appeals for a more positive view had had an effect. Some bishops believed that John Paul during his first trip had become too scolding and harsh. Extensive efforts were under way to increase the American participation in preparing those speeches, but the final editing would be done in Rome. Many Catholics expected that the performance of the bishops during the week-long meetings with the pope would greatly influence the outcome of that process.

Of the stops along the pope's way, San Antonio offered him especially rich sources of human warmth and festivity. There John Paul would find the kinds of crowds—many of them poor, devout Mexican Americans—that exuded the spirit of celebration and jubilation that had so often lifted his spirits in the third world. The southern swing would put the pope in touch with scenes that were the closest America came to reflecting that world.

Compared to areas of entrenched European Catholicism, the church in the Southwest struck a different tone. In keeping with its Hispanic character, it was less formal and institutional than, say, its Northeast counterpart. Priests were scarce; Hispanic priests much scarcer. In the Fort Worth diocese, for example, more parishes were without resident pastors than with them. Most Hispanic Catholics reared in Mexico had seen few priests and arrived without deeply ingrained churchgoing habits. In their new surroundings, much was the same. Leadership in Southwest parishes tended toward experimentation: pastoral teams composed of itinerant priests, nuns, and lay ministers.

From San Fernando Cathedral, Father Elizondo observed the complexities behind the monolithic appearances. On one hand, there was the continuing energy of Hispanic Catholicism that coursed through the cathedral itself. On Ash Wednesday, thirty-five thousand people streamed into the church to receive ashes. "We have a poor parish of maids, parking lot attendants, day workers," Father Elizondo said. "Very few professionals. We have forty to sixty baptisms every month and a big first communion class. Sunday at the 12:15 mass people get here fifteen to twenty minutes early just to get inside. The poor are welcome here. They have big family weddings and feel at home."

He paid tribute to the gifts bestowed by Hispanic spirituality: its folk piety; the religious significance placed upon the person, the family, and children; the emphasis on the Virgin Mary; its forgiving attitude toward sin. "To the Anglo mind, the whole concept of the law is that if you don't keep it you're a criminal," Father Elizondo said. "Hispanics think if you don't make it, it's a matter of human nature, and you can make an adjustment. They say, 'Father I'm human, and God is merciful.' To Hispanics, humanity and piety belong together, not piety and legalism.

"Hispanics also have marvelous shortcuts to God. Women especially focus on Mary. 'She's a woman,' they say, 'she understands.'" He recently spent a year reflecting on Mary with a group of women from the barrio. "To them, her virginity means that God has restored a ruined reputation. What God might call a prostitute God retains miraculously virginal. It conveys a sense of dignity to them in their hardship and poverty. Even if a woman is raped, God can protect her. That's a powerful message. I consciously claim Mary as co-redeemer."

Despite its richness, Father Elizondo said, Hispanic piety was still too often denigrated by Anglo Catholics and dismissed as ignorance and superstition. Increasingly Hispanics were turning away from Catholicism to Protestant traditions that ministered to their spiritual, emotional, and material needs. Father Elizondo had gained deep respect for the commitment and skills within these churches. They conducted worship in Spanish—offering an outlet for Hispanic music and feeling—while at the same time providing facilities for superb instruction in English. Their ministers were well educated. They capitalized on a feeling among many Hispanics that the Catholic church ignored or neglected them. While the Protestant challenge grew, Father Elizondo said, Catholic efforts lagged, due in large measure to lack of funds and priests. Catholicism was losing out.

A strong attraction to Protestant churches was the opportunity they offered for a layperson to exercise leadership. In the average Catholic parish, the priest held control, but the Protestants encouraged a wide assortment of lay activities and narrowed the distinctions between clergy and laity. "When the Protestants plant a church, they make everyone responsible," said Leonard Anguiano, administrator of the Mexican American Cultural Center. "They go into a neighborhood and plant a whole church. We plant an associated organization, a branch of the bishop. We have a broad-based church with one person in charge of everything."

Anguiano shared the view of many Hispanics that the alarm about attrition was spreading across the Catholic church but noted that, thus far, it had generated little solid commitment of resources to meet Hispanic needs. Without community action organizations like COPS, he said, the church's standing among Hispanics would be far lower than it was. But even the relatively visible and successful Mexican American Cultural Center, which was marking its fifteenth anniversary, was severely squeezed financially. The center's staff had shrunk from thirty-six to twenty-four by 1985.

The impending start of the federal amnesty program for illegal aliens (May 5) presented the church with an ambiguous chance to be of assistance. Many parishes, flooded with applicants who looked to the church as a trusted ally, found themselves wanting to help but distressed by the law's provisions. Though the church was a haven from unscrupulous agents poised to exploit naive aliens, the requirements for amnesty made their job difficult and exasperating. Procedures required proof of residency prior to January 1, 1982. Many Hispanics found it impossible to obtain the necessary documents. Moreover, strict enforcement of the law meant some members of a family would qualify while others would not. Church officials felt uneasy about becoming a party to family breakup. They were also disturbed by reports that some employers either refused to provide letters of employment to legitimate applicants or issued them only in return for favors.

With many problems bogging them down, church leaders looked to the pope's visit for a boost in the morale of the church in the region and much-needed affirmation of Hispanic Catholicism. "One thing I'm hoping for," said the Reverend David Garcia, chancellor of the San Antonio archdiocese, "is that the pope's coming may highlight religious questions—the idea of the church and its service to people. I hope we might experience some kind of surge.

"Hispanics are poised at the door of real leadership in the church," Father Garcia continued, "but we're not there yet. We've started coming into our own— we're proud to be Hispanic and Catholic, and the American church has started to recognize our heritage. But there are still obstacles. We still have to deal with structure. Our cultural background makes it difficult for us to work with rigid structures. I hope the pope's trip will help us in many ways."

Father caron was back at his desk after a five-day barnstorming tour of alumni groups in Billings, Montana; Boise, Idaho; and Salt Lake City, Utah. At each stop, the highlight was the evening routine: cocktails and dinner followed by a videotape about the college, his pep talk, and a round of questions and answers.

He liked mingling with the graduates and bringing them up-to-date. Most wanted assurance that Saint Ambrose's vital signs were robust and that the college was gaining ground in the race for prestige and blue-chip applicants. Like other alumni, Father Caron said, they believed that "the more visible the college, the more valuable their degree."

The heart and soul of a college president's job was, of course, to promote the institution in the best and broadest sense of the term. But the pressures to succeed had increased greatly. An abundance of colleges and universities were reaching out for a smaller number of high school students. Father Caron had looked reality in the eye. "There is tremendous competitiveness," he said, "as the market shrinks."

The powerful tools of the mass media also whetted the appetite for recognition and status. Marketing logic assumed that a higher profile brought tangible rewards: better students and more money. Public relations, in turn, depended largely on the bond among alumni, the school's ambassadors and its fiscal backbone. Taking these objectives into account, Father Caron considered the purpose of his get-togethers with Saint Ambrose graduates "not fund-raising but friend-raising."

On his return, a stack of mail awaited him along with a bundle of documents, memos, and phone messages. Time spent with alumni meant less time to give to the growing demands for his time and attention on campus. Juggling the two sets of obligations could be difficult, he said. "You're nobody if you don't go around visiting," he said, wearily, "but if you're away, people here don't think you care about them."

It was a relatively quiet March Saturday on campus, a chance for him to catch up and reflect. Several matters weighed on him.

During his travels, he had given thought to the newly released Vatican statement on reproductive technology. As an ethicist who taught a course in sexual ethics, it engaged him both as priest and as scholar. He had found in it little to cheer. Though he applauded it for underscoring the "human qualities of sexuality" and drawing attention to the "extensive moral problems created by the new reproductive technologies," Father Caron said the document had been far too negative.

"Rather than just pointing out all the ethical questions," he said, the statement had condemned everything too quickly, "especially that which enhances the product of love between a couple." Techniques for helping infertile couples conceive was to Father Caron legitimately "repairing what was gone." In declaring immoral nearly all scientific intervention in human reproduction, the Vatican had ruled out artificial insemination even among married partners using their own gametes.

"This is simply assisting a process that has gone amiss," Father Caron complained. "When you have a headache, you don't say that God wants you to have a headache, therefore you shouldn't intervene. God has placed in our hands ethically responsible ways of accomplishing these goals. Of course it's fraught with problems—the level of respect accorded the human embryo, for example. But we could find our way around these things."

The problem with such a document, in his opinion, was that it lumped together a range of issues from surrogate motherhood to freezing embryos and rejected them all without sufficient nuance and distinction. He guessed it would add difficulties in discussions with colleagues and students because it had further harmed the church's credibility. "Scientists themselves are concerned about the technologies," he said. "I wish the church were not trying to give answers to everyone, but I think the document comes off this way."

He would examine the statement in greater detail as time allowed. Making time for scholarship was always difficult, given his other roles, but scholarship was something he cherished. At Saint Ambrose, members of his religious order faced increasing pressures in trying to fulfill their teaching, research, and pastoral duties. There were fewer of them, and each was trying to do more.

As a priest who had helped develop services for Catholic homosexuals, he was also disturbed by the Vatican's latest pronouncement on homosexuality the previous October and the backlash he saw it creating. The statement had been "very disastrous," he thought. He saw a "clear plot afoot" to pressure bishops to expel Dignity, the largest Catholic gay organization, from parishes and official functions. Several chapters had already been ejected, and the climate was ominous. He had been distressed by the defense of the Vatican homosexuality statement by Archbishop Quinn of nearby San Francisco recently in *America*. "More gays no longer think that the institutional church represents the gospel," Father Caron said. "I hope some of the bishops will say that too. But I know there is fear prevailing. Among those it hits hardest are gays in the priesthood."

Closer to home, the continuing tensions over academic freedom in the church and the authority of bishops over Catholic colleges and universities insinuated themselves into his responsibilities as president. Fallout from Father Curran's ouster was still unclear, but Father Caron felt nervousness in the air. He assumed that the bishops hoped the controversy would be "quietly ignored." Meanwhile, he knew of no bishop seeking out college presidents like himself to discuss suspected dissent. "I hope it remains that way," he said. But a threat still existed so long as the church could move against Curran and Hunthausen as it had. It represented a "swing to authoritarianism" that he found distressing.

Before digging into the paperwork, he would take a break. He set aside his business and bounded down the hall toward the pool. After a good workout, he would return to work out more elusive kinks.

➤ ➤

ON MARCH 19, THE FEAST OF SAINT JOSEPH, THOUSANDS OF FLOWERS BLANKETED the entryway of the Cleveland parish church dedicated to the saint. Saint Joseph, the surviving Catholic church in a neighborhood whose honeycombed streets had once bustled with Germans, Italians, Irish, and Poles, had been living on borrowed time for six months now. The Diocese of Cleveland, under pressure from parish loyalists fighting to keep its doors open, had delayed action on a decision to demolish the landmark. It remained for the Friends of Saint Joseph to forge a rescue plan sufficient to pay for the vast repairs that the diocese judged too costly for a congregation that had dwindled to two hundred in a section of the city now nonresidential. The group had been granted a year to solve the problem. Otherwise, Saint Joseph would be reduced to rubble just as the other five churches of the neighborhood had been.

So far no such plan had been offered, though several were said to be under discussion. Most involved conversion of the adjoining Franciscan friary (which passed over to the hands of the diocese this month after a century of Franciscan custodianship) to residential or office use by a developer in some sort of financial arrangement that would provide the funds to keep the church standing. But nothing was definite. The Friends had won a stay of execution at the last minute the previous September, but the outcome was far from assured.

Though a practical solution seemed elusive, there could be no doubt that preservationist passions ran deep. Though most parishioners had long since hightailed it to the suburbs in the face of urban renewal and the lure of middle America, the news of the impending doom of Saint Joseph rallied them from their scattered outposts in the outlying hills of Cleveland. The thousands of flowers strewn by the loyalists under the face of Christ carved into the stone above the main doors testified to their sentiment. Many were those emigrants to the suburbs who had received first communion under those magnificent arches and had loaded their plates with pancakes at the famous parish breakfasts. It had implanted in them an image of "parish" that had been formative and impossible to supersede. Some had never found its equal.

But "urban renewal" had sounded the death knell in the 1960s, obliterating a whole section of the city in the name of progress, depriving the parish of its one indispensable resource: people. Saint Joseph had been entered in the National

Register of Historic Places since 1976. Its pedigree would not save it, however, without people to fill the pews.

Brother Xavier Kestler still lived in the friary and administered the Catholic school on the property. The K–8 school, financially independent of the parish, was all black and 85 percent non-Catholic. The Franciscan connection, which had been formally severed when the friary went over to the diocese, had been rich and deep, dating from 1867. Until recently, the thirty-six-room friary was a training facility for young men interested in the order. Such candidates were now few and far between. But not long ago, the friary had been buzzing with priests and brothers. It was their proud downtown Cleveland parish, the place Franciscans stayed when visiting the city.

A trim, spirited man with a full salt-and-pepper beard, Brother Xavier was of two minds with regard to the parish's fate. He agreed with the diocese that the parish was too tiny to justify the enormous repair costs (estimated as up to $1 million). But he also believed Saint Joseph might have been sustained with a little more creative foresight. Perhaps if all the people who now flocked to the cause of saving the parish had taken the trouble to visit the parish for mass even once a month, he guessed, the numbers might have stayed within the salvageable range. As it was, he said, they had come to the closing liturgy the previous September and admitted to paying no attention to Saint Joseph for twenty or thirty years. Where had those people been? he wondered.

Then there was the possibility that the area would become populated again if new high-rise apartments were built. Saint Vincent's Hospital triangle and Cleveland State University dominated the neighborhood now. More housing seemed logically the next step. No one could know for sure, of course, what would happen or what the implications for the Catholic church might be. But Brother Xavier and many parishioners had an aching feeling that things could have turned out differently.

The diocese's basic decision to shut down the parish had become clear at a closed-door meeting a year before (March 8) between Auxiliary Bishop James P. Lyke, himself a Franciscan, and the parish council. The news had leaked out by late spring. "For most of us," Brother Xavier said, "the decision to close the parish registered up here [pointing to his head], but we had trouble getting our hearts to agree with our heads."

Word about the impending demise of Saint Joseph had hardly gotten around when the mournful parish found itself faced with a problem of what struck some as shockingly disrespectful behavior. What they confronted was a polite form of looting. A variety of antique hunters saw a golden opportunity to cart away a piece of handcrafted treasure. Businesses, churches, and religious groups rushed to make their bids. Restaurants wanted pews, a designer had eyed the five hand-somely carved confessionals as potential telephone booths, and other inquiries had been made about the choir stalls, the statues, murals, paintings, stained glass windows, and the huge main altar, which was too big to be lugged out the door in one piece.

Sara Sedotti, a stalwart of the parish, captured the source of dismay many felt: "People on the periphery don't talk to you about people. They talk about saving statues and stained glass windows and wood carvings. We're asking, what happens to us as a parish?"

Others had more mixed feelings. In an op-ed piece in the *Plain Dealer* (October 8, 1986), George Eppley, a member of the faculty at Cuyahoga Community College, compared the church's fate to the rash of plant closings in the area. His fa-ther had been baptized in Saint Joseph, so he had direct ties. "But while I love the past," he wrote, "I am not an incurable romantic. I cannot expect the Cleveland diocese to subsidize my memories." Business and industry closings were far more devastating, he said. Though the church would be rightly mourned, he said, the announced coming of a United Technologies office complex near the Saint Joseph site offered hope.

So far, nothing had been moved and would never be if Larry Kruszewski had his way. He was a fifty-one-year-old sales and marketing executive who had grown up in the parish. His father died when he was five, and he was reared by his mother in a housing project. Saint Joseph had been "a home." There he said his first confession and received his first communion. He had been an altar boy. He now lived on the city's far east side, where he belonged to Saint Ignatius parish. But his heart was still with his boyhood church. Faced with this crisis, he said he would gladly make the twelve-minute trip to the church at least once a month if that would help keep the parish running.

Kruszewski was a gregarious, square-jawed man with graying hair and activist instincts. One of his prouder experiences as a young man was lending a hand in the presidential campaign of John F. Kennedy. Among other things, he had helped the Euclid County Democratic Club stage a JFK steer roast fund-raiser. He had been similarly stirred when he heard on television that Saint Joseph had been marked for the scrap heap ("I was dumbfounded," he recalled). He had orga-nized the Friends of Saint Joseph, a core group of twenty-five distant loyalists like himself, to lobby the diocese to change the verdict. Together with a cardiolo-gist and a restorationist, he took the Friends' case to Bishop Lyke. They made an impact. Though the September 14 closing liturgy had gone off as scheduled, be-fore a packed congregation of fifteen hundred, the wrecking crew had been stayed for at least a year.

Also in march there were other high-profile developments:

- There was movement in the Hunthausen case in March. The special commission formed by the Vatican to solve the Seattle dispute heard two days of testimony from those close to the situation. Witnesses who appeared March 6–7 at a seminary in Menlo Park, California, included eight bishops from the Pacific Northwest, five officials of the archdiocese, and the archbishop's board of consultors. Supporters of the archbishop were in a rosy mood after the session with the three panelists—Archbishop Quinn, Cardinal O'Connor, and Cardinal Bernardin—because they felt a favorable breeze moving through the proceedings. One witness, a strong backer of the archbishop, said he and others came away with "high enthusiasm" about chances for a desirable settlement. Another key Hunthausen partisan, Wes Howard, did not appear before the commission but told the *National Catholic Reporter* (March 20, p. 4) that chancery insiders told him that "things are going well" and that the archbishop was "quite pleased" with the course of the investigation. The week after the meeting in Menlo Park, Archbishop Hunthausen and Bishop Wuerl flew to Chicago for further talks with the commission on March 12.

- Father Curran took legal action in March in an attempt to regain his position on the active faculty of Catholic University. He had been suspended from the university after the Vatican stripped him of his license to teach as a Catholic theologian on grounds that he dissented from some church doctrine. In a civil suit filed in District of Columbia Superior Court and made public on March 2, Father Curran sought the right to offer courses in areas of the university that were outside the Vatican's direct control. His contention in the lawsuit was that his contract with the university allowed him to offer courses leading to civil degrees where no church license was required. That distinction applied even to the department of theology, where one-fourth of the students were enrolled in ecclesiastical programs and the other three-fourths were seeking nonecclesiastical, or civil, degrees.

  A Catholic University committee was still weighing the merits and implications of the Vatican's lifting of Father Curran's theological license. While awaiting the outcome of that review, the moral theologian had planned to teach civil-degree courses during the spring semester, but Archbishop Hickey, the university chancellor, ordered his suspension from all teaching at the school pending the outcome of the inquiry. The archbishop argued that despite the division of the theology department into separate degree programs, church and nonchurch, the theology faculty was, in effect, indivisible and required all instructors to have a special license.

In his lawsuit, Father Curran asserted that the suspension had violated his contract as a tenured professor and had harmed his "professional standing and reputation." The priest petitioned the court to permit him to teach civil-degree courses. His effort to seek redress looked to many like a last resort. Though there was much support for him in the church, the public outcry had faded (one church source said that for some who had abandoned Father Curran "guilt had turned into denigration . . . people didn't want to be identified with a loser"). Though his colleagues in the Society for Christian Ethics had urged the Vatican to rescind its action against him at its January meeting, fewer and fewer Catholic scholars seemed eager to press his case in the church. By seeking relief in the civil courts, Father Curran was signifying his conviction that he would not find it within the church. He seemed very much alone.

• Renew, the program for revitalizing parishes, came in for some modest criticism by a Fordham sociologist who had studied it under a Lilly Endowment grant. In the March 7 issue of *America,* Professor James R. Kelly applauded Renew's aim of fostering personal faith and closer parish ties. His research showed that it had achieved moderate levels of both, but only by steering clear of conflict. "When I first started my study of Renew," he wrote, "I could not imagine how a program of renewal could avoid the deep and pressing divisions within Catholicism that preoccupy its leaders and the press: questions about women's ordination, sexual morality, the scope of papal authority, and the like. I quickly came to see that, indeed, this nonjudgmental characteristic of Renew is one of the major reasons for its success. Amid the clamor of church controversy, many men and women seek mostly to deepen their attachment to the core elements of the average Christian life: the Scriptures, the Mass, prayer, uncomplicated fellowship and support" (p. 198).

Another of Renew's hallmarks, its avoidance of doctrinal and moral issues, he wrote, had invited charges of soft-sell permissiveness from the Catholic right. The program appeared to deepen awareness of human needs and justice issues but spurred little new social activism.

Overall, he said, Renew tried to "provoke piety, not passion," and to "enable people to love their church even in the midst of enormous institutional change and confusion." It hadn't ushered in "The Great Awakening of Catholicism," Kelly said, but its impact was "modest but real" (p. 199). All in all, it was a pleasant and useful but somewhat vapid variety of renewal—an assessment to which Renew advocates took sharp exception.

- The U.S. bishops and archbishops who would host the pope on his American tour emerged smiling from their Rome planning meeting with John Paul II and top church officials. They reported filling in the pontiff on several issues likely to raise hackles and perhaps even protests during his trip. Among them were the recent Vatican statement on homosexuality and the document on bioethics and reproduction. During their sessions, which they described as educational, they had also discussed ecumenism and the Vatican's controversial draft document on higher education.

  The bishops hinted that they had scored some public relations points by helping erase negative impressions planted at the Vatican by the Catholic right. No less an eminence than Archbishop Jan Schotte of Belgium, the Vatican official in charge of bishops' synods, seemed to confirm that apple-polishing had indeed taken place. "I would not hesitate to say," declared the archbishop at the closing news conference on March 21, "that the unanimous perception of the church in the United States is very positive here in the Roman Curia." Cardinal Bernardin, who attended along with the other cardinals, summed up the proceedings in his customarily sanguine manner. "It was primarily an informational kind of meeting, and we had a wonderful exchange."

  In response, many observers just assumed that the eager-to-please bishops had left out much of what Catholic America found objectionable about their church, preferring to omit such troubling topics in the company of the pope. Some had been asking whether the pope's visit to the United States would actually do anything to heal those rifts. Thomas J. Donnelly, president of the Mary J. Donnelly Foundation of Pittsburgh, raised the issue in the March edition of *Directions,* a newsletter to major Catholic philanthropists. Like others, Donnelly was struck by the "staggering price tag of the visit" and went on to ask if it could "improve communications within the Church." He hoped so because, he noted, "It is said that the Church in no other country has been so reproved for its policies and behavior." It was unlikely that the spectacular events along the pope's itinerary would produce the needed frankness and honesty, Donnelly said. A better means, he suggested, might be a few unstaged, spontaneous, and private conversations between the pontiff and a cross section of American parishioners. Others said the difficulty was that Catholic America didn't know what message it wanted to send to the pope even if it got his ear.

- The cardinals met in Rome to discuss the deepening financial crisis in the church's central government. After the meeting, the Vatican announced that the deficit for its current fiscal year was expected to be $63 million, $7 million higher than the previous year.

• Pope John Paul II published an encyclical on the Virgin Mary. Titled *Redemptoris Mater*, "Mother of the Redeemer," the 114-page encyclical was the pope's reflection on the centrality of Mary in the church's faith and theology. He elaborated on the role of Mary as the preexistent mother of Jesus Christ who was at the same time the model of obedience and trust, the model of faith who continued to lead the "pilgrim church." Just as the doctrine of her Immaculate Conception linked her with the origins of the church, the pope wrote, the doctrine of her physical Assumption into heaven pointed to her relationship with the coming Kingdom of God. For Catholic America, the encyclical was a call to renew devotions to the Virgin, which had sharply declined along with other forms of personal piety. The document echoed the pope's own deep devotion in vivid and persuasive terms.

It also posed immediate questions about ecumenical relations. Most Protestants objected strenuously to Marian dogma and practice as detracting from the sole Lordship of Christ. John Paul took care to underscore that the church saw Mary as the first among disciples and in no way a co-redeemer with Christ. Moreover, the first section of the encyclical, essentially a biblical meditation, seemed written with Protestant sensibilities toward Scripture very much in mind. By studying Mary, the pope said, the mystery of God's Incarnation was opened up; therefore, joint study by the churches could help bring them together.

Among the topics not covered by the pope that also held ecumenical interest were the implications of Mary's example for the place of women in today's church. Bishop William H. Keeler, chairman of the bishops' ecumenical and interreligious committee, quickly praised what he called the "positive ecumenical thrust" of the document. The pope said he wrote the encyclical in anticipation of the two-thousandth anniversary of the birth of Jesus, an event, he said, that also "directs our gaze towards his Mother" (Origins, April 9, vol. 16, no. 43, p. 747).

On the day the encyclical was issued, March 25, the pope announced that a Marian Year of devotion would begin on June 7, Pentecost Sunday, and continue to the feast of the Assumption, August 15, 1988.

AFTER THEIR SEMINAR WITH GILBERT, A KNOT OF NEATLY DRESSED YOUNG MEN, some clutching notebooks, engaged in spirited talk in a corner of a room lined with books mostly written by Catholic authors many centuries dead. The brisk exchange among these graduate students had carried on long after the seminar had ended. Often that happened. The object of study this day had been Aristotle's *Ethics*. Under Gilbert's tutelage, even the most arcane points of classical thought usually generated high levels of energy and curiosity and fueled prolonged discussion.

Gilbert himself had repaired to his tidy office a few steps away to attend to several matters that had accumulated on his desk. The seminar had pleased him. After a quarter century of teaching, he was not blasé about his experience in the classroom. He could still get as charged up by a rousing roundtable discussion as he had in his early days as an instructor, he said, perhaps even more so.

"I do essentially the same thing now as when I started," he said, his brown eyes shining. "It's a wonderful thing to do in the strange atmosphere of youthfulness." The biggest difference between teaching religious thought then and now, he said, was the relative lack of knowledge of religion nowadays among undergraduates. Their ignorance was "appalling," he said, and the blame, in his view, belonged on church education programs that dwelt too much on feelings and "entertainment" and too little on content. But Gilbert's grumbles stopped at the classroom door. He welcomed the students as he believed he always had. It wasn't *their* fault that they were ill informed. They represented—as they always had—his opportunity to impart the true faith.

Depending on who was evaluating Gilbert, he belonged either to the dying old Catholic order or to a long line of continuity that would ensure the church's future. To the Catholic left he was reactionary; to the right, prophetic. He eschewed the notion that he was an *agent provocateur,* but in fact he was usually, in a somewhat low-key, monotonal manner, setting off little storms of debate by his rigorous defense of Catholic orthodoxy as he understood it.

Lately he had been dwelling on the AIDS crisis, in part because of his concern for his students and in part because of his distress that some moral principles he cherished were being violated. He was especially troubled by two viewpoints that were appealing for public approval. One was that the disease should be divorced from the morality of homosexuality. The second was that the best means of prevention was to encourage "safe sex," primarily through the use of condoms.

Gilbert was certain that the church was on solid ground in its condemnation of sexual activity between members of the same sex. It was one of those absolutes for which he found convincing evidence in Scripture and tradition. Therefore, fighting AIDS to him meant asserting the church's unequivocal opposition to homosexual behavior. To accept it as normal or acceptable was a futile effort to expunge the stain of sin. That would countenance an attitude of permissiveness that, in turn, would only worsen the epidemic. No, he said, the disease could not be separated from homosexuality, for in the great majority of cases reported so far, homosexual sex was the causative factor. It would be far better to attack the problem at its root.

As for "safe sex," Gilbert, smoothing his hair back toward the crown of his head, was caustic. "We have a below-the-belt approach to everything," he scoffed.

"It's about as sensible as conducting a massive campaign to come up with a safe cigarette. To treat AIDS as an aspect of life that is just out of control is ethically bizarre. Maybe instead we ought to tell the potential victims to keep their pants zipped up." Condoms were the wrong solution for all the foregoing reasons and then some. He sided with the bishops who opposed them on moral grounds, not the least of which was the claim that they furthered a "contraceptive mentality."

Given his assumption regarding the immorality of homosexuality, he pushed his logic to the conclusion that gays with the disease were somehow ethically responsible for their tragic predicament. "What, after all," he asked rhetorically, "does it mean to use the term 'AIDS victim'?" Only those who were infected inadvertently through no sexual behavior could really lay claim to that description, he thought.

Not far away a town was embroiled in a dispute over whether to allow a child with AIDS into the public school. He felt sympathy for the child but not with the larger issue. The assumption was "that somehow AIDS is all over the public, and we have to accept it," he said. "Well, we don't. We don't have to load guilt on everyone who doesn't like people screwing around like that."

The church's principal teachers, its bishops, were by and large far too timid about promoting Catholic moral doctrine for Gilbert's liking. One place to start, so far as he was concerned, was to restore the sacramental view of Catholic marriage. He believed that since Vatican II there had been entirely too much loss of the holy. It had resulted in a "smudging of differences between the clergy and the laity, the sacred and the profane." Liturgy had lost its mystery.

An indication of this decline, he thought, was the sad state into which marriage preparation had fallen. To Gilbert it had become "extraordinarily secular, having mostly to do with how to get along and how to sexually excite your partner. How can it be taken as a sacrament when they get down to bodily plumbing right away?"

He had also given some thought to the upcoming papal visit. It was hard to tell what it meant that the pope drew such huge crowds. "What is really going on?" he asked. Pope Paul VI, he recalled, had wondered about that. For most Catholics, he suspected, the pope was an important reference point by which they defined themselves as Catholics. Unfortunately, an anti-papal mood had been fostered at many Catholic universities, including to a considerable extent his own. "It's become convenient to be anti-pope," he lamented.

On the brighter side, Gilbert found solace in the unshakable faith of many converts to Catholicism. They embodied an exemplary spiritual dimension, he said, and acceptance of the pope's role as Vicar of Christ seemed to them "perfectly natural."

He also was grateful during this season of Lent for the parish he often attended, a place "where the priest isn't a genius and the people are lower middle class, and they have bingo and regular adoration of the Blessed Sacrament."

Glancing out the window toward the campus, he fell deeper into reverie. "There's no sense of controversy there, no trouble, no question on their part about why they're there. I'd like to think that's more typical than what goes on at the university church. Parishes like that one I go to are so necessary. Those little ordinary parishes—they say something."

INSIDE THE CAMPUS THEATER OF SAINT JOHN'S UNIVERSITY IN COLLEGEVILLE, Minnesota, the audience of students, faculty, visitors, and townspeople was abuzz. The attraction was a debate on the following resolution: Women should be ordained into the priesthood. It was not a subject often debated at such a prestigious Catholic institution.

Arguing in favor of the motion would be the Reverend J. Robert Wright, an Episcopal priest and professor of church history at General Theological Seminary in New York City. Joining him on the affirmative team were Sheila Cracraft, a junior government major from Minneapolis, and Todd Ritter, a senior biology major from Menasha, Wisconsin.

The opposition was led by the Reverend Frederick M. Jelly, O.P., the academic dean and professor of theology at Mount Saint Mary's seminary in Emmitsburg, Maryland. On his team were Robert Christensen, a junior government major from Shakopee, Minnesota, and Jim Wise, a senior accounting major from Edina, Minnesota.

Accompanying Father Wright was a delegation of General Seminary students headed for a showdown on the basketball court against a team of seminarians from the Diocese of St. Cloud. The general group was also scheduled to talk some theology with the future Catholic priests during the visit. Among the Episcopalians were women preparing for ordination. Father Wright's job was to represent their case as best he could.

In accordance with the order set for the debate, the main combatants would follow the four student speeches as the main event on a boxing card followed the preliminary bouts. All the students were well prepared. Their appeals were framed by the prevailing concerns among Catholic Americans for justice, rights, and fair play.

Ritter exclaimed that "women want to be given the same chance" as men to test their call to the priesthood. Christensen countered that the church "believes in equal rights" but that "if God intended women as priests he would have chosen women apostles."

Cracraft stated that "Jesus accepted women into his ministry," contended that "humanity" rather than "maleness" was the key trait in a candidate, and concluded that it is unfair to tell women they are not called to the priesthood. Wise allowed that barring women might seem discriminatory but was based on the church's policy of "separate but equal" rather than "inferiority," emphasizing that all Catholics were given ministry by their baptism.

Father Wright described himself as a "representative of a catholic [sic] church that has ordained women." Vatican II itself had acknowledged that Anglicanism "contained elements of Catholic tradition," thereby conferring a measure of legitimacy not only on his church but, by implication, also upon decisions rendered by it. Areas of that Anglican communion had decided to ordain women.

In a deft show of erudition, Father Wright asked who among the Catholic luminaries had favored both the ordination of women and of married men? None other than the sainted Thomas More, he answered rhetorically. Men should admit that they had dominated the church. He noted that the official Anglican–Roman Catholic commission striving to reach a reunification agreement had concurred that the ordination of women wasn't "so contrary to the Gospel."

The church was, in its truest nature, always in dialogue with the culture in which it existed. It was "erroneous to say that nothing that has never been can ever be," he asserted. The church had once approved of slavery, forbidden cremation, and rejected ecumenical initiatives. All those positions had been officially and dramatically reversed. The same could be the case regarding women in the priesthood. Holding on to tradition itself had no basis in doctrine, he claimed.

True enough, Father Wright said with forcefulness and conviction, Jesus chose men as his disciples and never overtly countenanced the setting apart of women for ministry. But it would be a mistake to draw conclusions regarding that or other issues on the basis "of what Jesus himself *did not do*. He didn't declare the doctrine of the Trinity either. Doctrine develops." Tradition was to be upheld "unless it runs into problems," Father Wright insisted. "The problem now is that there is a new level of consciousness with regard to the position of women in the world." Polls would substantiate that most Catholics themselves would accept female priests.

As for the main reason against ordaining women given by the Vatican—that a priest must reflect the maleness of Christ—Father Wright said that in his opinion there was "no ground for saying women couldn't be images of Christ." The Christ whom the priest represented "transcends" all categories of "space and history," including, of course, such traits as maleness and femaleness. For the Catholic church, the question was a matter of discipline rather than doctrine, Father Wright reasoned. That is, the issue was mostly concerned with how the church was run and only secondarily with basic church teaching. The church had disallowed women. It could heed the voice of the modern age and ordain them. And, he was certain, there were sound reasons for doing so.

Father Jelly went right to the heart of the matter by declaring that the teaching, or doctrinal, issues were at least as important as disciplinary, or organizational, considerations. "Significant teachings in the Catholic tradition," he stated with delightful irony, "are related to the very nature of the church." The Vatican's 1976 declaration restricting the priesthood to men in fact counted for a great deal, Father Jelly suggested.

"In principle, development [of church teaching] is possible," he allowed, "but the declaration is authoritative now. It identifies the principle reasons of the magisterium [for not admitting women]." The essential reason was that the "church intended to remain faithful to the ministry of Jesus Christ. He did not entrust the apostolic charge to women, not even to his own mother. The apostolic church didn't accept the Greek practice of priestesses. Christ chose only men to be apostles. That's a descriptive rather than a theoretical argument," Father Jelly said.

As the "re-presentation of Christ," the priest signified both symbol of the risen Lord and the reality of the earthly Jesus. The maleness of the priest satisfied the need for that "natural correspondence," Father Jelly argued, drawing upon the Vatican declaration's logic. At the same time, he said, "men being men don't have the right to be ordained" as, for example, baptized Catholics have a "right" to the Eucharist. There is a distinction between those called to the priesthood and the "universal priesthood" that is bestowed on every Catholic at baptism.

He dismissed the accusation that refusal to ordain women was a denial of their inherent rights. "I don't see how that follows on the basis of Vatican II ecclesiology," he said. He hoped that in stating his position he had not insinuated "that there is anything at all defective about womankind," in answer to a question from Father Wright.

Father Jelly was not nearly as prepared to accept the verdict of opinion polls as his opponent seemed to be. He repeated that anything was "possible or probable if doctrine [with regard to the ordination of women] developed" but did not see evidence of such development at this point.

He favored two bold moves by the church with regard to the status of women. One was to undertake "some kind of exploration of the possibility of admitting women as deacons." The other was to separate "the power of ordination from the power of [priestly] jurisdiction." Those given the sacramental functions had heretofore ruled the church. But it didn't need to be that way, Father Jelly believed, because the sacramental and ruling functions, though melded together over the years, were separable. "I think we can recognize a tradition that has seen sexuality as a necessary sacramental symbol," he said in justification of the male-only priesthood, "but at the same time gives women the vote in councils and synods because that doesn't require ordination."

The two priests rested their cases. The audience, which had paid close attention to the debate, was allowed to vote for or against the resolution favoring women's ordination. It carried overwhelmingly.

— -

I TALKED WITH BISHOP SAWICKI ON TWO OCCASIONS. THE FIRST WAS A PHONE conversation on Saint Patrick's Day. He was wearing a green carnation, he said, and from his chancery office he could watch the merriment below on the street. Just then, he buoyantly reported seeing a half dozen young adults strolling light-heartedly along the sidewalk past the cathedral, decked out in bright green hats and trousers. At lunchtime, he said, he looked forward to taking in the annual Irish show.

"The Irish church—from the mid-twenties to the mid-forties—reinforced the home, and the home reinforced the church," Bishop Sawicki said wistfully. "It was a friendly church because people knew each other. They were always a mix of sad and glad. They were cheerful but always with a strain of nostalgia and regret—it was sort of a melancholy awareness that their country had been so dominated by England. They could recount the sad events [in the strife between the two countries] that happened in the nineteenth century as much as they could recount anything that happened last week."

Bishop Sawicki linked the fortunes of those Irish immigrants of yesteryear with the hardships of Hispanics, the most arrivals from foreign lands. The church must draw on the lessons of its own immigrant past and look to the special circumstances of Hispanics in order to provide urgent assistance. Much of that entailed striving for basic justice for Hispanics. To that end, he had worked with other bishops for a liberalized immigration policy. The outcome had not been favorable, however. The Simpson-Rodino bill, to which they had lent their vigorous support, had died in Congress. He had also joined bishops in supporting Cesar Chavez's drive to organize migrant laborers, recalling a particularly vivid moment when then Bishop Mahony of the Stockton (California) diocese "walked along the street with strikers, in his cassock and carrying a candle."

Yes, this was a good day to give thanks for the successes of the past and to look to the similar needs of today's frightened, impoverished newcomers.

The other encounter with the bishop took part during a break at an academic conference on a Catholic campus to which he had been invited as a resource person.

It was evening at the conference hotel, and Bishop Sawicki, clad in gray slacks and a plaid shirt, was relaxing in the lounge with two fingers of scotch and a quality cigar. A serious illness a few years back had induced him to savor such pleasures. He did so in moderate fashion, relishing the good things of life with quiet appreciation.

The conversation resumed roughly where it had left off on the topic of the maturation of Catholic America. On the level of parish life, he said, this process had resulted in a growing "democratic spirit" among the laity. Two-thirds of the parishes in his diocese had "people who know how to interact with priests" without "fear of speaking their piece," he said approvingly. The barriers that had set the clergy apart were crumbling. Laypeople were taking greater responsibility for the church, but largely in cooperation with priests.

Unlike that of Europe, the bishop noted, the U.S. church had "an absence of anticlericalism." About 50 percent of Catholics in the United States went to mass each week, a figure far higher than for any church in Europe, but that relative vitality he saw as no reason for complacency. Without vigilance, the same sluggish pattern could develop here, he said.

A conspicuous casualty of Catholic adaptation to America was the church's teaching on marriage. Like other Americans, "our people in increasing numbers find it difficult living with one man or one woman for life," the bishop said. "Those teachings are so difficult for some people that they get turned off and leave." The growing alienation of divorced and separated Catholics constituted a problem that left him without easy answers.

"In the past, we said, 'These are the teachings, and these are the conditions,'" Bishop Sawicki said. Now the struggle was to explain how God's love goes beyond the church and beyond the sacraments, for which many divorced Catholics would no longer be eligible. The pastoral solution, as he saw it, was to remind those who found themselves in abrogation of church law that God's grace was still available to them apart from participation in certain church rituals. Were he talking to a Catholic who had been remarried without a church annulment, what would he say? "I would want to be true to the gospel, to be reassuring that there is a way you can live in prayer and still be true to your faith community," he said.

"If we think of the total people of God," he said, "there are those who are in the nucleus, those in the next ring around, and those on the perimeter. Our hope is that over time those outside will come in."

Could church doctrine change regarding sex and marriage? Should it? Bishop Sawicki took a long draw on his cigar. His answer was ambiguous, shrewd. On the one hand, there was church law. On the other, the reaction to church law, either positive or negative, acceptance or rejection. Widespread rejection could be a sign that the current law inadequately expressed the "sense of the faithful," he said.

"The word *change* is hard for me to talk about," he continued. "It's one of the things we're talking about at this conference. Is [generally] accepted church teaching the same thing as the teaching that Rome and the current papacy proposes?

At the same time in moral theology we have what is called 'solidly probable opinion,'" he said, citing the concept that referred to an alternative or dissenting position.

"The role of a bishop like me is to recognize my responsibility for public church order in the church and to continue to present moral teaching accepted by the church, and to see that I give it with 'solidly probable opinion' that might well be accepted after my time. It would only happen over time, with ferment and changes in leadership."

Bishop Sawicki left room for maneuvering on some issues by adroitly distancing himself from official church stands. His method was almost imperceptible: while stating clearly what the Vatican had said in such and such a statement, he sometimes refrained from placing his own stamp of approval on it. He thereby affirmed what he could affirm and simply reiterated that the rest of it, indeed, was what the *Vatican* thought.

Thus, weighing the latest Vatican statement on homosexuality, he said it seemed to him "that traditional teaching had been restated with a new twist: that the condition itself was 'disordered' and wrong." He didn't object to the "clarity of the statement" (i.e., it said what it meant to say), but he wished it had been said "with a little more compassion." Did he consider it a disorder himself? "I'm afraid I'd have to punt on that one," he said. "I'm not well enough acquainted with the psychological data to contest [the Vatican's position]." On the question of whether nature or nurture was responsible for the condition, Bishop Sawicki ventured that "the Vatican hasn't decided yet."

The bishop had received the bioethics document from the Vatican as a good general statement on the "values that should control biological experimentation" and saw it as a sound starting point for discussion. "I think it was time for the church, with its long history in morality, to give its opinion across a spectrum of issues," he said, smiling broadly. "Others can react." That left the door open to further development. Once again, he raised a nonsubstantive question about "tone." The section addressed to world leaders sounded a little too much as if the "Holy See was dictating directly to governments," an approach he found regrettable.

Two items occupied much talk among the bishops these days, he said. One was the Hunthausen crisis in Seattle. He understood the ad hoc commission's work was going well. Things seemed to be moving ahead sufficiently to warrant giving "a green light to Rome to move Wuerl out."

The other was the formidable task of improving Catholic America's reputation in Rome. The pope's impending trip had made that task more urgent, Bishop Sawicki said, and it remained to be seen if the campaign to spruce up the American image had worked. The bishops hosting the pope on his U.S. tour had returned without giving a clear indication of how much they had dented certain negative stereotypes. It was a longer-range objective, requiring continuation of the twice-a-year visit by top officials of the U.S. bishops to "certain cardinals who keep putting us down." They would keep trying to send high quality priests to work in Rome to further polish the image and volunteer to act as intermediaries to clear up doctrinal problems.

PLANNING THE MONTH'S SECOND WEEKEND OF CONSULTATION ON THE FALL bishops' synod on the laity had left the organizers with a case of the jitters. The purpose was the same—to ask the laity what they thought—but the chemistry was unique. Unlike the other four dialogue sessions arranged by the bishops' laity committee, this one comprised disparate, sometimes feuding elements within the church that, so far as anyone knew, had never before been enlisted in a common project. And no one, most notably the planners, knew if and how they actually would get on when the opening whistle sounded on March 27 at the Shrine of Our Lady of the Snows in Belleville, Illinois.

Of the weekend gatherings, this was the most national and diverse, hence, almost by definition, the least predictable. Delegates to the other consultations had been picked by their bishops. These participants, by contrast, were chosen by an array of vibrant lay organizations. Sixty-three groups accepted the invitation to exchange thoughts with each other on their hopes for the synod. In all, they sent nearly a hundred representatives to the elegantly landscaped retreat center in Belleville.

The variety was stunning. It included the Blue Army of Our Lady of Fatima, Catholic Golden Age, Catholics United for the Faith, the Catholic Worker, the Christian Family Movement, the Cursillo Movement, Knights of Columbus, Maryknoll Lay Missioners, the National Federation of Catholic Physicians' Guilds, the National Office for Black Catholics, the Prelature of the Holy Cross and Opus Dei, Separated and Divorced Catholics, Pax Christi–USA, the National Catholic Committee on Scouting, and the Wanderer Forum Foundation.

Within this mix were stalwarts of both the Catholic left and the right whose views on the church clashed on practically everything. Between the poles was a large middle area occupied by service-oriented Catholics with no axes to grind. Several participants had been deputized by groups that focused on single issues such as peace, Catholic rights, or the conversion of Russia; others came from groups with many interests. Some knew others as critics of their own views only abstractly by dint of reputation or writings but had never actually laid eyes on them. By bringing them together, the organizers were understandably alert to the risk of uncorking old grudges or igniting long-smoldering combustibles.

If the Catholic church was in some sense a family, then this was the gathering of a far-flung clan whose distant cousins and estranged kinfolk sized up each other from the first with curiosity, caution, and suspicion.

Some liberals seemed especially on edge in the presence of the far right, represented primarily by the Wanderer Foundation and Catholics United for the Faith. These two groups, known for their aggressive and sometimes sensational attacks on everything they identified as lacking Catholic orthodoxy, struck fear and anger in many liberal hearts.

Al Matt, Jr., the *Wanderer* editor, appeared rather to enjoy his renown as a villain. His reputation for throwing a monkey wrench into the well-designed workings of the United States Catholic Conference served him well. It preceded him, psychically knocking things a little off balance whenever he entered a roomful of Catholics to whom he was a larger-than-life antagonist. It meant that he and his organization got credit for raising much more havoc than they actually did. He was the perfect nemesis, bellowing against perfidy in a deep, percussive voice, firing charges against the infidels.

None of the worst-case scenarios feared by the planners of the consultation came close to fulfillment. Some attributed the relative serenity to the protective intervention of the sainted patroness of the retreat center. Without discounting that explanation, others chalked it up to the same technique of social engineering that had ensured a safe outcome in San Antonio three weekends before. The operative word was *process,* and it was designed to move the group toward something called consensus by steering the flow of thought in certain useful directions. The key, as explained by Father George Wilson, the Jesuit "facilitator" for all the consultations, was to avoid conceptual conflict by dwelling upon the "lived experience" of the delegates. What they "felt" was often deemed more valuable to the consultation than what they "thought." To the Catholic right, this approach accented an egregious post–Vatican II flaw by supposing that subjective experience, individually and collectively, from the ground up, as it were, could displace the "objective" truth of the church's teachings from the top down.

Father Wilson survived an early challenge to his design. "We tend to jump into ideas and get into ideological conflicts when we don't start with lived experience," Father Wilson had told the group. Matt, along with some allies from both right and left, objected. The question, Matt huffed, was "whether or not you are sort of directing this so that the answers will be prefabricated." He proposed open-ended discussion.

Father Wilson defended his practice of using small groups. "I have the role of making the decision of how to run this meeting," he shot back. "I can't open this into a wingding of a hundred people." Such a free-for-all would in his opinion produce chaos. Replied Matt, "Then you have revealed your prejudice."

That threat having been turned aside, the meeting proceeded smoothly, under firm control. Monsignor Peter Coughlan, the undersecretary of the Pontifical Council for the Laity, gave a masterly keynote address on the vocation and mission of the laity. In a question period later, Father Coughlan, a British priest, observed that there was "a lot of distrust," "fear," and "manipulation" in the church that threatened to tear it apart. There was an urgent need, he said, "to speak to one another in Christian love and respect."

Dolores Leckey and Father Kinast, both continuing their road show for the bishops' committee, gave their instructive and insightful overviews. Since Father Kinast's talk in San Antonio, the volume of responses to the pre-synodical lay survey had climbed from 15,000 to 35,000, but the results, as he reported them, remained basically the same. All told, the weekend speaker scoreboard totaled five clergy and one layperson, and that, in its own way, begged the question of what a synod of the laity was really about.

Bishop Raymond Lucker of the Diocese of New Ulm, an alternate delegate to the synod, was responsible for summing up the mind of the weekend participants. For all the variety, and the chafing, the consultation had produced conclusions that pretty well matched those from the other meetings. Bishop Lucker, an astute, reflective church leader, was given high marks for accurately reflecting the main points.

He found eight emphases. First was the "yearning for spiritual growth" among the laity. Second was the need for "adult formation," including education and commitment. Third, laypeople felt their roles "were not taken seriously" and felt "treated as children." Fourth, greater collaboration was needed between clergy and laity. Fifth was the crisis of "polarization" that alienated clergy and laity, black and white, Hispanic and Anglo, young and old, male and female. The implicit appeal, the bishop said, was for greater unity and "reaching out to those who are hurting." Sixth was the role of women. Discussion had focused on "equality" rather than the issue of "ordination" as such. The call of women to church responsibility was not receiving adequate support. Seventh was the urgency felt by laypeople to "be the church in the marketplace," with all that implied. Eighth was the need for laypeople to be listened to.

By departure time on Sunday noon, the planners were breathing more easily. The building was still standing, no noses had been bloodied, and the church, so far as it appeared, remained intact, despite the contentious voices within the clan. The lay committee could feel good about pulling off a high-stakes gamble. If no grand alliances had been struck among differing members of the clan, at the very least they had supped at the same table together and perhaps revealed some humanity across lines. No one, it seems, had worn horns.

THE MARCH ISSUE OF THE *NEW OXFORD REVIEW* CARRIED A PROVOCATIVE SYMPO-
sium on the subject of whether dissent in Catholic America was acceptable, or
schismatic. Called "Roman Catholicism and 'American Exceptionalism,'" it drew
responses from a range of Catholic writers.

The journal asked respondents if the tensions surrounding the controversies
over Archbishop Hunthausen and Father Curran revealed the presence of a *de facto*
split with Rome. They asked if the "permissive practices" regarding sex, including abortion, should be considered "normative for or by American Catholics."
Should the same standard apply to "permissive American economic and nuclear
policies and practices"?

Some writers insisted that the widespread rejection of church teachings on sex
and related matters signified that indeed a break with Rome had taken place and
that Catholic America had fallen deeply within the clutches of paganism. One took
a more positive view, regarding dissent as a sign that the Holy Spirit was offering
new insights. Still others expressed chagrin at selective disobedience, whereby one
group clung to the church's sexual morality while shunning its social teachings
on nuclear arms and the economy, and another group did just the opposite.

The following are some choice quotes from respondents:

Walker Percy, novelist. "I frankly do not understand the behavior of Archbishop Hunthausen and Father Curran. I should have thought that these
men, both obviously intelligent, attractive, and well-educated, would, like
most Catholics, set great store by—indeed treasure—the primary of the Holy
See and its magisterium, both on scriptural and historical grounds. . . . In a
word, if I should discover, forty years after entering the Church, that I now
belong to a church consisting of a loose federation of flocks and bishops, my
first reaction would be that I could have saved myself a lot of trouble if I had
become a Methodist or an Episcopalian—no offense intended" (pp. 4–5).

Sheldon Vanauken, Catholic writer and lecturer. "'American Exceptionalism'
can only mean that we play by our own rules, whatever the Universal Church
says and whatever the lesser breeds may do. This is arrogance, not humility,
even as American Anglicans 'ordained' priestesses whatever Canterbury said
or the rest of the Anglican Communion did. The tail wagging the dog, as
rebel Catholics hope to do. Exceptionalism, surely, is nothing else but Protestantism in new clothing" (p. 9).

James G. Hanink, professor of philosophy, Loyola Marymount University,
Los Angeles. "One doesn't need a team of sociologists, armed with surveys,

to recognize a *de facto* schism in American Catholicism. Yet one must be clear about what the phenomenon means. At least this much: Catholicism has become a selective matter. Many Catholics now pick and choose among their church doctrines, visibly wincing when John Paul II reminds them of what they have jettisoned. . . . For if many pick and choose with respect to sexual ethics, many also claim a right to pick and choose with respect to Catholic social teachings. . . . 'Liberal Catholics' and 'conservative Catholics' alike protest one half but not the other of this destructive alliance" (pp. 11–12).

CALEB AND CINDY, IN FIVE YEARS OF MARRIAGE, HAD ACHIEVED ALMOST EVERY-thing they had hoped for. Things were pretty much on track. His optometry practice was expanding nicely, the children were healthy and happy, and the house was now basically furnished. There had been no major stumbles or setbacks. They were just an ordinary Polish-American Catholic man and a WASP-Methodist woman making their way in the dreamland of America.

During this Lenten season they had thought about their good fortune. "Sometimes when the kids are in bed, I express thanks for the children, for food, shelter, for all we have," Cindy said. "When we look at the hardships people go through, we're grateful we don't have those problems." For Caleb, thanks were due for "the job I can go to that presents countless possibilities and for my family that is well fed and well clothed."

Cindy said she often contrasted their abundance with the desperate suffering of so much of the world. "When I flip through the TV and see starving kids, I wonder why God would let that happen," she said with a grimace. "From another angle, why shouldn't we do something about it? It goes through my mind every day. I feel we haven't done anything to help the needy. We are starting to have the means to do something, even if it's something like taking in a foster child or sending money to feed people."

Caleb thought God had nothing to do with these miseries, attributing them to "man's free will. That's what causes these problems. I'm plenty angry at mankind." He said his wife was much more concerned about these tragedies than he was, and asked rhetorically, "Do I feel guilty? No. I see it. I acknowledge it. I feel my responsibility would be to make some contribution to an organization like Catholic Charities that distributes to the needy." He was convinced that doling out help firsthand to destitute people was impractical and probably a waste. "You never know what they're going to use handouts for," he said.

Until he felt more secure, he didn't feel free to consider giving his time, money, or talents to *anything* except his work and his family. Though Catholicism had been enormously influential in his life, his involvement in the church would be severely limited for the foreseeable future, he reckoned. Maybe someday. "When I get established and I'm not worried where my next patient is coming from, when I've paid my debts, maybe then I'll get back into it," Caleb said. "Then maybe I'll have to decide between the buck and the church. That's what it comes to." For all of that, Caleb felt the society around him was "sick" with materialism and gaudy show. His trips to the nearby mall reminded him of all he disliked.

Lent also tended to highlight the basics of the Christian faith they both held dear and to underscore the disparities instilled from their very different religious backgrounds. Caleb had received ashes at his parish on Ash Wednesday, a practice not observed in Cindy's Methodist tradition. Caleb felt guilty for not finding the time to observe more private devotions such as the stations of the cross, none of which were familiar to Cindy. "With much of Lent gone, I realize I've done none of the things I've wanted to do," Caleb said. Most of all he had wanted to attend one of the Lenten courses being offered by his parish priest. For Cindy, it was a time for reflecting on the trials Christ had experienced in his days on earth.

They had both grown up with an awareness of the season's emphasis on self-scrutiny and penance. This Lenten season, Cindy had singled out pettiness as the personal trait she most wanted to shed. Caleb had designated two flaws to work on: impatience and pickiness. Neither claimed to have made much progress.

They worshiped at their respective churches each Sunday and periodically attended one or the other as a couple. Each had come to appreciate much of what the other's services had to offer, but when it came time for communion, they felt worlds apart, alien worlds at that.

Caleb talked to his parish priest about the possibility that Cindy might be allowed to go with him to receive the eucharistic bread and wine. Officially the church barred those who were not in communion with the Catholic church, but exceptions had been made through accident or design. "He said that the point had seemed to be coming where that was feasible," Caleb recalled, "but that recently the church had slammed the door." At the same time, the priest told him of a Lutheran man who regularly came to the rectory to receive communion privately. Caleb interpreted this exception to mean that so long as it was out of public view and the person accepted Catholic dogma, it was all right. However, those were not conditions Cindy could accept for herself.

The same restrictions did not apply in Cindy's Methodist church. Caleb was eligible and welcome to share in the Lord's Supper. But he balked. It was wrong, even hypocritical, for him to do so, he thought. "I did it once and felt terrible," he said. "I was extremely awkward." He was afraid that his participation might signify to others that he approved a form of communion other than the Catholic sacrament itself, which to him held exclusive claim to manifesting the "actual body and blood of Christ."

Caleb's "one true church, one true sacrament" convictions hurt Cindy, pushed her to defend her church all the more and make a solid stand for her tradition.

Their spiritual lives were confined almost entirely to the time spent in church. They were not accustomed to praying together or praying very much in solitude. Caleb said there was one thing he did. Sometimes on a Saturday morning he arose early, put classical music on the stereo (usually Vivaldi's "Four Seasons"), and watched the sun rise through the back window. "That's prayer because I'm appreciating the beauty out there," he said. "I'd like to do it every morning, but that might spoil the special feeling." For Cindy, the closest to prayer she felt was a silent feeling of thankfulness when Susan and Paula were safely asleep at night.

In their own growing-up days, religious lessons had been learned both at home and school. Caleb's Polish immigrant parents and his brothers had lived across the street from the parish. A crucifix had been attached to their front door, as he explained half-kiddingly, "in case Jehovah's Witnesses showed up." He had been enlisted as an altar boy early on, the faithful, reliable soldier always on call for mass and "for everyone who died." It was this experience that fed his interest in becoming a priest, an ambition that faded during tenth grade in a private Catholic boarding school. His father often repaired to the church after work to pray, and his mother quietly said the rosary in the midst of the busy household. Private devotions were not so common now, Caleb said with a tone of disapproval, though he conceded that he found no time to do them himself. He also regretted that he had never read the Bible.

Cindy's religious education had come from weekly Sunday school, church worship, and especially from the example of her father, a devout man who took refuge early each morning in devotional readings and prayer. The family had joined hands each evening and said grace over dinner. The Bible had a prominent place in their home. In addition to weekly worship, she had taken part in the various programs of her church youth group. She remained active in a church music group and taught Sunday school from time to time. The children went mostly with her, but in keeping with her agreement with Caleb, they occasionally went with their father to his church.

Sunday morning often turned out to be long and, not infrequently, logistically rather complicated for the couple.

Though they were absorbed in the immediate day-to-day urgencies of their own lives, some events within the wider Catholic church did catch their attention. The bishops' letters on nuclear arms and the economy had eluded them, but their attention had been riveted briefly by the Vatican's statement on reproduction, a subject that concerned them greatly as parents. They both applauded the church for getting out front on the subject. Caleb, moreover, felt moved to comment as a man of science. "Science and technology are so advanced that moral and legal reasoning hasn't kept up," he said. "At least the Catholic church has the guts to make a statement." Cindy thought the Vatican had gone too far by rejecting *in vitro* fertilization, for, as she saw it, "God gave us our brains to use: if it helps a man and woman conceive, it doesn't disturb me." Caleb agreed with her. Both likewise found abortion immoral, including cases where the fetus was defective.

Did they see eye-to-eye on most values? "For the most part we're pretty well together on most things," Cindy said. And Caleb: "Usually without discussion it comes out we think the same way about most things."

April
1·9·8·7

I T WAS THE NIGHT OF APRIL 1, AND WILLIAM BULLOCK WAS MEET-
ing for the first time with all the priests and deacons of the
Diocese of Des Moines, about 150 in all. Next morning he would
become their bishop.

For the previous seven years, he had served as auxiliary bishop of St.
Paul–Minneapolis. Before that, he had guided the fortunes of the Catholic
preparatory school affiliated with the College of Saint Thomas. On this night in
the stately Iowa cathedral, he would hear the letter from the pope officially naming him to replace Bishop Maurice Dingman, who was retiring after nineteen
years to a chorus of affection and praise. Bishop Bullock, a man of impressive
stature in his own right, assumed his new duties with a tribute to his close friend
and predecessor, lauding Bishop Dingman as "the gospel ideal of servant—indeed
of greatness."

He then turned specifically to the priests and deacons. In the thirty-four years
since his own ordination, unforeseen changes had taken place, and still more
would follow in the years ahead, but this night he would focus on "three areas of
continuity in the priesthood and in the life of the church."

The first and "most basic truth," Bishop Bullock said, was that the priest was
"first and foremost a Catholic Christian, a man with a personal journey of faith to
make." This implied giving and receiving, a reciprocity between clergy and laity. It
meant not only that a priest should be aware of being a minister but that "you,
too, need the ministry of the church; that you, too, have a need to be forgiven, to be
blessed, to be fed, to be taught, to be consoled, to be anointed and finally, to be lovingly buried." Ordination had not made them immune to human foibles. Like other

Catholic Christians, he noted, they would face difficult moral decisions involving "honesty, money, sexual behavior, health care, threat of nuclear war, ambition, anger, and resentment." In addition, they would experience doubt and confusion. In light of their humanness, therefore, they would need forgiveness, encouragement, and blessings from those they served.

The second "reality of priesthood" to which he pointed was the need to be a source of learning and insight. What people needed from them, said their new mentor, was "a greater knowledge of the Christian faith and Christian life than they have had time to acquire." Laypeople wanted the priest to be conversant with the "research and findings of Catholic scholars" and to "have studied and learned enough to throw some spiritual light on the personal experiences and dilemmas which arise out of their families and work, their world."

By sticking to their area of competence, the bishop suggested, they might avoid false aspirations. For they would inevitably discover that "a lot of people are better Christians than you are. Many will pray more profoundly and intensely, labor more effectively for a just society and carry out the works of mercy with greater tact and generosity, or be better counselors and consolers than you . . . laypeople may outdo you in all those areas and they will not expect that measure of perfection from you."

Mindful of how they were perceived, they had best open their minds to ideas and stand ready to impart well-informed lessons in the history and teaching of the Catholic faith. "Studying, reading widely, taking an interest in new ideas, expanding the horizons of your mind and your knowledge of diverse cultures, clarifying your own thinking through argument and discussion, as well as reflection and prayer, are expected of us by the laity," Bishop Bullock said. "If you are intellectually alive, you have a much better chance of surviving the challenge to faith which will come from events and changes in the lives of those you serve."

An active, open mind helped ensure that the people entrusted to their care would not receive "just one way of looking at things, one style of faith, the only one you ever bothered to learn or the only one you have used in your own personal experience." Failure to cultivate the mind left the priest inept in the face of challenges from those whose beliefs did not fit the mold. "Those who encounter an unprepared priest will leave his presence quietly and politely," Bishop Bullock gently cautioned. "They may pray for him, but they will find that the church through its priest did not light their path or help in their life's journey." If they find a man familiar with "a variety of tenable theological, pastoral, and spiritual practices, they will listen."

Bishop Bullock concluded by assuring his priests of his "attention, fraternal love, and support." He, in turn, asked for their prayers. "Together we will do a great job of carrying on the wonderful work of my predecessor, Bishop Maurice Dingman."

The priests and deacons rose as one in boisterous applause.

OF THE MANY EFFORTS INSPIRED BY THE BISHOPS' PASTORAL LETTER "ECONOMIC Justice for All," none was more striking in style and poignancy than an ecumenical message, "Justice and the Economy" (Origins, April 2, vol. 16, no. 42, pp. 743–44), issued by the Catholic and Episcopal bishops of West Virginia.

The unusual collaboration by Bishop Francis Schulte, the Catholic bishop of Wheeling-Charleston, and his Episcopal counterpart, Bishop Robert Atkinson, took cues from the Catholic bishops' pastoral in addressing the worsening conditions in their economically hard-pressed state. Its unique feature was its form— free verse—a medium that expressed the elegance and power of the message itself.

West Virginia was surely a fit subject for elegiac appeal. In the rapture of the Reagan "boom," the "Mountain State" was one of those asterisked "pockets" of rising poverty and despair, largely ignored by heavy industry and idled by empty mine shafts. It was depressed and overlooked.

The two bishops, invoking words from the Catholic bishops' pastoral, emphasized that they were speaking as "pastors" and "moral teachers" and reasserted the earlier pastoral's standard for judging economic policies

by what they do to people
by what they do for people
and by how people participate
in them.

They implored the members of their two churches

to examine
the economic situation in
West Virginia
and seek solutions
that will be
just for one and all.

Their cry was couched as a "sense of urgency" brought on by too many people without jobs, slow economic growth, poor schools, and too little response by government to these chronic problems.

We note in all this
a feeling of hopelessness
among so many of our people.
What is worse,
this lack of hope
has fostered a frightening
complacency:
"That's the way it is . . .
and was and will be."

We cannot, must not, accept this.
Justice for all must prevail.

Justice, the bishops said, was predicated on "a change in attitude of both mind and heart." Seeking it meant, among other things, ridding society of "exploitation of the poor," hunger, and discrimination. People had a right to food, clothing, shelter, and health care, but these basics were denied to those

on the fringes of society:
    the unneeded and unwanted
    our children and our elderly
    the sick and the homeless.

They continued:

For justice to exist
not only is a change
in attitude demanded,
but solutions to the
problems must be found
and implemented.
We have no other
moral choice.

People of good will might differ about strategy, but the imperative itself was inescapable and multidimensional.

Justice is a
    social
    political

> *economic*
> *educational*
> *and above all,*
> *a moral issue.*

In their conclusion, the West Virginia bishops encapsulated their theme:

> *We affirm*
> *that what is demanded*
> *is a conversion,*
> *a change of mind and heart,*
> *a willingness to do*
> *what has to be done.*

MAUREEN GAZED PENSIVELY FROM BEHIND DARK GLASSES TOWARD THE OUTDOOR café table on which sat her glass of red wine. Her bulky red sweater and stylish accessories befit the outgoing nature she exercised during her workday as office manager for the academic dean. But a darker, tenacious inner self lurked just beneath that surface, stirring with perplexities.

She had been preoccupied in these final days of Lent with the prevalence of brokenness. She did not normally allow herself much time for brooding, she said, because there was too much to do at her job and at home. But she had found certain themes returning to mind again and again during her routines. One of them was brokenness.

A source of this preoccupation was her daughter Patrice. Sometimes it seemed to Maureen that she had spent her whole adult life worrying about her daughter. Patrice was five years old when Maureen and her husband adopted her. She had come to them "a very emotionally damaged person," and, in a household with two other children, she became unmanageable. Much of Patrice's childhood was therefore spent in a sanatorium, the cost of which depleted the family savings. Now, at age eighteen, she was off on her own, though her mother was hazy about some of the details. One thing her mother believed strongly was that Patrice had become a heavy cocaine user.

Maureen's story of her attempt to be a mother to Patrice was laden with remorse and revelation. She had come to a momentous turning point. "I learned a lot of things in dealing with Patrice," she said, "primarily that the best thing to do is back off. You can't just channel people's minds. You have to just be there and listen sometimes."

Until about a year ago, she said, "I had fought her bitterly—trying to save her. Then I decided to come to peace with her. The hardest thing to do is to walk away admitting that you can't help, that you have no control. The only control I have is how I handle things. I can't pretend to heal it."

The change had become possible because, in her view, she had accepted both her own limitations and those of the broken child she had taken in. "Patrice couldn't be touched when she came to us," her mother recalled. "She already had no self-respect. You just can't make up the void in someone who needed to be held as a child and wasn't. By five, it was already too late for some things."

Maureen felt deeply for her and with her. "For some reason I feel closest to Patrice of all my children," she said slowly. "I can really identify with what goes on with her. I feel the excruciating intensity of her pain. I can see why she's doing what she's doing. I know her extreme fear and pain. I'm over forty and a cripple in my own right because of things ingrained in me that are still there. I was never very secure. We were poor, and I was alone with nobody to rap with."

Maureen mourned for Patrice—whose body, she observed, "may never be able to carry her inner weight"—for herself, and for the broken minds, bodies, and spirits all around her. "I just hate injustice toward anyone," she said.

Maureen had been thinking about doing more for those in need. Perhaps now that the children were grown she should think about some other line of work, like social service. But she hesitated for fear that she would be overwhelmed: "You can't even make a dent in the problems—they're so vast."

Her consolation was the church where she had, as a lonely child, first found spiritual healing. There she encountered Jesus primarily as the physician of brokenness. "I realized recently that I had never been terribly connected with the organized church," she said, taking a sip of wine. "Religion to me was always a very personal thing. When I went to six-thirty morning mass as a girl, I didn't go because it was an organized church, I went to watch the sisters. They used to file in front of the candles to their pew. I'd watch them every morning. They had a spirit and a closeness to God that I wanted to attain.

"Then I'd follow the mass in Latin and say the prayers. That for me was *it*—and it still is. I can be upset with the ramifications of the rulings by the church, but things aren't going to change much for me in that way. In *The Name of the Rose,* which I've been reading, there's a debate over whether Jesus smiled. That's an interesting thought, but I remember that I have to get on with my own life, my own life, to see if I can do anything better.

"When I think of those nuns filing in, I think of the Byzantine art in that parish, the portrait of the 'Feet of the Deity' that don't quite touch the ground, I think again of shadows filing into a pew."

THE AIDS EPIDEMIC HAD PRESENTED CATHOLIC OFFICIALS WITH A PAINFUL predicament, testing the church's ability to fulfill Jesus' injunction to love the sinner while despising the sin.

The record showed that those stricken with AIDS were overwhelmingly homosexual and had contracted the disease through gay sex. The church considered those acts morally heinous, and the Vatican, in its statement of the past October, defined homosexuality itself as an "objective disorder." But at the same time, the gospel had imbued the church with a ministry of compassion toward the sick and dying. How to fulfill Jesus' mandate?

The appropriate reaction seemed obvious to most bishops: separate sexual causes from tragic results, and indeed church officials, for the most part, embraced it. Patients living out their last days in hospitals, homes, and hospices might be accorded the church's care in such a way that the moral questions about gay sex could be overlooked. It was a difficult pathway to tread, inasmuch as the Vatican letter's unequivocal condemnation of homosexual activity had embittered many homosexuals. Some bishops were privately dismayed with what they considered the letter's regressive content and chagrined by the timing of its release in the midst of the epidemic. As they saw it, the unhappy coincidence had also provided ammunition for those intent on seeing the epidemic as punishment for sexual sin. Others saw the church's teaching as more crucial than ever to stem the spread of the disease.

Inevitably, any discussion of AIDS by church leaders implicitly involved its teaching on homosexuality, so pastoral care could never completely be separated from moral strictures. But efforts were under way to minister in the name of mercy without pronouncing guilt. Often the effect seemed somewhat schizophrenic: bishops known for a hard line toward homosexuality visiting the bedsides of AIDS patients and urging their flocks to extend their understanding and support.

The first regional response came from the bishops of California. In a pastoral letter dated April 8, the twenty-eight bishops of the region proclaimed their overall objective: "We dedicate ourselves and our resources to spiritual support, to practical care and to educational efforts designed to reduce prejudice and to stop the spread of the disease."

Throughout their letter, the bishops exhorted Catholics to avoid assumptions of guilt. Drawing on the example of Jesus, they said, "our response to those who are ill should be that of compassion, not of judgment." Jesus had healed those who came to him "without judging individuals or imputing blame." Caring for AIDS patients meant doing away with irrational fears. To combat erroneous ideas about the disease's transmission and spread, the bishops commended the report by the surgeon general, Dr. C. Everett Koop. Inasmuch as Dr. Koop's findings were technical and scientific rather than moral, the bishops noted, they presumed to supply the missing precaution.

"And so," the bishops wrote, "avoidance of illicit use of drugs, sexual abstinence before marriage, and monogamous fidelity within marriage recommend themselves as medically necessary as well as morally responsible. The recovery of the virtue of chastity may be one of the most urgent needs of contemporary society."

Under separate headings, the bishops addressed various aspects of the problem. They appealed to parishes to include prayers for those with AIDS in the liturgical Prayer of the Faithful and encouraged individuals and groups to provide sufferers a range of services, from transportation and housecleaning to family support and counseling. The bishops acknowledged that many homosexuals had abandoned the church. "We regret this distance," they said, "and long to heal their wounds by offering our support and fellowship." Catholic hospitals that offered "non-judgmental and sensitive care" were praised, and hospice facilities for AIDS-infected prison inmates was underscored as a need.

Detection of AIDS may cause a family to discover that one of its members was a homosexual or a drug user, the bishops said, leading sometimes to "incredulity and rejection." They continued, "Our hearts must go out to those families weakened by anger or sorrow who cannot accept the reality of their loved one having AIDS. Reminding them by our ministry that human dignity comes from God, and that we believe each person is sacred—a unique reflection of God among us—we can encourage them to accept these persons with AIDS back within their embrace."

The crisis had inflamed fears and hostilities toward people who had already borne the bruises of prejudice, the bishops said. Catholics must help safeguard their rights and repel attempts to bar them from schools, housing, and medical care. Accurate information about prevention and spread should be provided to employers and school officials to guard against injustice. That included any effort to quarantine people with the disease or to violate their confidentiality.

When it came to the touchy question of whether the California bishops would endorse AIDS prevention programs that included information about the benefits of condoms, the prelates seemed to leave room for that possibility by remaining discreetly vague. The United States Catholic Conference had explicitly ruled out condom advertising. Archbishop Mahony of Los Angeles had the previous December refused to grant church facilities to an education program favoring condom use. But no national body of the church had ventured an opinion on whether offering information on condoms was licit if it was accompanied by clearly stated church teachings.

The bishops never used the word *condom,* nor did they set specific limits on education about AIDS. "We urge those engaged in educational ministries at all levels to cooperate with parents in developing interdisciplinary programs," the bishops wrote, "in conformity with the moral teaching of the church for the prevention of further spread of the virus." Health and school programs should be directed "toward the general public and also developed especially for those in high risk groups," the bishops said.

On April 9, one day after the California bishops issued their appeal for compassion, the Reverend Michael Peterson died of AIDS in George Washington Hospital in Washington, D.C. Father Peterson, forty-four years old, was a priest of the Archdiocese of Washington and a psychiatrist. He had founded the Saint Luke Institute of Suitland, Maryland, which treated priests and sisters for alcohol and drug addiction and sexual disorders.

Father Peterson had become nationally known for his work at the institute and for his exhaustive outreach to troubled clergy and religious in every region of the country. He had converted to Catholicism at age nineteen while a student at Stanford University. He had become a priest just nine years previously, after completing medical school.

The day he died, his ecclesiastical superior, Archbishop Hickey, released an announcement that Father Peterson had, indeed, succumbed to AIDS. It was the first such statement by an American bishop, though the disease had already claimed the lives of at least a dozen priests. The archbishop's statement echoed the California bishops' call for compassion. The difference was that the archbishop's words flowed from a powerful personal experience with one man, a priest under his care, day after day in the throes of death.

The two men had visited almost daily. The archbishop said he had counseled his priest to face the realistic possibility that the cause of his death would become public knowledge. Father Peterson had decided to disclose his ordeal to his fellow priests in the diocese and to the bishops. In his statement, the archbishop expressed the hope that Father Peterson's courage in facing the disease could strengthen fellow sufferers and inspire others to "reach out to those with AIDS with renewed conviction."

A throng of mourners filled Saint Matthew's Cathedral on April 13 for the funeral, a mass of Christian burial concelebrated by 180 priests. According to the *National Catholic Reporter,* the gathering included "scores of priests, a half-dozen bishops, the papal pro-nuncio, medical professionals, scholars, monks, women religious, gay activists and laity from around the country. Two chartered buses carried St. Luke patients to the funeral service."

Archbishop Hickey spoke, testifying again to the capacity of a personal encounter to instill deeper levels of understanding than strict readings of church law might permit. Calling Father Peterson "our brother," the archbishop said, "Our sadness is real today. Our own lives, our church and our community are diminished by the death of Father Peterson. . . . When I came to Washington, I got to know Michael as a brilliant and hard-working priest dedicated to the challenging ministry of assisting priests and religious in overcoming problems with alcohol and drug abuse or other difficulties related to their ministry. He combined the skills of a physician, the training of a psychiatrist, and the caring of a pastor in ministering to the special needs of troubled priests and religious. . . . I am proud of Michael's courage in sharing his illness."

The archbishop quoted from Father Peterson's recent letter to his fellow priests. "'For eleven months I have struggled, with the help of the eucharist and my own deepening faith and knowledge," he wrote, "that at my death I will meet him in the love that he has promised through the life, death and resurrection of his Son, Jesus Christ."

Elsewhere the debate continued over the Vatican's demand that dioceses prohibit groups that disagreed with Catholic teachings on homosexuality from using church property. Dignity, the Catholic national gay activist organization that had been meeting at parishes and other church facilities, was an obvious target of the ruling.

Several dioceses had evicted Dignity, though Seattle, where Archbishop Hunthausen's meeting with Dignity in the cathedral had been cited in the accusations against him, had so far not taken that step. Among the latest to evict the group were the dioceses of St. Paul–Minneapolis, overseen by the liberal Archbishop John R. Roach, and Richmond, Virginia, led by another liberal, Bishop Walter Sullivan, who was in no position to defy the order in the aftermath of a Vatican probe into his orthodoxy that had preceded the move against Hunthausen. Bishop Sullivan's act of compliance, however, sparked an embarrassing incident. The pastor from whose parish Dignity was evicted promptly resigned because of the order. The Reverend Vincent Connery had been at Sacred Heart Church in Norfolk for eight of the eleven years he had been a priest. He was highly respected by his fellow priests and close to Bishop Sullivan. After the order to banish Dignity was given, Father Connery protested in an op-ed article in the *Virginian-Pilot* (April 3) that he could not "lend tacit support to a church teaching which I believe is wrong." In the same article, he took issue with the church's views on sexuality, the bans against women priests and in vitro fertilization, and what he considered Rome's general heavy-handedness.

Referring to homosexuality, he wrote, "I do not question Rome's right and responsibility to articulate opinions on moral issues. Let us remember, however, that they are *opinions*—opinions about the way God sees things. Whether God agrees with them remains to be seen.

"What I do question is Rome's starting point; that any and all homosexual 'activity' (i.e., physical sex) is morally wrong. It's time for the Roman Catholic church to revise its teaching on this."

On April 3, the day the article was published, Father Connery met with his bishop. According to a statement released by a sorrowful Bishop Sullivan, the two had "mutually agreed that he would resign from the ministry. Father Connery has served with dedication. He has always had a deep concern for people, especially those on the margin of society."

EARLY ON EASTER MORNING, APRIL 19, IN SEATTLE, ARCHBISHOP HUNTHAUSEN huddled with his top advisers to craft a response to what they considered a disastrous turn of events. They were reeling from what seemed to them a rapid series of setbacks.

The crisis had been touched off by the archbishop's April 8 meeting in Chicago with Cardinal Joseph Bernardin. As he had headed off to answer the summons by the cardinal, one of three bishops appointed by the Vatican to investigate the Seattle tensions, he had exuded a mood of modest optimism. Indications were that the commission would resolve the dispute to his liking. The two days of open hearings by the three bishops in Menlo Park, California, back in March had, from all reports, boded well. The impression from the session was that the Vatican's largely negative picture of Seattle was giving way to a positive one.

But the cardinal had tossed him a bombshell. The commission had worked out a settlement, the cardinal told him, and proceeded to lay out the details. Under the plan, Auxiliary Bishop Wuerl would be removed, replaced by a coadjutor bishop who would, by definition, become the next archbishop when the seat was vacated. The appointment of a coadjutor was rarely done. Archbishop Hunthausen was being asked, in effect, to accept the presence of his successor within his archdiocese, a bishop to help straighten things out, until such time that he was gone.

The cardinal continued. Though a successor would be named, the archbishop's full authority would technically be restored in full. Unlike Bishop Wuerl, who had been invested with "special faculties" to curtail the archbishop's control over the Seattle church, the coadjutor would receive no such powers. Moreover, the archbishop would be allowed to approve the list of three candidates for coadjutor submitted to Rome. There was one more element presented by the cardinal: a commission evaluation or "assessment" of the situation in Seattle with respect both to the alleged "abuses" cited by the Vatican and the impact of Bishop Wuerl's assignment to restore order.

Archbishop Hunthausen had reacted to what the cardinal had to say with shock and disbelief. The idea of naming a coadjutor was rumored to be the pope's solution after the curia's proposal of sending an apostolic administrator to Seattle had run into stiff opposition. The coadjutor suggestion had been floated two autumns before when the Vatican issued its indictment of the archbishop, but the idea had been so stoutly resisted by the archbishop and his staff that it was assumed to be dead. Then Wuerl had been sent as an auxiliary bishop, a strategy no less objectionable in their eyes, but at least he was not a coadjutor. Now the coadjutor plan had been revived, much to the archbishop's dismay.

A further source of upset to Archbishop Hunthausen was the commission report. He had never publicly conceded the validity of the charges of laxity and abuse in the Vatican's long bill of particulars from Cardinal Ratzinger. That had been grossly unfair, in his view, but as he read the commission's version now before him, he considered it even worse, laying an even heavier burden of blame on his administration for wrongs he could not acknowledge. It bore the firm imprint of Cardinal O'Connor, the relative hard-liner on the commission, who felt the strongest that Seattle was an errant member of the clan that had to be treated sternly.

Recoiling from Cardinal Bernardin's terms of settlement on behalf of the commission, a deeply troubled Archbishop Hunthausen left the briefing without giving the slightest approval to the plan. To the contrary, he returned to Seattle furious with the commission proposal, in no mood to accept either a coadjutor or the assessment.

He arrived back in the archdiocese in time for Holy Week and another major development that the archbishop also took as a serious blow to his prospects. The latest issue of the *National Catholic Register,* dated April 19 but available several days earlier, carried a story reportedly leaked from a unnamed Vatican official that claimed a deal was in the making. The story had a twist that set the archbishop back on his heels. According to the *Register,* the Vatican would seek to "diffuse tensions" in Seattle not only by packing Bishop Wuerl off to his own diocese and naming a coadjutor, but also by forcing the archbishop to leave. The newspaper said the archbishop would be involuntarily retired "only after a grace period during which the archbishop would be officially restored to full episcopal powers."

Cardinal Bernardin's description of the settlement had contained no hint of a coerced departure. Indeed, the archbishop's sources insisted that there was no truth to that aspect of the story. But the news blackout had been broken, and speculation became rampant. Father Ryan, the chancellor of the archdiocese, sought to knock down the story in an April 15 press release. The release was plainly an effort to keep the lid on most of the main features of the proposed settlement. Father

Ryan knew, of course, when he issued the release that the newspaper had accurately reflected major features of the plan, with the notable exception of the "forced retirement" part of it. The chancellor's statement to the news media, was, therefore, somewhat disingenuous in a political effort to protect the archbishop from charges that the leak had originated in Seattle or represented a *fait accompli.*

"I urge you," said Father Ryan, the archbishop's alter ego, "to disregard the *National Catholic Register* article, because not only is it speculative, it is incorrect. The information that formed the basis of the article was apparently leaked to the reporter by an uninformed and irresponsible party in Rome or in Washington, D.C., a party who, it would seem, has little or no concern for the damage that unfounded speculation can do to our local church. . . . Meanwhile, I can assure you that the archbishop has not been asked to retire or resign, nor are any 'deals' being made in that direction."

The archbishop had most certainly dug in his heels against going along with the commission's propositions when he gathered his closest advisers on that early Easter morning. He was a man distraught. The Chicago heart-to-heart had made him angry. The *Register* article left him depressed. First, there was the problem of the publicity itself, which created bad will and suspicion about the possible motives of leakers. Second, there was the rush of paranoia stirred even by false reports. Given the level of distrust between the Vatican and the Seattle archdiocese, and within the U.S. church itself, even an off-base account of that kind had the whiff of plausibility to it. The idea that Rome would somehow push the archbishop out was a grim conviction in some quarters. It smacked of the inevitable.

During that Easter morning, the first blush of the celebration of the Resurrection, Seattle's prelate was locked in an inner struggle over the best course to take for the good of himself and the church. From his own vantage point, in the immediate aftermath of the Chicago meeting, there were several important thoughts and feelings to consider.

One was that the assignment of a coadjutor meant, symbolically, that the archdiocese was out of control and needed a watchdog of high rank to help apply a firm hand; therefore, acceptance of a coadjutor was out of the question. To the archbishop and many of his aides, such a concession would constitute an admission of guilt. They were not about to budge after holding out against the Vatican's finger-pointing for such a long time.

Another was that the archbishop had bad memories of the last go-around with the Vatican over the appointment of Bishop Wuerl. He had felt ill served by the process that delivered Bishop Wuerl and expected the same to happen again. Despite the promises from Cardinal Bernardin that he would get the right of approval of the candidates forwarded to Rome, he couldn't quite believe it would turn out well. There were too many loopholes and potential pitfalls built into the system that could betray even the best intentions. It hadn't helped, of course, that Bishop Wuerl, the last product of this sometimes arbitrary system of papal appointments (perhaps mostly for reasons that were purely circumstantial) was so widely distrusted within the chancery.

A third feeling that emerged in those initial discussions was a suspicion that the first evaluation handed to Archbishop Hunthausen by Cardinal Bernardin in Chicago was so at odds with the previous tenor of the inquiry as to suggest that it had been foisted onto the commission by someone else. The name that had immediately surfaced as the most likely ghost writer: Donald Wuerl. The auxiliary bishop had been in Rome the previous month, ostensibly to pursue his study of the North American College, and was known to have talked with the pope. Moreover, he had been reportedly peeved by not being asked to testify at Menlo Park on the technicality that he was not an official consultor of the archdiocese. These were the makings of the theory of a conspiracy to cast aspersions on Seattle. In fact, the report was a product of the commission. It bore the heavy stamp of the most disciplinary bishop, Cardinal O'Connor. But in the frenzied uncertainty of Easter, clues became calls to arms.

Though his set-to with the cardinal had ended without resolution, the archbishop let it be known that he would definitely keep talking to commission members, who were busy urging him to accept the settlement, and he would make a forceful written response to the first assessment. But as things stood, he was against giving in to the demand for a coadjutor. Around the archbishop's supporters swirled two nonnegotiable demands of their own: full restoration of the archbishop's power and dismissal of Bishop Wuerl.

The situation had hardened into a standoff. After a difficult, intensive look at the complexities, the commission had come up with the settlement as the best way out, assured that it had the pope's blessing. If the archbishop refused to go along with it, the consequences were obvious to all concerned. It would be the end of his activity as an archbishop. The Vatican would force him to step aside and replace him with an interim administrator.

Collectively, the commission was growing more exasperated by what they took to be the archbishop's willful and unreasonable behavior. Though the degree of feeling varied among the trio, they were growing more and more irritated by the seeming refusal by Archbishop Hunthausen to accept reality. In the first place, it was clear to them that pastoral practices in the archdiocese *had* steered around church law. Why couldn't Archbishop Hunthausen bring himself to admit it? Instead, he was prone to parry rhetorically, asking whether, in effect, any bishop did not have the very same things going on in his diocese? The answer was that certainly abuses went on everywhere—and that made it unfair to a degree—but the extent of it from place to place depended largely on the attitude of the episcopal leader. A bishop might encourage such breaches, wink at them tolerantly, or chase down the perpetrators, as Detroit's Archbishop Szoka had done in his pitched drive against general absolution. It was agreed that no bishop could entirely stamp out illicit practices, but there was wide variation on how much effort was put into containing the mischief. Within the hierarchy, Archbishop Hunthausen was clearly regarded as among the most permissive.

But the Seattle archbishop had, in some minds, gone over the line by refusing to play by the rules. Instead of accepting Rome's verdict, he had not only denied the validity of their charge that he had been permissive but appeared to consider some of the questionable pastoral practices as justified by local circumstances. The commission was miffed at this apparent duplicity. Why must he insist that they were somehow acceptable? Why must he play the Lone Ranger, writing his own laws and owing no accountability to the wider church? A breakdown of order was surely more than a matter of obedience to a higher authority? Church discipline mattered too. No, the commission couldn't buy his attempt to paper over real problems. They would insist that the Vatican's insistence on corrective procedures be taken seriously. They would have to overcome his stubborn resistance.

They were also well versed in church diplomacy. As they understood the political dynamics, Rome would approve the arrangement only if a coadjutor were appointed. There were no two ways about it. But "Dutch," as his colleagues and associates knew him, had proven well-nigh incorrigible. In a day when, as one observer close to the commission put it, "so many of our bishops are castrated," Dutch Hunthausen went his own way and was not a team player. Though he won a certain grudging admiration within the commission, he seemed increasingly to them to reject the very system of hierarchical authority and cooperation that he had pledged to uphold.

The commission understandably, then, felt in a bind. Even as the three bishops had worked hard for a formula that would calm the storm, the archbishop and his aides had continued to deny that anything was seriously out of order in Seattle and therefore scoffed at any effort that appeared to crack the whip.

The commissioners were in a jam of their own. Either they solved the problem and helped vindicate the claim that U.S. bishops should be given primary responsibility for keeping their own house in order, or they failed and became the brunt of ridicule. Other areas of the church might read such a calamity as a sign of Catholic America's persistent immaturity, while those within the U.S. church might regard it as the result of too little too late from the conference of bishops. The fallout from a spectacularly botched job might also put a grave damper on the pope's forthcoming trip to America. There was a lot riding on a successful outcome, and the commissioners, who took their assignments with utmost seriousness, had an un-cooperative archbishop on their hands who wouldn't confess and wouldn't accept punishment, even meted out in the most refined manner.

By the next day, a public anticompromise offensive had mobilized. The priests would be the shock troops. At an assembly of priests, Father Ryan asked their support for a statement of defiance that he had drafted. He secured ninety-two signatures, and during the next two weeks added another fifty-one, bringing the total to more than half the total priests engaged in active ministry in the archdiocese.

The statement captured the tenor of the previous day's discussions in the inner sanctum. In it, the priests repeated the widely heard complaint in Seattle that "our bishop has been evaluated improperly, inadequately, and unjustly." Against the allegations that he flouted church law, they lauded him as "a faithful teacher and orthodox teacher" who was a "compassionate, appropriately firm and loving shepherd after the model of the Good Shepherd, and a capable and competent church leader and administrator." The "judgment" that that impugned the arch-bishop's qualities as "a chief priest, teacher, and leader" is one that equally deni-grated their own, the priests said. They predicted that what they called the "grave scandal" that had ensued from the crisis would "take more than a generation to overcome or offset." Any fair evaluation in the future, the statement asserted, should be conducted by competent officials of the bishops' conference.

The prescribed "harsh and punitive remedies" had caused even greater harm, said the priests. The abuses they were intended to correct either did not exist or were, according to them, "more in the nature of pastorally motivated practices which, for sound reasons, have come to be accepted quite openly and generally in many dioceses of this country and beyond." The reform measures had been "forced upon him through a form of moral persuasion based more on coercion than on evangelical obedience."

Calling the current system that had been imposed on the archdiocese "un-workable and quite evidently destructive," they countered the commission with the two-pronged declaration that had become the rallying cry for the archbishop's defenders: return Archbishop Hunthausen to his full stature, and remove Bishop Wuerl. Then came their thinly veiled threat to the commission's proposal settle-ment. "In our judgment, to do any less than this will only further engage our church in the kind of compromise which appears to be based less on the concern for truth than on political considerations and imperatives; a form of compromise we find unworthy of Christians who follow a Lord who calls all of us to a radical honesty; a form of compromise, too, that has been predicted upon a woefully in-accurate judgment about our archbishop and about his government of and stew-ardship over the church of Seattle."

Another salvo was fired the next day by 120 nuns of the archdiocese in a statement that praised the archbishop and denounced the actions against him in terms similar to those used by the priests. An open prayer service that evening attended by nuns, priests, and hundreds of laypeople signaled the next stage of the struggle. The statements of resolve were read, and their messages, with the event itself, made the news across the country, resulting in this prosaic headline in the *New York Times* (April 22): "Priests Support Hunthausen."

As the days unfolded, another element began to work in the archbishop's favor. The *National Catholic Register* disclosure of a proposed deal had at first plunged him into gloom because of its assertion, an erroneous one as it turned out, that the Vatican intended to sweep him out of office as soon as the time was deemed ripe. The mere suggestion that Rome was acting deceitfully had stung him. But with that rumor apparently quashed, attention turned to the impact of the story itself.

To many Catholics, it seemed, the gist of the story cast the archbishop in the role of a victim coerced unfairly by Vatican bullies. The false claim that he would be forced out of office after a grace period, though apparently intended by a gleeful "leaker" to indicate that the archbishop's days were numbered, was instead stirring sympathy for him, a backlash that further strengthened his highly positive standing in the press. Ironically, the archbishop's opponents had given him a boost.

They had also given him unexpected leverage in his tilting with the commission. If the onus had been with the commission before, it was even more so now. Through this series of events, the archbishop was perceived even more widely as the wronged party in the clutches of Vatican operatives. The commission faced a delicate task in its effort to be an honest broker.

ON THE WEDNESDAY AFTERNOON BEFORE EASTER, PAUL AND THREE OF HIS COLlege buddies had piled into his weather-beaten blue Oldsmobile and sailed over the interstate to his parent's home in Illinois. His family had warmly welcomed friends of his who, for one reason or another, were unable to travel to their own homes for the holidays. The openness of his parents was one of the things he liked most about them.

He had looked forward to the break and had enjoyed it greatly. His mother had served up some of her best dishes to a tableful of guests who savored the home cooking. Leisurely talks between the generations lasted long into the evening. On Easter morning, they had gone to mass together at the family parish and returned to the house for a traditional ham dinner. Paul had felt festive and bolstered.

As he looked back a few days later, one comment in particular stood out. "Mom said she's seen a change in me," he recalled. "She said she likes it but can't quite figure it out. The way she put it was that I'd matured."

Paul felt himself filing occasions like that in his memory as his college days wound down. The hours of kidding and horseplay and camaraderie with his close friends meant more now, and he seemed to sometimes stand outside the experience, recording it for future reference. He did not want to forget. He wanted to hold on.

As the seniors looked beyond graduation from Saint Augustine, Paul saw himself between two groups. By far the larger number "were trying to get jobs that paid the most money," plain and simple, he said, while a small minority planned to do something more altruistic like serving in the Peace Corps. Most students had chosen courses "with the easy A's" and wanted the path of minimum resistance and maximum reward, he thought. Though he placed himself mostly in the monetary-payoff category, he also identified within himself a desire to serve the public. His goal was to enter the potentially lucrative field of law in a specialty such as labor negotiations that in his view made a valuable contribution to the community. In the back of his mind was also an eventual stab at politics.

By this time, late in the semester, the tempest over his inadequately footnoted term paper—for which he had been charged with plagiarism by the professor— had apparently blown over. He had redone the paper and handed it in to the professor's satisfaction, and that, from the university's standpoint, was the end of it. The campus newspaper hadn't received a single letter calling on him to resign from student government. The silence must have dismayed his political opponents on the newspaper who had gone to great lengths to magnify the incident, he noted with sardonic glee. The commotion had died down, and he had served out the remainder of his term.

In his final months as a student body officer, Paul had tackled three issues he found politically difficult. One involved student-faculty relations. He had long felt a growing distance between professors and undergraduates, due in part to the pressures on teachers to do research and writing for publication. As graduation neared, he said, many students were at a loss to find professors they knew well enough to ask for a recommendation for work or graduate school. But as he tried to address the problem, he felt the administration responded defensively and evasively. In his view, they had given him the runaround, and he had made no progress.

Another pressing need was to defuse rising tensions related to the growing army of students living off campus. Forty percent of the senior class now lived in nonuniversity housing, a percentage that had climbed sharply in recent years partly as the result, ironically enough, of stricter drinking regulations on university property. Residents of the community increasingly complained of drinking, rowdyism, and a general disregard for their neighborhoods. Raids on three recent late-night parties had netted more than a hundred students apiece on charges of drunkenness and disorderly behavior.

Paul believed that the university had for the most part "turned a deaf ear" to the problem. Accordingly, he joined a project to mediate between the neighborhood and the school that sought, among other things, to instill in students a greater sensitivity toward community needs. He felt they slowly made some headway.

A third source of political stress had been acrimonious debate over gay rights. Saint Augustine was, by Paul's account, "a very homophobic campus," still dominated by the legacy of many decades as an all-male Catholic college where homosexuality was unthinkable. But now, in keeping with the times, a gay and lesbian association had formed and requested official recognition from the student senate.

The university, eager to avoid any appearance of resisting the Vatican's campaign to rid the church of groups condoning homosexuality, opposed the application of this group on grounds that it violated a school rule against organizations based primarily on sexual orientation. In the face of that formidable obstacle, two votes favoring the group's request failed in the student senate, but the results reflected deep divisions within the student body. The first show of hands was an inconclusive tie; the second, with one member abstaining, turned down the request by the narrowest of margins, 8 to 7. Paul cast his vote against the resolution both times. He said he stood generally for the principle of gay rights but had been dissatisfied with the particular nature of the resolution. "I voted against it, because it was not a good proposal," he said. To his dismay, he said, the resolution appeared to signify approval of homosexuality itself rather than rights for homosexuals. He was not sure he could go that far.

Sexuality, not surprisingly, stirred much confusion, Paul said, and not the least the topic of homosexuality. He thought a lot of people on campus had "violent attitudes toward it," he said, "but there's also a lot of uncertainty in terms of how exactly homosexuals fit in. Is it a result of nature or nurture? A lot of people aren't quite willing to allow people to be just the way they are. The AIDS epidemic just contributes to the problem. People here say, 'Here's something that could kill us all and homosexuals have brought it.'

"There's another factor too," he continued, drawing a deep breath and wearing a tentative look. "In my age group we're trying to find ourselves and how we feel about our sexuality. Many don't know if they're homosexuals or not. That scares some people."

Paul had stepped down from his student government post after the annual election. His most concrete achievement, he boasted, was improving trash pickup at the dormitories. It was the kind of bread-and-butter issue that would serve him well in any future as an officeholder. And when all was said and done, he said, it had left him with a definite appetite for politics, scrapes and all. Right now there were class requirements to finish up in courses on marriage and family, international relations, political strategies in management, American social experience, and sports in American society.

And soon the fateful letters from the law schools would be landing in his mailbox.

FROM THE PULPIT OF THE CATHEDRAL OF SAINT ANDREW IN GRAND RAPIDS, Michigan, Bishop Kenneth Untener of the neighboring diocese of Saginaw delivered a lyrical call for a greater display of compassion by the church itself. Whereas the two bishops from West Virginia had called upon society to renounce callous attitudes toward the poor, Bishop Untener urged the church to spurn a certain hardness of heart of its own that he found creeping in.

The bishop had been invited to celebrate mass and give the homily on April 6 during the annual meeting of Michigan's Catholic educators. The Gospel lesson for the day, Jesus' encounter with the woman who had committed adultery, provided the springboard for his theme. Hearing the woman's confession, Jesus had responded with compassion and forgiveness, advising her simply to "go and sin no more." Within the early church there had been efforts to quash that story, Bishop Untener said, on grounds that it made Jesus look "too soft on sin." In the early centuries, as the church had imposed greater discipline, he said, "the more difficult it became to tell a story like this about Jesus. And so it was hushed up."

That temptation to get tough was showing itself now, Bishop Untener continued. "There is something in the church, sort of like a prevailing wind that makes us drift toward severity, away from softness," he said. He was not referring to individuals, he said, but to a kind of "corporate severity" church expressed "toward the world, toward our own people." All institutions drifted into rigidity and harshness, the bishop said, but the church was not just another organization founded by Jesus. It was called upon to "act as he did—not simply as individuals, but as a corporate body. That is why I worry about our drift toward corporate severity."

Though he did not specifically mention the church's handling of the Curran and Hunthausen cases as illustrations of such severity, to many who heard or later read the bishop's words the connection was unmistakable. Bishop Untener stuck to his more general theme that the church had neglected the works of softness. He chose examples at hand. The precious oils of anointing and healing had, until recently, been kept hidden. The softness of confession, the "tenderness" of Jesus toward sinners, had for a long period in the church been changed "into a severe closet, dark and anonymous, with the priest sitting as a judge." The succulence of bread had been reduced to "brittle and tasteless" communion wafers. The "warmth and fragrance" of wine had been removed from the Eucharist for centuries.

One test of the church's disposition was its treatment of marriage. "How would the people characterize our marriage tribunals?" he asked. "Would they identify them with Jesus in this Gospel passage or with the people who were demanding that the Mosaic law be carried out to the letter? It is a question of emphasis and the way we are perceived.

"We are perceived as severe. Not so long ago, if it was a mixed marriage you had to 'celebrate' it at a side altar or a sacristy. We are a church that, not so long ago, would not bury one of our own who committed suicide. Even today, in some of our new approaches and programs, we can be inflexible and rigid."

He urged the religious educators to embrace the softness of Jesus. "I dream of the day," he said, "when our religious education will so remarkably stress the gentleness, forgiveness, and love that Christians are called upon to live that this will be our trademark in the world.

"There is a lot of misery in our world and it desperately needs a merciful church. I pray that the church you proclaim will be a church manifestly filled with mercy."

As the start of the federal amnesty program for aliens neared, many of those who led efforts to assist applicants were frantic. Agencies created to help aliens complained of too little time to prepare for the expected crush. Advocates for the would-be applicants charged that many of the regulations set forth by the Immigration and Naturalization Service (INS) were unjust. Some felt the program itself was so ill designed that it should be scrapped.

Their growing apprehension fed on the widespread suspicion and distrust of the methods and motives of the INS. Rising tensions over U.S. policy in Central America, heightened by the emerging Iran-Contra scandal, had deepened bad feeling about the nation's intentions toward the region and its people. One activist described the amnesty concept as "a national psychic torture chamber." A Hispanic woman, asserting that the guidelines were "totally unrealistic," wondered if the program was "done just to keep us out."

Among many of the staunchest opponents of U.S. aims in Central America, immigration policy had largely become an instrument for political ends, particularly in El Salvador and Guatemala, where, it was thought by the activists, the Reagan administration sought to protect its support for repressive governments by denying that it was intolerable political conditions in those countries that caused people to flee. Part of that denial was the argument that these refugees were escaping only to improve their economic fortunes. Such disputes between activists and U.S. officials had spawned the spreading sanctuary movement, which was designed to harbor those who were earmarked for deportation by the INS on grounds that they were in this country to fatten their wallets rather than save their skins. These issues were intertwined among those closest to the centers of action for the amnesty plan.

The opening day, May 5, loomed ominously, therefore, to a large segment of volunteers and agency workers in charge of implementing the provisions of this limited opportunity for amnesty. Estimates of the potential pool of applicants ranged as high as 3.9 million. "We're at the tenth hour," Joe Murray, chairman of the North Texas Coalition in Dallas, told the *New York Times* (April 27). Underscoring the coalition's plea for a one-year delay, Murray said, "We are about to go over the dam, and we can't do anything about it. If the bill goes into effect, we will discriminate against the people we are trying to help."

Church officials were among those voicing the strongest outcries. Among the more visible protests was congressional testimony by Monsignor Nicholas DiMarzio on behalf of the United States Catholic Conference. Monsignor DiMarzio, executive director of migration and refugee services for the conference, appeared before the U.S. Senate subcommittee on immigration and refugee policy and delivered a ringing indictment of several aspects of the project.

The monsignor warned that the program would fail "if the course of events does not change dramatically" with regard to the rules governing the process. The church's foremost concern, he explained, was to keep families intact. INS regulations undermined that concept by threatening to deport as ineligible family members who arrived after the cutoff date of January 1, 1982. Moreover, the commissioner of INS, Alan C. Nelson, had indicated that there was "no national policy on family separation," a situation that, Monsignor DiMarzio said, gave rise "to disparity in treatment across the country." He urged that blanket amnesty be granted to all members of "such mixed households" who came forward together to apply.

He also found serious fault with the demands placed on applicants in order to qualify. The requirements were "excessively burdensome and restrictive," Monsignor DiMarzio told the Senate committee. Among other absurdities he cited was that an applicant who did not bring all the necessary proof to the immigration interview was not allowed to return with additional documents. In addition, he said, the INS had such a poor history of "losing files and documents" that it could not be trusted with the original records. Not the least of the difficulties was that the cost of preparing an application was beyond what many eligible poor people could afford (the basic fee to the government alone was $185; in addition, unscrupulous

lawyers were charging $1,000 or more for the *promise* of achieving favorable re-
sults; trafficking in forged documents was brisk). Altogether, he said, the whole review process had to become "less technical and stringent if this program is to
work."

Similar complaints were fired off in a pastoral letter from Archbishop Mahony.
The Archdiocese of Los Angeles not only contained the most Catholics of any in
the United States but the largest number of Hispanic church members. Already
265,000 people had preregistered for the amnesty program in parishes throughout the archdiocese. Archbishop Mahony, widely known for his support for migrant workers and for other chiefly Hispanic causes, took a forceful stand that
stopped just short of endorsing "sanctuary" as a form of civil disobedience.

"It is clear that many thousands of people will not qualify under the new law,"
the archbishop wrote. "There is also the danger of massive deportations and punitive actions against large numbers of people. Such actions would be deplorable
in our society and are unacceptable.

"There is no question that we must stand with our people. We have the moral
obligation to respond to those in our midst who will not qualify for the amnesty
provisions. The new law tells us that these people are now outside the framework of our concern as a society; our Christian tradition tells us the opposite.
The gospel itself and the teachings of our church call us to be most concerned
for those most needful and neglected members of our community."

Like Monsignor DiMarzio, the archbishop urged a change in rules to allow
that "if one family member were to qualify for legalization, other family members
should also receive derivative eligibility under the law." The application fee should
be lowered to fifty dollars. He also emphasized the need for a more vigorous plan
to protect employment rights of those who might be harassed under the new law
against giving jobs to illegal aliens. Already "anyone who is foreign looking or
has an accent" was more likely to suffer discrimination under the new regulations. Such violations must be closely monitored and INS raids on employers
halted during the amnesty period.

Finally, Archbishop Mahony vowed to rally behind those who, for various reasons, were denied amnesty. He refrained from directly pledging to break the law
by hiding illegal aliens, a practice of the sanctuary movement but promised, in
more vague terms, "to develop programs for deportation defense and advocacy for
those who may not qualify for legalization, including appeals for denial of amnesty
applications, legal representation in deportation proceedings and community
rights education programs." Refugees from Guatemala and El Salvador should, in
addition, be granted extended "voluntary departure status," he said.

The stand taken by Catholic leaders had certain evangelistic implications. At a
time when increasing numbers of Hispanics were joining evangelical and

Pentecostal churches, Catholicism's reputation among Spanish-speaking people depended in no small way on the degree of the church's advocacy on their behalf with the powerful interests of the INS. It was a major test case.

To facilitate amnesty applications, the INS had authorized a network of processing centers called Qualified Designated Entities. A major source of distress was that most of these centers had been approved in mid-April, leaving scant time to prepare. Each center was to be allotted about fifteen dollars for processing an application. Many in the church felt themselves in a dilemma. By establishing such centers, they reasoned, they could help refugees and offer them special sensitivity. But to do so meant working with the INS and taking the risk of being seen as government collaborators.

The quandary generated some agonizing debates and some contrasting decisions. In California, for example, three dioceses—San Francisco, Oakland, and Orange—refused to serve in that capacity, while Sacramento and San Jose joined the other dioceses in the state in going ahead with seeking designation after wrestling with the issue. An official of Oakland Catholic Charities gave to the *National Catholic Reporter* his view of why the diocese balked: "We operate in an advocacy role for our clients. Therefore, we don't want to be seen as operatives of the INS."

— ◄ ►—

AMONG LIBERALS, IN PARTICULAR, THE RUMPUS OVER LOYALTY AND DISSENT within Catholic America was blamed on the rising power of a conservative—some would say right-wing extremist—fringe that lobbied the Vatican much as a few self-appointed guardians of school decorum might petition the principal in an effort to straighten out classmates they considered unruly. Those accused most often of this sort of villainy were Catholics United for the Faith (CUF) and the publishing scourge of liberalism, the Wanderer Forum.

CUF's enemies portrayed it as a band of doctrinal desperadoes furiously attacking those they suspected of disloyalty. By reputation, they attacked their quarry (among them, of course, Curran and Hunthausen) by bad-mouthing them through a relentless letter-writing campaign directed mostly at the Vatican's top brass. They were believed to have many friends in high places who took their complaints very seriously indeed, giving them clout far beyond their small numbers.

As the casualties mounted in the struggle for Catholic America, the perceived influence of the alleged troublemakers magnified greatly among moderates and liberals, raising both the real and imagined power of the conservatives to new levels. They were suddenly being given credit for shaking the foundations of the church in the United States. Understandably, some of them delighted in this newfound notoriety after years of relative obscurity. All groups in this movement were tiny to begin with. Moreover, members of one group often belonged to one or more others, inflating the overall membership figures somewhat. Chuck Wilson, the executive director of the abuse-hunting Saint Joseph Foundation, for example, also sat on the board of CUF.

Inasmuch as this upsurge on the right was imagined among most Catholics as little more than a guerrilla army of the faith, the decision by *America's* editors to devote an issue to inspecting this development at closer range was significant. The two lead articles, both by Jesuits, addressed the issue. One, by the Reverend Patrick M. Arnold, S.J., a religious studies professor at Saint Louis University, examined the "Rise of Catholic Fundamentalism" in general. The other, by M. Timothy Iglesias, S.J., pursuing advanced theological studies at the Jesuit School of Theology in Berkeley, California, took a close look at the workings of CUF.

Father Arnold took as his premise that Catholicism in the United States was "even more severely threatened by the rise of its own distinctive brand of fundamentalism" than by any Protestant varieties of it. By the same token, he argued, "Though Catholic fundamentalism is a late and comparatively mild development within this trend, its rise can only be understood by comparing it with earlier, similar movements in other religions." In Father Arnold's opinion, the recent explosion of fundamentalism around the world accounted more than any other factor for the escalation of tensions in Catholic America. The bursting of right-wing religious groups onto the political stage during the 1980 presidential race, he said, signified the momentum that the movement had achieved (p. 298).

There were five "unhealthy characteristics" to this movement that Father Arnold held up for special mention (p. 298).

The first was its vengeful attitude toward perceived agents of change, an attitude fed by anger and fear. "In the United States, the phrase 'secular humanism' encapsulates all that is threatening to reactionary Protestants and Catholics alike," he wrote. Moreover, "Many Catholic fundamentalists even insist that the church itself has fallen prey to secular humanism, Marxism or atheism" (p. 299).

The second trait was closely related to the first. Frightened by change, Catholic fundamentalists retaliated against those believed to be the cause, mainly their fellow Catholics thought to have corrupted the faith rather than outsiders. The capacity of these self-appointed bearers of the true faith to "wound and intimidate liberal and moderate figures became undeniably evident in 1986," Father Arnold wrote, adding, "Theologians and religious women . . . have proved the most vulnerable to the purge" (p. 300).

The third was that Catholic fundamentalists, like their counterparts elsewhere, glorified an idealized past. It was, in their case, the halcyon days of the Holy Roman Catholic church before the convoking of the reform-minded Second Vatican Council.

The fourth earmark was the insistence upon "the absolute, infallible, inerrant and unambiguous authority of official religious texts." Protestant fundamentalists invested the Bible alone with such an exalted status; the Catholics instead gave reverence to the statements of the pope and the bishops. "Not only is defined dogma infallible," Father Arnold wrote, "but every teaching that proceeds from the Vatican is to be obeyed absolutely." In reality, he noted, some teachings received more attention than others. Those regarding "private sexual morality" were "given enormous weight," he pointed out, while those related to "social questions such as poverty, nuclear warfare, labor and human rights are, at best, regarded as matter for debate and, at worst, dismissed as 'interference with politics'" (p. 301).

The fifth characteristic was a deep involvement by the fundamentalists in right-wing politics that had developed during the 1980s. Father Arnold cited several recent incidents as evidence of the impact of this alliance. Among them was the alleged campaign by leading Catholics to discredit the 1984 Democratic vice presidential candidate, Geraldine Ferraro; the recruitment of Phyllis Schlafly, the successful crusader against the Equal Rights Amendment, to drum up Catholic support for the Strategic Defense Initiative ("Star Wars"); and the effort by the Catholic Lay Committee, led by prominent and wealthy Catholics, to damage the credibility of the bishops' pastoral letter on the economy.

The political reverberations of fundamentalism appeared especially disturbing to Father Arnold. The emergence of the church as a major defender of human rights and justice since Vatican II had challenged the "monopolies of political and economic power held by conservative groups, many of them Catholic," Father Arnold wrote. This had helped provoke an assault on liberals that resulted, among other things, in attempts to label them Marxist sympathizers or to impugn their theology and/or morality. "This latter tack, so far successful," he wrote, "has the effect of turning the church inward and making the members obsessed with questions of individual salvation and sexual morality. As a bonus, it has also left the American church divided and too exhausted to pursue much activity on behalf of social justice" (p. 302).

Father Iglesias's scrutiny of Catholics United for the Faith illustrated the difficulty of coming to hard-and-fast conclusions. The article was billed as a "case study in religious conservatism," and nowhere in it did the author define CUF as an example of fundamentalism. But the pairing of the article with that of Father Arnold left the impression that it had been intended as a subset of the larger universe of extremists.

Depending on the orientation of Catholics who might be asked, CUF was either the culprit behind the mischief against liberals like Curran and Hunthausen or the loyal, dogged guardian of the faith. Father Iglesias, described in the author's note as having been a student of economics and politics at Oxford and a community organizer in San Diego before returning to theology at Berkeley, emerged from his examination of CUF with Solomonic balance.

"By considering in turn CUF's Catholicism, its apostolate and its conservatism," he wrote, "I conclude that CUF is neither so wicked and dangerous as some of its opponents assume, nor the angel of light that it purports to be" (p. 303).

The facts of CUF's brief history were recounted. It was founded on September 26, 1968, in the wake of the revamping of Vatican II, by H. Lyman Stebbins, a retired stockbroker from New York. The aim, as set forth in the original statement of purpose, was "to be a rallying point, a point of unity, for the multitude of Catholics who have felt bewildered and blown about by the 1,000 winds of false doctrine being constantly puffed out by a 1,000 counterfeit teachers." CUF's membership, by its own admission, was fifteen thousand, the size of a single large suburban parish. The headquarters were in New Rochelle, New York (the same community where Opus Dei, that other thorn in the liberal flesh, was also located), and it had a staff of eleven. Nationally, full-time staff members were said to number about twenty-five. Even its harshest critics would have to admit it was a pretty small outfit to be supposedly raising that much hell.

Father Iglesias found the organization to be, not surprisingly, a lightning rod for angry and discontented Catholics looking for an outlet to vent their unhappiness with the church as it had metamorphosed since Vatican II. But he also discovered that CUF leaders moderated much of that frustration rather than fanning it. The group's stock-in-trade, of course, was promotion of its own understanding of orthodox Catholicism, summed up by Father Iglesias as fidelity to "truth and authority." Ignorance could result in confusion about the faith, but once the church's teachings were properly taught, CUF could make no excuse for dissent. Assent to the birth control encyclical was a key litmus test of commitment to orthodoxy, Father Iglesias added.

"CUF maintains that 'dissent' and the questions raised by 'dissenters' do not arise from intellectual rigor, ambiguity in key texts, sincerity, openness to one's experience or the struggle to evangelize faithfully in a wayward culture," he wrote, "but rather from a disordered mind or a disordered will" (p. 304).

Though CUF was committed to the teachings of church authority, Father Iglesias's microscope found inconsistencies and evasions to which any group of human beings was susceptible in applying theory to practice. CUF had gone out of its way to find justification for playing down the significance of the bishops' pastoral on nuclear war, for example, and in another case had worked against the *Christ Among Us* catechism, regarded as an atrocity among conservatives because of its teachings on sexuality, even though real bishops had put their stamp of approval on it.

On the question of whether CUF was out to build its own power base in the church, Father Iglesias found the evidence mixed. How much punch could the organization deliver? There could be no doubt that the group brooked no disagreement with its line and rejected any notion that there could be more than one interpretation of the truth and that it, like other groups, wanted good press.

He concluded, "Given the character of its participation in national campaigns and in offering input for bishops' conferences and synods, it is clear that, whatever else CUF is, it is a pressure group, and at times a very effective one. However, unlike special-interest lobbies, CUF is not seeking to promote its private interest so much as to influence the common policies of the church along the lines of its views of orthodoxy" (p. 306).

Was CUF, finally, a group of reactionary extremists or responsible conservatives? Father Iglesias looked at the group's strong emphasis on personal, spiritual renewal and its generally uncritical submission to authority. He reviewed its enemies list: "the liberal consensus, neo-modernism, secular humanism, developmental psychology, the religion of self-fulfillment . . . in addition to the ones a person might expect, such as the 'pro-choice' movement" (p. 307). All this had cast the organization widely as radicals beyond the pale.

But this was both a misreading of CUF's aims and a twisting of its record. In his view, the organization deserved better treatment. "Despite its past victories, its careful leadership and its good will," he decided, "CUF is not accepted by many as the legitimate, if conservative, group that it is" (p. 309).

━ ━

ON THE AFTERNOON OF APRIL 23, THE SMALL AUDITORIUM AT PRINCETON Theological Seminary was packed a full fifteen minutes before the start of the highly publicized lecture. The overflow crowd stood in the side aisles and at the rear of the room or squatted compactly in available spaces between chair legs, stacks of notepads and books, and feet. They eagerly awaited the arrival of the Reverend Charles Curran, Ph.D., professor of theology at Catholic University, *suspendus*.

Promptly at 1:30, the hottest Christian ethicist in the land was being introduced. He acknowledged the lavish praise with a self-deprecating grin and took his place at the podium to deliver what might best be characterized as the Curran stump speech, a scholarly brief on his own behalf against Rome's charges of illicit dissent, the generic statement of his case that had been given in various forms countless times before. The Princeton audience, made up largely of sympathetic Protestants and Catholics and not a few curious onlookers, greeted him with loud applause.

Father Curran stood tall and straight, wearing a dark gray suit, blue shirt, and striped tie. His black hair was, as usual, combed back, and he peered out toward his audience through metal-framed glasses. His head was large, his face open, and his features full. A high, broad forehead was anchored by a solid chin. His skin appeared sallow and soft, and he wore a wan look. Physical ailments had accompanied the stress of inquisition and public clamor. He had only recently spent ten days in the hospital for treatment of phlebitis. His voice, normally light-timbred, faded and cracked more than usual. He appeared tired and downcast, though not a shade less stalwart than he had all during the long ordeal.

A week before he had announced that he would teach at Cornell University during the coming academic year. The university had invited him to become its first visiting professor of Catholic studies. Meanwhile, his legal appeal for reinstatement as an active teacher at Catholic University was still awaiting a court decision.

In his lecture, Father Curran rested much of his case on the claim that the church had demonstrated a double standard. On the one hand, he said, the popes over the past century had considerably changed the church's teachings on social questions of economics and politics. But on the other, he continued, the church had refused to reform any of its principal teachings on sexuality. This showed, Father Curran said, that the church was not opposed to change itself, but that the changes were uneven and sometimes unacknowledged as such.

The framework for his analysis was the distinction, often invoked by Catholic scholars to help explain current tensions, between "classical" and "historical" ways of thinking. A classical consciousness, deeply embedded in Catholic tradition, understood the church as unchanging, absolute, and immutable, its teachings springing from eternal fixed, revealed principles. It was therefore deductive and largely objective. A historical consciousness, which marked the modern age, saw the church and its teachings as partial, changing, and contingent, conditioned by the "lessons" of historical experience. It was, by contrast, inductive and open to subjective, personal factors.

On social questions, Father Curran contended, Rome had moved from the classical to the historical. During most of the nineteenth century, Father Curran said, the church had fought against the drive for freedom and liberation throughout Europe, condemning capitalism, in his description, as "economic freedom gone wild." But a turnabout started with Pope Leo XIII's landmark social encyclical, *Rerum novarum,* in 1893. The gist of this and later response by popes to historical forces was to seek a middle ground between the extremes of collectivism and individualism. Not the least of these developments was the church's gradual acceptance of capitalism.

Moreover, as totalitarian regimes arising in the twentieth century became a threat to the sanctity of Catholic believers, Father Curran said, the church defended their interests by evolving a concept of personal rights ("Catholic tradition had talked not about rights but duties," Father Curran said). Such rights were explicitly defined by Pope John XXIII, father of the Second Vatican Council, in his famous 1963 encyclical, *Pacem in terris.* Two years before, in *Mater et magistra,* the same pope had defined an ideal social order as based on justice, truth, and character. Paul VI advanced the teaching further, declaring in his 1971 encyclical, *Octagesima adveniems* ("A Call to Action"), that among those rights were "equality" and "participation." The Second Vatican Council itself had broken sharply with church tradition by endorsing the principle of religious freedom. It had also heeded John XXIII's call to pay attention to the "signs of the times," the lessons that could be drawn from the passing historical scene. The church had backed away from claiming to have all the answers to the social question.

So the church's social teachings had obviously undergone great change over the past hundred years in light of the upheavals in the world around it, Father Curran said. Rome's views had not been inflexible. Not so with its morality, he added. In that department the church had remained rigid despite what seemed clear precedent for allowing a more historical approach.

There were three "models of moral life," Father Curran asserted. One was the teleological, which focused on the "goals to be attained" in the end. The emphasis was on final purposes. The second was "deontology," which had to do with "duties, laws, and obligations" that were inscribed in human nature from the first. The third was "relational/responsibility" toward "God, neighbor, and self," which underscored the subjective elements of morality.

Before Vatican II, the deontological model had prevailed, he said, resulting in a heavy stress on obedience to a set of eternal, external moral laws. Vatican II had helped shift the focus toward human experience as a source of insight and teaching to augment the church's objective standards. That direction had found its way into moral theology. The nature of human relationships, the intentions and consequences that went with moral choices, personal differences and the ends sought by certain actions, all had become part of the wider moral discussion. It was more this-worldly, concerned with particular circumstances and effects.

But Rome had effectively denied the legitimacy of the "relational/responsibility" model, thereby sticking to hard-and-fast principles. Historical consciousness might nurture social teaching, but it could not be allowed to affect personal and sexual morality. Father Curran tested his analysis against three recent moral documents, the 1976 statement on sexual ethics, the 1986 document on homosexuality, and the 1987 instruction on human fertility. None wavered from traditional conclusions, though the language of personalism and the awareness of historical circumstances could be found in all three, he noted.

"In these recent documents, the law model is primary," Father Curran said. "When we use a law model, something is either forbidden or allowed. There are no gray areas." By contrast, he said, the U.S. bishops' pastoral letter on nuclear war had left "a lot of gray areas which allow Catholics to disagree and still be loyal Catholics."

He continued, "It seems to me there is no doubt that historical consciousness and personalism are accepted in social teachings but not in sexual and personal teachings."

Nearing the close of his talk, he cited a common danger and his own greatest problem with the church. The danger was to assume that "tradition stopped fifty years before we were born." His problem with Roman Catholicism, as he saw it, "was not with its 'ands' but with its 'buts.'"

Those words condensed the theme of the lecture and the struggle of his professional and vocational life. His allusion to the inability of Rome to allow the "and" that signified ambiguity in a rush to close discussion with a "but" captured the difficulty in which he was trapped. His contention was that it was possible to hold fast to the sacred dogma of the church *and* at the same time to question the noninfallible teachings. The church's reply, in effect, was that it was indeed possible to speculate on the noninfallible teachings *but* necessary to submit to them nonetheless.

IN AN ADJOINING ROOM LINED WITH PORTRAITS OF PAST PATRIARCHS OF THE school, Father Curran reflected on his months under pressure from Rome and Catholic University. The place had made him think about the reaction to him ecumenically. Some had protested loudly in his behalf. But strangely, he said, some of those Protestant ethicists who stood by him during his first scrape with the Vatican twenty years ago were tacitly in Rome's corner this time. He suspected one reason was that they had been impressed by Rome's initiatives on human rights and other social issues and were "upset that the Catholic church was being embarrassed" now in this way.

Father Curran was described by colleagues as tougher and more durable than he might look, but by his own admission this had been a rough period. "Once I decided to go through this at the university, I knew it wouldn't be the most pleasant of times," he said. At this stage he was glad to have the option of going to Cornell for a year. He had been approached by the board in the winter of 1986 and had accepted last October. Though most of the faculty had supported him, he said, "I decided it would be good to get out of that situation, get some space and distance. I just haven't been able to concentrate. The negative side, of course, is that ultimately it becomes an adversarial relationship with the university." He said he'd tried to remind himself that pastors faced far greater difficulties every day in their parishes than he had had to go through.

He had seen the ax begin to fall "in the summer of '84 when the pope started his series of talks [on *Humanae vitae,* the birth control encyclical]." After one of the talks, Father Curran recalled, the head of the papal office for marriage and the family held an extraordinary press conference to name four theologians (including

Hans Küng and himself) causing problems for the church with regard to those issues. Cardinal Ratzinger had likewise complained publicly that "too many U.S.
theologians were dissenting from the church." The omens were much clearer
than messages on tea leaves.

The American bishops had "kept a low profile publicly" on the controversy surrounding him, he said. Cardinal Bernardin let it be known that he favored some
form of compromise, but otherwise, he said, "there was no public support by bishops at all. I've received letters from twenty bishops, most expressing support or
concern.

"What I say is that support never becomes a reality until bishops say at a public meeting, 'Pope, we love you, but you're wrong on this.'"

As it was, among many academics who felt powerless to do much more than
voice protests and church authorities who might have done more, he had been
set adrift, left to fend for himself. To those with influence, his was deemed a lost,
even unworthy cause, certainly not one worth risking reputation for. He would
go it alone save for some long loyal supporters.

APRIL ALSO BROUGHT THESE DEVELOPMENTS:

- A new version of the New Testament aimed at removing bias against women
  and Jews was published. It was a revision of the 1970 New American Bible,
  one of several approved for use in the church; it took a sixteen-member translation committee, including nine women, six years to complete. The effort
  was to be true to the Greek text in ridding passages of inappropriate male ter-
  minology. Generic words such as *persons* and *human beings* were substituted
  for male terms in several passages, and censorial references aimed at Jews
  were set in a fuller context of judgment on all humanity. God language remained masculine. The revision had been prepared under the auspices of
  the Catholic Biblical Apostolate with special attention to the needs of the
  ear. The reason was that its words would resound in parishes across the land
  each day. By default, the New American Bible had become the popular choice
  as the source from which the Scripture lessons were drawn for standard lec-
  tionaries (the other two authorized sources, the Jerusalem Bible and the
  Catholic edition of the Revised Standard Version, had fallen into disuse).

    The Reverend Stephen J. Hartegen, O.F.M., who headed the project, ex-
  plained the reason for recasting male references. "The question about dis-
  criminating against women affects the largest number of people and arouses
  the greatest degree of interest and concern," though he added that there was
  "little agreement about these problems or about the best way to deal with
  them." It was not possible, he said, "to please everyone," but the revisions had

been a start. *Commonweal* applauded the new NAB as a step forward but wished it had been even "more sure-footed and bold." Joseph Sobran, writing in the *Wanderer* (April 16), didn't see what all the fuss was about. "We go to church to get something permanent, not something trendy," he wrote. "We can get the trendy elsewhere. And I doubt that anyone is given scandal by a few gender pronouns."

- There was renewed protest by the bishops against the death penalty. On April 22, the Supreme Court rejected the claim by a Georgia man that the death sentence imposed on him was meted out unfairly to blacks such as himself and thus constituted "cruel and unusual punishment." The Court conceded that "sophisticated statistical studies" showed that the sentence was indeed applied in a racially biased manner but that more evidence was needed, and it upheld the right of Georgia to go ahead with execution. On April 24, the general secretary of the United States Catholic Conference, Monsignor Daniel F. Hoye, decried the decision on behalf of the bishops and reiterated the conference's moral objection to capital punishment. Regrettably, Monsignor Hoye said in a statement, the Court's ruling had, in effect, declared that even "where race is shown to be a significant factor" it was not weighty enough in itself to disallow taking a convict's life. The evidence in the case "strengthens our conviction" that the death penalty was handed out in an "irrational and discriminatory fashion," Monsignor Hoye said. "The system under which criminals are sentenced is such that race often plays a prominent role in determining whether they will live or die. Although there are equally strong reasons for its abolition, we believe that capital punishment under these conditions is surely 'cruel and unusual punishment.'"

- The leftist activist group Catholics Speak Out, an offshoot of the Quixote Center in Maryland, advised John Paul II to do more listening and less talking during his September swing through the United States. In their petition, copies of which were sent to thousands of constituents for their signature, the group urged the pope "to reduce the number or length of your talks by half and spend at least half of your time in each city listening to the voices of the Catholic people." The teach-in strategy, they argued, might help salve the wounds. "There are serious tensions and divisions within our church over issues such as dissent, the exercise of authority, human sexuality, and women in ministry and decision-making of the church," the petition said. "These tensions and divisions will not be resolved, or even dealt with, in the spirit of the Gospel, unless we respectfully listen to each other in ways that allow people to share the varied viewpoints that grow from their hearts and consciences. As you said well, *'Dialogue is the language of love.'*" (italics theirs).

Meanwhile, there was no sign that the pope was about to let up on his speechifying—his stock-in-trade—let alone cut it in half. Teams of Americans were frantically rewriting texts of those addresses to meet various suggestions and criticisms. Among those most personally involved in the process was Donna Hanson, a social worker from Spokane, one of those selected to speak to the pope as a representative of the laity. She had read a proposed draft from the advisory committee during the winter and found it "totally unlike what I would say." In an intense forty-eight-hour period, she had culled the results of a brainstorming session with her family and the themes from the committee draft and woven them into her own version of the speech. It pleased her. Host cities, too, were busily gearing up, and the bishops' conference was shipping out tons of preparation materials. In Miami, the first stop, the Reverend Thomas O'Dwyer, who was in charge of the visit, said the event was generating "an overwhelming amount of enthusiasm." In his two days in Miami, the pope was scheduled to give seven speeches.

• The trial of the Epiphany Plowshares defendants ended in a hung jury. The four antiwar activists—Lin Romano, Gregory Boertje, the Reverend Thomas McGann, and the Reverend Dexter Lanctot—had gone to trial on March 31 on charges related to their break-in at the Willow Grove Naval Air Station north of Philadelphia on January 6 (the feast of the Epiphany). In the incursion, the group admitted to hammering two helicopters and a P-3 prop jet and dumping blood on the damaged goods as a protest against the nation's nuclear policies. After weighing allegations that the group had engaged in trespassing, conspiracy, and damage to government property, the jury admitted on April 6 that it was unable to return a verdict. The four activists, members of a larger Plowshares movement that had staged many protests in recent years, contended that their actions were inspired by God's call to peacemaking. The two priests were still under suspension by the Archdiocese of Philadelphia for conduct considered violent and out of step with acceptable church behavior. A new trial was set for May 11.

• In Pittsburgh, there was a return of women to ceremonial foot washing. In 1986, Bishop Anthony Bevilacqua forbade women to take part in Holy Thursday reenactments of Jesus' act of humility in bathing the feet of his disciples at the Last Supper. The bishop drew on traditional thinking that such participation was potentially sexually provocative to priests doing the washing. Howls of protest arose in Pittsburgh and elsewhere on grounds that the prohibition was an indignity to women. An appeal to the U.S. bishops' committee on liturgy went against the bishop in March, and Bishop Bevilacqua announced that the decision would be left to "the prudent pastoral judgment" of each priest in charge. Many parishes went back to their standard practice of including women. The bishop himself, on the appointed day, April 16, presided at a Holy Thursday mass in a parish that had never made use of the rite. In his speech earlier in the month imploring the church to become more compassionate, Bishop Untener of Saginaw had noted with dismay that the foot washing ceremony was optional in parishes and asked rhetorically why it did not receive more attention. "Probably for the same reason that the apostle Peter had trouble with it at the Last Supper," he had told the religious educators. "It just didn't seem right for Jesus to be doing a thing like that."

- A warning shot was fired across the Vatican bows. The Reverend Richard P. McBrien, chairman of Notre Dame's theology department, delivered an ultimatum of sorts to Rome during a speech to the Notre Dame Club of Chicago on April 22. If the Vatican decided to push ahead with its schema governing institutions of higher learning related to the church, Father McBrien said, then Notre Dame would likely abolish its Catholic identity established under canon law and remain "Catholic" in a voluntary theological sense only. Notre Dame's outgoing president, Father Hesburgh, had been in the forefront of the opposition to the proposed schema, arguing that it could undermine the academic freedom and the autonomy of Catholic universities. But Rome's apparent insistence on such regulations—including one that would subject teachers of theology to hierarchical approval—had pushed tensions steadily higher. Father McBrien appeared to convey the full resolve of Father Hesburgh and many like-minded educators not to sit still for what they saw as Rome's unwarranted intrusion into their affairs. In the "worst case scenario," Father McBrien said, Rome would force universities to obey no matter what the resulting harm or quit being technically Catholic. For Notre Dame's board, he continued, that would mean either "remaining a university in the American sense of the word" or choosing to give up the "'honor' of being called a *Catholic* university in the *juridical* sense of the word. Father Hesburgh has assured me more than once that our board of trustees would follow the first course. Notre Dame would remain a university in the American sense of the word, and would also remain Catholic, but in the *theological,* not the juridical, sense of the word."

- Cardinal Bernardin dissented on the issue of artificial insemination—or was that *really* what he said? Speaking to medical students and researchers at the University of Chicago about the Vatican's guidelines on human reproduction—the first major prelate to do so since a storm of publicity greeted the statement's March release—the cardinal called on scientists to give the document a fair hearing. Its rejection of technological methods of procreation did not mean it deserved to be ranked on a level with the church's ill-advised scolding of Galileo, Cardinal Bernardin argued. On the contrary, he said, it was built on solid principles and sound reasoning to the effect that "love-making and life making" were inseparably linked. That ruled out all artificial means except those that aided an act of sexual intercourse itself to achieve that end.

But then, characteristically, he threw in something that sounded like a slightly convoluted disclaimer. Referring to his sympathy for childless couples who saw artificial insemination as furthering the church's standards of lovemaking and life making, the cardinal said, "My heart reaches out to them. Theirs is a difficult burden, and I share their pain. We must offer them love, support, and understanding. And in the end, after prayerful and conscientious reflection on this teaching, they must make their own decision."

Had he just said couples were free to make up their own minds? Didn't that put distance between him and the Vatican's absolute ban? The media thought so. A press release from the Chicago archdiocese attempted to clear up the flap over the comment, but appeared to do little more than leave the loophole open, albeit in fuzzier terms. Though the cardinal's remark had been interpreted as putting him at odds with Rome, the press release said, "the cardinal wishes to point out that the context of his statement makes it evident that he was not implying that the church's teaching in this instance is merely advisory, something which couples can accept or reject. In the final analysis, they must take the concrete decisions following the traditional norms governing the correct formation of conscience." Now, let's see. It was not okay to dismiss the Vatican's instruction, but maybe you could do so if you followed your conscience after having abided by the approved steps. Hmmm.

⬤ ⬤

ON THE PREVIOUS SUNDAY, CRAIG HAD FLOWN HIS MODIFIED MARINE CORPS JET fighter for the first time alone. The Skyhawk was "more of a hot rod" than the trainer aircraft he'd handled before, he said, and taking off was "like being in the end of a rocket." It had made him feel, he said, "like the most powerful person in the world."

Ahead lay lessons in flying closer formations with four or five other jets, more weapons instruction, a couple of cross-country instrument flights, and the toughest test of all, two weeks aboard an aircraft carrier practicing the most harrowing of landing patterns. Now two-thirds of the way through the year-long obstacle course, Craig had seen a couple of dozen classmates wash out for poor performance in the classroom and cockpit.

The Reverend Charles Curran, professor of theology at Catholic University, holds a news conference on August 20, 1986, in response to the Vatican action two days earlier stripping him of his right to teach Catholic theology. Curran lost his right to teach because of his dissent from the church's teachings on issues of sexual ethics.   (UPI/Bettmann)

Mario Cuomo, here receiving communion from Archbishop John J. O'Connor at St. Patrick's Cathedral in 1984, was a powerful, attractive symbol of a new independence among Catholic Americans.   (Religious News Service/Wide World)

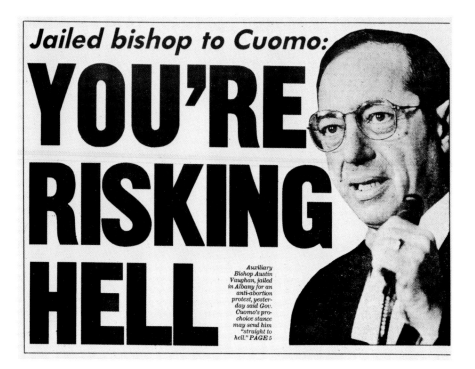

Jailed bishop to Cuomo:
YOU'RE RISKING HELL

Auxiliary Bishop Austin Vaughan, jailed in Albany for an anti-abortion protest, yesterday said Gov. Cuomo's pro-choice stance may send him "straight to hell." PAGE 5

In January 1987, Auxiliary Bishop Austin Vaughan, jailed in Albany for an anti-abortion protest, called Governor Cuomo a "Sunday Catholic" whose pro-choice stand may send him "straight to hell."   (Religious News Service)

Archbishop Raymond Hunthausen of Seattle tells reporters on November 14, 1986, that he has no intention of stepping down after his fellow bishops, meeting in Washington, gave him minimum support in his battle with the Vatican.   (UPI/Bettmann)

Bishop Joseph Howze of Biloxi, Mississippi, the nation's only black bishop in charge of a diocese, incenses the altar at Washington's National Shrine of the Immaculate Conception. Bishop Howze was the main celebrant at the opening liturgy of the National Black Catholic Congress on May 22, 1987, which drew delegates from more than one hundred dioceses across the United States. (Catholic News Service)

The Reverend John McNeill (right) and Dr. John Boswell (center) converse after a conference on homosexuality in the church held March 20, 1987, at Union Theological Seminary in New York, during which Father McNeill criticized the recent Vatican document on homosexuality. McNeill had been forced to leave the Jesuit order in January 1987 after refusing to give up his ministry to homosexuals. (Religious New Service)

Sister Francesca Thompson, professor of Afro-American studies at Fordham University, sounded a restive note in her keynote speech at the National Black Catholic Congress. "We have stood at the door of our church for many a year, timidly knocking, anxiously beseeching, and often begging for recognition," she said. "Now we come to insist on recognition." (Catholic News Service)

Rabbi Avi Weiss (third from left) and a group of U.S. Jews demonstrate in St. Peter's Square on June 24, 1987, against the pope's decision to receive Austrian President Kurt Waldheim. They wear prayer shawls over facsimiles of the uniform worn by inmates of Nazi death camps. (Reuters/Bettmann)

Austrian President Kurt Waldheim with Pope John Paul II during a private audience at the Vatican on June 25, 1987. (Reuters/Bettmann)

Molly Yard, (left) then president of the National Organization for Women, and co-protesters at a demonstration for women's rights outside the Vatican Embassy in Washington on August 26, 1987. (Reuters/Bettmann)

Demonstrators hold a candle-light vigil near the Vatican Embassy on September 2, 1987, calling for an end to discrimination against gay men and lesbians within the Catholic Church.
(UPI/Bettmann)

CATHOLIC
THEOLOGY
ON
GAY PEOPLE
IS
INTRINSICALLY
EVIL.

In Florida, thousands of worshipers, many waving Cuban flags, greeted the pope as he arrived at the site for mass on September 11. A persistent rainstorm with lightning and thunder later forced the pontiff to cut short his religious celebration for the estimated 200,000 who attended the mass.   (UPI/Bettmann)

A wind-whipped, grim-faced Pope John Paul II takes part in a mass at the University of New Orleans on September 12.   (UPI/Bettmann)

The pope is presented with an American eagle feather by Emmett White, a Pima tribe medicine man, during his visit to Phoenix on September 14.   (UPI/Bettmann)

Pope John Paul II hugs four-year-old Brendan O'Rourke, a San Franciscan who contracted AIDS through a blood transfusion, prior to services on September 17 at Mission Dolores Church. (UPI/Bettmann)

The everyday rigors sometimes got to him. "You can't possibly realize what it is to be graded every day of your life," he would tell his fiancée sometimes in frustration. But at other times he accepted it as normal routine. "As soon as you get your wings, you go to another school to learn another aircraft," he said stoically. "I view it as constant testing."

He had seen friends fail. How would he handle that fate? "If you don't fly well, people look down on you," he began. "I don't think I'd contemplate suicide, but I might run off to a mountain to think about things." He tried to remember that the pressure had a logic to it. "The skills we learn here serve well in places where there are huge stresses." In combat, for instance. Still, he tried not to become totally obsessed with performance. Watching others made him more circumspect. "Certain guys don't have balance," he observed. "They have great grades, but their lives are empty. I'm lucky I guess. My girlfriend and my family have encouraged me to have interest in other things."

Craig valued his independent mind. He subscribed to the *New Yorker, Atlantic,* and *Harper's* and read books as time allowed. He pursued history most avidly. In college, he saw himself as something of an academic beachcomber, following the lead of his curiosity and collecting thoughts, but only randomly buckling down to course work. In his collegiate freethinking style he saw shades of his father, an itinerant teacher with a lively, eclectic mind. Craig thought he would mostly go his own way as his father always had.

Politically speaking, a change in surroundings had accentuated his independent streak. As an undergraduate at Indiana University, he had been, by his own admission, "a right-wing Marine officer candidate." He had leaned that way partly in reaction against campus liberalism. In the Marine Corps, the heavy overlay of hawkish group-think had moved him closer to a peacenik stance. "Now," he chuckled, "I'm the young Democrat whose father supported Gene McCarthy against the Vietnam war."

Marine pilots and their superior officers formed his community now, and his place within it was becoming defined. He had sized up his companions. "Many of them have closed minds when it comes to what's going on in the world," he said. "Their first joking response to a world crisis is to send the carriers to clean it up. It may be a joke, but 75 percent of the guys believe that.

"Compared to most others, I think my views are different, though some of the instructors don't know how I feel about some things," Craig said.

The Reagan administration was continuing to threaten rebels in El Salvador and the Sandinistas in Nicaragua. Despite the uproar caused by the Iran-Contra scandal, saber rattling struck Craig as unrelenting. Imminent U.S. military intervention on the side of the Contras was often rumored within his squadron. Marine pilot-trainees had reason to be concerned.

"One instructor said he hoped I was ready to ship off to Central America," Craig recalled being told tauntingly. "I asked him what he thought acting tough like that was going to accomplish. That's when he stopped listening.

"I'm one of those who doesn't think Central America would necessarily turn out like Vietnam, but what would be achieved if we invaded?" he asked, begging the question. "What would be our goal if we did go for more overt military presence? It appears to me that the people there are leaning toward socialism because it looks like a better path to them. I think we should accept their ideas about how they want to run their country. I don't think we should be the world's policeman."

Craig scorned easy military victories designed "to make everybody feel good." He had aired such views and had gained, he felt, a reputation as "probably one of the only advocates of moderation" in his unit. But he had grown comfortable in that role.

"I don't any longer mind the comment that I'm not a Marine at heart," he said. "I don't think anybody should be."

Craig's repeatedly credited his father and his education for his penchant for ideas and cold analysis. The church, by contrast, figured nowhere in that development, so far as he knew. He had come to discover the church's intellectual side, but at no time during a childhood household steeped in Catholicism and all his years in Catholic schools had he been led to connect mind and faith. He still found it difficult to link the two. "When I think of the church," he said, "I don't think of that [intellectual] tradition. I think of it as trying to do good, trying to help people with problems and disciplining people.

"I would say that when I think of the church I think of Mother Teresa," Craig said. He had seen the movie version of *The Name of the Rose* recently, and it had caused him to reflect on the church's darker side. He remained basically at home in the church, but he put himself at some distance from some of its teachings, particularly those concerning sexuality and notably the ban on artificial birth control and premarital sex. He had also read recent reports of the church's stand against homosexuality. That bothered him.

"I'm not necessarily a supporter of gay life-styles," he said, "but I'm not a fag basher either. I'd like to understand it. The church needs to deal with the fact that there have always been gay people in the world. There are gay people in the military. Unfortunately, that has been covered up too."

May
1·9·8·7

— ~

SPRING HAD COME EARLY TO THE UPPER MIDWEST, USHERED IN by an unusually tepid, nearly snowless winter. For Anthony, it was the most joyous season of rebirth in many years.

Only three months before, he had resigned himself, at age fifty-six, to a few more uneventful years at Celestron before retirement. He had grown up with a burgeoning company that seemed to him sadly losing concern for its employees. The "promotion" he had received two years before felt more like a dead-end transfer—the kind of move intended to store a fading executive—than an opportunity to strut his stuff. He had been put on the shelf, he believed, and had to make the best of it.

But the picture had changed dramatically. A new group vice president had come in from Europe to reorganize the international division, and Anthony had become a prime beneficiary of the change. For some time, Anthony had tried to promote strategies for improving Celestron's share of the fire alarm security systems market. But nobody appeared to take his ideas seriously until the new man came to town. This vice president had heard Anthony out and given him the green light, going so far as to order his immediate boss to give Anthony a free hand to develop his concepts.

Within that division of the corporate universe, Anthony was suddenly a star. He felt on top again, like the young executive, full of pluck and promise, he once had been. His ego, starved for appreciation, had fattened up on heaps of attention. That stroke of good fortune had emboldened him, and it had paid off.

Relations with his boss had even improved after a rocky start several months before. "One day soon after he took over he told me he wasn't sure I'd fit in," he remembered. "I told him he needed me more than I needed him. I said, 'I've brought more recognition to this organization than anybody, including you.' He was stunned. I was in the dog house. But now he has come to realize that I know what I'm talking about."

In his thirty-second year with Celestron, he thought his stock had never been higher. "One of the veepees said I'd become an elder statesman," he reported proudly. "He said, 'Everyone knows you and respects you and what you say.' He thought I was the best known Celestron employee in the world. Even my boss said the other day that he's learned a lot from listening to me."

He was basking not only in the approval but in the satisfaction of seeing product sales take off around the world. Recently he had returned from the Far East and a seven-day, three-nation trip to Latin America. Europe was next. His normal routine was to meet with company representatives and give talks. It was not a chore, he said, "but a labor of love." That was true of his work in general now. Retirement was no longer an oasis Anthony yearned for. When to retire was now much more his decision, perhaps later, four or five years from now, than sooner. He was having fun. Newfound success had awakened his brash streak. Foreign sales were surging, closing the gap with the domestic side. "I've wanted to grow our market share, and I finally got the opportunity to do it. I'm gonna beat them," Anthony boasted.

The other fount of Anthony's well-being, his family, was also experiencing good times. In his exuberance, the virtues of his wife and his three grown adopted children stood out to him even more. The company's rediscovery of his worth translated into his renewed admiration for them. "People who know us well say we come as close to a perfect marriage as they've ever seen," Anthony said over breakfast one morning in a pancake house on the outskirts of the city. His eyes glistened, and his voice was choked.

On Mother's Day, the whole gang, including the newest baby grandchild, would be at his home, and he looked forward eagerly to it. "My whole work experience has allowed me to do well for my family," he said. "There's a lot to love here. We don't have a mansion, but I felt good when a business associate from a foreign country said how homey he thought our home was. My wife gets nervous about entertaining people like that now, but I tell her we're good enough just the way we are."

With all the blessings showered upon him, Anthony still experienced twinges of uncertainty. He had "far exceeded" his expectations at Celestron, making more money than he had ever imagined he might, yet he lapsed into moments when he was overcome by a sense of being undeserving. It lingered even when he reminded himself of his "super wife who understands me" and his "three good kids." He often used the word "lucky" to describe his circumstances.

That luck had begun in boyhood, he thought. Being the tenth and last child of an immigrant Italian day laborer had its advantages, he reckoned, inasmuch as the older children had suffered through grinding poverty that he had been largely spared. Losing his mother to mental illness when he was just three had been the severest of blows. They had taken her to an institution, never to return home. As a small child he had relied on the care of his older siblings and the kindness of neighbors. He had learned to do things for himself at an early age, something he counted as a decidedly mixed blessing. The church had also taken him under its wing, encouraging him to pursue his studies. Largely because of that support, he had been the only one in the family to attend college.

He did wonder why things had turned out that way for him, he said, whereas fate had treated his brothers less kindly. It wasn't reflexive for him to think God had ordained it that way. God, for Anthony, was personal but did not get involved in charting individual fates. "I don't think in those terms," he said. "I'm pretty practical. I hope I have a good relationship with God, but don't know for sure. I don't *feel* that I'm special, but I hope I am. I do know how blessed I am, and I hope the kind of life I've led reflects God's being pleased with that."

The boost in his prospects and morale had also led him to a major decision regarding his parish. He had stewed over whether his annoyance with the new, modernizing pastor was sufficient to cause him to leave. His friend the former pastor was long gone, as was, for the most part, the old-fashioned church he had represented. The new pastor was, understandably enough, a promoter of Vatican II changes in liturgy and other aspects of parish life. Congregational singing was one of those changes Anthony found most rankling. "They're doing more singing in the liturgy than when he first came," he said, with a sigh. "I didn't think that was possible."

But to Anthony, commitment to a parish was a matter of tremendous meaning. And his relationships to priests were crucial, dating from his youth and those years when he had entertained the idea of entering the seminary himself. He didn't intend for a moment to become less observant a Catholic; it was only a matter of where he would fulfill that commitment. Anthony measured a priest largely by his homilies, and there he found the new pastor a poor stylist. Still, he had to admit, he had been listening to the homilies more closely and had found that the young man sometimes "had a couple of good ideas," which unfortunately, added Anthony, himself a fairly accomplished speech maker by his own estimation, were delivered clumsily.

He had come to a conclusion after much contemplation. Several attractive parishes in the general area existed as alternatives, though they were no more traditional in the way that his own had been under the former pastor. Anthony considered those options, then decided to remain where he was. His protest would take the form of reduced offerings to the parish collection. It was his compromise. "I'm not giving what I could if I had a pastor I could work with better," he said solemnly. "Sometimes it's all quite frustrating."

ON THE MORNING OF MAY 5 IN THE BARREN NEVADA DESERT, TWO BISHOPS TRES-passed. Along with nearly a hundred priests, nuns, and lay Catholics from around the nation, they crossed into the Nevada nuclear weapons test site and thereby de liberately broke the law.

Bishops Charles Buswell, who had headed the Pueblo, Colorado, diocese before his retirement, and Bishop Thomas Gumbleton, the auxiliary bishop of Detroit, helped plan the symbolic act of protest to mark the fourth anniversary of the is-suance of the U.S. bishops' pastoral letter on nuclear war. Bishop Gumbleton had served on the five-bishop committee that wrote the pastoral. Pax Christi–USA, a Catholic peace group, organized the event, which started with a prayer vigil May 3, the actual day the pastoral letter had been adopted.

Bishop Gumbleton, president of Pax Christi; Sister Mary Lou Kownacki, the group's executive director; Bishop Buswell; and the scores of other protesters ig-nored a plea from Captain James Merlino of the Nye County sheriff's department to stay off government property. In keeping with their widely publicized intent, they trooped onto the test site. Accordingly, ninety-eight were arrested, clapped in plastic handcuffs, shuttled aboard buses, and hauled off for booking in the town of Beatty, sixty miles away.

It was the first time U.S. bishops had ever been arrested for protesting nuclear arms. An additional dozen other bishops had sent messages of support. Among them was Bishop Maurice Dingman, who had stepped down as bishop of Des Moines just a month before. Bishop Dingman, immobilized by a stroke, endorsed the protest as an effort to "help save the human race from total annihilation by a nuclear holocaust."

The rally in Nevada was, of course, very much a Pax Christi thing to do. The group was by nature antiwar and antiviolence of any kind. It was on the pacifist fringe, and certain bishops had taken certain risks with Rome by becoming ac-tive in it. Bishop Gumbleton, a member of the committee that wrote the peace pas-toral, was one; Archbishop Hunthausen was another. The fact that their views differed sharply from the church's prevailing "just war" theory had, in the opin-ion of many of the church's political pundits, cost both men dearly. The strong likelihood that Bishop Gumbleton would remain an auxiliary bishop forever, de-spite his manifest talents, and Archbishop Hunthausen's well-documented woes both testified to the price of bucking the establishment. Among their colleagues in the hierarchy, the Pax Christi bishops were radical peaceniks, sincere, and, at least under the current regime in Rome, perhaps, unrealistic and out of favor.

But the protest carried significance beyond that of civil disobedience on the part of a dovish group whose convictions and 1960s tactics were widely known and, among many Catholics, at least grudgingly respected. It was one of many indications that a major piece of unfinished business threatened to undermine the peace pastoral itself. It was a reminder that the bishops had only postponed the toughest question of all.

The arduous shaping of the pastoral, "The Challenge of Peace: God's Promise and Our Response," and its issuance had thrust the bishops into the public eye as never before. In the third and final draft of the statement, the bishops had condemned nuclear war as immoral. Weighing the possibility for destruction by the church's traditional criteria for the waging of a "just war," they had ruled out "first strike" strategy and proscribed any actual use of nuclear weapons.

But on the issue of whether the stockpiling of a nuclear deterrent could be ethically justified, the bishops found themselves in a wrenching dilemma. They debated long and hard. The first draft had bluntly described the mutual buildup of retaliatory weapons by the United States and the USSR as a "sinful situation." The phrase and the concept were cut from the final version. Also stripped from the final draft was this sentence: "As possessors of a vast nuclear arsenal, we must also be aware that not only is it wrong to attack civilian populations, but it is also wrong to threaten to attack them as part of a strategy of deterrence."

The bishops finally agreed to a formulation pressed upon them by Rome. The pope had declared in 1982, "In current conditions deterrence based on balance, certainly not as an end in itself but as a step on the way toward a progressive disarmament, may still be judged morally acceptable." The bishops, having had their arms twisted a bit by Rome, followed the pope's guideline. Deterrence could be approved as a temporary means of keeping the peace while agreements to disarm were worked out. Using that standard, they proclaimed a "strictly conditioned moral acceptance" of nuclear deterrence, adding that such defense "cannot be considered adequate as a long-term basis for peace." The condition for accepting the presence of fifty thousand nuclear warheads was that the United States show good faith efforts to bargain with the Russians to disarm.

Two questions had remained in the aftermath of the bishops' final acceptance of the pastoral letter. One was the unresolved issue of how it could be right to *threaten* to use nuclear weapons—the very premise of deterrence—if it was, to the bishops, patently wrong to actually use them? The other question was whether the U.S. government was sincerely pursuing arms reductions, the precondition the bishops had laid down as justification for temporary nuclear deterrence. It did not help those who claimed that America was fulfilling this requirement that President Reagan had overseen the most massive military buildup in the nation's peacetime history.

Just what kind of "good faith" evidence would suffice? And how much patience should the bishops exercise? How could bishops countenance a warehouse of weapons intended to deter an attack if firing such weapons was unthinkable? Didn't that invoke, as some conservatives believed, the "law of double effect"? That is, if immoral means (nuclear weapons) were permissible to achieve a moral end (both sides refraining from aggression), didn't that constitute the "double effect" or "lesser of two evils" situation rejected by Catholic moral theology? If that logic were extended to, say, the issue of abortion, some conservatives argued, the absurdity would be readily apparent. Could the church continue to condemn abortion but, in the absence of a legal prohibition, condone on a "strictly conditioned" basis (linked to the government's progress toward a ban, let us say) *some* acceptance of abortion?

Pressed by this unfinished agenda, the bishops at their fall 1985 meeting appointed an "ad hoc committee to assess the moral status of deterrence." A month later President Reagan met Premier Gorbachev in Reykjavik, Iceland, and generated a euphoric vision of eliminating all nuclear arms. The committee had been at work since then, and the two superpowers were engaged in talks aimed at ending intermediate-range missiles in Europe. Nothing concrete had yet emerged, yet there was movement. Was that enough to satisfy the bishops' condition? Meanwhile, nuclear weapons were still being detonated in the absence of a test-ban treaty.

Bishop Gumbleton sat on that committee along with two bishops on the original pastoral writing team, Cardinal Bernardin and Bishop Daniel P. Reilly of Norwich, Connecticut, and three other appointees, Archbishop John R. Roach of St. Paul–Minneapolis, Bishop Angelo Accera, O.S.B., of the military ordinariate, and Archbishop Mahony of Los Angeles. The group set no timetable for producing results.

Cardinal Bernardin, the chairman, did, however, outline the "four aspects of the arms race" under review: American and Russian policies on nuclear weapons, Star Wars (Strategic Defense Initiative, or SDI), the impact of military spending on domestic programs, and programs to modernize weapons systems by both sides. The announcement brought an acerbic response from one prominent critic of the bishops' stance on deterrence, Edward Doherty, a retired U.S. diplomat who had assisted the bishops in writing the pastoral letter. In a letter to the *National Catholic Reporter* (March 27), Doherty said the agenda sounded as if it had "been drawn up by the Arms Control and Disarmament Agency" (p. 19).

He added, "What the committee should be doing is to reexamine the proposition in the 1983 pastoral letter that 'nuclear deterrence is still morally acceptable.' That is, is it morally acceptable for the United States to threaten, and to prepare its strategic forces to use nuclear weapons in ways that the bishops themselves said could not be morally justified?

"The four aspects of the committee's review . . . will merely serve to distract attention from this basic question" (p. 19).

Over the past months, the tempo of debate about nuclear arms had been on the rise, spurred by recent moves in the arms reduction talks. The heightened concern had, in turn, focused renewed attention on what the Catholic bishops had said in 1983. After an initial splash, the pastoral letter had practically disappeared from sight. Now, after Reykjavik, it was resurfacing. Much of the discussion was conducted through articles, comments, and correspondence in the leading Catholic publications.

Michael Gallagher, a free-lance writer once employed by the bishops' conference, kicked off several pointed responses with a passionate rejection of the bishops' deterrence stance in the January 16 issue of *Commonweal,* provocatively headlined "Sidestepping the Challenge of Peace." Methodist bishops had recently denounced nuclear deterrence as "the idol of national security," Gallagher noted, and Catholic bishops were summoned to do no less. As it stood, he said, the bishops' position was "the moral equivalent of a blank check." The Reagan administration had done nothing significant on arms reduction policy, he concluded; therefore, the bishops' condition had not been met. Gallagher called on the bishops "to speak out in a time of decadence and moral confusion, and declare deterrence—the fixed intention to obliterate millions upon millions of human lives—an abomination in the sight of God and creation" (p. 13).

In a letter to *Commonweal* (April 24), Bishop Gumbleton agreed with Gallagher that willingness to use nuclear weaponry was intrinsically immoral. He referred to the "horrendous evil of intending to incinerate or even vaporize untold millions of people." In the minds of many opponents of deterrence, threatening to use was the same as intending to use, but Bishop Gumbleton did not explicitly equate the two as Gallagher clearly had. Treading a delicate line, the bishop turned from the argument of intrinsic evil to the procedure established in the pastoral for settling the matter. As a member of the committee that put the pastoral letter together, his deference to that procedure was understandable. It was a way of resolving differences among the bishops. A blanket renunciation of nuclear deterrence would please many people in the church, he wrote, but he can come to "appreciate the value of a church where all are respected as adult members" (p. 226).

By the standards adopted by the pastoral letter, Bishop Gumbleton said, "the conditions are not being met"; therefore, action was required. "We must refuse to support those policies [U.S. nuclear strategy] any longer," he wrote, "and perhaps even actively resist them" (pp. 252–53). It was not apparent whether the "we" meant that the bishops should, as a conference, reverse their official position on nuclear deterrence or simply that Catholics who came to that conclusion should band together and protest on their own. At any rate, Bishop Gumbleton invited those inclined to resist to the forthcoming Pax Christi rally in the Nevada desert.

The editors of *Commonweal* sided more closely with the bishops' moral approval of deterrence. Certain realities had to be faced, the editorial in the May 8 issue asserted. One was that nuclear weapons could never be entirely eliminated. Unilateral nuclear disarmament was an unacceptable goal, the editors said, because it would leave the United States vulnerable to the nuclear plots of "immoral nations" (p. 260).

There were ambiguities in the pastoral letter's thinking, most obviously the unclear distinction, morally speaking, between "threat" and "use." "Nonetheless," the editorial declared, "the moral case for deterrence needs to be voiced." In their debates in preparing the pastoral letter, the bishops had stopped short of ruling out "all use definitively, in particular retaliatory strikes against military and economic, not primarily civilian, targets that would not involve disproportionate noncombatant deaths" (p. 260). Whether such limited uses were actually possible were "empirical" questions that could never be fully answered. But they left certain theoretical doors open that should not be slammed shut. Perhaps there was room for morally acceptable use of nuclear weapons and perhaps not, but the editors thought Christians should engage in that analysis with some openness.

The editors said they spoke "with fear and trembling" about matters of such awesome consequence. But, they said, "unilateralism would create instabilities making nuclear war more, not less, likely. That, too, is a tremendous challenge to any conscience" (p. 261).

In conclusion, the editorial insisted that the "search for a moral nuclear deterrent is not equivalent to the acceptance of *any* deterrent. . . . Those who refuse to reject deterrence in principle face no small task" (p. 261).

WILLIAM CASEY, A CONFIDANT OF PRESIDENT REAGAN AND A PILLAR OF THE Diocese of Rockville Centre, died May 6 in Glen Cove, Long Island, at age seventy-four. He had directed the Central Intelligence Agency under President Reagan, and his activities had come under close scrutiny by investigators into the Iran-Contra affair.

Casey had stepped down from his CIA post on February 2 after undergoing brain surgery in December from which he never fully recovered. He died of pneumonia.

The funeral took place May 9 at Saint Mary's Church in the posh Long Island bay side community of Roslyn Harbor. President and Mrs. Reagan and Richard Nixon came to pay their respects. So did two Contra leaders, Adolfo Calero, who directed the rebels' political operations, and General Enrique Bermudez, their military commander. The Casey family had set up the William J. Casey Fund for the Nicaraguan Freedom Fighters to receive contributions.

Casey's death came the day after one of President Reagan's former top national security aides, retired Air Force Major General Richard V. Secord, told congressional investigators at the first round of Iran-Contra hearings that the former CIA director had approved shipping weapons to the Contras after Congress had barred such assistance.

Inside the parish in Roslyn Harbor, however, everything seemed in readiness to bestow nothing less than unqualified honors on Casey's prodigious accomplishments and the values he stood for. As it turned out, even there the mourners received a jolt of that other reality from an unexpected source.

The source was the usually mild-mannered head of the Rockville Centre diocese, John R. McGann, the celebrant of the funeral mass. Among his fellow bishops, he was counted most often a moderate and rarely spoke at meetings. He was numbered among the majority of bishops with low national visibility who plied their trade competently.

Bishop McGann began his funeral homily with a tribute to the man he described as a "respected colleague, distinguished public servant, devoted father and father-in-law and, above all, loving husband," praying that "as a believer in Jesus, Bill Casey will experience the fullness of the resurrection from the dead on the last day."

The praise became personal and apologetic. "The glare of public life sometimes obscures the human being who is the object of so much publicity," Bishop McGann told the gathering of 350 in the church and several hundred listening over a public address system in an adjoining hall. "For me, this funeral Mass is an opportunity to pray for a man I knew as someone who was willing to share his time and energy in service to the church of the Diocese of Rockville Centre."

Though he could have "excused himself from active participation in the church on the grounds of being too busy" with demands from "people in the highest ranks of the worlds of government and finance," Bishop McGann said, Bill Casey had chosen to serve. He had accepted a place among the bishops' lay advisers and had become a trustee of Catholic Charities, twice heading its fund-raising drive. While on the board of Saint Francis Hospital in Roslyn, he had led its successful development campaign. "He entered into all these efforts, not as a person who was just lending his name to them," Bishop McGann said, "but as a very real and active participant."

And, the bishop added, "His charity was not only done in public for all to see. He also did acts of personal charity, for example, putting young people through school."

The direction of the bishop's remarks continued in an upward trajectory. Bill Casey, with his "keen, bold intelligence" and "forceful personality who did not shrink from expressing his point of view" had likewise forsaken personal gain for public service, Bishop McGann asserted, for "he did not need public life to attain wealth or influence." Having reaped those harvests in private life, the bishop was saying, he had distinguished himself as chairman of the Securities and Exchange Commission, president of the Export-Import Bank, undersecretary of state, and, of course, CIA chief. The United States to Bill Casey had always been "the great bulwark of freedom and progress."

It could have ended there. Having extolled Bill Casey to the rafters as a great patriot and public servant, the bishop had fulfilled the mission expected of him. But he wanted to say something more.

"His conviction about the fundamentally moral purpose of American actions, I am sure, made incomprehensible to him the ethical questions raised by me as his bishop, together with all the Catholic bishops of the United States about our nation's defense policy since the dawn of the nuclear age.

"I am equally sure that Bill must have thought us bishops blind to the potential communist threat in this hemisphere as we opposed and continue to oppose violence wrought in Central America by support of the Contras.

"These are not light matters on which to disagree. They are matters of life and death. And I cannot conceal or disguise my fundamental disagreement on these matters with a man I knew and respected."

According to reports, the congregation, from Reagan on through, fell stone silent in stunned disbelief. The bishop's chiding had been gentle, perhaps, but chiding it was indeed, an eruption of conscience designed for maximum effect. The bishop had, for those brief moments, wrested control from the hands of politicians and passed it to the Catholic bishops. It was a passing that left the politicians in a vacuum. Someone else was setting the terms—for just a moment.

News of the bishop's genteel ambush of the solemn funeral gathering sparked an immediate uproar, mostly along politically partisan lines. Liberals hailed his action as a bold stroke; conservatives condemned it as disrespectful and wrongheaded.

Within the church, the Catholic right, as would have been expected, took greatest umbrage. It was that sector that complained most loudly about bishops taking up political and economic questions. By their understanding of God's economy, each order had its competence. Bishops and clergy in general were to stick to doctrine and liturgy and leave matters of government to the laity. Bishop McGann had incurred their wrath.

—◄ ►—

Vatican II had unleashed something called ecumenism. Roman Catholicism had long remained militantly aloof from other churches. But a new mandate inspired by the words and person of Pope John XXIII had brought about a dramatic departure, nudging the church toward the goal of Christian unity. Nowhere was this signal for openness and interchurch cooperation more welcome than the United States, the greatest marketplace of church traditions on earth, the apotheosis of pluralism.

The ecumenical spirit had burst forth across America like peace after a long, exhausting war. Catholics and Protestants and Eastern Orthodox followers met under each other's roofs as *Christians* after a great liberation. They talked, ate, and prayed with each other, often for the first time. It had all been so unthinkable. Catholics entered the previously forbidden terrain of Protestant sanctuaries. Joint weddings were permitted and celebrated. It was a time of excitement, festivity, and discovery.

But the curiosity had passed, the euphoria faded, and the glorious promise dimmed. The ecumenical "movement" settled into a scholarly "dialogue" stage, with teams of Catholics and others with specialties in such fields as liturgy, church history, and Scripture meeting in exotic spots throughout the world to unpeel the layers of their differences. They had made considerable progress. Many of those differences were, indeed, surmountable, the scholars said, if only the church leaders would say so and get on with it. The church leaders, for the most part, balked.

Popular interest in church unity was waning even as Karol Wojtyla ascended to the papacy in 1979 with very little zeal to add to ecumenical momentum. As Pope John Paul II, he had been much more intent on reasserting the exclusive claims of the Catholic church than pushing ahead with unity. Two decades after the ecumenical dream took shape in the Second Vatican Council's "Decree on Ecumenism," it lay in shambles.

But the pope would soon be visiting the nation with the greatest religious conglomeration in the world, so it seemed to many Catholics high time to fire up the ecumenical bandwagon. There were some obstacles Rome had placed in the way, however. Many Protestants who paid attention to church affairs had been deeply disturbed by the Vatican's action toward Father Curran and Archbishop Hunthausen. Both men had many admirers among non-Catholics. The issues in contention comprised one problem; the use of authority, another. Many Protestants winced at the style of hierarchical command they had seen increasingly exercised by John Paul II in those and other cases. It was not the style they expected of a church that was presumably ecumenical and consultative.

Because modern ecumenism was still in its infancy, old suspicions and insecurities remained very much alive. For Protestants, the issue was basically that of respect. Catholicism had held fast to the idea that it was the "one true church." The memory of Pius XII's ardent defense of that position right up to the remarkable turnabout of his successor lingered prominently in the minds of many church leaders.

Vatican II had shifted ground. Non-Catholic churches were suddenly recognized as having at least some valid characteristics of the one true church, even if none of them fully measured up. For Protestants, it was at least a sign of *some* respect, though it fell far short of theological parity in most Catholic eyes. The main thing was that there was movement. The Catholic church was no longer demanding that church unity depended on the "separated brethren" returning to the fold. In fact, the Vatican II fathers placed some of the blame for the Reformation split on Catholicism. Unity would involve a pilgrimage by the Catholic church along with the other ecclesial bodies, which were implicitly granted some degree of authenticity. The picture was one of walking together rather than one of the Catholic church knocking heads and insisting on conformity on its own terms. At least that was the theory.

But non-Catholics, of course, encountered many Catholics who had been unable to shed the deeply ingrained "one true church" thinking. To these representatives of the old order, Protestantism seemed at best well meant but woefully misguided and at worst spiritually poisonous.

Within the Vatican itself, tensions over the big ecumenical question—how much recognition to grant non-Catholic churches—were on the rise. Pope John Paul II had dedicated his papacy to reasserting the authority and uniqueness of the church of Rome. He had shown more interest in pursuing unity with the Eastern Orthodox, with whom he had become well acquainted in Poland, than with the Western churches of the Reformation. Even far-ranging agreements with the Anglicans, whose legacy and practice marked them more as Catholic kinfolk than the other Protestants, failed to produce practical steps toward unity. The pope put off action, asking for further clarification.

Moreover, the pope's theology was basically classicist, impelling him to see the church as possessing the means to salvation totally and exclusively. He was cordial to non-Catholic Christians and regularly held out the Vatican II promise of church unity, but he acted more in the fashion of earlier pontiffs who assumed the Catholic church had it all and that wayward Christians would sooner or later see the light and be welcomed back. In this view, non-Catholics had only the option of accepting the truth embodied first and foremost within the Catholic church; they did not themselves *contribute* to that truth.

Protestant qualms were deepening as plans for the pope's ecumenical visits during his American tour were reaching their final stages. In interchurch circles, there was considerable distress and nervousness about how to respond to the situation. The ecumenical highlight of the trip was set for September 11 in Columbia, South Carolina, where he was to appear at a prayer service with dozens of top leaders of a broad range of churches. For reasons apparently more linked to anti-Catholicism than displeasure over ecumenism, the president of the nation's largest denomination, the Southern Baptist Convention, had already turned down an invitation to attend the service, though the South Carolina state president had accepted. For that and other reasons owing to difficult interfaith relations, an uneasy climate hung over the event.

In the midst of preparations, the chief spokesman on ecumenism from the Vatican came to America as if on an errand to set some matters straight. Cardinal Jan Willebrands, president of the Secretariat for Promoting Christian Unity, was an architect of the Second Vatican Council, counted among those who most eagerly embraced the vision of John XXIII. Though the secretariat had effectively been downgraded, the cardinal remained a powerful figure in his own right and an enduring symbol of Vatican II values of ecumenism that were being largely ignored.

Cardinal Willebrands's trip seemed most clearly aimed at reminding Catholics what Vatican II documents *really* said about vital issues related to ecumenicism and to reassure non-Catholics that the basis of respect toward them lay intact. He set forth his themes in a major speech that he presented first in Atlanta on May 5 to the National Workshop for Christian Unity and repeated three days later to a Catholic University audience of students and scholars in Washington.

The Dutch cardinal, a round-faced, genial man who was a popular figure among church leaders, rehearsed the arguments at the Second Vatican Council about whether non-Catholic churches already had a share in the one, holy, apostolic church founded by Christ. The Council fathers, he recalled, had chosen to say that the true church of God "subsists in" the Catholic church but went beyond it too. The alternative was to say that the Catholic church "is" the true church of Christ, no more, no less.

The Council's "Constitution on the Church" had gone on to declare that "many elements of sanctification and truth" existed within the other churches, though the Catholic church alone had the full revelation, the cardinal said. Because God's grace was free to go where it would, Christ's body extended beyond Catholicism. "This means to say," Cardinal Willebrands said, "that the church of Christ is not limited to the visible structure of the Catholic church."

That may have seemed self-evident to those imbued with the Council's thinking, but to the many Catholics striving to return the church to the view that there was no valid church outside the Catholic church, the message was a stark reminder of what the authorities, the ultimate court of appeal, according to orthodox Catholics themselves, had actually said and why they had said it. The cardinal's speech was a rejoinder to those who would try to turn the theological clock back to Pius XII's position on non-Catholic Christians. It was also understood by some theologians as a mild rebuke to those at the Vatican who favored a more traditional view.

Under the new Vatican II mandate, the legitimacy of a church rested primarily in its communion with Christ, not its legal claims. "There is no question of declaring the Catholic Church self-sufficient or morally superior," the cardinal said. "It is enough to state that by the Spirit of Christ there has been deposited in it and is still to be found everything that makes it possible for the church of God to be what it is called to be." That neither precluded the spreading of God's goodness to other churches nor diminished its value in the Catholic church, he implied. Catholics could count their blessings without trying to compare themselves favorably.

Cardinal Willebrands knew, of course, that the Council's line of reasoning evoked the charge that it was improperly reducing the unique role of the Catholic church as a dispenser of salvation. Catholicism, said the critics, was being defined relatively as having all the truth, but not the truth exclusively, and that did violence, in their view, to the church's unique standing and mission. Had Catholicism become "just another denomination" as the critics charged? The cardinal thought not.

"Are we to conclude that *subsistit in* (subsists in) leads to an excessive relativization of the unique quality of the Catholic church?" he asked. "Some have thought so. But that would be to forget that the expression cannot be soundly interpreted apart from its context. The context shows plainly that there is no question of denying this unique quality of the Catholic Church, which the references to the hierarchy throw into more relief. Paragraph 14 speaks of full incorporation achieved *only* in the Catholic Church, as explicitly as could be wished."

On a practical level, Cardinal Willebrands saw "very deep and great progress" in the treatment Christians accorded one other but saw unity as remote. Many churches still clung to a conviction that theirs was the only way, the "one and only church" established by Christ. "But," he told his audience, "the theological problem is: what about the others?"

THEODORE MARTIN HESBURGH, C.S.C., THE IRREPRESSIBLE, SQUARELY BUILT PRIEST who had guided the rising fortunes of the University of Notre Dame for thirty-five years as its president, took leave of his post this month, showered with tributes befitting the best known and most heralded Catholic in America.

Father Hesburgh retired after Notre Dame's commencement on May 16, just a few days shy of his seventieth birthday, completing what *America* called "a career unequaled in the history of Catholicism." The previous weekend, he had reflected on that tenure during a closed-circuit television farewell beamed by satellite to 126 alumni gatherings. It was a triumph.

The farewell featured a sixteen-minute film summary of Father Hesburgh's life, with narration by Walter Cronkite, dozens of nostalgic scenes of the campus studded with rhapsodic testimonies to its reputed "mystique," and pep talks by prominent Notre Dame figures aimed at inducing nostalgia for the past and donations to the future. Father Hesburgh's words were fittingly sown with ideals and sentiment.

"To have been president of such a company of valiant, searching souls, to have walked at the head of this thirty-five-year-long procession, to have shared with you the peace, the mystery, the optimism, the joie de vivre, the ongoing challenge, the ever-youthful, ebullient vitality, and, most of all, the deep and abiding caring that characterizes this special place and all of its people, young and old, this is a blessing that I hope to carry with me into eternity, when that time comes," Hesburgh said.

In making Notre Dame a postwar Catholic university worthy of its name, Father Hesburgh had become an influential liaison between American Catholicism and America's political and cultural elite. At the time he assumed the presidency, Catholic officials had little visible access to these circles. Father Hesburgh's entry into the centers of power gave Catholics a real ambassador to pluralistic America who reflected back to them who they had already become and could be. He became a stalwart Catholic celebrity who visited the tents of the most high and returned telling charming stories about what had happened. He was more than a token. He was a forerunner.

THE THICK WALLS OF THE NATIONAL SHRINE OF THE IMMACULATE CONCEPTION shook with African-American rhythms. Near the altar, liturgical dancers acted out biblical messages. Prayers were raised up fervently in song. From the majestic pulpit Bishop Eugene A. Marino preached with fire. "We do not come here expecting to solve all of the problems of our society and church," he proclaimed, "but we must not be afraid of the challenge." After almost three hours, the opening mass of the first National Black Catholic Congress in nearly a century came to a triumphant close.

Celebrants in the shrine, completed in 1959 and site of a visit by John Paul II on October 7, 1979, included the eleven black bishops of Catholic America and two dozen of the three hundred black priests. Seated in the gleaming shrine, surrounded by massive slabs of highly polished marble, were fifteen hundred black Catholics from across the nation. It was a rare and august occasion to which cardinals and archbishops came to pay their respects. The last congress had taken place in 1894, when there was but one black priest.

Delegates traveled from 110 U.S. dioceses to attend the three-day meeting, May 21 to 24, at Catholic University to take stock of where blacks stood within the Catholic church and to ratify some plans for expanding their relatively small base. Of the 52 million Catholics in America, 1.3 million were black. The total population of black Americans exceeded 30 million. Though the number of black Catholics had increased nearly 400,000 in twelve years, the rise was mainly due to migration of black Catholics from other countries, mostly from Haiti. Catholic officials generally acknowledged that the number of American-born black Catholics had actually dropped. Their median age was now in the mid-fifties.

Attempts to tackle the problems had been stepped up. In 1984, the black bishops had issued an incisive analysis of conditions among blacks in general and black Catholics in particular, a pastoral letter called "What We Have Seen and Heard," but black Catholic leaders conceded that blacks were largely unfamiliar with it. In March, the National Office for Black Catholics presented a report on black Catholic contributions to the Synod on the Laity. It underscored many of the same points, noting dolefully, "Black Catholics have lived a shadow existence in the larger black community and in the larger Catholic church."

The congress, whose logo was the African acacia tree, had been called by four prominent black Catholic groups against the backdrop of a worsening crisis in the black community. During the Reagan years, blacks had borne the brunt of cuts in social programs. Poverty had fallen especially heavily on single mothers and their children. Drugs were exacting a terrible toll in lives and property; blacks were engaged in a desperate struggle to survive; neglect fell like an iron net around their neighborhoods. Jesse Jackson was increasingly cheered as the voice of hope for those caught in despair and frustration.

Despite the barriers still blocking blacks within the church and the frustrations born of unfulfilled expectations raised by stirring hierarchical commitments to justice, many black Catholics commended their church unreservedly to their unaffiliated brothers and sisters. They loved its spirituality and its sacraments, the worldwide, multiracial makeup of its family, and its long history of faith. The congress unloosed their devotion and their unease.

Sister Francesca Thompson, professor of Afro-American studies at Fordham University, sounded that restive note in her keynote speech. "We have stood at the door of our church for many a year, timidly knocking, anxiously beseeching and often begging for recognition," she said. "Now we come to insist on recognition." Sister Thompson said she was "appalled by my church. I am appalled by what it has done not to others, not to us, but to itself. It has denied itself what my people have to give it. To those who say, 'Take your time, change shouldn't come too fast,' we say, '1894 was a long time ago.'"

Five black Catholic congresses had preceded that last one in 1894. A combination of apathy among black Catholics and the hierarchy's general distrust of lay assemblies had put an end to them. Now that the idea had been revived, it was an occasion to do some business and some serious socializing. For many participants who were relatively isolated from other black Catholics, it was a time for camaraderie and solidarity, a chance to strike up new friendships and to share beliefs and ideas. The schedule left plenty of time to be social and festive. A gospel concert on Friday night and a jazz session at the close of the Saturday program provided experiences to balance the cerebral cares of the daily sessions.

The picture that emerged during the sessions was one of struggle. Several messages rang clear: that it was tough being both black in a white church and a Catholic among black Protestants; that the church had done too little to rid itself of racism; that the broader Catholic church had poor relations with the black community; that black Catholics, witnessing a deepening malaise in the church, needed to take hold of the means to win new members; that Catholicism had much to offer blacks but was doing an inadequate job of getting the word out; that there were too few black priests and bishops; that, sad to say, only one bishop was the head of a diocese; that the liturgy must better reflect black culture.

Though considerable criticism was leveled at society and the Catholic church in general for failing to combat the effects of discrimination, many leaders sought to bolster morale and exhort black Catholics to help their own cause.

Among them was the Reverend Clarence Williams, C.P.P.S., president of the Black Televangelization Network and a parish pastor. In a rousing speech, Father Williams challenged the delegates to take charge. Referring to the history of black Catholics, he declared, "For years we were outside trying to get in. Now we're inside and asked to lead." To do that well entailed paring down and boning up. It meant getting serious about the gospel and doing away with frivolity. Too many mixed motives now hampered this effort. In prophetic fashion, Father Williams preached repentance and revival.

"Half of our people want to go to church to have a good time," Father Williams said, "and half want to go in order to change the world. . . . We can't do evangelization without evangelism. We want to go in the name of the Lord, but we haven't come to know the Lord. There are more working for bingo than taking classes in Bible study. We're more concerned in the choir with the gospel on our lips than the gospel in our hearts.

"Because if we want to be a church that wants to reach out, we have to know who we are."

His audience nodded and clapped their approval of that diagnosis. There was plenty of room, it appeared, for self-criticism of efforts to win new souls while retaining the existing ones. Keeping young black Catholics *in* the church, for example, was a cause of growing worry. A survey conducted by the NOBC found that 73 percent of black Catholic respondents believed that "many of our young people" would be lost to other denominations.

But this was only part of the story Father Williams had come to deliver. Exposing weakness was only a means toward realizing enormous strengths.

Black Catholics had much to offer, Father Williams said, and could hasten the process by overcoming those shortcomings. "We haven't sold ourselves on ourselves," he said. "We have the largest church buildings in the black community, but we don't welcome anybody. . . . Black Catholics have to be sold on themselves. We have to say [to the unchurched] 'You've tried the rest, now try the best.'"

In earlier times, church leaders said, joining the Catholic church was largely a move to cross over into white society or to feel a cut above black Protestants. "It used to be very much that way," said Bishop James P. Lyke, the auxiliary bishop of Cleveland. "It used to be that a black becoming a Catholic became white. It was a sort of climbing Jacob's ladder that was driven by a deep sense of self-hatred turned around. But I think now that's in the past." The growth of pride in black culture had stifled that desire, he believed. Though in his view black pride had been waning, he said, "it's not eroding to the point where people are saying, 'If I'm going to make it, I'm going to join the Catholic world.'"

Bishop Lyke spoke between sessions. He was a youthful, handsome man, one of the rising leaders among the bishops, outspoken and refreshingly honest but not brash. He had coordinated the creation of a new African-American Catholic hymnal, titled *Lead Me, Guide Me*. He saw the hymnal as a vital resource in a drive to infuse more black music and spirituality into the Catholic liturgy.

If the Catholic church were ever to reach more blacks, many black leaders believed, the mass would have to reflect more elements found within black culture. Since Vatican II, the church had officially encouraged "acculturation," the adaptation of the liturgy to local customs and practices. Before the Vatican II, ethnic or "national" churches had served immigrants from such countries as Poland and Italy by melding aspects of their heritage into worship, so the idea wasn't new. But many blacks believed that for whatever reason that process had been slow in coming to black Catholics.

The obvious problem for black Catholics, Bishop Lyke said, was that discrimination inside and outside the church retarded full expression of black gifts and resources. Especially serious and chronic, he said, was "the classic clash in many cities between black people and white Catholics," with all the negative repercussions that had on black evangelization.

The archbishop of the nation's biggest city told the congress that he and others needed to do their part by paying greater heed to blacks. "Far too many of us white Catholics have heard too little and understood too little," confessed Cardinal John O'Connor to the Saturday morning gathering. "I weep over the fact that there are only 1.3 million black Catholics. We must remind Catholics all over the United States that they need not abandon their blackness by being Catholic."

For that, the cardinal received a standing ovation. Thunderous applause also greeted his pledges of support for evangelism and social action. Only a few hours before, he had stepped off a plane from Rome, where he and others on the special commission had held talks with the pope in a tense effort to solve the Hunthausen conflict. Though still groggy from his trip, he had lost none of his capacity for eloquence, adapting smoothly to his new setting. Cardinal O'Connor had a gift for both rhetorical flourish and empathetic involvement. He could be a spellbinder. With arresting sincerity, he bestowed his commitment to a better day for blacks. Should he fail to make good on his promise to them, he said, they were to hold him accountable.

The moment was at hand, according to Herbert Johnson, the director of black ministries in the cardinal's own archdiocese. "If the church doesn't begin to address our needs," Johnson told the Religious News Service (May 25), "we're not going to stay here. There are too many other faith communities in which blacks feel welcome." The same news service quoted Bishop Lyke as saying that the behavior of white Catholics deterred greater black participation. Bishop Lyke, by the RNS account, said black Catholics were discouraged by the specter of white Catholics who "go to mass on Sunday, take in the Eucharist, and then go back to their homes and say, 'We don't want you in our neighborhood, nigger.' They [black Catholics] feel it is phony, and it is."

On Sunday morning, the congress wrapped up business by approving a seventy-two-page pastoral plan of action. It called for a range of strategies for increasing black involvement and for enriching Catholicism with black culture.

The plan, which had been prepared by a steering committee and passed virtually untouched, called on the church to keep Catholic schools open for black children. Such schools were a major source of black converts, the document pointed out, and the closing of many of them for financial reasons posed a grave problem. The plan also urged the church to blend more black music, language, prayers, and revivals into the liturgy so as to better highlight the congregational character of black spiritual life. Pastoral training centers were also needed to acquaint clergy and laity with these and other aspects of black Catholicism, the plan said.

Other sections of the document commended the church's moral values as building blocks for black people caught in personal turmoil. In turn, the changing nature of the black family should be acknowledged by the church. Turning to young people, the plan urged parishes to attack the problems that often beset them: drugs, violence, and sex. Related issues of unemployment, economic conditions, and racism, as they affect young people and their elders, deserve increased attention by the church, the document said.

The vision was summed up this way: "We call upon black Catholic parishes to be beacons of hope to the community, through vibrant liturgies and a welcoming congregation, through enthusiastic and well- prepared homilies that teach biblical truths, through making the surrounding neighborhood feel at home in the parish or using its facilities, through the availability of programs that serve the needs of the poor."

In the months ahead, the pastoral plan was due to be circulated in dioceses around the country and presented to the pope. It would also serve as the blueprint for a new office of black Catholics established by the bishops and scheduled to open at the United States Catholic Conference in January. The spirit at the congress had been largely jubilant, but the huge scope of the challenge seemed nowhere underestimated. The delegates went forth with a look of pride in being black and Catholic and with the determination to continue the difficult march ahead.

—▬ ▬—

UNTIL A FRIEND HAD ASKED HANNAH TO JOIN HER ON A CHARISMATIC RETREAT, the idea had never appealed to her. But something about her friend's request seemed intriguing, so off she had gone, in the middle of May, to a Dominican convent. What she had found there left her astounded.

It was "nothing like I expected," she recalled, "not a lot of highly emotional stuff." Instead, the group of men and women were invited by the retreat leader, a nun, to "deal with inner healing and to come to terms with our parents and with the male/female parts of ourselves." Not everything was so intense. Meals had been leisurely, and a health spa offered a swimming pool and sauna for relaxation.

The highlight for Hannah had been an exercise that turned into what she described as "a real faith experience such as I've never had before." The following was her account of those powerful moments:

"The first evening, sister was talking to us about imaging and inner healing. She led us in prayer, especially concerning our parents.

"My father died when I was nine, and I don't remember much about him, but I've been discovering that there is something problematic in my intimate relations with men. From what sister said, I thought, 'Maybe this is where it comes from, my father.'

"Following her directions, I closed my eyes and put myself in the past, in a place in my childhood. I was five years old in an elaborate rock garden with a little pool and goldfish in back of my house.

"I went into the house and pictured my father in the house. I am bringing the Lord Jesus to him, to have the Lord touch him and fill him with the Holy Spirit.

"As I did that, a real revelation came to me—my father was ill all the time and was in need of healing.

"Tears broke in me. This was so real to me. I felt like a little girl, suddenly so cherished and loved. *I had his total attention,* like I had a relationship with him that never had been."

It had been part real, part imagined, all powerful. The two-week interval since the retreat had done nothing to diminish the powerful effects on her.

"I've felt more whole ever since. I'm still in awe of that happening. It was nothing like speaking in tongues or anything. Nothing prepared me for anything like that."

Much of Hannah's pressing mid-life search for herself centered on her need to feel loved and to be an adult on equal terms with other adults. More and more she recognized in herself a dependent child who had become overly "responsible" to earn the favor of grownups. She saw this pattern at work in her family background and in the church. As a Catholic, she had looked up to clergy and religious as superiors, as unequals. But it was also through the church that Hannah was starting to believe in the value of her own voice.

The concept of the basic equality of every baptized member of the church, be they bishops, monks, or short-order cooks, had taken on reality for Hannah during a period of time when she had been included in a special ministerial team at her parish. The pastor, a sister, and herself had worked together. Their functions had differed somewhat, of course, but she had felt a unique blend of personalities and talents and a shared sense of service. To her dismay, the team was broken up when both the priest and the nun were reassigned. The new priest showed little liking for the cooperative team approach, she said, preferring to be more removed. Some parishioners who had felt uncomfortable with the leadership of relative equals were relieved, she said, feeling that the country church "was Father's parish once again."

Hannah's diocesan duties had likewise exposed her to the challenge of seeing herself as an adult among adults. Having served on a high-powered committee reviewing the ministry and structure of the diocese, she had been asked to chair the group appointed to implement the committee's recommendations. She was nervous about the burdens it might entail. At the heart of the package of proposals by the committee was that issue of shared responsibility. If the suggestions were followed, the diocese of the future would be much more democratic than it had been. There would be stiff resistance to that sort of change, she thought, but it seemed right to her. It seemed right even though it still didn't quite seem "natural" to distribute decision-making power more evenly. Seeing things that way meant, to Hannah, growing up. But it wasn't easy.

"It breaks a lot of bubbles," she said, "like the one that says the Holy Spirit works from the top down. Maybe—but that's not the only way."

Her diocesan involvement had "brought home" to her "how human we all are," no matter what the rank or status in the church. "There comes a time," she said, "when you can no longer be a child in your faith. If a structure of the church keeps adults as children, then they'll never have the picture of Christianity we all ought to have. Yet I see models—I experienced one in my parish—that show me how beautiful it can be."

For several years Hannah had toyed with the idea of working full-time for the church, but now that possibility seemed real, and she didn't quite know what to think about it. She had already signed her contract to teach another year in the Olny elementary school when the diocese posted a job opening she could not ig- nore. It was a new position as coordinator for lay ministries. A growing number of parishes in the diocese were without priests, and laypeople were needed to pick up the slack. It was a job at the frontier of church life, fraught with risks, to be sure, but loaded with potential for developing lay ministers. Hannah studied the listing of qualifications. It sounded like her. She was making out her résumé.

A MEMOIR BY A NOTED LITERARY FIGURE WAS, OF COURSE, BY ITS VERY NATURE an event. When its contents turned out to be surprisingly religious, that drew a special kind of attention.

The author was Richard Gilman, professor of drama at Yale and former theater critic for *Newsweek,* the *New Republic,* and the *Nation.* His book, *Faith, Sex, Mystery,* offered an exotic mixture of elements that tantalized certain varieties of New York intellectuals.

By May, as the momentum of commentary continued, it was probable that Gilman's volume of confessions would become the *Catholic* book of the year among the highbrows. On the face of it, that might seem an ironic prize to award the story of a church dropout. But Gilman was no ordinary dropout, and his story was hardly commonplace.

Raised a Jew in Brooklyn, he had undergone a sudden conversion from atheism to Catholicism at age twenty-seven after reading *The Spirit of Medieval Philosophy,* by Etienne Gilson, in a single forty-eight-hour gulp. That was in 1952. Eight years later he left the church, no longer able to square his beliefs or his sexual behavior with the dogma and moral precepts of the church. Between his coming and going, he wrote for the Catholic publications *Jubilee* and *Commonweal,* maturing as a thinker and polishing his prodigious gifts as a writer.

Gilman's romance with the church was intense and transforming. Though he had felt it necessary to walk away from the church, he had not done so gladly. He had found nothing to replace it. Though he had won acclaim in the world of letters, he testified to being unhappy, yet unable to return to the faith and practice of Catholicism. Belief in God remained in him of a vestigial sort, though from his point of view, there was no active relationship behind it.

In telling his painful and candid tale, Gilman appeared to have awakened the sensibilities and insecurities of two kinds of readers in particular, both drawn irresistibly by spiritual adventurers who have wandered into the realms of true belief and back again with enticing reports from the front.

One was the group of Catholic intellectuals, who listened with fascination and trepidation. These were born Catholics, schooled in "reasonable" faith, who nonetheless doubted at times whether their faith held any appeal to the modern mind on its own merits. Was faith strictly a matter of parochial nurture, or could the outsider also find in it convincing arguments? Prestigious converts here and there offered reassurance, but they were few and far between, it seemed. Within the main currents of intellectual life, as they saw it, the chief tenets of Catholicism were considered mildly interesting, irrelevant, or ludicrous.

In *Faith, Sex, Mystery,* Gilman sent mixed signals to the Catholic intellectuals: showing profound respect for their faith but finally, unable to accept its tenets, breaking ranks with them, albeit with much melancholy. Some had reacted with anger, implying that his faith had been incomplete to begin with. Perhaps all "difficult" converts were susceptible to the charge that lack of Catholic upbringing made them misbehave this way. It was the Achilles heel of the convert, the latent "fatal flaw" that caused some to overcompensate by out-Catholicizing the cradle Catholics.

The other category of special reader fell within Gilman's company of lapsed Catholics. Church dropouts increasingly filled the top ranks of academic and cultural institutions. Many had bade their farewells to the church for a variety of sociological, economic, and moral reasons but without ever having *thought* their way out of the church with even a semblance of the rigor employed by Gilman. Lapsed Catholics with low-grade guilt feelings and unresolved theological questions were strewn all over the landscape of leading publications, universities, think tanks, and book publishers. These were highly educated people who had taken their Catholicism for granted, then given it up over something or other rather specific and tried to leave it at that.

But examples like Richard Gilman could rip the lids off those inner caldrons and cause them to spill over. Here was an esteemed Yale professor and critic, more than a peer, once a complete stranger to the church, who nevertheless totally capitulated to a mysterious power he found within it at one time in his life and had

agonized over it. The memoirs invited invidious comparisons. Had their decision
to leave been anywhere near as wrenching as his? Did they dare open up that issue
again—or for the first time? *Faith, Sex, Mystery* raised the possibility of faith even as
it discarded it. To the "former" Catholic, especially the one whose mind seemed most
firmly set against the church, a book such as this could spur intense curiosity.

— —

For THOSE WITH BOTH FEET FIRMLY PLANTED WITHIN THE CHURCH, THE UP-
coming Rome synod on the role of the laity seemed likely to offer some thoughts
of its own on faith, sex, and mystery. By early May, the working document for the
synod was widely available across Catholic America. The document was described
as a distillation of the contents of eighty reports from around the world. It was a
rough preview of the direction the synod might take.

Whereas many lay consultations on the synod had concentrated on areas of
tension and the need for sometimes drastic reform, the document predictably
stayed well within the realm of the very, very possible. As a homogenized product of many different viewpoints, none of which the Vatican allowed to be published individually, the themes opened up for discussion comprised a kind of least
common denominator, posing no apparent threats to the status quo.

Scarcely anyone believed the synod would somehow veer out of control and
call for radical change, but the document might have returned any wild-eyed
dreamers back to reality. As to the complaint that it would be a synod about the
laity run by bishops, Pope John Paul II reminded the world tautologically that
the thing was what it was. Though hailing the presynodical consultations as "excellent," the pontiff reminded two hundred lay leaders at the Vatican on May 23
that the synod was, to nobody's evident surprise, "essentially a place of sharing
for the bishops designated as synod fathers," meaning, of course, that rules were
rules.

Analysts combed the working document for any hints of subtle shifts in Vatican
thinking regarding the laity. Some claimed to find a few, among them these:

- Stress on "communion" rather than hierarchy as the basic model of the
  church, one that was more congenial toward organic, even democratic concepts

- Determination to keep lines between lay ministries and ordained ministries
  clearly drawn, but uncertainty about how to do that in changing circumstances relating to the rapid growth of laity in ministry

- A commitment to the essential equality between men and women, but a resolve to preserve the limits against women's full participation in the ministry of the church

- Affirmation of "basic Christian communities," the building blocks of church renewal in Latin America and the incubators of liberation theology

- Reassertion that the parish was the primary focus of the religious lives of Catholics, therefore assigning the so-called lay movements such as Opus Dei a secondary role

— ▬

To the general public, the pope's tour of the United States in September would mainly be a television spectacle full of touching and colorful scenes. In the eyes of many observers, Catholic and non-Catholic Americans seemed beset with a bad case of ennui, awaiting the next big show to keep them entertained and diverted from the nation's worsening problems.

Pope John Paul II was one of the world's most skillful users of television resources and one of the most telling critics of the slide from materialism to decadence. The pope's objective, assuredly, was to use the occasion of his wide TV exposure to shake this lethargy by appealing for self-examination and offering hope to those who, perhaps, in their torpor, were not even aware they were looking for it.

Meanwhile, for many Catholics most active in the church, the visit's significance would be as much audio as visual. Perhaps more than anything else, they envisioned the trip as a trail of speeches in which the pope would tell them what he thought of their church.

Though the pope's first journey to America had been a media smash, it had a somewhat disastrous impact on church morale. That was the widely held view in retrospect, at least. At John Paul's first stops in Boston and New York he had eloquently addressed the universal themes of human rights, poverty, and youth. Everything had been upbeat. But thereafter he had abruptly and dourly turned the bulk of his attention to divisive internal affairs.

During that second half of the trip, John Paul II had instructed the church in no uncertain terms. His message, sometimes scolding, was direct and unvarnished. Catholic America had received no dispensation, special or otherwise, from full obedience to moral doctrine and church discipline. If the church in the United States was having a hard time keeping the commandments, the pope told his people, then perhaps it was because affluence and individualism had induced waywardness. A chastening pope left behind many Catholics who chose to disagree rather than be chastened.

In the aftermath of the tour, many Catholic officials felt the pope had been too harsh on Catholic America in part because he had been inadequately informed about it. Subsequent actions by Rome against American bishops and theologians reinforced the conviction that John Paul was being misinformed about the church

in the United States (by the right-wing cabal) and had arrived at unwarranted conclusions. As the second trip approached, these officials vowed that this time the
pope would receive a fuller, fairer picture, one that would render his assessment
more sanguine.

Leading the campaign against disinformation were the officers of the bishops'
conference. In their recent trips to Rome, they had striven to put Catholic America's best foot forward. The visit to the pope by bishops of the cities hosting the
forthcoming papal visit pursued a similar agenda. Each time, they emerged from
these sessions with lavish assurances that falsehoods were being put to flight and
that Rome was looking ever more kindly on America. The latest was a buoyant
briefing from Archbishop Daniel E. Pilarczyk of Cincinnati on May 18 after talks
between officers of the bishops' conference and Vatican officials. The talks had
been "very useful," the archbishop said, and at no place did members of the curia
"give any indication whatsoever that they thought the church in the United States
was going down the tubes."

The alleged warming in relations had so far generated no obvious benefits for
Father Curran, Archbishop Hunthausen, and others charged with breaking Rome's
discipline, but the groundwork for averting similar cases in the future was supposedly being built.

The pope's batch of speeches would provide an important test of those claims.
If the tutoring of John Paul had succeeded, then, presumably, a revised, friendlier
version of the pope's assessment of Catholic America would emerge in September.

In quest of that goal, a ferocious paper chase had been set in motion. A flurry
of speeches drafted by hundreds of Catholics from many sectors of the church
landed in Rome. They included suggested topics and approaches for the pope's addresses plus texts of the talks that would be given by a variety of Catholics in the
pope's presence at the dozens of public gatherings.

Materials were being collected by the United States Catholic Conference. Then
everything had to be approved beforehand by the Secretariat of State at the
Vatican, a procedure that caused some grousing among those who felt the nonpa-
pal speeches should be allowed total freedom. Even with the screening devices, the
script was subject to improvisation. The most startling moment of the first trip
came when a nun, Sister Agnes Mary Mansour, abruptly challenged the church's
ban on women's ordination before a nonplussed John Paul.

With only three months to go before the pope's plane touched down in Miami,
the race to complete the texts was in high gear. Each host diocese had sent draft
speeches, and many church organizations whose constituencies would be specifically addressed by the pope had done likewise. The waiting game among many interest groups was to see whether the points they had done the most to promote
would make it into the final versions. Rewriting was in full swing, and decision
time was near.

Donna Hanson of Spokane, the head of the bishops' lay advisory committee, had basically shaped her talk to the San Francisco meeting of the pope and three thousand lay activists. The Reverend William Wood, head of the California Catholic Conference, had written a homily intended for use by John Paul in Monterey. Sixty members of the archdiocesan council in Phoenix had put their heads together to focus some thoughts on health care and other issues keyed to the pope's visit there. From San Antonio's preparation committee emerged a twenty-page report on the fine points of life in Texas for the pope's edification.

One of the speechmakers had drawn fire from the Catholic right. The Reverend Frank McNulty, a priest of the Newark archdiocese, had been chosen by the executive committee of the bishops for the honor of addressing the pope on behalf of the fifty-seven thousand priests in the United States. Father McNulty had, like the other speakers, consulted with many others before crafting his presentation. But the guardian of the far right, the *Wanderer,* found Father McNulty unsuited to the task. The May 16 edition of the newspaper carried an editorial that, in characteristic fashion, attempted to undermine the priest's credibility through the weaponry of unsubstantiated reports and insinuating description.

What it came down to, of course, was the *Wanderer's* usual obsession with anything that even came close to relatively liberal views on sexuality or women's role in the church, which in the newspaper's fury, were the same issue. Father McNulty had failed the *Wanderer's* shadowy litmus test on sex and was therefore unacceptable. The editors suggested yet another letter-writing campaign to Rome to protest Father McNulty's assignment.

Covering the hefty expenses of the trip continued to preoccupy many church officials. In Miami, Archbishop Edward McCarthy, faced with a $1.8-million outlay, attempted to mollify critics who believed the visit would absorb funds that might have gone to help the poor. The archbishop appealed to Miamians to contribute to their favorite charities to help forestall any shortfall. The highest price tag of any stop on the nine-city tour was posted by the Archdiocese of San Francisco. Due considerably to the high cost of fitting out Candlestick Park for the pope's outdoor mass, the archdiocese expected to spend a total of $3.3 million.

Though plans were moving ahead, all was far from ready. There was yet much nervousness and some large unresolved problems, most of all Seattle.

BY THE FIRST WEEK OF MAY, NEGOTIATIONS OVER ARCHBISHOP HUNTHAUSEN'S future in Seattle had all but collapsed. During the previous three weeks, incessant talks between the archbishop and the three commission members had steadily soured, making a settlement seem more elusive.

The terms of the proposed pact from the commission, conveyed to the archbishop by Cardinal Bernardin, remained the same: the archbishop would be restored to full power but at the price of accepting his eventual successor, a coadjutor bishop named by the Vatican to replace Bishop Wuerl, who would be reassigned. It also meant accepting the commission's official report on the state of the archdiocese.

Archbishop Hunthausen and his aides had resisted the coadjutor concept before, viewing it as a tacit admission that things were indeed so amiss in the archdiocese that special Vatican assistance was needed to clean it up. They had never fully acknowledged the existence of the laid-back climate described by Cardinal Ratzinger in his 1985 indictment of the archbishop's leadership, and they were no more inclined to give ground now. In addition, the archbishop and his advisers were shocked by the commission's preliminary evaluation of the archdiocese. Not only did its dour tone surprise them, but its criticisms seemed to some even harsher than Cardinal Ratzinger's censure. From previous dealings, they had read the commission's attitude as highly positive. But the evaluation shattered that optimism.

The archbishop had long felt misunderstood by Rome but had reason to expect better treatment from his fellow American bishops. His hope suddenly crumbled when the cardinal, the supposed mediating influence on the commission, had handed him the proposed settlement, including the evaluation. As April wore on, he and his advisers were running low on that most indispensable ingredient, trust. At one low point, he even denounced the process as "evil."

Meanwhile, the proposal remained on the table. Under the provisions spelled out by Cardinal Bernardin, the archbishop would have partial control over the selection of a coadjutor. The three names normally forwarded to Rome by the papal pro-nuncio, Archbishop Laghi, would be approved by the archbishop. That did not mean he would pick all three, only that he go along with whatever names made the final cut. Having had Bishop Wuerl forced on him, the archbishop was opposed to letting the commission make any of the choices. For the moment he was buying nothing, only testing possibilities. With the wall of distrust thickening, he was increasingly isolated and alone.

As a means of keeping his options open, he forwarded to the commission three preferences of his own: Bishop Michael H. Kenny of Juneau, Archbishop Francis T. Hurley of Anchorage, and Bishop William S. Skylstad of Yakima. The commission scratched Bishop Kenny as too much a liberal in the Hunthausen mold. Archbishop Hurley was crossed off because, according to church protocol, the move to coadjutor would be considered a demotion for someone already an archbishop. That left Bishop Skylstad. After much jockeying, the commission agreed to submit two names, Bishop Skylstad, of the archbishop's choosing, and Bishop Thomas J. Murphy of Great Falls–Billings, Montana, a man the archbishop liked and respected but had some immediate qualms about placing in that role.

The question was still whether acceptance of any coadjutor constituted, in principle, an admission of guilt that he could not make in good conscience.

The commission had also considered criticisms of its first evaluation and was busy revising it to rectify the tough-minded quality imparted to it by Cardinal O'Connor. Under its mandate, the commission had to measure progress or lack of it regarding the charges brought by the Vatican. Cardinal Ratzinger had cited a range of illicit practices within the archdiocese. They included allowing Catholics in irregular marriages to take communion, general absolution, sponsorship of groups that opposed church teaching on homosexuality, permitting children to receive communion before going to their first confession, serving communion to non-Catholics and letting former priests take parish roles forbidden to them. Behind all those separate complaints, however, was the main issue of Archbishop Hunthausen's integrity as a church leader.

Rome's severest blow was to judge him unfit. In its "chronology" of events released the previous November on the eve of the showdown over the Hunthausen case at the annual meeting of bishops, the Vatican had asserted that although the archbishop had been "an effective leader in many respects," he nonetheless lacked "firmness necessary to govern the archdiocese."

By the first days of May, the tension between the archbishop and the commission was at the breaking point. The archbishop remained adamant that his acceptance of a coadjutor was contingent on his choice of both nominees. The commission refused to back down from its offer. At this point, the four of them were wearing down each others' nerves daily during long, grueling conference calls.

The commissioners were reaching the end of their rope. They had appealed to the archbishop's loyalty to the church and to the pope. They had tried to convince him that the appointment of a coadjutor was the absolute requirement for suing Rome for peace and a restoration of his authority. But their goal had proved vexingly beyond their reach.

Though the settlement seemed rational, even generous, to them and the Vatican, it did not strike the archbishop that way. As the commission tried to seal the deal, an exasperated archbishop threatened to go over their heads by flying straight to Rome, only to have the Vatican put the kibosh on his plans. There would be no meeting with the pope or top Vatican officials, they informed him, without what amounted to a signed confession and a pledge to mend his ways.

As patience wore thin, the commission feared that an erratic archbishop would circumvent them in another way by taking his story directly to the press. His popularity would virtually assure him a groundswell of support. Efforts to reach an accord would likely collapse and with it the chance that U.S. bishops could show that they could best keep their house in order without Rome's meddling. From the commission's point of view, the failure of this opportunity would fall not only on their heads but on the larger movement toward a collegial resolution of problems by the bishops' conference. It was in the midst of such failures that Vatican power might reassert itself.

As the pressures to accept the commission's settlement increased, Archbishop Hunthausen became more solitary and downcast. He did not welcome the commission's argument that if he loved the church he would submit. He believed that through sleight of hand by the commission or the Vatican he might end up with a coadjutor who would be no more satisfactory in the long run than Wuerl had been. He could not be sure about Murphy as coadjutor. He could not be sure about anything. If a successor were to be appointed, what would be the sense in carrying on anyway? He couldn't see how it could possibly work.

Alarm was growing on both sides. But from the commission's perspective, the jittery impasse could not go on much longer. What resulted amounted to an ultimatum: accept the assignment of a coadjutor, agree to submit the names of Skylstad and Murphy, and go along with a final, revised assessment. He held out for the choice of both names. Without agreement, the settlement talks would break off. The consequences appeared dire. Archbishop Hunthausen would be forced by the Vatican to leave the archdiocese.

On May 4, all indications were that Archbishop Hunthausen would reject the package and, in effect, quit. To do otherwise, some of his associates believed, would be to accept defeat and egregious compromise. The settlement looked dead, the commission's good-faith work in vain. Those close to the negotiations described it as a dark, frightening time when all hope seemed to vanish.

Three days later, to follow through on the death-and-resurrection imagery employed by those closest to the scene, everything had come to life. On May 7, the archbishop had accepted that which he had nearly spurned. The deal was struck. The two names would go forward, one chosen by the archbishop, the other by the commission.

What happened to bring about the change? Witnesses described the reversal in transcendent terms, as the product of a spiritual transformation that swept over the archbishop. Both the archbishop's partisans and those involved with the commission spoke of the intervention of the Holy Spirit in bringing about what the human principals could not. Archbishop Hunthausen's supporters attributed the change to his ability to place the dictates of the gospel above his own wishes. In the end, they said, he also believed he owed it to the church in Seattle and most especially to his loyal backers to stay. It was God's will as he understood it. To those who saw the situation more from the commission's vantage point, the success had been largely due to the commission's heroic forbearance.

The process of reconciliation had been aided in no small measure by the ministrations of a skilled lay intermediary who helped the archbishop sort through the tangle of factors involved in the dilemma. On the purely human side, that assistance was credited more than any other single element with saving the settlement. The archbishop was counseled on his way to a new vision.

To the weary commissioners, word of the archbishop's change of heart, coming when it did in the depths of their gloom, predictably produced a huge collective sigh of relief. That breakthrough was not quite the end of the process, however. The commission must still go to Rome to submit the package to the pope. They had been in touch with the Vatican all along, of course, but without the pope's final approval, nothing was official.

With the archbishop's acceptance in hand, the commission scheduled a trip to the Vatican to talk it over and nail down additional details. On May 19 and 20, they met with top church officials and the pope to review the terms of the settlement. Cardinal Ratzinger reluctantly signed off on it. The pope exuded more enthusiasm. If this was what the commission had worked out, John Paul said, then the settlement had his confidence. The deal was done.

Under the provisions of the settlement, Archbishop Hunthausen would be restored to full authority in his archdiocese, and Bishop Murphy would become coadjutor bishop to assist him in ending the abuses cited by the Vatican. The commission would complete its assessment and stay on for a year to monitor those efforts. Bishop Wuerl would leave for a yet-unspecified assignment elsewhere.

Bishop Murphy was notified of his impending reassignment on May 23. He was at Archbishop Hunthausen's side at a May 27 news conference in Seattle where the agreement was made public.

The announcement included release of the commission's assessment. Most significantly, the report tied abuses to a "climate of permissiveness" fostered by the archbishop. Simply doing away with aberrations would not be enough, the report said, adding, "it is the overall attitudinal 'climate' or psychological and ecclesiastical orientation of the archdiocese which is the ultimate key to the situation." Though nothing like the "lack of firmness" accusation cropped up in the report, the commission had laid blame for a chronic condition squarely at the archbishop's feet.

That grim diagnosis notwithstanding, a smiling archbishop opened the news conference by giving the settlement his blessing. "The result is a good one," he told a throng of reporters in the chancery. "I have no difficulty accepting it." But his satisfaction dimmed in response to a question about the assessment. He said that he disagreed with "some important aspects" of the commission's report and, more astonishingly, declared that he could not support it.

In a letter to his priests the day before (the National Federation of Priests' Councils earlier in the month, by a 121 to 3 vote, backed the majority position among Seattle priests for total, no-strings restoration of the archbishop), he had stated the apparent paradox directly: "I want you to know that while I am not in agreement with a number of important aspects of the assessment and am therefore not prepared to endorse it, I have nonetheless come to the point of accepting the commission's proposed resolution to our situation."

At the news conference, Archbishop Hunthausen stressed that Bishop Murphy would have no special faculties. That is, the Vatican had vowed to refrain from deputizing Bishop Murphy to take over certain of the archbishop's functions. It was the archbishop's forced surrender of five areas of the archdiocesan operation to Bishop Wuerl that had touched off the rebellion the previous fall, and the Vatican apparently did not intend to rub that raw wound again. Coadjutors normally were given special faculties, but Archbishop Hunthausen said he was sure an exception had been made in this case.

He also flatly denied that he had agreed to step down after a certain time in return for being restored to power. "There has been *no* deal," he said. "I can't say that emphatically enough." But it was also a fact that the commission would be keeping an eye on things for at least a year. The question the archbishop was unprepared to answer was, What would happen if the Vatican decided a year hence that the archdiocese had failed to shape up to its liking? Would he be asked to leave at that point?

The archbishop's supporters looked at the plus side. It was a compromise, they admitted, but some gains had been achieved. Their two most important objectives, the return of the archbishop's full authority and the departure of Wuerl, had both been accomplished. They knew relatively little about Bishop Murphy, but what they knew they liked. In general, he seemed to share an outlook similar to the archbishop's, but only time would tell. Perhaps the most crucial aspect of the agreement, many supporters said, was that in their view the Vatican had backed down. It had forced Wuerl on them, and that had sparked a rebellion that had caused Rome to retreat.

On the basis of the reinstatement of their archbishop and the arguments put forward by his supporters, Seattle found much reason to rejoice, though the celebration was tempered by lingering suspicions. Until Bishop Murphy became known and unless the air was cleared of rumors of secret deals and covert Vatican schemes, the atmosphere in this archdiocese, small in numbers and unmatched in geographical splendor, seemed likely to remain uneasy. The archbishop's army of devoted followers vowed to be vigilant and watchful.

Drawing on the same evidence, the far right, those who objected most strenuously to the archbishop's "pastoral" leadership, proclaimed the settlement a crushing defeat for the church. The *Wanderer* declared it "a clear victory for the 'Americanist' wing of the U.S. Episcopacy which has long campaigned for more input into the resolution of 'tensions' between the Holy See and the local Church. . . . While many observers view this latest settlement as a compromise, others see it as a retreat by the Holy See in the face of determined and organized opposition from Seattle dissidents supported by a network of Americanist allies throughout the country" (June 4).

It was perhaps natural that the far right, which had rallied its forces nationwide to urge the Vatican to discipline Archbishop Hunthausen, should see the outcome as a triumph by a far-flung network of "Americanist" conspirators. At any rate, there was gloom in the St. Paul, Minnesota, offices of the *Wanderer*. "In all candor," bemoaned an editorial in the same issue, "it must be said that the so-called compromise decision regarding the case of Archbishop Raymond Hunthausen, recommended by the 'Bernardin commission' and accepted by Pope John Paul II, seems to us as making a bad situation worse." The archbishop's "prophetic" leadership represented to the *Wanderer* crowd and those like them the kind of bullheaded, self-styled individualism that was hammering the church like a wrecking ball.

In the eyes of many, disaster had been averted. The commission had squeaked by. The archbishop could go on with his job under a new mandate. The brinkmanship was over for the time being. There was a something of a new start in the Seattle archdiocese. The ambiguities would have to work themselves out over the next months, but at least for now, the heartbeat of the church in Seattle was returning closer to normal.

FROM ACROSS THE CONTINENT, SISTER RUTH REJOICED OVER THE OUTCOME IN Seattle. Since December, when she joined a nationwide protest against the Vatican's treatment of Archbishop Hunthausen, she had prayed daily for him and his return to full authority. Sister Ruth was among those who felt the resolution was a victory by the Catholics of Seattle and a tacit admission by Rome that it had blundered. Like many others, she savored what seemed to her a humbling setback to the haughty Vatican. The gains might be short-lived, or it might even be a Pyrrhic victory, she allowed, but for the moment the results felt good.

She was approaching age eighty, still moving at a full clip. A few weeks before, she had led a retreat for laypeople in Indiana. What struck her was the increasing parish responsibility assumed by laypeople, partly to compensate for the steady drop in priests. She found lay Catholics from rural Indiana were coping as best they could. "Fewer parishes have priests," she said, "so the people are implementing church services in whatever way they can, taking a lot more on themselves." The irony, she said, was that while the Vatican was making such a fuss about the niceties of church law in Seattle, because of this manpower shortage, in more and more areas churches were being left pastorless and relatively unmonitored.

Leading spiritual retreats and health-care seminars along with her own hospital chaplaincy continued to occupy the bulk of her time. To these various activities she brought her own vision of ministry, heavily influenced by an abiding concern for women. That cause had been strengthened by her study of the Scriptures. In approaching the Bible, her eyes and ears were attuned to the voices and insights between the lines written long ago by men using predominantly male imagery. Sister Ruth had been awakened to a spirit just beneath the surface of those passages, a feminine voice straining to be heard.

Among the references she cited was a Genesis account in which God, speaking to Eve after she and Adam were expelled from Eden, refers to childbirth. The common translation, Sister Ruth said, was, "In sorrow you shall bring forth children." "Sorrow" and "pain" were the standard terms, used synonymously. But she had recently discovered that the original text yielded another definition: "hard work." There was a "vast difference between 'pain and sorrow' and 'hard work,'" Sister Ruth exclaimed. The traditional meaning implied punishment and victimization, she said, whereas "hard work" conveyed a more noble meaning. To her, the oversight was all too typical of male presumptions in biblical scholarship that bore tragic results for women.

"Translations that are selective cause so much unnecessary pain," she said. "There are valuable obscurities that can be surfaced with adequate scholarship and truly human experience. What the problem comes down to is that we are usually not getting the total picture. We base a great deal on Scripture and tradition. I agree in general with that, but I have reservations. The church has received a great deal that is slanted."

Her thoughts were still spinning from something she'd seen the other day on television. The Reverend Hans Küng, the Swiss theologian who had been censured by the Vatican for his doubts about papal infallibility and other renegade views, was the guest on a talk show. Father Küng, as Sister Ruth heard him, had talked about the church dominating lives and causing suffering, claiming that the church as we knew it was not the church of the gospel but a medieval church.

"I can identify with that," Sister Ruth said. "When I hear about tradition, I wonder what is meant by tradition, who are the people who have been called on to represent that tradition. Certainly not women for the most part. It's been one-sided. But as women read and reflect, they write about their own experience of Scripture and of God."

A prophetic voice was being spoken through that voice, one that Sister Ruth believed the church neglected at its peril. "The women I talk with seem to have greater sensitivity toward the faith," she said in her lilting, inviting tone. "But women are not recognized. The spirit is coming through them, through the grass roots. That says something about the Holy Spirit." Then with a spritely laugh, "Even the church can't withstand the Holy Spirit."

She was trying to ignore the drumbeat of publicity over the pope's trip, thankful, she said, "that it's something I don't have to do anything at all about." The talk she heard was mostly griping about the cost of the trip. Two physicians she knew were very upset about the money, she said, but to her it was something to become detached from.

By contrast, she had become increasingly involved in the care of AIDS patients. She paid regular calls on three, aged nineteen, twenty-six, and thirty-four, all close to death. Two of them were women. She had begun to understand more about the disease through her retreat work. Relatives of patients and sufferers themselves had taken part in prayer and soul-baring. Then those with the disease had entered hospitals to which she made herself available for visitation and spiritual counsel. She had grown particularly close to the three patients.

"I've learned so much from them," she said. "One thing I found in common among them is the terrible fear of what would happen to them *before* they die.

"I try to be honest. AIDS is something I don't know as much about as they do. Nobody knows much. I do know that if you can't pinpoint fear it becomes worse. If fear is free-floating, you can't do anything with it.

"They are afraid, and I don't have pat answers. I have some faith and some hope, but it's not my place to try to mouth a lot of words that don't even make sense to me. I try to be honest and sincere. I say there is no certainty of what happens before they die. I can only say, 'I'd be as afraid as you are'—and that I'll stay with them."

STILL OTHER DEVELOPMENTS IN MAY:

- As of May 1, a fund called Mary's Pence would provide an alternative to that other, traditional, collection for the pope, Peter's Pence. The idea sprang from Chicago Catholic Women, a group comprising five hundred lay and religious women. Sister Kay Ashe, prioress general of the Sinsinawa Dominicans, was named to lead the nine-member national board. Its purpose, organizers said, would be to raise resources for women afflicted by violence, poverty, and other hardships. The new campaign—conducted through ads, direct mail solicitations, and appeals to groups—would come on the eve of the annual passing of the hat for the pope. Though the leaders emphasized that their drive was not intended to compete with Peter's Pence or other church collections, the timing of the new charity was intriguing. Could Mary's Pence become a vehicle for protesting the papacy? Catholic officials were already worried that June's appeal for the pope might suffer from the recent conflicts between Rome and the U.S. church. Due largely to better promotional methods, the American sum between 1982 and 1986 had shot up from $5 million to $13 million, nearly half the total raised by the church worldwide for a deficit-ridden Vatican. Mary's Pence organizers said their collection would offer a means of giving to those special needs of women that had long been underfunded by the church. Among the first contributions was a thousand dollars from the Association of Chicago Priests.

• Amid many complaints, the amnesty program for illegal aliens got off to a slow start on opening day, May 5. A total of 107 centers authorized by the Immigration and Naturalization Service, a sizable number sponsored by the Catholic church, began a year of receiving applications for temporary citizenship. To qualify, an applicant had to prove residence before January 1, 1982. Each center was equipped with a 310-page book of regulations, which many critics considered far too stringent. Church officials continued to appeal for a change in the program to make it possible for family members who could not pass the test to remain with those who did. It was believed that many qualified people stayed away for fear the INS would deport their spouses, children, and other relatives. On May 7, the president of the bishops' conference, Archbishop John L. May, called for President Reagan's "personal intervention" to grant "special status" to the nonqualifying family members so as "to remove the uncertainty facing these individuals and convince all eligible undocumented aliens to come forward and obtain the legal status the law envisions." Other officials of the bishops' conference kept protesting what they considered exorbitant fees imposed on applicants.

Neither the White House nor the INS had shown any indication of budging. The begrudging attitude surrounding the amnesty program—and the wariness about how it would actually be implemented—only deepened distrust of the INS among the potential applicants. The May 23 issue of *America* noted "an uneasy suspicion abroad that the amnesty program has not been working smoothly so far and that even when all the glitches have been eliminated, the program will retain sinister possibilities of working misery in some cases . . . aliens have not much reason to expect geniality from the INS, which has already indicated that it expects to be rejecting millions of the applications." Somewhere between 2.5 and 3.9 million people had been expected to seek amnesty, but in light of the scant turnout in the first weeks, estimates were falling.

• The Gallup Poll asked Catholics, "Looking ahead ten years, do you think the Roman Catholic church will be stronger in the world than it is today, or not?" The results: yes, 23 percent; no, 46 percent; the same, 22 percent; no opinion, 9 percent.

• The Catholic bishops formed a task force on AIDS headed by Bishop William Hughes of Covington, Kentucky, to help coordinate policy and establish consensus on several aspects of the escalating epidemic. Compassion, sexual morality, and practical assistance were key aspects of the church's response, though the weight assigned to each element differed according to the outlook of whoever was doing the responding. The May *Columbia* magazine of the Knights of Columbus included some thoughts by columnist Russell Shaw, secretary for public affairs for the United States Catholic Conference. Shaw's unmistakably conservative views honed in principally on AIDS as a symptom of moral degeneracy. "Although there are many ways of viewing the AIDS crisis," he began, "it should be clear among other things that the individual and social consequences of the so-called sexual revolution are coming home to roost in a spectacular and disastrous way." AIDS sufferers deserve sympathetic treatment, Shaw said, and "punitive, panicky measures merit no encouragement" (p. 4). But the key now was prevention through repudiation of error and vice. Referring to the reported cases of priests with AIDS, Shaw identified the cause as two decades of liberal opposition to mandatory celibacy and approval of gay sex. "You cannot spend 20 years encouraging people to play with fire," he wrote, "and expect no one will get burned." The answers lay in reclaiming "self-discipline, abstinence, a return to traditional values and standards of behavior." The scourge might represent "the last gasp of the discredited permissiveness which has done so much harm to individuals and society," Shaw said. "If so, the country has paid a terribly steep price just to reach this point" (p. 4). It was undoubtedly a conclusion that was widely shared across Catholic America.

- The two-pronged effort by the Quixote Center to bring relief to Nicaragua forged ahead on strengths it often did not know it had. Politically, the Mount Rainier, Maryland, center lobbied hard for an end to aid to the Contras and peaceful relations between the Reagan administration and the Sandinistas. Specifically, the Quixote staff pressed ahead toward a goal of matching the $100 million in congressional aid to the Contras by raising an equivalent amount in humanitarian assistance for the Nicaraguan people. A "socially conscious" telephone fund-raising agency had been hired to solicit funds for shipping goods. It was yielding encouraging results. On the morning of May 22, for example, the staff reported pledges of nearly $17,000 from the calling blitz the night before. Another $1,000 check from a religious order had come in the mail. The Nicaraguan "Quest for Peace" total stood now at $36.8 million.

- The *National Catholic Reporter* (May 8) published some findings from a comparative study of priests. The results were reported by a team of Catholic University sociologists: Dean R. Hoge, Joseph J. Shields, and Mary Jeanne

Verdieck. The data compared attitudes of priests in 1970 with those in 1985. Generally, the group concluded, the priesthood has grown more liberal, though young priests have become more conservative. Nearly three-fourths (71 percent) in both samples believed ordination conferred on the priest "a new status of a permanent character which makes him essentially different from the laity within the church." Conversely, only about one in five (18 percent in 1970, 20 percent in 1985) believed "there is no ontological difference between the priest and the laity." About half in each sample thought celibacy should be optional, and an overwhelming percentage (87 percent, 85 percent) agreed, "The Catholic church is the one true church established by Christ, with Saint Peter and his successors at its head." Belief that "God's word" came through such figures as Mohandas Gandhi or Martin Luther King, Jr., had increased from 58 percent to 65 percent, as had the idea that a person should sometimes put "personal conscience above the church's teaching" (from 52 percent to 61 percent). The spirit of pluralism and freedom of conscience was alive and appeared to be gaining ground even among priests. Between the two measuring years, 14–16 percent of diocesan priests and 17–20 percent of religious priests had resigned, the study said.

• Once again, in the third week of May, a trial against the four defendants in the Epiphany Plowshares trial in Philadelphia ended in a deadlocked jury. The group of two priests and two laypeople had admitted their trespass onto the Willow Grove, Pennsylvania, naval air station on January 6 to conduct an antinuclear protest that left Army and Navy aircraft damaged. They had appealed to higher conscience. The first jury also was unable to reach a verdict. Meanwhile, the National Federation of Priests' Councils at its annual meeting voted 89 to 37 to ask Cardinal John Krol to reinstate the two Plowshares priests. The cardinal had suspended them after they were arrested for conducting the raid. A third trial was set for July 13.

• Like a once-prosperous nobleman looking frayed but no less dignified, venerable old Saint Joseph parish still stood its ground in a decaying part of Cleveland. But its extinction, lamentable though it was in the eyes of the diocese, seemed a step closer. The diocese could not justify spending $1 million to refurbish an admittedly grand Gothic structure that had no congregation any longer. It had bought the attached friary from the Franciscans, and the last members of that order had moved out. Now the premises were starkly empty. The Save Saint Joseph coalition, however, was nowhere ready to concede defeat. Vowing to raise the funds needed to permanently stay the diocese's demolition order, the group said it was reviewing alternative uses for the buildings but was not discussing details of any concrete plans.

CARL WOULD SOON BECOME A DEACON. HE WAS WINDING UP HIS THIRD AND final year of studies this month at the seminary. Ordination by the bishop came next. At that point he expected to step down as president of a small company that made parts for computer printers.

At age sixty-seven, Carl said he felt that "the Lord has called me to do something more, to expend the energy I can to serve." He was drawn to social ethics, he said, in particular "the relationship between moral decision making and economics, where I feel I can help." To him that meant, among other things, focusing on the gap between rich and poor. He had heard the bishops' letter on the economy as a clarion call and wanted to help implement its message.

He was among nearly 1,900 American men preparing for the diaconate. Since the tradition had been revived by the Second Vatican Council, more than 8,400 candidates had been ordained in the United States, far more than in any other country. According to statistics from the bishops' conference, nearly nine in ten deacons (88 percent) were over the age of forty; slightly more than a quarter of them were over sixty. Eight in ten (82 percent) were white, 13 percent Hispanic, and 4 percent black. Nearly all (93 percent) were married, 4 percent were celibate, 2 percent widowers, and 1 percent divorced.

Deacons had become increasingly visible, though their status was still somewhat murky. To many Catholics, they came across as fascinating hybrids, somewhere between laymen and priests, living secular lives with their families and taking on clerical roles in the church. Deacons performed a variety of functions within parishes. They read Scripture lessons, did baptisms, visited the sick, taught religious education classes, and generally helped the pastor. Forty-three percent of ordained deacons were under contract by parishes or dioceses, of whom just 4 percent received pay.

The precise identity of the deacon remained foggy in much of Catholic America. His duties were often defined by the priest in charge, but varied immensely from place to place. And many found it difficult to distinguish between deacons and full-time lay ministers, many of whom had received similar training. Deacons were allowed to preside over all the sacraments except penance and the Eucharist (consecration of the host), so they had considerable latitude. They were being used more and more to take the place of nonexistent priests, but to many parishioners they seemed neither fish nor fowl.

Carl echoed that concern. "The diaconate is not too well understood," he said, seated next to his wife, Lois, in the modern living quarters of the suburban Minneapolis rectory adjoining their parish. "The bishops have done a poor job defining deacons, who wound up being not much more than lay ministers. But I don't personally place great value on ordination anyway. The more I see what the 'People of God' means, the less credence I put on ordination."

That one theological concept, "the People of God," had turned the church upside down and Carl along with it. As proffered by Pope John and woven into the Second Vatican Council, it was the horizontal counterpoint to a vertical church, proclaiming democracy in the midst of monarchy, defining the church first and foremost as the people rather than the hierarchy.

For Carl, the idea was overpowering. As the Council was ending, he, Lois, and their six children were living in Milwaukee. Their parish priest had held special meetings to explain the Council's message. Up to that point, Carl recalled, he had clung to the view that "being a Catholic meant following rules and regulations. I thought solutions came from the church above and that the church and the world were separate. So naturally I could separate my business from my life." The Council's thinking overturned his own, he said, bringing about a "reawakening," a conversion that he described as "greater than switching religions."

In 1965, the final year of the Council, Carl remembered thinking that "for forty-five years of my life I had believed that rules and regulations were going to be my salvation. The 'People of God' concept took me from rules and regulations to the belief that *we* were the Kingdom of God." About the same time he became involved in the civil rights movement under the leadership of the Reverend James Groppi. He also resolved to apply the insights from Vatican II to his role in the family. So long as he had pictured the household as a reflection of a church centered in obedience to authority, he had been a taskmaster, he said, "very results oriented." With the shift toward his new thinking, he said he had "given up acting like an authoritarian father."

Carl, a rangy man with kindly features who chose his words well and carefully, had entered the Army during the Second World War after his graduation from Dartmouth. Upon his return from the service, he began a series of successful corporate moves within the electric engine industry. He had ventured into his own enterprises more recently but planned to retire after his deacon training ended.

Lois was thoughtful and spirited. She had been raised a Lutheran. She and Carl had been married after the war in a church rectory because "Carl's parents wouldn't come to the church. Protestants were treated like second-class citizens." She converted to Catholicism after the birth of the couple's first child. Lois had done the lion's share in raising their six children. They were scattered among the occupations: lawyer, doctor, engineer, banker, and book editor. One was still in school. Two had married Catholics and one a Protestant, and three were unmarried.

The couple had gone through deacon's preparation together. Lois had signed up for all the requisite courses and was fully conversant with many fine points of current theological debate. The two of them had followed the Curran case with keen interest. Both believed he had been dealt an unjust blow by the Vatican. "We feel moral theologians have to have the opportunity to speak their minds," Lois said. "There's not a seminary in the country that doesn't have a Charles Curran."

With her knowledge came growing irritation that she was barred from becoming a deacon herself. "It infuriates me that I don't have the choice," she said. "I've taken all the classes, worked on all the projects, and taken all the hospital pastoral training." Her awakened convictions about women in the church had broadened. She now believed women should be admitted to the priesthood as well as the diaconate. "There are such qualified, spiritual women who'd make the most wonderful priests," she said.

As Carl looked back over his diaconate training, he thought the basic "People of God" theology had served him well. He was convinced that the hierarchically ordered church of his youth was no longer either possible or desirable. "My theology was well founded before the diaconate program," he said. "During our first session together as a class, we were told we were a Vatican II diaconate and that anybody pre–Vatican II had no place in it." In a word, he said, "We can't be forced back to a church we no longer believe can save us in the ways we thought."

There were eight in his class. After ordination, they would take on various assignments. Carl would stay in his community and work with his parish and perhaps with the wider church. No plans were yet definite. He would work closely with Lois, he said. They were already a team, like some other diaconate couples who, some argued, helped prepare the ground for acceptance of a married priesthood.

Carl hoped he could combine his social justice interests with his skills as an administrator. The possibility seemed real because of the parish's eagerness to develop new programs and its record of strong lay involvement. His experience with that vitality had confirmed his belief that such lay-centered parishes were on a collision course with efforts to reimpose hierarchical authority. Such efforts would be futile, he thought.

The parish's openness to initiatives such as he proposed was accompanied by tough challenges. Carl and Lois lived in an upper-middle-class community where they felt strong resistance to the church's teachings on social justice. The moral climate of the community had changed, they said, in the direction of greater materialism and greater isolation from the wider world. The much-discussed epidemic of greed had struck. "Things have gone in a progression here," Carl said, "from individual selfishness to group selfishness." Social problems existed there, he said, "but they're more hidden."

Carl considered the bishops' pastoral on the economy a good starting point for his work in the diaconate. The premise of the bishops' letter was reaffirmation of a common humanity in which no walls of privilege divided some from others and all were entitled to certain economic rights. Carl's goal was to get that message across. Deacons should be used to better effect, he thought, and he would soon find out what it was like to test those limits.

"We're an affluent parish," he said. He continued with an application of the "People of God" concept that had sustained him since his rebirth in the church. "We can't touch the problems of people in the center of Minneapolis unless we can get people to understand what it means to be the body of Christ of which we are all a part. We can touch some of those problems when we realize that what we do is not charity but part of social justice."

━ ━

WITH THE TWO-HUNDREDTH BIRTHDAY OF THE U.S. CONSTITUTION PASSING rather quietly, an archbishop submitted an ambitious tribute from his particular vantage point in Catholic America. Archbishop J. Francis Stafford of Denver issued a pastoral letter on May 28 that combined a salute to the Constitution with a celebration of the archdiocese's centennial and anticipated the bicentennial of the founding of the U.S. Catholic hierarchy.

The archbishop had gained prominence among the rising young Vatican loyalists in the hierarchy, and his pastoral letter reflected both the new orthodoxy and a neoconservative political slant. The format suggested a scholarly approach to the question of what it meant to be Catholic and American. Allusions to church tradition mingled with quotes from the Founding Fathers and principles of church-state relations from that once silenced but now venerated Jesuit, John Courtney Murray.

Though the pastoral took on this somewhat formal structure, its contents hardly represented a detached outlook. The archbishop had some things to say, and say them he did. Among his points were these:

> The bishops in the last century developed a theology of democracy while combating anti-Catholic nativism and came to see the American republic as an instrument of God's purposes.

> The American experiment was threatened by rampant individualism, which had reduced freedom to "simple license" and elevated personal gain over the common good.

> The best hope for promoting the democracy's health was to return to the medieval concept of fostering common virtue, an idea the archbishop traced to the Founding Fathers and to Father Murray ("the founders and framers,

whether they acknowledged it or not, were reflecting Christian medieval concepts of the right ordering of society, culture and polity," the archbishop claimed).

In sum, pernicious individualism stemmed from the revolutions of modern times, starting with the anticlerical French, whereas the redeeming vision of a just, well-ordered society of virtue was the gift of the medieval church.

It was time for Catholics to take advantage of their strength of tradition and growing influence on America to help restore the moral life of virtue necessary to keep the promise of American democracy.

Catholic theology with regard to human nature contained the vital balance between hope and realism needed to steer a true moral course for the future.

Better government was less government insofar as the medieval church taught that "only a virtuous people could be free and just: and that human rights were not benefits distributed by the state, but were in fact inviolable personal claims that the state had to respect."

The nurture of virtue was the indispensable ingredient in a healthy society ("The integrity of our moral culture is the essential condition for the continued development of the American experiment according to the standard of liberty and justice for all").

Freedom was the antithesis of acting on impulse, rather, taking Lord Acton's definition, it was "not the power of doing what we like, but the right of being able to do what we ought."

A diligent search for the "oughts," the moral laws that should obtain in a society, was overdue.

Roe v. *Wade,* legalizing abortion, was a "reactionary decision" because it violated the desired harmony between "individual liberty and the common good."

Family values, as taught by the church, and free enterprise, the gift of democratic capitalism, were critical foundation blocks in the building of a good and just society ("The entrepreneur who creates hundreds of new jobs is performing a morally good act").

America should boldly espouse responsible freedom and oppose tyrants "of either the traditional or modern stripe" (an endorsement of the Contras in their fight against the Sandinistas, often construed as the nearest and most

dangerous of totalitarians by the neoconservatives, seemed implicit here, perhaps in response to Bishop McGann's censoring of William Casey earlier in
the month).

In short, Archbishop Stafford stood tall for the Constitution and exhorted Catholics to help repair the morally chaotic republic that he saw disintegrating under
it. The forces of the modern revolutionary had overtaken the sane values of the
medieval church, and it was time, with the church's help, to engender virtue to
save the American character and guide it into the next century. It would require,
he thought, a combination of relatively unrestrained economic freedom and voluntarily restrained moral freedom. Government could not do the job. It would
take the resources of those private institutions, perhaps mostly the church, to ensure the preservation and fulfillment of those precepts embodied in that noble
Constitution, our most precious political document.

June
1·9·8·7

——

THE ANNUAL RITES OF SPRING HAD BROUGHT THE ACADEMIC
year at Saint Ambrose to a close. Final grades had been recorded after the usual crunch, students had packed their belongings, and seniors stayed on to receive their diplomas at festive
graduation ceremonies presided over by Father Caron.

Two items attracted special attention among alumni, parents, and students. One
was the plan by the college to introduce coed housing in the fall. The other was the
announcement of an $11.5-million gift to the endowment.

Both developments had, in different ways, required Father Caron to balance the
needs of contemporary education with traditional values of the church.

The proposal to open a residence for both men and women was high on Father
Caron's personal agenda, aimed in part at bringing Saint Ambrose up-to-date.
Before becoming president of the college five years before, he had taught at an-
other Catholic institution where coed dormitories had existed for a dozen years.
Such arrangements were a commonplace feature on campuses, a factor that Saint
Ambrose had to consider in order to compete for high-quality applicants.

Students favored the idea, faculty committees endorsed it, and the trustees
seemed poised to give it a thumbs up. But the alumni board balked, arguing that
such a move would foster sexual hanky-panky. Given the importance of the
alumni, the board's objections threatened to derail the orderly process by pro-
longing the debate. To avert a stalemate, Father Caron explained, he had exercised
his legitimate authority to approve the plan "by fiat." Among the arguments he advanced in its favor was that "statistics show that there is less promiscuity in coed
dorms." But many conservative Catholics were not convinced, he conceded, and
their opposition could still hamper smooth implementation.

The eye-popping gift to the endowment carried moral implications of a much different sort. Like any college president struggling to make ends meet, Father Caron was thrilled by this sudden infusion of capital. But he also felt the call of the church's cry on behalf of the poor. He had absorbed the bishops' pastoral letter on the economy with an eye toward what it meant for Catholics like himself who oversaw the handling of large sums of money. He sensed both the opportunity and the responsibility of the $11.5-million bundle that had landed on his doorstep. It focused his attention on the church's "preferential option for the poor" (the phrase introduced by Pope Paul VI in an encyclical on justice) and conjured new projects in his mind. It struck him as a blessing and a potential temptation to go astray of the church's pledge to the downtrodden.

Father Caron puzzled over how money and other resources might help fulfill the church's teaching. He noted the tension between giving handouts and attacking systems. "When we talk about the option for the poor, we are creating the seeds for social change," he said. "I have no problem with those doing direct service to the poor, but how does that weigh against the need for more structural change? We tend to forget the impact we need to have on social change. And we forget what sacrifice means. Giving out of largesse is far different from breaking into the core of the widow's mite."

A program to help students and faculty become more aware of social justice and human need was getting under way. Volunteers were being enlisted, professors and students were getting firsthand experience living among homeless and impoverished people, and academic courses exploring the bases of poverty and injustice were in the formative stages.

Exposure to the underside of life in America helped open the question of "how we're special as a Catholic university," Father Caron said. He had come back from a recent excursion into the city's slums with students and faculty. After the brief, shocking foray, they had talked. "We discussed what it means to be an ethical person," he recalled. "We got into the questioning of the structures of our society as a whole, especially as it's built on our sense of competition. At the end of our session, we talked about what corporate society regards as success as compared to what the gospel regards as success."

Partly as the result of the bishops' letter and direct contact with these problems, he had become more aware of the ethical dimensions of the economy. "I had not been teaching those things nearly as much as the subjects of sexuality and war and peace," he wrote. The balance was shifting.

Hefty contributions to the endowment made programs in social justice more possible, Father Caron reasoned, but he was not sure how far to press this cause. The fact was, big donors, as a rule, frowned on projects that raised serious questions about the system that had produced their wealth (to the point of favoring redistribution of that wealth—a most unwelcome outcome) and were among the likeliest foes of the bishops' views of economic justice. In contrast, they generally favored charitable activities that provided direct services. Father Caron had no intention of soliciting gifts under false pretenses. He had both academic and church values to pursue, and that required both honesty and daring. That is, it demanded loads of diplomacy.

Scouting funds entailed rubbing shoulders with the rich and the mighty. "The only way we [Saint Ambrose] are going to be successful," he said, "is to excite the people who have the resources and are prepared to be very generous. As president, I need to be in that setting where they are living a very, very successful life-style. I must be as comfortable with it as possible."

The danger Father Caron saw in himself was not that he would feel aversion toward luxury but that he would like it too much. "I like nice things," he said. "That helps me to know I could be attracted to such things. Knowing the materialism in yourself helps you recognize what you can get sucked into. I like to go first class. People like me get first-class tickets on the airlines. If I didn't, would it be more attractive or less? Does it make it harder to understand what it means to be poor? I happen to have university credit cards. What is university business? How do I balance things for the good of the university?"

Two other matters were occupying Father Caron's attention: preparation for the course on sexuality he would be teaching again in the fall and the Damoclean sword from the Vatican that still hung over academic freedom in Catholic universities.

On sexuality, he intended to follow his established pattern of mixing doctrine with dissent. "I feel a responsibility to teach what the church teaches," he said firmly, "and also what scholars see as inadequate in it." The most troubling aspect was homosexuality. The Vatican's document on the subject the previous October—labeled derisively as "The Halloween Statement"—had immediately struck him as a step backward. Further reflection had confirmed his dismay. "It's part of a pattern of retrenchment by the Vatican," Father Caron intoned angrily. "Part of me sees it as a vindictive thing. The Vatican seems to be feeling its oats, bringing all the baggage of AIDS and the fear that gays will rape children to bear on this issue. But I can't understand why they felt such a need."

Previously he had taught the church's official distinction between homosexual nature, not considered bad in itself, and sexual expression of it, which was condemned as sinful. But with the new document the distinction had been erased, and homosexual nature itself was declared "inherently disordered," that is, disposed toward sinful acts. That made Father Caron's teaching assignment tougher. "At what point does it become sin?" he asked. "Maybe that means friendship between homosexuals is no good."

The effort to shove Dignity, the largest organization of gay Catholics, out of church premises was itself "a disaster," Father Caron said, even though in his view Dignity's stance was too militant. For all its faults, he said, Dignity was a meeting place for gays who would otherwise shun the church. As it stood, the Vatican had done an immense disservice to them, he believed, to wit: "Imagine saying to people that their nature is cursed."

On the academic freedom front, he was hearing rumors that the Vatican might either shelve its document on higher education or scale it down to make it acceptable. Like other Catholic college presidents, he was most concerned about the emphasis in earlier drafts of the statement that encouraged more direct involvement by the hierarchy in internal policies. Such a step, the presidents feared, might give bishops the power to remove faculty members and thereby constituted a threat to the separation of church and state.

Giving the hierarchy a role as guardians of orthodoxy on campus could create a cramped, anxious climate, Father Caron thought. He accepted the view that attempts to suppress unpopular views only gave them more credibility. So far he had experienced no problems with the local bishop, but the Vatican attempt to issue a document had planted the worry.

Father Caron was looking forward to the summer schedule of few meetings and only a handful of public appearances. He wanted to read and think about things that tended to get put off during the hectic school year. Was it a lonely job? "Yes," he said softly, "especially being unmarried. My religious community is there, but of course as faculty members they have their own ties to the university, and as president I have to be cautious in relating to them. They've been pretty good about it.

"Expectations come to me from all the various constituencies, and sometimes they conflict. It's a heavy job."

LIGHT FROM THE BRIGHT SATURDAY MORNING SUN STREAMED THROUGH THE round transparent roof of Our Lady of Fátima Church, bathing the bronzed figure of the risen Christ behind the altar in a soft luster. The concrete-and-wood structure, situated in a thickly settled, middle-class section of Seattle, was about to take part in an event that dramatically placed modern technology at the service of pious tradition.

Two giant video screens—several feet apart—faced the congregation. Soon, if all went as planned, those screens would carry live pictures of the pope entering Saint Mary Major basilica in Rome to recite the rosary. Millions of Catholics around the world would be watching and following along.

The $2.6-million television spectacular, financed by the Bic corporation and other commercial sponsors, was designed to help usher in a year devoted to the Blessed Virgin Mary. John Paul II had announced back in January that a Marian

year would officially begin on Pentecost, June 7, preceded by the rosary the day
before. Preparations were extraordinary. Not only would the pope be televised live,
but gatherings of Catholics in sixteen locations around the earth, all of them
shrines to Mary, would be interconnected. The project required the use of eighteen
communications satellites working in unison. Altogether, thirty-one countries,
including, of course, the United States, would be able to receive the telecast.

Thus, places with names that evoked mystery and miracles—Knock, Lourdes,
Czestochowa, Fátima, Guadalupe—would be linked together in a great space-
age prayer chain. Gatherings at Marian sites in Paraguay, Senegal, the Philippines,
and Portugal would join those in many other scattered locations to watch the pope
in the grand basilica in Rome speak five languages as he led them in the familiar,
soothing cadences of the paean of praise, "Hail, Mary, full of grace . . ."

In Our Lady of Fátima, technicians were making the final checks before the
vast, intricate system was set in motion. Because the local CBS affiliate was facilitating the relay, a signal from the station played on one of the screens as a way of
testing picture quality. As it was Saturday morning, the affiliate was carrying the
regular fare, kids' cartoons. The effect was surreal. In the solemn atmosphere of a
parish awaiting the pope, animated figures cavorted recklessly and boisterously
across the big screen, snookering, clobbering, and chasing each other with their
regular madcap frenzy and indestructible daring. People seated in long wooden
pews watched as silently and impassively as might a group of children inured to
the sheer zaniness of it all. The other screen was blank.

Just before the stroke of ten, Archbishop Hunthausen quietly entered the sanctuary, strode down the side aisle, and sat in the front pew facing the right-hand
screen. He wore a white robe, white stole, and red skullcap. When a similarly
white-robed John Paul II suddenly appeared in muted colors on both of the
slightly concave grainy surfaces, the archbishop led the congregation to its feet.
Later, he knelt in prayer with his people, facing the luminous image of the pope.

Science had brought these two formidable church leaders into eerie communion only weeks after a dispute threatened to dissolve their hierarchical bond. The
pope, in obvious agreement with the criticisms made of his bishop in Seattle,
had set forth the terms of discipline and settlement of the crisis. The archbishop,
after balking at the terms and warning that he would try to take his case directly
to the pope, had backed off and accepted the slightly amended pact. The pope had
endorsed it. The archbishop had announced the package at a May 27 news conference, just ten days before. Bishop Thomas Murphy had been named coadjutor
archbishop, the unpopular auxiliary Bishop Donald Wuerl dismissed as the
Vatican's enforcer, and the archbishop restored to his full powers.

The one-way viewing of the pope was the closest the archbishop had come to
a face-to-face encounter with his ecclesiastical boss since the Vatican's disciplinary action against him had erupted into a major conflict. The opening of the

Marian year offered an ideal occasion for displaying solidarity in faith. Mary represented unconditional humility and love. She was common ground between pope and archbishop, the model they both aspired to, the intercessor to whom they both prayed. A Marian year promised both renewal and hope.

In a six-minute homily, John Paul reflected those sentiments: "This, brothers and sisters scattered from one end of the earth to the other, is the message which the Virgin brings to each of us at this special moment: God is love! Whoever you are, whatever your life may be like, God loves you. He loves you totally."

At the conclusion of the rosary, cameras panned the sixteen Marian shrines, where participants sang together the "Salve Regina." Among the faces was that of Archbishop Hickey from the jammed Shrine of the Immaculate Conception in Washington. The picture stirred another memory of the Seattle ordeal. Archbishop Hickey had been sent by the Vatican in 1983 to investigate the charges against the Seattle archbishop.

As the singing brought the prayerful hour-long pageantry to a close and John Paul left the basilica, Archbishop Hunthausen joined the wave of applause arising in Our Lady of Fátima parish and feeding in from the sites around the globe.

The archbishop then arose and faced the people for some comments of his own. He looked tired but flashed a broad smile. His face bore an expression of reverie and meditation.

"For me, it has been a marvelously moving moment," he said. Perhaps as an expression of his yearning for unity, he saw in the Marian year the seeds of healing. "I hope," he continued, "that it will draw us closer together as a human family, as sons and daughters of the same God." He always felt "close to the Holy Father," he said, "but saying the rosary with him—with the rosary he gave me several years ago—in a special way has drawn me closer to this experience."

He had been dazzled by the magnitude of the event made possible by advanced technology. "It is fair to say that this morning we've experienced the fruits of a revolution that has begun to change the way we see ourselves," he said. "It's so important that we use the media to draw us closer together as a people."

The archbishop asked for a deeper understanding of Mary's role in the life of the church. He asked for her intercession for those who suffer and for peace, "not just in the arms race but in misunderstandings which lead to conflict." He urged "all to use devotion to Mary as help and hope in these troubled times. Thank you."

Spirited applause rose up from the pews as the archbishop made his way out of the church. The next day, Pentecost Sunday, he was scheduled to return to the Trident nuclear submarine base in Bangor, Washington, to commemorate antinuclear protests. He had been a regular at such protests, and, though this was not billed as a protest itself, he felt the call of duty in honoring those who had put themselves on the line, sometimes at a considerable price.

In the aftermath of the settlement, a sizable number of Seattle Catholics remained convinced that Rome's actions against the archbishop were the result of his highly visible protests against nuclear weapons.

A fresh piece of circumstantial evidence stoked those suspicions. Catholics from the archdiocese traveling in Poland had heard about the agreement from Polish church officials several days before the news was made public in the United States. The Seattle visitors surmised that Polish church leaders were keeping close tabs on the situation because of their belief that it had implications for U.S. military policy.

According to this view, the Poles feared that antinuclear protests such as those in which Archbishop Hunthausen took part might lead to a weakening of the U.S. nuclear deterrent against their communist nemesis, the Soviet Union. The analysis assumed that the pope, who had approved of deterrence as a step toward disarmament, had likewise been susceptible to pressures from the American government to curb the peacenik Hunthausen. By coincidence, the pope had met with President Reagan at the Vatican on the day of the worldwide telecast of the rosary.

Allegations that the archbishop had been victimized by the Vatican at the behest of U.S. officials had been repeatedly denied by both church and state, but the conspiracy theory refused to die among many of Seattle's Catholics. Why else, they continued to wonder, would Rome move against him? Lapses in church practice and weaknesses in leadership could be found anywhere. What made the archbishop different, they believed, was that he spoke out against the pride of the Navy's nuclear defense and refused to pay taxes to the U.S. government for the portion he felt went to defense. He had stood out as a nagging voice of conscience, and the government had enlisted the church to slap him down. That account of the matter had widespread currency in Seattle despite the vigorous denials.

In the days after Archbishop Hunthausen stood together with Bishop Murphy at the landmark news conference, Seattle was still sorting it all out. The air was filled with caution. Many were glad the ordeal was over but still felt violated and skeptical. Bishop Wuerl had been sent to Seattle as an auxiliary but, as it turned out after months of smoldering confusion, had been authorized to take over some of the archbishop's powers. Who was to say Rome was on the level this time? Trust had worn thin. Many were bitter about the diagnosis of the archdiocese that the special commission had handed down at the time of the news conference. It had spoken of a "climate of permissiveness" that the archbishop had allowed to prevail in Seattle. It was this attitude, the commission said, that must be cleared up in order to eliminate the irregular practices cited by Cardinal Ratzinger. Archbishop Hunthausen had himself publicly rejected the commission's conclusions.

The archbishop appeared to have gained even greater stature in the eyes of his flock as the result of the controversy. Such was his high standing that the charges by Rome were largely sloughed off as nonsense or condemned as persecution. By now, it was generally accepted that his popularity had forced the pope's hand. When Rome had struck its hardest blow by sending Bishop Wuerl to usurp some of the archbishop's authority, it had been the huge outcry from the archdiocese that had led the Vatican to negotiate a settlement. They had staged a popular uprising on the archbishop's behalf with apparent success. From that, they felt some sense of victory.

There was, then, acceptance of the settlement but little enthusiasm for it. Many in Seattle indeed felt their Catholicism had been impugned and predicted that the wounds would not heal quickly. "There's been a lot of pain and suffering," said Mary Pat Olson, a lawyer active in Catholic Network Northwest, a pro-Hunthausen group. "It will not be wiped away by an announcement of an agreement." Others saw the agreement as a grudging compromise at best or even a ruse. Concerned Catholics believed the struggle was far from over. They vowed to keep watch.

"This is an interesting chapter," the Reverend Michael McDermott, director of administration for the archdiocese, told the Seattle Post-Intelligencer soon after the settlement was announced, "but it's not the final chapter."

THE DAY BEFORE WHIRLING SATELLITES DELIVERED THE POPE TO SEATTLE, A LEADing Jesuit theologian arrived in a Seattle University lecture hall to expound on the subject for these times, "Dissent in the Church."

The Reverend Richard McCormick, S.J., had become one of the most respected and widely quoted moral theologians in Catholic America. Through his many books, scores of talks, and decades of teaching at Georgetown University and, more recently, at Notre Dame, Father McCormick had honed a distinctively progressive outlook in assessing the array of moral problems that confronted twentieth-century Catholics.

His topic, dissent, might have seemed inflammatory in the emotionally charged atmosphere of Seattle, but it actually had little to do with the roots of the Seattle conflict. Archbishop Hunthausen had been accused of allowing practices that implied or even encouraged dissent, but he had never been charged with dissent himself. The quarrel in Seattle, overtly at least, was about *authority*. The archbishop was repeatedly portrayed as a doctrinal loyalist. The case of Father Curran, Father's McCormick's blood brother in moral theology, was, of course, a wholly different matter. It was about the church's right to compel total doctrinal conformity. He had been suspended for refusing to bend, for refusing to abandon his disagreements with church teaching. That clearly *was* about dissent.

Father McCormick began by citing the traditional distinction, alluded to by Pope John XXIII in opening the Second Vatican Council, between the pure and ineffable "substance" of belief and its "formulation" in human words, which was "always subject to improvement." Believers, then, were limited by language but might come closer to expressing the "substance" of their faith over time. Formulations changed, Father McCormick said, and as the new replaced the old, tensions arose.

"Distancing from past formulations is what I mean by dissent," Father McCormick said. During such transitions, he said, the focus usually shifted away from the moral issues themselves toward matters of ecclesiastical conflict over change and conformity. Analysis of the problems and the search for better answers generally took a backseat to squabbles over who should control the church's future. Such a shift, he said, had thrown the current church into wrenching turmoil.

Attitudes toward dissent depended on "one's image" of how the church defined its teachings, Father McCormick continued. That rested on how much weight was given to the "experience and reflection of the faithful," that is, the collective wisdom of the people.

Two distinct views had emerged, he said. One maintained that, of course, the people of faith "have to be listened to, but those in authority must determine the truth." The other believed that "the experience and reflection of the faithful was essential to a binding proclamation of truth. If many don't see the wisdom of a proposed teaching and it is not understood by the people, then it may be improperly formulated, poorly expressed, perhaps even wrong."

Father McCormick continued, "A bishop of the first view tells people what is right in an authoritative statement of certainty and clarity." By comparison, a bishop of the second view believed in "discovering together what is right, in doctrinal development, in doubt and questioning and the ordinary processes of human learning."

One way of discerning teaching was vertical; the other, horizontal. One saw teaching from a model Father McCormick described as "descending" from the top; the other was "ascending" from the bottom. The first had prevailed in the pre–Vatican II or "preconciliar" church; the second had arisen on the wings of the Second Vatican Council and marked the "postconciliar" church.

The preconciliar outlook employed a "pyramidical model" whereby "truth and authority descended from above" and whereby the term "church," to all intents and purposes, meant "a small group in authority," Father McCormick asserted. It tried to protect the people from the complexity of moral and spiritual issues, viewing education as a "highly defensive" activity that expected docility and passivity by students and people. Authority was "highly centralized," and "the only ones with education were clerics." Thomistic philosophy provided a uniform system of unquestioned thought. Non-Catholics were seen as "adversaries." Theologians were assigned to "mediate the teachings of the hierarchy."

There was "undue distinction between teaching and learning," Father McCormick said. "Undue emphasis on the 'right to teach' [by church authorities]. Undue isolation of one function—the decisive word, the hierarchical issuance of authoritative decrees."

From the other direction, the postconciliar church matched up very favorably indeed in Father McCormick's estimation. It was a perspective well suited to Catholic America's democratic creed. It was rooted, Father McCormick said, in "a self-definition of the church as the 'people of God,' concentric not pyramidical, with the people as a source of revelation and wisdom, where there is two-way communication" between people and clergy. Complexity of mind and faith was encouraged ("Catholics have become immersed in cultural and intellectual life as never before"), authority was exercised collegially at all levels ("at least in theory"), education was open to all, and non-Catholics were sought out "as sources of wisdom."

Under the guidelines of openness and participation, education under postconciliar auspices became something radically different from the preconciliar variety. It emphasized "student engagement and involvement" and relaxed Thomistic hegemony in favor of "pluralism in philosophy." Good education required that "the learning process be essential to the teaching process, that teaching be a multi-disciplined function and that it involve the competence of all of us."

Furthermore, the "proper response" to good teaching was "not exactly obedience," Father McCormick explained, but an attempt to "assimilate the teacher's wisdom, a docility of mind and will eager to make the wisdom of the teacher my own with readiness to reassess our own opinions." As a moral theologian of the church, he would hesitate to disagree so as to cast disrespect on others in public forum. However, that did not rule out taking a stand after much soul-searching. "If I dissent," he concluded, "it's the end of an arduous, prayerful, reflective process.

"The response of dissent is an end and a beginning. It's the end of an arduous process; it's also the beginning of a new reflection in the church.

"If a large group of demonstrably loyal people find themselves unable to assimilate [a teaching], the church should respect them . . . dissent should be accepted as a nonthreatening contribution to the process of knowing."

Father McCormick might have been referring to the large-scale dissent within Catholic America over the church's teachings on artificial birth control, divorce, and several other issues. In the postconciliar climate he was describing, such refusal might constitute a vote of no-confidence that has its own legitimate authority. Father McCormick and other theologians appealed to the tradition of *sensus fidelium*, by which no teaching is authentic unless it is received positively by the people.

Before concluding, Father McCormick alluded to several aspects of debate in the church. Regarding the recently released document on bioethics, he questioned the narrow range of consultation by the Vatican in preparing the wide-ranging statement and added, "Wouldn't it have been wonderful if they had invited all the churches to an ecumenical dialogue on these issues." He noted that the text made "no reference to any other documents, just previous statements of popes."

Regarding the Curran case, Father McCormick saw the church in danger of "overplaying its hand . . . by equating all ordinary teaching practically with infallible teaching—we're paying a great price for that." Father Curran had been chastised for claiming the right to dissent from noninfallible teaching. "He is loyally committed to the magisterium even though he disagrees with it," Father McCormick said. "That is the way we ought to have dissent in the church today."

Neither divorce nor homosexuality was a closed matter, he believed. In each case, he said, "I don't think the church really knows what it wants to do."

Mindful of the upheaval in Seattle, he ended with a tribute. "I look at this archdiocese as a model," Father McCormick told an appreciative audience of students, laypeople, sisters, and priests. "It has a climate of giving people space, elbow room and encouragement. That's what we need."

THE ONSET OF THE MARIAN YEAR STIRRED HOPES OF A REVIVAL IN THE PERSONAL and communal devotions to Mary. Such expressions of Marian piety as the rosary, novenas, processions, and celebrations had been at the very heart of Catholic life prior to Vatican II. But these practices had faded, even vanished, in much of Catholic America. In the renewed church, they were widely regarded as quaint, perhaps even superstitious, vestiges of an antiquated Catholicism. Weekly liturgical celebration, in which Mary was prominent, had became the almost exclusive setting for Marian devotion. Meanwhile, within the annual liturgical calendar, eighteen feast days honored Mary.

Church leaders agreed that the recitation of the seven-hundred-year-old rosary, the centerpiece of Marian devotions, both communally and personally had suffered a particularly precipitous decline. No survey figures measured participation rates before Vatican II, but a high proportion of Catholics (women far outnumbering men, as in all Catholic religious observance) was believed to say the rosary either privately or during the Latin mass. Five years after the conclusion of the Second Vatican Council, Gallup found that 40 percent of Catholics said they had prayed the rosary during the previous month. That level has held steady. During 1986, it was 38 percent. According to the Notre Dame study of regular church attenders, 61 percent never took part in the practice, and another 15 percent did so only once a year. Catholics raised in the post–Vatican II church were especially unlikely to become involved.

Defenders of Catholic orthodoxy tended to blame much of the disarray in the family and church on this sharp drop-off in Marian observances. Though there was nothing inherently conservative about the devotions themselves, the ardent and almost exclusive promotion of these practices by the Catholic right, through rosary "crusades" and other means, had certain political implications. To a degree, the espousing of Marian devotions, rather than dedication to the devotions per se, had become a mark of reaction to despised "modernism." Conservatives had frequently invoked their Marian attachments as an implicit means of standing for the Old Church against the New Church. A counterreaction was found on the Catholic left. Resistance to Marian devotions signified—unconsciously, one suspects—defiance against pressures to return to the Old Church. It was subtle, to be sure, inasmuch as those across the church's political spectrum deeply venerated the Mother of Christ.

Feminism within Catholic America had also had an impact. For many Catholic women awakening to that movement, the church's image of Mary had been too distorted by a long patriarchal imprint to be fully embraced without substantial reexamination. It was the picture of an extremely passive, subservient Mary that they objected to. The pluralistic climate in America had also tended to reduce popular Marian practices. Many Protestants regarded the church's treatment of Mary as a sort of idolatry that detracted from the central place of Christ. The resulting friction did not accord with the renewed spirit of ecumenism. The Catholic downplaying of this part of their tradition was at least salient in this regard, moving the church closer to the nation's Christian mainstream.

The flood of Hispanics had likewise placed the discussion in a new framework. Hispanic devotion to Mary was well known as both a folk tradition and a powerful dimension of the organized church. In certain settings, the Mary of Hispanics took on the attributes of liberation theology, bestowing dignity on poor women.

Pope John Paul II, who brought to the papacy a compelling personal witness to Mary, was scheduled to visit San Antonio during his September tour. He was expected to draw on the strength of Hispanic devotion to Mary to encourage a broader return to Marian practices throughout Catholic America.

The pope had sounded that note with regard to the rosary during his telecast recitation to begin the Marian year. "May the rosary *once more* [emphasis mine] become the accustomed prayer of that 'domestic church' which is the Christian family," the pope said during his six-minute homily. "The prayer of the rosary will bring to our world, with the smile of the Virgin Mary, the tender tones of God's love for the brave but anxious humanity of the twentieth century."

Archbishop John May of St. Louis called for greater awareness of Mary in a statement that coincided with the inauguration of the year by the pope. He recounted the close ties between Mary and the church in America: John Carroll, the first bishop of the United States, was consecrated on the Feast of the Assumption, 1790; Pope Pius IX named her patroness of the nation in 1854; the National Shrine of the Incarnation in Washington was dedicated to her in 1959. He lauded her as "the most perfect model of readiness to receive Christ when he comes" and "the greatest example of the spiritual attitude that each of us ought to have."

However, while urging Catholics to heighten their awareness of Mary, the archbishop seemed to be sounding a cautionary note to those who tended to foster cults of the Virgin apart from the mainstream life of the church. "I therefore encourage special efforts during this Marian year to practice both liturgical and private devotions to Mary *in a balanced way,*" he said. The veneration of Mary should be kept within the boundaries of the church's liturgical guidelines, the archbishop seemed to be saying, not spin off separately so as to become staging areas for interest groups.

The appeal for Marian renewal took a different tack and a sharper edge at a conference June 13 in Louisville, Kentucky, sponsored by two stalwarts of the Catholic right, the Cardinal Midszenty Foundation and Catholics United for the Faith. The theme of the annual Church Teaches Forum was "Mary and Her Immaculate Conception." As reported in the *Wanderer* (June 25), several speakers stressed that a return to Marian devotion could reverse the corruption of both church and society.

Foremost among them was Cardinal John Carberry, the retired archbishop of St. Louis. Belief in the Immaculate Conception, the cardinal said, could cure the "painful effects of the diabolical secularism . . . even in groups that call themselves Catholic." He continued, "How desperately modern men and women need to be reminded: We are not rugged individuals, but the Body of Christ. The Immaculate Conception teaches us who we are, how we must be focused on God and the Church, and how dehumanizing sin is; how it alienates us from God and one another" (p. 1).

The Reverend Bernard Luedtke, O.M.V., bringing with him what the *Wanderer* described as "a beautiful gold reliquary containing a fragment of the Blessed Virgin's veil," traced various crises to a root cause. "The problems in society are due to problems in the family," Father Luedtke said; "the problem of vocations is the family; the problem of the whole world is the destruction of the family; the problem is love. Mary teaches us what love is. Mary shows us Jesus. We will have love when we let Jesus into our hearts" (p. 8).

A Benedictine abbot drew a connection between the neglect of Mary and moral collapse that was even more graphic. "The documents of Vatican II impelled us to look to Mary, to ask her to intercede for us," said the Reverend Edmund McCaffrey, O.S.B., "but there has been a decline in devotion to Mary, and we have seen a subsequent decline in morals, values, and the family."

"What happens to a home where the mother is absent? We begin to see disorder in the house, and after the disorder, the vermin come out, the rats, and maybe that's the way it has been in the Church. We got rid of Mary, and the vermin came out. If you want order in the house, put the mother back in!" (p. 8).

FOR SEVERAL MONTHS, THE FOUR BISHOPS ELECTED BY THEIR PEERS TO REPRE-sent Catholic America at the October Synod on the Laity in Rome had received a good deal of advice on issues lay men and women themselves wanted the synod to pursue. The bishops' committee on the laity had, among other things, brought one or more of the bishops face-to-face with groups of laypeople in five locations around the country. As expected, even these relatively controlled and structured sessions uncovered some blunt complaints about problems felt by lay Catholics. The fact that such two-way discussion would stop at the synod door—where bishops alone took part—became, not surprisingly, an underlying tension during the consultations. It was as if government agricultural officials were meeting to ponder the fate of the farmer without the active presence of actual farmers, whose nonbinding opinions had been solicited beforehand.

Having met with this sampling of a few hundred of the laity and collected opinions from as many as a hundred thousand American Catholics, the committee on the laity brought the education of the bishop-delegates to a conclusion at a closed symposium June 7 to 9 at Saint Mary's College in South Bend, Indiana.

Father Robert Kinast, who had kept tabs on the questionnaire widely circulated among the laity, gave his final summary of results to the assembled bishops, lay consultants, theologians, and other specialists. The affable priest, a theologian on the faculty of the Washington Theological Union, told the seminar that the findings from the total survey agreed closely with the partial samplings he had reported at earlier consultations.

Several results stood out. The laity believed that all Catholics were given a ministry by their baptism and flatly rejected "any dualism within the people of God" between either church and world or clergy and laity. Therefore, it followed that all Catholics took part in the single mission of the church, clergy and laity functioning separately but equally in different roles. Though laity claimed that the church's mission embraced both church and world, they showed little grasp of what it meant for them to conduct that ministry in the worldly settings outside the family in which they spent a large share of their public lives: work, neighborhood, politics, and so on.

"In short," Father Kinast concluded, "the theology of Vatican II, at least in its salient features, has been well appropriated by these faithful [those sampled]. What is lacking is a practice consistent with this theology. The greatest benefit of the synod for the church in the United States would not be to clarify or reassert theological principles . . . but to urge their consistent implementation, if not to recommend specific changes and initiatives which would do just that."

Having summed up the thoughts of the American laity, Father Kinast turned his attention to the newly released Vatican working paper for the synod, which purportedly reflected these and other concerns from around the world.

Released at the end of April, the working paper attracted attention in at least two ways. One was because it punctured any lingering fantasies that controversial topics such as women's ordination even to the diaconate might somehow creep onto the agenda. The consultation procedure had been carefully controlled to prevent such subjects from entering the pipeline, but the working paper put the would-be reformers on notice just in case. The other source of interest and debate, of course, was what topics had made it into the working paper. Because it was technically a trial balloon, response to it might cause some shift in the focus of the synod. In that spirit, presumably, Father Kinast made his comments, judiciously noting that he was "not offering a critique of the working paper (which would be unfair), but more of an imagined dialogue between the laity in the United States who participated in the consultation and the drafter(s) of the working paper." In other words, this was what the laity might say if they *were* doing the talking.

The document had pluses and minuses, though, on balance, the minuses in Father Kinast's "dialogue" came out ahead.

First, the strengths. The document would be applauded by the laity for starting from the human situation and welcoming their increasing participation in the church's ministry. Furthermore, "The working paper clearly wants to avoid suggesting that ordination or religious vows constitute a superior class of Christian." Likewise, the emphasis on merging faith and real life and on marriage, family, and work as "key areas for exercising the apostolate" would be welcome. The affirmation of parish and pastoral councils seemed fitting to Father Kinast, as did the stress on liturgy, Scripture, and need for greater attention to the needs of women and young people.

That was all to the good. But there also were some serious gaps, Father Kinast thought, between the working paper and results of the consultation of the laity. Among the most distressing was the tendency he saw in the document to revert to the old habit of placing clergy on a level above the laity. He referred at one point to "an unmistakable, hierarchy-centered perspective which gives the impression that the laity are being looked at rather than lived with." Again: "The repeated insistence that there is an essential difference between the ordained (ministerial) priesthood and the priesthood of the baptized would strike many of the laity in the consultation as contradicting the fundamental equality of baptism." Likewise, he said, the laity would balk at being described as secular in contrast to the religious and ordained. "Secularity is not how laypeople distinguish themselves," Father Kinast said. "They speak rather of baptism and gifts of the spirit."

He continued, "Laity in the consultation would question the need always to be reminded that 'no charism [gift] dispenses a person from the jurisdiction of the bishops of the church. . . . It often seems that official documents take away with such statements what they have just asserted and what laypeople know in their experience—they are gifted by God and not likely to go astray if they do not always check in with ecclesiastical authorities."

Father Kinast detected this dual streak throughout: positive statements about the renewed place of the laity and statements that implied that they were inferior and reliant on the clergy, even childlike. This split-level thinking extended to the synod itself, he said, especially to "the impression that the laity are dependent on the synod to determine how the laity can overcome the separation of faith from life." He added, "The laity in the consultation do not want to assign blame and are not anticlerical, but they do want to be taken seriously in their frustration with clergy who retard the renewal of the church."

From several vantage points in Father Kinast's dialogic response the problem boiled down to unfinished business between priests and laity. "By eliminating almost all mention of the clergy's relationship with the laity in actual experience," he noted in conclusion, "the working paper sidesteps one of the most pressing concerns of the laity in the consultation."

Overall, he ventured, the Vatican document would probably cause little commotion. "If I were to hazard a guess, I think most of the laity in the consultation would find the working paper inoffensive, generally affirming, and not very challenging. I think they would also expect more from the synod itself."

Various other observers of lay Catholicism expanded on themes touched upon by Father Kinast. Among those delivering parting shots to the bishop-delegates were Professor Edward Sellner, chairman of the National Association of Lay Ministry and theologian on the faculty of the College of Saint Catherine in St. Paul, Minnesota, and Professor Michael Warren of Saint John's University in New York City, Professor Lisa Cahill of Boston College and Professor Doris Donnelly of Saint Mary's.

Professor Sellner asserted that the laity have difficulty believing in the spiritual depth and validity of their experiences in everyday life. He applauded the working paper's refusal to separate world from church, priest from layperson, life from faith, but noted that the laity in the consultations had "some degree of distrust" about finding spiritual meaning in their daily lives. The problem as he saw it was that "many laity do not trust the revelatory power of their own experiences nor realize that their own gifts and wisdom can be resources for spirituality."

The laity needed exemplars of the faith from their own ranks to emulate, Sellner said, "We ask the question why the only models of holiness the church seems to be giving us as declared saints are priests and nuns. If asceticism is any criterion, what about the daily asceticism of the laity: our struggles to care for families, to maintain jobs, to sustain elderly parents, to find meaning, to persist, to let go?"

Professor Warren, an instructor in catechetical ministry, spoke about young people. In his experience, he said, the crisis of "youth and faith" was first and foremost a "problem of credibility," adding, "Their problem is not the gospel but its embodiments in church polity and actual local communities." Young people tested the church to see if it lived up to its beliefs. Generally speaking, he said, youth ministries succeeded when they allowed young people to "become coproducers of their own religious culture" and failed when they reduced young people "to the status of consumers."

Accordingly, the parish that adopted "the values of the wider, secular culture . . . overlaid with a thin religious veneer" held far less appeal than that which took "risks and is willing to suffer to follow the gospel" thus becoming "a true sign." Further, "The parish . . . least troubled by the gospel's call for justice will be the same one least able to tolerate the questioning, struggles or the occasional tentative scoffing of young people."

Warren counseled the bishops to seek to lead by example rather than new pronouncements. "Instead of lofty statements of ideals, youth need the sacramental embodiments of the gospel life in living groups." Young people should be taken in as full participants with a full voice. "Suppose in talking with youth about the church," Warren said, "we stopped telling them what the church is supposed to be and stopped claiming that these ideas are what the local church really is despite, at least in some instances, clear evidence to the contrary? In other words, suppose we stopped asking youth to believe in the church and instead asked them to examine the lived belief of the church?"

The challenge to young people would be thus: "Go find the groups of disciples of Jesus who best follow his way of siding with victims and whose life-styles exhibit nonviolent love, patterns of sharing and compassion, and a concern for the future of this world of ours, given to us as a sign of God's love. Find those who have risked something to follow Jesus' way and ask them if you can walk along with them in doing the works of justice and mercy. Don't worry about what denomination they are with, just join their life."

Warren asked, "If we proposed such a catechesis to youth, would they pick your parish? Would they pick a parish in your diocese? Would they pick a Roman Catholic parish at all? These are questions we as a church must face."

THE U.S. BISHOPS' CONFERENCE, WHICH HAD PROCEEDED WITH CAUTION ON THE AIDS crisis, announced on June 8 the formation of a team to explore the epidemic. The news itself was indicative of the bishops' hesitation. The task force had been named back in March but had been kept under wraps. It became public only after the National Catholic News Service got wind of the move in late May.

In February, the bishops' conference had spoken out against condom ads on television but had thus far developed no comprehensive set of policies and guidelines regarding AIDS. The administrative board of the hierarchy had then formed the task force under the aegis of Archbishop John L. May of St. Louis, president of the bishops' conference.

As outlined by Archbishop May, the team would cover four areas related to "the challenges this dread disease poses." One was the nature of the malady itself. A second was sex education, which included the subject of condoms as preventives. A third was the volatile issue of health clinics in high schools. The fourth was "media treatment of AIDS, including advertisements and public service announcements."

Heading the task force was Bishop William A. Hughes of Covington, Kentucky. The other members were Cardinal Joseph Bernardin of Chicago, Bishop Raymond W. Lessard of Savannah, and Bishop Anthony G. Bosco of Greensburg, Pennsylvania. After completing its study of the various aspects of the disease, the task force was expected to deliver a set of recommendations to the bishops' conference.

Though a national response was still down the road, action continued on the local level. A coalition of New York Catholics, believed to be the first such lay group to address the issue, called for a stepped-up program of AIDS testing, and the bishops of New Jersey unveiled a policy statement on several aspects of the disease.

The New York group, called the Catholic Social Policy Coalition, had convened the previous fall at the instigation of Cardinal O'Connor, who saw it as a means of promoting involvement in social policy, and it existed within the framework of the archdiocese. It was made up of delegates from more than two dozen traditional lay groups such as the Holy Name Society, Knights of Columbus, fraternal groups of police and fire personnel, and the Legion of Mary. The combined constituency was estimated at two hundred thousand.

In a report, the coalition called for required AIDS tests on applicants for marriage licenses and patients admitted to hospitals. Likewise, the coalition said, reporting cases of AIDS from such screening to public health officials should be mandatory, and confidentiality should be strictly observed.

The archdiocese, which had said nothing one way or the other about mandatory AIDS testing and showed no interest in doing so, remained noncommittal toward the proposals.

The New Jersey bishops, in their June 18 statement, made no mention of the issue of required testing but concentrated instead on four areas where the church touched the lives of AIDS sufferers and their families: "as pastoral minister, as employer, as educator and as social service provider."

Each diocese must provide "at least one pastoral minister" to oversee the care of those with AIDS and their families. Among the functions of the minister would be to educate pastors who were "reluctant to serve persons with AIDS."

AIDS patients must be assured of their right to receive the sacraments and "Christian burial in accordance with the provisions of the Code of Canon Law," the bishops said. Pastoral ministers must, in addition, make every effort to protect the anonymity of sufferers.

The bishops also insisted that the church scrupulously follow the law in refusing to discriminate against people with AIDS in hiring and employment. In cases where the person could no longer reasonably perform work duties because of advanced illness, the bishops said, counseling and support should be made available. Similarly, children with AIDS were welcome in church-run schools except in unusual cases entailing health risks. In such circumstances, the bishops said, "A student with AIDS who is excluded from school shall be provided with appropriate educational programs as well as catechetical instruction at the proper level."

In certain key respects, the New Jersey bishops were chiming in with bishops from other parts of the country to forge some practical measures to meet the spreading scourge. The broader set of guidelines would wade into the more controversial areas, but for now the local bishops were on patrol at the gate, devising pragmatic responses to a fierce enemy.

FROM HIS RUST BELT DIOCESE, BISHOP SAWICKI READ THE TEA LEAVES IN FAR-away Seattle. Like other bishops, he had sensors finely tuned to church politics. Drawing on the facts as he knew them, Bishop Sawicki scored the Seattle outcome as a modest win for the forces of Archbishop Hunthausen.

Given the complexity of the case, the verdict was less than clear-cut in the bishop's mind, but his seasoned eye read the clues as Vatican face-saving. Confronted by a rebellion, Rome had, in his opinion, done its best to cut its losses. In talking to other bishops, he said, the "general reaction was that, given the circumstances, the Vatican made the best possible decision."

He welcomed the restoration of full authority to the Seattle archbishop, an old friend of his, and saw the removal of Wuerl as "a clear indication that Rome knows the situation was not working." Further, "naming Tom Murphy coadjutor indicates the sensitivity of the Holy See to choosing someone who was compatible with Hunthausen." Just as Rome had tried to set things right, Bishop Sawicki said, so had the archbishop shown goodwill by his "acceptance of a coadjutor." He had nothing but praise for the three commission members. They had "exhibited great statesmanship," he said.

Thus, in Bishop Sawicki's opinion, the Vatican had made the best of a bad situation without leaving heavy footprints. Nowhere could he see where Rome had bowed explicitly to the wishes of the bishops' conference in handling the case. It had appointed the three-member commission to work out a settlement without directly acknowledging the move as a response to the bishops' November 1986 offer to help. The Vatican had also insisted on a tough-minded assessment of the archdiocese and had left unclear what tests the Seattle archdiocese would still have to pass in order to remove itself from probation. Rome had retreated under pressure, Bishop Sawicki surmised, but had kept the situation under its thumb. It had exercised prudent damage control.

Like many other prelates, he regarded the Seattle case as a warning about the havoc that right-wing Catholics could raise. He was sure that the barrage of complaints from the right had caused Rome to react against the archbishop. "Their initial response was to reign him in," Bishop Sawicki said. "Now they acknowledge that there are some irregularities [in Catholic practice], but they are not so grave as to prevent him from exercising full authority."

He cautioned against drawing too many conclusions from the Seattle agreement. The naming of the three-bishop commission to mediate the dispute seemed to him a new development, and he assumed the Vatican might think twice before lowering the boom on a bishop in similar fashion in the near future. Beyond that, he discouraged predictions. "I don't see Seattle teaching us any more than that, within our unity there is diversity," he said circumspectly. "The Holy Father has to tolerate extremes of the far left and the far right."

"This was a kind of mop-up operation," he continued, "so it's difficult to see what will happen. Will the Holy See in the future be more secretive? Or more exhaustive in attempts to reach agreement through the American bishops, short of sending someone to investigate? I don't know. My guess is that because of the huge publicity and upheaval over this one, any church administration would be very chary about moving along the same path."

Bishop Sawicki had his own busy rounds to tend. The life of a bishop was far more varied than it used to be, he observed. Since Vatican II reforms had kicked in around 1970, he said, the bishop's role had been redirected. There were many more church organizations and a greater number of community concerns that fell under his ministry. "I have more than twice as many meetings as before 1970," he said. Perhaps more significantly, he added, the bishop was now expected to participate rather than simply oversee things, stay above the battle, as in the past. He was often now in the midst of give-and-take.

The day before, he had met with a group of charismatic Catholics to discuss a special celebration. "In an earlier day, I would have been concerned almost solely with the liturgy and ritual," he said. "I would have presided over the meeting, watching and observing. Now they want me to be involved in the development of what they are doing."

Across his schedule, more of his activities were demanding a greater investment of himself, and, overall, he found the experience both draining and stimulating. He offered a sample from his calendar of recent days. He had attended a day-long conference on the impact of a large industrial plant closing. A group had asked to meet with him about raising salaries of teachers in Catholic schools. Upcoming was a session of the diocesan pastoral council to talk about closing or consolidating Catholic elementary schools, followed by an open forum for senior citizens on the need for housing and social activity, a meeting of a national board on aid for missionaries, a convening of the seminary board, and the regular meeting of the diocesan priests.

The plant-closing conference best illustrated how his role had shifted, he said. The aim of the conclave was to devise strategies for softening the blow on the community. Alternatives ranged from emergency help to families in need of services to legislative remedies. "At an earlier time, they might have asked for my endorsement of what they had decided," he observed. "Now I was expected to be part of the dynamic developing the response, to be part of the intellectual interplay.

"I gave a brief presentation on what had happened to another community when another plant had closed. But I was not any kind of authority. I realize that many people there knew more than I did and that my views didn't adequately express the views of many other people. But I welcome it because I am part of framing the questions and some *possible* answers. I do enjoy that interplay. I see the need to be a learner as well a teacher.".

—◆ ◆—

In June, there were some noteworthy developments in the story of the church finances. On June 8, the Reverend Andrew M. Greeley released a study that showed a striking decrease by Catholics in their giving to the church. The findings were reported in a new book by Father Greeley, *Catholic Contributions: Sociology and Policy,* which included an epilogue by Bishop William McManus, the retired bishop of Fort Wayne–South Bend.

Father Greeley linked the steep decline to "resentment about what Catholics perceive as insensitive church teachings and authority" regarding, in particular, artificial birth control and other aspects of sexuality. "People thought that Catholics would either 'knuckle under' or leave the church," Father Greeley said. "But neither happened. And the result is a protest through money" (*New York Times,* June 10, p. 22).

The percentage of personal income donated by Catholics declined by half over twenty-five years, from 2.2 percent to 1.1 percent, according to the priest-sociologist, while Protestant giving had remained at a 2.2 percent level.

The conclusions were drawn from comparisons of surveys by the Survey Research Center of the University of Michigan in 1960 and 1975, the National

Opinion Research Center of the University of Chicago in 1963 and 1974, the Gallup Poll in 1982, and Yankelovich, Skelly and White in 1984.

In dollar figures, the average Catholic contribution was $320 in 1984, compared to $580 for Protestants. The study found the downward trend most prevalent among those who had more schooling, tended toward a liberal outlook, and had a strong commitment to the church. Catholics who were poorer and less educated were the only group to keep pace with Protestant giving.

Bishop McManus, in his epilogue, noted the financial squeeze suffered by lay employees as a result of the decline. The situation was especially critical, he said, for lay teachers and staff in Catholics schools, who worked for wages far below those outside the church. "If all salaried Catholics paid two to three percent of their salary income for the support of their parish and diocese, the church would have more than enough to pay all employees adequate salaries and benefits," the bishop wrote (p. 22).

To counteract the downward spiral, Bishop McManus and Father Greeley both urged the church to inform Catholics better about the needs of the church and to bring more laypeople into the budget process.

Information and participation had also become key factors in the Vatican's effort to pay its bills. Having disclosed a $67-million deficit earlier in the spring, Rome was quietly meeting with influential American Catholics in an effort to raise big money. The plan called for soliciting $100 million from the Americans to be set aside as an endowment to pay off Vatican debts.

In its initial stages, the campaign had failed to meet with great success. Two formidable obstacles stood in the way of enthusiastic cooperation by wealthy American Catholic laypeople.

One was the continuing shadowy saga of the scandal involving huge losses by the Vatican Bank centering on charges by the Italian government against the bank's president, Archbishop Paul C. Marcinkus. The church's response to the situation ran against the grain of American jurisprudence and good business sense. Rome had so far refused to honor Italian subpoenas for the archbishop and had turned aside requests for its own open inquiry into the scandal. The Vatican had also rebuffed demands that the bank be turned over to a group of Catholics who were expert in international finance. On the contrary, the archbishop and his key advisers remained in place, to the chagrin of many of the very American Catholics who were now counted upon to bail the Vatican out. Reform of the bank was virtually a condition of support among many of them.

Commonweal (June 19) was among the voices demanding the facts: "Vatican finances have become more open and accountable under the present pope, but more needs to be done . . . a cloud of suspicion will linger over the Vatican unless there is a full airing of the Ambrosiano affair and a pinpointing of responsibility. It is time for Peter to make a full accounting."

The other stumbling block was the Vatican's reluctance to make full financial disclosure. Leading prelates from America had been warning Rome with increased volume that the success of fund-raising appeals was contingent on compliance with what Catholics in the United States understood to be sound accounting procedure. Many dioceses in the United States, in response to this pressure, had begun issuing annual budget statements that, depending on the diocese, were more or less detailed. Thus far Rome had made no serious effort to satisfy that need. To American eyes, their attempts had been laughable. As part of an effort to coax substantial contributions from a group of well-heeled Americans, the Vatican had trotted out a balance sheet. The Americans dismissed it as totally inadequate and nonsensical.

No wonder, then, that the $100-million trust fund had gotten off to such a slow start. The Americans were inclined toward money matters the way Jesuits once were toward theology. It was their lifeblood, and they did not appreciate being left in the dark about a subject they understood perhaps better than any other. Objections by the wealthy against what they regarded as a lack of Vatican accountability was a particular sore point, inasmuch as such resistance was costing Rome potentially big contributions. A leading Catholic financier and contributor called the drive nothing less than "a referendum on John Paul II's pontificate" and predicted that it would fall far short of its goal.

The most immediate concern among many of the church's top brass was whether the assortment of discontents might reduce contributions to the annual Peter's Pence collection at the end of the month. The American total had hovered around the $13-million mark in recent years, nearly half the sum collected around the world for the pope's discretionary use. In the face of a string of Vatican budgetary shortfalls, the pope had been exercising that discretion by placing the Peter's Pence money into curial operating expenses rather than using it as a reserve for outside charities.

In addition to the possibility that Catholics dismayed by one thing or another might skip the collection, there was Mary's Pence, the alternative campaign established by Chicago Catholic Women for ministries to women and children. Leaders of the fund discouraged descriptions of the drive as a rival to the pope's appeal, but it was commonly perceived as such. In fact, the fifteen-hundred-member peace and justice group Chicago Call to Action was calling upon Catholics to support Mary's Pence instead of Peter's Pence. The Association of Catholic Priests in Chicago had also endorsed the drive, but without calling for a boycott of the collection for the pope. Among the objectives of the new fund was help for poor women, released prison inmates, and victims of battering.

The hefty tab for the pope's visit was the other major item on the church's fiscal agenda. Bishops along the pope's itinerary had been given until October, a month after the trip, to make final their financial plans for defraying the costs within their dioceses. For some, such as the bishop of Monterey, the task was staggering.

With a final cost expected to reach $30 million (including the $2 million it would cost the bishop's conference, to which the Knights of Columbus had contributed $250,000), every bishop was under pressure, partly because some Catholics questioned whether the expense was necessary or worthwhile. A variety of fund-raising efforts were under way, including, of course, appeals for large gifts from affluent Catholics and non-Catholics.

In Miami, the pope's first stop, Archbishop Edward McCarthy sought to placate critics who charged that the $1.8-million price tag on the visit would drain funds that were earmarked for the poor. Without denying the allegations, the archbishop proposed a strategy for making up the loss, calling on Miamians to make donations to such charities as the United Way and the Salvation Army that provide direct social services. "If we can get a million people to respond at an average of $5 apiece," Archbishop McCarthy reasoned, "there will be $5 million going to the poor."

THE GLOSSARY USED TO DESCRIBE PEOPLE WHO HAD SEVERED THEIR TIES WITH the Catholic church was growing. Not long ago, the term *lapsed* would have sufficed to cover most of them. It had a passive sound, denoting an absent-minded, desultory drifting away into the church's storage compartment of inactive souls. In the post–Vatican II church, however, new words were needed to define the growing number of Catholics who found themselves outside the church by choice rather than default or who refused to leave the church despite their disagreements with its teachings. Those in the latter category, who dissented from the church's views on matters such as birth control and divorce but still considered themselves within the fold, had come to be known as "communal" or "cafeteria" or "pick-and-choose" groupings of "disaffected" Catholics. The total outsiders, on the other hand, might still prefer to think of themselves as lapsed, suggesting happenstance, but might also identify themselves somewhat more assertively as "alienated."

According to a recent Gallup Poll, 80 percent of people born Catholic said they were members of the church, an indication that perhaps as many as one in five baptized into the church was not active in it. The loss was most striking among younger people. Of the Americans surveyed by Gallup, 36 percent of those under age thirty said they were raised Catholic, but only 31 percent now considered themselves part of the church.

Reasons for the estrangement felt by many people toward their former church were fairly widely agreed upon. Most often cited were conflicts around the church's rules on sexuality, marriage, and divorce. There were an estimated 8 million divorced Catholics, 6 million of whom had remarried. Under liberalized annulment procedures, it had become easier to have a marriage declared invalid, thus permitting a Catholic to embark on a marriage recognized by the church. But according to church officials, only about 10 percent of divorced Catholics applied for an annulment. That meant that millions of Catholics who had been divorced and remarried without an annulment were ineligible by common theological understanding to receive the sacraments of the church. From that source alone sprang much of the alienation.

The growing numbers of aggrieved Catholics had sparked concern among bishops and priests and was reshaping some of their attitudes toward this group. No longer were the outsiders to be pitied as misguided, delinquent apostates who had wandered, at their peril, beyond the safe confines of Mother Church until and unless they returned as penitents. By contrast, the recent trend favored reaching out to the defector with warmth and understanding instead of scolding or judgment. Many bishops had begun sponsoring "Welcome Home" campaigns at Christmas and Easter aimed specifically at people who, for one reason or another, had left the church and/or felt rejected by it. These reconciling efforts conveyed the message that there was no personal problem too big to be ironed out by clergy sensitized to the hurts of the alienated, even allowing that harmful behavior by the church might have caused the rift.

A further development in the drive to win back the disgruntled was a program called Alienated Catholics Anonymous, reported in the June 13 issue of *America*. The article consisted of an interview with the founder of the program, Monsignor Thomas P. Cahalane, pastor of Our Mother of Sorrows parish in Tucson, Arizona. Its purpose, Monsignor Cahalane explained, was to offer "an environment of hospitality and an invitation for renewal of relationships with Christ and the church." Those interested in mending fences were asked to join together for four sessions to explore their qualms with the pastor. Since the idea was introduced at Christmas 1985, Monsignor Cahalane said, between twenty and thirty people had turned up for the start of each series. How would he describe those who signed up? They had never "been successful at moving away totally from Catholicism," he noted, adding that they harbored a desire to return but were unsure whether they would be accepted (p. 477).

The meetings were informal, personal, and open, Monsignor Cahalane said, giving the wary former members an opportunity to speak about their hopes and fears. They were asked, among other things, why they had responded, how they felt toward God and the church, and what apprehensions they brought with them. The answers provided the grist for discussion. Throughout, the monsignor said, he stressed "the themes of the healing, forgiving, reconciling church." The most common sources of alienation, he said, were "their own personal choices [divorce and remarriage, feeling that the church was not meeting their spiritual needs]. Others were hurt by encounters with parish leadership. And still others found themselves suddenly alienated from the church in terms of their understanding of the church" (p. 480).

Success in dealing with such problems, Monsignor Cahalane said, depended on the ability of such a program to provide the experience of "a caring church." Evaluation forms from sessions at his parish had yielded a list of the program's "strengths": "program based on individual needs of the group, clear explanations, dialogue between people before and after the sessions, excellent rapport between priest and people, sharing and really caring, clearer understanding of the changes in the church coming from Vatican II, a step-by-step explanation of the Mass as it was celebrated, nonjudgmental acceptance of people and an invitation to them to express feelings. There never was the slightest pressure—only encouragement" (p. 479).

At the conclusion of the latest sessions, the "graduates" whooped it up at a "Prodigal Sons and Daughters Banquet." On the Sunday following, each one came forward to the altar, where Monsignor Cahalane introduced them, welcomed them, and blessed them.

AT THE CATHOLIC THEOLOGICAL SOCIETY OF AMERICA'S FORTY-SECOND ANNUAL convention, the late Thursday evening session was set aside for hearing resolutions. Called the "information meeting," it followed the organization's awards banquet in an austere hotel ballroom of the Society Hill Sheraton in Philadelphia.

Predictably, between a quarter and a third of the society's thirteen hundred members had turned out for some or all of the four-day convention, June 10–13. Though the format of panels, speakers, and workshops had remained basically the same over the past decade, the ranks of the CTSA had changed considerably. The normal badge of entry was still a doctoral degree in a theological discipline, but beyond that the society bore little obvious resemblance to what it had been thirty years before.

Into the early 1970s, CTSA had been simply an all-male club of priests, most of whom taught in seminaries, attending meetings in clerical collars. Now, after a period of tension, the society's rolls included a sizable number of women and nonclerics, and many were on nonseminary faculties. Women religious and priests still composed three-fourths of the membership, but during the bustle of the convention only a few wore the distinctive garb of religious life. Without much alteration, the group might easily be taken for a professional gathering of historians or sociologists. In the view of many long-term members, two factors had considerably reshaped the society during the past decade.

One was the fallout from a clash over a statement on sexuality. A special CTSA committee delivered a report in 1976 that took issue with many aspects of the

Vatican's defense of traditional sexual ethics the year before. The committee state- ment touched off a furor within the society that resulted in CTSA voting to "re- ceive" but not adopt the statement as its official stance. Most conservatives had dropped out in protest, some going on to form a rival group, the Fellowship of Catholic Scholars. The controversy and the split gave CTSA a decidedly liberal stamp, though its membership could not be stereotyped quite so easily. Father Curran, under fire for his liberal views, and Father Avery Dulles, the prominent Jesuit centrist, were both members, after all, and both were in attendance. But the rift had been serious and lasting. Most significantly, it had, in effect, deprived the society of vigorous debate, sundering theologians into two separate camps.

The other, more subtle influence had been the steady increase of members who had earned their doctorates at non-Catholic institutions such as Chicago, Berkeley, and Harvard. Of the applications approved for CTSA membership this year, for example, twenty-six had graduated from Catholic schools, sixteen from nonchurch universities.

The implications were difficult to trace, but some assumptions had taken hold. One was that graduates of ecumenical graduate schools were less grounded in the church's tradition than their counterparts from Catholic universities, hence showed less interest in the institution itself. This trend, in turn, was believed to have accelerated the drift from Rome. Father Dulles had, in fact, commented re- cently that American church theology, for various reasons, was the least self-con- sciously Catholic theology ever done in church history. "Formation" remained an important precept in Catholic theological education, and those outside the parochial framework had presumably missed much of it. That caused some to worry. On the other hand, there were acknowledged benefits from Catholic par- ticipation in prestigious ecumenical academic settings. It was a sign of growing theological inclusiveness whereby Catholics could both avail themselves of intel- lectual riches and contribute to them.

Father Curran's predicament had jeopardized the goodwill needed to carry on cooperative theology. Curbing dissent had a chilling effect among both Cath- olic and Protestant theologians and revived the specter of Vatican repression. There was talk that newly minted Catholic Ph.D.s were thinking twice about ac- cepting teaching positions at Catholic universities, Catholic University in partic- ular, for fear that their scholarship might be impaired. On the other hand, the climate of foreboding prompted attempts to lure outstanding professors away from Catholic University. Notre Dame was very much in the market, having somewhat embarrassingly been unable to fill endowed chairs in its theology de- partment. The school courted a half dozen CU faculty notables but scored no successes.

The judgments against Father Curran since the last CTSA meeting—the strip- ping of his license to teach as a Catholic theologian and his suspension from

Catholic University—cast a dense cloud over this convention. He was, after all, one of them, a compatriot, a fellow professional held in great affection and esteem. A joint statement of support by former presidents of the CTSA and the College Theological Society said, "We can think of no Catholic theologian in this country who is more well-liked and personally admired than Charles Curran." An attack on him was an attack on them. If Rome could strike at him, they reasoned, no one was safe.

In 1986, the membership, by a 171–14 vote, had urged that "no action be taken against Charles Curran that would prohibit him from teaching on the theology faculty at the Catholic University of America," but that appeal, along with others, obviously had the collective impact of spitting in the wind. In October, after the Vatican's revocation of his license, the CTSA board took the further step of submitting a brief on his behalf to Catholic University in an effort to defend his place on the faculty. The special committee looking into it favored retaining Father Curran, but to no avail. Father Curran's suspension from the university had been carried out against that recommendation on orders of Archbishop Hickey and remained in effect. The brief by the CTSA board had envisioned any disruption of Father Curran's right to teach at the university as "incomprehensible on professional grounds, unjust in the singling out of this one scholar from many of his peers with similar opinions, and indefensible in the light of traditional understanding of what a theologian does."

Father Curran, notwithstanding stalwart support from the mainstream theological club, now had a suit pending in the courts. CTSA had unequivocally upheld Father Curran's right to teach, but in face of the setbacks to him, what else could it say? The Thursday evening information session became the forum for weighing at least some options.

The focal point became academic freedom. Professor Monica Hellwig of Georgetown University, president of CTSA, reported that the American Association of University Professors, "prompted by the Charles Curran case," had sent along a copy of its forty-seven-year-old statement on academic freedom for the society's approval. The question, Professor Hellwig said, was whether the society wanted "to endorse it or deliberate a year?"

Adopted by the AAUP in 1940, the statement was a foundational document in support of "full freedom of research and in the publication of results" and of the system of tenure. In its original form, the statement contained a clause that allowed religious institutions some leeway in imposing limitations on academic freedom but insisted that any such restrictions "be clearly stated in writing at the time of appointment." In 1970, the AAUP supplemented the document with a set of "Interpretive Comments" that virtually erased that exception. The relevant section read, "Most church-related institutions no longer need or desire the principle of academic freedom implied in the 1940 Statement and we do not endorse such a departure." The statement represented a powerful consensus among educators but, of course, was itself not binding on any college or university.

Dozens of learned societies and professional associations and other educational organizations had endorsed the document, among them the American Catholic Historical Association (1966), the American Catholic Philosophical Association (1966), and CTSA's next of kin, the College Theological Society (1967). But CTSA had balked, largely because of doubts about how academic freedom, strictly speaking, related to the seminary setting where so many of them taught. Did the Curran situation warrant a setting aside of those reservations for the sake of affirming a basic right?

The ensuing floor debate was dominated by the concept of "appropriate" or "legitimate" freedom, that is, academic autonomy that somehow respected the right of the church to expect its teachings to be affirmed. Finding the formula had proved elusive, to say the least. It was a conundrum. Academic freedom implied no limits. Fidelity to the church implied, in some cases, no freedom. There was strong feeling that the Catholic church needed some kind of dispensation from the raw freedom the 1940 AAUP statement asserted. But there was also pressure from the ranks to do something in view of the Vatican's "unjust" action against Father Curran.

Frustration rose against the bulwark of ambivalence. Some argued that indeed it was time to throw caution to the winds by standing firmly behind the statement. "If we say 'no, it's not expedient for us to endorse it,'" said one theologian impatiently, "it almost sounds as if we believe the opposite." Another said he felt "embarrassed" that the CTSA had wavered so long. Still another reminded the body that for those embarking on careers in teaching "the question of academic freedom is crucial."

Counsels of moderation quickly enveloped the more radical sentiments, coaxing the group once more to the more familiar ground of ambivalence. A member from California summed up the working dilemma: "One option is to do nothing. That would be interpreted by some as endorsing violations [of academic freedom]. Or we can vote to accept [the Statement] as is—which is unacceptable. What can we do?" The next response brought forth the first suggestion of a strategy for resolving the question. "If this body cannot say something to move the conversation forward," said a slightly exasperated cleric, "then I don't think we are theologians of repute. I think we should support the Statement in principle and, second, say that we have more to say than is here in the Statement."

Having been provided what politicians called "wiggle room," several members rushed to insist that their hesitance in embracing the Statement *in toto* was in no way ducking. "This needs more study from all of us," said one. "I don't think we're backing off." Said another, "I'm concerned that we don't get stampeded into seeing this as a litmus test. I don't think our refusal to back the Statement even in principle should in any sense be interpreted as backing off." And so forth. Though there would be more talk, the matter was essentially settled. Despite some objections at the end, the group settled on a two-part resolution that would recognize the importance of the principle of academic freedom and would correlate that with, in the words of one speaker, "our own sense of the responsibilities of theologians."

The resolution submitted to the business session on Friday afternoon read:

> Whereas the CTSA is on record as supporting the principle of legitimate academic freedom and wishes to make clear that support, and whereas the CTSA has been offered the AAUP 1940 statement, with its 1970 interpretations, for endorsement, and whereas the AAUP text may not respond accurately, adequately, and/or sufficiently to the complexities of our varied settings, be it Resolved that the CTSA reaffirms its commitment to and support of the principle of legitimate academic freedom, and directs the Board to take steps to study this matter, to support initiatives currently in process, and report back to the Society at the June 1988 meeting.

The resolution passed, minus the third *whereas,* thus putting the CTSA on record in favor of the principle behind the 1940 Statement but not the Statement itself.

Some related the CTSA restraint in speaking more boldly on academic freedom to the hopes attached to the society's pursuit of a mediating role in averting clashes between theologians and church officials. The Reverend Leo O'Donovan, S.J., had chaired a committee that, with representatives of the Canon Law Society, had produced a statement aimed at settling future disputes between theologians and bishops. The unpublicized document, "Doctrinal Responsibilities," had already been approved by the bishops' key committee on doctrine and would be submitted to the entire body of bishops for approval in November.

Before concluding its business the CTSA also adopted a motion that the entire body put its stamp on the pro-Curran testimony forwarded to Catholic University by the CTSA board the previous October. Though the testimony could affect no tribunal now—the negative outcome against Father Curran having been rendered months ago—it was another vote of confidence in one who walked among them.

━ ━

DURING THE CONVENTION, HELLWIG TOOK TIME FROM HER DUTIES AS THE CTSA president to reflect on the uncertainties brought about by the Vatican's stepped-up campaign against dissident theologians.

She was a woman through whose pleasant features shone an unusual intelligence and a deep store of generosity. She spoke with calmness, firmness, and assurance. As a highly respected theologian at prestigious Georgetown, she moved among a broad range of theologians. She was distressed by the way many of them had been treated. To her, the most unsettling case histories documented Rome's intrusion, directly or indirectly, into the academic lives of priests and nuns. They were, in her opinion, cause for alarm.

In one situation a university was seeking a dean for its theological school. The search committee made its selection and offered the candidate the job. "He was then invited to meet the local archbishop," Hellwig said. "He meets with the archbishop, and they have what appears to be a pleasant conversation with no problems.

"The next day the rector tells the man, 'Nothing doing.' The man has difficulty getting a reason why. The problem turns out to be that a small point of ecclesiology has emerged from this man's nineteenth-century research—and the archbishop doesn't think this is the way it should be. The rector finally says that the university was vetoed by the archbishop."

Another case involved a "well-known priest" who taught theology at a seminary. Trouble arose when the priest asked his bishop in another locality for laicization (formal transfer to lay status) for the purpose of getting married. "The seminary foundation has no problem with that," Hellwig recalled, "but the bishop who oversees the seminary doesn't like the sound of it. So he tries to find a technical flaw in the man's tenure—and the academic structures of the seminary won't cooperate with him, because the objections he has raised are, in their view, ridiculous.

"Then the bishop contacts the bishop of the man's home diocese, successfully getting him to hold up the laicization until the priest has resigned from the faculty."

A more direct means of achieving that end was devised by a "prestigious university," Hellwig explained, by writing faculty contracts with clerics in such a way that "if they get laicized, they lose their jobs."

Another case of intervention involved a theologian at a university whom Hellwig described as "making a name for herself in her field." But someone found something "displeasing in her research" and complained directly to Rome. "She is a member of a religious community," Hellwig said, "so Rome, instead of going to the university, starts writing letters to her Mother Superior" demanding the professor's removal from the university. "The Mother Superior, by virtue of her obligation of obedience to the pope, does remove her without telling her why."

Though moves against theologians were hardly new, Hellwig said, reactions had changed. When "John Courtney Murray was told to keep quiet about his research, he simply obeyed. I think what has changed is that in the last decade or so scholars who have received such an order haven't necessarily conformed without protest. So the prohibition has tended to go to the rector of the institution or to the bishop of the place." She had felt the sting herself. Her own appointment to a faculty position at Catholic University had been blocked, she said, by the university rector, who balked at hiring a former nun (she had left her religious community long before). "It is repression," she said tersely.

Despite her aversion to outside intervention by Rome in a school's academic affairs, Hellwig ardently held to the idea that Catholic universities should do their utmost to keep their religious identities. "We have to keep alive the ecclesial [church] dimension," she said, "though this doesn't immediately equate with ecclesiastical control."

She had great hopes that the joint committee (CTSA, College Theological Society, and Canon Law Society) would hammer out a set of procedures that would protect theologians from arbitrary intrusion from outside church officials. Though no such rules would be binding, they might set an example that would become the prevailing standard. Guidelines might also diminish the power of vigilantes of the Catholic right who had fired off accusations to Rome against theologians they deemed heretical or immoral. They had achieved apparent success in stirring Rome to take disciplinary action. Formal procedures, allowing for due process and careful sifting of evidence, might forestall these efforts by arch-conservative self-appointed kangaroo courts.

But as much as Hellwig wished to curb the influence of the far right, she also believed that the time had arrived for a lowering of theological voices and efforts at mending fences. "We can accommodate people who teach the Baltimore Catechism and want Latin masses," she said. "Only by fostering solidarity can we realize our potential. Where dissent arose, she said, it should be voiced with respect and discretion. "It requires courage, prayerfulness, and gentleness. Rome cannot be seen as the enemy but as fellow Christians taking positions according to their consciences, positions we see as having to be challenged. It takes humility and compassion and a certain politeness."

— ◆ —

SEVEN MONTHS HAD PASSED SINCE THE BISHOPS ISSUED THEIR PASTORAL LETTER on the U.S. economy. But promoting it within the church had been arduous. Its moral rebuke of economic inequities marched into the teeth of Reagan triumphalism among Catholics and non-Catholics alike. Resistance, especially among Catholic business leaders, was mountainous. Because the pastoral was official policy, however, social revisionists had acquired a powerful new tool that could not be simply brushed aside. Slowly it was feeding into the vast circulatory system of the church.

One evidence of this steady outflow was found in the June-July issue of the *San Francisco Catholic,* the magazine of the archdiocese. A cover headline, "Economic

Rights: The Bishops' Pastoral in Action," flagged the issue's main theme. Contents included five articles related to the pastoral and its practical consequences. It was a package aimed at spreading the word about the bishops' statement and looking at areas where it applied locally.

In a crisp introductory piece, assistant editor John Godges referred to the pastoral hyperbolically as "an earthquake of a document, the rumblings of which are just beginning to reshape our social landscape," and "perhaps the most outspoken and comprehensive statement about social justice ever issued by any national committee of bishops." He reviewed the letter's salient points: that the scope of poverty in America was a moral scandal, that the military budget should be cut and social programs increased, that economic growth should not be gained at the expense of the environment, and that everyone was entitled to at least a sufficient portion of the world's goods. These aims rested, Godges said, on six principles stated by the bishops: human dignity, solidarity, participation, option for the poor, and subsidiarity, the principle that problems should be solved by the competent authority closest to the scene (p. 21).

Insisting that the "bishops do not call for socialism," he continued, "In an age in which the richest two percent of families in the United States hold an estimated 28 percent of the nation's net wealth, in an age in which the minimum $3.35 hourly wage commits a family to an income well below the poverty line, in an age in which affordable housing is disappearing even for the middle class in the Bay Area while 'executive' homes proliferate, in an age in which the Church itself has failed to secure retirement benefits for aging nuns, in an age of Wall Street insider trading scandals, the bishops' pastoral letter on the economy comes as an urgent reminder that an unbridled profit motive is incompatible with human dignity and Christian community" (p. 21).

The accounts that followed highlighted responses to concerns voiced by the pastoral. One focused on the Family School, an interfaith center serving the educational, social, and employment needs of single mothers. Another, on health care, looked at the efforts by the California Association of Catholic Hospitals to win state legislative approval for "incentives to hospitals to accept indigent, uninsured patients and spread the burden more equitably." The program would be funded by raising the cigarette tax from ten cents to twenty-five cents. Still another examined the role of Catholic Relief Services overseas.

Another analysis by Godges, "Employment and a Just Wage," also pointed up some of the tensions generated by the pastoral. The Justice and Peace commission of the archdiocese was studying the tangle of problems related to unemployment. George Wesolek, executive director of the commission, was quoted as saying that the pastoral letter had stirred "tremendous interest on the part of the business community, which usually doesn't participate in Catholic issues." Reading on, it was also clear that interest did not necessarily mean support (p. 24).

Norman Berryessa, described as a financial consultant at a San Francisco investment firm, was cited as a backer of the letter. He had spoken for it at a June 1 mass in the city's financial district. Berryessa, as depicted in the article, saw no conflict between the bishops' message and good business practice. "There are not two worlds but one world," he was quoted as having said, "and we can't separate them. It's possible to invest and think about doing something significant for the benefit of mankind and still make a profit. Everyone wants to make money, but you can make it and not take from the poor or damage the environment or do something that fosters an oppressive government" (p. 24).

Berryessa had been named to an *ad hoc* group by the Justice and Peace commission to promote the teachings of the pastoral letter. He had told Godges that he expected to encounter rejection of it "among wealthy Catholics who think this is a left-wing deal when it's simply interpreting the gospel. A lot of the opposition comes from Catholics who feel their power is being taken away if you're talking about a just wage. The letter is saying let's not only make a profit, but let's share it with others and let others participate in the profits, too. . . . The pastoral has alienated a lot of people, but not a lot of people understand it, and we're trying to get the word out that this is not a radical piece of writing any more than the gospel is" (pp. 24–25).

Commending the pastoral as a tame footnote to an equally easy-listening gospel did not appear to be what Godges had had in mind when he described the bishops' handiwork as an "earthquake." But the effort to present the pastoral as a congenial appendix to the capitalist credo suited Catholics in business who wanted to accept the lessons of the bishops without tampering substantially with the system wrought by Reagan free enterprise. Theirs was an earnest and sincere effort to interpret the pastoral in a way that rendered it both manageable and harmless. Chances were, they knew many of their fellow Catholics rejected the pastoral outright as a socialist threat to that system and were trying to find a respectable middle way. It was not easy.

The same article carried comments attributed to Art Pulaski, identified as executive officer of the San Mateo AFL-CIO Labor Council. Pulaski had, according to Godges, found much to cheer. His reading of the document took a much different slant from that of Berryessa. Pulaski, who had also been appointed to the *ad hoc* group, was quoted as saying that the pastoral "strikes right at home for us. . . . It says some impressive things about how everyone needs to have their just rewards economically in this world. . . . With multi-national conglomerates, corporate buyouts and mergers, employers are solidifying their power, and it's even more important to organize. There is more union-busting, and the letter firmly opposes that. The bishops have made a very bold move" (p. 25).

The pastoral letter had become a screen onto which many agendas were being projected. Meanwhile, there remained the formidable task of educating the church at large about its actual contents.

— ⁓

IN HIS RED CARDIGAN SWEATER, BLUE OXFORD SHIRT WITH OPEN COLLAR, AND crisply pleated slacks, Gilbert the fastidious professor might have been taken for an off-duty priest. He was, in fact, a high priest of Saint Thomas's philosophy, a modern scholastic of daunting reputation. Meticulous in all things official and unofficial, he was a man for whom sloppiness in thought or behavior verged on sinfulness.

On that bright, chilly spring day, Gilbert paused in his university study to review the roots of his quarrel with the modern age, to wit, its elevation of the self as the measure of all things. The governing credo said that truth was defined by the individual. Gilbert's rebuttal had begun to take shape early in his life, reaching a critical stage of formation while he attended graduate school more than three decades ago.

Back then, as an apprentice scholar, he became occupied with the widely held observation that "young people were underwriting subjectivity." Rather than accepting it as an irreversible turn in human consciousness, Gilbert thought "subjectivity itself" needed to be examined objectively. The traditional concept of "objective" religious truth that stood no matter what anyone believed had become increasingly quaint (though absolutism took other guises, as, for example, a set of unalterable principles in the human rights and feminist movements). In a cultural climate where truth was the creation of individuals, he wondered, was there any way of "appraising subjectivity" that would not be just another relative, personal opinion, that wouldn't "involve the imposition of just another point of view?"

As he pursued the question, he felt a certain kinship with Søren Kierkegaard, the nineteenth-century Danish philosopher and religious thinker who had said of himself, "I am the corrective not the norm." Kierkegaard, using his immense literary skills, had run against the cultural and religious grain. Gilbert's discomfort with the currents of his own age put him in somewhat similar tension with it. Unlike Kierkegaard, Gilbert could fasten on to the Thomistic pre–Vatican II church to gird himself. But he would find too much of the modern world in the post–Vatican II church to claim it any longer unconditionally as an ally. He would become more an outsider both as a Catholic and as a philosopher holding out against a vastly changed world of thought.

The issue that had absorbed him in graduate school continued to be a major focus in his teaching. "Kids talk as if there are no objective criteria for anything,"

he said. "I say to them that if I find something objective, then I have another level
of appraising what I do both before and after I act." But among many students, talk
of "fixed" truths met strong resistance as an illegitimate attempt to impose one
set of views on everyone else, Gilbert said. To make his case, he appealed to the
church's theology of "natural law," wherein, it was argued, God's binding moral
precepts were evident through ordinary reason within the course of everyday life
for anyone in any cultural setting. They were the natural laws to which all human
beings were accountable (the sense of justice and fairness, the immorality of artificial birth control, etc.). So said the church.

Gilbert invited students to take that approach and suggested that these precepts
were already part of their common existence. "In the structure of our actions," he
stated in summary, "there are laws, shared assumptions, we can't escape. It's important to show people that they already hold them." A belief in natural law obviously undermined the idea that every person invents the truth, or, as Gilbert put
it, "prevents people from acting out of radical subjectivity."

He remembered a formal debate at a philosophical society meeting in which
he had been pitted against a man who scoffed at the notion of natural law. "He
wanted to be right, and so did I," Gilbert said. "We shared that assumption."
Gilbert was sure the man had thereby unwittingly proved his point. "The natural
law view is evident even in the worst person's retention of wanting to do right,"
he said. "Rationalization is a sign of that."

But Catholic America was veering farther from its heritage of objective truths,
he felt, in its lapse into an individualism that was essentially Protestant in origin.
"Just the other day a Protestant minister who has been studying philosophy here
told me that he'd decided that most people who call themselves Catholics are as
Protestant as he is," Gilbert recalled. "'Like me, he said, they have problems with
Marian dogma, are not accepting of the moral dogma of the church, and question the pope.' That was an extremely interesting observation." Vatican II had
dusted off and reaffirmed the right of personal conscience, to be sure. But in their
eagerness to claim that right, Catholics were forsaking the authority of church
teaching.

"People think that if they reflect on something conscientiously and come to a
conclusion that it's wrong, they must follow their conscience," Gilbert said carefully.
"Obviously that is part of our tradition, but it's not the end of the story. It does not
exonerate you. It's possible you might be wrong. It's true that you're obligated to follow your conscience. But it doesn't mean one conscience is as good as another."

Gilbert, the guardian of orthodoxy, the man out of step with much of Catholic
America, saw the church in the United States as splintered and seditious, where
fewer assumptions were, in fact, held in common and where "people now like to
think Rome is the enemy." Did the many conflicts within the church constitute "a

debate among Catholics or functional Protestants?" he wondered. "What criteria do we use for deciding whether views of Catholics are properly *in* or *out?*. . . People [in the church] argue about *in vitro* fertilization as if there is no moral framework, but that they have a right to decide this for themselves." Subjectivity through and through. The term "Catholic" had become "equivocal" in Gilbert's view. It was for him a replay of the nineteenth-century "Americanist heresy"—the movement to harmonize the church with American values that was squashed by Pope Leo XIII in his 1899 encyclical *Testem benevolentiae*—making a staggering comeback.

Gilbert mourned what he saw as a drift within his own university from its Catholic moorings toward the mainstream of secularism. To compete favorably for professors, the school had broadened its hiring standards, downplaying the importance of a candidate's Catholic identity. As the result, he said, "there are a lot of people on the faculty for whom [Catholic] tradition doesn't make much sense." The effect of that pattern was discovered too late, he felt, and though there had been a recent effort to redress the balance, he doubted that the damage could be repaired. He didn't expect "any big change in the drift." Perhaps in all honesty it should drop its Catholic designation as "no longer a place where you go to receive Catholic instruction. I don't think our theologians would object to that. If you were to ask them if they saw themselves as retailers of what Catholics believe, I think the majority would say no."

Gilbert the "corrective, not the norm" had made a name for himself as a deft polemicist, but the jousting sometimes brought him up short. "Things keep coming to me, all sorts of controversies I've been caught up in—and I long to be free of those things," he said.

"God did not choose to save his people through dialectics," he said somberly. "I just want to take care of my own garden. But it's not just a matter of winning arguments. It's about eternal life—all the things this place [the university] is made for are about eternal destiny and the life of the mind. Kids come in here and say that they've been told the Catholic position is that Jesus didn't rise from the dead." To counter that kind of thing required forceful argument, he thought.

"But to think of arguing to demolish somebody can be a real distraction," he said, "because you can do it for rotten reasons. Maybe it's just that we get caught being human.

"I used to nurse the illusion that everyone liked me. In recent years I'm aware that things I say infuriate people. I'd rather not have people think I'm saying things to taunt them. I don't know how I got into this—do I have a right to cancel out?

"There are days when I'd just as soon not have to feel displeased because of what one of my colleagues has said about me. It is painful. But I'm a Papist, a *Roman* Catholic at a time when lots of people don't want to be true to that. But I don't know any other way to be."

No MEETING IN MEMORY HAD AROUSED SUCH EMOTION AND BITTER CONFLICT IN advance. Finally, it took place, on June 25 at the Vatican. Pope John Paul II shook hands with Kurt Waldheim, the embattled president of Austria. The occasion had all the trappings of an official state visit. For thirty-five minutes, the two men spoke privately in the pope's study, sealed away from cries of "shame, shame" outside Vatican walls. The deed had been done.

Many outraged voices had implored the pope to shun the Austrian leader. Waldheim, a Catholic, was laboring under the dark shadow of accusations that stemmed from his World War II record as an officer of the Third Reich. He had been specifically charged with knowingly aiding efforts to ship Jews from Greece and Yugoslavia to the Nazi death camps. Though Waldheim had repeatedly denied the charges, the American government had found them sufficiently credible to bar the former United Nations general secretary from entering the United States. The reaction had been different at the Vatican. Waldheim's request for a formal meeting with the pope had been granted.

Notice of the agreement earlier that month had sparked a fire storm of protest from Jews and others who saw the pope's move as a callous affront to the memory of the Holocaust. In reply, the Vatican asserted that the pope was simply following normal procedure in receiving the duly-elected head of a friendly nation with strong Catholic ties. It was a matter of recognizing the Austrian people, Vatican officials said, rather than conferring moral respectability on their leader.

Critics refused to be assuaged by such arguments. As the day arrived, tensions mounted. The Vatican was ringed with extraordinary security. The National Catholic News Service described the scene:

> As the Pope and Waldheim were meeting several hundred demonstrators from the Federation of Young Italian Jews and from several left-wing Italian parties gathered about a hundred yards from St. Peter's Square. A few protesters were wearing the striped uniforms of concentration camp prisoners, and some camp survivors showed the numbers tattooed on their arms.
>
> In an unusual move, Italian police had totally closed off the square to pedestrians. Helicopters whirred above as demonstrators yelled "executioner," erected a mock gallows with a noose hanging from it, and waved signs reading, "Waldheim go home" and "What kind of a pope is this?"

By custom, details of the pope's private talks were not made public. In his prepared statement after the meeting, John Paul referred neither to the allegations against Waldheim nor to his previous denunciations of the Holocaust. He did, however, extol his guest as an exemplary diplomat. "All your activities in international circles as a diplomat and foreign minister of your country and through your difficult and highly responsible activities in the United Nations were dedicated to achieving peace among peoples," the pope said. Later, Waldheim told reporters that the charges of war crimes against him had been discussed with the pope "in a marginal way."

Before and after the meeting, the issues surrounding it became a major test of Jewish-Catholic relations in the United States. The Waldheim imbroglio followed on the heels of debate over the pope's beatification of Edith Stein, a German Jew who became a Carmelite nun and was put to death by the Nazis. Though John Paul had praised her as a "great daughter of the Jewish people," there was lingering irritation among those who felt that she had been unfairly depicted as a Catholic martyr rather than a victim of her Jewish roots. And some Jews felt that the elevation of a convert demeaned Judaism. The other piece of unfinished business between the two faiths was the Vatican's refusal to grant diplomatic recognition to Israel. That sore point had been highlighted the past January during Cardinal O'Connor's problematic trip to the Middle East.

But the Waldheim incident touched a much deeper nerve. Several large Jewish groups urged the Vatican to call off the meeting. Among those entering pleas was the head of the American Jewish Committee. "It would be altogether a matter of personal conscience were the pope to receive Dr. Waldheim as a private Catholic communicant seeking pastoral solace," said Theodore Ellenoff, president of the committee, in a statement June 17. "For the supreme pontiff, as head of the Holy See, to receive Kurt Waldheim as president of state makes a mockery of truth and justice." Calling the Austrian president "an active participant in the Nazi war machine" who had "lied to the international community [about his activities] for 10 years," Ellenoff cautioned that the pope stood to diminish his "extraordinary record" on human rights and social justice by going through with the meeting.

In anticipation that the Vatican would go ahead undeterred, a hastily called strategy session of twelve of the most influential Jewish groups, including the American Jewish Committee and the Anti-Defamation League, decided to play their trump card, threatening to boycott the meeting scheduled in Miami between John Paul and prominent Jewish leaders during the pope's trip to the United States in September. Both sides had placed great value on such a high-visibility event as a sign of progress in relations between the two faiths, but for many Catholics concerned about the recent Jewish discontent, it was especially crucial to the church that the meeting succeed, as a means of showing Catholic goodwill and calming Jewish anger.

Archbishop John L. May, president of the bishops' conference, moved quickly to salvage the September 11 papal event in Miami. Like other American bishops who addressed the issue, Archbishop May avoided criticism of the pope while suggesting that Jewish-Catholic relations in the United States should be treated separately from events in Rome. Above all, the archbishop hoped that preparations for the September 11 meeting would continue smoothly. In a June 22 statement, the archbishop voiced confidence that the bond between Jews and Catholics was "strong enough to overcome any specific difficulty of the moment." He praised the cooperation that had already gone into the plans for the event and, holding out a carrot, noted optimistically that the format in Miami would include "a significant statement addressed to the Holy Father by a representative of the Jewish community and a response by the Pope."

The questions raised by the Waldheim episode were so serious, said the leaders of the American Jewish Congress, that the ability of the established Jewish-Catholic dialogue to handle them was doubtful. One thing was clear to the congress: "The meeting scheduled for September 11 in Miami is not where these questions will be addressed," their letter said. "It is therefore not where we can be."

It remained to be seen whether other Jewish groups would boycott the Miami event as decisively if they achieved nothing through negotiation. No matter what the outcome, formal relations between Jews and Catholics appeared to be on shakier ground than at any time since interfaith talks began after the Second Vatican Council.

CALEB'S PARENTS, TONY AND SOPHIE, HAD DRIVEN OVER FROM THEIR HOME JUST a few miles away on a Sunday. Cindy's parents were almost as close, so visits with the in-laws were common. The two sets of grandparents had generally paid separate calls, however, except for a few ritual occasions such as Caleb and Cindy's wedding itself nearly six years before and baptisms of the two children. The bigger gatherings had by all accounts been pleasant, but the parents had too little in common to sustain much social life. Caleb's folks were working class people grounded in small town ways, immersed in the customs and practices of Polish Catholicism. Cindy's mother and father, devoted United Methodists, were molded by the influences of urban mobility and professional life.

Across differences of class and denomination, Caleb and Cindy had both inherited a powerful commitment to family and church. With regard to the home, they both held traditional values. Accordingly, the man was the primary breadwinner and head of household maintenance, the woman responsible for nearly all cooking, cleaning, and child rearing.

Lately the system had broken down somewhat under pressure from Cindy's efforts to complete her master's degree in education. She was required to be at the university four times a week for two hours. Three of those days, the children were cared for by a babysitter. But because Wednesday was Caleb's regular day away from his optometry practice, it made sense for him to cover her absence then. He admitted that he had done it grudgingly.

Caleb's father, Tony, was a spare man with a shock of gray hair, swept back, and sharp facial features that had been passed along to his son. He wore dark, thick-framed glasses that set off the ruddiness in his slightly sunken cheeks. His eyes exuded kindness through a layer of impenetrable sadness. His wife, Sophie, a fellow Polish immigrant, had a shy, fearful look and a taut manner. She was a small woman with an tense mouth and darting eyes. Her hair was tied back in a bun, and she wore a red print dress with white shoes. Her demeanor suggested wariness and profound agitation.

Both Caleb's parents held the same impression of him as a boy: in a word, exacting, needing little discipline. "He'd see a messy or dirty spot and would start cleaning the whole house," his mother said. Caleb himself acknowledged that he was still hard to please and tended to be "picky," regarding that more as a virtue than a vice. "I used to think I was a good housekeeper," Cindy sighed, "until I met him." Caleb's rigor had found ample application in other areas of his life, notably in his attitude toward religion.

Though Caleb physically resembled his father, he reflected his mother's temperament, a pervasive dismay over the way things were. Sourness combined with disdain into a mood of disillusion. Tony and Cindy, by contrast, exuded a honey-like sweetness. Father-in-law and daughter-in-law were children of the light, positive and sanguine, both having subordinated themselves to their more dominant mates, quietly injecting notes of hopefulness and open-mindedness. A spiritual harmony linked them.

Tony, neatly dressed in a blue shirt, gray slacks, and brown shoes, talked about his days as a young man during World War II in Poland when he had been confined for two years in a Soviet labor camp "loading barges and sleeping on a slab on the floor." Before that, he said, laying his plate down, "I had a strong vocation; my dream was to be a priest." The war had derailed that ambition and tested his spirit ("Faith was the only thing that saved me").

After the war, he had migrated to America, married, and started a family. But the memory of the labor camp was still painful, evoking a visible, haunting pall from the core of his unsearchable melancholy. He had worked as a skilled machinist (he believed the occupation represented his proper station in the work world) and kept devout allegiance to the church (praying always, he said, for a clear mind with which to approach his problems). His close friendship with a Methodist neighbor had opened the door to the legitimacy of other churches. "I feel completely that being a Christian comes first," he said in a near whisper, "before being Catholic." Both his daughters-in-law were non-Catholics. "We love them both," he said, then surprisingly, "yet spiritually they are like enemies.

Church unity is what I want most. But it's not coming." Long hours of Bible study had convinced him that *"agape*—that means love"—was the paramount requirement for followers of Jesus.

Sophie saw much darker forces at work in Catholicism, masterminded by a liberal cabal of trendy, permissive priests bent on throwing tradition to the winds. If she had a chance to speak with the pope during his trip to America, she would tell him "he ought to discipline bad priests who are following secular ways on abortion, birth control, homosexuals, and other things." The mass media only made matters worse by "never interviewing the loyal priests, but always the dissidents, always the liberals." She decried what she saw as all sorts of aberrant behavior taking place in parishes near and far. One that was "especially bad," she said, was the "polka mass," a liturgy punctuated by the folk music of Eastern Europe. She had gone to the priest beforehand with a magazine article that denounced such practices as illicit, but to no avail. "My faith is Catholic—I'm conservative," she said solemnly. "But all around me I see radicals and liberals. The problem is very serious."

Her son agreed with her conclusion that the church had fallen into laxness and waywardness. "It took centuries to get the church all messed up," Caleb chimed in apocalyptically. "It may take decades to straighten it out." Too many Catholics were "wishy-washy," and that "had been overlooked for too many years. The church needs to take hold and say, 'This is the way it is.'" Half of those at church "don't want to be there," Caleb believed, and he was downright sick of the "apathy." It was time to enforce tough membership standards. In the long run, he thought, "The church would be better off with smaller numbers who showed greater participation." Caleb would advise lazy Catholics to try harder to get something out of church. Giving up was the worst sin in Caleb's list of commandments.

The kind of person Caleb had in mind for restoring some backbone was a friend he and the family had known since childhood. The friend had entered the major seminary but for reasons unclear to Caleb and Tony had dropped out. Tony, who said he felt like a father to him, knew that the cause had something to do with the young man's conservative views, but they had never spoken about the exact nature of the dispute. The friend had gone on to college and returned to town.

One Sunday in the choir together at mass, Tony recalled, he saw the young man react against something a visiting missionary said from the pulpit. "I looked at him and said, 'What are you waiting for? The Holy Spirit is calling you. He took me seriously,'" Tony said. The young man at once searched for a religious order that would accept him and had recently been ordained a priest. "Deep inside I knew he was going to do it," Caleb said, professing a touch of envy. "He'll be excellent. He's totally honest and opinionated, but at least you'll know where you stand with him."

Cindy had gone to the ordination with the rest of the family a few weeks before. She had been impressed by the pageantry, the long line of priests in the procession, the "beautiful music," the dignity of it all. She was becoming gradually more familiar with the world of Catholicism, taking it in with guarded appreciation. Cindy said she felt less the outsider, but an outsider nonetheless. Her attention was mainly directed these days at finishing her master's degree. "I'm thoroughly enjoying school," she said, while her mother-in-law began clearing the table. Suppressing momentarily an impulse to jump up to help, Cindy went on, "The course is only five weeks, so it's really crammed. Three more to go. This is my last course, then I take the comprehensive exam and research two topics. Then I should get my M.A." She smiled broadly at the prospect of attaining this goal of her own that could allow her to expand her horizons. Her goal was to teach. "I just hope," she said adventurously, "that someone out there wants me."

Some other highlights in June:

- Figures from the 1987 *Official Catholic Directory,* the annual publication of P. J. Kenedy and Sons, showed that Catholic America had grown by a tiny one half of one percent to a total of 52,893,217 over the twelve months ending January 1, 1987. The number of diocesan priests stood at 34,471, a drop of 2 percent, while the total of religious order sisters declined one percent to 112,489. Meanwhile, a surge continued in the ranks of deacons, up 5.5 percent to 7,981 from 7,562 the year before. Catholic schools again lost ground. There were seven fewer parochial and diocesan high schools (850), three fewer private high schools (558), and ninety-three fewer elementary schools (7,772), with 2,030,598 students, a decline of 70,000. Los Angeles retained the title of largest U.S. diocese, with 2.6 million Catholics, followed in size by Chicago, Boston, New York, and Detroit. The most recent estimate of the number of Catholics worldwide, from the Vatican's *Statistical Yearbook,* was 866.7 million, 18 percent of the earth's population.

- The executive committee of the bishops' conference took action to completely withdraw United States Catholic Conference funds invested in firms doing business in South Africa as a protest against that country's policy of apartheid. Already $18 million of the USCC's assets had been divested at the request of the bishops' administrative board the previous September. The board stipulated that the remaining $5.3 million be withdrawn unless a subcommittee of bishops judged that South Africa had made significant progress toward ending apartheid by May 1, 1987. In its report, the sub-committee, headed by Auxiliary Bishop Joseph Sullivan of Brooklyn, ruled that no substantial improvement had taken place. On that basis Archbishop John L. May, president of the bishops' conference, and the other four members of the executive committee on June 2 set the final phase of divestment in motion. In their decision in September 1986, which authorized divestment, the bishops on the administrative board declared that "change must come within South Africa" on "human, moral, and political grounds." All "nations and institutions which have a relationship with South Africa are part of the political and moral drama being played out in that nation," their statement said. They urged all Catholic dioceses, health care facilities, universities, and colleges to withdraw South African investments in accord with that mandate.

- "Homosexuality and the Priesthood," an article by the Reverend Richard P. McBrien, chairman of the Notre Dame theology department, in the June 19 issue of *Commonweal,* declared that the time had come for the church to examine, above board, questions about gay seminarians, priests, and bishops. How many were there? Had the percentage increased in recent years? Was the size of that group related in any way to "the increasing visibility of child-molestation cases involving Catholic clergy?" (p. 380). Was there a discernible gay culture in seminaries and among priests in dioceses? Were undeclared gay priests and bishops even tougher on avowedly homosexual priests than their colleagues? Were gay priests more conservative or liberal than heterosexual priests? Any more or less inclined to favor or oppose obligatory celibacy? More or less likely to promote the church's social teachings? To these and other questions, Father McBrien suggested no answers, only that the need for information was pressing. "The alternative," he wrote, "is leaving them to gossip, to unexamined, closed-door decisions, or to policy by default" (p. 380). Father McBrien did offer one opinion: that the best way to improve the quantity and quality of priests would be to make celibacy optional.

◄ ►

To MARK THE TWENTY-FIFTH ANNIVERSARY OF THE OPENING OF THE SECOND Vatican Council, which formally convened on October 11, 1962, *U.S. Catholic* magazine asked Catholic Americans "what's happened to your church in the last 25 years?" A variety of responses formed the substance of a special June issue.

The magazine's regular monthly unscientific reader survey was devoted to questions related to changes brought about by Vatican II and how well they had been received. Most results generally paralleled those culled from more rigorously scientific studies. The vast majority of Catholic Americans in the *U.S. Catholic* survey liked the changes. But there was also evidence of confusion between the newer mode of elasticity and the older style of strict conformity.

"The American Church in particular," wrote Tim Unsworth in an overview of the survey, "now seems more divided between those who prefer legal rigidity and precise canonical definitions, and those who would view the church as helping individual people 'where the rubber hits the road,' as one layman put it" (p. 6).

Reforms most noted by the respondents added up to "a terrifyingly large number," Unsworth said. They included many of the obvious: the English mass, the presence of laypeople in the liturgy and as eucharistic ministers, greater availability of annulments, ecumenical activities, and an enhanced role for women. The "list was even longer," Unsworth said, in reaction to the question of what had been the most difficult to adjust to, though, he added, the items were, for the most part, "relatively small ones." They included ending the meatless-Friday obligation, disappearance of Latin from the mass, the sight of women in the sanctuary, the attenuation of the confessional, and abolition of the expectation that women would wear hats in church (p. 7).

"If *U.S. Catholic* readers could reclaim one thing from the pre-1962 church," Unsworth wrote, "it would be the 'smells and bells.' Many cited a measurable loss of awe—a loss of solemnity, reverence, and mystery that grew out of the Latin rite. There were numerous appeals to restore traditional Marian devotions and a surprisingly large number of people who wanted to see restoration of clerical dress and religious habits." In assessing these sentiments, Unsworth thought "faith and nostalgia become so intertwined that it's hard to tell the difference." And what reforms would these readers most like to see ahead? Optional celibacy and the ordination of women both received much support, the author reported. Though the church in the United States "remains confused" a quarter century after Vatican II, he wrote, *U.S. Catholic* readers on the whole would "rather live with the confusion than revert" (pp. 7–8).

Specific aspects of the historic turnabout were explored in separate articles.

Mary O'Connell examined the influence of feminism on the church. The twenty-five years since the inception of the Second Vatican Council had coincided closely with the tremendous upsurge of feminist thought and activism. Betty Friedan's landmark book, *The Feminine Mystique,* appeared the year after the Council fathers rolled up their sleeves and went to work. Though the Council had opened possibilities for greater participation for women in the church, O'Connell found, women had largely taken on more of the workload but had remained outside the circles of church authority and decision making. "That may

mean that the church is becoming more feminized, but not feminist," she quoted
the sociologist William McCready as saying in response (p. 15).

Among the issues creating dissension and division were abortion, on which disagreement existed among Catholic women as well as between feminists and the hierarchy, and the ordination of women. Though some women pressed for the
ordination of women itself, O'Connell said, others saw it more as a symbolic
issue than an actual goal, inasmuch as they believed that a wholesale reform of the
priesthood was a necessity before women could legitimately take part in it. At least
half of Catholic America now favored ordination of women, she reported, though
the bishops insisted that the door was closed.

The Women-Church movement had meanwhile become a way station for
women who felt alienated by many of the church's teachings but refused to leave
Catholicism. Women-Church groups met to pray and partake in liturgies outside
the framework of the official church. It was a network of Catholic women in
semi-exile awaiting greater reforms in the church. On the other side of the fence,
a group called Women for Faith and Family had appealed to Catholic women to
be loyal to the church's teachings on "all matters dealing with human reproduction, family life, and roles for men and women in the Church and in society" (p.
18). The leader of the drive, Helen Hull Hitchcock of St. Louis, wife of the
Catholic historian James Hitchcock, had helped write "An Affirmation for Catholic
Women" containing the pledge of loyalty. It had garnered thirty thousand signatures since it began circulating in 1984, O'Connell said.

Most American Catholics found themselves somewhere between the positions
of Women-Church and Women for Faith and Family, O'Connell wrote. "They
mostly support the feminist changes that have coincided with Vatican II reforms,"
she stated, "where feminism clearly challenges institutional Catholicism they are
less certain though still sympathetic to many feminist concerns" (p. 18).

The impact of social and economic pressures on Catholic family life over
twenty-five years was the subject of an article by James Breig. "So what happened
to Catholic families?" Breig asked. "A lot of things. Some of them bought into the
American Dream and found the price to be their integrity, marriages, or faith.
Many heard the church asking them to do more than they were willing to do,
while others haven't heard the church say anything sensible. Some blame society;
others point to themselves. Still others ask how the Catholic family could have
remained the same in a world in which the role of women changed and the nation in general became altered by such shocks as Vietnam, Watergate, the sexual
revolution, escalating drug use, and a thousand other crises" (p. 53).

And in a piece that asked whether American Catholics were "hammering out
a do-it-yourself morality" (p. 54) in defiance of the church, Robert T. Reilly saw
greater independence, which stopped short of full-scale rebellion. A trend among

Catholics to do more of their moral thinking for themselves was unmistakable and irreversible, Reilly noted. Vatican II had restored the role of personal conscience in forming moral decisions. At the same time, the values in the surrounding society had shifted.

"Twenty-five years ago Catholics embraced stability, family unity, commitment, more conservative sexual mores, and the sublimation of individual aspirations," Reilly wrote. "Today, according to Father Val J. Peter, director of Boys Town and a former theology professor, the prevalent values are 'self-fulfillment, creative growth and integration, personal autonomy, living in harmony with the modern world, and the celebration of pleasure'" (p. 55). There was no turning back to a day of uniform adherence to church rules, Reilly asserted. Catholics were more inclined to form their consciences on the basis of their experience and their relationships, lamentable as that may be to some church leaders.

"The Catholic Church must learn how to deal with the phenomenon of dissent," Reilly concluded, "must be more compassionate and more evangelical, and must find ways to communicate more effectively. And the laity, still uncertain even while increasingly autonomous, must learn how to order their independence and better inform their conscience" (p. 58).

Altogether, the special issue could be read as a brief for Catholic America against charges from Rome and the Catholic right that the church in the United States was a renegade, prodigal child. In the weeks before the pope's scheduled arrival, debate about the character of Catholic America—Was it loyal or morally and theologically dissolute?—was expected to heat up. The special issue argued that it was energetic, sometimes inclined to spawn dissent, but fundamentally faithful to Catholic tradition. "I say once again," wrote Robert E. Burns in his regular page-two column that often set the tone for the magazine, "that the whole church, The People of God, laypeople, religious, priests, bishops, and the Pope, have reason to be proud of American Catholics. More than any other group of Catholics, perhaps, they have kept the faith" (p. 2).

July
1·9·8·7

M IDWAY THROUGH THE SUMMER AND NEARLY THREE MONTHS after receiving his B.A. degree, Paul was already glancing back at his college days as if through a rearview mirror. In a final cascade of events, he had finished up his course work, plunged into exams, and emerged smiling in the center of the family picture on the sprawling green campus at graduation. To Paul, the tall oaks and the familiar, dappled pathways of Saint Augustine had never looked better. His place in that long, proud procession of graduates had been certified, and he remembered feeling elevated by it all.

The festivities had been made sweeter by mid-April notices that he had been admitted to law schools. As he had expected, he had been accepted at those second-tier schools that ranked just below the most prestigious institutions. His choice was a school in Washington, D.C., where he hoped to mix law training with some close-up education in national politics. Though looking forward to it, he wondered how he would deal with the adjustments and pressures after coasting through the last year of college where everything was so relaxed and familiar.

Meanwhile, he was in the midst of the summer hiatus. His first preference for a job, an internship in a Dallas law firm, had failed to pan out, so he had accepted the offer by a friend of his father to do computer work in a New England drug company. There he monitored experiments done by doctors with various drugs. In this first week of July, he was compiling the "thirty-five nonhypertensive things that hypertensive drugs were being used for." Paul liked the office atmosphere because it gave him a chance to observe how he performed in the adult work world. He was a good team player, he thought, even pretty decent managerial material. But then again, he found himself sharing his father's aversion to office politics. He wasn't sure he could tolerate "the game playing—and I see a lot going on."

His fly-on-the-wall status in the office had yielded some special moments of insight. One was especially vivid. "One day the boss calls me in and tells me to enjoy this part of my life because later on I'll get lots of responsibility," Paul recalled. "He seemed to be saying, 'Don't work here or any place like it, because it will just wear you down.'" Still, he thought that "in the right circumstances" he could envision himself fitting into such an operation. His student government experience had given him confidence in his ability to handle tough, weighty situations, so perhaps, he thought, he could be his "own person" in the midst of corporate complexity. Maybe.

If his thoughts about his future sounded somewhat tentative, he explained over a hamburger and beer after work, it was because he had three weeks earlier received a terrifying jolt. A phone call had brought the awful news that one of his college roommates, Mike, lay near death in a French hospital after being hit by two cars on a Paris street. The caller was another roommate. "Is he going to die?" Paul remembered asking. The roommate said he didn't know. To Paul it had been a horrible blow, "the worst in a long time. That song 'Only the Good Die Young' kept ringing in my ears."

While Mike clung to life far away, Paul had paced the hallways at work and at home "talking to God, saying, 'What's going on?' For a couple of days I believed he was going to die. When I was a child I guess I'd asked God for things for myself. But during those couple of days it was different: I prayed for wisdom. I reached this resolution in my mind, that somehow he was going to be blessed. That's how I prepared for him dying. Thank God he didn't."

To the jubilation of family and friends on this vigil, the coma lifted after nine days, and soon Mike returned to his parents' home in Maryland to recuperate. Paul had been to visit him and saw his friend making sure, steady progress with the help of a wheelchair and heavy medication.

As Paul looked ahead to a seemingly boundless future, the incident had reminded him that his life, too, had an unpredictable final limit. "Death is a strange thing to come to terms with at this age," he said. The crisis had also heightened his admiration for Mike, a mechanical engineering student who didn't hide his emotions. "He's really a good person, sort of naive, very honest with his feelings," Paul said. Mike's sensitivity had played a role Paul now valued more. "He was a catalyst," he recalled. "When he felt something, he said it. He could say 'I love you guys,' and we were all a little embarrassed by it. He'd go out with a girl a couple times and fall head over heels in love with her."

Meanwhile, Paul himself had been smitten by a young woman he had met during the summer. "Since high school I haven't felt this strongly about anyone," he exulted. "I think I've been hit by the L-word, as we called it at school." He predicted the romance would make it past the swoon of seasonal warmth into the fall. By then he would be settled into a new place going to a new school. It tasted like adventure, and in light of the scare he had experienced during Mike's peril, he said he felt very grateful indeed. He would try to remain thankful for the day and not look too far ahead, he said. A future in law, politics, whatever, would have to be built on a life that meant something, he believed, and Mike's brush with death had reminded him of things like that, things like God. He had hope.

"I'm eager to be back at school," Paul said, eyes flashing, "because I love school. I'm getting ready for life."

THE GUESSING OVER PRESIDENT REAGAN'S CHOICE TO FILL THE VACANCY ON the U.S. Supreme Court left by Justice Lewis Powell's retirement ended on July 2 when Reagan introduced Robert Bork as the nominee at a Washington news conference.

Among those most delighted by the president's choice were the "pro-life" forces, which included, of course, a large slice of Catholic America. Judge Bork had publicly denounced the *Roe* v. *Wade* ruling by which abortion had been made legal and, according to the opponents of abortion, could therefore be counted upon to cast the crucial vote to overturn it. The Knights of Columbus quickly urged confirmation, as did several other groups, including the American Life League, which rushed two hundred thousand petitions of support into the mails. The *Wanderer* also launched a spirited drive to drum up backing.

The Bork debate would most certainly intensify until the confirmation hearings, set to begin September 15, and from early indications it would be a bare-knuckles brawl. The triggering event at the White House set in motion a quarrel over the meaning of the Constitution, the timing of which was uncanny. President Reagan's announcement, with a grinning Judge Bork at his side, fell just two days before the Fourth of July, and the hearings would commence during the culminating events celebrating the bicentennial of the Constitution.

The July 4 holiday afforded noted Catholics an opportunity to reflect on the historical significance of the remarkable set of guiding principles that emerged during those intense days of the Constitutional Convention two hundred summers ago.

From Washington, the United States Catholic Conference issued a statement on July 2 jointly with the National Council of Churches and the Synagogue Council of America that saluted the Constitution's enduring principles, especially the "protections of religious liberty," and challenged the nation to a "renewed commitment to achieve full equality and true freedom for all the peoples who make up this nation." It continued, "Only then can we fulfill the spirit and promise of the Constitution."

On Sunday, July 5, Monsignor John Tracy Ellis, the most honored historian of Catholic America, stood in the pulpit of Saint Matthew's Cathedral in Washington to deliver his own paean to that centerpiece of democracy housed in the National Archives. Monsignor Ellis, now in his eighty-fourth year and still a lecturer at Catholic University, appeared more frail with the passing of time but never less distinguished.

The monsignor's address reflected his awe of those remarkable events in Philadelphia two centuries earlier and his reverence for the Catholic church's place in that legacy, the dual allegiances from which his own inspiration had been drawn over the decades. As twin exemplars of this glorious past, he focused upon George Washington and John Carroll, both luminaries in the constitutional period. Washington's inauguration as the first president in April 1789 was followed a month later by Carroll's selection by his fellow priests as Catholic America's first bishop. Both men, said the monsignor, had been "role models" noted for their "personal integrity, for their sterling moral characters, and in the face of formidable obstacles for their courageous defense of the truth as they perceived it."

This was a moment to give thanks for these two leaders and for the "singular blessings that have derived for all Americans from that fundamental set of laws crafted two hundred years ago," Monsignor Ellis said, most especially for religious freedom guaranteed by those laws. Before independence, Catholics had been denied citizenship in most of the colonies, he reminded his hearers, so the issue of religious liberty was hardly moot to the thirty-five thousand members of the church (of a total population of four million).

Before John Carroll's elevation to bishop, while serving as superior of the Catholic community in the new nation, he had for good reason, therefore, ardently embraced the concept of religious freedom. "It was a position from which Carroll and his successors never swerved," Monsignor Ellis intoned with pointed irony, "even if the official teaching of the Church remained otherwise [in opposition to religious liberty] until the passage of the Declaration of Religious Freedom of Vatican Council II in December 1965."

Had America lived up to the high standards of character and conduct established by Washington and Carroll? "In some aspects I think we can answer in the affirmative," Monsignor Ellis ventured, "but in others honesty compels one to admit that in recent years there has occurred an increase in disquieting factors such as abortion, divorce, sexual permissiveness, to say nothing of child abuse, drug addiction, theft and lying on levels both high and low—all this to a degree that thoughtful citizens have felt cause for alarm."

Despite these signs of degradation, the monsignor counseled hope as the only appropriate disposition. "Meanwhile," he said, "each of us can do his or her share in support of the time-honored principles of our federal Constitution, just as we are called to do by our religious faith in support of the Church's teachings."

ALSO COINCIDENT WITH THE CELEBRATIONS OF THE FOURTH OF JULY AND THE bicentennial was yet another test of the Constitution's durability and practicality in the dramatic unfolding of the Iran-Contra investigation. Nine months after the first disclosure that Reagan administration officials had conducted secret arms sales to Iran and illegally funneled profits to the Nicaraguan rebels, the inquiry into the case by Congress was in full swing, highlighted by public hearings.

There were two major issues. One concerned the constitutional separation of powers. Congress had specifically forbidden aid to the Contras during the time when income from arms sales to Iran, allegedly carried out to help free hostages in Lebanon, was being siphoned to them under White House auspices. It appeared, then, that the president, or those appointed by the president, had violated the Constitution's restrictions on the executive branch.

The other issue had to do with the pattern of lies and deceptions used by administration officials to carry out their covert project, including the conveyance of deliberate falsehoods to members of Congress. The scandal was widely seen as the greatest threat to the rule of law since Watergate. But the outcome was far from clear.

Robert B. McFarlane, President Reagan's former national security adviser, who had apparently attempted suicide in the wake of the scandal, appeared before the joint House-Senate panel in June, revealing nothing startlingly new. The nation awaited the appearance of Lieutenant Colonel Oliver North, the White House contact who ran the operation, therefore the star witness.

After much wrangling over what could legally be included or excluded from his public testimony, Colonel North answered questions in a one-day secret session with the congressional committee on July 1. Six days later he strolled with ramrod bearing into the crowded hearing room bathed in television lights and packed with excited onlookers to begin his jousting with the panel and its lawyers in full view of the nation. The colonel looked resplendent in his Marine Corps dress uniform, medals shining, every inch the picture of loyalty to his country.

For six grueling days, Colonel North confounded the best-laid plans of his interrogators by parlaying that image of rectitude and patriotism-at-any-cost into a fabulously popular pitch to the galleries. By the end, he had explained away his breaking of the law as necessary to fulfill a higher calling to rescue the hostages (which had not occurred) and to keep the hopes of the Contra "freedom fighters" alive by keeping them supplied. The fact that he had lied to Congress, received private funds from a weapons' supplier, and shredded key documents paled in the glow of Colonel North's rugged piety. The American public flocked to his side, polls showed, and enshrined him in sudden heroism.

The Catholic right (North had been raised Catholic, like McFarlane and other principals in the affair, including former national security adviser Admiral John Poindexter and the late CIA director William Casey, but now belonged to a Pentecostal church) rallied behind the fresh-faced colonel partly in support of the Contra cause. Cardinal Obando y Bravo, head of the Nicaraguan church, was a staunch opponent of the Sandinista government, accusing it, among other things, of impeding the free exercise of religion. The fact that the regime smacked of Marxism also incited the Catholic right to embrace the Contra drive. Many were still fuming over Bishop John McGann's criticism of U.S. aid to the Contras during William Casey's funeral in May. To the extent that Colonel North's performance conferred religious legitimacy on the Contra cause, the right saw him as a vindicator of its special interests.

Typical was this tribute: "You might wonder why I have written this column," wrote the Reverend Enrique T. Rueda, a New York priest, in the July 23 issue of the *Wanderer.* "I usually write about Church affairs. The question is legitimate. I have several reasons for writing about the North affair. I would love to say Mass for him and his family when this is all over. A Mass of Thanksgiving would be in order, one at which we would pray for the late director of the CIA William Casey, the unsung hero of the entire story. A Mass, incidentally, in which I would also attempt to make up for the disgraceful behavior of Bishop McGann, who offended the memory of Bill Casey in front of his family at his funeral Mass.

"By writing this column, I wish to thank Lt. Col. North for what he has done for America and for Nicaragua. To the extent that the policies he implemented succeed, the Church in Nicaragua will be free to serve the people in a truly evangelical way."

At the very least, the hearings and the Iran-Contra media hubbub had underscored the debate over whether Congress should fund the Contras and, if so, in what manner. It was a policy fight in which Catholic leaders, standing against the religious right, had developed an increasingly strong position against American military assistance to the Nicaraguan rebels. The U.S. bishops had long favored nonviolent solutions to conflicts in Central America. Their dissent from Reagan administration policy was widely seen as a sign of the growing confidence within the church that Catholics no longer need prove their patriotism by displaying unstinting support for any and all policy options labeled anticommunist. Further, the close ties between many U.S. Catholics and the church in Central America allowed views from that region to gain an influential hearing.

In keeping with that special relationship, in the midst of heated congressional debate over renewing arms shipments to the Contras, five U.S. bishops traveled to Costa Rica to meet with ten bishops from Central America and Panama from July 21 to 23. Auxiliary Bishop Joseph Sullivan of Brooklyn headed the group in his capacity as chairman of the bishops' Committee on Social Development and World Peace.

The bishops issued a joint statement after their talks that bluntly declared that "U.S. relations with Central America must give clear priority not to military aid, but to economic assistance for development." It continued, "We are in complete agreement that the solution to the conflicts afflicting Central America need to be sought through political measures." Though applauding what they called "the rise of democratic processes" in the region as "a sign of hope," the bishops urged that democracy be "not limited only to political life but should be economic and social as well."

From Boston, Cardinal Bernard Law reinforced the nonmilitary approach. To those who were accustomed to the cardinal's unwavering conservatism on doctrinal and ecclesiastical matters, the force of his statement against Contra aid came as a surprise. Liberals especially welcomed the support of a churchman like the cardinal who was greatly admired by the Catholic right.

In his statement, published in the July 24 issue of the archdiocesan newspaper, the *Pilot,* Cardinal Law recalled his trip to Nicaragua the previous November and judged that "the situation of the church there has, if anything, worsened. The cause of human rights generally has not improved in Nicaragua." The Sandinistas were clearly to blame for this state of affairs, the cardinal asserted, and he had no doubts that the regime must be reformed in order for things to improve. Having tried to reassure those who might mistake him for a Sandinista sympathizer, he asked how the needed reform could be best accomplished. The most obvious strategy was to arm the Contras. Two popular pictures of the Contras had dominated discussion, the cardinal said. One portrayed them as remnants of Samoza's national guard, thugs who had terrorized the country before the dictator's downfall in 1979. The other pictured them as liberators and bearers of freedom.

"Is our government limited to a choice between these two caricatures?" Cardinal Law asked.

> I think not. While it is legitimate to be concerned about the present orientation and drift of the Sandinista regime, I question whether the only way in which permanent change can occur is through military pressure exerted by the Contras. To be effective in changing the situation, military pressure must be overpowering. That would seem to demand that U.S. armed forces be directly involved. This I would consider to be most ill-advised.

Furthermore, the effectiveness of the Contra struggle as a lever for change must be weighed against its cost. The armed struggle in Nicaragua has taken too many lives already. Non-combatants have been rendered refugees in their own land by the civil strife. The fighting has contributed to the deterioration of an already faltering economy. Our policy cannot and should not be built on continuing aid to the Contras.

The cardinal endorsed other measures for ending the strife. They included support for the peace process introduced by the four-nation Contadora alliance (Mexico, Venezuela, Colombia, and Panama) and an assistance package offering loans to farmers, food to the hungry, and economic incentives in return for human rights improvements. Not surprisingly, Cardinal Law's statement attracted considerable attention. Owing to its source and its pungency, it had unusual influence in projecting the Catholic church into the tense controversy.

For maureen, the summer pace in the dean's office no longer slowed as much as it had before the push to make maximum use of university facilities year round, but she welcomed the more relaxed atmosphere stimulated by the warm weather and the seasonal informality.

On impulse, she had decided to drive to Boston for a long July weekend with her daughter Karen, recently divorced and starting a new job. Maureen had always felt close to Karen, the child of her first marriage, and had relived the pain of her own divorce during Karen's ordeal. But she had strained to keep herself from interfering in her daughter's life. Now, as Karen was entering a new phase, Maureen felt no limits in offering Karen support and encouragement.

Karen's life had taken another sharp turn, her mother learned upon arrival in Boston. She had met a man who had swept her off her feet, a man she literally spoke of as a gift from God. Maureen had been astonished. Karen, the professed nonbeliever, the religious rebel, had startlingly become the born-again convert. "She said she'd asked God to please send her someone she could start a new life with and help get her through," Maureen recalled. "Then she said, 'He did that for me,' and started thanking God."

The answer to her prayers was, as it turned out, a "rather orthodox Catholic," as Maureen described him. Given his strong convictions about the sanctity of church teachings, Karen said she had been reluctant to mention her first marriage at all. But the possibility of a life together had loomed so suddenly that she was compelled to tell him about it. Whereupon he asked her to seek an annulment. Karen, flushed with gratitude for her deliverance, had "decided she'd do it for his sake, though she didn't care much for the idea," Maureen said.

For nearly a year, Maureen had been weighing the same question in response to her husband's request that she take steps to have her first marriage declared invalid. Her immediate reaction had been to refuse on grounds that it would insult her first husband, whom she held in high regard. But she thought it best to take more time with the decision. Making the move now seemed to her "out of the question." She explained: "I don't see myself as being a better Christian by knocking down a person I have a lot of respect for. It would be wrong for me to do it." She regretted acting against her husband's wishes. "Normally I don't put myself first," she said, "but I had to because it means making a charge against another person, my former husband."

Karen's newfound faith, her euphoria over the man in her life, and her resolve to seek annulment combined to leave Maureen somewhat stunned and concerned but determined to accept her daughter as she was. At the same time, she felt good fortune in other areas of her life, mainly in her relations with two of her other children.

Patrice, now a young woman, had been emotionally tormented from her first days as an adoptee. Maureen had long struggled to connect with Patrice, with little success until recently. "I started dealing with her differently," Maureen said, searching for an explanation. "I had always said how much I cared for her, but I started listening more to her instead of giving so much advice. She responded differently: she didn't become volatile. Patrice finally believes I love her. It was a huge milestone. She now feels she has a mother who really loves her. We can go on from there to deal with anything."

Her bout of acute ambivalence toward the Catholic church—whether to stay or leave—had also resolved itself, somewhat to her amazement, in the direction of abiding loyalty to the church. "Maybe in *some ways* I've left," she joked, "but I'm going and enjoying it more."

She went on, "I'm amused at myself at what's developed. I hear people who are angry at the church and find myself saying, 'You're not going to leave the church, are you?' I wish I had a tape of that. I can't believe it. People say they don't feel the same way, and I say, 'Let's talk it through'! There are things wrong with the church, but that has nothing to do with your faith. A friend who's a banker said he was very angry with the church because those who run it don't do what they say. I actually caught myself saying, 'Now Bill, stay with your faith, don't judge the church by the priests, I think that faith is a victory in itself.'

"No denomination is going to offer me more than the Catholic church. Maybe I don't belong there, but I'll have to keep my fingers crossed that when I die I'll come up on the great computer with enough credits to pass."

Among other reasons for staying in, Maureen thought, was "so as not to desert the Charles Currans of the world who try desperately to work on the fringe. I don't feel I honor my own commitment by leaving them alone to do my work."

Maureen's allegiance to the church had risen in conjunction with her renewed appreciation of the Blessed Virgin Mary. Through some reading and discussions she had come to see Mary "as very strong, maybe the first Catholic feminist," who had "probably for all these years been a role model for me without my really knowing it." Perhaps as the result of her own recent experiences with her children, Maureen saw Mary as a mother "who was able to listen to her Son just as we all need to listen to our children." She had tried to see Mary "not so much as visionary but as one who made footprints in real life—that makes me feel better about her. She is a more direct route to God—woman to woman. I always saw her strength, I guess, but I never applied it to myself. I never felt an affinity."

For Maureen, the Virgin Mary opened a way into the church. Largely because of her childhood and her divorce, the question of who was approved or disapproved, who was "in" or "out" of the church had haunted her. She had found enough voices of approval to sustain her. The figure of the Virgin Mother added immeasurably to that feeling of acceptance.

On her way home from visiting Karen in Boston her car had broken down, and the results had been fortuitous. During the two-hour wait for the tow truck, she had picked up the book she had brought along, the colossal best-seller *The Road Less Traveled,* by M. Scott Peck, and plunged into the final section on grace. It was a word and a concept that had always seemed strangely alien to her. For reasons she couldn't grasp, she had never felt that the promise of God's grace had been fulfilled in her life. "For all the religious introspection I had done," she said, "I didn't have it, and I didn't know how to find it. But I longed for it."

The scales had fallen from her eyes as she read the book and invested its message with her own thoughts. What struck her as a blinding insight was that grace was the presence of God in every person, warts and all. It was acceptance of oneself as flawed but imbued with God's spirit. "I think I had been looking for something bigger than that," she said, "some halo that would signify it. But it's not that. It's a strain of God that lies within each of us." It was more everyday and pedestrian than she had imagined. It was something other than human perfection. To the contrary—it was a divine spark in the midst of the mundane world. That had appealed to her immensely. It was something you just *had,* not something you earned.

"The Catholic church teaches us that we all have grace," she continued, "but I didn't believe we all could find it. That isn't so." Perhaps the greatest implication of that insight to Maureen was that the church could not deny the presence of grace to anyone. It could not finally determine who had it and who did not. Grace was just as available to dissenters such as Hans Küng and Charles Curran as it was to those who never uttered a contrary word or disobeyed a single rule. The idea had rejuvenated and freed her.

"I can't be silent about that," she said briskly, "even though that kind of thinking might run against the grain." Then, sheepishly, she added, "I get splinters from running against the grain sometimes."

Some things had come together over these months. "I tried real hard when I was a child to do things right—and I didn't think anyone ever noticed," she said wistfully. "Now all these good things come from God. People don't have to do them for you."

FATHER TOM HAD JUST WADED INTO HIS HOMILY WHEN MOLLY, A BEAMING, BUBbling infant, suddenly spit up all over her father's neatly pressed shirt. Don, the dampened father, threw a grin of helplessness in Molly's direction, stood up halfway, and started toward the restroom in haste, doing his best to avoid disturbing anyone, cradling his daughter a discreet distance from him.

Hardly anyone in the sanctuary of Holy Apostles batted an eye. Among the worshipers, there were babies and toddlers aplenty, most of them bunched near the exit to allow their parents to respond quickly to nature's various calls. As Don stealthily made his way out, he passed a mother nursing her child and another feeding carrot sticks to a ravenous little tyke in yellow Oshkosh britches. Meanwhile an unflappable Father Tom preached on—taking as his theme the need for Christians to become the Body of Christ—with an enthusiasm that seemed to feed off the energies and normal chaos of young families.

The sanctuary was plain and simple, devoid of statuary except for Jesus on the crucifix and a small figure of Mary, and the 150 or so people were dressed casually. They greeted one another warmly before the opening procession began, creating a friendly, festive mood such as might be found around an evening campfire of backpackers. A table in front of the altar, which was draped with a white cloth and held two red candles, contained a bouquet of mixed flowers and the arresting inscription, "Feed the Hungry."

Holy Apostles at Sunday mass was *informal* to say the least, and parishioners loved it that way. The interior of the eighty-year-old French Gothic structure in the sizable West Coast city had been redesigned to serve that purpose. To affect the sense of mutual participation in the liturgy and to reduce the distance between clergy and laity, some front pews had been uprooted from their positions facing forward toward the altar and replaced across from one another on opposite sides of the center aisle. At the same time, the altar was moved out of the chancel down into the congregation. The result was a modified church-in-the-round, with people seated on three sides of the altar. The design spoke a "people of God" theme and was the mark of a parish that not only had embraced the reforms of the Second Vatican Council but might want more.

The remodeling marked the abrupt shift at Holy Apostles not quite two decades ago that had almost totally transformed its character. Until then, it had been a rather sedate parish, withering slowly from the flight of its members to the suburbs, partly in retreat from the influx of blacks and Hispanics. A neighborhood inhabited mostly by descendants of European immigrants had rapidly become populated by poor nonwhites who had migrated from various parts of the country. When racial disturbances reverberating from other urban settings rocked this city in the late 1960s, tensions were felt acutely within the parish bounds, exposing the gulf between itself and its neighbors. Faced with the parish's irrelevancy and eventual extinction, the archdiocese had agreed somewhat reluctantly to an emergency rescue strategy. A priest with enormous talents and a penchant for risk taking was given the assignment of saving Holy Apostles. It was the beginning of a remarkable rebirth.

The new pastor was an inspired preacher with an overriding conviction that the church's message entailed serving social needs. Under his leadership, Holy Apostles began operating an expanded food bank and clothes closet, a medical clinic, and, by the late 1970s, a legal center. Its neighborhood center became a welcome haven for young people from surrounding streets with nowhere else to go. There they could shoot hoops, practice art, and get help with their schoolwork. Assisting the parish in all these ventures was a contingent of recent college graduates who had enrolled in a Catholic equivalent of the Peace Corps. The parish attracted new groups of them periodically and relied heavily on their volunteer skills and efforts. Moreover, with the pastor's full backing, the parish had eagerly adopted the spirit of the Second Vatican Council and implemented its provisions with gusto. The parish council had been invested with considerable authority from its earliest days, and laity generally had a strong role in the church's affairs. Parish retreats were both spiritual and social.

All of the changes would have meant little without a fresh supply of parishioners to shore up the sagging parish. As it happened, the new image of Holy Apostles as socially concerned and "progressive" attracted an influx of new members. They came largely from outside the boundaries of the parish (upwards of two-thirds of the total), and many were liberals who had become disaffected with the Catholic church in varying degrees. Holy Apostles became a magnet for those who had dropped out or existed as nonconformists at the fringes of other parishes. Many of them were those who objected to the church's teachings on sexuality or complained that its involvement in social justice was woefully inadequate.

For diverse reasons, then, by the mid-1970s Holy Apostles became the refuge for well-educated Catholics who felt uneasy or unwelcome in a conventional parish. It was the lively, slightly renegade alternative where the *elan* of the sixties held forth and where sticky issues such as divorce and single parenthood, though not ignored, were played down. In the words of the pastor who oversaw it all, it had become the parish of "the Volvo set," Catholics scattered among various professions, some of whom had sought jobs that suited their sense of social responsibility. During his tenure, which ended in 1983, the membership rolls grew from two hundred to six hundred, a fifth of whom were blacks, including some from the neighborhood, and the parish had attained a distinct, if somewhat controversial, reputation throughout the archdiocese. Though many applauded Holy Apostles' resolve and its many achievements, some worried that it was too permissive.

Going from East to West in Catholic America was to experience, in general, a steady moderating of church tradition and a drift toward less formality and legalism. Thus, Catholics on the East Coast tended to adhere most closely to prescribed practices and patterns, the Midwest less, the West Coast least. The parishes sampled during this year more or less exemplified those differences in conformity.

Saint Benedict's, in an eastern seaboard city, emphasized religious observance and institutional concerns, and its activities were firmly in the hands of the pastor and his two associates. Incarnation parish, in a suburban Midwest community, showed similar respect to the pastor but less deference, voiced more dissent from church teachings, and exhibited much greater lay participation in designing programs and goals. Holy Apostles, though hardly typical of any region in certain key respects, nonetheless mirrored the West Coast's overall inclination to minimize the gap between clergy and laity and to center relatively more than other areas on lay leadership, partly in response to a greater shortage of priests. Power sharing between priests and people, virtually nonexistent in the East, increased at Incarnation and rose still further out West.

The agenda of the parishes varied greatly and was less obviously conditioned by geography. Saint Benedict's sought primarily to serve members' religious duties, thus was most inward-looking; Incarnation, through the Renew program, had turned its gaze somewhat more outwardly; and Holy Apostles had staked its very identity on reaching out to the needs of others. Of the three parishes visited, only Saint Benedict's was territorial in the true sense. At Incarnation, and even more so at Holy Apostles, a big chunk of the membership lived outside the parish lines—even outside church law.

Father Tom, finishing his homily that overcast July morning in a snappy eleven minutes, had taken over at Holy Apostles four years ago. Fortunately, most people resisted comparing him with the former priest (those who remained, that is; 15 percent of the parish had left at the time of the change, some following him to his new assignment). To the contrary—the parish liked Father Tom for himself. They applauded his prayerfulness, his quiet demeanor, the quality of pastoral care with which he touched people, and many more of his traits. Furthermore, they generally conceded that a change in pastors had been a good, even necessary, thing.

The fact that Father Tom's leadership was far less commanding than that of the former pastor was considered a big plus by many members, inasmuch as it prodded the laity to take on greater responsibility for their parish. Holy Apostles had become in many respects a lay-focused island unto itself, removed from many reminders of the wider church, conducting itself more as if it were an independent congregation than part of a hierarchical structure, made up of people who, in the quasi-Protestant style that had become the hallmark of American religion, had *chosen* to be there and, as volunteers, felt free to claim the parish as their own.

Members almost uniformly spoke of their parish with deep affection and pride. But mingled with the exuberance and optimism was a deep strain of anxiety. Holy Apostles had remained steadfastly on the course set at the start of the 1970s and had been pretty much on automatic pilot into the 1980s. The inevitable self-scrutiny that had accompanied the change in pastors, however, had exposed the need for some sort of recharging of the batteries.

The social programs that had been started with a burst of purpose and adventure had long since become agencies that functioned smoothly on their own with less direct involvement by members. The success of these projects had led in some cases to incorporation into citywide services and in general required less participation by church members themselves. Understandably, the excitement that attended the parish's rebirth as a center of social ministry was running out of steam, even though the power of its vision continued to attract the self-selected few. And nothing had replaced or redefined that mission. The parish was living off the vitality of the past, and some members had momentary twinges of apprehension that its best days might be behind it unless something sparked renewal.

To say that the parish reflected the times within both the nation and the broader church was no overstatement. As an enclave of liberal Catholics with an active interest in social programs, its members felt great alienation from both Pope John Paul II's doctrinal firmness and Ronald Reagan's antipathy toward government-sponsored social welfare. Like all liberals, they were on the defensive, somewhat captive to the thinking that prevailed in the days of Pope John XIII (or "Good Pope John" as he was often called) and the "Great Society" of Lyndon Johnson. Holy Apostles was in something like paralysis, then, trapped by its nostalgia for the past without quite knowing where to go.

The neighborhood itself would continue to impose a big part of the agenda for the congregation. Poverty and squalor had deepened among the adjoining blocks of mostly single-family homes. An infestation of drugs, particularly crack, had driven up the crime rate and caused an epidemic of fear to sweep the streets. Many dilapidated houses were abandoned; squatters lived in many others. Unemployment had shot up. Violent gangs had invaded the territory. By one corner of the church a knot of volatile men milled around the local outlet for fortified wine, talking loudly and occasionally jostling one another. Holy Apostles had found it more difficult over the years to serve with compassion while keeping its guard up ever higher.

Perhaps it was partly the feeling of futility in the face of these monstrous problems that had led some parishioners to seek a more spiritual direction for Holy Apostles without sacrificing its social activism.

Chris, a university administrator, father of two youngsters and a Holy Apostles booster, was one of those who thought that way. "We have a bias toward action," he explained in his office on Monday morning, "and our need is for contemplation in order to get balance. At this point, I just want to stop and feel that other half." Father Tom had just the right skills to help inculcate spirituality, Chris thought, without neglecting the service programs. To Chris, a better balance could help Holy Apostles attain that new lease on life everyone wanted. But no shot in the arm would be worth the loss of the parish's special character, Chris thought, so caution was essential.

Chris and many others at Holy Apostles were proud of the parish's ability to work out its own destiny beyond the tighter controls and conventions of the larger church establishment. In truth, it was a "mission" parish heavily dependent on the goodwill of the archdiocese for financial survival. But for some time, obviously, Holy Apostles had been given a long leash and had enjoyed something of a dispensation. It sometimes made them heady.

The executive committee of the parish council convened early in the week to review several items. A new parish secretary was needed by September. A search was also under way for a full-time youth minister. Planning was needed for the annual fall meeting on the parish budget. The woman in charge of the parish auction had resigned. A replacement must be found for Larry as head of the executive committee. An insurance advisory had come from the chancery that required attention. Time must be allowed to talk about the last parish retreat. The committee of three, along with Father Tom (just "Tom" here) moved through their business with dispatch. Much of their work was to shape these various items into an agenda for the next meeting of the twelve-member council.

Larry, an energetic lawyer, had to rush off, but the two other members, Pat and Barb, stayed to discuss their faith and their parish.

Pat, a cheerful, outgoing woman in her mid-thirties, had been raised in a well-heeled New England family. Her mother was "a traditional Catholic," she said, while her father had dropped completely out of the church. Going away to college had exposed her to the reality that "there were two sides of the tracks, and that I was on the endowed side," she said. She had looked into the Peace Corps, but upon discovering that the agency was "not pleased that some of my motives were Christian" enrolled instead after graduation in a Catholic volunteer service. That experience had taken her to an Eskimo mission in Alaska along with twenty-four other young people.

At the end of her two-year stint, Pat stayed on the West Coast near friends who knew of Holy Apostles. By then, she said, she had "dropped out of the middle class." To her great relief and surprise, she said, she walked into a parish whose concerns for social ministry were close to her own. She had met her husband there, and the couple had two small boys. Professionally, she held a position of considerable responsibility as assistant head nurse at one of the city's major hospitals.

Barb, a few years older than Pat, had grown up in the city and after finishing college signed up happily with the Peace Corps, doing public health education in the Ivory Coast. On her return, she acquired a master's degree in social work, which had led to work first with adolescent girls and more recently with Southeast Asian refugees.

Raised Catholic, Barb had gone through a "crisis of faith" as a young adult that caused her to leave the church. "When I worked with teenage girls I was very anti-church," she said. "I told nobody I was Catholic." At the same time, sensing the need for "a spiritual component" in her life, she tried Buddhism, then Mormonism. Eventually a friend who attended Holy Apostles coaxed her into trying it. She began to attend occasionally, but soon, she said, she was hooked. That was three years ago. Among its appeals, she said, was "the greater percentage of single people here than in other parishes and the atmosphere of tolerance and acceptance. They didn't ask me if I was Catholic."

The attachment both women felt to the church was bound up very particularly in this parish. It contrasted with their general distrust of Rome. Holy Apostles, in their experience, stood as something of an exception to the rule imposed by the Vatican on a universal church. "There are certain things I can't tolerate," Pat said. "but I still believe. I just couldn't defend the Catholic church as an entity, because I pick and choose, and here it's more possible to do that. The problem is that the global church doesn't always act Christian."

Barb also had lingering reservations. "I have a lot of problems with the institution," she said. Chief among her criticisms was that the church "didn't utilize the gifts of people, particularly women, but men too. It doesn't give people credit for spiritual depth." She also noted in many of Rome's public pronouncements a "lack of compassion and understanding of other peoples' needs. Look at how they deal with people who dissent. They squash them."

Holy Apostles offered a meeting ground for acting out the faith with fewer encumbrances. For Pat, it was the place "the neighborhood saw as its advocate," which drew people "who are willing to pull back from the American mainstream—from the life-style of 'the self' espoused by TV. . . . The core of people are here for much more than simply what feels good to them." For Barb it represented "an opportunity to practice what I believe" in terms of fighting poverty and injustice, particularly as it affected single women with children. Neither woman regarded her choice as between Holy Apostles and a more orthodox parish; it was Holy Apostles or nothing at all.

Nearly everyone connected with the parish, including these two leaders, worried about the declining neighborhood and the tapering off of social involvement by parishioners, however understandable. Efforts were made to take the pulse of both parish and neighborhood on a fairly regular basis. Within the church, there were gatherings that mixed partying with serious jawboning about the state of the parish. Likewise, "listening teams" periodically fanned out through the streets to hear people's concerns.

Sometimes the passion for justice burning in a young outsider such as Carole, a recent college graduate serving Holy Apostles as part of the group of volunteers, became a reminder of the fires that once burned more fiercely and pervasively in response to social crises.

Carole was bright, high-spirited, restless, impatient, and idealistic. She ran the food bank and helped in other areas but stayed away from mass in protest of the Catholic church's refusal to ordain women and eliminate sexist language. Before signing up for the volunteer service with her husband, the couple had spent time in a Catholic Worker community. They had been active in campaigns against nuclear weapons, racial injustice, and hunger.

She did her job gladly, she said, screening those who came seeking food, gathering supplies, and packaging items for distribution. As parishes went, she said, she rather liked Holy Apostles, but she felt the parish had grown to rely too much on volunteers like herself, sponsored by a national religious order, "as a cheap way to get the tasks done. Holy Apostles gets more out of this than the clients who come for help." Her view of her fellow volunteers was equally unsparing. "I thought they'd really be into social justice and simple living," she said. "But that wasn't necessarily so. Most just wanted a break from their studies before they go to graduate school."

Carole's decision to avoid mass left her uneasy, especially when well-intentioned people in the parish asked her about it. But she was steadfast. "Sexism is there, and people don't realize it," she said. "I feel I'm being left out. I'm told that semantics don't matter. They *do* matter. I don't think it's true that because I'm a woman that I'm not good enough to consecrate the Eucharist. I don't think Jesus thought that either.

"I really like the early church, where small groups shared their belongings," she continued. "But of course when you talk that way you're labeled a socialist." Accordingly, her bent was toward radical remedies for social problems that went beyond the options most parishioners considered reasonable. In that sense,

Carole's "radicalism" stood out in bold relief against the backdrop of familiar, well-integrated responses to social needs. She made the parish seem downright ordinary and uneventful.

Sexism was one issue on which Carole's views did converge with those of many parishioners. Complaints about male-exclusive language in liturgy and church discussion reflected growing anger over the exclusion of women from the clergy and from high councils of the church. A particular source of friction were two banners hung prominently in the church. One read, "By the Peace Among Our People Let Men Know We Serve the Lord." The other featured the words of Martin Luther King Jr., "I Have a Dream," surrounded by four summonses to "Love," "Equality," "Peace," and "Brotherhood." Many churchgoers found the words *Men* and *Brotherhood* constant irritants that they could not ignore.

Feminism had raised especially troublesome and divisive problems for the parish. To many women, a mere couple of words on banners might seem trivial, but they symbolized a certain intransigence and a streak of bias that ran through the church. Several capable, dedicated women had already left Holy Apostles over the issue, and that trend had tripped a quiet alarm.

Though Holy Apostles prided itself on the extent of its lay-centeredness, the clergy came in for a large share of the blame when things were out of kilter. Thus, Father Tom and the former pastor were widely criticized for the use and continuance of sexist language and practice. Both were described, in fact, as "antifeminist" by some members. But at the same time disgruntled feminists had made no concerted effort to change those things outside prescribed liturgical and church practice, such as banners, that were optional.

Like Catholics in other places, those at Holy Apostles, where lay status was accorded unusual respect and power, often showed a deeply paradoxical strain of passivity toward church authority, displaying considerable deference, waiting for the clergy to make the moves without raising a challenge. In reality, of course, even in the most liberal parishes the laity was allowed only about as much collaboration as the clergy and hierarchy permitted—and lay advice was just that, advice—but the reluctance by the laity to test the limits could be startling. Resentful women bolted Holy Apostles rather than organize protest. The upshot was, however, that neglect of the problem had cost a great deal already and impeded the parish's desire to renew its mission. Everyone, it seemed, was still waiting for the laity to take matters more into their own hands. Perhaps, some thought, they were really waiting for Father Tom to do it for them.

In other respects, personal initiative was celebrated. Parish members were, on the whole, unusually receptive to things like human potential exercises and various therapies. They were, therefore, naturally given to gazing inward at parish behavior. Analyzing the strengths and weaknesses of Holy Apostles and envisioning the parish's future were major extracurricular activities. It was done with obvious love and concern.

On Thursday evening, with a light, cool breeze rustling the leaves outside, a group met to talk about the particular crossroads at which the parish had arrived. The six women and two men responded eagerly to the invitation to a free-flowing, open-ended discussion. They exuded a profound affection for and loyalty to Holy Apostles that was both touching and unusual. *All* had chosen to join, and *all* said they had a great stake in the outcome of the transition the parish was obviously going through.

They were a mixed group that included two couples in their thirties with small children, a grandmother, a single parent, a housewife approaching retirement, and a young mother with three children in grade school. They touched upon many topics with a striking degree of consensus. Without exception, they spoke of the parish as a source of strength and fellowship.

The feeling was expressed most poignantly by the single parent. "I just went through a bad year," she said, "with a divorce and a very sick daughter. Without the people at Holy Apostles I could not have survived physically or spiritually or financially." Her daughter's condition had been diagnosed as incurable. Yet, because of the parish's ministry to them both, "nobody was better prepared to leave this life" than her daughter. "Sometimes the parish seems like a huge sponge that spills fresh water over everyone," she said.

Her testimony prompted an earnest but somewhat inexplicably defensive response from one of the men. "I wouldn't apologize to anyone for this parish community," he said. He held out a closed fist. "It's not this," he said, then opened it and extended an open hand, "but this." Said one of the older women, "My husband is not Catholic, but he went to church with me. Eventually we drifted away, but we were drawn back because of how close everyone was."

The idea of service to others remained at the center of the parish's appeal to this group. "I've been with visitors to the church who, halfway through the mass, ask, 'Are you *sure* this is a *Roman* Catholic church'?" said another woman, "And I say, 'Yes, Roman Catholic.' You have to be a seeker of the Word and be willing to put it into action. We have an opportunity to live the gospel by being involved in social justice issues." The direction taken by Holy Apostles didn't make the parish better, the group insisted, just different. It was right for them.

Their fierce ties to Holy Apostles contrasted with their weak, at best, affinity for the universal church. Theirs was a form of congregational Catholicism that tried its best to ignore the overarching presence of a worldwide institution. "It's as if at times the parish weren't even aligned with the Catholic church," said one of the young mothers. "What we have here is a universal church led by those who are, after all, only human beings given authority and power who try to run the whole organization. When it gets down to us, it doesn't mean much." Said another, "Many people just try to hang out in our church and [on matters of church teaching such as birth control] just do their own thing."

In fact, the consensus among them was to play down their Catholicism (though they also felt ineradicably Catholic). A contributing factor was the relatively low percentage of churchgoers on the West Coast. Faced with large numbers of unchurched people with little or no grasp of Christian tradition, churches were under more pressure to show a united front on issues, and denominational or church labels held less meaning than in areas where entrenched traditions had long ago dug in their competitive heels.

"My identity is more rooted in Christianity than Catholicism," said one group member. "I have a hard time saying what it means specifically to be Catholic." Another participant said that if "I stopped going to the Catholic church, I wouldn't go at all," because of her belief in the "real presence of Christ in the Eucharist, which is vitally important to me." Otherwise, she said, "The Catholic church itself is not important to my life. . . . Religion is not what people need; it's spirituality."

Regarding the future, most had anxieties but few concrete suggestions to alter the course of Holy Apostles in better or more enlivening directions. One person thought it might be time to give stronger emphasis to "meet the needs of families" inasmuch as she "thought of Holy Apostles as adult, issue-oriented." Another stressed ministry to women. Most had thought about what might happen if Father Tom were to leave. They knew of no priest who might meet their needs, but they did have candidates. One was a layman who had been a spark plug in the parish; the other was Sister Celia, the sole nun remaining on the staff, who had seen many changes over the years. Either one of them could take over the parish with their blessing.

And how did their faith relate to their private and work lives?

One of the men said he tried to bring his faith to his job on a daily basis.

"With three young kids, I can't concentrate on anything very long," added a mother, "but I do want them to grow up respecting the fact that not everyone is like them, that there is a need to understand everyone's perspective. We're all bombarded by lots of things. It's hard to maintain simplicity."

The other man worked in an alcohol and drug treatment center. "There are days when I feel that I add Christian balance to my current boss, who's a priest. There's a constant call to use my faith. Some days I do that very poorly. . . . I think I have a mission to help treat those who can't get treatment elsewhere, to give them a chance to recover. That takes some degree of faith."

Another woman recalled her wedding vows, which contained "a statement of our faith that we would help each other see Christ in the people we meet. . . . It also helps me see the faith and compassion in my husband."

Still another woman said she tried "to be Christ-like to everyone I meet" but found it tough to do in the large corporation where she worked in market research. She hoped eventually to switch to some kind of nonprofit enterprise.

The evening wore on, cake and ice cream were served, and the concerned parishioners of Holy Apostles spent the last portion of their evening together carefree and contented with one another's company, letting the future for the moment take care of itself.

Through the week, the parish church itself was notably quiet, its people engaged elsewhere in practical, workaday Christianity.

By late Friday afternoon, Sister Celia had finished most of the duties she had assigned herself for the day and, with warmth and graciousness, reflected on her experience at Holy Apostles. A dignified-looking woman in her sixties, Sister Celia had arrived at the parish soon after the former pastor had taken the place by storm. By happenstance she had become principal of the parish school, but she had stepped down after four years because she "felt too old to do the job right." The archdiocese had soon thereafter shut down the school, a decision bitterly opposed by the parish. Its abandonment by the archdiocese signaled to many members a callousness toward inner-city poor children. How could the bishops be talking about economic justice, some parishioners wondered, and at the same time allow such resources for the underprivileged to be shut down?

Sister Celia had stayed on after the closing to direct the religious education program and to oversee a host of projects. Her effectiveness, enthusiasm, and spirituality had left a deep mark on the parish. The previous pastor had been "a fantastic priest" in her estimation, but she joined those who believed that it had been time for him to step aside to help the laity overcome its reluctance to "take full responsibility." The goal was far from being accomplished yet, she allowed, but the people had gotten a better handle on some things such as finances, which had been in the former priest's control. Among in-house priorities, she ranked adult education, youth work, and Bible study as the chief needs. Laypeople, especially women, should give more homilies at the Sunday masses, she thought. She had given many herself.

Her sights also continued to be set outward toward the needs of the neighborhood. Sister Celia had been a constant voice of conscience. Many poor children had come to the school because of her, and she lamented the end of that experience. "One of my sadnesses," she said, "is that we don't have better evangelization to the black community." Human needs were mounting daily, she said, and the parish must keep on the case. In many respects she embodied the past while looking to the days ahead. She believed her outlook had remained that which took root in her early years at Holy Apostles.

"Every day," she said slowly, "I used to cry for the poor."

THE VERY NOTION THAT ANYONE WOULD CANCEL A HIGH-VISIBILITY MEETING with the pope as an act of protest was totally contrary to normal assumptions about the way things were supposed to work. But such an eventuality was in the offing. American Jewish groups pressed their threat to pull out of their scheduled Miami meeting with the pope on September 11 in reaction against John Paul's June 25 welcome of Austrian president Kurt Waldheim at the Vatican.

The pope had a great personal investment in his relationship with Jews. His visit to a Rome synagogue in 1986 had been an emotional and spiritual high point in his effort to strengthen those bonds. The Miami meeting was viewed as another, one that would attract enormous attention. But in the wake of the pope's Vatican reception of Waldheim, who stood accused of complicity in Nazi war crimes, those ties were under severe strain. American Jewish leaders, outraged by the pope's action, quickly seized on Miami as a pressure point.

The meeting was to be about forty-five minutes, consisting of an address by Rabbi Gilbert Klaperman, president of the Synagogue Council of America, and a response by the pope. Plans called for about two hundred people to attend.

The first warnings that the ceremony might never take place had come from the Synagogue Council and the American Jewish Congress, both of which stated flatly that a Miami get-together now seemed out of the question without at the very least some sort of face-to-face rapprochement between Jewish leaders and the pope. The two other organizational sponsors of the event, the American Jewish Committee and the Anti-Defamation League, were only somewhat less forceful. It appeared that the Jewish leaders would insist on some kind of amends-making session between themselves and the pope as the quid pro quo for keeping their appointment in Miami (though, of course, it would never be implied that the pope owed them any kind of apology). Meanwhile, the process of drafting Rabbi Klaperman's speech had been stopped. The climate remained highly charged.

On July 10 came the first indication of diplomatic maneuvers, when the United States Catholic Conference reported that the day before, the Vatican secretary of state, Cardinal Agostino Casaroli, had met with four Jewish leaders. Cardinal Casaroli was said to have been in the United States on an unofficial visit and squeezed some time out of his schedule to meet with the Jewish representatives at the behest of the American bishops.

The bishops' press office released a statement by Archbishop May, president of the bishops' conference, asserting that the group of four Catholic officials including himself had briefed Cardinal Casaroli on Catholic-Jewish relations in the United States "especially as they have been impacted by recent controversies and allegations that the Catholic Church is insensitive to the memory of the

Holocaust." Further, he said, the group had facilitated the meeting the next day between the cardinal and the Jewish leaders. About that meeting Archbishop May would only say that it had been "informal in nature" and "serious, cordial, and reflective of mutual trust and concern."

All participants had agreed to remain silent about the meeting, but one Jewish leader, Rabbi Marc Tanenbaum of the American Jewish Committee, said the parley had "covered all the outstanding issues" and that he regarded this "as part of a process leading to other meetings with the pope." Archbishop May was already on record, on behalf of the bishops, favoring some kind of talks with unspecified church officials in an effort to iron things out.

In addition to signaling movement in the stalemate, the account by Archbishop May appeared aimed at boosting the credibility of the American bishops. As the debate over the Waldheim visit had exploded, the bishops had been criticized for their refusal to dissociate themselves in any way from the pope's action. The archbishop's account had the sound of a face-saving move, portraying the bishops as key mediators and imputing to them a measure of virtue for giving Cardinal Casaroli the lowdown on the controversy, implying that they had stoutly represented Jewish interests. At any rate, the Casaroli penultimate summit got the ball rolling.

The process was carried a step further later in July when Rabbi Tanenbaum flew to Rome as a liaison for the Jewish groups. He came away sounding optimistic. "I have the impression," he said, "that they [Vatican officials] are actively considering some kind of gesture or statement that would seek to improve the situation."

Meanwhile, from the Catholic side, opinion about the Waldheim affair varied sharply. Some believed the pope had acted properly as an international leader whose credentials as a friend of Judaism were impeccable; therefore, in their view, the matter had been blown far out of proportion. Others believed that the dignity accorded to Waldheim was an affront to the memory of the Holocaust and added fuel to charges that the Vatican had acted too timidly against Nazi war crimes in the first place.

FROM ALL INDICATIONS, THE POPE WAS STILL COMING TO AMERICA, POTENTIAL glitches notwithstanding. A sure sign was the July 10 notice by the bishops' conference that a thirty-minute film, *America Prepares for the Pope,* was ready for distribution.

In the film, designed as a preview of the themes that would be highlighted at each of the nine stops on the tour and narrated by Charlton Heston, a ninety-second spot by the pope included a salutation that touched all bases. "I greet you

with joy and affection: Catholics, Protestants, Jews—all believers and nonbeliev-
ers alike," the pope said. "I look forward to being with you again."

The central motif of the tour, "Unity in the Work of Service, Building the Body
of Christ," seemed agreeable and innocuous enough to satisfy a broad Catholic audience, but the ever contrary *Wanderer* found something to grouse about. The
right-wing newspaper was in sour mood anyway because the pope had not
cracked down enough on liberals to suit its taste for order. Now Gary Potter, one
of its regular sharpshooters, found something in the theme to make him dyspep-
tic. The concept of unity "seems undercut by the fact that the 'dialogs' scheduled
for John Paul include ones with such particular groups as Black bishops and Black
Catholic leaders in New Orleans . . . and Native Americans in Phoenix," Potter
wrote in the July 9 issue. "Segregating the meeting with Black Catholics appears especially questionable two decades after passage of the Civil Rights Act."

With regard to actual preparations, the dioceses hosting the pope were working feverishly to tie up sometimes rather elusive loose ends. Most urgent was the
need to find the money to finance the visit. The host bishops were expected to
raise the funds on their own. A survey by the *National Catholic Reporter* (July 3)
turned up a variety of strategies for filling the coffers.

Some bishops took the celebrity route, building a high-visibility campaign
around wealthy and powerful citizens. San Francisco, which expected a price tag
of $3 million, New Orleans ($2 million), Phoenix ($1.5 million), and Charleston
($473,000) relied especially on committees of rich and powerful people to spear-
head their drives. In other cities, notably Los Angeles ($3 million), Miami ($2 million), and San Antonio ($275,000 as part of a joint effort by Texas dioceses to split
the bill), the bishops themselves became, in effect, their own chief fund-raisers.
Every diocese, in fact, used a mixture of methods: diocesewide collections, big-
donor appeals, and solicitations from corporations and foundations.

Certain efforts had gained notoriety. Glitzy San Franciscans turned out in force
for a $250-a-plate dinner at the home of the Jewish mayor, Dianne Feinstein
(criticized by some Jewish groups for doing this in the aftermath of the Waldheim
incident); the Gallo wine family made a substantial gift to Los Angeles (San
Francisco hoped also to cash in on the family's benevolence); Bishop Thomas
O'Brien of Phoenix coaxed $100,000 from Charles Keating, the real estate mag-
nate; and, with a single deft phone call, Archbishop Roger Mahony persuaded
the religiously oriented Dan Murphy Foundation to part with $500,000. The
Schuff Steel Corporation of Phoenix donated to the papal mass a sixty-five-foot
bronze cross weighing seven tons; the gift of a sixty-pound silver bar—said to be
the biggest in the city—was melted down into coins bearing the likeness of the
pope, which were on sale for $29.95.

Even with all the promotions and big-name campaigns, planners were considerably worried about falling short of the goals and being saddled with a deficit.

Most anxious was the small, relatively insulated diocese of Monterey, which was looking at a $2-million tab with few large resources to tap. Monterey's quick fix proposal—to auction off television rights to the mass at Laguna Seca speedway for a big windfall—had been quickly shot down by church higher-ups, so the outlook was rather bleak. "In the pit of my stomach, there is a deep fear we won't make it," an official of the diocese told NCR. "But there is also great faith and a line of credit."

Much had been made of claims that the pope's first trip to the United States in 1979 had short-changed ecumenical concerns. At that time, the pope had made a brief appearance before a group of church leaders at Trinity College in Washington, D.C., and had been the only speaker. This time much more care had been taken. The ecumenical gathering planned for Charleston on the pope's second stop was to be a far more significant event, complete with two-way conversation between John Paul and a selected group of twenty-eight officials from Protestant and Orthodox churches (including two women) and a joint prayer service in the stadium of the University of South Carolina.

Enthusiasm for meeting with the pope was not uniformly high among the non-Catholic Christians. The Vatican's actions against Archbishop Hunthausen and Charles Curran and its March document on biomedical ethics, among other things, troubled many Protestants, who felt that principles near and dear to them had been attacked. Some of the same leaders also felt increasingly at odds with the Catholic church over abortion. Ecumenism was at a very low ebb, in part because John Paul had been so intent on emphasizing aspects of Catholic identity that set it apart. Nonetheless, for the sake of goodwill and church unity, the consensus among the non-Catholics was that it was better to put differences aside and greet the pope in South Carolina with modest hopes.

One priest involved in planning the papal trip was convinced that John Paul was in for a disappointing reception. He was dismayed by the apparent lack of excitement by Catholics only seven weeks or so before the visit was to start. Moreover, he sensed a negative mood. "Everyone seems to think, 'Well, he isn't the king; this isn't the Middle Ages when he comes visiting the vassals.' There are left-over tickets all over the place, and money for the trip is coming in very slowly. Many priests and nuns are against his coming. They're trying to create a new kind of church and want to be left alone. . . . They don't understand the benefit of the extra-rational dimension of spirituality that the pope opens up. America deeply needs a hero and needs unifying, but won't hear a word he says as a prophet of the poor and as a man of prayer."

On the other hand, the priest predicted that the pope would get an earful from Catholic America in behalf of women's ordination, optional celibacy, and other issues. "All the talks to the pope this time are written by us," he said. "This is the first time we've talked to him. He'll hear the truth, couched euphemistically."

AFTER WATCHING COLONEL NORTH SPAR DEFTLY WITH MEMBERS OF CONGRESS, Craig and some of his Marine Corps buddies argued about the colonel's testimony and the whole Iran-Contra affair. He agreed with his fellow pilots in training that their Marine comrade had done a masterly job of winning public confidence "by knowing what people wanted to hear." But they were divided on what to make of the performance.

"Most of my friends were saying that what he did was good," Craig recalled. "I said I respected him for Vietnam but that others on the [congressional] panel had just as distinguished records, so he couldn't just win the argument on that account in my opinion. I said 'I'm a Marine and North's a Marine, but he still broke the law.' I said I felt it was unfortunate that people were willing to break the law to get what they wanted done. We argued quite a while."

That exchange had taken place little more than a week ago and had churned in Craig's mind since. Given his situation—consumed by military routines night and day—this nationally sensational case of a high-ranking officer testing the limits of both the military code and the law was compelling, to say the least. It wasn't just Colonel North's admitted violations in the name of higher duty he found questionable. He had become more skeptical of President Reagan's denials that he had committed any wrongdoing. "How could the president not know what was going on?" he asked, resting in his small Texas apartment after a long Sunday of training. "Jimmy Carter even knew who was playing tennis on the White House courts. This is so big I can't imagine the president divorcing himself from the issue."

But implicating the president could not excuse Colonel North's actions, Craig felt. Impelled to choose between his attachment to the Corps and allegiance to the law, he had held fast to his original instinct. "My overall feeling," he said angrily, "is that North's allegiance is without exception to the Constitution. If you want to get down to it, any Marine at his swearing in says he will be loyal first to the Constitution."

Craig himself never wanted to take part in covert operations, he had decided, but he retained the belief that there were times "when dying for ideals and having to kill other people for those ideals" was "not wrong." Likewise, he felt there "were times when it was not wrong to use nuclear force." Rather than look for reasons to justify power, Craig thought in terms of exceptions to the presumption against its use.

Such matters had become more clear to him over the long months of learning to fly. He found himself standing somewhere between more militant comrades and a certain reference point in his mind: his father's strain of pacifism. Like "some of the young Christian types" he had known in college, his father doubted that people died in war for worthy reasons. His father's favorite movie was *A Man for All Seasons,* Craig said, because it showed Thomas More's refusal either to succumb to wrong or to resist it.

After almost a year, flight training was nearing an end. Schedule delays had set back completion of their training from late August to mid-September. Craig would be glad when it was over. Nearly twelve months of high pressure had worked wonders on his confidence and skills, but he looked forward to a break before the next phase of training. And by the time he moved on, a pair of gold wings would testify to a proud achievement. Of two hundred candidates who had comprised Craig's original group of would-be pilots, fifty had been accepted. Of that fifty, ten to fifteen had been washed out in the first stage of training, another four were dropped for academic reasons, three or four failed to perform well enough at the controls of propeller-driven aircraft, and two or three were disqualified in jets. That left roughly two dozen survivors. An elite group, eligible, among other things, to attend the next Tailhook Convention for all those who had ever streaked to a stop across the deck of an aircraft carrier.

With graduation nearing, he and Karen had settled on a wedding date the Saturday before Christmas. The site would be the Methodist church where Karen's father was the minister. Craig's tradition would be represented by a Catholic priest who would assist in the ceremony. "We're real excited," Craig said. "The church has a real nice congregation, and I'm very comfortable there. It won't be too big a wedding, I don't think, but Karen and her mother are planning it so I'm not sure about that."

He and Karen were still undecided about what to do about attending a church. "I've been so busy, it really hasn't been a big deal," he said, "but I think that will change now with getting married and eventually having children."

On a visit home not long before, he had again felt his parents' unhappiness with the fact that he and Karen had been living together and had been "talked to about getting married." Moreover, his mother, a convert to Catholicism, had urged him, her youngest of five sons, to stay within the church. Reminding him that none of his brothers any longer had ties to Catholicism, she had told him, "You're our last shot at it. And they [the church] have done so much for you." At the same time, Craig explained, his parents liked Karen a great deal and had great respect for her parents.

Perhaps the two of them would compromise and attend an Episcopal church. Sometimes that felt right to Craig, though he had reservations about leaving the Catholic church. "It might all come to a terrible head about the time we get married," he said sardonically. "All I know is that when we're married we want to worship together on a regular basis. But I don't know quite how that's going to work out."

THE SYNOD ON THE LAITY WAS ALSO FAST APPROACHING. DURING THOSE CLOSED-door sessions within the Vatican, the hierarchical delegates would be pondering the place of laypeople in the church, one of the great pieces of unfinished business advanced by Vatican II. At least a substantial minority of laypeople in Catholic America, drawn into the invitation to take part more fully in the life of the church, cared deeply about the outcome. Even those who scoffed at the very idea of synodical bishops presuming to pass judgment on laypeople in their absence tended to see the outcome as an important milestone in a protracted struggle.

In addition, thousands upon thousands of Catholic Americans had done something to help prepare for the synod. The bishops' committee on the laity had provided the means by which they could express their thoughts and feelings about the topics the synod should take up—primarily through questionnaires and consultations—and the volume of response had been enormous. There were those who argued that the process was weighted too heavily toward affluent, middle-class Catholics whose church activity was far above average, thereby leaving out the many whose relative inactivity often reflected far greater dissent than found within the church mainstream or the self-defined "orthodox," but it was generally conceded that the bishops' team had made a serious and strenuous effort to gain lay advice.

The question of whether the synod would grapple with anything of real significance to laity had persisted. Powerful doubts had extended even into the chambers of a presynod planning meeting two months before in Rome. One hundred fifty laypeople from fifty-six countries, many of them distinguished scholars and professionals, had exchanged candid views on the state of laypeople. To one observer, the most critical question to arise was not, so far as anyone knew, on the synod's agenda: how to enable the laity to connect their faith with their lives, including their work.

The problem, as he saw it, was not just that laypeople had to overcome resistance by clergy, but equally that they had to erase the lay reluctance to take responsibility. Too many laypeople seemed content to leave things the way they were, he said, for fear of upsetting the status quo. On the one hand, he said, the Rome meeting evoked a feeling that laypeople shouldn't take the bishops' synod seriously "if they don't take our lives seriously." But the colloquy also displayed the depth of lay passivity. "There was a sense," the observer said, "that the laity looked at themselves as renters rather than owners."

Pressure to turn away from discussion of lay roles *within the church* to one aimed at linking faith and life was being applied with special force by the National Center for the Laity in Chicago. Entirely too much attention had been given to what laypeople could and should be allowed to do under clergy aegis in the institution, according to this thinking. The desired alternative was to help the laity think theologically about their circumstances of home, work, school, and so on. Such theology would be developed by laypeople themselves rather than be imposed by the church. This option had gained a wide enough hearing to form a kind of counterpoint to the generally accepted main agenda of the synod: that is, whether laypeople would "be allowed" to do more within the church.

This option was so sufficiently established that it arose in most discussions on the future of the laity. The Chicago group posed their alternative as a substitute for the other with some apparent success. But some bishops and many of the laity tried instead to reconcile the differences by wrapping the two objectives—in-house and worldly—into a single program with dual emphases. Whatever the reaction, the Chicago center's proposal had helped make an impression that many felt might carry over into the synod.

Strong suspicion that the synod would do little or nothing either to or for the laity was accompanied by the fears on the Catholic right that the conclave would be hijacked by liberals. Grist for their conservative mill had been supplied by the extensive consultations. The findings contained a powerful democratic note in the form of appeals for more inclusive leadership. The laity, and women in particular, were asking for a stronger voice in church affairs. The right quite correctly understood this message as a threat to the authority of the hierarchy, as they interpreted that authority, and worried that the bishops might bend to those democratic impulses as a means of assuaging the masses.

One faction, therefore, struck back. The National Catholic Coalition, as the group called itself, aimed its attack at the two lay advisers the bishops had named to the synod. One of them, not coincidentally, was Dolores Leckey, head of the bishops' lay committee, who directed the consultation process. She had unearthed the results the right had found so unnerving. The other adviser was Lucien Roy, the director of lay ministry training for the Archdiocese of Chicago.

In a July 20 letter to Archbishop May, president of the bishops' conference, the coalition called for the removal of these advisers and suggested a pair of substitutes, Phyllis Schlafly, best known for her tireless and successful campaign against the Equal Rights Amendment for women (and more recently publicized for asserting that AIDS was God's punishment against its victims), and Professor Charles Rice, a law professor at Notre Dame. The coalition followed up the letter with a July 22 news conference in Washington attended by the group's two nominees and two prominent conservative Congressmen, Henry Hyde of Illinois and Robert K. Dornan of Ohio.

From the outset, of course, the coalition knew that the bishops would never accede to any such demands. The news conference was aimed instead at calling attention to the grievances of the right. As theater, it worked, attracting considerable press coverage with its lineup of colorful, outspoken crusaders. Kathleen M. Sullivan, the coalition's executive director, said at the news conference that the group's "paramount objection" to Leckey and Roy was that they were employees of the church who were, therefore, unable to represent the laity, especially "loyal, orthodox Catholics." After making their case for new advisers, members of the group seized the opportunity to criticize the bishops' pastoral statements on the economy, nuclear arms, AIDS, and U.S. policy toward Nicaragua. Not a strategy that a group expecting to attain its goal might use.

The coalition had taken pains to submit a compromise of sorts. In her letter to Archbishop May, Sullivan had added: "Should you deem it impossible to make the replacement, we suggest Mr. Rice and Mrs. Schlafly be included on the team to insure that expertise on all segments of the laity be available to the Bishops."

A week later, Archbishop May replied. In a July 27 letter to Sullivan, he politely but firmly assured the coalition that the bishops would stick to their original choices. In case the group had missed the fine political distinctions, the archbishop noted that Roy and Leckey were "not delegates to the synod representing and speaking for the Catholic laity of the United States. They are serving as staff people to the bishops who are delegates to a synod made up entirely of bishops." He was sure that Schlafly and Professor Rice were "richly qualified" to speak for the U.S. laity. But since that was not the role of the advisers, he was equally sure that "Neither one . . . would want to serve as a day-to-day member of the bishop delegates' staff." He hoped that they had both taken the opportunity to make their sentiments known during the consultations. If not, he counseled, there was still time, and the bishop delegates were all ears.

The archbishop also gave the two advisers a vote of confidence. Leckey, as co-ordinator of the consultation for the bishops, was "the most informed person in the country as to what our Catholic lay people have said to their bishops who will be participating in the synod," he wrote. And he commended Roy "as a lay theologian with rich background in the role of the laity in the church."

ARCHBISHOP MARCINKUS, THE BELEAGUERED HEAD OF THE VATICAN BANK, HAD remained behind the walls of the Vatican since February to avoid being arrested by Italian officials. An Italian court still wanted him and two aides for questioning on conspiracy charges in connection with the 1982 ($1.3 billion) collapse of Italy's then biggest bank, Banco Ambrosiano, but the American archbishop and his aides had not budged while the church challenged the legitimacy of the arrest orders. Under international law, Italian authorities could not enter the sovereign state of Vatican City to carry out the arrest orders, so a stalemate had ensued.

From the first, the Vatican had stonewalled the request (stunned that it had happened at all, convinced as the Vatican Bank officials were that their $240 million "voluntary contribution" to Banco Ambrosiano's creditors in 1984 had mollified the accusers), but had produced no detailed rationale for its defiance. Meanwhile, the crisis had not receded in the least. Because of Rome's heavy dependence on support from the church in the U.S., the archbishop's business was very much the business of Catholic America. Financially, a lot was riding on the outcome of the case.

Now came evidence of a more formal defense. The Italian Catholic weekly, *Il Sabato,* reported in its July 4 issue that, based on a document it had obtained, a Vatican tribunal concluded in April that the efforts to extradite the archbishop and his aides violated the 1929 Lateran Treaty between Italy and the Vatican. According to the newspaper, the tribunal claimed that the three church officials were protected under Article 11 of the treaty, which stated that "central entities of the Catholic Church" were immune from "every interference on the part of the Italian state." As for the charges, the tribunal described them as merely "in part conjectural and contradicted by some of the documents produced by the defense." Moreover, *Il Sabato* noted, the Vatican had no extradition agreement with Italy.

In a surprise announcement on July 17, the Italian Supreme Court essentially accepted the tribunal's reasoning and quashed the arrest warrants against the archbishop and his two bank assistants. They were free to leave the Vatican. The court's decision, which could not be appealed, agreed that the Vatican Bank constituted one of the "central organs of the church" off-limits to Italian authorities under terms of the Lateran Treaty.

The decision relieved the Vatican from legal pressure but did nothing to clear up the accusations against Archbishop Marcinkus. As a friend and business partner of the late Roberto Calvi, who had been head of the now defunct Banco Ambrosiano and who had hanged himself after the collapse, the archbishop had produced documents to help shore up Mr. Calvi's sinking ship. The allegation was that the archbishop's intervention knowingly perpetrated a fraud by making the Italian bank seem healthier than it was. But for now, at least, Archbishop Marcinkus remained solidly at the helm of the Vatican Bank, and there was no indication that any change was likely to take place soon.

The persistence of the scandal was having a crippling effect on the increased drive to raise huge sums in America to defray the bulging Vatican debt. An emissary sent to the U.S. from Rome with the intention of igniting the still-secretive $100 million U.S. bail-out of the Vatican ran headlong into Marcinkus-related resistance. Wealthy Catholics sounded out about making big contributions wasted no time expressing their distress with the scandal in particular and the Vatican finances generally. Unless the archbishop and his team were removed and an international commission of top financial people installed to oversee the church's central fiscal affairs, the Vatican could expect no pile of hefty gifts from rich Americans, the emissary was told.

The stunned emissary returned to Rome with the dismaying news. There would be no fat financial package to announce to the Pope when he got to America; no substantial downpayment on a $100 million campaign.

In the shadow of the high drama of big money, Mary's Pence, the fund that posed a modest yet graphic alternative to Peter's Pence, in effect if not by design, kept plugging along two months after it was started by Chicago Catholic Women to aid ministries to women and poor people. Fund directors reported raising $10,000 so far.

⸺ ⸺

WHEN THE PHONE CALL HAD COME FROM THE TRAVEL AGENT WITH A TRAVEL offer, Sister Ruth was ready to go. The agent had wondered if she would like to recruit a group of tourists and lead them on a pilgrimage to the two most renowned shrines to Mary, Lourdes and Fátima, in connection with the celebration of the Marian year? In return for her efforts, of course, her trip would be free of charge.

She had jumped at the chance. As she began her eighties, she still brimmed with wanderlust, raring to pack her bags at the right suggestion. Within a few weeks, aided by notices placed in parish bulletins, she had enrolled five couples, enough to meet the need.

To prepare for the pilgrimage, she had exerted herself with typical diligence and thoroughness, combing religious works, historical texts, and travel guidebooks to bone up on both the sacred and the secular aspects of the sites where the group would travel. "I did a lot of homework over the first part of the summer," she said. "Before we left, we visited with each other and I gave them lots of background."

Her specialty was the spiritual lore of the shrines. Looking back on the tour just after returning, she was amazed at how foreign those places had seemed. As Catholic Americans and middle-class parishioners, they had found themselves in an earlier age of piety surrounded by practices that seemed to belong to an alien religious tradition. The shock had initially registered at the spectacular Portuguese setting of Fátima. There, in an area the size of eight football fields, pilgrims approached the shrine painfully on their knees, fervently calling on God for help. "Some of the people with me were deeply disturbed by this," Sister Ruth recalled.

"That gave me an opportunity to talk with them," she continued. "I explained that we were in the midst of a medieval theology of the transcendence of God which says that no act of penance is too much. That's their theology. We don't have to buy into it. It's not ours. Ours may be more reaching out to others, more in the way of penance through social justice. It was a help to them to see the difference within the same Catholic church. It was important not to condemn others while still being true to our culture."

The group itself had become molded into a tightly-knit unit; they looked out for one another and took mutual heed of lessons to be learned. They traipsed around together, worshipped together, ate together, and explored thoughts together. An example of this solidarity had stood out to Sister Ruth. One of the men was disabled, she noted, but "the other men didn't let him miss a thing."

If on the one hand she had been "impressed most with the spirit of people to help a handicapped person," she had also come away more convinced than ever "that there was no way I accept the spirituality they practice there—saying the rosary all afternoon, standing in an open plaza for four hours without a bench or a tree, rain falling or sun scorching. I don't feel called to do that."

There were some contrasting interludes. On their way to Lourdes, they had paid a weekend visit to Madrid. At an elegant parish near the University of Madrid, they had inquired when they might attend mass. "The people we asked said 'Saturday evening at 7, 8, 9, or 10'. None on Sunday," she said. "It was done like that for the sake of the students. Those who went to church liked to go early Saturday evening, then go dancing all night. The architecture might have been medieval but the practice was not."

The symbolism inside the sanctuary had also been memorable. The space looked "more like a stage than a traditional sanctuary," she remembered. "There was a statue of Our Lady of Mercy in front of which were broken chains and a broken fence. She is the patroness of all the imprisoned. The broken chains and fence represented release from slavery of all kinds, including drugs. I think that meant a lot, especially in a university setting."

Just as the piety at the shrines had given the group something to think about, Sister Ruth had become an object of curiosity to a Portuguese woman who had served the group as a guide. "She said she couldn't figure me out," she chuckled. "I didn't seem like a nun to her. I wasn't wearing a habit and she said I didn't seem to think or act like nuns she knew. 'Are you really a sister?' she asked me. 'Why, yes,' I told her. 'I work mostly in hospitals'. She asked me some more questions, then she burst out, 'I think it's wonderful. I never met a sister like you'."

The reality of her vocation had struck as soon as the tour was over. Awaiting her at home was a message from the director of the county nursing association. Of all aspects of her work—teacher, retreat director, women's ordination advocate, social activist, religious community leader, health professional—none commanded more of her time and devotion than care of the sick. While she could not identify with divine intervention as it was sought at Lourdes and Fátima, she resolutely believed that God's healing presence could be conveyed by ministers of love.

The phone message turned out to involve a request. The nursing director asked Sister Ruth to pay a call on her associate who was described as "having a tough time because her son-in-law is dying of cancer." She was now visiting regularly with both the woman and the young man. "I think," she said cheerfully, "that the Holy Spirit is still around."

—◂ ▸—

LIKE AN AGING LEADING LADY TURNED OUT IN HER FINEST FOR WHAT MIGHT BE her final audition for a starring role, St. Joseph Church had been primped for one last bid to win the hearts and minds of those who had been disposed to write her off as a discardable relic. The entire gothic 114-year-old interior had been scrubbed clean, the altar pieces and fixtures buffed to vintage lustre, the sanctuary bedecked with flowers, and the burned-out ceiling bulbs replaced. St. Joseph looked every inch the elegant dowager of downtown Cleveland churches that indeed it was. And the occasion for which it had been so lovingly fitted out marked the high point in the drive for its survival.

For over a year, St. Joseph had been earmarked for destruction, a victim of adversity stemming from urban renewal and the scattering of parishioners to the suburbs. No one questioned the special beauty of the structure or the treasured memories of generations of German immigrants that it held, but with only a handful of people still coming regularly to mass and the cost of building repairs soaring, the diocese had decided reluctantly that it could no longer justify keeping St. Joseph open.

Though the final liturgy had been celebrated the previous September, a diehard group, "Friends of St. Joseph," had managed, with the help of the city landmarks commission and other community leaders, to keep the building from being destroyed. The diocese agreed to give the twenty-five-member group a year to come up with an alternative proposal for saving the church. Nothing concrete had yet emerged, though the group's ebullient leader, Larry Kruszewski, refused to wave the flag of surrender, keeping open the possibility that the church might be used for either religious or non-religious purposes, anything acceptable so long as the landmark itself remained intact. Time was running out, however, and prospects were dimming.

The one largely untapped factor that could make a big difference was public sentiment in favor of preserving the architectural gem, which was cited as a Cleveland landmark in 1973 and three years later listed in the National Register of Historic Places. Tapping into that support could buy time and perhaps prompt sound suggestions for its continued use.

With those feelings in mind, the "Friends" planned an open house for Sunday, July 19, and had spiffed up their beloved old house of worship to welcome what they hoped would be a big crowd. The idea was that people who, like Kruszewski, had been reared in the parish, perhaps baptized, confirmed, and married at that very altar, would once more enter those portals and touch base again with precious memories that could be galvanized into solid support for preservation. Media attention was also expected to be a boon.

Everything was in readiness. On display were the chalices and vestments used over the years. A local beverage distributor had donated six thousand cases of soda to the cause and a baker had contributed thousands of cookies. The St. Joseph organist for the last forty-four years before its closing, Marcella Basel, now seventy-nine years old, was enlisted to play once more as the visitors strolled through from noon til 6 P.M.

The day was hot and humid but the turnout was heavy. Groups explored the large spaces and snug crannies of the church, watched a videotape of its history and reminisced. By the time it was over, more than three thousand people had filed through the building. Kruszewski served as master of ceremonies. He recalled the highlight of that afternoon. "There I was, looking up at those huge arches and vaulted ceilings," he said, "then very dramatically, they turned the lights on in sequence and we saw those miniature lights like jewels." He had introduced a member of the city's historical society who spoke for a while. "Then I told them to go home," Kruszewski continued, "and, if they couldn't pledge money to help us, then they could write a letter to the bishop. If they didn't do at least that, then we failed."

Keeping the edifice standing might still be a pipedream, despite the outpouring of devotion and emotion that day and the extensive media coverage which gave the plight of St. Joseph heightened visibility, but Mr. Kruszewski saw some genuine cause for hope. The diocese had cooperated in the open house and had made no dire threats of carrying through with demolition when the year's reprieve was up. The "Friends" were cautiously confident that their drive was whipping up public opposition to razing the building to the point where the diocese had to take it into account. "If we can get three thousand people out on the hottest day in July, then get many of them to make out a pledge," said Kruszewski, the irrepressible optimist, "then the diocese has to realize that people really care."

The open house had been "well staged" if he did say so himself. Then with a chuckle, "If I'd gone through there myself that day, I think I would have been very impressed."

SIX MONTHS AFTER BEING TOSSED OUT OF THE JESUITS FOR HIS OPPOSITION TO the church's teaching on homosexuality (and his refusal to quit his ministry to them), the Reverend John McNeill looked back with irony. Life had gone on for the man who had called the Society of Jesus his religious community for forty years. He had been unceremoniously shown the door by his superiors (with the reluctance of men following orders from *their* superiors, he observed); he had been served the harsh penalty of banishment. Yet, he asserted in a telephone interview, the dismissal had turned out to be a blessing in disguise.

"To my great surprise," he declared, "a tremendous sense of joy and liberation came from my separation from my religious family. I had feared that it would turn me into a deep depression, but the exact opposite happened: grace, peace, and joy.

"I realized that I'd been guilty of idolatry of the church," he continued. "I felt a direct, personal relationship with God that was not mediated by the church."

His years of obedience to a Jesuit order to keep silent about homosexuality had been broken when the Vatican issued its tough stance against both homosexual inclination and activity the previous October. Like many others in the forefront of the drive to improve the status of gays in the church, Father McNeill, who described himself as gay, judged the Vatican document a terrible setback and felt he could no longer keep from speaking out. He did and was expelled as the result.

The sequence of events, as he saw it now, had brought certain matters to a head. He had come to see "*hubris* in the church, thinking that it can speak to everyone about everything," whereas "gay people really have something to say *to* the church." The meaning he saw in the October statement was "that God made the church fallible." What gay Catholics had needed, he concluded, was "a sign like this of how fallible the church is." It set them free to see the church, not as a strict parent whose authority was unquestionable, but as an institution with flaws, he thought. That liberated gays to step back with a clear conscience, "make their own decisions about their lifestyles," aware that there was nothing absolute about the church's views.

His busy practice of psychotherapy included many priests and seminarians struggling with those issues. Some along the way had gone beyond seeing the church with clay feet to rejecting it altogether. "I'm discovering," he said, "that a lot of these people realize that much of the real work of God cannot take place within the institution." The Gay Men's Health Crisis and other service agencies, such as drug rehabilitation centers and homes for retarded people, "are loaded with ex-priests and religious" seeking an alternative, he said.

His own work, he noted wryly, had always been "greatly enhanced by anything Rome does against me." Since his ouster, he was in even greater demand among gay-rights groups. As the author of the best-known book in its field, *The Church and the Homosexual,* which explored the subject from the perspective of biblical scholarship, he had won a wide and respectful hearing. As a priest who qualified as a senior citizen, he exuded the calm, contemplative air of a man who has learned much from experience. Among gay activists, Father McNeill was an elder statesman and a source of counsel. His framework was more ecumenical than ever, he said, and he was thankful for the benefits gained from stronger ties with people from other churches. The burst of energy stemming from the crisis had also set him to writing again. He had completed more than two hundred pages of a new book on gay spirituality.

Many of the thoughts on that subject had grown out of his contact with AIDS sufferers. "Something extraordinary is going on there spiritually," he said. "These people are learning to live with death through hope and faith in the resurrection. Dying men are praying together with the men who love them and experiencing a peaceful death through total trust in God's mercy."

The dread disease had wrought its own theology, its own ethic, he said, offering, among other things, "a means of escaping the dualism of 'immortal soul' and 'evil body.'" Gays believed in the goodness of the body "and of sexual love for its own sake," in spite of the ravages of the flesh that AIDS brought. "If God could let his word become flesh," Father McNeill said, "then we have to let our word become flesh" in the face of "new realities about death."

Spiritual, emotional, and physical love belonged together, Father McNeill thought, and the church's attempt to separate sexuality from other kinds of love for gay people was folly. Regarding the place of sex in gay relationships, he said, "You can't build a relationship on grounds that as we grow healthier we have to give each other up"—which was precisely, he added, what the Vatican expected gays to do.

He was looking forward to the annual meeting of Dignity, the ministry to gay Catholics that he had helped organize eighteen years earlier. This year it would be held in Miami in conjunction with the yearly convention of the Metropolitan Community Churches, a network of non-Catholic gay congregations.

The Vatican's policy statement last October had explicitly forbidden all forms of church support for groups opposed to Catholic teaching on homosexuality, an ultimatum that between the lines spelled *Dignity* with a capital *D*. Since then, 13 of the 108 chapters of the organization had been ejected from their meeting grounds on church premises by orders of the bishops. What disheartened many Dignity members was that expulsions were carried out by some bishops considered most sympathetic to gay ministries, specifically Francis J. Mugavero, head of the Brooklyn diocese, and Walter Sullivan of Richmond, Virginia.

Recently a new tactic had surfaced. Archbishops Daniel Pilarczyk of Cincinnati and John R. Roach of St. Paul–Minneapolis demanded that chapters within their diocese sign a statement agreeing with the church's teachings on homosexuality or be removed from church property. The Dayton chapter, under Archbishop Pilarczyk's jurisdiction, complied with the edict and was allowed to stay; the Cincinnati chapter refused and was kicked out, as was the chapter in Minneapolis, which balked at Archbishop Roach's order.

Among the questions on the agenda of the Dignity convention in Miami—which began Wednesday, July 22, and continued through the week—was whether to take action against the Dayton chapter for caving in to the pressure. In the end, the delegates chose to respect Dayton's right to decide for itself and dropped the matter.

But the organization expressed its collective outrage against the October statement by separating itself even further from church views on homosexuality. Dignity had been somewhat ambiguous on the morality of sexual activity between homosexuals. The expression of sexuality should be "consonant with Christ's teaching," said the organization's original statement of purpose. To most interpreters, that might have implied abstinence, but it allowed some flexibility. Not so the new statement of purpose adopted by the convention. It read, "We affirm that gay and lesbian people can express their sexuality physically in a unitive manner that is loving, life-giving, and affirming." It further declared that Dignity "emphatically disagrees with and calls for a reexamination" of church teachings on homosexuality.

The explosion of applause that accompanied the overwhelming approval of the revised statement sent a powerful signal. In the wake of the Vatican's most recent declaration of its policy toward homosexuality, common ground between gay activists and the church had virtually disappeared. Distrust and enmity had replaced an uneasy truce. Positions on both sides hardened. The murkier middle had almost totally evaporated. "Dignity has been keeping Catholics in the church at least minimally," Father McNeill had said in the interview, "and should have been embraced one hundred percent by the church." No longer did it seem possible that the organization could be anything like a way station or holding area for gay Catholics.

Members of Dignity also seemed ready to shed any remaining ambivalence about the morality of homosexual acts. A draft of a document on sexual ethics, presented to the convention, referred to physical love among homosexuals as "the holy gift of God" and pointed to the goal of bringing "our spirituality and sexuality together and to express Christian faith in our sexual lives." Moreover, it declared categorically that those members of Dignity who were sexually active "have found that we are more at ease with ourselves, more fulfilled in our relationships, more productive in our work and service."

Fired anew with resolve, Dignity leaders vowed to take their grievances to the pope during his trip to the United States. The convention called on members to participate in peaceful protests, masses, and prayer vigils. Father McNeill had been invited to be principal celebrant of a "counter-mass" at John Paul's stop in San Francisco, but he was disinclined to do it. The challenge, as he saw it, was to balance respect for the papal office with a nonconfrontational demonstration of dissent against Vatican policy. What made the San Francisco situation more complex for many gays was that plans called for the pope to visit with AIDS patients, a high-visibility show of pastoral concern that was widely supported.

Attitudes toward AIDS and homosexuality were, of course, as entwined within the church as in the broader society, perhaps even more so, given the particular moral doctrine of Catholicism. Action on one front invariably had implications on the other.

Though the U.S. bishops had denounced the suggestion that AIDS was somehow divine punishment for immorality, the judgment continued to crop up on the religious right. "For many thousands of U.S. men the wages of sin in recent years has been AIDS," wrote Gary Potter in the July 30 *Wanderer* in the course of a diatribe against a priest accused of giving aid and comfort to homosexuals.

From another source came an attack on the church's drive against Dignity. "I, for one, find it scandalous that, one by one, Catholic dioceses have been hanging out a 'Not Welcome' sign for chapters of Dignity. . .," wrote Robert E. Burns in his regular column in the July *U.S. Catholic.* "How else is such a cold and insensitive action to be interpreted by Dignity members but as designation that they are beyond redemption? A group of homosexuals is, like any group of us, composed of sinners and saints. And what mere mortal is empowered to say which is which? What an arrogant presumption for any one of us to sit in judgment on any other!

"The AIDS plague and the concomitant question of homosexuality, it seems to me, offer us a splendid opportunity to save our soul. Or lose it" (p. 2).

The sensitive relation between the two issues was also evident when, on July 23, President Reagan named a thirteen-member commission to fight AIDS. Among those picked was New York's Cardinal O'Connor, whose concern for AIDS sufferers stood alongside his staunch defense of the church's views on homosexuality. Three days later, during Sunday masses, three hundred demonstrators marched outside Saint Patrick's Cathedral to protest the appointment of the cardinal to the commission. Protesters cried, "Shame," and pointed to the cardinal's alleged "anti-gay" record: his opposition to the distribution of condoms as a strategy to fight AIDS, his stand against a proposed city gay-rights bill the year before, and his vigorous upholding of the church's laws against homosexual practice. Critics dismissed the cardinal's maintenance of a hospital, a hospice, and a dental clinic for AIDS patients as an inadequate response to the crisis.

The Catholic bishops of Pennsylvania joined forces with the state Council of Churches to appeal for compassion for AIDS sufferers and their families. Declaring in a July 31 statement that it was "time for us to speak together as Christian leaders," the ecumenical group said it was "not our intent to render judgment, but simply to point out clearer directions for our pastoral and practical concern." The leaders called on the churches to contribute "presence, time and energy to ease the isolation" of sufferers. They also urged that more private and public resources go into caring for those who were afflicted and for finding a cure, cautioning that such an effort "may involve reordering of society's priorities."

"AIDS must concern each one of us," the statement said. "AIDS kills. The numbers of those affected by AIDS appear to be growing rapidly. Faithfulness to God means we care."

WHILE FATHER CURRAN'S APPEAL FOR REINSTATEMENT TO THE CATHOLIC University faculty made its way through the courts, the cries in support of academic freedom grew stronger across the breadth of church-related campuses. Whether or not those who spoke up believed Father Curran had been mistreated, the overwhelming sentiment among them was that the right to conduct scholarship without interference was well-nigh sacred.

Father Curran's dissent and the punishment meted out by Rome—stripping him of his license to teach as a Catholic theologian—together with the Vatican's proposed schema for imposing firmer control over Catholic colleges and universities had caused educators and other prominent Catholics to rethink their stand on freedom and authority. The result was an outpouring of carefully reasoned essays and speeches.

A common theme in these ruminations was pride in the distinctive design and quality of the system of secondary education built by Catholic America and gratitude for the democratic ideals that made it possible. Writers and speakers who sang the praises of the founders of Catholic higher education invariably paid tribute to the political climate that had allowed Catholic universities and colleges to blossom and prosper as nowhere else in the world. The crisis brought on by the Father Curran episode and the schema had apparently awakened many of those in the forefront of Catholic education to the special benefits America had conferred upon them. They were tenacious about holding fast to these principles and to the character of their 235 institutions of higher learning in the face of challenges from Rome.

America being America, protection against encroachments on academic freedom did not logically stop at the door of theologians. Theologians were generally believed to be entitled to the same American guarantees of liberty granted every scholar, even though their situations were often different, in the sense that they were accountable principally to the church. But how to draw the line? The Catholic Theological Society of America had just the month before put off a decision on whether to endorse the statement by the American Association of University Professors on academic freedom, citing as the reason for its demurrer the unique conditions under which theologians worked: with one foot, as it were, in the academy and the other in the church. The theologian's commitment to the faith of the church presumably placed understandable limits on pure, unadulterated freedom, and the CTSA wanted more time to think through the issue.

One indication of the attention such problems aroused was that the summer *Current Issues in Catholic Higher Education,* published by the Association of Catholic Colleges and Universities (ACCU), was devoted fully to the discussion. It contained a dozen recent addresses on academic freedom, the character of the Catholic college, theological dissent, relations between bishops and theologians, Vatican policy toward Catholic universities, and the age-old tension between the hierarchy and scholars. Contributors included bishops, theologians, college presidents, and leaders in Catholic higher education. Several had taken part in the colloquy on a similar range of topics the previous January at the University of Notre Dame.

Solidarity existed on several fronts. Everyone agreed, for example, that Catholic sponsorship of a college or university held great positive potential so long as the church refrained from any kind of direct or indirect interference in the internal affairs of the university. Among those who made that point most forcefully were the Reverend Timothy S. Healy, S.J., president of Georgetown, and the Reverend William J. Rewak, S.J., president of Santa Clara University. Within the American legal framework, Father Healy reminded his audience, "a catholic university is not a form of the Church's life, but a secular entity (like a city) in which the church lives, functions and exercises her influence on the lives of its members and even upon the processes of teaching and learning" (p. 37).

Half of the presidents of the 235 Catholic colleges and universities had gone on record as stoutly opposed to those provisions in the schema that required tighter church controls over their institutions, including formal approval of theological faculty members by the presiding bishop. If the Vatican went ahead with that demand, several institutions had signaled (Notre Dame among them) that they might discard their "Catholic" identity in protest. Among the other threats was the danger that the imposition of church control could jeopardize government funds. The writers included in the ACCU journal amplified a widespread conviction.

The right by theologians to dissent received a somewhat more qualified endorsement. At issue were several questions. Was dissent permissible? The consensus was yes. Were there conditions attached to a theologian that were not applicable to other faculty members? "Probably," owing to the particular responsibility to the church by those who purport to expound its beliefs, but not such as to squelch disagreement. Was dissent healthy? "Perhaps" or even "definitely" if carried out with love for the church and a large dose of "docility" toward the collective teaching of the church. An individual should never presume his or her wisdom superior to that of the tradition. How could a bishop deal with dissent? "Variously," without resort to juridical sanctions, except, some argued, in the most extreme cases. (One entry in the volume, a response by Archbishop Rembert Weakland, O.B., to Dr. Daniel Maguire of Marquette University, consisting of a public statement of opposition by the archbishop to Professor Maguire's dissenting positions on abortion and homosexuality, illustrated the point—it was possible to dissent from the dissenters without trying to fire them.)

Father Rewak provided an especially vigorous defense of dissent. In the broadest sense, he wrote, "in order to protect the intellectual vitality of the Church's understanding of itself, responsible dissent is not only allowed, it is required" (p. 48). A maverick with totally unacceptable beliefs might turn up every once in a while, but the risk did not justify destroying the greater principle of intellectual freedom. "The alternative is unreasonable," Father Rewak wrote, "for to stifle such an aberration, with some form of censorship, is to put in jeopardy that far greater good of theological development" (p. 48). For Rome, development meant issuing prescriptions from headquarters; Americans preferred advancing through dialogue.

"In summary," he continued, "we are being true to our mission as a Catholic university (1) only if we are engaged honestly and unrestrictedly in intellectual inquiry; (2) only if we are allowed to dissent—and the dissent is couched in sincere terms of dialogue—in order that our understanding of our role in the Church's mission can grow, and so that the Church's understanding of itself can grow; and only if we embrace pluralism. . . . So we should not be afraid of taking risks with our intellects, with our ideas and our criticisms" (p. 49).

Like many of his colleagues, Father Rewak felt constrained to point out that Catholic University, because of its direct pontifical degree-granting relationship with the Vatican, belonged to a category apart from all Catholic institutions of higher learning in the United States Were the scalp of a Santa Clara dissenting professor to be demanded by the Vatican, he declared, "we would not be able to comply with it." He added, "But it is also true that The Catholic University of America, since it, too, is subject to accreditation and empowered by the state to give civil degrees, will certainly have a difficult time if it decides to heed the Vatican directive" (p. 49).

Not everyone, of course, was enamored of the rise of pluralism and scholarly independence on Catholic campuses. Many conservatives deplored a trend they interpreted as capitulation to secularism and apostasy. They welcomed the Vatican's moves to bring errant theologians into line as well as its effort to reinforce the Catholic character of universities through the schema. One champion of the Vatican's cause was the Saint Joseph Foundation, whose motto, "To defend Catholic truth and uphold Catholic rights," signified its inclination to get involved with such issues. Chuck Wilson remained steadfast at the helm of the small but gritty organization, taking on the complaints of those who felt their rights had been violated within the church. So upset were Wilson and his colleagues at the foundation by the drift of Catholic higher education that they might have filed a class action suit on behalf of Catholic students if that had been an option.

A headline in the foundation's newsletter, *Christifidelis* (vol. 5, no. 1), read, "Just What Is a Catholic University Anyway?" The accompanying article, not surprisingly, raised grave doubts about whether many fit the qualification of being guided "by authentic Catholic teaching." Any Catholic university worthy of its name must be expected to submit itself to the oversight of the hierarchy in areas set forth by canon law and conditions spelled out in the proposed schema.

"Most 'Catholic' colleges and universities in this country, we suspect, would fall far short of these standards," the article said. "For example, one can scarcely imagine an academic community truly characterized by 'Christian inspiration' where faculty members openly dissent from magisterial teaching and sign pro-abortion advertisements, where contraceptives are distributed in the classroom, where the Holy Sacrifice of the Mass is trivialized by continuous liturgical abuses, where public officials who openly favor abortion are given honorary degrees or elected to boards of trustees and where sexual license by students is tolerated if not actually encouraged by lax discipline. It is no secret that these and similar aberrant activities are commonplace on many so-called Catholic campuses" (p. 7).

It concluded as follows: "Either *be* Catholic or cease claiming to be, one or the other" (p. 7).

Meanwhile, the attempt by scholars to nudge the hierarchy into adopting guidelines for settling disputes between theologians and bishops was inching along. An *ad hoc* group from the four major Catholic learned societies had met with the doctrinal committee of the bishops' conference with no visible results thus far. A document outlining procedures for ensuring due process for scholars accused of wrongdoing had been forwarded by the *ad hoc* group to the bishops almost four years before but had elicited no response. In light of the anger and suspicion aroused by the Curran case, the bishops were disposed to do something to ease the tension, but they moved with great caution. A set of guidelines—the result of collaboration between the scholars and the bishops—was in the pipeline. There were hints that it could be presented to the bishops at their next meeting in November.

— ◄ ►

Around the little plains town where Hannah lived, the third week of July was harvest time. Not far on any side of her house, giant combines roamed the vast fields, gobbling thick clusters of wheat, corn, and soybeans in the annual ritual of gathering nature's miraculous yield. Exceptionally favorable weather conditions had blessed the farmers this year. Hot sun had fostered a last good spurt of growth, and the dreaded lightning storms had so far left the crops alone. The effect on Hannah and her neighbors was to induce that feeling of thankfulness and enduring, if improbable, hope that people close to the land often understood best. In this case, abundant fields made them forget the financial hardship that had plunged so many farmers into despondency and ruin in recent years. Hannah's livelihood was directly affected by the plight of farmers on this land; her husband earned his keep at a local grain elevator.

Hannah hadn't planted a vegetable garden in her back yard this year, though she had managed to tend a few tomato plants. Much of her free time during the summer was devoted to a correspondence course on children with learning disabilities offered by the state university. In one sense, it was old hat. She had become familiar with much of the theory during the many years she had taught such students in the local public school. But in the reading materials she had also come upon much that was new to her. Most important, she felt it had broadened her understanding of "how to meet their needs and accept their differences."

She had signed up for the course not knowing whether she would be returning to the school for another year. Her application for the position of director of lay ministries for the diocese had been on active file since spring. She had alerted her principal to the possibility that she might be leaving but until the previous week had heard nothing. It had been on her mind constantly. As the next school board meeting approached, her principal had again asked in a friendly way what was going on. Hannah had felt pressured and tense, left in suspension too long for her good or the school board's.

At that point, she had taken the initiative by asking a diocesan official in charge of filling the position if any decision had been reached. "It's down to two of you," she recalled him telling her, "and we'll make the choice tomorrow." Her hopes soared. On her way to a peace and justice workshop the next day, she pressed someone close to the situation, a longtime confidant, for what he knew, and he delivered a shock. "The committee has narrowed the list down to three," he reported tersely, "and you're not one of them."

Her friend's version, which she trusted, left her stunned. From the moment Hannah had seen the job opening, she had felt almost as if it had been made for her, the culmination of a long preparation process, the chance to apply her skills to the needs of the church. Just before hearing from her friend that she was out of the running, she did remember feeling a spasm of hesitation but had discounted it.

"The night before I was so sure it would be offered to me," she said, "that I was actually starting to get cold feet. When I got the news, I was consumed with a sense of relief. I was surprised how good I was feeling. There was something saying that the job really didn't apply to me after all. I wonder if it will hit me with a real sense of loss later on. I am really curious about what criteria they used and why I was eliminated. And I sure don't have a lot of trust in that guy who told me I was still in. I never want to be in a position of asking him a favor. Do I really want to work in such a situation anyhow? Maybe I'm much better off. I know I've got to react somehow to all this in ways I haven't yet."

For the moment, at least, her impulse to do some kind of full-time church work had been quelled. "It's nice to have this behind me so I can do other things," she said. She would stay in the classroom, where she felt almost convinced that her teaching · was, indeed, her God-given ministry. Yet something kept her from being certain about that. The church was her extended family, and she felt drawn to it as to no other place, through thick and thin. Those who had most shaped her life were employees of the church, so it was natural for her to think that greater rewards came to those who were total insiders. But something also kept her from wanting that kind of involvement. As an outsider, professionally at least, Hannah felt she could speak her mind more freely, take risks, avoid the political games employees play.

Right then, it seemed to her that her Christianity might develop better if she were a gadfly on the fringe of the establishment. "If I operate well, out of integrity," she said with a touch of whimsy, "I might just crash into some walls. Nobody wants to crash, but it's what happens sometimes when you take leaps of faith. It's sometimes in the crashes that we grow most spiritually."

She was already looking ahead to the start of school. On her request, she had been assigned younger students. "I'm at the age where I like to be with little children who accept me without question," she said. "It shows in their faces. I'm nurtured as much as I hope the kids are." The other day she had been thinking about the last batch of parent conferences the previous year, especially how concerned they had been. "In the course of that day, many of them showed real emotions about their children," she remembered. "It deeply impresses me just how much they care about them and how so many feel unable to do what they want for them. Family situations are really pretty depressing around here, particularly for farming people."

Something else had also roused her enthusiasm: the idea of starting a project to teach immigrants to read. A nun who ran such a project in a nearby city had piqued Hannah's interest. Reading skills were one of her specialties, and she was aware of a growing need. Hispanics were becoming more plentiful, and refugees from Southeast Asia were moving in to take jobs in meat packing plants. Not long before, a group of German Mennonites had arrived from Canada, and she had taken part in a reading project for the mothers in that group.

As usual, the commitment had a personal dimension. Through her parish, she had come to know a Guatemalan man who wanted to learn English. "I've been picking him up for mass every week," she said. "He lives all by himself in a trailer behind the farm house. He works on the farm. On our way to church, we go back and forth, Spanish and English, and he wants to know more." Offering tutoring was, among other things, she thought, a path out of the kind of isolation in which this man was trapped. She had discussed with some local people the possibility of getting a program going soon and believed prospects were good.

With twenty-five years of marriage behind her and her three grown children far from home, Hannah looked back at her life a great deal, especially at the rough spots. After her powerful experience at the charismatic retreat a few months before, she had tried to keep her attention focused on its theme, "Healing Life's Hurts." She had located a major wound that weekend in a dreamlike encounter with her father. She was exploring further with the help of a book by John Sanford, *Dreams—God's Forgotten Language.* "What it's done for me," she said, "is to help me respect that part of myself. Dreams show us that we have urges to be whole and healthy."

Hannah believed her future lay in recovering her past through the coded language of dreams. She had uncovered much that was painful but had found the means to make it better. "I get to the stage where I project Jesus into the situation," she said, "so that real healing of memories can come about."

"Sometimes, mostly at night, I get tired and discouraged," said Hannah, reflecting still the quiet restlessness that nearly drove her to Haight-Ashbury during the social revolutions of the 1960s, "but then comes daybreak, life is good, and I am grateful."

OTHER JULY DEVELOPMENTS INCLUDED:

- A survey of Notre Dame alumni was released that reflected Catholic America's absorption into a kind of libertarian mentality that had grown during the Reagan years. Compared to a similar poll conducted by the university ten years earlier, 37 percent of Notre Dame alumni now identified themselves as Republicans, up from 22 percent from the previous decade, while the Democratic minority remained steady (17 percent), and the percentage of "independents" fell to 40 percent from 57 percent. The proportion of self-described "conservatives" rose sharply to 41 percent from 31 percent, while the liberal bloc shrank from 35 percent to 26 percent, and a consistent one-third of respondents marked themselves as "moderate." The rightward drift politically was accompanied by greater resistance to Rome's directives (the church equivalent, perhaps, to the widespread, Reagan-inspired aversion to government intrusion of any kind). Just half now believed the pope to be infallible "when he speaks *ex cathedra* on faith or morals." Support for allowing divorced Catholics to remarry in the church had jumped to 79 percent from 57 percent, and 56 percent favored ordaining women (up from 31 percent). Three-fourths (75 percent) thought abortion was morally right under certain conditions (they split evenly on whether "abortion on request is immoral for everybody"), and 83 percent approved of artificial birth control. Two in five (43 percent) thought Vatican II had introduced enough change, but a growing proportion (40 percent compared to 31 percent ten years before) wanted more. Three-fifths (60 percent) objected to the idea that the university should take religion into account when hiring faculty; only two-thirds (65 percent) agreed with this statement: "Notre Dame can be a Catholic university and be independent of control by the church." Family income reported by the 3,832 respondents (of the 5,309 sent out): 22 percent between $15,000 and $34,999; 40 percent in the $35,000 to $74,999 range; one-fourth over $75,000, and 10 percent over $100,000. Given the dual swings in alumni attitudes—toward the political right and away from church conformity—it became all the more striking that 89 percent "credited Notre Dame with helping develop their values, moral standards and commitments to life."

• Another in a series of efforts was made to acquaint regional and local groups of Catholics more fully with the bishops' pastoral letter on the economy. Nearly a hundred California church leaders from schools, parishes, and chanceries met in Los Angeles to discuss many aspects of the letter, including those criticisms of the U.S. economy that had raised the hackles of some of the most ardent Catholic backers of free-market capitalism. The gathering was reminded by the Reverend David Hollenbach of Woodstock Theological Center in Washington, D.C., that the letter was aimed at prodding Catholics to resist the prevailing American "privatization of religion" and to choose, instead, to apply the church's values to their roles in the world. The man most recently responsible for dramatically underscoring the concept of "privatization of religion" was also on hand. Dr. Robert N. Bellah of the University of California at Berkeley, an Episcopalian, was principal author of the 1985 seminal work on the subject, *Habits of the Heart*. He told the group that capitalist stress on competition and self-gain made the bishops call for cooperation and sacrifice, "something the majority of Americans would rather not hear right now."

• There was evidence that the amnesty program for illegal aliens was off to a slow start. Since May, when the provisions of the Immigration Reform and Control Act went into effect, only a small number of aliens had come forward to apply for legal status. The Immigration and Naturalization Service had projected the total potential applicants at two million but reported on July 2 that so far, two months into the twelve-month grace period, only 213,174 had done so. Directors of application centers established by Catholic dioceses had reported processing very few (Los Angeles, with twenty-two centers, had forwarded only two hundred) and cited many causes for the paucity.

Among the reasons given: widespread distrust of the INS among aliens, too much red tape in filing applications (the preregistration screening form was seventeen pages long), too little effort by the government to help aliens obtain needed documentation (they had to show that they had arrived in the United States before January 1, 1982), and confusion about what kind of records were needed. The INS shrugged off the complaints as incorrect or insubstantial and insisted that the response so far to the program was roughly in line with its expectations. Immigration officials argued that the low numbers from the Catholic centers were due more to their own ineptness than to any obstacles posed by the INS.

• The fate of Epiphany Plowshares defendants took another turn. Since the group of four had been brought up on charges of delivering hammer blows to aircraft at the Willow Grove Naval Air Station near Philadelphia on January 6 to protest U.S. nuclear arms policy, two trials had ended in hung juries. In June, the two priests, the Reverend Dexter Lanctot and the Reverend Thomas McGann, both under suspension by the Archdiocese of Philadelphia as a result of the charges, pleaded guilty. Their sentencing date was September 7. The two laypeople, Lin Romano and Gregory Boertje, were brought into court for a third trial. It ended abruptly July 15 after supporters of the defendants created courtroom havoc by loudly appealing for divine justice and decrying nuclear war. The judge ruled in favor of the prosecution's request for a mistrial. A fourth trial was set for September.

• Archbishop Mahony made an assault on X-rated movies. Referring to the seat of his archdiocese, Los Angeles, as the "pornography capital of the world," the archbishop called on its citizens to boycott all stores that rent X-rated material and to patronize those that don't. "By supporting your pro-family video dealers you will be making a strong statement," Archbishop Mahony told a conference on obscenity sponsored by the archdiocese. "By committing your family not to give one more dollar of profit to those who degrade humanity, your position is made bottom-line clear." He described pornography as "a training manual for how to get or give AIDS." Two statistics indicated what tough sledding the archbishop faced. A Video Software Dealers Association survey of eight hundred dealers showed that 77 percent carried X-rated films, which accounted for 13 percent of their total sales. And a *Los Angeles Times* poll the previous summer found Catholics much more tolerant of pornography than other faith groups. Only 35 percent of Catholics favored legal barriers on pornographic materials, compared to 61 percent of self-described fundamentalists.

From seattle, the news was, in a nutshell, so far so good. in the month since the Vatican-approved settlement had returned Archbishop Hunthausen to full authority, removed Bishop Wuerl, and installed Bishop Murphy as a shot-gun-riding coadjutor, things had gone ahead a little better than generally expected.

The biggest factor in this modest swing toward optimism was the disarming first impression left by Bishop Murphy, formerly of Billings, Montana. At his first meeting with priests of the archdiocese, he had won them over with modesty and his apparent affinity with the spirit and purposes generated by their popular archbishop. At the official welcome in July, he captured further affection with his warmth and intelligence. It was a dazzling start in the estimation of the Reverend Michael Ryan, archdiocesan chancellor and chief Hunthausen partisan.

"Things are going very well," Father Ryan said. "Initial reaction to Bishop Murphy is very positive. He's fit right in—done everything right. Not in a staged way. His instincts are right." Father Ryan had been solidly opposed to the con-cept of a coadjutor bishop when it was proposed by the three-member commis-sion appointed by Rome to solve the dispute. Like others in Seattle, Father Ryan saw a coadjutor as a permanent infringement on Archbishop Hunthausen's au-thority. But he had acceded to Rome's demand and, moreover, admitted to being pleasantly surprised by the commission's candidate.

That pleasing turn could not erase the bitter reaction in Seattle to the com-mission's final assessment, which impugned Archbishop Hunthausen's leadership in a number of areas and insisted on remedial efforts under the direction of the commission. The commission met with Archbishop Hunthausen and Bishop Murphy in late July to discuss details of the timetable for correcting the problems over the next year. According to participants, the meeting went smoothly. Things seemed to be off to a good beginning. One element in the plan had not come to fruition: the expected visit to Rome by the two bishops as an act of homage and reconciliation. Fatigue and time pressures were cited as chief reasons why the mis-sion was not carried out.

Archbishop Hunthausen kept a busy schedule around the archdiocese in the weeks following the settlement, but his emergence from a sort of self-imposed exile within his own precincts came on July 31 when he gave the keynote ad-dress to the Catholic peace organization Pax Christi in Chicago. Rumors that the archbishop's problems with Rome had stemmed from his peace activities, partic-ularly his antinuclear protests at the Trident submarine base in Bangor, Washing-ton, had persisted despite denials by the Reagan administration and the Vatican. Many Catholics took it as an article of faith that the U.S. government had gained Rome's cooperation in clamping down on him in an effort to curb such activities.

The conspiracy theory had never been publicly proved to be true, but activists of course assumed that underhanded means had been used to suppress the evidence.

Among the peace activists, then, Archbishop Hunthausen had come through the period of tribulation as a more credible spokesman for peace than ever, a martyr who had not forsaken the cause despite reprisals. He had continued trekking to Bangor to decry nuclear submarines. Now he would stand before his friends in the peace movement, the Pax Christi, people with whom he shared a special bond, to light their lamps of enthusiasm.

The night was hot, in the nineties, and the hall at Loyola University was packed with a thousand supporters. Archbishop Hunthausen entered like the pacifist equivalent of a conquering hero to a cheering crowd. He quickly signaled that he remained at the forefront of the antinuclear bishops. He had not retreated in the least.

He spoke for twenty minutes and was interrupted nine times by applause, according to Robert McClory of the *National Catholic Reporter* (August 14), including five standing ovations. He denounced the escalating arms race and declared that the "doctrine of nuclear deterrence cries out for condemnation."

In their 1983 pastoral letter against nuclear war, the bishops had accepted deterrence on a "strictly conditioned" basis, namely, that it was a stopgap measure while the United States and the Soviet Union pursued options for disarmament. An earlier draft of the document had rejected nuclear deterrence outright as immoral, and Archbishop Hunthausen, in his speech, indicated that he believed the bishops should have stuck by that earlier position. The unrestrained arms buildup since the bishops adopted their letter had made a shambles of the "strictly conditioned" provision, he asserted. Furthermore, he argued, possession of such terrifying weapons implied an intention to use them—and that in itself was sinful.

"In my view," he said, "we are rapidly approaching the point where our courageous pastoral letter will no longer be seen as the challenge it was meant to be; it will become, instead, the nuclear equivalent of a blank check. Should this happen, I would regard it as a deeply tragic conclusion to the peace pastoral."

That contention—and the broader exhortation from the resurgent archbishop from Seattle—received resounding approval.

August
1·9·8·7

T HE VIEW FROM VIRGIL C. DECHANT'S OFFICE ON THE TOP
floor of the twenty-three-story Knights of Columbus headquarters offered unobstructed sights of downtown New
Haven and its far outskirts. Anchored by four dark brown columns,
the dense, brooding building was master of its surroundings even
as Dechant's presence towered over Catholic America's most powerful fraternity. He was Supreme Knight over an organization with
1.4 million men and $2 billion in assets that wielded enormous in-
fluence. The Knights' renowned loyalty to church authority, their
pouring of vast sums of money into projects to promote church
aims, and their vast amount of volunteer work were among the traits
that had endeared them to the Vatican and won them praise among
bishops, priests, and millions of ordinary parishioners.

It was mid-July, about two weeks before the start of the 105th annual meeting
of the Knights of Columbus, and Dechant was getting his reports in shape. At age
fifty-six, he was in his tenth year as the elected head of the order, a Kansan who
had prospered by selling cars, farm equipment, and real estate, businesses that
he still owned. To his job as head of the complex order, he brought an ample
store of understated shrewdness and know-how to go with his Kansan common
touch. These qualities had served him well in his dealings with powerful prelates
and politicians in efforts to further Knights of Columbus goals that, by definition, were identical to those of the Vatican. Dechant, like his predecessors, had had
access to popes and presidents by virtue of the order's financial might and the
collective, hence political, force of its convictions. By most estimates, he had
proved more than equal to the task.

Virgil Dechant exuded the geniality of his midwestern upbringing and bore a composed, reserved look. First impressions were of a man both informal and formidable, ordinary and distinguished, polite and cautious. He was a rangy six-footer with a face smooth and doughy, a full head of thick, graying black hair, and soft eyes behind clear-framed glasses. He wore a black suit with red pinstripes, a red handkerchief, white shirt, and red striped tie. He sat at a modest wood desk, polished to a high gloss, in an open, airy space with a floor of glistening marble tile. Behind him was a painting of the Madonna and photos of his wife and family.

Insofar as the Supreme Knight reflected the mood of the sprawling order, much of it was a throwback to the climate of earlier, simpler times, the 1950s perhaps, when unflagging trust in church and state came easily and naturally; when one set of Christian values pretty much prevailed; when the nuclear family was snugly ensconced at home; when religion and society taught that men alone were divinely ordained to head household, church, and community; when God was assumed to be on America's side because America was good; and all, save communism, seemed pretty much right with the world. Though it was tougher upholding such a vision against the waves of disillusion and dissent, Dechant's leadership made it possible to retain much faith in those ideals within the fellowship of friends and Catholic comrades. He provided that crucial reassurance that the Knights of Columbus mix of patriotism (practically synonymous with anticommunism), service, and religious commitment had not become passé. His was, for the most part, a low-key, good natured, benign conservatism, without the stridency and snarl of the upstart new right, and it seemed perfectly in tune with the mood of the order.

"We're average Americans," Dechant said. Like most popular fraternal groups that dotted towns and cities across America, the Knights of Columbus had drawn the bulk of its strength from the working class. Councils reflected aspects of the church, the locker room, and the saloon, a refuge from home and women. With the advent of television and other diversions, recruitment had become more difficult. The order had managed to grow 15 percent in the ten years Dechant had been at the helm. Through its ads, thousands of inquiries came in each month, of which some became serious seekers. The number of councils had increased over the same period from 6,200 to 8,700. They served a membership that was growing older and somewhat more removed from the mainstream of Catholic men.

The financial backbone of the organization, the source of its largesse, was its life insurance business, one of the nation's most vigorous. As of July 1, the value of its written policies topped the $12-billion mark. About one in three Knights (35 percent) was insured by the company. During 1986, income from premiums alone was $294 million (total intake was $383 million from all sources, or $1.5 million each working day), and $92 million was disbursed in dividends. The number of Knights of Columbus insurance agents had climbed to 1,113 by the end of 1986, up from 667 a decade before. The order was proud of its record. *Best's Insurance Reports,* the industry's most respected rating service, gave the Knights of Columbus insurance operation an A plus for "Superior" performance.

From that immensely successful enterprise along with the other sources of income from dues and fund-raising events flowed huge stores of funds for charitable work. During the previous year, the Knights of Columbus reported giving away nearly $68 million and devoting 24 million hours to volunteer services. Among the principal recipients were churches, students, schools, the poor and disabled, and victims of natural disasters.

Nothing loomed larger in the order's sense of mission than its continued role in strengthening the structures and aims of the universal church. Much of that attention had been focused on shoring up or modernizing the Vatican. Its funds had paid for renovation of the entire facade of the pope's church, Saint Peter's basilica, along with the magnificent statues of Saints Peter and Paul in Saint Peter's Square. The completion of the project had been blessed by John Paul II in February, with beaming Knights of Columbus leaders in attendance. The Knights had also provided a satellite uplink system for the Vatican Television Center, constructed a chapel to Saints Cyril and Methodius (co-patrons of Europe and especially revered by the pope) in Saint Peter's grotto, helped keep solvent the North American College in Rome, and annually sent the pope earnings from a $10 million "Vicarius Christi" fund set up in 1982 to be used at the pontiff's discretion ($6 million had been forwarded so far).

Closer to home, the Knights were no less active in attending to the needs of the church under the guidance of trusted members of the hierarchy. A grant of $2 million had been made to defray costs of the new headquarters for the bishops' conference in Washington; $1.8 million had been earmarked for seminaries, another half million to seminarians; $150,000 was allocated yearly to support natural family planning offices (in addition to funding a center for research in Nebraska); $250,000 was helping pay for the pope's trip to America; millions continued to be set aside for student loan programs; millions more were lent at low interest to churches and dioceses; a $900,000 fund paid for the upkeep of the Catholic network of military chaplains; and sizable outlays went to help stamp out abortion. Among its more recent outpourings of patriotism was a $1 million gift to help refurbish the Statue of Liberty.

Dechant was, in effect, head of a big philanthropic agency in addition to being the bishop-equivalent over a fraternity and an overseer of a welfare operation. He was one of the most sought-after figures in Catholic America, endowed with the power of the purse strings. With a trace of helplessness, he said, "I have on my desk at any moment at least $30 million in requests." Once in a while he got "snookered" by someone ("it's more difficult when it's a cardinal"), he confessed, but over time he had felt better able to detect a schemer or a bogus venture. The one bidder who never went away empty-handed was the Vatican. "We have yet to turn down the Holy See," he said, adding, "We have a relationship with Rome that is the envy of many." He had been a prime mover in the drive to establish a $100-million American fund to help the Vatican regain solid financial footing. "I'm to meet with [Cardinal] Krol," he reported. "I don't think we'll have much problem."

From his command post, surrounded by portraits of past Supreme Knights, Dechant reflected an easy, solid confidence. It spoke of permanence and stability, money and control. The storms within the church seemed far away and unreal. Beneath the surface noise in the church, he believed, lay a bedrock of stability that the Knights helped maintain. "I don't see dissent among the rank and file in the U.S. any more than in other parts of the world," he said. "Our press and some leaders of the church exaggerate it." Despite problems with birth control and other areas of sexuality, "still the teachings go on," he said, "leaving much to be desired, perhaps, but it's not all that bad. Differences should be minimized. I think the greatest hope is the willingness of American Catholics to support their church financially . . . and to practice their faith, though many have difficulty living up to [the church's] principles."

He saw other positive signs. The ongoing Marian year declared by the pope would bolster commitment, he was sure, and from the information he had seen, "attendance at mass is up and Catholic schools have ceased to close . . . we have over three million children in Catholic schools. There's nothing like that in the entire world. It's a tremendous demonstration of faith." The facts could be questioned; the enthusiasm and the certainty were beyond dispute.

With the annual meeting at hand, the Supreme Knight offered a preview of what might be in store. There was little guesswork. By tradition, the Supreme Knight, along with other top leaders, shaped the major resolutions beforehand, and the delegates went along with them. Overshadowing all other business this year was the move to win the convention's endorsement of Robert Bork as President Reagan's nominee to the Supreme Court.

No issue engaged the Knights more passionately than its drive to overturn the 1973 *Roe* v. *Wade* Supreme Court decision legalizing abortion. So central was this concern that the campaign to attract new members increasingly focused on the order's antiabortion activism.

The drive had picked up momentum. The previous year's meeting had gone on record in favor of President Reagan's antiabortion choices of William H. Rehnquist as chief justice and Antonin Scalia as associate justice. Both had been confirmed by the Senate, and Dechant had been invited to their induction ceremony. Like many other abortion opponents, the Knights reckoned that a Supreme Court majority in favor of reversing *Roe* was now just one vote away, and Robert Bork looked like the answer. Though the Knights of Columbus described itself as apolitical, therefore justified in receiving its tax-exempt status, the order did enter public debate on certain issues such as abortion and pornography that were judged to be primarily moral rather than political.

Buoyed by the relatively easy confirmations of Rehnquist and Scalia, Dechant expected a tough fight over Bork but seemed reasonably optimistic. He had no doubt about the convention's will. "Bork's nominee resolution will get adopted," he firmly predicted, "and within forty-eight hours we can contact a million and a half members."

Convincing pro-abortion Catholics to reconsider their views required more understanding than judgment, Dechant believed. "From the beginning," he said, "I've learned that you have to appreciate every Catholic point of view because you don't know what factors caused him to arrive at his position. Nor can you back people into a corner. People change. That's where I have a problem with people in the pro-life movement who just write off people who don't agree. I think you can persuade people to change their minds. Some on the right strike out at everybody."

But with the Supreme Court seemingly on the verge of throwing out *Roe,* the first priority was to apply the Knights' hefty leverage on Bork's behalf in the larger game of power politics and to postpone the art of gentle persuasion.

The time for mobilization arrived the first week of August. By the morning of the Fourth of July, the New Orleans Hilton Riverside was bustling with two thousand delegates from the United States, Canada, the Philippines, and Central America. The site was just blocks from where Pope John Paul II was scheduled to stop during his tour of the United States in just a little over a month. The mood was festive and exuberant. Under Dechant's urging, the Knights had recently broken with tradition to bolster their profamily message by encouraging wives to accompany their husbands, and many of them did, modifying ever so slightly the Knights' image as a male stronghold, though, of course, the women were not part of the convention's official business.

During the opening session, the pope and the president of the United States reassured delegates of the high respect in which the order was held in Rome and Washington. The pope appeared on big screens with a prerecorded message, thanking the order for restoring Saint Peter's basilica and hailing the Knights of Columbus as "an excellent example of the contribution which the laity can make by working together." President Reagan sent similar remarks by tape and letter. On the videotape, Reagan offered greetings to "my friend, Supreme Knight Virgil

Dechant," referred to the Knights as "a very special organization for America," pledged to continue his fight against abortion, and expressed his gratitude for "your support for our judicial nominees."

Covered in the Supreme Knight's annual report were an upbeat assessment of the order's insurance business, a mixed view of membership trends, a summary of charitable activities (including word that the pope would be handed another $1 million from the order's special fund during his stop in San Francisco), and a challenge to the Knights to step up their combat against pornography and especially against abortion.

Calling for the rejection of *Roe* v. *Wade,* Dechant showed his greatest indignation: "Abortion-on-demand spits in the face of God, the Creator and Giver of all life. It was God who said, 'Increase and multiply.' It is man who says, 'No! My comfort, my convenience come first.'"

At the opening night's "States Dinner" the Supreme Chaplain, Bishop Thomas V. Daily of Palm Beach, Florida, served up a rousing call to arms as the evening's main speaker. Bishop Daily delivered a portrait of John Paul II as a warrior pope, the embodiment of good, against an army of worldly evil. His portrayal of the pope was dualistic, Manichaean. The children of the light understood the source of his supreme authority and were obedient; the children of the darkness doubted.

Referring to the pope's election on October 16, 1978, Bishop Daily said, "Divine Providence forged a thunderbolt and hurled it at our contemporary world—a world that oftimes does not want to hear the truth about good and evil. . . . We cannot help but know that in all our endeavors we truly will be strengthened by his presence and enlightened by his message. For he comes to us, to everyone everywhere, not merely as the 'pilgrim pope.' He is Peter. He is the rock foundation— the holder of the keys of the Church—the shepherd of the whole flock. . . . He stands in place of the Lord Jesus Christ for the Church."

Bishop Daily hailed the Knights for their dedication to the church and expressed confidence that they would help John Paul bring about the "restoration of the church." Though some "criticize or even dare to defame [the pope] and his leadership," Bishop Daily knew the order would not let the pope down or fail to acknowledge his "singularly blessed pontificate."

On the third and final day of the convention, the proposed endorsement of Judge Bork came to the floor along with the rest of the resolutions. There had been some hints that the move to support Bork might be opposed by those who felt that the Knights of Columbus would thereby violate its claim of political neutrality. But no resistance drive took shape, and the resolution sailed through. Its language dressed up the reason for the Knights of Columbus backing, which was predicated solely on his presumed vote to dismantle *Roe,* by couching its endorsement in terms of his being "exceptionally well-qualified for the position, . . . having the

proper judicial temperament, intellectual power and breadth of legal experience."
The Knights urged his speedy approval by the Senate.

Nearly a half dozen other resolutions were concerned with abortion. It was
the issue on the minds of delegates as they departed, though the growing reality
among them was that they would have to be prepared for something less than a
total ban. They should be ready to accept a series of state-legislated restrictions
rather than expect a constitutional ban in the near future. It might be a long, difficult haul, but they were many and strong, and they believed that even the slower
tide was running in their direction.

GILBERT, LOOKING AHEAD TO THE FALL SEMESTER, WAS IMMERSED IN ARISTOTLE,
rereading portions of the ancient Greek's treatises on ethics and philosophy.
Aristotle had nourished Saint Thomas, who ushered in the age of scholasticism
that formed the bedrock of Gilbert's Catholicism.

Summer was Gilbert's time to prepare and to renew himself in the baths fed
by the wellsprings of his faith. Aristotle was among those sources who refreshed
his understanding and reconfirmed his belief that there was but one set of truths
for all humanity.

The Iran-Contra hearings had reminded him how far America had wandered
from any such standard of truth. He heard in the testimony a loud strain of liber-
tarianism—"that there is only process and no content." To Gilbert, the libertarians cared only that individual rights were protected (the "process") and rejected
any concept of universal truth. It was up to each person to form the content of
belief, or live without it.

Gilbert had attended many meetings of traditionally conservative groups at
which libertarians had begun appearing in greater numbers. In many respects,
they shared ideas. Both fought to minimize the role of the state, and both trum-
peted the cause of free enterprise. But on other issues, such as religion, they
tended to part company radically in the groups Gilbert attended and in the influential circles of the Reagan administration. Religion was an especially divisive
issue. Conservatives generally, Gilbert in particular, cherished religion as the cumulative wisdom of the ages and the primary glue of civilization. Libertarians, on
the other hand, had little or no use for any challenge to individual autonomy,
which most forms of organized religion imposed through the exercise of authority (none more obviously than the Catholic church), and were highly skeptical at
best about the existence of fixed religious principles.

The libertarians Gilbert encountered had elevated the right of "conscience" to a
level of sacredness but had changed its traditional meaning. Whereas conscience
had been accountable to the objective dogma of the church, under the libertarians

it meant only that people could use it to legitimize their own subjective belief in anything. "The latest thing," he lamented, "is appeal to conscience as a nondiscussable way of holding any moral view. People use this appeal to cover their moral theories. They don't want it questioned, because they feel they just have a right to hold it—except if you hold a general view that it's all right to beat your wife. Then people say, 'Let's look at it to see if it's a reasonable view or a wrong view.' But they won't do that with other beliefs.

"Within the church, people try this formula—their right to conscience—as a smokescreen so you can't get down to what they're really saying, can't get down to cases. They then believe their views are just as good as the magisterium's and that they're just as free to call themselves Catholics."

From his right-wing redoubt, it was all further evidence of the sorry state into which both church and society had fallen. The Iran-Contra crowd paraded before the microphones and justified breaking the law on the murky grounds of conscience. So did dissenters in the church. Both kinds just sort of made it up as they went along and sanctified it in the name of conscience. There was no more glaring example of this shift than in attitudes toward confession. "In order to go, you had to have some moral certainty," Gilbert said. "But many, perhaps most, people don't think such certainty exists and therefore don't think they sin anymore. We've smudged standards in the church to the point where people don't actually know they're falling short."

That reminded him of another indication of how bad a fix the church was in: the excitement about various polls that purported to take the pulse of Catholics in anticipation of the pope's visit. They showed vast disagreement with church teachings and a growing streak of independence, none of which Gilbert wished to deny or argue with. What he found disturbing was the assumption by many in the media *and the church* that these opinion profiles should be used in a political sense to determine policy. That smacked of the tendency to equate church and America as only different forms of democracy based on egalitarianism and the rule of the majority. "That's not the kind of society the church is," Gilbert said, "and if it ever happened that policy was developed that way, I'm afraid it would be all over."

He continued. "What is the whole point of being a Christian? Isn't it to be holy? How would you know when that's working? Certainly there's no test for it."

As the polls got cranked out, the church got measured in secular terms, he felt, "many seeing it as just another subsidiary society within the state, like the United Nations, modeled along political lines. But that leaves out the extraordinary things—like the way people respond to the pope—which are hard to reduce to a function of polling."

In other respects, Gilbert thought the church was bending too close to the secular realm by confusing its own mission or listening to exaggerated reports.

One alleged example he cited was misuse of the phrase "signs of the times," emphasized by the Second Vatican Council at the inspiration of Pope John XXIII. Certain elements in the church had usurped it for their own purposes by insisting that it meant "that the church should pick up the prevailing winds of the world and go with them. But it seems to me that it was meant to be used to say that the church should analyze the times in order to more effectively preach the gospel."

Gilbert believed that far too much of the erroneous worldliness had fed the bishops' pastoral letters on nuclear war and the economy. "Bishops ought to stand in judgment of the world," he said. "But the last two bishops' pastorals have done the exact opposite by catching hold of big prevailing issues in an effort to gain approval. They got into things that change, that are very evanescent—instead of transcendent things—as though they are endorsing one side in a debate. That trivializes church leadership."

If that development stemmed from a distortion of a key concept, the current uproar over women's place in the church had in Gilbert's estimation been blown totally out of proportion. "The number of women in the church who think there's a problem is minuscule," he said dismissively. "The preponderance don't want to be priests and altar boys. Some say they are abused unless they can participate in decision making. And they want what they now call empowerment. My God, it all sounds like they belong to a corporation. Power in the church? What would that mean?"

His question, of course, was a statement of incredulity. How could anyone mistake the church for just another institution in which ambitious people jostled with one another in the struggle for leadership and policy? How could anyone imagine such a thing? The question might have seemed less of a put-on in someone with far less savvy and practice of church politics than Gilbert (he was an expert sniper in a band of robust guerrillas garbed in orthodoxy). But given his acumen and aplomb, the incredulity toward the women seemed like pure posturing, hinting that he felt much in common with them, as one who, like them, aspired to a greater share of influence. Things were not going his way either, and he was doing his level best, through his speaking, writing, and, yes, politicking, to move things in his direction.

It was in Gilbert's nature to see the church under siege by hostile forces and to minimize the danger. Taking the challenge from women lightly, therefore, was equivalent to according it great seriousness. Likewise, he spoke of the gay "threat" as a monstrous peril while dismissing it as an overstated force that had been exaggerated by the media.

A priest who was a fellow faculty member had committed suicide recently. Rumors circulated immediately thereafter that the priest was an active homosexual. Gilbert, who said he was inclined to believe the rumors, was stung by the incident. He regarded practicing homosexuals as nothing less than "perverts" and favored rooting them out of the faculty. Self-avowed homosexuality exhibited the sin of pride as surely as did theological dissent. Both tried to make virtue out of vice. He had been disturbed by a growing number of reports claiming that the percentage of gay priests was climbing. He scoffed, but he was afraid it might be true. Worse, he envisioned the church's softening its stance against homosexuality in the face of this reality and the pressures within the church to accept it as "a perfectly valid alternative life-style." That would be another victory for subjectivism.

So even during this interlude on the quiet campus, there were many fronts on which Gilbert felt called to struggle in the name of Aristotle, Saint Thomas, and the rest. The new academic year would begin soon. He vowed to continued fighting the good fight. There was refuge in his family, his writing, his tucked-away parish where they celebrated mass as much as they could the old-fashioned way.

He probably wouldn't spend too much time watching the pope on television. He couldn't trust the commercial networks to convey that sublime encounter between pope and people. To counteract all the hype and all the filters, he would have to see the light of faith sparkle in the eyes of those whom the polls seemed to miss. And he knew that the light emanating from those places would catch up with him wherever he was.

━ ━

IN AUGUST, THE BACKSTAGE DIPLOMACY BETWEEN THE VATICAN AND JEWISH leaders aggrieved by the Waldheim incident yielded its first noteworthy results.

On August 4, the pope asked Jewish leaders to meet with him and Vatican officials in Rome later in the month to air their differences. The invitation was extended by Cardinal Jan Willebrands, the official in charge of the Vatican's relations with the Jews, in a phone call to Rabbi Mordecai Waxman in Great Neck, New York, chairman of the International Jewish Committee on Interfaith Consultations, the umbrella organization for dealing with the Vatican. The cardinal assured the rabbi that the meeting would be "substantive," a key word because it promised serious debate beyond polite gestures.

The move satisfied a key demand by Jewish leaders. Since the June 25 reception of Waldheim by John Paul, many prominent Jewish spokesmen had insisted on a face-to-face session with the pope as the essential precondition for attempts to repair frayed relations. For the Jews, only such a personal encounter would allow them adequately to express their anger over Waldheim. For the Vatican, the price for failing to answer the demand might be high. Distrust would most certainly corrode the reserve of goodwill, and many Jewish leaders might carry out their threat to skip the scheduled meeting between Pope John Paul and Jews in Miami. Under those pressures, the Vatican gave the green light. Within a day major Jewish groups had accepted.

The sessions would be held August 31 and September 1. Topics would include the Holocaust, recent eruptions of anti-Semitism, and Vatican policy toward Israel, in addition to the Waldheim visit.

The movement toward allaying Jewish protest and anxiety picked up still greater momentum when a related initiative by the pope came to light eleven days later in the form of a letter from John Paul to the U.S. bishops' conference president, Archbishop John May. The overt purpose of the letter was to thank the archbishop for sending a copy of *Pope John Paul II on Jews and Judaism,* a compendium of papal statements that, fortuitously, had been published jointly by the bishops and the Anti-Defamation League shortly before the Waldheim visit. But the pope used the occasion to express his condemnation of anti-Semitism and the Holocaust, statements obviously meant for public consumption. Describing Jews, as he had done often, affectionately and reverently as "our elder brothers in the faith of Abraham," the pope reiterated his support for the changes in the Catholic-Jewish relationship inaugurated by Vatican II.

He spoke emotionally about how that evolving relationship affected the Church's view of the Holocaust. "With our hearts filled with this unyielding hope, we Christians approach with immense respect the terrifying experience of the extermination, the *Shoah,* suffered by the Jews during World War II, and we seek to grasp its most authentic, specific and universal meaning," the pope said.

"As I said recently in Warsaw, it is precisely by reason of this terrible experience that the nation of Israel, her sufferings and her holocaust are today before the eyes of the Church, of all peoples and of all nations, as a warning, a witness and a silent cry."

Not everyone was rejoicing at this series of Vatican attempts to mollify Jewish outcries. Some Jewish critics were appalled by what they saw as a failure by self-appointed Jewish representatives to stand up to the Vatican over the Waldheim incident. The critics argued that the tightly knit group of interfaith dialogue experts compromised the interests and attitudes of the wider Jewish community by letting the Vatican too easily off the hook.

The meetings in Rome finally took place according to plan and yielded no big surprises. Nine Jewish officials sat down with an equal number of members of the Vatican's Commission on Religious Relations with the Jews for the first round of talks in the office of Cardinal Willebrands, the commission president, on August 31. The discussion began at 9:30 in the morning and ended at 6:30 P.M., with a long break for a kosher meal at midday. Four Jewish leaders had been delegated by their colleagues to each address one of the topics on the agenda: the Holocaust, anti-Semitism, Catholic teachings on Jews and Judaism, and Vatican policy toward Israel.

The exchanges included some strong criticism. On the subject of Catholic attitudes toward the Jews, Rabbi Alexander M. Schindler, president of the Union of American Hebrew Congregations, said in his prepared text that Jews were "pained and puzzled" by several homilies in which "the charge of Jewish responsibility for the death of Christ is revived, Jews are rebuked for their continuing rejection of Christianity's fundamental premise, and the validity of Judaism as a living faith is brought into question." Rabbi Marc Tanenbaum's statement on the Waldheim visit referred to it tartly as the "capstone" of "revisionist tendencies" in the church that "minimize or obscure Jewish martyrdom." In reply to the protest over Waldheim, the Vatican delegation defended the visit on grounds that the charges against the Austrian president had not been proven and that a refusal by the pope to see him would have wrongly implied guilt. For their part, the Vatican representatives complained about the stinging attack after the Waldheim visit by the American Jewish Congress.

Cardinal Willebrands announced during the meetings that his commission had been authorized to prepare a document on the Holocaust, the historical causes of anti-Semitism, and its continuing presence in the modern world. The Waldheim visit had refueled the debate over the adequacy of the resistance against the Nazis by the Vatican in general and Pope Pius XII (accused of "silence" toward the Holocaust by critics) in particular. The prospect that Rome might now produce a rigorous document that included an account of the church's role during that period raised the possibility that new material might be brought to light.

From responses by Jewish leaders at day's end, the chance to be heard seemed to outweigh by far the lack of any progress in resolving key matters. According to the participants, the talks were marked by cordiality, respect, and openness. Cardinal Willebrands said he hoped that the Vatican could maintain closer ties with the Jewish groups, perhaps, though he did not say so explicitly, so that Waldheim-type crises might be avoided in the future.

On the next morning, the delegations paid a call on Cardinal Agostino Casaroli in his office at the Vatican secretariat of state. According to reports, the joint delegations reviewed the scope of the talks with the cardinal.

At the close of that briefing, the Jewish group was whisked fifteen miles away to Castel Gandolfo, the pope's summer retreat, and were seated in a fourth-floor room of the seventeenth-century palazzo. Promptly at noon, Pope John Paul entered the room and shook the hand of each guest using the greeting "shalom" ("peace"). He spoke a prayer in Hebrew; his guests prayed in kind in Latin. John Paul then offered some introductory remarks. From there on, the meeting became truly historic. It was the first time in memory, perhaps ever, that a pope had agreed to an open, spontaneous discussion with Jewish leaders in which there were no formal texts or prewritten speeches. The pope and the Jewish leaders more or less "winged it" for the next hour or so.

The Jews unburdened themselves of the profound anguish among Jews over the Waldheim visit and expounded on the other topics covered the day before. Originally, they had been advised that the Waldheim affair was off-limits, but they later explained that in the end no restrictions had been imposed, a move they saw as a concession. By the same token, the pope was under no obligation to respond to these complaints, and he did not. Participants said he never mentioned the incident or made any sign of apologizing for it.

John Paul did touch on Nazi horrors by reminiscing about his days as a young man in a Poland occupied and terrorized by the Third Reich. He put his enthusiastic personal support to the plan to produce a document on *Shoah,* the Hebrew term for the Holocaust. By all accounts, the session was both intense and warm. At its close, the pope took time to greet them again with his personal remarks and expressions of respect and esteem.

The Jewish leaders emerged pleased with the nature of the talks and confident that they could drop their objections to taking part in the Miami ceremony. They felt that the Vatican had taken them seriously and made significant moves to respond to their grievances. The pope had given something, yet stood his ground. The Jewish leaders had voiced the outrage of their people in full view of the world's media. In the continuing saga of Catholic-Jewish diplomacy, it was sufficient face-saving on both sides to permit the bumpy ride to go ahead.

JUDGE BORK'S LEONINE VISAGE, SAD-EYED AND SCOWLING, HAD BECOME A FIXTURE in the media as the clash over his nomination to the Supreme Court became more furious. Well in advance of the scheduled September 15 start of the Senate Judiciary Committee's confirmation hearings, major liberal and conservative forces, along with politicians, were fighting for and against the nominee. Liberals scorned him as a right-winger intent on letting his politics override constitutional rights. Conservatives hailed him as an upholder of traditional values whose presence on the Court would form a conservative majority to overturn *Roe* v. *Wade* and reverse or stop other liberal moves.

Among the nearly two hundred liberal groups lobbying against Judge Bork were the AFL-CIO, the Leadership Conference on Civil Rights, and producer-director Norman Lear's People for the American Way. Conservative backers of the nominee included the American Conservative Union, Concerned Women for America, National Right to Work Committee, and, of course, the Knights of Columbus.

Organized Catholic campaigning was overwhelmingly pro-Bork for the same reason the Knights of Columbus had backed him. He seemed a good bet to cast the deciding vote against *Roe,* not an absolutely sure thing, maybe, but the next best thing, based on his outspoken disdain for the Court's decision in that case. Though formal Catholic groups worked for President Reagan's choice, individual Catholics were divided. Many prominent church members, among them Senator Edward M. Kennedy, were pushing hard to defeat Judge Bork out of concern for retaining abortion rights and for other issues. Senator Joseph Biden, the Catholic chairman of the Judiciary Committee and a Democratic candidate for president, shed his neutrality early on by vowing to fight the nomination partly on grounds that Judge Bork posed a threat to legal abortion.

Not that the judge's more informed supporters believed he would prove to be a panacea on the abortion question. Even if he did vote to overturn *Roe,* they knew, that would only begin the struggle. A column by Joseph Sobran in the traditionalist *Wanderer* (August 6, 1987) reflected this sober realism, summarizing the thoughts of another conservative writer, George Will. "Even if his presence on the Court helps reverse *Roe v. Wade,*" Sobran wrote, "most states at this point would probably keep abortion legal. After all, many of them fund it. And state courts could also strike down anti-abortion laws" (p. 5). The most Bork could do would be to remove the federal government as a protector of abortion rights.

Though the results of a successful drive to install Judge Bork might be less than ideal to antiabortion activists, it was a cause that seemed well worth the effort, a partial triumph in an area where victories were scarce.

With that energy and outlook, Catholic groups had gone out to campaign for the judge. The vast Knights of Columbus network went into full swing to promote the nomination. "Senators listen to institutions," one state officer of the order remarked, "and on a close vote like this we could make the difference." Petitions were being cranked out, and phone lines hummed. A group called the American Life League took space in the August 27 *Wanderer* to appeal for endorsements of its statement. "Bork's confirmation could not, of itself, stop abortion-on-demand . . . but it's another step in the right direction," the appeal said in part. Summing up, it said, "For the sake of the babies—Help American Life League get Judge Robert H. Bork onto the U.S. Supreme Court" (p. 2).

ON THE HAZY SATURDAY AFTERNOON IN AUGUST, ANTHONY WAS BABYSITTING his two granddaughters, aged two and seven months. He loved his new role as grandpa. Of Anthony and Lynn's three children, all adopted, two were married and on their own. The two grandchildren under Anthony's care were the offspring of one son and his wife. The other daughter-in-law was pregnant. It was all working out as well as Anthony could have hoped, just about everything he imagined that a family could be.

He had returned to the Midwest that week from a business trip to Brussels and London, where he had continued to ride a wave of sudden success. Under his direction, Celestron's gains in the overseas alarm system market were phenomenal: a breathtaking 330 percent over their goal already for the year. Most of that zoom had happened in the astonishingly brief period of nine months, and Anthony's reputation had soared with it. As the executive whose ideas had fueled the growth, he had become the globe-trotting ambassador to foreign outposts, the roving consultant boosting the product in such a way that, as he put it, "when I get done they think it's their idea." The good word about Celestron's alarms "was passing around the world like wildfire," he exulted.

All this activity had launched him into a fast-moving schedule and given him entre into top-management circles. Over lunch Friday, his boss had conveyed a request that he pay a call on the company's operations in Pakistan along with the aside, "You don't know how much you're in demand." Another executive had told him that the product line under Anthony's command "was the most significant thing happening to this business right now."

The flattery would have been enough to swell anyone's ego, but Anthony resisted feelings of cockiness. He was still awestruck that after floating as a relative unknown in the sea of middle management for so many years he had become— nearing age sixty—an overnight sensation, transformed almost magically from status as the class plodder to class genius. But his Catholic upbringing, he insisted, had instilled in him a habit of looking at life as full of ambiguity and paradox, guarding him against illusions of grandeur induced by the elixir of high praise.

"In my work, I'm meeting a lot of big guns, and it would be easy to start thinking you're more important than you are," Anthony mused, "especially when it's been so long in coming. I've never had that trouble before, but I've got to be careful. Things can really get out of perspective if you don't watch it. I always got more recognition outside my home office, in the field, than in it. Now it's coming from everywhere. And now if I say something, people listen. It really is neat. I can feel the difference in these last nine months. Next year should be even bigger."

For balance, he turned to "wife, family, kids, church," not necessarily in that order. There was also a slightly haunting "there but for the grace of God" sensation that helped him keep perspective. "Take those people whose careers are heading downhill," he said, patting the infant to sleep. "It usually has nothing to do with the quality of their work or their ethics. They just drew short straws from somebody above them who just pushes them aside. It's just the way corporate America is. I'm just lucky."

As a reward, he had been offered one of the juiciest plums at Celestron. A group vice president had suggested that the company send Anthony and his wife on a foreign assignment of their choosing. "It would be a golden opportunity to have fun in your last years with the company," the vice president had told him. Once he had coveted such a chance, but, oddly enough, he said, it held no appeal at the moment, largely because of the couple's desire to stay close to the family. He politely declined the offer.

The decision to remain at company headquarters, though less exciting, perhaps, did keep him in the running for one final promotion, something that only a year before would have seemed impossible. His heart was not set on getting the job, he insisted, but recent events had stoked the old fires of competition within him. He would watch with one eye, he guessed, while trying to look unconcerned.

Sticking to the midwestern city where he had grown up and the company where he had spent his whole working life also meant persisting in his loving fight with his parish. The whippersnapper of a new pastor, with his Vatican II theology that made Anthony edgy, would never replace the pastor Anthony had revered for his refusal to cotton to the new ways. Anthony had been forced into a crisis of whether or not to remain in the parish and swallow the bitter pill, a move unthinkable in the days of his youth, when parish-shopping was unheard of. So over the past few months, Anthony had agonized. He had gone from wanting to quit to hanging in there out of a sense of duty to resolving to outlast the whippersnapper.

"The way he does things, the way he is, is more than painful," Anthony blustered. "It makes me so damned mad I'm going to stay, attend his going away coffee, and tell him I'm glad he's leaving."

And while he was on the subject of the trip, he had a few thoughts on the pope's upcoming U.S. visit. As a traveling man himself with loads of experience in a corporation, albeit not the size of the Roman Catholic church, he had drawn some comparative observations. In his corporation, he said, the top brass made a concerted effort to go around visiting and consulting with the troops in the field, a strategy not unlike the pope's travels to the far corners of the earth to see his people. The difference, he thought, was that the corporation executives "tried to find out what the lower echelon executives were thinking in order to make things better," whereas the pope did the talking and didn't seem to solicit advice. Instead, as Anthony saw it, John Paul was "making the rounds of the branch offices trying to reinforce the rules and increase control."

Though hugely respectful of the papacy, Anthony did not regard the pope's method as a sound style of management. "I don't know if he's a delegator—at least I don't think he's a Reagan-style delegator whose advisers tell him what to do.

He appears instead to be rather autocratic. No, he's probably no delegator. And I don't know that he has tried to solve problems but keeps wanting to reinforce those rules.

"People in the church have been telling the Vatican for a long time that they should have married priests and birth control and other things," he continued. "Maybe they're listening, but they're shutting their eyes to the problems."

What it came down to, Anthony surmised, was that "the church doesn't have any competition. Corporations change because of competition."

But from another place in himself, Anthony wanted to be in the crowd as John Paul made his way across America. The pope was for him "an esteemed person," the chief priest of the church that had brought him through the tough early days and helped propel him to the future that was now panning out so gloriously. He wanted to see the pope respond to the expected protests—he anticipated John Paul handling them deftly. He would have liked to be in that number. But while the pope journeyed across this land, Anthony himself would be on assignment in a faraway country.

"Although the voices of women are being heard in a significant way for the first time in both church and culture," wrote Professor Francine Cardman of the Weston School of Theology in the summer issue of *Church,* "there is still much more to be said and many more women to be heard from" (p. 53).

That observation, at the conclusion of Professor Cardman's survey of feminist theology, suggested both progress and restiveness. The beginnings of the movement, auspicious as they were, she implied, should not obscure the long journey that lay ahead.

Scholars whose ground-breaking work had placed them in the vanguard of feminist theology and spirituality figured prominently in the analysis by Cardman, who, in addition to teaching at Weston, was active in the Women's Theological Center in Boston. Among these leading scholars: Carolyn Osiek, Sandra Schneiders, Mary Jo Weaver, Charlene Spretnak, Phyllis Trible, Elisabeth Schüssler Fiorenza, Barbara Wildung Harrison, and Rosemary Radford Reuther.

Many of the writings by these authors, while grounded in Western Christianity, were not confined or limited by it. A notable feature of feminist theology was its eclecticism, its tendency to reach beyond the classical church disciplines to realms of non-Christian and nonrational experience. Not only were these scholars attempting to unmask the distortions imposed by male progenitors of religious tradition, they were pointing the way to new forms of spiritual experience, inviting women to participate in their own spiritual quest, sometimes, as in the case of the

"Women-Church" movement, apart from men. Theology and practice increasingly fed each other: scholars providing the intellectual grounding, and worshipers creating settings where those insights found resonance within a larger framework of faith communities.

Cardman's overview of feminist scholarship with regard to the church, spirituality, Scripture, theology, and ethics witnessed to the growing body of knowledge and theory that was undergirding the movement and inspiring further efforts at research and creativity. It was clear that the foundation was being built.

Meanwhile, the Catholic hierarchy was attempting to placate the increasing discontent among women in the church who saw outright sexism in certain ecclesiastical attitudes and practices. In good "pastoral" fashion, bishops collectively and a few individually had initiated open hearings to give some women the opportunity to express their opinions on a broad range of church issues. In 1983, the bishops voted to begin the process of writing a pastoral letter on women, against the advice of many leading Catholic feminists. The problem as the feminists saw it, in addition to their refusal to accept such a document written solely by men, was that the bishops could only go ahead with such a project with their hands tied. There was no way they could respond freely to a sincere study of ordination for women, which was the largest symbolic issue at hand, at least. They were under prior restraint, bound to uphold Rome's total ban on women clergy and several less obvious defined policies. But the bishops had forged on ahead, weighing the potential damage against the need to do something to allay the protest by women.

Looking ahead to the pastoral letter, several localities across Catholic America established sounding boards for the concerns of women, among them the Archdiocese of Los Angeles. In 1985, under Cardinal Timothy Manning, more than twenty-five hundred women in the archdiocese met to voice their thoughts and specify their complaints. It fell to the new head of the archdiocese, Archbishop Roger Mahony, to place those exchanges in his own perspective.

He did so by issuing a pastoral letter to Los Angeles Catholics on August 14. In his introduction, he struck a conciliatory note, conceding that "all too often in our Christian history men have been slow to listen to what women have been saying." Women in the hearings had expressed gratitude for aspects of the church, he wrote, "but they added that at times many still experienced alienation and rejection in the church."

From there, he got specific:

1. Certain groups of women still experience alienation in a particularly acute manner: divorced women, single mothers, single women and those who have had less opportunity for education. Many of the women in these groups feel that there is no place for them in the church.

2. Women in professional groups lament the rejection of their gifts, especially gifts for leadership. Professional counselors, educators, administrators, health care professionals and business executives too often encounter a patronizing and, indeed, authoritarian resistance in some of their parishes where they suggest ways in which their gifts might be used for the welfare of the community. These professional women sense a widespread exclusion of women from policy-making positions in the church.

3. Many women still find that some clergy view them with suspicion and fear. They find that the cultural stereotypes of women prevent honest communication and mutual respect between themselves and some of their parish priests. The latter at times seem to project a patriarchal attitude and are unable to treat women as ministerial colleagues.

4. Many women continue to feel oppressed by a system of church laws which has been created by men through a process in which women have had no decisive role. They are confused by and often resent certain rules and practices governing annulments and the lack of a clear and understandable distinction between important beliefs and practices in the church.

5. In many cases, liturgical roles not reserved to the ordained have not easily or graciously opened to women. This and the exclusion of women from lesser liturgical roles such as that of altar server as well as the exclusive use of "sexist" language still prevalent in liturgy make public worship for some women a painful experience of alienation rather than a joyous and freeing experience of salvation.

The archbishop then offered some prescriptions, noting that "we need to recognize that cultural changes have brought both society and church to a new recognition of the equality of men and women, and that this recognition must find new expression in our ecclesial life."

One priority would be to eliminate "what has come to be called 'exclusive' or 'sexist' language." Archbishop Mahony recommended that "all of the church's official prayer books, liturgical books and rituals be reviewed with the goal of maximizing inclusive language," lest some women be left to "wonder whether the fullness of salvation is really theirs if the language does not include them." He criticized those who were "inclined to trivialize the issue because, in their minds, these are 'only words.'" Inclusive language should be used increasingly to reflect sensitivity toward women.

The other major proposal was to encourage women to enter the ministries of the church, especially those opened by Vatican II in parishes and dioceses. "We need to recover a greater sense of men and women working collaboratively, side by side," the archbishop wrote. "Women must increasingly be placed in policy-formation and decision-making levels within the church." Such positions included chancellors of dioceses, seminary professors, editors of diocesan newspapers, directors of diocesan family life, and pastoral ministers.

In conclusion, Archbishop Mahony acknowledged the tension over the roles of women as one of several crucial problems in the church that must be honestly faced. And without alluding directly to groups such as "Women-Church" with separatist leanings, he appealed for unity and warned the clergy to curb sexist ways. "It would be tragic for any group, impatient for change, to split off and attempt to form its own church," the archbishop said, on the one hand. And on the other, "It is equally tragic for the pastors and bishops of the church not to listen to the prophetic voices which speak with such good will. That is why the voices of women in the church must be heard."

Though the pastoral letter's call for ending sexist language and bringing more women into church decisions received much favorable comment, an icy blast blew from the *Wanderer.* Archbishop Mahony, an ally of the Catholic right on some issues, found himself the object of polite scorn for his words on women. The problem, wrote Frank Morriss in a muted attack in the September 10 issue, was that the archbishop, perhaps inadvertently, had given credibility to the charges against the church by women, therefore "indirectly accepts those complaints and recognizes them as having substance." Behind these moves was a grab for ordination, Morriss feared. The archbishop's letter at worst suggested "that the Church will and should conclude that things are just as these women say, and that we should accept their testimony and act upon their suggestions."

THE BEST-KNOWN WOMAN RELIGIOUS ON EARTH, MOTHER TERESA, HAD FINISHED her meeting with her order's superiors earlier in the month and paid a visit to Scranton, Pennsylvania, on Sunday, August 16. There, as everywhere she traveled, throngs mobbed her, hailing her as a saint-to-be and clinging to her every word. As it turned out, the former seat of a coal mining empire in northeast Pennsylvania would be a jumping-off point for her first journey to the Soviet Union. She would leave Scranton for New York, Rome, and Moscow, arriving there on Thursday if plans held. Her declared mission was to win permission from Soviet authorities for her order to establish a facility near Chernobyl to care for victims of the nuclear disaster.

The tiny, wrinkled founder of the Missionaries of Charity had been crisscrossing Catholic America frequently in recent years, elevated to heightened prominence by a Nobel Peace Prize in 1979 and growing adulation within the church as a holy figure who displayed extraordinary care for the poor and dying. Among Catholics in the United States, she struck deep chords.

Perhaps to most, including many bishops, she exemplified a fading ideal, combining simple loyalty to church authority and dogma with surpassing personal compassion. A variation on that theme was that she was a badly needed reminder of self-giving to a society in which self-seeking was supreme. In that sense, she was a visible challenge to do what "looking out for number one" American culture increasingly dismissed as quaint at best, lunacy at worst. To some, Mother Teresa was a strangely welcome, if stylized, reminder of things they were not prepared to do. They were glad someone was still keeping the flame of sacrificial charity alive.

And wittingly or not, the seventy-six-year-old nun had become a factor on the American political scene and in the skirmishes between the right and left wings of the church. Her presence at antiabortion rallies and her remarks in support of total allegiance to the pope and church teaching set a powerful example. She was much in demand among Rome's staunchest allies in their struggle against "Americanism," though she stoutly denied taking sides herself either theologically or politically.

The Scranton stop, her only speaking date on her current trip, had been designed as a display of support for Pope John Paul II, particularly his firm defense of the church's ban on women priests. A school secretary in the Diocese of Scranton, Mary Dorothy Walsh, had set the wheels in motion by pursuing an invitation through a letter to Mother Teresa at her center in Calcutta. Fulfillment came to the woman in Scranton eighteen months later when the nun in the white sari with blue trim actually arrived.

Her three-hour visit began with a short news conference where she sketched hopes for her Soviet trip. Her order wanted to offer "tender loving care" to those suffering from nuclear contamination. Asked about women priests, she said, "No one has been a better priest than our Lady. The role that a woman has no man can fill. Every woman has something special." On the duty of the well-heeled in the United States to help the poor, "I find many rich people speak to the poor. It is a great change, there is great concern. There are many, many poor people here in the U.S. You don't see it so clearly as you do in Africa. There is much to do." On her most joyful achievement: "I have helped hundreds of people, made many people feel wanted and loved, who would have died unwanted and unloved."

Then came a ceremony at the University of Scranton where, in a ritual at once understandable and improbable, she received an honorary doctorate in social science. Her speech was twenty-one minutes long and focused on abortion and loyalty to the pope. "Abortion has become the greatest destroyer of love, the greatest destroyer of peace," she declared. She urged those with unwanted pregnancies to give the children to her missions. "I want that child. Don't destroy it," she pleaded. She also observed, "Homelessness is not only not having a home made of bricks, homelessness is being unwanted and unloved." On her way out of the auditorium crammed with four thousand cheering admirers, she handed religious medallions to two boys, Tommy Gaylord, seven, and his brother, Timothy, five, both victims of muscular dystrophy. Her message was bright as the shining day.

WITH THE POPE'S VISIT IN THE OFFING, SUMMER WAS BUSIER THAN USUAL FOR most of the bishops. Though Bishop Sawicki's diocese lay far from John Paul's route, he was called upon to give his share of support to the venture. He did not envy the host bishops. For all the honor the visit brought, he explained, the headaches were enormous and the benefits marginal at best. If to him it was a decidedly mixed blessing, he noted how some others of his brethren, convinced that the advantages far outweighed the liabilities, had campaigned hard to win the privilege. To him, there was no simple accounting for such hierarchical differences.

Like most people, the good-natured, ruddy-faced bishop marveled at the pope's stamina in embarking on these world ventures. He remembered well John Paul's first whirlwind trip to the United States in 1979. In the interim, he knew that the pope's advisers had lobbied for shorter trips and fewer, briefer speeches ("They're too long for anyone to listen," Bishop Sawicki concurred). But John Paul had shrugged off such counsel, maintaining his bone-wearying schedules and delivering his encyclopedic talks.

At the one stop Bishop Sawicki planned to attend in person, the pope's meeting with the U.S. hierarchy in Los Angeles, the format would be strikingly different from that followed on the earlier trip. The adjustment had been made in part to erase a snub.

"Back in '79," the bishop recalled, "we [bishops] were supposed to meet him at 8:30 in the morning, and he never showed until 11:30. Then he read his speech, went out to eat lunch, then went to mass. There was no chance to talk to him. This time we selected four speakers among our members and had a hand in choosing the topics they would speak to him about. It's very good for the people we serve to be aware that we do tell the pope what our people feel."

He hoped the pope would listen to his brother bishops, but he knew there was no way of ensuring that. Bishop Sawicki sized up John Paul as a loving man who could be tough to please and impossible to budge. This quality of compassionate sternness could jolt the bulk of Americans, who seemed to hanker after approval, the bishop felt, and contribute to a misunderstanding of the pope's message. That distortion sprang especially, he thought, from John Paul's orthodoxy and its implicit criticism of so much about the behavior of Catholic America.

"There is the impression, unfortunately, among some American Catholics and non-Catholics that the Catholic church here is deficient because it doesn't measure up to the ideals the pope enunciates," Bishop Sawicki said. "There is an uneasiness Catholics experience from him because he seems not satisfied with us. In fact, he's not satisfied with anybody." He added with a chuckle, "We don't, needless to say, get a perfect report card."

The bishops were no more immune from this critique than anybody else, he noted. They might get to speak their piece, but they would more likely hear some sour notes in return. Otherwise, he didn't expect the pope's return engagement to kick up as much excitement as the first ("not as novel"), and he forecast "short-term interest" in it inside and outside the church.

Polls on beliefs and practices of Catholic Americans were popping up all over the media to dramatize the pope's trip. All in all, Bishop Sawicki considered them accurate and useful. "It helps us to see ourselves better," he said. "I saw a quote from another bishop that called them biased. I disagree with that. It's a defensible sociological device we can use to good benefit. Take the surveys of clergy, for example. The clergy I meet with don't say, 'We're not like that.' We have to minister to that reality."

He did think too much was made of "dissent" reported among Catholics. To Bishop Sawicki it was a misnomer. Technically speaking, he said, most Catholics who were described that way actually broke laws they *agreed* with rather than formulated alternative, or dissenting, positions. "People we serve may disobey, but they don't dissent," he said. "They are disobeying the teachings and see themselves that way. To dissent means that learned persons in the church have thought and talked about noninfallible teachings and say they have difficulty accepting them."

The events on the national church stage had preoccupied the bishop during these weeks, but he remained cheerfully detached, resonant with an awareness of transience, attendant to the things close at hand. He was, in fact, more absorbed by a particular challenge at his door, that of enabling laypeople to "live out their faith life in home, office, and so on."

He had been inspired by the Chicago Call to Action conference the previous fall that urged laypeople to develop and refine theology of their own experience rather than look primarily to the church to provide them institutional ministries such as membership on parish councils or service as eucharistic ministers. It was at home or on the job that the real work of inculcating faith was done. Here the laity had to help themselves. Clergy knew next to nothing about it.

His own ministry remained highly personal and had attained an unusual degree of credibility. One recent incident was illustrative. A couple of days before, he had read an op-ed piece in the local newspaper that had taken him to task for his views concerning the city's economic disarray. Bishop Sawicki had been impressed with the quality of the piece. He dropped the man a note inviting him to call to talk about their differences. The man had called.

OFFICIAL PREPARATIONS FOR OCTOBER'S SYNOD ON THE LAITY HAD BEEN wrapped up in June at a closed-door symposium at Saint Mary's College in Indiana. That was not quite the end of it, however.

A loud footnote was sounded in the August 20 issue of the *Wanderer.* On page one, under Gary Potter's byline, began a lengthy article allegedly based on a fourteen-page personal report on the Saint Mary's meeting by a disgruntled participant identified only as an "orthodox theologian" (p. 1). According to Potter, the unnamed theologian's account proved that an elite clique at the bishops' conference had rigged both the process of synod consultation and its outcome by excluding "orthodox" voices such as his own. The more sensational hook was a comment attributed to Archbishop Weakland during the symposium that denounced the right-wing *Wanderer* as "vicious people."

Potter explained that the insider's account had been written as a letter to friends of the unidentified theologian and insisted that neither the *Wanderer* "as such or this writer [had] been in contact with him concerning the document" (p. 1). The name of the letter writer was easy to detect, given the evidence within the letter itself. It was Professor Germain Grisez of Mount Saint Mary's College, a widely known conservative writer and one of the select group invited to take part. Subsequently, Grisez acknowledged that the newspaper had never asked his permission to publish his account nor had a third party been authorized to act in his name. It had been leaked evidently by someone who believed that Grisez's version of the Saint Mary's meeting would help blow the cover off a liberal conspiracy.

In Potter's hands, the letter confirmed many suspicions. Among them: that the bishops had become putty in the grip of church bureaucrats intent on undermining Catholic morals and doctrine; that radical feminists were making headway in their drive for the ordination of women; that subjectivism and relativism were gaining ground against objective truth; that top church officials were disloyal to Rome. The synod consultations had been carefully designed to exclude disagreement, it was alleged, and to funnel responses into predetermined molds. From that standpoint, the whole process had been fixed.

"Now," read a section cited by Potter from Grisez's letter, "consultation is being used in a very different way, to provide a *pseudo-sensus-fidelium* justification for positions which either do not pertain to the Church's teaching at all or are at odds with it. Obviously, any consultation, even if conducted in the fairest possible way, will elicit much more from activists than from other segments of the faithful. So the sample is hardly representative and, in addition, minority contributions are being treated as if they expressed the mind of the faithful at large. Rigged like this, consultation is a manipulative device for those who control the process" (p. 8). The entire Saint Mary's symposium, Grisez was quoted as saying, "actually was constructed to make it seem that more people were contributing than really were, and to make the views of the organizers seem to come from a larger group than they did."

The *Wanderer* article also included other provocative tidbits that Potter allegedly excerpted from the letter. For example, Cardinal Bernardin was said to have told the theologian that synods of bishops hadn't achieved much and that "the Church is really granting divorces but not admitting it, and that most of the people and priests don't accept the teaching on contraception" (p. 9).

In keeping with its reputation, the *Wanderer* had seized upon *some* facts and *some* evidence as a pretext for rehearsing bitter attacks against those who strayed from its notions of orthodoxy. With regard to the synod, the newspaper's avid followers were not alone, of course, in feeling like outsiders to the consultation process. Many on the left had complained as well that the synod consultation had precluded them and their causes. Such had been the dilemma of synod officials: how to structure discussion to keep it within realistic boundaries. Exposure of the Grisez letter was only the latest, and perhaps last, exercise in frustration to emerge from the process.

Grisez, his private musings made public by a right-wing partisan newspaper, now had another grievance, which he made known in a letter to *Wanderer* editor Al Matt, Jr. The fourteen-page missive was never intended for publication, he insisted. It "was not, did not pretend to be a scholarly work. It was, rather, like diary entries which I wished to share with friends—an expression of my impressions, reactions, observations, and reflections—hastily written shortly after an emotionally draining experience and tiring trip home." He did not challenge the accuracy of the quotes from the letter, but added that its informal character could have resulted in "more or less serious misunderstandings and factual misstatements" (he did not point out examples). Certainly he "would never have published the letter as I sent it to friends," he wrote, "for to do so would have been reckless about the truth concerning very important matters and several people's reputations."

Farther along, he continued in the same vein: "Again, even insofar as what you published of my letter communicates some truth to your readers, it nevertheless harms the reputations of several participants of the meeting. In writing my friends, who regularly move about in academic and/or ecclesiastical circles, I foresaw little harm to anyone's reputation, and I believed there was a just cause to accept this slight harm."

The *Wanderer* had thus contributed to this character assault, Grisez asserted, and violated the confidentiality that participants had a right to expect. The newspaper had "published substantial parts of what I wrote about the meeting although its private character was obvious." The usual arguments thrown up by secular media in defense of their decisions to print confidential materials—principally the public's "right to know"—did not stand up under these conditions in a nondemocratic church, Grisez contended.

Not the least of his grievances was that the letter's publication had been a blow to his good name. "You also have wronged me," Grisez wrote. "My relationship with bishops and people who work for them, including those who participated in the symposium, is of great value to me, not in the view of some selfish interest, but precisely in view of my commitment to be an orthodox theologian. I cannot serve the Church by making some contribution to the study and teaching of the bishops or the Holy See unless I deserve their respect and trust. Your wrongful publication of substantial parts of my letter has gravely damaged my respectability and trustworthiness."

The *Wanderer* did not print the letter, nor, according to Grisez, did he receive any kind of reply.

ON AUGUST 22, HUNDREDS OF THE FAITHFUL ARRIVED AT BLESSED SACRAMENT chapel of the national shrine of the Blue Army, otherwise known as the World Apostolate of Fátima, to celebrate the Feast of the Queenship of Mary.

The shrine was set in hilly country amid dairy farms and thick groves of trees interspersed with modest wood-framed dwellings. An apron of rich green turf dotted with buildings sloped gently upward to a flat crest on which stood an eye-catching structure with pleated roof and sharply pointed peak that resembled a leprechaun's hat.

The chapel roof, which looked from afar like the folded brim of the hat, symbolized the mantle of Mary covering and protecting her children. From it rose the four-sided tower topped by a crown that stood for Mary's queenship. Atop the entire structure was the statue of the Virgin herself.

The location of the shrine, tucked away in a forest off the beaten trail, both preserved it in a state of serenity and symbolized the organization's place at the fringes of mainstream Catholic America. Its enthusiasms, though earnest, solemn, and deeply reverential, bespoke pieties either never learned or long forgotten by most Catholics across the nation.

For decades, the recruits to this army had been pursuing a special assignment that they believed had been imparted to them in a series of appearances by the Virgin Mary to three shepherd children near Fátima, Portugal, in 1917. The focus of that mission was the conversion of Russia. An account of Mary's message made public years later by Sister Mary Lucy, the only one of the three children to survive childhood, contained this apocalyptic mandate:

"If my wishes are fulfilled, Russia will be converted, and there will be peace; if not, then Russia will spread her errors throughout the world, bringing new wars and persecutions of the Church; the good will be martyred and the Holy Father will have much to suffer: certain nations will be annihilated, but in the end, my Immaculate Heart will triumph. The Holy Father will consecrate Russia to me, and she will be converted, and the world will enjoy a period of peace."

To help avert disaster and assure a happy outcome, Sister Mary Lucy reported that Mary had instructed her followers to perform certain acts of devotion. Not only would these acts of piety hasten the conversion of Russia, it was claimed, but they earned the penitent means by which they could obtain the "Sabbatine Privilege," quick release from purgatory after death.

Fulfilling the requirements entailed a few central practices. One was praying the rosary daily. Another was observing chastity appropriate to the single or married state. A third was wearing of the scapular, a religious article consisting of two patches of brown cloth, each about half the size of a credit card, connected by two strings and worn over the shoulders, one piece hanging down the front of the body, the other down the back. It was a scaled-down, abstracted version of the centerpiece of a Carmelite monk's habit and was worn beneath outer garments. To be effective, the scapular had to be blessed by a priest or qualified layperson. The person was then "enrolled."

Members were also expected to participate in a series of devotions on the first Saturdays of five consecutive months ("The First Saturday" regimen as it had become known) and to perform daily acts of sacrifice for the sins of the world. The Blue Army claimed that the Virgin's challenge had been taken up by some 5 million Catholic Americans, 25 million Catholics worldwide, though exact figures were impossible to come by.

The army's passion for converting Russia was, quite understandably, inextricably bound up with virulent anticommunism. Within Blue Army tradition, utter disdain for Marx had quickly become the flip side of devotion to Mary. The combined theme became the army's trademark and a powerful rallying cry for many Catholics in the darkest period of the cold war following World War II. Though Pope Pius XII had given the cult the papal blessing in 1942, church leaders in recent decades (with the exception of some of the most conservative bishops) generally had paid little attention to it, treating it more like an eccentric, even fanatical, relative than a close member of the family. At the same time, however, the shrine at Fátima had remained a popular center of spiritual renewal.

All the sharp edges of the Blue Army's crusade could be found in its literature, but in reality the gatherings of loyalists took on a musty, anachronistic air of ceremonies belonging to a dim past shrouded in mystery and hints of Armageddon.

Blessed Sacrament chapel, the focal point of the shrine, was a striking nod to modernity in a pristine setting governed by tradition. Other buildings on the grounds included an exact replica of the chapel at Fátima and "Holy House," whose dimensions were said to match those of the home where Joseph, Mary, and Jesus lived. Flower gardens displayed thick clusters of daisies, carnations, marigolds, zinnias, mums, and roses. Overhead the sky was cloudy and the air sultry.

Two hundred people, nearly all older women in black mantillas, moved slowly behind a statue of Mary borne by four men in dark suits, a priest and two acolytes. As their line made its way around the grounds toward Blessed Sacrament chapel, they sang "Ave, Ave Maria," the Fátima Ave, and lovingly fingered rosary beads;

many of them looked transfixed. Through a loudspeaker system, the rosary was being recited to all corners of the shrine.

The procession took its purposeful time, eventually reaching its destination, where dozens of others had arrived for the program. They were there to celebrate a style of Mariology that was coincidentally a statement about their attachment to an older theology of the miraculous bordering on the magical. To show respect, they were expected to abide by a dress code: no shorts for men, women, or children, no sundresses, no halters, no low-cut dresses, mandatory shirts and shoes. A woman with a V-back dress was brought a white shawl by a nun to cover up.

John M. Haffert, the cofounder of the Blue Army, welcomed them. "A queen has rights over her subjects," he reminded them. He told of a miracle by which Mary had once spared Rome the plague. He exhorted them to give Mary special honor during the Marian year, quoting Pius XII's words that devotion to her was "the best hope for peace."

He introduced Bishop George W. Ahr, retired bishop of Trenton, a tried-and-true friend of the army, with a backhanded compliment. "There'll be no eulogies, no great biographies for Bishop Ahr," Haffert said, "but he has a monument in our hearts." Bishop Ahr took over, first placing a blue cape over the head of the statue of the Virgin, then topping it with a gold crown. The army was consecrated to her Immaculate Heart.

In his homily during the mass, the Reverend Roger Mary Charest, managing editor of *Queen* magazine, portrayed the significance of the feast day in the images of royalty. It was all in Scripture, he told his listeners. "The Kingdom of Christ is in the heart of every human being," he said. "If Christ is King, Mary is Queen in her own restricted way . . . they have the right over our minds as well as our hearts."

Submission of mind and heart to the Sacred Heart of Jesus and the Immaculate Heart of Mary was the true meaning of consecration, he continued, as a roar of thunder rolled across the sky. His voice rose a level in intensity as he declared, "The Blue Army is fighting spiritual warfare against the powers of evil."

There were prayers for the pope's upcoming trip to the United States, for Mother Teresa's visit to Russia, and for the Marian year. After communion, the statue was processed through the chapel, the way strewn with flower petals. The Blue Army pledge was recited, and those receiving scapulars were duly invested. From every vantage point, the army's appeals struck the eye in messages spelled out boldly in banners: "Jesus Wants to Use You." "Obedience." "Wear the Scapular." "Say the Rosary."

WITH THE POPE'S PASTORAL VISIT AT HAND, THE NEWS MEDIA WERE BUSY WORKING up special reports on the state of Catholic America that became forecasts of what John Paul was likely to find. These "curtain raisers," as they were sometimes called, dwelt largely on tensions between Rome and U.S. Catholicism, building an aura of suspense that would presumably keep many people glued to their newspapers, radios, and television sets from the moment the pontiff set foot in Miami.

Even before the final deluge of articles and documentaries had been unloaded onto the public, Archbishop May sent a clear signal that, as president of the bishops' conference, he thought things had gotten just a little out of hand. In a statement issued August 11, the archbishop indicated his considerable annoyance with the hype and the focus on dissent. Apparently smarting from several notions making the rounds, he wanted to set some things straight.

First of all, he said, claims that interest in the trip was sluggish and disappointing were ill founded. Requests for tickets to papal events and for media passes had, in fact, equaled or surpassed the volume before John Paul's first trip. "Anyone who imagined that the 1979 visit had taken the edge off the 1987 visit," he asserted, "was mistaken."

Further, all the attention on doodads and protest groups (like gays and advocates of women's ordination) threatened to obscure the real meaning of the trip. "I have no quarrel with stories about souvenirs and the other trivia associated with the papal visit," the archbishop insisted. "I realize that minutiae have a fascination of their own. And I am not surprised by, even if I don't exactly welcome, the evidence that various special interest groups have decided to use the visit to call attention to their particular grievances. . . .

"I hope, though, that fascination with trivia and interest in the slant that third parties wish to give the visit won't entirely distract attention from what the visit is all about."

As he understood it, the purpose of the visit was fourfold. For one thing, it was "a pastoral visit to Catholics," no matter how much it might also serve the needs of other Americans. Closely related was the objective of manifesting the "essential unity of American Catholics with one another and with the Holy Father."

He added, with a defensive edge, "You will remind me of course that there are many conflicts among Catholics in this country as well as tensions between some elements of the Church here and the Holy See. No doubt that's true. In the Roman Catholic system, however, the papacy is a vital and irreplaceable principle of unity among all the elements and members of the Church. Pope John Paul's presence among us will make that principle visible and operative in an especially dramatic, welcome way."

The visit would also give Catholics an opportunity to "affirm their religious identity" and to explore what it meant to "believe like a Catholic and to live like a Catholic—in a wealthy, consumerist, nuclear-armed, secularized country like this one in 1987," Archbishop May said. There was a "certain amount of confusion" over that, he said. Finally, the trip was "extremely important" to Catholic

America, the archbishop said, much more significant "than the news of trivia and the agendas of special interest groups would suggest."

But even as Archbishop May tried to refocus attention toward more positive concerns, news organizations were putting final touches on results of surveys and field reports that pointed in far less cheering directions. In late August and early September the media would unfurl its analysis of Catholic America, which, reduced to a single word, read "crisis."

A three-part series in the Detroit *Free Press* (August 16, 24, 30), based on a Gallup Poll of Michigan laypeople, priests, and religious, reflected elements common to other regional and national surveys of Catholics. Among the findings: the pope was immensely popular and highly regarded as a spiritual leader (upwards of 90 percent responded so); at the same time, about three-fourths rejected the church's ban on artificial birth control (79 percent) and its bar against allowing divorced members to remarry (74 percent); and smaller but substantial majorities favored married clergy (56 percent), women priests (54 percent), and non-Catholics being admitted to communion in Catholic churches (54 percent). The pattern was now increasingly familiar. American Catholics loved the church and its hierarchy on their own selective terms, affirming its central theological convictions but making up their own minds about those issues about which they felt some personal competence. Increasingly, they were stepping out of line on issues such as divorce and birth control without feeling that it made them "bad" Catholics.

Other surveys highlighted particular aspects of this disposition. A Yankelovich Clancy Shulman poll for *Time* (published in its September 7 issue) found, for example, that 93 percent believed "it is possible to disagree with the pope and still be a good Catholic." Slightly more than half (53 percent) thought the pope infallible when speaking on dogmas such as Christ's divinity but only 37 percent when ruling on morality. An unusually comprehensive survey by Gallup for the *National Catholic Reporter*, reported in its September 11 edition, expanded on other studies in several notable directions. One was to document the deep longing among laity (nearly 70 percent of whom said they would never consider leaving the church under almost any condition) for a greater role in church decision making, especially on the parish level (including how money was spent and choice of parish priests). Another was to show how relatively few Catholics said they had even heard of the bishops' highly publicized pastoral letters on nuclear arms (29 percent) and the economy (25 percent).

NBC packaged this widely accepted view of Catholic America in a special, "God Is Not Elected," hosted by Maria Shriver and broadcast the evening of August 25. Much of the hour-long report explored sources of friction among American Catholics resulting from church teachings on homosexuality, *in vitro* fertilization, divorce, contraception, and other matters. Bishops were given time to make brief responses, but the shape of the program made their task well-nigh impossible.

Sparks flew from the Catholic right. A reaction from conservative columnist Joseph Sobran was printed in the September 10 *Wanderer*. Sobran called Shriver's account "an inane attack on the Pope." He was "embarrassed," he said, that the "scion of America's most famous Catholic family [the daughter of Eunice Kennedy and Sargent Shriver and the niece of President John F. Kennedy] should display such utter incomprehension of her; and my, religion." Doctrines were true no matter what Catholics thought about them, he declared. Rather than being chastised for refusing to conform to worldly ways, Sobran submitted, the pope should be applauded. "The glory of the Catholic Church," he wrote, "is that it has always managed to stay behind the times" (p. 4).

Likewise, the gadfly pamphlet *eye* (August 21) predicted triumphantly that the pope would stick to his guns. "The Pope will soon make his long-awaited second U.S. tour," wrote the editor, John McFadden. "This time, he is unwelcome to many. Gays. Feminists and (alas) Jews chief among them. So be it." Though hounded by calls for changes in church teaching, McFadden was certain John Paul would not budge. He wrote, "Our pilgrim Pope wills to *redeem* the times, not appease them. He may fail, but he's right: appeasement won't *work*."

One person's sacred tradition was another's heresy. There were those who saw "signs of the times" as corruptions and threats; others who saw them as beckonings of the Holy Spirit. For their part, the small cadres of agitators who understood their mission as awakening the church to its true purposes of liberation were preparing to take to the streets with their campaigns while the pope made his way across America.

A day after the NBC broadcast, about a hundred protesters marched on the Vatican embassy in Washington to voice their objections to church policies that in their view harmed women. Several carried a banner bearing the inscription: "A Message to the Pope—Women's Rights Are Human Rights." Twelve, including Eleanor Smeal, former president of the National Organization for Women, and Frances Kissling, president of Catholics for a Free Choice, were arrested for demonstrating inside five hundred feet of the embassy while delivering a basket of protest statements to the door.

At the sites where John Paul would appear, the uncompleted details of preparation seemed endless. San Antonio presented perhaps the most troublesome set of problems. An outdoor mass was expected to draw half a million people to a treeless stretch of land where they were threatened by scorching heat and inadequate supplies of water. Recently the city's health commissioner, Dr. Katherine Rathburn, had resigned in protest over what she considered unsafe conditions. "It's too dangerous," Dr. Rathburn said. "And for the love of God, don't bring your children." The warnings prompted cancellations at San Antonio hotels and general nervousness within the diocese. But church officials, keeping their composure, went ahead with plans, attempting to reassure the faithful, including the tens of thousands expected to stream over the Mexican border to see the pontiff, that adequate precautions were being taken. After resolving a myriad of hitches and snags on their way to this, the eleventh hour, an emergency of this kind seemed to them quite manageable.

A HURRIED TRIP IN THE MIDST OF SUMMER HAD GIVEN FATHER CARON A LIFT. IN the brief span of two weeks, he and another priest had touched base in Greece, Italy, Sicily, Paris, and London, where they ended with a lunch at Westminster Cathedral. He had returned tired but refreshed.

Greek ruins and Michelangelo's masterpieces were of a far different order of contemplation and remoteness, of course, from thoughts of college dormitories and drug addiction, but he had quickly slipped again into the practical routines of the college presidency.

That co-ed housing unit that had raised such a fuss a few months ago was taking shape nicely. Due mostly to his enthusiastic backing, it would open up in the fall semester as the first of its kind at Saint Ambrose. The outcry from distressed graduates who saw a co-ed dorm as an invitation to moral depravity had stopped. Father Caron had deftly pushed the idea to completion, and everything was set. A respected priest had agreed to serve as resident rector. Rooms in the building had been immediately snapped up. Several students had already moved in, and as far as Father Caron could tell they were "interacting with each other as we'd hoped."

There were other promising breezes wafting across campus at this time of new beginnings. For one thing, recruits to a special honors program were arriving to begin an experiment aimed at upgrading the college's academic climate. Father Caron had helped raise enough scholarship aid to make the project feasible. It was his hope to "attract high-caliber students who will not be isolated from the student body." With funds secured, the college went out and enrolled twenty-five gifted young people within the entering class.

Another development was the opening of a center of Asian studies encompassing language study, culture, and business and underwritten by a major foundation. These days, Asian studies were on the cutting edge of academia. Saint Ambrose could place itself in the thick of competition for students eager to pursue the blossoming interest in practically anything Far Eastern.

Other signs of vitality included a bigger baseball stadium and plans for a new science building that would be implemented as soon as the funds had been raised.

On the worrisome side of the ledger was student drug use. It was not abuse of marijuana or crack or heroin, of which Father Caron and his eyes and ears around campus saw little evidence. The problem was alcohol, pure and simple, Saint

Ambrose's "drug of choice," he said. Like many similar Catholic schools, Saint Ambrose had been all male for most of its history, and, as at virtually every men's school, drinking had fueled social life. It was a tradition that held fast into the age of coeducation. Now that states and localities were tightening up drinking laws and the public was growing more conscious of the dangers of alcohol, the time seemed ripe for a stepped-up campaign of education and help for the problem drinker. Under Father Caron's guidance, the school had formed a team to intervene with students who were troubled by alcohol.

"We're really trying to address drinking in a comprehensive manner," Father Caron said. "We have good control over dorm drinking, but lots of kids go off campus. We're not trying to instill prohibition for those who are old enough to drink, but we do want them to have the right information, and we want to preclude harmful behavior that results from drunkenness. It's not easy, though the tide of society seems more in the direction of doing more examination of this area, especially as it concerns drunk driving. We've done some things here to provide an alternative for those students who don't want to get into that kind of drinking. Not long ago when some students were holding a big toga party we sponsored a kind of Diet Coke cocktail party. Quite a few kids came."

With the challenges of college life drawing him in so many directions, was it possible to remain Catholic-centered in any real sense? Father Caron thought it was, though he conceded that the line between Catholicity and universalism could be thin indeed. Inclusiveness was the watchword of the modern university. When did a college focused on being "Catholic" become instead a place where many religions held forth? There was no easy answer, he knew, but the lack of any certainty could not, in his mind, justify either too much withdrawal from the world or too much endorsement of it.

Father Caron's goal was to preserve Saint Ambrose as "a mainstream Catholic university," itself a necessarily ambiguous objective. In a nation as pluralistic as America, where change was transforming all institutions all the time, there was no absolute image of what a mainstream Catholic university was or might be in the future (once nearly all Catholic, Saint Ambrose's percentage of Catholic students had held steady in recent years at about 60 percent). That for Father Caron was both the challenge and the strain of being the president of a Catholic university. He loved the job for all its ambiguity.

He would soon be involved again in one of those sticky situations in which loyalties rubbed against each other. His class in sexuality would convene in less than two weeks. Exhibit number one would be the Vatican's recent statement on bioethics that ruled out nearly all techniques of reproductive technology, including artificial insemination between childless husbands and wives. The techniques were rejected by Rome for introducing dehumanizing elements.

Father Caron was a churchman and an administrator, but when he entered that classroom he intended to be foremost a scholar. "We will read the church's document carefully," he said. "We will also review contemporary research on reproduction. As we go on, I hope we'll give the subject a lot of thought. I will tell the students to be careful about identifying the actual causes of dehumanization. I will tell them to think it through for themselves."

He was also a proud brother. The start of the school year would coincide with the wedding of his sister. He would travel to the East Coast to perform the ceremony. He was looking forward eagerly to it. He saw his life full of glowing facets for which he felt deeply thankful.

EVERY SO OFTEN, DURING HIS LONG DAYS IN THE SALVATORIAN MISSION WAREhouse, Brother Regis Fust's mind flashed back to an incident years ago that still baffled him.

Two men had come to see him. They had wandered through his sprawling warehouse, gazed upon the towering stacks of supplies, and heard about the cries from the pits of human deprivation. When they were finished, one man had walked away silently, never to be heard from again. The other had wept inwardly, and from that day on had handed over as much as $165 a week to help Brother Regis do his work.

To the Salvatorian brother, the story was a parable that somehow explained why his relief mission existed at all and likewise accounted for its fragility. Why did some, like the old woman in the Gospel who offered her all, her "mite," respond so freely at the specter of hunger and disease while others, like the rich young ruler described elsewhere by Jesus, simply turn away?

Brother Regis did not normally brood over that question, either to boast or to feed self-pity. He went about his daily chores, from hoisting huge cartons with a hand lift to hosting a visiting bishop, in humble gratitude for the cheerful giver. But there were moments of seeming fruitlessness and exhaustion when, for example, his appeals for crucial relief supplies fell on deaf ears and funds were in short supply—as they were here in late August—that the question haunted him.

Brother Regis's base of operations was the 25,000-square-foot warehouse, an austere cement block structure that sat inconspicuously across from a dog food plant and a shoe factory in the sleepy Wisconsin town of New Holstein, eighty miles northwest of Milwaukee. Six days a week, he and a team composed of four other Salvatorian brothers and four nuns assiduously pressed on with the work. One nun, Sister Dora Zapf, was a Salvatorian from Germany who shared with him the chief responsibilities for running the mission. The three other nuns had placed themselves at the disposal of the mission after retiring from decades of service in other religious orders. The little community, gathered in somewhat makeshift fashion, shouldered each others' burdens and fulfilled their prosaic duties with obvious stoutheartedness and joyous spirits.

Volunteers, nearly 150 of them, were indispensable allies. Every weekday they busied themselves on assembly lines, packing more goods into less space to cut down on shipping costs, which were based on volume rather than weight. Two cartons of children's aspirin from the manufacturer could be squeezed into one. As much as twenty tons could be stuffed into a twenty-foot shipping container, so every crack and crevice counted. Most volunteers were retired people from the area. As they prepared goods for the long voyage, they joined in lively chatter. They said what they most liked was getting their hands on a project whose impact was so tangible.

Paid employees didn't exist. Costs were cut to the bone.

The warehouse was a product of utter, hard-headed devotion, a rather drab monument to the stubborn ambition of a self-effacing religious brother who labored in relative obscurity with his loyal associates to do the best job he could— which was, from all appearances, really good. Their record of getting the job done was superb, though relatively unknown. In the realm of relief work, suffused with heartache, little noticed except at times of calamities like earthquakes and famines, Brother Regis and his companions had few equals.

In the twelve months ending in December 1987, this shoestring operation expected to ship 11 million pounds of sorely needed supplies overseas, mostly to remote outposts in Africa and Central and South America, through a variety of Catholic orders and Protestant church agencies. The volume of supplies had multiplied tenfold over the past decade. There were, to be sure, bigger and much better known relief agencies. But perhaps none bore more indelibly the human and spiritual imprint of those who had kept it alive.

According to the most recently published figures from the Agency for International Development, voluntary agencies alone delivered $1.8 billion worth of relief supplies in 1985. Brother Regis measured his contribution to that total in pounds instead of cash because, he reasoned, dollar figures often included overhead and could thus be misleading. The mission was certainly a small player in the overall cause of relief, a relatively tiny drop in that bucket. But like all relief agencies, its true rating was based on what it accomplished with what it had. And on that score perhaps no agency scored higher.

Among the dozens of shipments included in a recent mission report were these: 27,160 pounds of various supplies to the missions in Paraguay at a transportation cost of $2,069.14; 34,460 pounds of mostly medical help to Gombo Leprosy Control Center in Ethiopia at a cost of $5,118.59; 62,350 pounds of clothing and miscellaneous health and hygiene resources to the clinics in Nicaragua at a cost of $13,300.

Brother Regis was an American original, a fifty-five-year-old native of nearby Wausau who cobbled the mission together through trial and error, mostly by his own lights. He had entered the Salvatorian Fathers and Brothers, now a dwindling order, straight from high school, bringing with him a desire to make use of his life and a supply of rugged self-reliance. Most of his learning about relief operations had come through doing. He had benefited from no instructors and no manuals, he said. He had felt driven by the enormous needs out there.

"They didn't have a theology for what I'm doing," he said with a wry grin. He fine-tunes his function thusly: "I don't prescribe. I don't dispense. I beg."

He would ship for any group whose intentions were to alleviate misery. Though the political ideology of a donor or a recipient did not stand in the way of his providing service, he did not hide his disdain for Marxist-socialist regimes that, in his view, obstructed progress. Even on a personal level, however, he could overlook ideology for the greater good. In the warehouse's small conference room, for instance, hung a picture of himself and Sister Dora in Tanzania with the former president of the nation, Julius Nyerere, a Catholic and avowed socialist. Sister Dora had taught one of Nyerere's children in a mission school, and the former president had been a good friend to the warehouse. Brother Regis pointed to the affectionate inscription on the picture, spoke admiringly of Nyerere, and grumbled about his politics.

The one unforgivable sin that a government could commit, from Brother Regis's standpoint, was to delay the shipments by placing roadblocks at customs or trying to extort bribes from recipients.

Shipping bills in excess of $1 million crossed his desk the previous year, requiring constant hat-in-hand appeals. For a man who was the very antithesis of the slick self-promoter, an introvert if there ever was one, soliciting charity would have been inconceivable without a mammoth incentive. Even with one, he conceded, it was plenty difficult. The specter of the mission's constantly depleted checkbook certainly helped him stay on the case. Fresh in his mind were the most vivid memories of escapes from fiscal peril. The mission by its nature lived on the edge. When he spoke of relying on faith to make up the deficits, his deep basso voice shook with credibility.

The small Salvatorian religious order from which the relief mission sprung had its roots in this dairy region of Wisconsin, and it was on the site of the warehouse that in 1959 Brother Regis went to work in a print shop run by the order.

At that time, the Salvatorians were sending a trickle of goods to their mission stations in Tanzania. As requests mounted, Brother Regis began squirreling away more supplies in his corner of the shop, shipping them when and how he could. He felt compelled to do more and, in 1963, with no solid guidance from superiors to fall back on, devoted himself full time to the task.

In operational terms, the mission worked something like this. Corporations and other donors stepped forward or were otherwise prodded to donate products that ranged from worm medicine to construction nails; contributions were sought from individuals, religious groups, and foundations to pay for shipping. Mission workers unloaded the semitrailer trucks that arrived almost daily, repacking supplies into more compact units and cramming them as tightly as possible into containers. From New Holstein the containers were hauled to the Port of Milwaukee, where they were either loaded aboard ships or sent by rail to other ports.

Mounds of assorted supplies filled the cavernous warehouse, awaiting consignment. Among the assorted goods: kosher matzo (excellent for making tortillas in Central America), powdered milk, cold capsules, skin lotion, anti-itch cream, aspirin, soap powder, four motorbikes—whatever corporations chose to give away. Some were products that had been judged obsolete in the competitive market or had been displaced by a newer line. Behind every charitable donation, Brother Regis was well aware, lay a considerable tax benefit to the company.

Being a charity meant taking whatever was handed out. Mission needs did not always match up well with what came in, unfortunately. And there were always a few white elephants, like hair mousse and lawn fertilizer. Finding a proper place for the odd items often required tact and ingenuity. "But sooner or later we find use for most anything," Brother Regis said.

Each twenty-to-forty-foot shipping container, which could be hitched up to a truck cab for transport, usually contained a mixture of goods, depending in part on what had rolled in. For a long time, Brother Regis sought a supply of intravenous equipment, without luck. Then came a huge shipment.

"That's how it is when you're getting donations," he said with a trace of frustration. "You want something, and there's nothing. Then you get lots of it. It's totally unpredictable."

Brother Regis knew how to deliver the goods. His record for getting cargo past customs obstacles to the rightful recipients was extraordinary. He found the loopholes and developed deft strategies largely by his own wits. He detested bureaucracies, preferring to keep the operation simple and personal. He kept in his head who was asking for what and stayed in touch with them from a hopelessly cluttered office.

"Sometimes it's easier to be smaller," he said during a short, preoccupied coffee break. "The bigger some places grow, the more directors and managers they get. If a big request comes in, they've got to have a board meeting to decide about it. If I get a call, all I do is walk over to Sister Dora and ask her if she thinks we can do it."

The most recent mission report noted some of the bigger donations that had come in: 1 million antibiotics, 3.5 million children's pain tablets, ten semitrailer loads of medicine and hospital supplies, 400,000 pounds of food, and 2.5 million cold capsules.

Along with these statistics, the report included some of the letters from those on the receiving end. They overflowed with gratitude and graphic reminders of life on the front lines of human survival. Invariably, they provided a look at how most any basic provision that landed at the mission door could be put to good use.

From Tanzania: "We thank God daily for you and to be the happy recipients of such useful and badly needed medicines and supplies. . . . The drips as the resistant Malaria increases are just invaluable, and have saved many a life. The food items, Baby food, cocoa and breakfast bars kept us alive during the sugar shortage. . . . The bandages material, wool ends, toothpaste and brushes . . . and I cannot describe how useful the big tin of screws has been."

From Guatemala: "I wish you had been here at 4:00 this morning as we loaded our car with so many of the wonderful things the last shipment brought. . . . Shortly after the first shipment of Similac arrived a very distraught father came to us telling us his wife had just died in childbirth. Whatever would he be able to feed the infant? Imagine his relief when we were able to give him a case of Similac."

Brother Regis treasured such letters as testimony to the many calls for help that the mission had answered even as he agonized in the face of the large pile of requests in front of him. Enter the imponderables.

Why, he asked, hadn't more corporations responded to his appeals with donations? Why, after a television appearance on a national cable religious program, were there only eight offers to help? "The audience was pretty charismatic," he recalled. "They think prayer will take care of everything. The Bible also says prayer without good works is dead."

Without insider connections, he said, it was impossible to get a foot in the door of most big corporations even to discuss the possibility of aid. But so long as the chasm of destitution and illness yawned, he vowed to keep trying. "What choice is there?" he asked rhetorically. The fact that so many turned him away did not deter him. His doggedness had been the gift that had kept the supplies rolling.

Meanwhile, he intended to remain at his station, a touch curmudgeonly, grimly hopeful. His spirituality was grounded in earthly sustenance, feeding the hungry, clothing the naked, and easing the pain of the sick. Was he an idealist? "I suppose," he replied with an impish grin. "But, then again, I might not be." He didn't know exactly. But of one thing he was sure and his eyes brightened as he said it: "I'd like to see a lot more people get involved."

— ◂ ▸

ECONOMIC AND HUMAN RIGHTS CONCERNS MARKED SEVERAL KEY DEVELOPMENTS
in August:

- Church efforts to assist those who had left poor countries for a better life in
the United States included a request to Congress for financial support for
them and an appeal to the Immigration and Naturalization Service for a
change in work rules. In testimony to a House subcommittee on immigration, Monsignor Nicholas DiMarzio, director of migration and refugee services for the United States Catholic Conference, urged a change in the law
to permit some monetary assistance to the new arrival who would not be a
"public economic burden," the phrase the government used to define a long-
term dependent. The appeal sought a change in that part of the reformed
Immigration and Nationality Act that pertained to employment. By that act,
the recently initiated amnesty program required illegal aliens who were looking for work or who had begun employment after November 6, 1986 (the
day the amnesty law was adopted by Congress) to obtain employment au-
thorization from the INS before an approaching September 1 deadline.
Church officials, already upset with many of the program's provisions, complained that the deadline imposed unreasonable demands on applicants and
placed too great a burden on the government's processing machinery. Making
the case forcefully for other bishops, Archbishop Mahony of Los Angeles suggested that the deadline be moved back to coincide with the May 4, 1988,
end of the amnesty application period.

- The Quixote Center in Washington reported that its drive to aid Nicaragua
had reached $65 million, two-thirds of its goal. The center's intention was
to match the last infusion of U.S. assistance to the Contras, $100 million in
supplies approved by Congress the previous year. The response by the
Quixote staff was to send an equivalent amount of food, medicine, and clothing to the Nicaraguan people. Meanwhile, events in the region were reshaping the debate over the war. On August 7 a Central American peace plan
was signed by Costa Rica, Guatemala, Honduras, Nicaragua, and El Salvador,
the achievement largely of Oscar Arias, president of Costa Rica. But proponents of Contra aid were set to press Congress in September for $310 mil-
lion to help keep the rebels in business. Welcoming the peace plan but fully
expecting the bitter conflict to continue, the Quixote Center pushed
doggedly ahead toward its goal.

- In Dayton, Ohio, Archbishop Daniel Pilarczyk gave a glowing assessment of
the church's revised method for teaching and baptizing adult converts in a
August 25 talk to his Cincinnati archdiocesan priests. Ever since Vatican II

had authorized the wholesale revamping of the practice, called the Rite of Christian Initiation of Adults (RCIA), the new procedure had been taking shape, not without controversy. Before the Second Vatican Council, converts had been taught the rudiments of the faith and baptized privately, but under the Council's mandate this became a public function of the whole church community. In the fall of 1986, the text to be used by parishes in carrying out the RCIA had been finally approved by the U.S. bishops, so the program was now official policy for all parishes.

Archbishop Pilarczyk, noting that 90 percent of new Catholics are baptized more or less automatically as infants, said the RCIA focused attention on those adults among the remaining 10 percent who chose to be Catholics as adults and praised the program as an effective and meaningful means of welcoming many more potential converts. "We are saying that the renewed RCIA calls the community to an awareness that the church grows not just through the baptism of children who already believe," the archbishop said, "but also through the baptism and reception of adults who are from outside its fellowship. We are saying that the growth and strengthening of the church are the responsibility not just of church ministers, but of the whole community. We are saying that fellowship in the church is not just a matter of accepting certain truths but of opting into a common worship. We are saying, finally, that this process of reception into a worshiping community is not a secondary activity of the parish community, but part of its ongoing regular activity."

The current rancor in the church, Archbishop Pilarczyk said, should not been seen as a deterrent but instead testified to its vitality, to wit, that "in spite of the family quarrels there is a depth of meaning and understanding and potential and joy and ultimate fulfillment in the Catholic Christian faith which is not available anywhere else."

• Invoking key points in the bishops' recently completed pastoral letter "Economic Justice for All," Auxiliary Bishop Joseph Sullivan of Brooklyn issued the annual Labor Day statement on behalf of the United States Catholic Conference on August 28. Bishop Sullivan, chairman of the conference Committee on Social Development and World Peace, highlighted the pastoral letter's call for cooperation by business, union, and government leaders in creating economic programs grounded in justice and human dignity. Among its appeals were for joint efforts to help workers make the transition from manufacturing to service industries and job training for those in special need, especially welfare recipients and minority young people. Labor Day 1987 came at "an important and challenging moment for American workers and the unions that represent them," Bishop Sullivan said. He recapped the church's strong backing for the rights of workers to a living wage, safe working conditions, protection against arbitrary dismissal, and "adequate health care, security for old age or disability, and unemployment compensation." And he repeated the church's support for labor unions, quoting from the bishops' pastoral: "no one may deny the right to organize without attacking human dignity itself. Therefore we firmly oppose organized efforts, such as those regrettably seen in this country, to break existing unions or prevent workers from organizing."

CALEB AND CINDY'S CHILDREN WERE SETTLED DOWN FOR THE NIGHT IN THEIR upstairs room, where a soft summer breeze blew through the windows. Paula, nearly a year old now, had been carried to bed by her father after falling asleep on the living room rug. Her sister Susan, three years older, buoyed by summer's nighttime electricity, stayed awake with her last bit of gusto, finally lulled into slumber by her mother's reading of bedtime stories.

Their parental duties done for the day, Cindy and Caleb leaned back into the sofa with a relieved, gratified look. Their thoughts lingered on the uplift they received from the fresh prayers Susan spoke before she went to sleep that always came straight from her heart.

"She's a real inspiration for me," Cindy said tenderly. "The way she prays is incredible. She doesn't memorize anything. It's spontaneous—a little miracle every night. Sometimes she prays for people not having enough clothes or housing or for children going to bed hungry. It's cute, sure, but they're gifts given to us to appreciate. It's more heartwarming than adult prayers are supposed to be for the children."

"I had one from my childhood—a memorized prayer," Caleb chimed in, "but I'd rather have her go off on her own. She gives thanks for all the worms on our driveway so the birds can eat. Then she closes her eyes, and she's off."

Their daughters did all the out-loud praying in the house. For Caleb and Cindy, prayer was mostly something done in church. Otherwise, on those rare occasions, they had explained, they offered up their own thoughts and feelings silently and alone. In Caleb's Polish Catholic upbringing, the family had prayed words handed down by the church both at mass and at home. The rosary was a fixture in family devotions. Though Caleb had not recited it for many years, he did repeat the familiar prayers of the church at the Sunday liturgy. Cindy's Methodist parents had taught her certain "standard prayers," she recalled, but "we always felt that prayer should be more conversational." In those private moments when she did utter a brief message to God, she said, it was indeed conversational. She wanted her children to approach prayer in a fashion that reflected their autonomy.

"I want them to be individuals, to stand on their own two feet," Cindy said resolutely. "I want them to think this through carefully like everything else and to make logical decisions. I was always on the fence—I still am often—and I want them to be sure and firm." It followed, then, that she gave them wide latitude to chart their own courses in life, with one notable barrier. "The girls can do anything they want," Cindy said, "except if one of them wants to be a nun."

As a couple, they appeared sure and firm, secure in a spacious suburban home with two lovely, healthy girls, accumulating a nest egg from Caleb's expanding optometry practice, tightly woven into their respective families, habituated to a traditional husband-wife division of labor. Cindy had completed her master's degree but could not see herself as a working mother. Perhaps she would when the children were grown, she conjectured. Caleb's career was, correspondingly, his consuming interest. From almost every angle, they were the young adults on the steadily upward trajectory of affluence, content to fulfill their roles determinedly if not gleefully. It was the life they had chosen, and they believed they had chosen well.

Cindy was pretty much where she had expected to be, perhaps a bit beyond. "After Susan was born," she confided, "I was in love with my child, though I didn't really see it that way at the time. It was a new love in my life, one of the only breaks in a kind of continuity. I'm better off than I thought I'd be at this stage of my life, not just in material things." She grinned sheepishly, glancing at Caleb, "If I'd married who I once thought I would, it would have changed me for the worse."

Caleb nodded, threw a knowing glance to his wife, and added a capsule adult biography of his own. "I'm farther along than I thought I'd be in my profession," he said tersely, "though I didn't expect all the diddly-poo problems I've run into."

There were, of course, cracks in the solid foundation brought about by the very circumstances of that ordinary middle-class world. Most of those pressures were, like those on Catholic America itself, beyond their control, sometimes beyond their full grasp. The complexity wrapped in the seeming simplicity was itself staggering. Life in the suburbs was, for all its outward serenity, bedeviled by its own separateness, its own set-apart quality that mirrored the gaping divides between home and work, men and women, commitment and freedom—a microcosm of the world beyond. The home and its green little pasture somehow symbolized stability and longing, dreams realized and dreams suppressed, settledness and restiveness.

Cindy and Caleb were where they thought they were supposed to be and didn't allow themselves much room to speculate on how their lives might be different. But once in a while fragments of old dreams did push through to consciousness.

"Every so often," Caleb said, "I think about going to Yale to study forestry and working someplace by myself where I wouldn't have to talk to anyone and I'd be outdoors listening to the world." Cindy also had a recurring fantasy: "When the kids are grown up, I think about joining the Peace Corps."

But the excursions into these chambers of the imagination were few, they said. They expected to be right where they were years from then. Caleb saw himself a decade hence having better mastered the endless details of business that exasperated him no end but not rid of them. Cindy saw in the same elapsed time the girls passing through the last stages of childhood.

They worried about the world their daughters would enter. They wondered whether exposing Susan and Paula to the beliefs and traditions of both Catholicism and Methodism would imbue them solidly enough with the right values. Not that they expressed regrets about their "mixed" marriage and the extra effort involved in providing two tracks of religious education—far from it. If anything, they hoped that it would strengthen certain convictions, especially teachings about right and wrong, that the two churches held pretty much in common. They hoped that their daughters could learn enough to form their own minds and consciences, but would it be sufficient to steel them against worldly forces?

"We are in the midst of a generation of me-people of loose morality," Cindy thought. "Maybe things have begun to turn around and society has begun to tighten up a little. There aren't enough people out there holding onto strong morals. Sure, you have to push to get ahead, but there's a point where you say, 'Enough is enough.' Where do you draw the line?"

Her question looped back to herself and Caleb, to their own difficulty deciding where to draw that line for themselves. Their own drive for success sought balance with those other, sometimes elusive values that were thought to nurture home and family. Late into the evening, Caleb was pensive. "I'd like to have a few consecutive days off with no schedule, no paperwork, no answering service, no social obligations," he said, "so we could do some simple things together. It seems like we're getting caught up racing to get things done whether there's a time problem or not."

Cindy lovingly took his hand in hers. "It does get more complicated," she said calmly, embarking with sure footing across terrain that encompassed some of their mutual wishes and anxieties. "Part of me says that it would be great just to pick up and start somewhere new. The other part of me says I'm a family person and I'd have a hard time doing that. On the whole, I guess, I'm a little more content, a little more relaxed, than Caleb."

September
1·9·8·7

T HE GLEAMING WHITE FIGURE OF POPE JOHN PAUL II ALIGHTED
from his chartered Alitalia 747—dubbed *Shepherd I*—into
blistering 100-degree Miami sunlight at 2:15 on the afternoon
of September 10. Descending the ramp, he smiled broadly as he
waved his first salutations, his blue eyes sparkling, his robust, ruddy
features projecting a manly vigor that stood up to the ethereal quality of his robes. Striding to a canopy on the broiling tarmac, he was
greeted by an ebullient President Ronald Reagan who, accompanied
by his wife, Nancy, had flown in earlier on *Air Force One.*

Thus began John Paul's much heralded ten-day visit to Catholic America, a journey that, if the media forecasters were to be believed, would be mostly uphill.

From his twenty-four-hour stay in Miami, where a series of tone-setting events
were scheduled, he and the papal entourage, pursued by hundreds of reporters
aboard *Shepherd II* and *Shepherd III* (could the *Wolf* squadron be far behind?),
would proceed full-steam to Columbia, South Carolina, New Orleans, San
Antonio, Phoenix, Los Angeles, Monterey, and San Francisco, ending the tour with
a stop in Detroit. Twelve thousand miles in all, and the airline would give the pope
full frequent-flier credit.

Television would monitor his every move. Multiple crews were mobilized to
trail him through every city, and a joint venture by the Catholic Television
Network of America and Mother Angelica's Eternal Word Network promised "arrival to departure" coverage. Practically every detail of the trip was, accordingly,
planned with television in mind.

It was John Paul's thirty-sixth trip outside Italy, his second to the United States,
since being elected the 263d successor to the throne of Saint Peter in 1978. He had
touched down in sixty-eight countries. In keeping with the regular practice of

this most widely traveled pope in history, he announced himself as "a pilgrim." The Catholic faithful knew him as Christ's representative whom God had anointed to lead the church at this crucial hour. Security forces, an army of seven thousand police, National Guard, and Secret Service agents, the sheer size and complexity of which spoke volumes about American anxieties, knew him by the code name Halo.

John Paul was certainly not a pilgrim in any ordinary sense, no simple soul pressing ahead toward a distant shrine. Rather, he was, by dint of his office and personal aura, a sort of moving shrine himself to whom the faithful made a pilgrimage, a source of refuge for those who felt hard-pressed or in search of spiritual sustenance. He came to them not as a seeker after truth but as the dispenser of it, bearing answers rather than questions—in short, the Rock.

That rocklike certainty was blessing to those who hungered for such assurance and bane to those who argued for greater discussion of basic church positions. Both types were surely among the viewers who watched on television as John Paul stepped from his plane. They were among the many groups he had come to reach. In the coming days he would worship, pray, and speak to anguished dissenters, staunch defenders of the faith, and throngs of ordinary believers who felt blessed simply by the pope's presence. In addition, he would speak to non-Catholic America, that vast religious and secular hodgepodge that was fast losing any semblance of a common moral or spiritual language.

Themes for that message to America at large arose naturally out of historical circumstances. By design, John Paul would be touring the nation in the very week that marked the two-hundredth anniversary of the completion and signing of the Constitution. Commemorations were planned for Washington and Philadelphia, providing the occasion for reflecting once again on such pillars of constitutional democracy as freedom, truth, and civic duty, ideas that lent themselves superbly to the pope's purposes.

With so many audiences along his path—insiders and outsiders, liberals and conservatives, reformers and reactionaries, the aggrieved, the angry, and the spiritually fatigued, the despairing, and all others who awaited from him a healing word or touch—John Paul, the chief pastor of Roman Catholicism, faced a daunting task.

Within his far-flung flock there were distinct problems that were tougher and more threatening than any single difficulty he might find in Catholic America. Europe remained notably more anticlerical and atheistic, Latin America was more fractious and theologically radical, Africa less bound to traditional Christian concepts of family, and Eastern Europe, including his beloved Poland, more beleaguered. But the difficulties in Catholic America loomed larger because America mattered more to Rome. America's political and economic dominance in the community of nations had conferred upon Catholic America a visibility and influence far out of proportion to its numbers within the universal church. Its wealth was vital to Vatican interests, and its behavior, for better or worse, was projected around the globe by the American media. It had acquired, then, as far as Rome was concerned, an unfortunate capacity to shape belief and behavior in other sectors of the church. The Americans' well-advertised feistiness and dissent, fed by affluence and free choice, had therefore commanded the pope's special attention. It threatened unity and challenged the pope's authority. Given Rome's recent actions to squelch this streak of American rebelliousness, it was reasonable to predict that John Paul would press this effort further, trying to curb it before other Hunthausens created more Seattles. But it was one thing to identify the mischief and quite another to curb it.

The pope would make his case through his forceful character and his satchel full of forty-eight speeches. The process of writing the talks had differed markedly from that employed before his first U.S. trip, to the Northeast and Midwest in 1979. The speeches for that trip had been crafted in Rome with virtually no help from the American bishops, giving rise to widespread complaints that the messages betrayed a serious ignorance of the U.S. church. Partly in reaction to that criticism, U.S. churchmen were given a much stronger hand in drafting key texts this time around, subject, as always, to final Vatican judgment.

The other major change was that several American Catholics would get a chance to voice their concerns directly to the pope through ten "structured dialogues" during which the Americans and the pope would trade prepared remarks. In deciding what he would say at these formal exchanges, John Paul had access to what his dialogue partners would say; the Americans were obligated to send their texts to Rome for approval far in advance of the trip. The pope's contribution, by contrast, would be unavailable to the Americans beforehand. And there would be no chance for cross-examination. Despite these handicaps, Catholic leaders had for the most part welcomed the idea as a method by which Americans could share the platform in some way with the pope and speak their minds. The U.S. church would, it was argued by advocates, thus get at least some sort of hearing.

BEFORE GETTING ON TO THOSE IN-HOUSE MATTERS, HOWEVER, JOHN PAUL HAD formalities to conduct with President Reagan. The welcoming rituals, brief but important, would give John Paul a succinct opportunity to sketch broad themes that would appear throughout the trail of speeches he would leave behind.

President Reagan greeted the pope on behalf of the nation and the small gathering of invited guests. Noting the Constitution's bicentennial, the president imparted his own lesson in civil religion. "From the first," he said, "our nation embraced the belief that the individual is sacred—and that God himself respects human liberty, so too must the State. In freedom, we Americans have in these two hundred years built a great country—a country of goodness and abundance. Indeed, your Holiness, it is precisely because we believe in freedom—because we respect the liberty of the individual in the economic as well as the political sphere—that we have achieved such prosperity."

The president tempered his message of triumph with a profession of humility and deference: "Yet—and yet we Americans admit freely to our shortcomings. As you exhort us, we will listen. With all our hearts, we yearn to make this good land better still."

The pope's opening words melded piety and diplomacy in a tradition of evangelistic goodwill that stretched back to Saint Paul's letters. Greeting "all the people of this land," John Paul declared that his first objective was to proclaim "the Gospel of Jesus Christ," adding that he also came as "pilgrim in the cause of justice and peace," "pastor to the nation's Catholics," and "friend" to "people of every religion," the poor, the struggling, the lost, the sick, and the dying.

He also picked up the Constitution theme, praising it as a "great document" of freedom and urging Americans to donate from the prosperity they had attained under its rule to help the world's needy.

Later, after an hour-long private meeting with the president at Vizcaya, an Italianate palace owned by Dade County, John Paul returned to the subject of the Constitution's promise of freedom, investing it with a meaning that formed an important subtext for his trip. "An experience in ordered freedom is truly a cherished part of the history of this land," he said in a joint appearance with President Reagan in the lush gardens of the palace. But, the pope continued, "The only true freedom is the freedom to do what we ought as human beings created by God according to his plan. It is the freedom to live the truth of what we are and who we are before God." Freedom, he said, was "fragile," adding, "Any distortion of truth or dissemination of non-truth is an offense against freedom; any abuse of authority or power, or, on the other hand, just the omission of vigilance, endangers the heritage of a free people."

The link between freedom and truth had undergone changes in definition. Vatican II had abandoned the established premise that "error has no rights," a weapon that had been once widely used to bolster Catholicism as the privileged state religion, as the result of the American-inspired initiative to support religious liberty. Other faiths, indeed, those with no faith, were accorded the same rights by the Second Vatican Council. But John Paul's words were reminders that the old disposition lived on, though reformulated. Now it was not that freedom exercised in its true sense meant choosing Catholicism, but, as the pope defined it, choosing "truth," though it was reasonable to suppose that for him the two were one and the same.

Before ending his remarks, the pope also reinforced his message that a rich country like the United States had a great responsibility to help the world's poor. President Reagan's reply to this pontiff, who was suspected of socialist leanings by many of the nation's most ardent capitalists, including prominent Catholics, plugged free enterprise. "Generous aid from the wealthier nations to the poorer is certainly of great importance," the president said, "but in the long term it's even more important to share the conditions—the moral causes of prosperity, including respect for the economic rights of the individual."

JOHN PAUL WAS WHISKED FROM THE AIRPORT THROUGH A CITY IN WHICH SECU-rity precautions included the sealing shut of manhole covers and the placement of armed forces everywhere. His first customary stop was the local cathedral or an-other principal church, in this case Saint Mary's Cathedral, where he could feel the comfort of familiar spiritual trappings and speak to his people, as he did at the large masses, in a common religious language. The pastoral work, the mission of encouragement and theological bolstering to the inner core of ordinary Catholic Americans, would go on largely in the cathedrals and at the huge outdoor liturgies.

To the media, much of this religious talk would seem esoteric, utterly devoid of news value. But to John Paul these were the staples, the meat and potatoes, of his message to fellow Catholics, his most personal and heartfelt reflections. These talks to "insiders," to those who often had traveled far and endured hardship to see and hear him, comprised a moving seminar in the essentials of the Catholic faith that was remarkably nuanced and comprehensive. It might be the only exposure to an encompassing system of thought that most reporters would ever hear in the course of their rounds.

Very little of what the pope had to say on these occasions referred uniquely to Catholicism. In pluralistic America, he preached something closer to generic Christianity, reaching out as an evangelist. He emphasized the salvation brought by Christ and the need for personal growth in the Spirit. Among the topics he explored, in separate homilies, was a series on "mystery": the mystery of the Holy Trinity, the church as mystery of communion, and the mystery of the Kingdom of God. Other themes included the sacrifice of the Cross, devotion to Mary, penance, and the place of Scripture.

The first of these meditations, on the importance of personal prayer, was de-livered at Saint Mary's. He addressed the packed cathedral after emerging from a period of praying by himself at a side altar, monitored by television crews with commentators speculating on how long he would remain alone on his knees. "Dear brothers and sisters," he told them, "we must never underestimate the power of prayer to further the Church's redemptive mission and to bring good where there is evil. As I mentioned earlier, we must be united in prayer. We pray not just for ourselves and our loved ones, but for the needs of the universal church and of all mankind." It was an appeal that he would make again and again.

THE HARMONY AND UNITY OF THE CATHEDRAL WOULD SOON GIVE WAY TO THE pope's first taste of tension a short distance away during his meeting with representatives of the nation's diocesan priests. At Saint Martha's Church, the first of the structured dialogues would likely indicate what could be expected from these exchanges. The priest chosen to speak for his colleagues was the Reverend Frank J. McNulty, a sixty-year-old pastor from suburban Roseland, New Jersey, well known for his writings and conferences with clergy. The dialogue would produce the most enigmatic moment of the trip.

Father McNulty's speech, entitled "If Priests Could Open Up Their Hearts," was a model of shrewd, diplomatic protest. He painted a picture of American priests as dedicated and pressed to their limits by heavy demands. A particular source of stress among them, he said, was the difficulty of promoting the church's "moral message." "It troubles us that people often do not perceive the Church as proclaiming integral truth and divine mercy, but rather as sounding harsh, demanding." Perhaps the fault lay in the style of some of the church's moral documents or in a "false perception" of moral doctrine. Though never mentioning a third possibility—that Rome itself was to blame—Father McNulty recalled Pope John XXIII's appeal for "the medicine of mercy rather than severity," continuing, "As we go about trying to heal the wounded it saddens us that many have a different image of the Church we love and serve. It saddens us that the Church is not as credible to those within it, and to those outside of it, as we would like it to be." The man most responsible for credibility sat behind him, head down.

Father McNulty extended his purposeful ambiguity—code talk—to the question of celibacy. The sharp drop in candidates for the priesthood had both worsened the work load for active priests and highlighted the reason most often cited as the cause of the problem, the bar against a married priesthood. Recent polls showed a majority of priests opposed to mandatory celibacy. "Its value has eroded and continues to erode in the minds of many," the priest gamely told the pope. "This is of great concern to us because it has serious implications for the Church. We know, Holy Father, that you have been unequivocal in your support for the celibate commitment which thousands of priests in the United States have made and intend to keep.

"For your support we are grateful because it is not easy to strive to be warm, loving, and affective men and yet be faithful to that commitment. We can only ask you to continue along paths of support and exploration . . . exploration of how the discipline of celibacy can be most effectively implemented today." Father McNulty had again tiptoed up to the edge of outright dissent before artfully stepping back. The pope had his right hand cupped behind his ear as if to hear better. He showed no expression.

The priests' spokesman then saluted theologians in what could be taken as a thinly veiled defense of the Reverend Charles Curran, who was still fighting his expulsion from Catholic University's theology department. "Theologians have a charism too, and we are grateful for their gift," he said to loud applause. "When they function with freedom and fidelity, we priests are supported in our pastoral efforts."

Lastly, Father McNulty urged his ecclesiastical boss to seek the advice of his brethren on issues they knew best, including the question of who best qualified as bishop material. From there he went one step further to push, almost, for consideration of women for the priesthood. He endorsed the idea of women's service that the pope had espoused, adding, "We would also be greatly encouraged if the Holy See, together with the local churches, would continue to explore the range of service that women might appropriately offer the Church."

Controversy was unavoidable if priests were to be candid with the pope, Father McNulty said. Questioning was built into the American character. "We treasure freedom—freedom of conscience, freedom of religion, freedom of expression. . . . Priests know well that there are no easy answers but want to face the questions with honesty."

As he drew to a close, he recited a poem called "Thought's Resistance to Words," which the pope, with a half-embarrassed smile, recognized instantly as his own creation. "Thank you," the pope said. It was encouraging, Father McNulty said, "that we have a pope who is also a poet, because poets know the human heart."

The priest finished, turned toward the pope, received his embrace and, according to Father McNulty's later report, a private greeting that sounded both gracious and perfectly noncommittal: "You found good words." Praise for the form if not the substance, or was it a wry reference to the priest's "good taste" in including a poem of his in the speech? During these brief moments, the audience of black-suited men cheered. They sang, "Here I Am, Lord, It Is I, Lord, I Have Heard You Calling in My Life." Then, a thick hush fell as they awaited John Paul's first words.

He began, not with the speech, but with a seemingly improvised phrase that appeared to arise out of a deep reverie. "I remember a song," he said in his heavily accented English: "It's a Long Way to Tipperary."

The remark set heads spinning. Was it a sardonic reference to a great distance he saw between his views and Father McNulty's? Was it the comment of a weary traveler far from his home base? Was it some sort of Freudian slip or a highly coded piece of free association? Whatever it was, nothing John Paul said during his entire visit would be as intriguing or inexplicable.

His speech, by contrast, was decidedly straightforward. In essence, the pope told his cherished field workers to place their trust in Christ and that with the help of the Holy Spirit their difficulties could be surmounted. Christ would take care of recruitment of seminarians, so, by implication, the celibacy issue was not crucial. If the priest kept himself centered in his ministry of Word, sacrament, and pastoral care, everything else would be all right. Place great faith in the "mystery of ecclesial unity," he told them. Be confident that the church safeguards the truth.

The two men had not exactly talked past each other; neither had they talked to each other. In that regard, those who hoped for some livelier sparring went away disappointed. There was little likelihood that anything of the sort would take place in the other nine exchanges. If John Paul was not about to debate here, with his ecclesiastical next of kin, chances were that he would not get into it with groups from which he stood at a greater distance.

◄ ►

First thing on the pope's docket on friday morning was the much-debated public meeting with American Jews. Outrage over the pope's June 25 reception of President Kurt Waldheim of Austria, an accused Nazi war criminal, had nearly derailed the session. The emergency meeting in Rome a week before between Jewish leaders and the pope—at the behest of the Jews—had apparently patched up things enough to prevent a major disruption right at the start of the papal visit. Differences might have been papered over but they were hardly resolved.

Jewish leaders were divided both on attending the affair and on the contents of the statement to be read to the pope. Some were also torn between an inner impulse to snub the pope and a desire to play a visible, public role in shaping the Catholic-Jewish dialogue. Two Orthodox Jewish organizations had already announced that they would boycott the meeting. Both belonged to an umbrella group, the Synagogue Council of America, which also included Reform and Conservative Jews. The council's president, Rabbi Gilbert Klaperman, bowed to pressures from his fellow Orthodox brethren and withdrew from his appointed role of attending and reading the joint statement to the pope. In his place would be Rabbi Mordecai Waxman who belonged to the Conservative movement.

The final draft of the statement itself, the only speech during the papal visit that the Vatican would not see in advance, had been hammered out by a dozen Jewish leaders during a five-hour session three days before. Some of its architects and those close to the process were optimistic that the pope would make an important breakthrough, perhaps even announce the Vatican's willingness to grant diplomatic recognition to Israel.

Meanwhile, the pope had broken his public silence about his Vatican welcome of Waldheim during a session with reporters aboard his flight from Rome to Miami. The visit had been "necessary," he said, "to show the same appreciation and the same esteem for every people. He came as a president democratically elected by a nation."

At the Dade County Cultural Center, two hundred Jews awaited the pope and greeted him warmly. Despite all the unease and uncertainty surrounding the event, it had actually materialized. The speeches contained nothing remarkable. Rabbi Waxman led off, reading the joint statement. Its tone was generally conciliatory. With reference to the Waldheim incident, it said, "Obviously, the differences expressed at last week's meeting have not been resolved." But it hailed the opportunity to "express the pain and anger of the Jewish community" to the pope out in the open. Before Catholics and Jews could cooperate in curing the world's ills, Rabbi Waxman added, "we must first mend ourselves." Throughout the talk, complaints were routinely paired with assurances of goodwill on both sides and claims of progress in Jewish-Catholic relations. Among the familiar grievances were that bolder efforts were needed to erase Christian roots of anti-Semitism and that the Vatican had refused to grant full diplomatic status to Israel.

The statement was a barometer of how much the Waldheim affront had reopened accusations that Rome, particularly Pope Pius XII, had done too little to save Jews from the Nazis. The statement welcomed the forthcoming Vatican document on the church's response to the Holocaust and the broader area of anti-Semitism in general that the pope had set in motion at the Jewish summit meeting the previous week.

"While your sensitive concerns and your noteworthy pronouncements about *Shoah* [the Hebrew term for Holocaust] have been heartening," the statement said, "we have observed recent tendencies to obscure the fact that Jews were the major target of Nazi genocidal policies." But the statement went on to approve the pope's letter on the Holocaust to the head of the American bishops in August for showing "a deep level of understanding of that terrible period."

The pope, in his address, affirmed his affection for Judaism and reverence for its "immense spiritual resources." Referring to *Shoah* as "that ruthless and inhuman attempt to exterminate the Jewish people," the pope reaffirmed his intention to have the Vatican search its own records to produce a thorough document on the period and added a peremptory defense. "I am convinced," he said, "that history will reveal ever more clearly and convincingly how deeply Pius XII felt the tragedy of the Jewish people, and how hard and effectively he worked to assist them during the Second World War."

John Paul also took the occasion to repeat his support for a homeland for both Jews and Palestinians. He ended with a call for continued collaboration and his pledge to uphold the dignity of people everywhere. There was no mention of Waldheim.

It was over. After all the anguish, threats, protests, and patient diplomacy, a peaceful, relatively innocuous gathering of pope and Jews had come to pass. The pope had given away nothing, held his ground, made no apologies for Waldheim, defended Pius XII. The Jews had couched their complaints in an agreeable context, refrained from voicing their anger too sharply, voted to trust a process of exploration that had opened at Vatican II. Faith in that process had finally outweighed their disdain for the Waldheim visit.

FROM THE CULTURAL CENTER, THE POPE WAS SHUTTLED STRAIGHT ACROSS TOWN from east to west to his final stop in Miami, a mass in Tamiami Park. The scorching sun had driven the thermometer into the nineties by late morning when the Popemobile (a custom-built Mercedes Benz 230G, fourteen feet long, nine feet high, with a benzene-powered 2.3 cc engine, power steering, power brakes, air-conditioning, and cassette player) made its way through the cheering crowd, thick with Cuban Americans, toward the altar dominated by a hundred-foot cross. The liturgy had begun, and the pope was into his homily, when the tropical elements took over. Dark clouds swooped in, lightning knifed through the air, and thunder crashed. When the drenching rain began, John Paul was forced to retreat, completing the mass with thirty priests in a sheltered section of the park. He reemerged to bless the sopping crowd after the storm had passed. He then left for the airport and the short trip to Columbia, South Carolina.

THE COLUMBIA LEG OF THE JOURNEY WAS DEVOTED TO ECUMENICAL RELATIONS and was intended to compensate for what had been considered a serious deficiency of John Paul's 1979 visit. During the earlier trip, the pope had had a brief meeting with leaders of other churches at Trinity College in Washington, but he had kept the leaders waiting a long time and had done all the talking. It had been perceived widely as an empty, even triumphant gesture, and many feathers had been ruffled. This time ecumenism would not receive short shrift.

Shortly after the start of his five-hour stay, twenty-six representatives of U.S. Protestant and Eastern Orthodox churches sat down for a closed session with the pope. Among them were Presbyterians, Methodists, black Baptists, and Antiochan Orthodox. Bishop Philip R. Cousin of the African Methodist Episcopal Church greeted the pope and read a statement on the group's behalf that pressed the issue of how the growing stack of recent agreements stemming from talks between Catholic theologians and scholars from other churches might actually lead to something. Despite the apparent success by scholars in defusing and unraveling centuries-old barriers to church unity, little had been done to move toward unity, causing many ecumenists to grow impatient. Rome was seen as particularly adept at dragging its feet.

"Based on the considerable and careful work since the [Second Vatican] Council," Bishop Cousin asked, "how can we work with the Roman Catholic church in concrete ways to take practical and responsible steps now to manifest this *koinonia* [communion]?"

John Paul offered little direct encouragement. Agreements were fine, he said, but far from sufficient to switch on the green light. "Indispensable as the work of dialogue is, and even though the act of dialogue itself begins to improve relations between us," he said, "our ultimate purpose goes beyond the statements and reports of ecumenical commissions." As his previous thoughts on ecumenism showed, the pope believed church unity would come about only through a deepening of prayer, holiness, and understanding of the meaning of the church.

The pope was no more ready to give quarter to Bishop Cousin's implied criticism than he was to the Jews' irritation over Waldheim. "Ecumenism is not a matter of power and human 'tactics,'" he said dismissively in reference to calls for church authorities to act on the basis of the agreements. "It is a service of truth in love and humble submission to God. Similarly, our collaboration in the important areas you list is not a matter of measured calculation."

The pope sent mixed signals again at the colorful stadium prayer service, surrounded by clerics in an array of vestments that exhibited the history of schismatic Christianity, from the richly embroidered robes of Eastern prelates to the simple black garment of the Baptist preacher. John Paul embraced them as a fellow sojourner in the faith and a brother in service. He was gracious and generous, neither eager to press the regal claims of his office nor in any way disrespectful toward those whom he would not, for formidable theological reasons, admit to his communion table.

But along with his abundant humanity and Christian goodwill went his hardline approach to ecumenism. His speech to the assembly underscored the divisions among them instead of pointing to new possibilities for convergence. Its focus was the well-being of the family, a subject close to the heart of all the churches, but one that provoked intense theological and moral debate. Everyone believed in family, to be sure, and the churches felt caught in the throes of enormous social change, but the topic involved such areas as sexuality (artificial birth control being the most prominent), abortion, and the role of women, around which some of the fiercest interchurch conflicts had flared. But that was the pope's theme for the ecumenical prayer service, and he took the occasion to insist on adherence to Catholic doctrine.

John Paul affirmed the "common faith" they shared in Christ and acknowledged the centrality of Scripture for the church (words that many Protestants found especially to their liking). He then turned to marriage and family, which he called "sacred realities" and followed with a proscription against divorce. "Because God's love is faithful and irrevocable," he said, "so those who have been married 'in Christ' are called to remain faithful to each other forever."

The rest of the speech was largely devoted to upholding the sanctity of that teaching and, by implication, the cluster of Catholic doctrine related to the family. Demands of modern living threatened the "lifelong interdependence" of couples, and unspecified "sins against love and against life are often presented as examples of 'progress' and emancipation.'" Was the pope casting aspersions here on the challenges posed by feminism? These "sins," said the pope, were nothing else than "the age-old forms of selfishness dressed up in a new language and presented in a new cultural framework."

Further, John Paul decried "a false notion of individual freedom" that defied tradition and refused to restrain passion. By contrast, there was the "true freedom" to choose the truth as understood by the church. It was the theme to which he had alluded before, combining an American byword with Catholic necessity. "America," he declared, "you cannot insist on the right to choose, without also insisting on the duty to choose well, the duty to choose the truth. Already there is much breakdown and pain in your own society because fundamental values, essential to the well-being of individuals, families, and the entire nation, are being emptied of their real content." Any of these points might have sparked spirited debate between John Paul and the rank of clergy seated behind him.

Afterward, ecumenical figures spoke appreciatively of the pope's initiative in meeting with them—and welcomed the display of mutual regard and respect that it graphically signaled—and some rated it a solid plus for interchurch relations. But others confided privately that they felt that the pontiff had done nothing to move ecumenical discussions off dead center and may have even set them back by avoiding some topics and speaking mostly in nonnegotiable terms.

— ◆ —

JOHN PAUL FINISHED UP IN COLUMBIA WITH A PRIVATE VISIT TO FORMER PRESIdent Jimmy Carter. The ecumenical tent was struck, and he was off to New Orleans that same night. Upon arrival at 9:46, he was met by a delegation of church and state dignitaries and escorted to the residence of Archbishop Philip M. Hannan for the night.

Saturday's agenda was heavy, beginning with a stop at Saint Louis Cathedral in the heart of the magical French Quarter shortly after 8:00 A.M. and ending twelve hours later with a call at Notre Dame Seminary. In between were an appearance before eighteen hundred black Catholics, structured dialogues with church educators and young people at the Superdome and with college presidents at Xavier University, and an outdoor mass at the University of New Orleans. Pope watchers had often wondered why he took on such punishing schedules, but John Paul seemed to thrive on them, driven as if there were so little time to cover all the bases he felt obliged to reach, consumed by duty.

After giving one of his more esoteric theological talks on the Holy Trinity to an understanding, reverent congregation of priests and religious in the cathedral, John Paul rode in a motorcade to the Superbowl over a parade route that included a stretch of famed Canal Street. From the Popemobile, John Paul strode into a hall resounding with cheers from black Catholics. As he often did in the midst of people with a legacy of oppression, he looked comfortable, most at home.

The pope's special recognition of the importance of blacks in the church took place against the backdrop of the influential National Black Catholic Congress four months before. Blacks active in the church were pressing harder for elimination of racism within all areas of Catholic life, more black bishops, and greater reflection of black culture in liturgy. A bulky pastoral plan of action in pursuit of these and other aims had emerged from the congress.

Bishop Joseph Howze of Biloxi, Mississippi, the nation's only black bishop in charge of a diocese, introduced the pope, recalling that a recent pastoral letter by black bishops had decried the "stain of racism" as not only a "major obstacle" but "the opportunity to work for the church's renewal as part of our task of evangelization.

"Black Catholics want to express our faith, reflecting our unique identity and experiences," Bishop Howze said. "Yet, at the same time, we want our expression of faith to become ever more a part of the Christian Catholic tradition, already rich in diversity and redemptive in Jesus Christ."

John Paul, seeming to draw strength from his vibrant audience, raised his voice in thanks for the many gifts to the church from the black experience. "I express my deep love and esteem for the black Catholic community in the United States," he said with emotion to thunderous applause. "Its vitality is a sign of hope for society . . . there is no black church, no white church, no American church. But there is and must be, in the one church of Jesus Christ, a home for blacks, whites, Americans, every culture and race." And he denounced the causes and effects of racism.

"Even in this wealthy nation, committed by its Founding Fathers to the dignity and equality of all persons," the pope said, "the black community suffers a disproportionate share of economic deprivation. Far too many of your young people receive less than an equal opportunity for a quality education and for gainful employment.

"The Church must continue to join her efforts with the efforts of others who are working to correct all imbalances and disorders of a social nature. Indeed, the Church can never remain silent in the face of injustice, wherever it is clearly present." The response through the hall was deafening.

Continuing, the pope paid tribute to the Reverend Dr. Martin Luther King, Jr., and the nonviolent movement that he led.

As for what blacks could do to help themselves, the pontiff returned to familiar themes, warning against worldliness, which he called worse than the "terrible burden of slavery" and urging blacks to "rediscover the spirit of family life which refuses to be destroyed in the face of even the most oppressive forces." On the one hand, he warned, "consumerism, mindless pleasure seeking and irresponsible individualism" were "shackles of the spirit which are even more destructive than the chains of physical slavery." On the other, blacks should shun "positions which weaken or destroy the family," allusions presumably to such practices as divorce and abortion. Finally, he said, "Black Americans must offer their own special solidarity of Christian love to all people who bear the heavy burden of oppression."

From the jubilant outburst of the crowd it was clear that John Paul had touched these black Catholics deeply. He had shown empathy and an acknowledgment of their situation. It was his most powerful and effective speech so far on this trip. Except for the fact that he announced no plans to increase the number of black bishops or to name a first black archbishop—a development many hoped for but few expected—he had not left them disappointed as he had Jews and ecumenical leaders. This speech had been an unqualified success.

From that triumph, John Paul was swiftly escorted to the crowd of Catholic teachers and principals, where he would hold the first of the day's three dialogues. As he entered the hall, a high school choir broke into Handel's "Halleluia Chorus." There followed four speakers in succession—a nun who served as principal of a Massachusetts high school, a laywoman who was religious education director of an Illinois parish, a monsignor who ran the school system in the Diocese of Brooklyn, and a layman who was principal of a school in St. Paul, Minnesota. They dutifully reviewed the U.S. Catholic school system, detailing for the professorial pontiff both strengths and weaknesses. He, in turn, took the occasion to commend their dedication, praise the role of parents in raising their children Catholic, and exhort the educators to inculcate the "full truth concerning the human person"—the church's "full truth," the whole truth, nothing but the truth.

From that session with teachers it seemed only natural that the pope should next meet with the forty thousand students seated around the Superdome stadium where the New Orleans Saints would open their National Football League season the next day. Aboard the Popemobile, John Paul emerged through a stadium portal and slowly circled the field, waving to the wildly cheering throngs of youngsters both in the grandstands above and on the field, while, onstage, a Christian rock group pumped out a song with an explicit spiritual message: "I know we shall come together to build up the body and the kingdom of the Lord."

After receiving ceremonial gifts and hugging some of the bearers, the pope began to speak to them as a doting uncle might. His advice was that they should use their freedom to make the only choice that mattered: the truth as taught by the church. It was the now-familiar theme reaching a new crescendo. The word *truth* appeared exactly two dozen times in the text of the speech; *true,* another four times.

"Let no one deceive you about the truth of your lives," the young Catholics were told by their Holy Father. "The opposite of deception is truth—the person who tells the truth, the person who is the truth. Yes, the opposite of deception is Jesus Christ." And the "truth of Christ" meant that a divine plan existed for each and every one of them, a plan that ruled out egotism. Pausing to add emphasis, he told them that "there is no room in the church for selfishness. There is no room in New Orleans for selfishness. It destroys the meaning of life; it destroys the meaning of love; it reduces the human person to a subhuman level." Rather, the plan called them to a life of "justice and fraternal love."

Partnership with Christ and his plan meant practicing the values of the Beatitudes—among them meekness, mercy, and peace—and heeding the church's proscription of sex outside marriage. No matter how much the world might scoff at these limitations on sex, the pope said, "the message of Jesus is clear: purity means true love and it is the very opposite of selfishness and escape. Love is purity. Purity is love. I thank God you are understanding that."

The "truth of Jesus" applied to all of life, he asserted, his voice rising in urgency. "The world will try to deceive you about many things that matter: about your faith, about pleasure and material things, about the danger of drugs," he warned them. "And at one stage or another the false voices of the world will try to exploit your human weakness by telling you that life has no meaning at all for you. The supreme theft in your lives would be if they succeeded in robbing you of hope. They will try, but not succeed if you hold fast to Jesus and his truth." He urged them to pray. It would get them out of themselves and open them to God's plan.

Prime elements of John Paul's theological outlook had come through with crystal clarity. The world was risky, full of dangers and calumny, a grand deception, lost without the full revelation witnessed to by the church. By implication, the vices and delusions were harder to detect in America, where freedom and affluence painted an alluring picture of the "good life." The speech was a succinct summary of his evangelistic appeal, preached fervently to those who faced crucial choices about the direction of their lives.

Four speeches and countless smiles into the day, John Paul repaired to the home of Archbishop Hannan, on a street festooned with ribbons in the papal colors of yellow and white, for lunch with two dozen prelates that featured New Orleans specialties, gumbo and grits, from Antoine's, one of the city's famous eateries.

By mid-afternoon, skies were darkening over the grounds of the University of New Orleans where the papal mass was to begin at 4:00. Those inclined to find omens had cause to be on high alert. In Miami, a fierce storm had cut short the outdoor mass in the middle of the pope's speech. On the same day, twin twelve-story towers had been wrecked by another violent downpour at the site of the scheduled mass at his next stop, San Antonio. Now, just prior to the start of the second public liturgy, high winds drove sheets of rain into the shelterless crowd amid slashes of lightning and sharp claps of thunder. Frightened worshipers scurried every which way for protection.

By the time the dark clouds had rolled away, allowing the colorful liturgy to begin, the temperature had dropped from an early afternoon high of 103 degrees to a more comfortable 75. The musical trimmings of the mass were top drawer. Al Hirt, whose trumpet was a signature of New Orleans jazz, played an evocative rendition of "Ave Maria," and another of the city's stars, Pete Fountain, played the black spiritual "Just a Closer Walk with Thee" on his clarinet. "I have always heard about the beautiful music of New Orleans," John Paul said in response. "Today I have been able to hear it and admire it personally."

In his homily, the pope exhorted the damp crowd to show mercy toward others, as Jesus taught. They must practice justice, he said, but mercy went beyond justice. In what appeared to be a rebuke to the death penalty, which Louisiana had taken a leading role in practicing, he said, "Christ is very clear: when we ourselves are without sympathy or mercy, when we are guided by 'blind' justice alone, then we cannot count on the mercy of . . . God—God before whom we are all debtors." All people were indebted to God for his forgiveness, the pope said, and should express their gratitude for his mercy by forgiving others. But many people today "especially those caught up in a civilization of affluence and pleasure, live as though sin did not exist and God did not exist."

The exercise of loving mercy was needed nowhere more than within families, the pope said, taking the opportunity to put in another forceful word for the church's refusal to grant divorce. Lack of forgiveness can put marriages under great strain, he said, adding a defense of church law on pragmatic grounds. "No doubt some people will object that Christ's teaching about the indissolubility of marriage, as it is upheld by the church, is lacking in compassion," the pope said. "But what must be seen is the ineffectiveness of divorce, and its ready availability in modern society, to bring mercy and forgiveness and healing to many couples and their children, in whose troubled lives there remain a brokenness and a suffering that will not go away."

More than two hours elapsed before the mass concluded. Evening was at hand, and John Paul still had one more appointment, a highly anticipated meeting with the presidents of Catholic colleges and universities at Xavier University, the only one among the 235 church-affiliated institutions founded for blacks.

Xavier was the most logical setting for the pope to speak to the two internal church issues that had raised the loudest alarms among Catholic college officials: the shape of the Vatican's much-debated policy document on higher education, which in its latest version proposed much more involvement by bishops in university affairs than most administrators could accept, and the role of theologians in the wake of the cancellation of Father Curran's license to teach in the name of the church on grounds that he improperly dissented against Catholic teaching in several areas of sexuality. Father Curran had argued all along that he had exercised a legitimate right by disagreeing only with noninfallible teachings. Controversy raged over whether theologians were entitled to any forthright dissent and, if so, under what circumstances. The opportunity to speak to the issue was one that the pope was believed to be unlikely to pass up.

John Paul offered his thoughts from under an umbrella. Rain had moved back into the area, soaking the crowd in the open quadrangle before tapering off to a steady drizzle during the pope's speech. Though nearing the end of a marathon day, the pope looked stalwart and spoke resolutely.

He praised the work of the church's colleges, reminded his listeners (among them Father Caron) that theirs was both a human and a divine task and encouraged them to bolster the Catholic identity of their schools. The linchpin of the university, he recalled, was the church's confidence that reason never conflicts with faith. "Faith and love of learning have a close relationship, a basic compatibility," he said. The pluralism of ideas in the modern academy did not "exist for its own sake," he insisted, but must be "directed to the fullness of truth." It was this need to keep faith in steady dialogue with reason that for him made the hierarchy's involvement so crucial.

"The Bishops of the Church, as *Doctores et Magistri Fidei,* should be seen not as external agents," the pope said, "but as participants in the life of the Catholic university in its privileged role as protagonist in the encounter between faith and science and between revealed truth and culture."

It was the question of how bishops were to be "participants" that had raised so much anxiety among the college presidents. The Vatican's draft of its schema on higher education included a provision that would give bishops the right to approve faculty positions in theology. Most presidents had read this as permitting church meddling in the internal life of the university, a practice that would, in the estimation of the majority of presidents, breach church-state separation and thereby disqualify their schools from receiving public funds. Government aid, which had gone a long way toward keeping their schools afloat, was given on the condition that the university be free of outside interference by church officials, therefore independent of external controls. The pope's words left open how far he thought bishops should go, but seemed clear that he had something in mind that was closer to the intent of the draft schema than the wishes of the presidents. At the very least, it appeared that the strenuous pleading by the presidents for a change in Vatican thinking on this point had so far made no obvious impact.

John Paul also had something to say about theologians. Combating "intellectual and moral relativism," the pope said, required a "metaphysical approach" in which "theological science has a special role" and was "much more than an academic discipline." Theology, he said, was "truly a search to understand ever more clearly the heritage of faith preserved, transmitted, and made explicit by the Church's teaching office." The bishops, in concert with the pope, were ultimate guardians of theological truth and needed theologians to assist them in this process.

"But theologians also need the charism entrusted by Christ to the Bishops and, in the first place, to the Bishop of Rome," he continued in a key passage. "The fruits of their work, in order to enrich the life-stream of the ecclesial community, must ultimately be tested and validated by the Magisterium. In effect, therefore, the ecclesial context of Catholic theology gives it a special character and value, even when theology exists in an academic setting."

The pope concluded his talk by calling on the presidents and administrators to awaken social concerns among their students. "University students," he said, "are in a splendid position to take to heart the Gospel invitation to go out of themselves, to reject introversion and to concentrate on the needs of others." He encouraged student involvement in the "whole social order," including "economics, politics, and human rights and relations."

Close to 9:00 P.M. the pope's motorcade pulled into Notre Dame Seminary, where the pontiff wished a group of Polish Americans a good night. Then he continued next door to the archbishop's residence to call it a day.

Two aspects of the New Orleans visit were especially striking. One was that none of the three structured dialogues had stirred any debate. Young people, college presidents, and Catholic school leaders represented groups with grievances toward Rome in one form or other. They were all part of the "American problem." Yet the contributions from those who spoke for them gave not the slightest hint that they were among the constituencies of Catholic America whose allegiance to the Vatican was, to varying extents, tenuous.

It was also evident by New Orleans that the pope was generating far less excitement along the tour route than he had his first trip. From the start crowds had been much smaller than expected. Church officials continued to cite a cluster of factors—including ubiquitous television coverage, bad weather, and the media's exaggerated reports of logistical difficulties—for holding down the turnout. But nearly everyone agreed that there was more to it. The spark somehow wasn't there.

Figures from New Orleans provided the latest documentation of the expectations gap. The bleachers outside Saint Louis Cathedral that morning had not been full. The stadium at the Superdome was prepared to handle 71,500 young people: 46,000 came. Upwards of a quarter million were expected at the open-air mass, but just 130,000 showed. Church officials complained that the press was making too much of crowd sizes, but it was plainly news when the response to the pope fell so far short of the church's own estimates.

Still, New Orleans had been eventful for the church in America, the pope's encounters with key groups significant. New Orleans was now history. Texas lay over the horizon.

SAN ANTONIO WAS THE BUCKLE IN THE SOUTHERN HISPANIC BELT, THE HEARTland of Spanish-speaking Catholic America. Seventy percent of the city's Catholics were Hispanic. Among them were the first Hispanic mayor of a major U.S. city, Henry Cisneros, and the first Hispanic in the nation to head an archdiocese, Archbishop Patrick Flores. It was home of the influential Mexican-American Cultural Center and San Fernando Cathedral, founded by the Spanish more than 250 years ago. The visit by the pope was intended to highlight the growing Hispanic presence in Catholic America.

That formidable presence—up to a third of all U.S. Catholics and increasing rapidly, accounting for most of the church's numerical rise in recent years— though seen as a blessed source of new life for Catholic America, had been accompanied by nagging and chronic problems. Hispanics complained of being shunned, neglected, or taken for granted by the church. In various ways, they were putting church officials on notice that, despite their Catholic origins, the church could not simply count them as loyalists no matter what. Nearly a fourth of them had joined other churches that specialized in meeting personal needs. Others, reared with a Latin attitude that viewed church-going much more casually than did North American Catholics, kept their distance from the institution.

Added to that were the relative hiddenness of so many Hispanics, whose poverty or illegal status consigned them to the margins of society, the wounds borne by immigrants in the throes of culture shock, and the paucity of Hispanic priests. These difficulties composed a picture that was staggeringly complex. The net effect for the church was that Hispanics were somehow loosely within the Catholic-American fold but not part of it to any degree proportionate to their numbers. They constituted a huge group of outsider insiders, whose future, it was widely assumed, would largely shape the U.S. church.

Here in San Antonio, the crucible in which churned the most fervent hopes and the most distressing problems of Hispanic life in the United States, the pope would need all his gifts as an evangelist as he sought to woo the lost sheep home and uplift those who had never left.

After landing at Kelly Air Force Base, John Paul was whisked away in a closed limousine to the site of the outdoor liturgy, a 114-acre pasture in Westover Hills, a natural cup in the earth twelve miles northwest of downtown San Antonio that had been donated for the purpose by a Jewish businessman.

Round-the-clock efforts had cleared away the debris left in the wake of the ferocious storm that had struck the area Friday. The high winds had sent the twin twelve-story staging towers crashing to the ground, damaging sections of the altar construction. Designers and crews responded immediately, improvising by hoisting banners on cranes behind the altar.

The welfare of the crowd had continued to worry planners, though the public clamor had eased off since the city's former health commissioner, warning that hundreds could die from intense heat and shortage of water, had abruptly resigned earlier in the summer. The day was indeed hot, with temperatures soaring into the mid-nineties. But the crowd was again—perhaps mercifully—smaller than expected. The prediction had been 500,000; the actual figure was about 300,000, the largest reception the pope had so far received. Included among them were an estimated 10,000 Mexicans, far fewer than expected, who had crossed over the border, 150 miles away, on visitor passes.

The bulk of the faithful had come well equipped with protective gear and water containers. From his papal throne, John Paul could gaze out on a vast array of umbrellas that looked like a field of newly sprouted mushrooms.

In his homily, the pope returned to the theme of penance. Sin was certainly not a subject the pope reserved for the United States, but he was lending it urgency during these days, as if bent on reminding this boisterous, proud country that it, too, fell prey to transgression and that it paid a great price if it ignored that fact. "Today, on this Lord's Day, I wish to invite all those who are listening to my words not to forget our immortal destiny," the pope said: "life after death—the eternal happiness of heaven, or the awful possibility of eternal punishment, eternal separation from God, in what the Christian tradition has called hell."

The practice of confession had suffered "a great neglect" in certain parts of the world, the pope noted. He urged bishops and priests to "do everything possible" to emphasize the sacrament. And in an implicit criticism of the growing practice in the United States of "general absolution," during which the entire congregation collectively received absolution, the pope said, "Just as sin deeply touches the individual conscience, so we understand why the absolution of sins must be individual and not collective, except in extraordinary circumstances as approved by the Church." Entered into properly, the sacrament of penance led to trust in God's forgiveness and to the possibility of the "vibrant renewal of the whole Catholic Church."

Confession, as the pope was defining it, was not primarily a checklist of iniquities or an institutional mechanism of control through guilt. It was instead a means whereby people could discover responsibility for themselves and their society, a process by which they uncovered God's love and compassion as the prelude to finding their roles in society.

As a consequence of God's mercy, the pope said that those who had been forgiven were obliged to bring "hope and love wherever there is division and alienation." He singled out those who took risks to aid refugees from Latin America for special praise in advancing that cause. Referring to "the movement of people northward" from Mexico and other countries, he said, "Among you there are people of great courage and generosity who have been doing much on behalf of suffering brothers and sisters arriving from the south. They have sought to show compassion in the face of complex human, social, and political realities. Here human needs, both spiritual and material, continue to call out to the Church with thousands of voices, and the whole church must respond by the proclamation of God's word and by selfless deeds of service. Here too there is ample space for continuing and growing collaboration among members of the various Christian Communions." By serving the "needy and the persecuted," the pope said, America lived up to the values of justice and freedom embedded in the Constitution.

That passage would create the media headlines for the day's coverage of the papal trip, sounding as it did like a veiled endorsement of the sanctuary movement. That interfaith effort, centered in the Southwest, had run afoul of the law for helping refugees escape what movement activists considered political oppression in countries south of the border. Short of outright support for that effort, the pope had at the very least given his general backing to the refugees and those who worked with them at a time of sharp debate over whether immigrants from Central America should be admitted and intense dispute over the one-year alien amnesty program. Some church officials had loudly assailed that program as badly flawed and totally insufficient. Catholics who worked with newcomers on either front could feel bolstered by the pope's words.

As the mass concluded, the pope blessed the crowd in Spanish and English, and Beethoven's "Ode to Joy" flowed over the rolling terrain. The throngs began their long trek to the buses, some walking fully two miles. The pope went to eat lunch and rest at the seminary before giving a major speech to the annual convention of Catholic Charities.

Before the pope took the platform at Municipal Auditorium, the executive director of Catholic Charities USA, the Reverend Thomas J. Harvey, put some zing back into the concept of the structured dialogue. His lively contribution reflected a change of direction in the organization he headed.

Catholic Charities, a network of 633 member agencies, had established itself as a highly respected social service arm of the church, meeting the needs of individuals and families with compassion and efficiency. But in recent years, in keeping with the church's increasing focus on attacking the root causes of injustice, the organization had begun to devote more of its resources to social change. Because the newer role often entailed working for political reform, Catholic Charities had drawn criticism from those who objected to such activism. But agency leaders had refused to back away from what they regarded as responsible advocacy.

Speaking to the pope on behalf of his colleagues, Father Harvey proved to be the most candid, challenging dialogue partner since Father McNulty had spoken for priests in Miami. Chiding the nation for neglecting the poor, Father Harvey declared that "we in Catholic Charities lament the lack of commitment today to include ever more people in the opportunities of this nation. Millions of homeless persons live in our streets. Thirty-four million Americans live below the government-defined poverty line. One quarter of our children, one quarter of our nation's future, lives in poverty. . . . Our ministry is to transform society into an environment worthy of the enhanced dignity Jesus conferred on all people."

Calling on bishops, pastors, and the laity to help "build a fully humane and just society" by working to improve conditions for the poor, Father Harvey added tersely, "Do not be deceived by the perception that the only enemy which threatens this country is one which challenges the common defense. Poverty, unemployment, and the erosion of family stability also attack our nation from within."

Father Harvey then turned his attention to the pope. Urging the pontiff to continue campaigning for justice and human rights, the priest added an appeal for a more open-minded approach to issues *within* the church as one means of helping enhance the church's social ministry.

"Where people are suffering from such debilitating problems as divorce, diseases such as AIDS, and the ambiguity of changing life-styles," Father Harvey said, "we ask patience of the Church's teachings so that we do not close the door to opportunities for better solutions to these pressures of our changing world than our present wisdom easily affords."

His suggestion that the church's answers to moral issues such as divorce were inadequate and that "better solutions" could emerge under more flexible circumstances was in sharp contrast to what the pope had taught. John Paul understood the church's moral teachings as divinely revealed fixed truths rather than temporary, historically conditioned precepts that could be improved. With Father Harvey's appeal, the debate had been joined on behalf of the great numbers of

Catholic Americans who apparently agreed that "better solutions" were possible and desirable.

The pope's response made no mention of Father Harvey's challenge to leave some slack in the church's moral reins. It was a nuanced statement of John Paul's understanding of the church's rightful role in combating poverty and injustice. Christ had enjoined his followers to reach out to all who were afflicted with love and acts of charity, to enhance their dignity, the pope said. He invoked the New Testament story of the haughty rich man who was cast into the torments of hell for ignoring the pleas of the poor man, Lazarus, who lay at his doorstep during their earthly existence. The condemned rich man now gazed enviously upon the poor man exonerated in paradise. It served as a dire warning not only to wealthy individuals but to rich nations who fail to heed the cries of the poor. It obviously served the pope's mission to the United States very well.

"In his kingdom the poor have a special place," he said. "The Church cannot be any different." But poverty was a broad concept, he added, more than just "a matter of material deprivation." It also included, he said, "spiritual impoverishment," the "lack of human liberties" and the consequence of "any violation of human rights and human dignity."

"There is a very special and pitiable form of poverty," he continued, "the poverty of selfishness, the poverty of those who have and will not share, of those who could be rich by giving but choose to be poor by keeping everything they have. These people too need help."

Relieving suffering must include "direct action" toward those in need while helping them attain "the dignity of self-reliance," the pope declared. Moreover, he said, "Service to the poor also involves speaking up for them, and trying to reform structures which cause or perpetuate their oppression." Concern for this task further required Catholics to ponder "the relationship between rich societies and poor societies."

Though giving thumbs up to an institutional approach to social change that had a liberal bent, John Paul's conclusions had a decidedly conservative tilt. "The organizational and institutional response to needs, whether in the Church or in society, is extremely necessary, but it is not sufficient in itself," he said, adding, "In the final analysis . . . we must realize that social injustice and unjust social structures exist only because individuals and groups of individuals deliberately maintain or tolerate them. It is these personal choices, operating through structures, that breed and propagate situations of poverty, oppression, and misery. For this reason, overcoming 'social' sin and reforming the social order must begin with the conversion of our hearts."

Social action had a place in the pope's thinking, though the exact nature of that involvement remained vague. The American bishops, in their pastoral letter on the economy, had argued that government should take the lead in erasing poverty, but the state figured nowhere in the pope's speech. He cited the bishops' letter in one brief, unrelated quote. He placed importance instead on spiritual remedies, specifically on personal conversion. The pope was wary of organized efforts for social change in the name of the church. His years of deprivation under avowed Marxists had turned him against anything that smacked of class warfare, social engineering in the name of "the people," or violence. As he insisted in his speech, "Force and manipulation have nothing to do with true human development and the defense of human dignity."

In closing, John Paul extolled American generosity, expressed gratitude for the achievements of Catholic Charities, and gave a nod to the Constitution, whose birthday was fast approaching. "By working for a society which fosters the dignity of every human person," he said, "not only are you serving the poor, but you are renewing the founding vision of this nation under God."

Before moving on to a Hispanic parish on San Antonio's west side, the pope paid a call at the picturesque San Fernando Cathedral, the nation's oldest, founded in 1731, where the Mexican General Santa Anna had waved the bloody flag to signal his troops to take no prisoners at the Alamo. Gathered in the cozy church were 825 men and women from Texas dioceses studying for the priesthood or religious orders. They gave him a rousing reception, shouting *"Viva El Papa"* and *"Papa Juan Pablo, todo el mundo te ama"* ("John Paul, the whole world loves you"). His face was radiant, reflecting the special joy of being at home with those to whom he felt special ties.

He took the occasion to assert what he called an "essential difference" between clergy and laity, which he summed up as "the truth that Jesus entrusted the Twelve" (the putative original priests), and which thereafter belonged exclusively to the ordained, namely, "the authority to proclaim the Gospel, celebrate the Eucharist, forgive sins, and provide for the pastoral care of the community." It was John Paul's "high" view of the priesthood, which tended to maximize the distance between holy orders and the laity. Though paying respect to the Second Vatican Council's conviction that all Catholics were called to a life of holiness, he quickly made it clear that laypeople had a "mission which is uniquely their own" and should not be confused with that of the clergy. In Catholic America, of course, those lines were becoming increasingly blurred.

The pope also commended celibacy to the youthful congregation, calling it "an enhancement of your life," an opportunity for "greater closeness to God's people," and "a gift of yourself to God." He went on, "Humanly speaking, this sacrifice is difficult because of our human weaknesses; without prayer it is impossible. It will also require discipline and effort and persevering love on your part. But in your gift of celibacy to Christ and his Church, even the world will be able to see the meaning of the Lord's grace and the power of his Paschal Mystery."

The pope's next stop, Our Lady of Guadalupe, in the heart of the city's west side *barrio,* had been immaculately scrubbed, polished, and painted for the visit by the pope. It would be his only scheduled appearance at a parish on his tour. The site chosen was significant in that it both honored Hispanic Catholics and dramatized the growing alarm at their rising rate of attrition from the church.

Excited parishioners and visitors, numbering about three thousand, were packed into the plaza in front of the church to welcome the pope. A procession of singers, dancers, and various music makers provided hours of entertainment for the festive, joyful, sun-baked audience. When the pope entered, he was showered with shouts of *"Viva Papa,"* the crowd buoyed by the vigorous strains of a mariachi band. John Paul blessed his well-wishers, then paused to admire the vibrant mural that bordered the stage. It depicted the Blessed Virgin appearing as Our Lady of Guadalupe hovering over the parish and its environs. The pope studied the mural intently, nodding in approval.

The sun was setting, and a cool breeze wafted over the plaza as the pope began to speak. His words of greeting, his endearments, his speech were entirely in Spanish, the sole occasion on his pilgrimage when that would happen. His mission was wrapped in affection and lightheartedness, but it had a serious purpose. John Paul was there to do some heavy-duty Catholic evangelism in response to what he saw as gaps in the widely held Hispanic style of Catholicism and a more general neglect of many parish-based activities across the nation.

Among the features of the Hispanic style was a certain casualness toward the institution and its rituals, an openness to mixing elements of Catholicism with other religious and folk traditions in varieties of home-based shrines, and, of course, apparently a growing inclination to discard formal Catholic allegiance for other churches. By normative European and North American church standards, Hispanics placed far less emphasis on the parish and its ritual obligations, but their spirituality ran deep and flowed abundantly. The question for many church leaders was, How could this spiritual fervor be directed into standard parish channels? That was the assignment that the pope had taken on. Every major point in his speech was linked to something church authorities perceived as a problem that contributed to the loss to other churches. Though directed principally at Hispanics, his words had broad application across Catholic America.

Spanish-speaking people were the first evangelizers of the region, the pope noted at the outset. His central message, he said, was that parish life was the prime locus for continued evangelism today. That same parish that so many Hispanics viewed from a distance was vital in John Paul's vision of redemption. The first point he wanted to make was that the parish was utterly indispensable for the nurture of the Christian life. It alone provided the essentials for full religious practice.

Second, he asserted that the church's teaching cannot be done free-lance or *ad hoc;* it has "an objective content." "We cannot invent the faith as we go along," he said, implying that many, in fact, did just that. "We must receive it in and from the universal community of faith, the Church to whom Christ himself has entrusted a teaching office under the guidance of the Spirit of Truth." That primary educational unit, the family, must, above all, heed the "authentic teaching of the Church."

John Paul's third point was that the parish must intensify its efforts to strengthen families, which he called the "living cells of the parish," and to mend those that were broken. This service involved "proclaiming the whole truth about marriage and family life," the pope said, "the exclusive nature of conjugal love, the indissolubility of marriage, the Church's full teaching on the transmission of life, and the respect due to human life from the moment of conception until natural death, the rights and duties of parents with regard to the education of their children, especially their religious and moral education, including proper sex education." Makeshift Catholicism was unacceptable, the pope insisted.

Fourth, the sacraments were a "fundamental aspect" of the parish and an absolute necessity for living God's plan. In an apparent allusion to the sizable number of Hispanic couples (and non-Hispanics as well) who married outside the church—or lived together unmarried, or got divorced—the pope singled out the sacrament of matrimony for special mention. "Without it," he said emphatically, "Christ's design for human love is not fulfilled; his plan for the family is not followed. It is precisely because Christ established marriage as a Sacrament and willed it to be a sign of his own permanent and faithful love for the Church that the parish must explain to the faithful why all trial marriages, merely civil marriages, free unions, and divorces do not correspond to Christ's plan."

Likewise, the Eucharist and penance were sources of God's grace that the baptized could scarcely do without. These gifts were, by implication, available exclusively in the Catholic church. Trying to find them elsewhere, no matter how congenial other churches might be, was, not surprisingly, unimaginable to John Paul. Wayward or indifferent Hispanics were thereby put on compassionate notice.

Like a true American revivalist, the pope even concluded with his equivalent of an "altar call": "Jesus commands us to serve our neighbor, to reach out to those in need," John Paul said. "And I ask you especially to reach out to those brothers and sisters in the faith who have drifted away because of indifference or who have been hurt in some way. I invite all of you who are unsure about the Church or who doubt that you will be welcome to come home to the family of families, to come home to your parish. You belong there!"

On his way back to the residence of Archbishop Flores for the night, he took a slight detour to greet one thousand citizens of Panna Maria, Texas, who had driven sixty miles to see him. Unlikely as it might have seemed, Panna Maria claimed the distinction of being the oldest permanent Polish settlement in the nation, dating back to 1834. The former archbishop of Cracow met them at the Assumption Seminary, smiling broadly as the people lavished praise on Karol Wojtyla, toasting him in Polish. He spoke informally, telling his delighted listeners that the tale of their town was well known in Poland. He then waded among them, taking their hands in his, blessing them with words of joy and hope.

BEFORE DAWN ON MONDAY, A SIXTY-MEMBER MARIACHI GROUP POSTED TWO blocks from the pope's residence split the morning air with a rendition of *"Las Mananitas"* ("The Dear Little Tomorrows"), a Mexican song used to serenade distinguished visitors. It was 6:00 A.M., and John Paul was preparing to leave San Antonio for Phoenix. On his way to Kelly Air Force Base two hours later, he was sent off by fifty more musical groups, the path of his motorcade strewn with hundred of flowers. Thousands waved good-bye, many with tears rolling down their cheeks.

Phoenix was something else, a garden blooming in the desert, the symbol of urban life in the far Southwest. It was as newly created a city as John Paul would ever set foot in, a commingling of Indian, Spanish, and Anglo cultures. Of the 1.9 million population in the metropolitan area, 27 percent were Catholics (on the same survey of religious identity, 15 percent checked "none").

A certain brashness came with the young, resettled territory. On the day of the pope's arrival, for example, an editorial in the Arizona *Republic* boldly expounded on the divisions within Catholic America. The laity wanted more clout, the newspaper declared, but the church was neither a democracy nor "a theological debating society." Dissenters were "naive" to blame their troubles with Rome on the pope's failure to grasp the divisive issues. "He simply has a markedly different conception of the church and the timeless, unchanging quality of Catholic dogma and moral theology," the editorial said. "Doctrine, in the pontiff's mind, is not subject to majority vote or the vagaries of the latest Gallup poll." Neither Rome nor the contrary Americans could be expected to change to suit the other, the newspaper confidently predicted.

Fittingly in this boomtown, the pope took a hard look at "development" in a public address from the balcony of Saint Mary's Basilica, the city's oldest Catholic church, to a noontime crowd in the civic square. His enthusiasm for the burst of growth was more than a little tempered by critical questions about the spiral of self-indulgent enterprise that had gripped the entire nation during the Reagan years. As usual, the pontiff carefully chose his terms for defining the problem, using diplomacy and inference. "In the past forty years, in particular, you have experienced remarkable progress and development," he told the Phoenixites. "And this brings with it increased obligations and responsibilities."

Most of the rest of the speech strongly implied that the pope considered those duties largely unfulfilled. Referring to "On Development of the Peoples," the major social encyclical of his predecessor, Paul VI, John Paul noted that though the "temptation toward avarice" was common to all humanity, "Yet, does not the temptation present itself more forcefully to those who have received a larger share in the material goods of the earth?" He continued, "As you look with gratitude upon the high standard of living that many of you enjoy, at least in comparison to the rest of the world, may your hearts go out to the less fortunate. May your hearts and hands be open to the poor, both within your own society and in developing nations of the world." Development that is authentic, he insisted, "contributes to the good of every person everywhere."

Before reaching Saint Mary's, the pope had spent a morning immersed in the issues of health care. From the airport, he had gone directly to Saint Joseph's Hospital, where he walked the corridors, chatting with awe-struck nurses, attendants, and doctors and visiting, among others, a fifteen-year-old boy with brain cancer, a girl of six who had been hit by a drunk driver, paralyzing her from the neck down, and a diminutive two-and-a-half-month baby girl, born prematurely at one pound, five ounces, whom John Paul cradled in his arms.

From the hospital the pope went to a meeting of Catholic health professionals for another structured dialogue. The other half of the dialogue team this time was John E. Curley, Jr., president of the Catholic Health Association, who had had some pointed things to say about the rising struggle to provide health to the needy while staying afloat financially. There was the problem of making up for the loss of nuns and male religious who had been the mainstays of the 620 Catholic hospitals and 300 facilities for long-term care. It was the nation's "largest system of health care services under a single form of ownership," he noted; through it every year passed 40 million people and $22 billion.

Competition and soaring costs were making their job tougher, he said, squeezing limited resources. Meanwhile, the health needs of those the church was called to serve, the poor and the elderly, those whom, he said with irony, "few are competing to care for," were rising. "Our institutions and services are increasingly caught in a tension between our call to care and the need to survive in a potentially ruinous economic climate," Curley said. "Our challenge is clear. We must remain financially viable if our ministry and our witness are to continue."

Still another source of stress was the challenge of moral questions introduced by advances in medical technology. It was in the health institutions, where science offered new responses to medical problems, that such questions were raised most urgently for the whole church, Curley said. He asked the pope to hear his organization's "special concerns" in this area.

"Our nation's health-care environment increasingly poses ethical dilemmas that defy simple answers," he asserted. "Our ministry may well be placed in jeopardy if it cannot come to terms with issues such as: genetics and genetic engineering; technologically assisted human reproduction; organ procurement and transplantation; foregoing life-sustaining medical treatment; human experimentation, and so on.

"The list of ethical issues facing the Church and its health-care ministry seems endless. We do not raise these issues for discussion during your brief pastoral visit. Rather, we raise them to underscore the serious problems confronting our ministry as we approach the twenty-first century."

Though Curley never explicitly mentioned the controversial instruction on biomedical ethics issued by the Vatican in the spring, he had implicitly denied that it had decided the range of ethical matters to the satisfaction of health-care professionals. The instruction had, among other things, forbidden in vitro fertilization for childless couples, along with all other forms of technologically assisted procreation (including artificial insemination) and had called for laws banning all fetal experimentation.

Curley tried to allay any fears of dissent with an assurance of goodwill and a muted warning that the church would suffer if nothing were done. He said of his appeal, "We do so in love, in faith, and with a certain trepidation about the future."

John Paul came as close as he had yet to replying outright to a dialogue partner by restating his theology of health care. Caring for the ill was an extension of Christ's ministry of healing, he told them, and had two important dimensions. One was practical. Catholic hospitals must continue to strive to "ensure that everyone has access to health care" without concern for "social and economic status," he said, adding that the "inalienable dignity of every human being is, of course, fundamental to all Catholic health care." The other function was pedagogical. As part of the church's spiritual mission, Catholic treatment centers were called upon to become teachers of "moral truth, especially in regard to the new frontiers of scientific research and technological achievement."

This brought him to the brink of direct response to Curley's appeal for flexibility with respect to some of the emerging tough issues posed by medical science. The pope again rested his case on the truth as pronounced by the magisterium.

The church questioned breakthroughs in medical technology not to "judge harshly those who seek to extend the frontiers of human knowledge and skill," the pontiff insisted, "but in order to affirm the moral truths which must guide the application of this knowledge and skill." In defending the dignity of the human person, the church and its agencies must protect "the life and integrity of the human embryo and fetus," uphold life from conception to death, combating abortion on one end and euthanasia on the other. The instruction had been issued with exactly those goals in mind.

"Once again it [the instruction] affirmed the sacred and inviolable character of the transmission of human life by the procreative act within marriage. It explained that new technologies may afford new means of procreation, but 'what is technically possible is not for that reason morally admissible.' To place new human knowledge at the service of the integral well-being of human persons does not inhibit true scientific progress but liberates it. The Church encourages all genuine advances in knowledge, but she also insists on the sacredness of human life at every stage and in every condition."

There would be no need for retreat from the instruction's conclusions so far as the pope was concerned. The case was closed. Science was helpful as long as it left the church's divine revelations unperturbed. In a showdown between science and the church, the church rested solidly on a higher truth. Catholic health workers were enlisted in the church's cause. "You must always see yourselves and your work as part of the Church's life and mission," the pope told them, emphasizing that "there be close and harmonious links between you and the Bishops."

John Paul also invoked the example of the Good Samaritan to urge them to reach out to AIDS sufferers. It was his first public statement on the disease and came just three days before he was scheduled to meet AIDS patients in San Francisco. "Today you are faced with new challenges, new needs," he said. "One of these is the present crisis of immense proportions which is that of AIDS and AIDS-Related Complex. Besides your professional contribution and your human sensitivities toward all affected by this disease, you are called to show the love and compassion of Christ and his Church."

As he had in other cities, the pope lunched and rested at the residence of the local prelate before returning to the press of events. Late in the afternoon, he was back on track, stopping first at a gathering of ten thousand Native Americans in Veterans Memorial Coliseum. They had come to Phoenix for a three-day meeting of the Tekakwitha Conference, a group that fostered Catholicism among Native Americans and named for Kateri Tekakwitha, a seventeenth-century Mohawk woman who was expected to be made a saint soon.

The church's checkered history of relations with Native Americans, of course, went back to the earliest European incursions. Stories of forced conversion, abuse, and enslavement riddled the early accounts of missionary priests, and only gradually and unevenly had things improved. But old wounds still festered. One particular sore point was the effort to canonize the eighteenth-century founder of the original California missions, Junípero Serra, a trailblazing Spanish Franciscan whose behavior had become the focus of sharp dispute. Many Native Americans, drawing on the evidence collected by some historians, claimed Father Serra had condoned beating, forced labor, and desecration of their traditions. But other scholars examining the same record viewed Father Serra, who died in 1784, as a relatively enlightened, even exemplary figure who opposed the fierce religious, racial, and ethnic prejudices of his times. Under John Paul, he had already been declared "venerable," and the pope had been expected to advance his cause by beatifying him (the step before canonization), during a scheduled visit to Father Serra's grave at Carmel Mission in California. But the Vatican had announced before the start of the trip that preparations could not be completed in time for that to happen. This spawned speculation that the delay was caused more by protests and a desire to avoid the embarrassment of fueling the bitter dispute than by red tape. Meanwhile, the controversy had continued to flare.

An estimated 285,000 Native Americans were Catholics, among them twenty-five priests and one member of the hierarchy, Bishop Donald Pelotte of Gallup, New Mexico. In contrast to the campaign to elevate Father Serra, which had stirred much resentment among them, the process of canonizing Kateri Tekakwitha evoked overwhelming pride and enthusiasm. She had succumbed to smallpox in 1690 after a heroic life in Canada devoted to caring for the ill.

The pope entered the coliseum with Bishop Pelotte at the end of a long procession of Native Americans in native clothing, their steps animated by drums and gourds. The sound of a group of men singing native music in union bore an uncanny resemblance to Gregorian chant. The pope, following the line, twice circled the wooden revolving stage, eagerly reaching out to touch hands, arms, heads, cheeks, shoulders. Above the stage hung a magnificent banner done in Native American patterns in bright turquoise, red, and orange. There were more songs and dances and cheers for the beaming pope. In a graceful ceremony, he found himself in the unusual position of being subject to the ministrations of another. Emmett White, a Pima medicine man, carried out the ritual of presenting John Paul with an eagle feather, the symbol of peace, justice, and righteousness. In commanding fashion he held it over the bowed pope's head, shaking it gently, intoning chants, offering it as a gift.

Alfretta M. Antone, a Pima woman, provided a rousing introduction, welcoming the pope and urging him to exert his influence to aid Native American causes. "Upon initial contact with Europeans," she declared, "we shared the land given us by our Creator and taught others how to survive here. History, however, stands as a witness to the use and abuse we have experienced in our homelands."

She asked the pope to intervene in behalf of "Native peoples" to help secure, among other things, equal treatment, self-determination, an end to racism, fulfillment of broken treaties, and compensation for land. He could also assist those who embraced the Catholic faith by promoting the use of more Indian culture and language within the church, she said, and by hastening the sainthood of Blessed Kateri Tekakwitha. "In the name of all Native Americans," she said, "we ask your Holiness for your blessing and guidance as we walk together with God as we live here on Mother Earth and for all time to come."

To the astonishment of some in the crowd, John Paul offered a stout defense of Father Serra. Acknowledging that the first Europeans had left "a harsh and painful reality for your peoples" and that the "cultural oppression, the injustices, the disruption of your life and of your traditional societies" had indeed taken place, the pope turned to what he believed to be a brighter side. Many early missionaries had "strenuously defended the rights of the original inhabitants of this land," among them Father Serra, whose efforts deserved "special mention," the pope said.

"He had frequent clashes with the civil authorities over the treatment of Indians," the pontiff claimed. "In 1773 he presented to the Viceroy in Mexico City, a *Representacion,* which is sometimes termed a 'Bill of Rights' for Indians. The Church had long been convinced of the need to protect them from exploitation." He added, "Unfortunately not all the members of the Church lived up to their Christian responsibilities. But let us not dwell excessively on mistakes and wrongs, even as we commit ourselves to overcoming their present effects . . . we are called to learn from the mistakes of the past and we must work together for reconciliation and healing."

Not surprisingly, the pope's reading of that history was a highly preferred one that believed the good far outweighed any bad, a conclusion obviously necessary to justify Father Serra and his cause for sainthood. The audience of Native Americans sat through the apologetics in polite silence, though some later said they had been stunned by what they considered a whitewash of Father Serra and an effort to erase the historical sources of grievance.

John Paul was otherwise lavish in his praise for the dignity of Native American customs and urged the church to honor them. He called the gospel of Christ "the greatest pride and possession of your people." The biggest roar from the crowd followed his mention of Kateri Tekakwitha, whom he described as "the best-known witness of Christian holiness among the native peoples of North America, a true daughter of her people."

To improve the plight of Native Americans, the pope recommended self-help, working together to solve "common problems of unemployment, inadequate health care, alcoholism, and chemical dependency. You have endured much over hundreds of years, and your difficulties are not at an end. Continue taking steps toward true human progress and toward reconciliation within your families and among your communities, and among your tribes and nations."

As evening settled in and temperatures dropped to comfortable levels from the daytime highs in the nineties, John Paul found himself at yet another football field, the home turf of Arizona State University.

It was the feast of the Triumph of the Cross, an occasion that allowed John Paul to speak passionately about a subject that moved him deeply, the power of redemptive suffering and the mystery of Christ's salvation through offering himself up to death. At the close of the mass, two dozen people with various ailments were pushed in wheelchairs by Boy Scouts to the baptismal font. The pope thereupon closed out his day in Phoenix much as he had begun it, by touching the ailing. One by one, he anointed those brought to him with oil, laying his hands on them to bestow the sacrament of the sick.

A day after the pope had hailed the "courage and generosity" of those who helped refugees "arriving from the south," praising their "compassion in the face of complex human, social, and political realities," the Immigration and Naturalization Service requested a clarification. Was the pope, in fact, endorsing the sanctuary movement, whose defiance of regulations in protecting refugees who would otherwise have been deported had made it an irritant to the INS? Many close to the movement thought he had indirectly done so. In response, the Vatican spokesman, Dr. Joaquin Navarro Valls, said no.

"In his homily in San Antonio on Sunday," Dr. Navarro said in a prepared statement, "the Holy Father addressed the phenomenon of undocumented immigration on the moral, not legal, level. While expressing compassion for undocumented aliens and admiration for those who seek to aid them, he did not endorse any specific movement or group nor did he encourage violation of the civil laws as a solution to this problem." Each side appeared to get what it wanted. The sanctuary activists seemed satisfied that they were certainly not excluded from the pope's support, and the INS had its disclaimer.

Los angeles beckoned. the nation's second most populous urban area was not totally unfamiliar to the pontiff. Eleven years before, as a Polish cardinal, he had paid a quiet call on the city. Now he was returning on a highly conspicuous errand.

There he would set foot in the largest of all U.S. archdioceses, 2.9 million Catholics spread over nearly 8,800 square miles, an area otherwise teeming with spiritual traditions. A vast garden of religions dotted the Southern California landscape. Images of their assorted leaders, from saffron-robed Buddhist monks to richly tailored TV preachers, passed regularly across the public's field of vision. Yet L.A. was triumphantly worldly. Celebration of the things of this world was its hallmark. It was the symbolic home of the secular spirit. Religion, it seemed, like all things there, was removed from normal, everyday existence. This was the Culture of Fringe. In this realm of the brazenly worldly, this secular frontier, the pope was going to preach the gospel.

The short flight from Phoenix brought the pope to Los Angeles at about 10:00 A.M. From there, he sallied forth on the obligatory motorcade, a 7.2 mile trek to Saint Vibiana's Cathedral during which the Popemobile was at some points clocked at nearly twenty miles per hour. Some of the three hundred thousand spectators (the police were ready for at least a million) along the route complained that the pope had whizzed by in a blur. Many sent white and yellow balloons wafting in the air as he passed.

One parish along the way had prepared a greeting that fired both religious and political passions. Our Lady Queen of Angels, also known as La Placita and "The Mission Church," was the center of a thriving Hispanic ministry in downtown L.A. whose roots went back to 1781. Each weekend, more than ten thousand worshipers flocked to eleven masses, and two hundred babies were baptized. Besides spiritual succor, the mission also helped supply food, clothing, shelter, and job counseling. It had a special concern for new arrivals from Central and South America. As one of the area's main cogs in the sanctuary movement, the mission took in a steady stream of illegal aliens, housing an average of thirty-five at any time. Its priests and active laypeople openly took risks. Having placed itself in legal jeopardy, the mission found that it could not count on unstinting support from the archdiocese. Archbishops had sent mixed signals.

Mission workers had come to idolize Oscar Romero, the archbishop of San Salvador who had been assassinated after demanding that the government of El Salvador cease violence against the people. The slain archbishop symbolized both the struggle for freedom in that region and protest against U.S. policies toward the war-torn area.

To express their sentiments to the pope, a group of La Placita activists arose early the morning of the pope's arrival to make ready their display. By the street in front of the mission where John Paul was due to pass by, they hoisted a huge picture of Archbishop Romero with a banner that read: "John Paul II. The People of Oscar Romero Greet You. Bring to Us Peace and Justice." They also made artificial flowers to wave as he passed: black ones, which stood for injustice, green for hope, and white for justice. Police received rumors that mission people would try to halt the Popemobile by rushing out into the street. The local precinct captain warned them against it, and the Secret Service told the pope not to halt.

The moment arrived. Down the street came the motorcade. As the pope neared, he caught sight of the martyred archbishop, lifted his arms high as if to embrace it and made the sign of the cross toward the knot of mission loyalists. They took it as a great blessing on themselves and their cause.

Choral music filled the cathedral as the pope entered and slowly made his way to the altar. After he had greeted the congregation and blessed Los Angeles, a woman's voice broke the silence. "God bless *you*, Holy Father," she shouted. A surprised pope responded good-naturedly, "Thank you for this blessing," which, in turn, evoked loud laughter. He continued revealingly: "It is true that the pope and every bishop has a special mission to bless, but at the same time it is also true that all of us—and the pope in a special way—needs the blessing of the people of God."

In his talk, the pope plunged directly into the urgency of braving the powers of darkness in a climate of spiritual warfare. As Christians, they were united in their faith in Christ's redemptive love, he told them. As Americans, they were able to live out the implications of that faith. "However, freedom to follow your Catholic faith does not mean that it will be easy to 'speak and act' in the name of the Lord Jesus with a conscience formed by the word of God authentically interpreted by the Church's teaching. In a secularized world, to speak and act in the name of Jesus can bring opposition and even ridicule. It often means being out of step with majority opinion." But suffering for the sake of the gospel was not in vain, he assured them, because Christ had conquered the world.

By mid-afternoon, the pope's next audience was getting into high gear. Some six thousand young people aged fifteen to twenty-five packed the Universal Amphitheater, and another twelve thousand were tuned in by satellite hookup in Portland, Oregon, St. Louis, and Denver. It was the fanciest high-tech spectacle along the pope's trail, and tour planners wanted to make the most of it to show that he, and by inference the church, could excite young people, a group whose disaffection with Catholicism appeared to be growing.

Before the pope arrived, the amphitheater crowd had been coached like a game show audience in the fine art of pandemonium by nothing less than a television director, Marty Pasetta, whose credits included staging the Academy Awards. The young people were told to forget all about hushed reverence when the pope got there, but to relax and whoop it up.

They took their cues when John Paul's bleached white presence appeared from behind bright crimson curtains. Yelling, foot-stomping, whistles, and hand-clapping produced a tumult. The pope, grinning easily, taking energy from their exuberance, walked along the rim of the stage, reaching down to touch his ecstatic followers. From the outset, with the youngsters shouting, "We love you," he seemed to be having a good time with those he found easy to accept, with whom he felt no edge.

Because this was a big television event, his talk was shorter than the one he had given to the young people in New Orleans so as to permit more time for him to interact with them spontaneously and personally. He spoke to them about hope, asking them to consider where it came from.

"Why does it sometimes happen that a seemingly healthy person, successful in the eyes of the world, takes an overdose of sleeping pills and commits suicide?" he asked. "Why, on the other hand, do we see a seriously disabled person filled with great zest for life? Is it not because of hope? The one has lost all hope; in the other, hope is alive and overflowing. Clearly, then, hope does not stem from talents and gifts, or from physical health and success! It comes from something else. To be more precise, hope comes from someone else, someone beyond ourselves."

In the interest of promoting vocations, he also asked, rhetorically, why he had become a priest. It was "a mystery," he said. "Yet," he said, "I know that, at a certain point of my life, I became convinced that Christ was saying to me what he had said to thousands before me: 'Come, follow me.' There was a clear sense that what I heard in my heart was no human voice, nor was it just an idea of my own. Christ was calling me to serve him as a priest."

Then, from a red chair, he fielded prepared questions from his live and teleconference audience. In response to some, he spoke of his mother's death during his boyhood and of the dark days in Poland during the Nazi occupation. Others evoked playfulness.

The peak moment came at the end when Tony Melendez, a singer born with no arms who played the guitar with his feet, sang for the pope, "Never Be the Same." So touched was John Paul that he leapt off the stage and embraced and kissed the twenty-five-year-old performer. Melendez, a native of Nicaragua, lived in Chino with his mother, two sisters, and a brother. He used his right foot to strum the guitar and the left to press the frets. With his acquired skills, he directed music in two parishes and sometimes played for change in public parks. The sight of the emotionally overcome pope kissing his cheek was the most arresting of the trip. Gasps of joy and awe arose from the audience.

"Tony, you are a courageous young man," the pope told him. "You are giving hope to all of us."

The pontiff's next engagement, with media bigwigs, was right next door at the Registry Hotel. Movie moguls, television executives, publishers, actors, producers, directors, and other Hollywood notables had been invited to hear the pope size up their industry. Among the invitees were Bob Hope, the director Oliver Stone, Charlton Heston, Phil Donahue and his wife, Marlo Thomas, the producer Norman Lear, Paramount's chairman Frank Mancuso, and the new-age guru Shirley MacLaine. Altogether 1,450 media movers and shakers had turned out.

As the shape and style of his tour amply demonstrated, John Paul's interest in media was far from that of a detached observer. His papacy was the first that had aggressively sought to exploit communications tools to further church aims. The remarkably photogenic pope with the knack for making the deft gesture at the right moment had done very well by television—as his appearance with the young people had demonstrated—and under him the Vatican had explored new avenues for promoting the messenger and his message. A church camera crew now followed the pope on all his excursions. So for all its criticism of the media as the devil's playground, Rome was well aware of its power and its usefulness.

The media celebrities jumped to their feet with applause when the pope entered the ballroom. John Paul began his speech by paying his respects to the skills and resourcefulness of the assembled luminaries, noting their immense influence on public attitudes and behavior. The church vigorously supported their constitutional right to speak freely, but with that freedom came both dangers and opportunities. "Communications products can be works of great beauty, revealing what is noble and uplifting in humanity and promoting what is just and fair and true," the pope said. "On the other hand communications can appeal to and promote what is debased in people: dehumanized sex through pornography or through a casual attitude toward sex and human life; greed through materialism and consumerism or irresponsible individualism; anger and vengefulness through violence or self-righteousness. All the media of popular culture which you represent can build or destroy, uplift or cast down."

That responsibility meant accountability, the pontiff said, "accountability to God, to the community and before the witness of history. . . . In a sense the world is at your mercy."

The freedom to speak implied a commitment to "truth and its completeness" and a resolve to shun "any manipulation of truth for any reason." The truth of a piece of work was measured by the extent to which it upheld human dignity, the pope said. They must ask themselves, he said, if what they communicated was "consistent with the full measure of human dignity. How do the weakest and the most defenseless in society appear in your words and images: the most severely handicapped, the very old, foreigners and the undocumented, the unattractive and the lonely, the sick and the infirm? Whom do you depict as having or not having human worth?"

Society depended on their "goodwill," John Paul said. They had been entrusted with much, and he wanted them to know that the church was "on your side," supporting "all your worthy aims." To fulfill this high moral and spiritual duty, they would need to care first for their own souls, he told them. Speaking as a pastor, he offered them counsel on avoiding the vain seductions of money and glamour. "You must cultivate the integrity consonant with your own human dignity," he said caringly. "You are more important than success, more valuable than any budget. Do not let your work drive you blindly; for if work enslaves you, you will soon enslave your art. Who you are and what you do are too important for that to happen. Do not let money be your sole concern, for it too is capable of enslaving art as well as souls. In your life there must also be room for your families and for leisure.

You need time to rest and be re-created, for only in quiet can you absorb the peace of God.".

Finally, the pope offered them his encouragement and blessing. "As communicators of the human word," he said, "you are the stewards and administrators of an immense spiritual power that belongs to the patrimony of mankind and is meant to enrich the whole of the human community."

The celebrity-studded audience thanked him with thunderous applause. Just how much the message would affect their work was something else again. The movies, for example, had shown no sign of calling off their heavy reliance on sex and violence, not exactly the pope's formula for fostering human dignity. Among the summer's top hits: *Beverly Hills Cop II, Predator,* and *Robocop,* all larded with uses of deadly force, and the sex-drenched *Witches of Eastwick.*

That evening, the pope celebrated mass in the Los Angeles Coliseum, using a liturgy that honored Mary, Our Lady of Sorrows, in continuation of the feast of the Triumph of the Cross. The theme of his homily was that the sorrow and compassion of Mary gave meaning to human suffering. At the foot of the cross, the pope said, Mary experienced her greatest suffering yet remained obedient and merciful. It was a message close to the pope's heart in a land he felt that, on the whole, knew too little about darkness and suffering. This was the word meant for the spiritual army that valiantly resisted the secular, the relatively few eager to search the inner mysteries of the faith in the pope's rich meditation. "In bitterness and alienation from God and our fellow human beings we will never find the answer to the question—the 'why?' of suffering," the pope said. "Calvary teaches us that we will find an answer only through the 'obedience' mentioned in the letter to the Hebrews."

California was "beautiful and prosperous," he said, but these blessings had not erased sorrow and suffering. Modern advances, including technology, sometimes added new problems. "No amount of economic, scientific, or social progress can eradicate our vulnerability to sin and death," he insisted. "On the contrary, progress creates new possibilities for evil as well as for good. Technology, for example, increases what we can do, but it cannot teach us the right thing to do. It increases our choices, but it is we who must choose between evil and good."

Compassion such as Mary showed must find expression in every aspect of their lives, John Paul said. They must be Good Samaritans. It was "a virtue we cannot neglect in a world in which human suffering of so many of our brothers and sisters is needlessly increased by oppression, deprivation, and underdevelopment—by poverty, hunger, and disease." The world of John Paul was full of sorrow and misery that human effort, including science, could alleviate but not explain or solve. The answers for the pope were in the Paschal Mystery, from the cross to redemption.

EARLY TUESDAY MORNING, THE THREE HUNDRED AMERICAN BISHOPS MET WITH the pope for an intense session at Our Lady Queen of Angels Seminary. Four bishops had been chosen to report to John Paul on the state of Catholic America: Cardinal Joseph Bernardin of Chicago, Archbishop John Quinn of San Francisco, Archbishop Rembert Weakland of Milwaukee, and Archbishop Daniel Pilarczyk of Cincinnati. They would approach the pontiff as a team of lawyers might represent clients, pleading the case for their fellow bishops and the wider church in general, hoping for a sympathetic response. The real content of their pleading, of course, had been in the pope's hands for many weeks. His response was prepared for delivery.

The Hunthausen controversy cast its long shadow over the meeting. It had been just over a year since the Seattle archbishop announced that the Vatican had stripped him of some of his key powers on grounds that he had failed to adhere strictly enough to the church's rule book on matters such as barring non-Catholics from communion. He had been censured, over the heads of the U.S. bishops, for piloting his ship too loosely. That had not set well with the bishops. The popular archbishop had been restored to full authority in May, after mediation by a Vatican-appointed committee of American bishops led by Cardinal Bernardin, but the conflict had left a legacy of distrust and had left a sharper edge on the U.S. hierarchy's dealings with Rome.

The discussion of affairs of state would also take place against the backdrop of polls and surveys reporting areas of widespread dissent among American Catholics on several issues of vital interest to Rome, including artificial contraception, divorce and remarriage, a married priesthood, and women's ordination. The Gallup survey for the *National Catholic Reporter* (September 11 issue), for example, found that 90 percent believed they should decide birth control for themselves; 70 percent felt similarly about weighing the morality of divorce. Two-thirds felt they could be "good Catholics" while dissenting on birth control, and 58 percent felt they could claim the same status though they disagreed with the church on divorce.

The prelates began the morning with prayers in the splendid old San Fernando Mission, following which the pope spent forty-five minutes greeting the bishops one by one, shaking their hands and imparting a personal word. It was then time for business. The bishops went first.

The subject of Cardinal Bernardin's brief was Rome's relationship to the U.S. church. To grasp that better, the cardinal felt it necessary to understand the profound influence of a free society on Catholics. "We live in an open society where everyone prizes the freedom to speak his or her mind," he said. "Many tend to question things, especially those matters which are important to them, as religion is." This led them to "almost instinctively react negatively when they are told they *must* do something, even though in their hearts they may know they should do it" and to vent a "certain rebelliousness." But tension in itself was not a bad thing, Cardinal Bernardin contended. The key was to attain "a proper balance between freedom and order."

As he saw it, trouble arose from "two unfortunate tendencies." One was the habit among many Catholics of regarding Vatican directives as regressive and unreasonable. The other was the Vatican's inclination to accuse those who questioned "how a truth might be better articulated today" of apostasy. "As a result," the cardinal said, "both sides are sometimes locked into what seem to be adversarial positions. Genuine dialogue becomes almost impossible." To make matters worse, some misunderstood the pope, alleging that he failed to comprehend "the actual situation in which the Church finds herself in the different parts of the world today." Though not agreeing, neither did the cardinal exactly exempt himself from this viewpoint that was so widely held in Catholic America.

Cardinal Bernardin's prescription for improving relations was based on the quintessential American faith in working things through together as relative equals. He called for a climate in which bishops could speak to each other and to Rome "in complete candor, without fear." There was room for conflict, he believed. "Even if our exchange is characterized by some as confrontational," he said, "we must remain calm and not become the captives of those who would use us to accomplish their own ends." Such a process must finally allow for the possibility of change, "for growth and development in certain areas of the Church's life and ministry."

The practice of collegiality—sharing authority in a quasi-democratic manner—was the key to the cardinal's vision. The concept had enlivened and strengthened bishops' conferences to a degree that Cardinal Joseph Ratzinger, head of the Vatican's department of dogma, worried that such regional conferences had begun to encroach on Rome's authority. John Paul shared those reservations. During his U.S. visit, the pope had noticeably played down the bishops' conference, granting it and its chief accomplishments, the extensive pastoral letters on nuclear arms and the economy, only passing recognition.

Knowing full well the ongoing struggle for the integrity of the bishops' conference, Cardinal Bernardin put in a good word for it, describing it as a boon to Rome's interests rather than a threat. "I believe that we are learning how to balance this dimension of collegiality with the collegiality of the bishops of the universal Church," he said in exemplary code talk, "in union with you as head of the episcopal college."

It fell to the scholarly Archbishop Quinn to talk about how the church's moral teachings were affected by "new realities." The Second Vatican Council had underlined the importance of interpreting moral doctrine in light of the "signs of the times," the archbishop established as a premise. In the midst of new moral circumstances, bishops were called upon to persuade American Catholics that "the revolutionary changes which have occurred in personal and societal life in the twentieth century are not grounds for dismissing Church teaching as outmoded" and at the same time to encourage in them a "conversion of the heart" that brought home the "reality that the Christian moral life is challenging, but not onerous . . . is not a set of abstract rules designed to constrict our lives, but a call to pilgrimage and conversion that can enrich our lives."

Among the new realities Archbishop Quinn enumerated were rising divorce rates, increased affluence and educational attainment among Catholics, advances in medical technology, greater knowledge of human sexuality, and dramatic shifts in the roles of women. Though the church's "moral imperatives" provided firm guidance in meeting these challenges, Archbishop Quinn said, there should be room to maneuver in coming up with practical answers. Old remedies would not suffice, he insisted, because "we cannot fulfill our task simply by an uncritical application of solutions designed in past ages for problems which have qualitatively changed or which did not exist in the past."

Moreover, he said, "moral theology must respond to these new human realities in a manner which at once reflects what newness there is in these issues, the legitimate development of the human sciences, the enduring nature of the human person, the tradition of moral wisdom in the Church, and the absolute claims of the Gospel."

The archbishop was alluding to a method used by the U.S. bishops in writing their major pastoral letters that offered Rome a way out of its moral absolutism. That is, he drew a distinction between binding moral principles (e.g., that life is sacred) and the specific application of these principles to concrete cases. Though there could be no dispute over the precepts undergirding moral teaching, the pragmatic solutions were open to question as conditions changed. He and his fellow bishops were concerned that American Catholics "of good will" dissented from church teachings. Not all of it could be blamed on the "permissive, narcissistic and consumer qualities of our society," though he allowed that some of it was. The problem was so pressing, the archbishop said, that the bishops considered it "a continuing incentive to search more carefully for more effective ways of translating the Church's teaching into more attractive language—even when presenting the difficult or corrective teachings of the Gospel."

In rewording or reformulating practical ethical guidelines, Archbishop Quinn commended the method of dialogue the bishops had used in preparing their major pastoral letters. It was precisely that process of consulting a variety of people throughout the church that the Vatican had often been criticized for ignoring as it prepared important moral statements. "Dialog and discussion, of course, are never a substitute for the decisions of the Magisterium," the archbishop said. "But they are . . . its indispensable prolegomenon."

Reading the archbishop's message one way, it seemed innocuous. But its hints pointed to a more ambitious agenda, one that would take complaints of dissidents as the starting point for looking for better moral teachings. Viewed that way, it was revolutionary. The archbishop understood the consequences of prodding the Vatican. At the Rome Synod of Bishops in 1981, he had subtly proposed a reexamination of birth control—by suggesting that 40 million or so American dissenters might not be wrong—and had felt not so subtle heat from the Vatican to clarify his stand so as to align himself squarely with church teaching.

Archbishop Weakland, another of the brainiest of the bishops, contributed to the cordial gripe session by reporting about the laity. They constituted the "largest number of educated faithful in the world," he said, quickly laying claim to their credibility. And they were, by and large, a faithful lot who examined church teachings for themselves. Like Cardinal Bernardin, the archbishop underscored the deep influence that the spirit of liberty and free inquiry had made on their lives. They were, he said, "jealous of their tradition of freedom and deeply resent being told how to vote on an issue or for which candidate to vote. In fact, any interference might have just an opposite effect." More to the point, the archbishop stated bluntly that "an authoritarian style is counterproductive, and such authority for the most part then becomes ignored."

The laity wanted several things rather urgently, he continued. One was a spiritual means of bridging the gaps between work and family, their public and private selves, that "does not condemn the technological world in which they live and work, that helps them sift the good from the bad." Another was the desire for greater roles in the church, where, in reality, they often felt "held back by a fear that can look like clericalism or clerical control on the part of Church leadership."

Women, in particular, wanted to be "equal partners in sharing the mission of the Church," but, he lamented, many felt they were treated as "second-class citizens." Acknowledging the church's ban on the ordination of women, he continued, "Women do not want to be treated as stereotypes of sexual inferiority, but want to be seen as necessary to the full life of a church that teaches and shows by example the co-discipleship of the sexes as instruments of God's Kingdom. They seek a church where the gifts of women are equally accepted and appreciated. Many of them do not yet see the Church imaging such a co-discipleship but fear that it is still one of male superiority and dominance."

The fourth speaker was Archbishop Pilarczyk on the subject of ministry in the U.S. church. As he presented it, the picture was decidedly mixed. The downside was well known: the numbers of vocations to the religious orders of women and men had plummeted, as had recruits for diocesan seminaries. The influx of laypeople into church responsibilities had touched off turf questions: When did the laity become too clerical, and vice versa? Celibacy was a nagging issue that just wouldn't go away. The secular tide meant that society was "increasingly inhospitable to Christian belief," he told the pope, "with the result that ministry to believers and unbelievers alike is more demanding than it was in the past." On the plus side, the archbishop said, were the many benefits of increased lay participation, the rise in the ranks of deacons and an upsurge of spiritual-renewal programs.

Some concerns, he confessed, were a "source of great anxiety for us bishops." Would there be enough priests to go around? And, enigmatically, "How can we better identify and address the real questions of church order and doctrine which face us?" Could the church provide benefits for its workers? But there was also cause for rejoicing, he said. Despite problems, Archbishop Pilarczyk said, "we welcome the developments which are making the Church in our country a church of ever deepening participation and collaboration instead of a gathering of the active few and the passive many." As the result, he concluded, "Catholic people in our country have available to them depth and variety of ministry in the Church far greater than ever before."

It was a ringing endorsement of the ministry of the laity. The ministry in the U.S. church was surely in "turmoil and crisis," he conceded, "but it is not the turmoil and crisis of death and decay, but of development and of life."

Then it was the pope's turn.

He began by thanking his brother bishops for their "daily toil" and their "partnership with me in the Gospel." He went on to deliver the longest speech of the trip, a twenty-two-page response that restated his basic theology of the church.

That theology was, as the bishops were well aware, decidedly "classical" in its heavy emphasis on a pyramidical conception of authority flowing downward from the Holy Trinity through the pope and bishops to priests and finally to the people. Transcendence and permanence were key features: the otherworldly and the mystical took precedence over mundane affairs, and dogma were immutable fixtures implanted by divine revelation.

Examining Cardinal Bernardin's look at the frayed relations between Catholic America and Rome, John Paul found the cardinal's analysis seriously deficient. The cardinal had been on the right track in stressing that bishops were bound to the pope through the "notion of *communio*" (participation together in a special way through Christ's grace), but the rest of the pontiff's remarks implied criticism of the cardinal's plea for greater collaboration among various elements of the church.

It seemed to the pope, for example, that since Vatican II the "vertical dimension" of the church had been neglected in comparison with the "horizontal." It was significant that the pope never once in the speech referred to the church as the "people of God," a central theme of Vatican II and a term especially favored among

Catholic liberals. The vertical dimension was the key to grasping the divine order of church government "with the Roman pontiff as its visible head and perpetual source of unity." The bishops did well to remember that "you are, and must be, in full communion with the Successor of Peter." Papal authority was clearly supreme in every local church, and for his part, he said, he had "endeavored to fulfill my role as Successor of Peter in a spirit of fraternal solidarity with you." In bolstering the vertical, the pope clearly ignored Cardinal Bernardin's appeal for more participatory "conciliar" forms of decision making to which U.S. Catholics, as devotees of democracy, were naturally partial.

The pope moved on to assess the thoughts on moral theology by Archbishop Quinn, who had noted dissent from church teachings by Catholics "of good will" and had suggested that old solutions did not necessarily fit new ethical dilemmas, adding that the church could learn much from the social and physical sciences. The dissent issue evoked an especially sharp reaction from the pontiff.

"It is sometimes reported that a large number of Catholics do not adhere to the teaching of the Church on a number of questions," the pope said in a curiously detached manner as if his own archbishop had not just brought one of those reports, "notably sexual and conjugal morality, divorce and remarriage. Some are reported as not accepting the Church's clear position on abortion. It has also been reported that there is a tendency on the part of some Catholics to be selective in their adherence to the Church's moral teachings. It is sometimes claimed that dissent from the Magisterium is totally compatible with being a 'good Catholic' and poses no obstacle to the reception of the Sacraments. This is a grave error that challenges the teaching office of the Bishops of the United States and elsewhere."

Not only had John Paul assailed the pick-and-choose style of Catholicism practiced widely in America, he had defined it as an affront to hierarchical authority that could result in excommunication.

So far as the pope was concerned, moral dilemmas were not to be resolved through large-scale consultation within the church, drawing insights from secular disciplines. Being Catholic meant submission to the teachings of the hierarchy, pure and simple, because they derived from God. The church's task was not to open these issues to reexamination but to teach the doctrine effectively.

"To accept faith is to give assent to the word of God as transmitted by the Church's authentic Magisterium," he proclaimed. "Such assent constitutes the basic attitude of the believer, and is an act of the will as well as of the mind. It would be altogether out of place to try to model this act of religion on attitudes drawn from secular culture.

"Within the ecclesial community, theological discussion takes place within the framework of faith. Dissent from Church doctrine remains what it is, dissent; as such it may not be proposed or received on an equal footing with the Church's authentic teaching."

Bishops should discuss with theologians the "legitimate freedom of inquiry which is their right," the pope continued, but that right was strictly limited. Theologians should be encouraged to perform their valuable task of serving the "community of faith" always "subject to the authority" of the bishops. "In particular your dialogue will seek to show the unacceptability of dissent and confrontation as a policy and method in the area of Church teaching." Moreover, in order to properly insure that Catholic colleges and universities were faithfully imparting true doctrine, the pope said bishops would need "frequent contact with teaching and administrative personnel."

Archbishop Weakland's reflections on the laity, which had included a warning against "authoritarian" leadership and an appeal for full equality for women in the church, drew a less pointed reaction from the pope, with a notable exception. As he waded into the topic, he picked up on the archbishop's description of the American laity as "the largest number of educated faithful in the world" and treated it with irony. That being the case, he mused sardonically, what kind of effect were those educated Catholics having? How was an American culture "evolving today" as a result of their intervention? he asked. "Is this evolution being influenced by the gospel? Does it clearly reflect Christian inspiration? Your music, your poetry and art, your drama, your painting and sculpture, the literature that you are producing—are all those things which reflect the soul of a nation being influenced by the spirit of Christ for the perfection of humanity?

"I realize these are difficult questions to answer, given the complexity and diversity of your culture. But they are relevant to any consideration of the role of the Catholic laity," which comprised, he repeated, "'the largest number of educated faithful in the world.'" There might be a correlation between education and devotion to the church, the pope had allowed, but he seemed to have his doubts.

Bishops could serve laity best through the sacraments and "preaching and teaching the word of God with fidelity to the truth." They were to support family life as prescribed by the church, he said, striving "to present as effectively as possible the whole teaching of the Church, including the prophetic message contained in *Humanae vitae* [the birth control encyclical]." He praised the bishops for promoting peace, fostering justice, and defending human life.

On the topic of women, the pope said the church's aim was "to promote their human dignity," which, he emphasized, was "equal to that of men's dignity," but he stopped far short of endorsing Archbishop Weakland's call for a redress of injustices against women or for new forms of co-discipleship. "As I have stated and as Archbishop Weakland has pointed out," the pope said, "women are not called to the priesthood. Although the teaching of the Church on this point is quite clear, it in no way alters the fact that women are indeed an essential part of the Gospel plan to spread the Good News of the Kingdom."

John Paul's thoughts on vocations took note of Archbishop Pilarczyk's assessment of the difficulties posed by increasing secularism, but he counseled the bishops against falling prey to the "prophets of doom" who foresaw the inevitability of drastic shortages of seminarians. "We must resist them in their pessimism," the pope implored them, "and continue in our efforts to promote vocations to the priesthood and religious life. Prayer for vocations remains the primary way to success."

Though welcoming the increasing participation of the laity, he carefully avoided using the words *ministry* and *vocation* to define their roles (which implied equal standing with the ordained). Nor did he support the archbishop's idea of exploring new ways of expanding those traditional concepts. It was important to him that the role of the ordained retain its distinct and separate status. The "ministry" of the priest and the "involvement" of the laity in the mission of the church were complementary rather than consistent with each other, the pope explained. "Just as the priestly ministry is not an end in itself, but serves to awaken and unify the various charisms within the Church," he said, "so too the involvement of the laity does not replace the priesthood, but supports it, promotes it, and offers it space for its own specific service." To the degree that Archbishop Pilarczyk spoke for those American Catholics who saw the drop-off in recruits as an opportunity for the laity to step forward in new areas of service, the pope was registering his disagreement. For him, a more active laity was not the answer.

He exhorted the bishops to keep a close watch on seminaries in order to safeguard the "dogmatic and moral teaching of the Church." He stressed that their involvement in seminary training "can never end. It is too central a task and too important a priority in the life of the Church. The Church of tomorrow passes through the seminaries of today."

At the close of the speech, the pope issued instructions on a few other concerns, including another warning against abuse of general absolution and a reminder about the church's stand on homosexuality. "I wish to encourage you also in the pastoral care that you give to homosexual persons," he said. "This includes a clear explanation of the Church's teaching, which by its nature is unpopular." All Christians were "always worthy of the Church's love and Christ's truth," he said. A day hence he would be in San Francisco where that teaching had encountered particular opposition.

The meeting adjourned, and the pope joined the bishops at lunch. In the aftermath of their unusual exchange, two impressions stood out. One was that the bishops, through their appointed spokesmen, had gained something by being allowed to voice their concerns to the pope but, as a practical matter, had come away empty-handed. Nearly everything they had commended about the U.S. church as well as their suggestions for substantive change had been ignored or rebuffed by John Paul. The other impression was that the pope had firmly re-asserted his control of the church by vigorously upholding his hierarchical un-derstanding of authority and demanding total allegiance to it. That was exactly the kind of stand-up proclamation of Catholic orthodoxy that buoyed conservatives and allayed their anxieties about what they saw as resurgent "Americanism."

Later, Archbishop Pilarczyk, speaking to reporters on behalf of the bishops, said on an upbeat note that the meeting had demonstrated that "collegiality is alive and well." With regard to the pontiff's warning that those who disobeyed church teach-ings could not be considered "good Catholics" and might, in fact, be denied the sacraments, the archbishop took an equally sanguine view. "It's very clear to me that you can't in good conscience pick and choose among teachings, then contend you're in good standing," he said, "but I don't think the pope is saying that every-body practicing birth control should leave the church." Deciding something so im-portant should be done on a case by case basis, he thought. And he didn't feel the bishops had been scolded or that the pope's statements implied any "displea-sure with the church in this country." The bishops had simply been told that they were expected to teach hard truths no matter what the consequences, the arch-bishop concluded. "The purpose of the church is not to have lots of people in it," he said. "the purpose is to teach the teachings of Christ."

From doing the most serious business with his bishops, John Paul moved to a more playful setting, a classroom full of Catholic schoolchildren. Accompanied by Nancy Reagan, the pope talked and joked with twenty-one students at Immaculate Conception School, tenderly imparting advice and answers to their prepared questions in his broken English, looking thoroughly delighted. The children were excited and entranced. Before leaving, he gently hugged and kissed each child.

There remained for him in Los Angeles a visit with eight hundred representa-tives of non-Christian religions at the Japan Cultural Center and a final mass at Dodger Stadium.

The interreligious gathering included Hindus, Buddhists, Muslims, and Jews, though some Jewish leaders refused to attend in protest over the Waldheim inci-dent. The leader of Roman Catholicism urged joint religious efforts to achieve human rights, justice, and peace on the strength of their mutual foundation in conscience. He paid respect to each of the four faiths and pointed to the existen-tial challenge posed to them and the church by the secular mentality. "Dear broth-ers and sisters of these religions and of every religion," he said, "so many people today experience inner emptiness amid material prosperity because they over-look the great questions of life. What is man? What is the meaning and purpose of life?. . . These profoundly spiritual questions, which are shared to some degree by all religions, also draw us together in a common concern for man's earthly welfare, especially world peace.

"The fragile gift of peace will survive only if there is a concerted effort on the part of all to be concerned with the glaring inequalities not merely in the enjoyment of possessions but even more in the exercise of power," the pope said.

At Dodger Stadium a record crowd of sixty-three thousand rose to its feet sounding a tumult as John Paul, robed in red, entered in the Popemobile and circled the field. The joyous throng waved handkerchiefs, hats, bandanas, anything available, to show their affection.

In his homily, the pope underscored the unity among Catholics and their need to take unpopular stands. Though they belonged to the one church in Christ through the working of the Holy Spirit, he told them, that did not mean sacrificing their distinctiveness. "In the Church in Los Angeles," he exclaimed, "Christ is Anglo and Hispanic, Christ is Chinese and Black, Christ is Vietnamese and Irish, Christ is Korean and Italian, Christ is Japanese and Filipino, Christ is Native American, Croatian, Samoan, and many other ethnic groups." There was "unity in diversity." The crowd cheered its approval.

It was the feast day of two third-century saints, Pope Cornelius and Bishop Cyprian, he noted. They had fostered unity during "a time of painful dissension" in the church, he said, drawing what appeared to be a shrewd parallel with the situation he had found in Catholic America. "How appropriate," he said, "that we should observe their feast on the day when the present Successor of Peter is meeting with the Bishops of the United States. The feast focuses our attention on a basic truth, namely that the unity of the members of the Church is deeply affected by the unity of the Bishops among themselves and by their communion with the Successor of Peter."

At several points in his homily, the pope switched to Spanish, to the great delight of the large Hispanic contingent. They also applauded wildly when he praised those who had helped millions of resident aliens gain their citizenship.

Coming to the end of his stay in trendy Los Angeles, the pope somberly exhorted his people to resist secular temptation even if it exacted a price. "The Church faces a particularly difficult task in her efforts to preach the word of God in all cultures where the faithful are constantly challenged by consumerism and a pleasure-seeking mentality, where utility, productivity and hedonism are exalted while God and his law are forgotten," he said. "In these situations, where ideas and behavior directly contradict the truth about God and about humanity itself, the Church's witness must be unpopular. She must take a clear stand on the word of God and proclaim the whole Gospel message with great confidence in the Holy Spirit." It could be a lonely task, he knew, for only a minority grasped it. Sometimes, for the sake of the gospel, he believed, smaller was better.

—◣ ◢—

On thursday, september 17, the papal entourage left los angeles for seven hours in Monterey before moving on to San Francisco. Monterey had been chosen to allow the pope access to the 217-year-old Carmel Mission where Junípero Serra, the controversial Franciscan saint-in-waiting, was buried. As originally conceived, the pope would have declared him beatified at that time. But because that step had been postponed, for what the Vatican attributed to procedural snags and others saw as a retreat in the face of Native American anger over Father Serra's candidacy, attention had shifted to the papal mass at Laguna Seca Raceway that would precede his trip to the mission.

Laguna Seca was in the midst of an agricultural region that, like the nearby Central Valley, provided some of the nation's most abundant and valuable crops. Appropriately, he would take agriculture as his theme. The barren brown hills overlooking the raceway made a natural grandstand for the seventy-two thousand worshipers. The focal point was on the plain below, a cross-shaped altar built of interlocking fruit and vegetable crates, covered with plywood.

Interest in the pope's homily on agriculture had been running high in this region of fertile soil. Relations between growers and laborers had been often uneasy and tense. During the late 1960s and early 1970s, the state's Catholic bishops had played a partisan role, siding with Cesar Chavez and the United Farm Workers in the movement's successful effort to organize a union. Issues of pay, working conditions, and housing had continued to flare up. In addition, the specter of mounting farm bankruptcies had become a major national crisis. The pope's words, therefore, would be carefully scrutinized.

He opened his talk on a note of foreboding, quoting Moses: "Be careful not to forget the Lord, your God." Moses knew, he said, that God was, in fact, "easily forgotten," and nowhere was that more true than in wealthy nations. "In our own day," the pope exclaimed, "are we not perhaps witnesses of the fact that often in rich societies, where there is an abundance of material well-being, permissiveness and moral relativism find easy acceptance? And where the moral order is undermined, God is forgotten and questions of ultimate responsibility are set aside. In such situations a practical atheism pervades private and public living."

He went on delivering the most stinging jeremiad of his trip so far. "In these closing years of the twentieth century, on the eve of the Third Millennium of the Christian era, a part of the human family—the most economically and technically developed part—is being specially tempted, perhaps as never before, to imitate the ancient model of all sin—the original rebellion that expressed itself saying: 'I will not serve.' The temptation today is to try to build a world for oneself, forgetting the Creator and his design and loving providence. But sooner or later we must come to grips with this: that to forget God, to feign the death of God, is to promote the death of man and of all civilization. It is to threaten the existence of individuals, communities and all society."

The redemptive alternative from the Scriptures beckoned the human race to remember the Creator with humility. God, creator of the land, was its ultimate source of growth, hidden within nature, the pope said. Human labor that brought forth the fruit of the land in consciousness of the Creator was, he said, quoting Pope John XXIII, "a vocation, a God-given mission, a noble task and a contribution to civilization."

God had blessed America with some of the richest farmland in the world, which had been tilled with remarkable success, he noted, but in spite of this record many farmers had suffered poverty and indebtedness, and many of the poor lacked food. The bishops listened respectfully to growers' difficulties over rising costs and fair pricing and laborers' grievances over pay and working conditions. Though the church had no specific answers to the larger problems, the pope said, it did teach the principle that "the dignity, rights and well-being of people must be the central issue. No one person in this process—grower, worker, packer, shipper, retailer or consumer—is greater than the other in the eyes of God."

Speaking with urgency and verve, John Paul appealed to all sides to cooperate in finding solutions: "Each one of us is called to fulfill his or her respective duties before God and before society. Since the Church is constrained by her very nature to focus her attention most strongly on those least able to defend their own legitimate interests, I appeal to landowners, growers and others in positions of power to respect the just claims of their brothers and sisters who work the land. These claims include the right to share in decisions concerning their services and the right to free association with a view to social, cultural and economic advancement. I also appeal to all workers to be mindful of their own obligations of justice and to make every effort to fulfill a worthy service to mankind."

John Paul, whose service in the Polish church helped keep him mindful of the struggles of small farmers, was placing himself squarely behind the aspirations of those migrants who worked the land in California, including firm support for their right to organize, without casting aspersions on growers and landowners. He had added an important element to the unstable mix. The clusters of farm workers gathered on the slopes of the hill burst out in applause. On a related matter, the pope praised the benefits that had accrued from the one-year amnesty that allowed some illegal aliens to gain citizenship, a view that clashed somewhat with the growing criticism of that law from the American hierarchy.

In concluding, he returned to his basic caution. For the great harvest of America, he gave thanks. "But may your abundance never lead you to forget the Lord," he added, "or cease to acknowledge him as the source of your peace and well-being."

After distribution of communion to the sweet-tempered crowd by dozens of eucharistic ministers, among them laywomen in straw hats, the pope gave his dismissal and was soon bound for the Carmel Mission in a helicopter provided by President Reagan. He went immediately to the restored basilica, packed solid with 450 dignitaries and mission regulars. There he prayed at the grave of Father Serra and again lauded the founder of Carmel and twenty other California missions, while, outside, two dozen Native American demonstrators denounced the eighteenth-century priest as unfit for sainthood.

The pontiff made a brief appearance in the courtyard of the mission, where twenty-five hundred onlookers had bought thirty-five-dollar tickets and waited five hours for a fleeting glimpse of him. As was his wont, he approached the crowd, kissing schoolchildren and reaching out to a group of thirty disabled people.

John Paul then ate with a group of bishops, rested a while, and climbed aboard his helicopter for San Francisco.

From Crissy Field in the Presidio, the pontiff and his welcoming party, headed by Mayor Dianne Feinstein, sped straight for San Francisco's most famous landmark, the Golden Gate Bridge, majestic in the thin shroud of the late afternoon fog. He paused to gaze meditatively upon this conjunction of human and natural design, commenting softly to the resident archbishop, John Quinn. Then he stepped into his bullet-shielded vehicle for a 1.8-mile ride down Geary Street, which was lined with fifty thousand spectators, a tiny fraction of the million or so expected, to Mission Dolores, the basilica dedicated to "Our Lady of Sorrows," where for the first time he would encounter victims of AIDS.

This meeting, in the city known for its flourishing gay culture and for its devastating AIDS epidemic, primarily among gay men, had been nervously anticipated for months. Setting the stage was the Vatican's release of a document on homosexuality the previous October that had toughened the church's stand on the subject by calling even the homosexual "inclination" a "more or less strong tendency ordered toward an intrinsic moral evil." Because the revised policy appeared to place the church against both the orientation and the behavior, many Catholics concerned with AIDS denounced it as unwarranted, harsh, and insensitive. Protests against it arose immediately and had persisted. One of the most prominent critics, the Reverend John McNeill, had been silenced years before by his Jesuit order for writing on the topic of the church and homosexuality. When he broke the gag order, the Society of Jesus expelled him.

Until this trip, the pope had never spoken about AIDS, adding even greater discontent and feeding speculation about how he might link a hard line on homosexuality with an expression of compassion for victims of the dread disease. On the flight to the United States, he had told reporters that homosexuals belonged "in the heart of the church" and refused to support the idea that AIDS was punishment for

sinfulness, but added, "The church is doing all that is possible to heal and especially to prevent the moral background of this," a comment widely interpreted as
ascribing the cause of the illness to illicit behavior. On the Phoenix leg of the trip,
he made his first public mention of AIDS, appealing to health care workers to "show
the love and compassion of Christ and His church" to those who had contracted it.

Inside Mission Dolores basilica, a gleaming white adobe church built in 1791,
sixty-two AIDS patients sat together among the nine hundred congregants waiting
for the pope. All were Catholic and carefully chosen to attend. When the pope entered, cheers and clapping resounded through the arches while the choir sang "*Dios,
te salve Maria*" ("God, Save Mary"). John Paul moved slowly down the main aisle.
Approaching the section where the AIDS patients stood, he began at once to reach
out to them, marking some on the forehead with the sign of the cross, touching others on the head, cheek, shoulder, arm, or hand. The most dramatic moment occurred when the white-robed pontiff wrapped his arms around Brendan O'Rourke,
four years old, who had contracted AIDS through a blood transfusion. The pope
moved among the terminally ill with gentleness and serenity.

His words to them were more measured in certain key respects. In this pope,
theological reasoning often seemed to stand in tension with displays of pastoral
love such as he had just shown. His message was about loving the sick and dying,
but it was couched in terms of sin and forgiveness. The proof of God's love, he
said, was that "he loves us in our human condition, with our weakness and our
needs." Christ came to save sinners and the "love of Christ," he asserted," is more
powerful than sin and death. . . . This is the Good News of God's love that the
Church proclaims throughout history, and that I proclaim to you today: God loves
you with an everlasting love. He loves you in Christ Jesus, his Son."

Tellingly, he recalled the story of the prodigal son, which, he said, demonstrated
that God was "always ready to forgive, eager to welcome us back." That compassion, he said, "enables us to hope for the grace of conversion when we have
sinned." The pope never mentioned homosexual activity or any other specific item
in the church's catalogue of sins, but neither was it excluded.

God's love knew no bounds, John Paul proclaimed. "God loves you all, without
distinction, without limit. He loves those of you who are elderly, who feel the
burden of the years. He loves those of you who are sick, those who are suffering
from AIDS and AIDS-related complex. He loves the relatives and friends of the sick
and those who care for them. He loves all with an unconditional and everlasting
love."

The message was bold and bracing and doctrinally correct. It had conveyed the
pope's enormous personal warmth and caring along with pastoral encouragement informed by the Scriptures without diluting the church's teachings on the
sinfulness of homosexual sex. It was a masterpiece of compassion and diplomacy.

About a block away from the mission, two thousand demonstrators organized by gay, lesbian, and feminist groups protested against the church's stand on homosexuality, shouting such phrases as "Shame, shame" and "Pope, go home." It was the largest protest staged so far during the papal tour. Only a smattering of opposition to various church positions had materialized along the way despite predictions of sizable turnouts. There was a rough parallel between protests and crowds coming to see the pope. Both witnessed to indifference.

Awhile later, 150 members of Dignity, the Catholic gay rights organization that had been barred from using church property in several dioceses since the Vatican's letter on homosexuality last October, conducted their own Eucharist at the Palace of Fine Arts. The two-hour mass began with a candlelight procession from the city streets into the building. Priests and nuns took part in the liturgy, which was built around an appeal for liberalization of church views toward homosexuality.

Another 150 protesters against the Waldheim visit camped outside Saint Mary's Cathedral, where the pope's final appointment of the day was with three thousand representatives of men's and women's religious orders.

Religious communities had made more waves than any other single sector of the church. Within their semiautonomous structures, they had pushed many of the Vatican II reforms to new limits and tested Rome's tolerance. Many practiced aspects of democratic rule, stressing collegiality and downplaying hierarchy. Religious men and women had been in the forefront of both liturgical reform and social activism in behalf of peace and justice causes. As a result of their relative boldness, some, like the Jesuits, had felt the Vatican's hand of reprimand for allegedly going too far.

Nuns were, on the whole, the most creative, educated, dauntless leaders of the church, often ignored but never diminished. They had often exhibited remarkable courage in speaking out against church policy. When the pope last visited the United States, Sister Teresa Kane, then president of the Leadership Conference of Women Religious, had stunned a Washington, D.C., audience by departing from her prepared text to ask the pontiff seated behind her to consider "the possibility of women being included in all ministries of the church." Though John Paul had not responded to her point, she had raised it dramatically, some even said brashly. On his return to the United States, the case of the twenty-four nuns who signed the 1985 *New York Times* ad supporting a diversity of stands on abortion—an act of sacrilege to some and heroism to others—was still alive, though most of the Vatican's ejection procedures against them had been quietly resolved by Archbishop Quinn. Despite these tensions, religious orders had recently been given a clean bill of health. Results of a study undertaken by a U.S. bishops' committee on behalf of the Vatican, released last November, concluded that "in general religious life in the United States is in good condition."

At Saint Mary's, the sleek, glittering modern cathedral, two speakers were ready to represent the voice of religious communities in dialogue with the pope: the Reverend Stephen Tutas, a Marianist priest and president of the Conference of Major Superiors of Men, and Sister Helen Garvey, president of the Leadership Conference of Women Religious.

Father Tutas reviewed the profound changes that had reshaped men's communities, their relationship with the church and their dealings with the world around them. "While we feel called to oppose many currents in our culture," he said, "we also recognize values and gifts in American culture which we find especially rich for the Church today. We see the need to help build the Church in the United States in a way that responds to the needs of the American people and in a style that is appropriate to our culture, which values equality, freedom, openness and participation in decision-making that affects our lives." He also praised the increasing involvement of laypeople and emphasized that his fellow priests and brothers were "especially hopeful about recognizing the rightful role of women—religious or lay, married or single—in the Church in the United States."

The operative term was "rightful role," a blank slate that could mean many things, from Rome's version of "separate but equal" to a feminist's understanding of full equality that included ordination to the priesthood.

Sister Garvey became fairly specific. Wearing a blue suit, her back to the congregation facing the pope, she sketched brief, moving portraits of women religious devoting their skills to an array of needs in prisons, homes, communities, and universities. God spoke to sisters through their *experiences,* which, in effect, imbued their experience with a source of truth as real and authoritative in its own way as formulated dogma. With that as solid ground to stand upon, she said, "We desire for ourselves, and for all believing women, complete incorporation in the Church." Boisterous applause filled the cathedral. She continued, "In its critical decision-making responsibility, the church needs the fullness of women's gifts and the strength of women's commitments." Again loud applause. A stumbling block was a particular form of "sinfulness in our church" that she described as "the inability to dialogue with an openness born of love." How could issues as crucial as those concerning women ever be resolved, she had asked, without genuine give-and-take? Obviously, no such dialogue was going on at the moment in Saint Mary's. As her words had made implicitly clear, this was closer to an exchange of monologues. "How can women participate completely in the life of the Church and in the life of society?" she asked toward the end of her talk. "How can their rich, generous, loving spirit influence the great issues of our time, the great mission of our Church?"

By their response, the congregation in the cathedral showed that they apparently thought those questions pertinent indeed.

Significantly, the pope had again been pressed on the subject of women and, as on the two other occasions during his trip—first by Father McNulty in Miami, then by Archbishop Weakland in Los Angeles—not by laypeople but by full-time servants of the church.

John Paul spoke graciously to pew upon pew of nuns, priests, and brothers, expressing his gratitude for their devotion and service, empathizing with their struggles to renew their communities. He was aware that their efforts to breathe new life into their orders had yielded such fruits as "a God-given spirituality" and "a deepening of personal and liturgical prayer," he told them, and that such renewal necessarily entailed "risks and errors . . . undue impatience on the part of some and undue fears on the part of others." Healing those divisions, he knew, had become a crucial part of their mission. He also expressed thanks for their service to the poor, the neglected, and the oppressed.

He was likewise cognizant, of course, that they were suffering declining membership. Have courage and trust, he counseled. "Your own essential contribution to vocations," he said, "will come through fidelity, penance and prayer, and through confidence in the power of Christ's Paschal Mystery to make all things new." To facilitate the process, it was important that they be models by practicing their vows of chastity, obedience, and poverty.

Living up to those vows unavoidably led to clashes with the values of the world, John Paul said. Learning how to approach the world with the "saving message of the gospel" in their various ministries required meticulous sorting out. "No person or group of people can claim to possess sufficient insights so as to monopolize it," he said. Social ministries were open to inclusive participation. All who were baptized need to heed the Holy Spirit's guidance. "And since the Holy Spirit has placed in the Church the special pastoral charism of the Magisterium," he added as no small proviso, "we know that adherence to the Magisterium is an indispensable condition for a correct reading of the 'signs of the times' and hence a condition for the supernatural fruitfulness of all ministries in the Church.

"You indeed have an important role in the Church's dialogue with the complex and varied cultural environment of the United States. The first law of this dialogue is fidelity to Christ and to his Church."

He had once more played the "authority" card, which carried an assumption of total obedience to the hierarchy as the starting point for any further discussion of service to the world. The kind of dialogue to which he referred—among various constituencies in the church for the sake of shaping a mission to the world—was something quite different from Sister Garvey's call for honest exchange *within* the church about its own teachings.

The pope also appealed for "a true understanding of the values involved in America's historical experience." The Christian meaning of "the common good, of virtue and conscience, of liberty and justice must be distinguished from what is sometimes inadequately presented as the expression of these realities." To guard against falsehood, it was incumbent upon them to "proclaim the full truth about God—Father, Son and Holy Spirit—and the full truth about our human condition and destiny as revealed in Christ and authentically transmitted through the teaching of the Church." They should not, in other words, fall victim to moral and religious relativism, but cling fast to the whole truth preached by the church.

The pope's long day, which had begun in Los Angeles and continued in Monterey, had now come to an end with a short walk to the cathedral rectory, where he would spend the night.

Friday morning he returned to the cathedral for a session with three thousand laypeople from dioceses across the nation. In advance of the upcoming Synod on the Laity in October, the subject of the laity's relationship to the church had received unusual attention. John Paul's strategy had been to encourage lay participation within the limits he found within the Vatican II documents while retaining clear separation between the place of the laity and the place of the ordained. The breakdown of these categories, in the view of the Vatican, had prompted much attention in recent years. This issue had loomed large in the background of Rome's disciplinary action against Archbishop Hunthausen in Seattle. It had figured in cases where clerical authority was challenged by nuns. It had helped create the climate of "thinking for oneself" that had made Father Curran a threat. The Saint Mary's colloquy with laypeople was, therefore, a venture into unsettled terrain, where answers acceptable to both sides were hard to come by.

Donna Hanson spoke first. She was the director of social ministries in the Diocese of Spokane, chairwoman of the U.S. bishops' lay advisory council, married and the mother of two teenage sons. Her background included past membership on the Junior League's national board, three decades of social work, and leadership of the U.S. bishops' national lay advisory board. Seated up front in Saint Mary's were her husband and sons, with whom she had rehearsed her twelve-minute talk. She had written the final draft herself in a marathon forty-eight-hour session in her home. Her delivery of it would electrify those in the cathedral and the vast television audience. It would become a signal moment in the ten-day tour.

"We American Catholic laity, 98 percent of the Catholic Church in the United States, welcome Your Holiness, to our land of rich diversity," she began, speaking deliberately. She had talked with many laypeople about what she should say, she explained to John Paul, who sat motionless, arms folded over his chest. She would speak principally from her experience, but had consulted many others. Though the laity was a very mixed lot, she could assure him that "unity, not division, is our goal; service, not power, is our mission."

Taking as her theme a piece of Native American wisdom, she offered her own variation: "Never judge another's life until you have walked in their shoes for a day." She would attempt to help him walk in the shoes of Catholic America. That meant, first of all, grasping the concept that Americans believed that raising questions was a good means of measuring whether the country's practices lived up to its ideals. "Today, my culture compels me to keep questioning those in leadership positions. . . . Not to question, not to challenge, not to seek understanding is to be less than a mature, educated and committed citizen."

She continued, sounding each word with care, building drama: "When I come to my church, I cannot discard my cultural experiences. Though I know the church is not a democracy ruled by popular vote, I expect to be treated as a mature, educated and responsible adult. Not to question, not to challenge, not to have authorities involve me in a process of understanding is to deny my dignity as a person and the rights granted me both by church and society."

The church needed to reach out to all elements within the country as Jesus welcomed diverse people in his day, she said. Could a full welcome be extended to "women, our inactive clergy, homosexuals, the divorced and all people of color?" she wondered. Special attention was likewise needed for "single parents, widowed and divorced." It was incumbent on the church to mirror the great variety of laypeople and to understand their circumstances.

Lay men and women already active in the church yearned for something similar. They were the "most highly theologically trained in the world," but too little "spiritual formation and education" was available for them, and they lacked "structures in which to truly share responsibility." In addition, she said, "Lay ministers are involved as never before, but full acceptance by both clergy and the people of God has not been fully realized." However, she assured John Paul, resting his head in the palm of his hand, that these obstacles had not kept lay ministers from cooperating with other parish leaders.

How to accomplish these goals? She suggested they walk in each other's shoes. For her part, she would step into his slippers by endeavoring to understand his burdens: how he saw things in his various roles as world leader, supreme teacher, and convener of conclaves such as the Synod on the Laity.

"Your Holiness," she continued, "please let me know that you are also willing to walk with me. Accustomed as I am to dialogue, consultation and collaboration, I do not always feel that I am heard. In my cultural experience, questioning is generally not rebellion nor dissent. It is rather a desire to participate and is a sign of both love and maturity.

"Walk with me. My family experiences daily remind me that example speaks louder than words. It is imperative that both we parents and the church witness the gospel we preach, and, above all, that we be just, compassionate and forgiving.

"Please walk with each one of us. As you, we have given our lives in service to the church. As you, we must also seek forgiveness seventy times seven, but we truly believe that we are all gifted and that the Holy Spirit speaks uniquely to

each of us. Like you, we are children of God; may we please continue this walk together?"

A frenzied ovation broke out as the congregants rose to their feet. This final
show of approval, following five other outbursts during the talk, signified the
depth to which her message tapped both their frustrations and their longings.

She approached the pope. He greeted her with a warm smile, placed his hand
on her head to bestow his blessing, and said, "Yours was a good talk."

Hanson had sketched lay hopes in broad terms. Following her to the podium
was a man whose purpose was to focus more narrowly on a touchier topic.
Patrick S. Hughes, the director of pastoral ministries for the Archdiocese of San
Francisco, would speak on the ambiguous place of laypeople who worked as professionals within the church. In parishes and dioceses, laity were increasingly
serving as administrators, teachers, coordinators, and in other functions that
had been performed primarily by priests and nuns in the past. These "lay professionals" belonged to something like a hybrid species between laity and clergy
that had difficulty earning trust on either side. That they tended to think of their
work as a "vocation"—a term once solely applied to priests and religious—was
troubling to church leaders, who echoed the pope's insistence that nothing
should smudge the clear lines separating the two worlds. The word *minister,*
which was commonly used among the lay professions, raised similar objections.
On the other hand, fellow members of the laity were often reluctant to grant them
the same authority or respect they accorded clergy and religious with similar responsibilities. Others thought the newcomers were themselves too inclined toward their own brand of "clericalism." But with all the growing pains, the
emerging order had become indispensable. A widening of the scope of lay involvement by Vatican II in conjunction with the loss of so many nuns and priests
meant the church could scarcely do without them. All indications pointed to a
rapid increase in their number in the near future. It was, therefore, incumbent on
the church to help clarify their status and to assist them in staking out acceptable boundaries.

Hughes had some specific requests on behalf of his colleagues. The first on his
list was for greater recognition of their special call. "It is important that diocesan
vocation offices promote the universal call to ministry, including the call to full-
time lay ministry, as a vocation and value to the church. It is important that we
publicly and ceremonially celebrate the ministry provided by laypersons." A vital
means of showing such support, he continued, was to provide more and better
training that reflected the diversity of lay experience along with financial aid to
those who needed it to pursue their studies.

The large proportion of women involved in lay ministry deserved better treatment, Hughes asserted. Recognizing that there had been "some progress in the

church as more women have moved into significant ministerial positions," he declared that "sexism remains a major issue among those who work for the church" and called for more strenuous efforts to erase it.

He had two more items for the pope to ponder. One concern had to do with working conditions. Many lay professionals had sacrificed financially to take church jobs at lower pay than they could have earned outside, but this should not deter the efforts to set "equal and just salaries for men and women." Likewise, church employees needed to be protected by fair labor practices regarding hiring, promotion, and firing, and grievance procedures. His second concern was about the problems caused by the clergy shortage and contained an apparent plea to consider opening the priesthood to those other than male celibates. "We affirm the dignity and worth of all ministries," Hughes said, "and encourage the ongoing discernment of what is the nature of ordained ministry and who should be called to it." Ending shortly thereafter with the rousing approval of the audience, Hughes likewise received an affirming reception from the pope and sat down to hear his reply.

In that reply, John Paul invoked once again the picture of a perfectly ordered hierarchical church where everything had a place and there was a place for everything. In this design, there was no confusion, no overlapping of responsibility, only the most tranquil interdependence where nothing substantial needed to be redefined. Bishops and clergy took their irreplaceable responsibilities in leading the flock, and the laity was the bridge to the world. It was a beautiful vision of splendid harmony where issues raised by Donna Hanson and Patrick Hughes seemed beside the point.

The great work of salvation included a "specific contribution to the Church's mission" by the laity, the pope said. Hierarchy and laity shared a "true equality," though their functions, as assigned by the Holy Spirit, were different. They were to partake in church activities as time permitted, he emphasized, but their main task was to spread the Word in their daily routines.

"You are called to live in the world," he said, "to engage in secular professions and occupations, to live in those ordinary circumstances of family life and life in society from which is woven the very web of your existence. You are called by God himself to exercise your proper functions according to the spirit of the gospel and to work for the sanctification of the world from within, in the manner of leaven. In this way you can make Christ known to others, especially by the witness of your lives. It is for you as laypeople to direct all temporal affairs to the praise of the Creator and Redeemer."

The primary arenas for exercising this lay mission were work, especially in positions of secular influence, and the family, where parents educated children and Christian values were put into practice. He specifically noted the "difficult situation"

of those who existed outside the ideal family: single parents, the elderly and widowed, and separated and divorced Catholics. Though the church could not offer
communion to those who divorced and remarried, the pope said, "she assures these
Catholics too of her deep love."

Women had contributed greatly to the mission of the laity, the pope said, particularly "in partnership with their husbands, in begetting life and in educating
their children. . . . The Church is convinced, however, that all the special gifts of
women are needed in an ever-increasing measure in her life, and for this reason
hopes for their fuller participation in her activities. Precisely because of their equal
dignity and responsibility, the access of women to public functions must be ensured. Regardless of the role they perform, the Church proclaims the dignity of
women as women—a dignity equal to men's dignity, as revealed as such in the
account of creation contained in the Word of God."

Dignity was assured within John Paul's framework of distinct and inviolable
responsibilities. There was equality in dignity, he had said, but that did not imply
interchangeable roles.

Both lay men and women had helped renew the Vatican II church. Of the recent surge of lay participation he said, "I rejoice with you at this great flowering of
gifts in the service of the Church's mission." Then came the yellow flag of caution.

"At the same time," he began, "we must ensure both in theory and in practice
that these positive developments are always rooted in the sound ecclesiology
taught by the Council. Otherwise we run the risk of 'clericalizing' the laity or 'lai-
cizing' the clergy, and thus robbing both the clerical and lay states of their specific meaning and their complementarity. Both are indispensable to the 'perfection
of love,' which is the common goal of all the faithful. We must therefore recognize and respect in these states of life a diversity that builds up the Body of Christ
in unity."

Laypeople were most urgently needed in the front lines of the church's struggle to meet and overcome "new challenges and new temptations" both within
themselves and the wider society. The perils included "insidious relativism" that
waters down "the absolute truth of Christ" and reduces it to just another set of
beliefs or opinions; "materialistic consumerism," which promises ease "at the price
of inner emptiness"; and "alluring hedonism," with its shallow thrills "that will
never satisfy the human heart." "Once alienated from Christian faith and practice
by these and other deceptions," the pontiff said, "people often commit themselves to passing fads, or to bizarre beliefs that are either shallow or fanatical."

So the laity's principal duty was to combat the evils that rose up from every
side. The threat was never more ominous. "It is up to you the Catholic laity to in-
carnate without ceasing the gospel in society—in American society. You are in

the forefront of the struggle to protect authentic Christian values from the onslaught of secularization. Your contribution to the evangelization of your own society is made through your lives. Christ's message must live in you and in the way you live and in the way you refuse to live."

With the stakes so dire, talk of walking with laity as the first step toward internal church reform or of new initiatives to promote lay professionals seemed relatively unimportant, even superfluous. In that beautiful, classic design of the church held by the pope, each component had its own designated duties. Time and energy were, by implication, better spent by the laity in keeping its special trust than in seeking to cross over into new territory.

The cheers for John Paul were hearty and frequent during his talk. He had brought a vision that differed considerably from that offered by Donna Hanson and Patrick Hughes in several respects, but it had a strong and familiar place in the collective memory of the church. It, too, won applause.

Under bright blue skies at Candlestick Park, the pope closed out his San Francisco stay by presiding over a mass that featured a chorale and prelude composed by the noted jazz musician Dave Brubeck. The pope's throne sat in the midst of a simple cube-shaped structure from which he could look out upon the elegantly spare platform and altar.

In his homily, John Paul revived the theme of the cost of discipleship. Christians who remained true to the values of the gospel would reap scorn and spurning, he told the seventy thousand people in the stands. As he had indicated many times during his trip, those who were "fully Catholic" would find themselves a stalwart minority. In a world of wickedness and apostasy, his message of consolation was that suffering was indeed redeemed.

"To be identified with Christ means that we must live according to God's word," he said. "For this reason the Church never ceases to proclaim the whole of the gospel message, whether it is popular or unpopular, convenient or inconvenient. And the Church is ever mindful of her great task to call people to conversion or mind and heart, just as Jesus did."

He went on with this prophesy of trial and pain: "Christ remains today a sign of contradiction—a sign of contradiction in his Body, the Church. Therefore, it should not surprise us if, in our efforts to be faithful to Christ's teachings, we meet with criticism, ridicule or rejection." Rejection, thus considered, became a sign of true discipleship, a wound inflicted by the world that was counted righteous by God.

For the visibly worn pope, the trip from Candlestick Park to the San Francisco airport was mercifully short. There he boarded *Shepherd I* for the 2,083-mile journey to Detroit, his final U.S. stop.

$\textbf{F}$OR THE PAPAL PLANNERS, DETROIT WAS SOLID, RELIABLE CHURCH GROUND. IT shared the heritage of European immigrant Catholicism with the rest of the Northeast quadrant of the country. Originally the pope was to have wound up his tour in San Francisco, but planners feared that the protests there might end the trip on a sour note. So Detroit, which was bypassed in the pope's 1979 Northeast travels, had been added with confidence that it would provide a more fitting farewell.

The pope touched down at 9:04 that night and after a brief official welcome left by helicopter for the Cathedral of the Most Blessed Sacrament by way of Sacred Heart Seminary. Entering the cathedral beneath its twin spires to a bracing chorus of trumpets, he strode slowly up the center aisle, pausing to bestow his blessing as waves of applause reverberated through the Gothic rafters. Archbishop Edmund Szoka formally introduced his guest of honor. As he neared the end of his remarks, his voice grew halting, and tears flowed down his cheeks. The pope embraced his old friend, a fellow Pole by heritage, and said warmly, "I have been looking forward to this happy moment when in this Cathedral, the Mother Church of the Archdiocese of Detroit, I would have the opportunity to express my love for all of you in Christ."

After reminding them that the church was "more than an organization with moral influence" but rather "an instrument of redemption," John Paul told Detroit Catholics that he had "come here today with the desire to strengthen you." Completing his brief talk, the pope retired to the archbishop's residence for the night.

Saturday, September 19, John Paul's last scheduled day in America, began at 8:00 with a nostalgic visit to the heavily Polish community of Hamtramck, a 2.1-square-mile city within the boundaries of Detroit. Of its twenty-thousand residents, about half were of Polish origin. The pope had visited the enclave as a Polish cardinal and clearly delighted in his return, invigorated by a touch of the homeland. Polish flags, signs touting the Polish "Solidarity" movement, and women in Polish ethnic dress lined the path of the pope's motorcade. The crowd cried, "Witamy" ("Welcome") and sang lustily the familiar "Sto lat" ("May you live one hundred years").

John Paul spoke to Hamtramck in Polish from a pavilion constructed in a field. Behind him was a ten-by-six-foot painting of the Polish patroness, Our Lady of Czestochowa, created by a Detroit artist, Dennis Orlowski. In his talk, the pope paid glowing tribute to the generations of Poles who brought their heritage to America, most especially their Catholicism. They had accomplished much, he said, and built strong spiritual foundations in their new home. Preserving those ethnic roots, he added, made them better Americans.

"The more you are aware of your identity, your spirituality, your history, and the Christian culture out of which your ancestors and parents grew, and you yourselves have grown," he said, "the more you will be able to serve your country, the more capable will you be of contributing to the common good of the United States."

Many in the small but rapt crowd of forty thousand (three hundred thousand had been expected) were moved to tears by the sight of the leader they hailed as one of their own, a native son. They wore expressions of reverence and responded with restraint except when it came to singing some of the great songs of the Polish church. Then the sound rose up in a mighty swell. The effect was both powerful and tender. As the pope gave his blessing and prepared to leave, they broke into "*Boze, cos Polskie*" ("God for Poland").

The papal caravan sped off straightaway for the Ford Auditorium and a rendezvous with 2,800 permanent deacons and wives from 144 dioceses. With the deacons dressed in business suits and their spouses in Sunday finery, the assembly might have been mistaken for a meeting of Protestant ministers and their spouses. Since the permanent diaconate had been restored by Pope Paul VI in 1968, married and single men had been ordained to a ministry that left them free to enjoy their families and carry on secular work while serving the church, a life not unlike that of many Protestant clergy. Deacons could marry couples and baptize children, preach and teach, counsel, visit the sick, and assist the poor in the name of the church. Consecration of the eucharistic elements of bread and wine was reserved for priests alone, as was the authority to pronounce forgiveness of sins, but the deacon otherwise had a broad array of discretionary assignments. A film presented before the pope spoke showed them working with the elderly, giving guidance to young people, and assisting at mass. Picking up the unofficial theme song of the U.S. diaconate from the film, the audience sang with great emotion: "Whom shall I send? Here I am, Lord . . . I will go, Lord, if you need me; I will hold your people in my arms."

There were now eight thousand deacons attached to parishes and church agencies throughout the United States—more than anywhere in the world—and many were still regarded with some confusion by laypeople and priests, who were unsure where to place them in the scheme of things. Bridging the gulf between priests and laity, taking on certain aspects of both, some deacons felt that neither understood them well and complained of having a murky identity. Their status was expected to clarify over time as their roles became more familiar. In the process, they were becoming in the eyes of many Catholics an unwitting pastoral model of a married priesthood, paving the way for the day the church would take that step.

The pope began his remarks to the deacons by saying, "I give thanks to God for the call you have received and for your generous response. For the majority of you who are married, this response has been made possible by the love and support and collaboration of your wives."

For married deacons, the ministry was an outgrowth of the sacred bond between the couple. "So intimate is their partnership and unity in the sacrament of marriage," the pope explained, "that the Church fittingly requires the wife's consent before her husband can be ordained a permanent deacon . . . the nurturing and deepening of mutual, sacrificial love between husband and wife constitute perhaps the most significant involvement of a deacon's wife in her husband's public ministry in the Church. Today, especially, this is no small service." On the need for mutual spiritual growth: "You who are wives of permanent deacons, being close collaborators in their ministry, are likewise challenged with them to grow in the knowledge and love of Jesus Christ."

Hearing the pope wholeheartedly endorse a concept of the husband-wife ministerial teams that involved women intimately with the designs and purposes of ordination was remarkable. Given the sacramental indivisibility ("the two became one") assumed in the marriage union, it seemed plausible that the husband's ordination was in some sense also the wife's. The pope's words hinted at such a conclusion without going that far. There could be no doubt that he saw the wife as a partner in the deacon's mission, albeit a subordinate one.

Perhaps more than in any other talk on the tour, John Paul was on the theological frontier, where the way was not fully charted but evolving, where the premises opened up new possibilities perhaps not foreseen by the Vatican. Changes were already afoot. In advance of the Synod on the Laity, for example, there was considerable conjecture over whether the bishops would consider ordaining women as deacons.

For the deacons seated in Ford Auditorium, however, the focus was more concrete. The pope had come to bolster them and to spur them forward. He accented the dual nature of their mission by describing the "heart" of the diaconate: "to be a servant of the mysteries of Christ and, at one and the same time, to be a servant of your brothers and sisters." The deacon was a witness to the gospel in both church and world. Ordination provided him grace "even as his secular occupation gives him entry into the temporal sphere in a way that is normally not appropriate for other members of the clergy. At the same time, the fact that he is an ordained minister of the Church brings a special dimension to his efforts in the eyes of those with whom he lives and works."

But the call to impart the gospel, he reminded them darkly, as he had other groups in other ways, could be arduous. "The task is seldom an easy one," he said. "The truth about ourselves and the world, revealed in the gospel, is not always what the world wants to hear. Gospel truth often contradicts commonly accepted thinking, as we see so clearly today with regard to evils such as racism, contraception, abortion, and euthanasia—to name just a few."

Shortly after 11:30, John Paul arrived at Hart Plaza to deliver a speech that had been promoted by the United States Catholic conference as a major statement on social justice. Moreover, the conference said, the speech would extol the American bishops' recent pastoral letter on the nation's economy, which harshly assailed treatment of the poor. The outdoor plaza was near the site commemorating the European founding of the city by the French in 1701 and a short walk from the site of the United States Catholic Conference's bell-ringing 1976 "Call to Action" conference, which honored the nation's bicentennial. Once again, the crowd of thirty-five thousand fell far below estimates, some of which had gone as high as half a million. Even in the reliable, loyalist Catholic stronghold of Detroit, the apparent lack of interest in catching a firsthand glimpse of the pope was indeed striking.

From a platform constructed thirty-five feet above Hart Plaza, sealed in a bulletproof booth, the pontiff delivered his highly anticipated speech on social justice to a crowd treated earlier to the music of the Aretha Franklin and others. The speech fell far short of its advance billing. Rather than adding a distinct new page to the church's social teachings, it was mostly a loosely bound set of the pope's well-known convictions, focusing on the need to end human misery through Christian action and international cooperation. The bishops' economic pastoral received no mention at all. And the pope proposed no new specific remedies for injustice, nor did he criticize existing economic systems as he had before (both communism and capitalism having come under his censure for what he considered their excesses).

It was an appeal for compassion and generosity that grew personal. He reminded them that during his first papal trip to America he had alluded to the Gospel story of the rich man and Lazarus as a parable that reflected Jesus' imperative to help the poor (he had referred to the same story repeatedly during this trip to drive home the same lesson). "I now ask you today: What have you done with that parable? How many times in the past eight years have you turned to that parable to find inspiration for your Christian lives? Or have you put it aside thinking that it was no longer relevant to you or to the situations in your country?" The persistence of poverty made it necessary to "discover the poor in your midst."

Modern know-how could worsen suffering and injustice, he insisted, once again speaking skeptically about the capacity of technology to bring about true human progress. He spoke to a city where automation and plant retooling had cost thousands of jobs. Unemployment stood at 8.8 percent. "The introduction of robotics, the rapid development of communications, the necessary adaptation of industrial plants, the need to introduce new skills in management—these are but some of the factors that, if not analyzed carefully or tested as to their social cost, may produce undue hardship for many, either temporarily or more permanently," he said.

Interdependence had become a fact of life, he emphasized. It was time for "a new world conscience" and for "a new worldwide solidarity." The United Nations was the key organization in helping attain those goals through its pursuit of peace and human rights. Its history had underscored the need for an "international authority" to guide and direct the nations toward harmony and justice.

"America is a very powerful country," he said. "The amount and quality of your achievements is staggering. But by virtue of your unique position, as citizens of this nation, you are placed before a choice and you must choose. You may choose to close in on yourselves to enjoy the fruits of your own form of progress and try to forget about the rest of the world. Or, as you become more and more aware of your gifts and your capacity to serve, you may choose to live up to the responsibilities that your own history and accomplishments place on your shoulders. By choosing this latter course, you acknowledge interdependence, and opt for solidarity. This, dear friends, is truly a human vocation, a Christian vocation, and for you as Americans it is a worthy national vocation."

Pontiac Silverdome was John Paul's final appearance at an American sports shrine. The $200,000 altar, like the others on which the pope had celebrated public masses on the tour, was massive. The Detroit *Free Press* estimated that the wood to build it would have been enough to construct four averaged-sized new houses.

The pope's valedictory homily was a sweet, irenic, pastoral summons to be grateful for the bounty of God's love and to live in a manner worthy of the gospel. No Christian could ever be worthy of God's benevolence, he said, but through faith and repentance it could be experienced. The only fitting response to that gift was the offering of oneself to God. Christians partook of two worlds. "We live in this visible earthly life," he said, "and at the same time the life of the Kingdom of God, which is the ultimate destiny and vocation of every person." In closing, he said, "And so, my brothers and sisters, 'Conduct yourselves in a way worthy of the gospel of Christ,' that is to say, measure the things of this world by the standard of the Kingdom of God. Not the other way around! Not the other way around!"

Communion served, the pope stepped to the microphone for an impromptu expression of thanks for the welcome given him by Detroit and the nation during his stay. In turn, he said, looking exhausted, sounding somber, "I hope and I wish that this visit will be spiritually fruitful." His tone suggested that his own expectations were not very high. Soon he was bound for the airport and a brief, closed meeting with Vice President George Bush before boarding his flight to Canada. With him would go a $10-million donation from wealthy contributors to help restore the Vatican's fiscal health. It was intended as the first installment of a wider drive to raise as much as $100 million from Catholic America.

Emerging from the short session with Bush, the pope stood before the cameras and waded into the forty-eighth and final text of his ten-day pilgrimage. In condensed form, the speech was a splendid John Paul blend of honey and vinegar, a paean of praise to America and a reproof of its policy toward abortion. The United States overflowed with natural and human resources, he rhapsodized, and its manifold gifts were worthy of great praise. Its geography was wondrous, its people generous, its achievements awesome, its freedoms the envy of the world. "Yes, America, all this belongs to you," he said. "But your greatest beauty and your richest blessing is found in the human person: in each man, woman and child, in every immigrant, in every native-born son and daughter."

He then turned critical. The supreme test of America's "greatness," he said, was "the way you treat every human being, but especially the weakest and most defenseless ones.

"The best traditions of your land presume respect for those who cannot defend themselves. If you want equal justice for all, and true freedom and lasting peace, then, America, defend life!"

Life must be protected from conception to natural death, John Paul insisted, ending with a pungent flourish. "Every human person—no matter how vulnerable, no matter how young or how old, no matter how healthy, handicapped or sick, no matter how useful or productive for society—is a being of inestimable worth created in the image and likeness of God. This is the dignity of America, the reason she exists, the condition of her survival—yes, the ultimate test of her greatness: to respect every human person, especially the weakest and most defenseless ones, those as yet unborn.

"With these sentiments of love and hope for America, I now say goodbye in words that I spoke once before: 'Today, therefore, my final prayer is this: that God will bless America, so that she may increasingly become—and truly be— and long remain—one nation, under God, indivisible. With liberty and justice for all.'

"May God bless you all.

"God bless America."

Epilogue

W ITH THE POPE'S TOUR, THIS YEAR IN THE LIFE OF CATH-
olic America came to a close. It had been a time of remarkable ferment and challenge.

Questions with long-range implications had been put to various elements in the U.S. church. Bishops had anxiously observed the ordeal of their colleague Archbishop Hunthausen. Was it an isolated case or a chilling portent? Priests were called upon to add the Vatican's total ban on reproductive technology and the nettlesome document on homosexuality to their already difficult task of promoting unpopular teachings. How would they, a shrinking corps, reconcile the often conflicting needs of hierarchy and laity? Theologians had been put on notice by Rome's actions against Father Curran. Did that signal a broader crackdown on dissent and academic freedom? Laypeople, meanwhile, had been widely consulted in preparation for the upcoming Synod on the Laity. Had that process heightened their expectations for change? Those were only some of the issues that lingered as the curtain rang down on the year. Many other individuals and subgroups faced dilemmas and uncertainties of their own.

Catholic America had rarely if ever experienced more turbulence in one year across such a wide spectrum of constituencies. The sweeping reforms that emerged from Vatican II had produced years of high drama, to be sure, but in general that period had been marked by astonishment and exuberance, with dismay as a traditionalist subtext. By contrast, the stretch of time covered in this book was defined principally by profound disquiet within every major sector of the church. Even the Catholic right, which cheered the pope's effort to curb reform, viewed the U.S. church gloomily as being mired in disarray.

Part of the reason for the disquiet was societal. An increasingly edgy national mood exacerbated the uneasiness in Catholic America. The United States was in the throes of a downturn. The Reagan presidency, which had been flying very high, began to lose altitude, largely because of the Iran-Contra scandal. Criminal charges of insider trading and other financial swindles against Wall Street kingpins were exposing the seamier side of the bullish 1980s. On a broader scale, the topic of moral decline caught the attention of the media. At the same time, the fiscal fortunes of the nation appeared to be faltering. The United States was falling deeper into debt and further behind the Japanese in capturing valuable foreign markets. All this took place as America was celebrating the two-hundredth birthday of the writing down of its constitutional principles. Catholics celebrated those republican ideals even as they felt new pressures from Rome to abandon those same democratic assumptions when they entered the church.

Forces from within and without the church had, therefore, brought about among Catholics a period of renewed self-examination of how their national and religious identities fit together. Much of that scrutiny was prompted by the events of the year we have reviewed. Those experiences have continued to shape the discussion.

Because real life does not conform neatly to arbitrary time frames, an account of a single year will necessarily leave many stories incomplete. People and issues moved ahead, of course, sometimes toward resolution or dramatic twists. In anticipation of questions that might naturally arise concerning the outcome of this or that "story," the remainder of this space will be used to provide some answers.

THE SYNOD OF BISHOPS ON THE SUBJECT OF THE LAITY GOT UNDER WAY promptly on the first of October and ran until the thirtieth. In attendance were 230 voting bishops and 60 nonvoting lay observers, including Virgil Dechant, Supreme Knight of the Knights of Columbus from the United States, and 20 theologians picked by the Vatican.

During the first half of the synod, bishops in succession delivered eight-minute prepared speeches interspersed with twenty-minute talks by some of the laypeople. Further discussion took place in the small groups broken up by language. Themes that emerged from this process basically coincided with the concerns voiced by Catholic Americans. On the whole, for example, the testimony favored opening up the roles of altar server, acolyte, and lector to females. Though girls and women had filled these functions in the United States and other countries, of course, such practices had never been approved by Rome. The American delegates saw this as a realistic goal and a step in the right direction. Canadian bishops, known for their relative independence, went a bit further, asking that women be ordained as deacons. On another matter, lay ministries, the bishops likewise found widespread agreement. Within reasonable limits, they believed, such ministries should be strengthened, recognized, and expanded.

But a strange thing happened on the way from this initial stage of the synod to its completion. Neither the proposal concerning women nor that boosting lay ministries made it into the final set of fifty-four propositions that the synod sent to the pope for his disposal. Not a shred of either popular idea remained. Instead, the synod presented a packet of innocuous suggestions, mostly regurgitations of Vatican II themes that stressed lay consultation and participation. Where women were mentioned, their innate "dignity" was reaffirmed, and their involvement in church decision making was encouraged, though there were no specifics.

The bland, abridged results were greeted by Catholic journalists with a mixture of "what can you expect?" cynicism from liberals and "thank God it did no harm" relief from conservatives.

This thin-gruel outcome reinforced church scholars and prelates who maintained that synods were impossibly hamstrung to begin with, overcontrolled by the Vatican and unable to do more than give highly disposable advice. But some proponents of greater lay involvement weren't ready to write off this synod as a total loss. If this meeting had broken no new ground on issues important to them, they argued, neither had it tried to reverse the progress initiated by Vatican II. At least the bishops had explored pertinent issues with one another in the very visible presence of laypeople, the activists asserted, and that was no small accomplishment.

Virgil Dechant was not around for the end of the synod. In the wake of the record one-day stock market crash on October 19, he had rushed back to oversee investment strategy for the sizable Knights of Columbus portfolio.

As always, the last word on any synod belonged to the pope. He was free to accept the counsel of his bishops in whole or in part or to totally ignore it. This time John Paul's response came a little more than a year later in a document titled "Christifidelis laici" (Lay Believers in Christ), dated December 30, 1988. It generally reflected the themes brought forth by the bishops and offered nothing substantially new. But those looking for signs of change noted approvingly that the pope made conspicuous use of the expression "lay ministry." As demonstrated on his visit to the United States, he had hitherto applied the word *ministry* strictly to the work of the clergy. The distinction between the ordained and the unordained remained fundamental to his analysis, but the concept of "ministry" had apparently been stretched.

FATHER CURRAN WAS TEACHING AT CORNELL AS VISITING PROFESSOR FOR THE 1987–88 academic year. At the same time, he was pressing his civil lawsuit against Catholic University in an effort to overturn his suspension the previous January. The suit charged that the action by the university had violated his contract as a fully tenured professor. His suspension by the university's chancellor, Archbishop

James A. Hickey of Washington, followed a 1986 ruling by the Vatican that found Father Curran "neither suitable nor eligible to teach theology" because of his dissent from the church's teachings on birth control, homosexuality, and other issues. Even before ordering Father Curran suspended, the archbishop had initiated moves to revoke the priest's "canonical mission," the church license required to serve on faculties accredited by the Vatican.

A special faculty committee assigned to study the suspension recommended in early 1988 that the priest be restored as a fully tenured professor "in the field of his competence," though the committee acknowledged that the university had a right to withdraw his canonical mission. If that happened, the committee said, Father Curran should be permitted to teach his subject somewhere on the faculty that did not fall under the Vatican's direct jurisdiction. On January 26, 1988, the trustees of the university flatly rejected the committee's findings, voting to cancel Father Curran's canonical mission without offering an equivalent professorship in a department not Vatican-supervised. School officials later raised with him the possibility of some sort of faculty position outside the field of religious studies on condition that he refrain from teaching Catholic moral theology, a restriction that, not surprisingly, Father Curran found totally unacceptable. He would stick with his legal challenge for full restoration.

In April 1988, a civil court judge denied a motion by the trustees to quash the suit. By the end of the year the court proceedings were under way. The trial was an unusual, even arcane, spectacle. High-ranking prelates, including Archbishop Hickey and Cardinal Joseph Bernardin of Chicago (president of CU's trustees), took the stand to testify in favor of the university's action. Fine points of church law were entered into evidence. Superior Court Judge Frederick Weisberg was called upon to enter the murky terrain between church and state.

On February 28, 1989, Judge Weisberg handed down a decision that went against Father Curran and for the university. Nothing in his contract gave him "the right to teach Catholic theology at CUA in the face of a definitive judgment by the Holy See that he was ineligible to do so," the judge wrote. The opinion was based on the judge's conclusion that Catholic University's pledge of academic freedom was compromised by its special ties to the Vatican. "On some issues—and this case certainly presents one of them—the conflict between the University's commitment to academic freedom and its unwavering loyalty to the Holy See is direct and unavoidable," the judge wrote. "On such issues, the University may choose for itself on which side of that conflict it wants to come down, and nothing in its contract with Professor Curran or any other faculty member promises that it will always come down on the side of academic freedom."

Having never been promised full academic freedom, the judge reasoned, Father Curran had no right to expect to be protected by its safeguards. In the final analysis, the judge decided, Catholic University had never aspired to be "a full-fledged American university."

Father Curran accepted the ruling stoically, vowing that "this was the last battle" he would fight with the university. He was still a moral theologian with no university to call home. He was then on another visiting professorship, this one at the University of Southern California. Catholic colleges such as Notre Dame and Boston College that would have clamored for his services a few years earlier now made him no offers. In late 1990, he accepted a tenured university professorship at Southern Methodist University.

The case deepened the concern for academic freedom at all church-related institutions of higher learning. Catholic University *was* special because of its pontifical charter from Rome. But could the hierarchy claim other grounds for limiting this freedom elsewhere? Judge Weisberg had only exposed the dilemma in a different way.

In September 1991, the Amercian Association of University Professors voted to censure Catholic University on the grounds that Father Curran's academic freedom had been violated. Later that fall, the university's board of trustees adopted a new policy on academic freedom. It upheld the right to scholarly inquiry but required that theologians "give assent" to church doctrine.

THE GROWING DESIRE TO HEAD OFF BITTER PUBLIC QUARRELS BETWEEN THEOLOGIANS and bishops had prompted a move from both sides to draft a set of norms that they hoped could resolve conflicts reasonably and fairly without outside help. The combined efforts of the Catholic Theological Society of America and the Canon Law Society of America had proposed such norms in 1983 to the doctrine committee of the bishops' conference. The product of their joint venture was presented to the business meeting of the bishops in November 1987. Reflecting "due process" American style, it included a careful, judicious step-by-step method for settling everything from a simple misunderstanding to a major disagreement.

The package reached the floor near the close of the bishops' final session and was roundly attacked by Archbishop Stafford as "fatally flawed." He and other conservatives claimed that the procedures usurped the supreme teaching authority of bishops by seeming to put theologians on a par with the hierarchs. The term used derisively to describe this alleged trespassing was *parallel magisterium.* When it came time to vote, so many bishops had already left the meeting that a quorum was lacking. The guidelines were therefore returned to the doctrine committee.

A second roadblock stopped the proposal from reaching the bishops' meeting a year later. At the last minute, the Vatican Congregation for the Doctrine of the Faith intervened with objections similar to those voiced by the conservative U.S.

bishops. The head of the doctrine committee, Archbishop Oscar Lipscomb of Mobile, Alabama, ironed out the differences with Vatican officials at a March 1989 meeting in Rome. A slightly modified form of "Doctrinal Responsibilities," which now met with Rome's approval by giving greater emphasis to hierarchical supremacy, easily won acceptance by the American bishops the following June. Bishops were free to use them or not. Proponents said the norms remained basically intact. Afterward, Archbishop Lipscomb said, "I would like to think that the Curran affair might have had a different outcome if such a process had been in place."

Two other elements stirred things up. One was the Vatican's surprise announcement that theologians, along with other academics and church administrators, would be required to take a new loyalty oath that covered virtually everything the church taught, fallible, noninfallible, and so on. Announced February 25, 1989, in *L'Osservatore Romano* and put into effect March 1, it went far beyond the previous pledge, which consisted of the Nicene Creed. The replacement, which caught those most affected off guard, retained the creed, but added the following:

> With a firm faith, I believe as well everything contained in God's word, written or handed down in tradition and proposed by the church—whether in solemn judgment or in the ordinary and universal magisterium—as divinely revealed and calling for faith.
>
> I also firmly accept and hold each and every thing that is proposed by that same church definitively with regard to teaching concerning faith or morals.
>
> What is more, I adhere with religious submission of will and intellect to the teachings which either the Roman pontiff or the college of bishops enunciate when they exercise the authentic magisterium, even if they proclaim those teachings in an act that is not definitive.

Further constraints were imposed by the "Instruction on the Ecclesial Vocation of the Theologian" issued by the Congregation for the Doctrine of the Faith on June 26, 1990. The most publicized feature of the document was that it forbade theologians from publicly opposing any church teaching. "One cannot speak of a 'right to dissent' in the church," the document said, "inasmuch as the freedom of the act of faith is linked to the moral obligation to accept the truth which the interventions of the magisterium intend to serve."

For theologians, the room for intellectual maneuvering seemed to be quickly shrinking.

➤ ➤

ON A RELATED MATTER, THE VATICAN RELEASED ITS FINISHED SCHEMA ON HIGHER education on September 25, 1990. The document, which provided principles for fostering the Catholic character of church-related colleges and universities, was greeted by a collective sigh of relief from Catholic educators. Earlier drafts had, among other things, raised the possibility of greater involvement by bishops in church-affiliated schools, a prospect that had worried and angered both faculty and administrators. That their loud complaints had been effective, surprisingly so, was evident in the content and tone of the final version. Legalisms had been largely replaced by general guidelines. Its voice had changed from didactic to uplifting. On the particularly touchy issue of resolving disputes between bishops and theologians, there was still some ambiguity that could raise issues concerning a university's freedom from hierarchical interference, but in one key respect it was different. In the final documents, methods for resolving such disputes were to be worked out primarily at the local and regional levels rather than by higher authorities, permitting areas of the church such as America to incorporate their particular traditions in solving the problems.

Some of the college and university presidents who had been most alarmed in earlier drafts by what they saw as threats to the independence and integrity of their institutions were among the biggest boosters of the finished product. Though they allowed that certain implications of the document still needed to be ironed out, they were breathing easier, certain that they could live with it quite well. It was widely hailed among the educators as a triumph of consultation and cooperation.

━ ━

ARCHBISHOP HUNTHAUSEN CONTINUED TO PICK UP MOMENTUM IN HIS EFFORT to return the archdiocese to the zestiness that had distinguished it before the damage inflicted by the Vatican's investigation of the archbishop's pastoral practices. Among the most visible signs of increasing vitality, said his supporters, was the recent celebration of the twenty-fifth anniversary of his consecration as a bishop. On August 30, 1962, he had formally entered the hierarchy with responsibility for the Diocese of Helena, Montana. In honor of the occasion, the archbishop was feted by a thousand at a cathedral dinner where he toasted Archbishop Murphy, the newly arrived and already popular coadjutor archbishop, for coming to Seattle to make peace with Rome possible; by smaller gatherings of well-wishers in various regions of the archdiocese; and by six thousand members of Seattle's religious community at a gala ecumenical dinner, many of whom wept openly as Rudyard Kipling's "If" was recited in tribute.

Though much had improved since the months preceding the settlement, the climate was notably more cautious and reserved than it once had been. The *modus operandi* of archdiocesan leaders was prudence and avoidance of risks that might provoke more trouble from Rome. The archbishop had been through an ordeal that had left him without some of the moxie that had made him such an unlikely church frontiersman over the years. For reasons that made perfect sense to his legion of admirers, he had become less bold, more subdued—though unbowed. The overriding need was to play it relatively safe by cooperating with the three-bishop commission charged with making sure that certain "abuses" it had found were corrected.

On April 11, 1989, the "all clear" was sounded when Rome's ambassador to the United States, Archbishop Pio Laghi, announced that the commission's oversight of Seattle "is completed." After more than five years of inquiry, a wrenching conflict between Seattle and Rome, a barely agreed-upon resolution, and five follow-up meetings between the archbishops and the commission during the period of probation, it was over.

Responding to the news the next day at a news conference, Archbishop Hunthausen flashed traces of his old upbeat, unfazed, unapologetic self. He looked older, his hair having turned whiter, but his doctors had recently pronounced him fit nearly three years after his cancer surgery. "I am grateful for the announcement of closure," he told reporters. "We don't really feel that we compromised on anything. We very deliberately examined what we were doing, reviewed and updated some guidelines, but there were no substantial changes made as a result of the inquiry." And he vowed to remain at his post for eight more years until he reached the mandatory retirement age of seventy-five.

By the spring of 1991, however, the archbishop had had a change of heart. On June 18, he announced that he would retire on his seventieth birthday, which fell on August 1.

FOR RETIRED NUNS, WHOSE DESPERATE ECONOMIC STRAITS HAD BEEN UNCOVered by the *Wall Street Journal*, some help began to arrive. In response to the startling revelation that $3 billion would be needed to provide for the aging nuns, the U.S. bishops authorized an annual collection for ten years at their November 1987 session. Under the accompanying guidelines, 90 percent of the income was to be distributed directly to religious congregations. During the initial Retirement Fund for Religious campaign in 1988, more than $25 million was taken in (the highest amount ever collected by the bishops in a single appeal); in 1989, the total was $29.5 million.

THE DRIVE TO RAISE $100 MILLION FOR THE VATICAN'S SHRINKING TREASURY had rougher sailing. In October, the Vatican projected its 1987 deficit as $59.3 million, down from its $63 million estimate earlier in the year but still a record. Americans remained stoutly resistant to the idea of handing Rome large amounts of money without the assurance of thorough fiscal disclosure (a demand that had increased in the wake of the scandal involving the Vatican Bank, whose head,

Archbishop Paul C. Marcinkus of Cicero, Illinois, stepped down on October 30, 1990). There was also debate about strategy: whether such a drive ought to be aimed at big-money Catholics or broad-based, whether primarily by high-powered professional fund-raisers or more through in-house facilities. In November, Archbishop Laghi met with thirty-five key advisers at the Vatican embassy. Various concerns were voiced, and a steering committee was appointed that included Virgil Dechant. None of the dinner guests made financial pledges of their own at this stage.

THE QUIXOTE CENTER, ON THE OTHER HAND, ANNOUNCED AT A NOVEMBER 14 news conference that it had successfully attained its goal of $100 million in relief supplies for Nicaragua. Thus the feisty, leftist center, friend of the Sandinista regime, made good on its vow to raise a dollar's worth of aid for every dollar Congress provided in military assistance to the Contra rebels. Meanwhile, the Jesuit order initiated the process of expelling the Reverend William Callahan, S.J., a key Quixote leader, over his strong protests.

TWO OF THE FOUR MEMBERS OF EPIPHANY PLOWSHARES WHO OPENLY CONfessed to carrying out an antinuclear protest at the Willow Grove Naval Air Station were sentenced to jail. The Reverend Thomas McGann and the Reverend Dexter Lanctot, both priests of the Philadelphia archdiocese, had pleaded guilty in June to misdemeanor charges, including trespassing, for their role in hammering aircraft at the base. Two previous trials of all four defendants had ended in mistrials. On September 7, the priests were sent to jail for a hundred days and fined five hundred dollars apiece. They served the time and were later restored to active priesthood in the archdiocese. After a third trial in July of the other two participants, Lin Romano and Gregory Boertje, which was also halted when onlookers disrupted the proceedings, both were convicted in a fourth trial in September. Both filed appeals. Romano was retried for a fifth time in November 1988, on lesser charges, found guilty, and given two years' probation. Boertje was later jailed for failing to show up for sentencing and was committed to jail for two years. He was not retried.

IN CLEVELAND, SAINT JOSEPH PARISH WON AN INDEFINITE STAY OF DEMOLITION. With membership under two hundred and upkeep gobbling up scarce resources, the diocese had closed the Gothic landmark at a tearful final mass attended by hundreds of former parishioners in September of 1986. Plans called for leveling the structure, but in the face of protests the diocese allowed opponents a year to come up with a better idea for this monument to urban immigrant Catholicism. Intense lobbying by the Friends of Saint Joseph, culminating in a successful open-house during the summer, had paid off. On September 26, the diocese announced that it was suspending the demolition plans in order to entertain proposals for making the buildings available for alternative use. Bringing the facilities up to safety codes would cost a minimum of seven hundred thousand dollars, the diocese reminded preservation enthusiasts. Both commercial and nonprofit uses were under consideration.

SAINTHOOD FOR MOTHER KATHARINE DREXEL, A PHILADELPHIA NATIVE WHO DIED in 1955, came closer to realization. Pope John Paul II beatified her in a ceremony on November 20, 1988. For the heiress-turned-nun who established a network of schools for black and Indian children, canonization was just one step away. She would be the second saint born in the United States, after Mother Elizabeth Seton. The cause of Father Junípero Serra remained stalled, however. Whether principally due to red tape, to strenuous protests by those who accused him of mistreating Indians, or to some other factor, his cause had still not moved ahead.

THE AMERICAN HIERARCHY'S EFFORT TO ADDRESS A PASTORAL LETTER ON THE subject of women bogged down under the weight of the problems it generated. From its inception by vote of the bishops' conference in 1983, it had seemed an impossible task. But the committee in charge had listened to testimony from representatives of dozens of women's organizations and written a first draft that was generally well received when issued in April 1988. Among other things, it used extensive quotes from those who opposed certain Catholic practices and teachings affecting women (for example, birth control and the ban on women's ordination) and recognized unjust treatment of women by the church. It called for a "radical conversion of mind and heart" as a remedy for the "sins of sexism" and stressed the need for more women in places of responsibility throughout the church.

Critical reaction to the text from fellow U.S. bishops and Roman authorities resulted in a pared down second draft, made public in the spring of 1990, that more strongly asserted the importance of heeding the birth control encyclical and the Vatican's reasoning against admitting women to the priesthood. It was much leaner than the first draft (99 pages compared to 164) and far less willing to advocate a reopening of controversial issues. One example of a line that appeared in the first draft but was dropped in the second: "Consulting with women on matters pertaining to birth control will contribute to church teaching on sexuality."

Ironically, the success of both drafts in making a persuasive case for a wholesale condemnation of sexism as a "sin" became the project's chief obstacle. Critics claimed that the letter's convincing arguments against sexism made official church restrictions on women insupportable and hypocritical. In a surprise move, seven bishops petitioned for a halt to the attempt to finish the pastoral letter on grounds that it had lost credibility. Leaders of many women's groups, including the influential Leadership Conference of Women Religious, likewise urged the bishops to give it up. In September of 1990, Archbishop Daniel Pilarczyk, president of the bishops' conference, announced that action on the pastoral had been postponed indefinitely. The archbishop attributed the delay to a Vatican request that the U.S. bishops consult with other hierarchies around the world before making a decision about their document.

A third draft, slimmer still at eighty-one pages, was made public on April 9, 1992. Sexism was once more condemned as sinful, and equal treatment of women under the law and in the workforce were vigorously affirmed. With regard to women in the church, the document was more conservative than its predecessors, dropping, for example, the previous pledge that the bishops would encourage "participation by women in all liturgical ministries that do not require men." Critics, still urging the bishops to discard the project, saw the third draft as evidence of further concessions to the Vatican. Supporters saw it as sounder and better balanced. The bishops were due to debate the pastoral in open session at their spring meeting. In the nine years since the pastoral was authorized, it had never been discussed in plenary session. Some bishops were determined to finish the task; others still called on their brethren to abandon it.

THE COMPLETED PASTORAL LETTER ON THE ECONOMY WAS, A YEAR AFTER ITS PASsage, making slow headway at best in reaching the mainstream of Catholic America. From the modest $525,000 allocated by the bishops for implementation of a pastoral, a national office was opened in Washington to oversee promotion of the document. By the fall of 1987, 130 dioceses had appointed full- or part-time directors of implementation, and six dioceses had issued pastoral letters of their own on how the bishops' teachings could be applied to local conditions. Hundreds of thousands of copies of the full text or summaries of it had been distributed, dozens of seminars and workshops had been devoted to it, and various other media resources had spread the word.

Despite these efforts, resistance to the pastoral's sharp critique of the American economic system (foes sometimes attacked it as socialistic) remained strong, and ignorance about it was widespread. A Gallup Poll in August for the *National Catholic Reporter* found that only 29 percent of Catholic respondents knew that the pastoral even existed.

THE SAINT JOSEPH FOUNDATION REMAINED ON CALL AS THE DEFENDER OF THOSE who complained that their right to orthodox Catholic practices had been violated by abuses introduced into liturgy and other areas of church life. Chuck Wilson, the chief paladin of the San Antonio–based conservative operation, reported late in the year that progress was slow in efforts to resolve cases the foundation had taken on. One case in Pittsburgh had been decided against him. A parish whose members were mostly elderly had been closed in conjunction with the opening of a new church nearby. The members resisted the closing on grounds that it imposed a travel hardship on them and deprived them of their rightful worship. The Vatican Congregation for Clergy sided with the Diocese of Pittsburgh's decision to shut it down.

THE SUBJECT OF AIDS PROVOKED FURTHER DEBATE OVER HOW TO RECONCILE A ministry of compassion with a morality of absolutes. Tensions flared among the bishops over where they stood collectively on the issue as the result of a statement by their administrative board in December. In addition to urging stepped-up efforts to care for sufferers and their families, the statement by the forty-eight-bishop board allowed for information about the use of condoms as part of a broad program of education to prevent the disease. Avoidance of drugs and adherence to the church's teaching against any sex outside marriage were the surest means to avert spread of the disease, the December 10 statement said, but inasmuch as some people rejected Catholic morality, education about AIDS "could include accurate information about prophylactic devices." They were not "promoting the use of prophylactics, but merely providing information that is part of the factual picture." The statement met with the approval of several leading moral theologians, who pointed to the legitimacy within Catholic tradition of choosing the lesser evil (condom use) over the greater one (the greater risk of exposing a sex partner to a fatal disease).

But others saw red. Cardinal O'Connor led the assault against that part of the statement, denouncing it as "a grave error" for allegedly violating the church's ban on artificial birth control. Condom information would be forbidden within his archdiocesan AIDS programs, the cardinal declared, and other bishops followed his lead. Archbishop May, president of the bishops' conference, was perturbed over the public display of feuding among his brethren and announced that the bishops would discuss the matter further at their next meeting in June 1988. There the conference achieved harmony by retaining the board's statement, with its allowance for condom education, and ordering up another statement that would carry the endorsement of the whole conference, by inference, then, out-ranking the board's or at least diminishing its authority. The second document was approved in November 1989. No less committed to compassion for sufferers, it made no mention of prophylactics as a means of prevention.

REVIEWS OF THE POPE'S VISIT WERE POURING IN BEFORE HIS DEPARTING FLIGHT got off the ground. Apart from subjective readings of what had happened, a few observations were widely accepted. One, there had been far less excitement over the pope this time than when he had arrived as a papal newcomer in 1979. Small crowds and modest interest attested to that fact. Two, the pope had to share the spot-light with those who spoke for Catholic America and was sometimes upstaged by them. Three, the strains between Rome and the U.S. church, far from being resolved, had been dramatized. John Paul had again imparted to the American Catholics his unequivocal expectations. American bishops had been pressured anew to stamp out dissent within their flocks, where disaffection on some issues ran high, while remaining true to their own commitment to show pastoral understanding. Four, the trip had saddled many of the host dioceses with a burdensome debt.

Along more partisan lines, the assessments divided sharply. Many on the right took particular comfort from the pope's emphasis on the interior life and his in-sistence on obedience to church teachings on sex and other matters they consid-ered essential. The rightists weren't so happy with his seeming endorsement of the sanctuary movement and were mostly silent on his preachments about poverty and against greed. Leftists embraced those social commandments, while often overlooking his spiritual message, and decried what they saw as his refusal to en-gage Americans in fruitful dialogue. The structured exchanges had featured speak-ers pleading for more discussion of issues, the leftists argued, but the pope had ignored their appeals and tried, instead, to shut off debate by repeating answers he falsely believed to be full and final.

Tensions over dialogue had crested in Los Angeles in his meeting with bish-ops. There the pope had unleashed his most stinging rebuke, warning that dissent risked excommunication. That directive meant something immediately translat-able to bishops seeking to do Rome's will. It signified, among other things, that they could, with papal permission, declare open season on politicians who took a pro-choice stand on abortion policy. Otherwise, John Paul had had virtually nothing direct to say about the cluster of challenges posed by the four bishops who spoke on behalf of their colleagues and constituents.

During those ten days, the commentators seemed to agree, John Paul had done little to heal the frictions between the United States and the Vatican, though in stops along the way he had given hope and vitality to an array of audiences gathered under various church auspices. He had reached out to Hispanics, blacks, health care workers, college presidents, AIDS sufferers, the laity, nuns, Indians, media moguls, young people, priests, non-Catholics, and an assortment of other groups. Most had taken away something of personal value that went beyond the struggles of the moment.

If the trip had changed anything, it was perhaps nothing detectable in the everyday life of Catholic America but rather something political at the level of church leadership. The pope had shown his determination to hold his ground against all comers. It was perhaps clearer that bishops and priests either belonged to the pope's party or not. Making that decision had graver consequences than ever before. The visit might have reinforced those political alignments and made them count for more; to that extent, it held a potential for affecting how clerics related not only to Rome but to each other as well.

The 1979 visit had been a triumph for the pope alone. The return engagement belonged almost as much to Catholic America. This trip did not stir nearly the excitement; its importance was not evident in parades and motorcades. But something more dramatic happened. The church in America discovered its voice and let it be heard—candidly, not rudely, personally, not individualistically, loudly, not shrilly. The Americans were not speaking *against* the pope but *for* their conception of Catholicism. They weren't going to be dismissed for belonging to the rich First World. From Father McNulty in Miami to Donna Hanson in San Francisco, that voice came across as committed to the church but uncertain about the sufficiency of some of its lessons and practices. The voice did not shrink or falter, nor forsake politeness or honesty. Long after most of the pope's four dozen speeches were long forgotten, the memory of a handful of Catholic Americans would endure in images even more than in words. Eighteen months after giving her dramatic talk to the pope, Donna Hanson's desk was still piled high with mail from admirers. She had been in constant demand by colleges, churches, and television studios to reshow her speech to John Paul and to expand her thoughts.

The consensus among those close to church leadership was that the pope would not make another tour of America. He had brought his message, proclaiming the gospel and inviting Americans to reflect critically on their privileged circumstances, and it was obvious from the disappointing response that the papal capital that could be spent on those aims had been pretty much depleted. So when *Shepherd I* soared out over the Michigan skies, Pope John Paul II had probably seen the last extended tour of a country that seemed to sadden him unlike any other.

As the pope bade farewell, the ten Catholic Americans who had shared their thoughts, feelings, and experiences with me during the course of the year were following their special pursuits from their various vantage points. Some had paid close attention to the trip; others had caught only brief glimpses. All were in one way or another caught up in the quickening rhythms of fall.

Maureen was at her post in the university's administrative hub, but her mind was divided. One of her former bosses had become head of an organization that championed freedom of thought for Catholics and had advertised for an assistant. She had leapt at the chance, convinced that "the job description sounds like it's written for me." She expected to hear something soon. Meantime, at home, she had been responding to a personal appeal for religious liberty from her teenage son, Kevin. He no longer wanted to attend mass. Maureen was inclined to go along with him, inasmuch as her son's ambivalence toward the institution resembled her own, and her reluctant husband had finally relented. With her permission, she had given some advice to her religiously emancipated son. "I told him," she said, "that it was important for him to hear people with a spiritual message. I left it at that."

Paul was ensconced in new quarters near the Washington law school in which he was now enrolled. The new Saint Augustine alumnus was nostalgic about his college days even as he strove to meet the demands placed upon him as a first-year law student. Labor law was on his mind, partly because of the highly publicized strike by the National Football League players' union. He imagined himself on the "tricky ground" between players and owners. Things were going "pretty well" with his girlfriend, he said, but he was trying to avoid "getting into a situation where I get hurt." There had been reminders of issues posed by the church. One of his friends, a college classmate and a Washington neighbor, had recently gone on a retreat on sexuality. She had told the priest leading the retreat that taking birth control pills left her feeling "confused." By her account, the priest had told her not to worry about it. He felt himself better able to live with such ambiguity, adding, "I've grown tremendously."

Sister Ruth kept up her brisk pace as autumn took hold. There were retreats to guide, patients to visit, classes to teach, weary and troubled souls to comfort, causes to uphold. In the company of other nuns in her community, she had seen segments of the pope's trip on television. The four bishops who made forceful statements to the pope in Los Angeles had impressed her. "Our bishops did not back down," she said proudly. "Now it's important if they can hold their own ground and not capitulate." She had given more than five decades to full-time church work, and among the things it had taught her was that change had many roots. "A lot of people influence the future of the church," she said jauntily. "For younger generations today the church is moving too slowly. But looking back someday, people will be amazed at what's happened."

Craig sported a brand-new pair of gold wings on his Marine Corps uniform. Flight training had ended in early September, and graduation, with his parents in attendance, had followed two weeks later. He was elated. "I completed something challenging that somebody saw fit to spend lots of money for," he said. "Now I'm wearing wings of gold. I'm not just a nobody." But the bravado would be short-lived, he reckoned. He would soon start the next phase—six to eight months learning to fly a Harrier fighter—once more as a beginner. It was humbling, he said, to think there was so much to learn. The assignment would take him and his fiancée to North Carolina. Both the location and the challenge excited him. The Harrier was second only to the F-18 as the preferred choice of graduates. Plans for the December wedding were shaping up nicely, he said. Catching a few glimpses of the pope on television, he had been impressed by John Paul's mastery of crowds. In those moments, though his own thoughts "weren't always in tune with [the pope's]," he felt a tugging from his deep ties to the church. He said it had felt real good.

Hannah was back in her classroom in the Olny elementary school. Early in each school year, she explained, she had always felt enchanted by the new cluster of fresh faces placed under her care. Harvest time on the surrounding plains was for her a season of renewal ushered in by children. In those first weeks, there were the usual frustrations and frayed nerves, she allowed, but they were fewer and took a far lighter toll than did the stresses of later, wearier months. At the start, in the midst of brimming eagerness, all seemed possible. She had received a letter from her daughter Lynn, the oldest of her three children, who lived in Phoenix. She reported having been deeply touched by seeing the pope during his stop there. That surprised and pleased her mother, who knew Lynn as a very "critical Catholic, an *NCR* [*National Catholic Reporter*] reader." Yet in her letter she had said "there was something symbolically good about his coming." She also enclosed a snapshot taken of Hannah's niece, a nurse, standing behind the pope as he visited her floor in the hospital. Lynn had graduated from college, was working at a savings and loan, and wanted to pursue a master's degree in theology and teach. Soon she would be married, and Hannah thought the couple might start a family right away. "I wouldn't mind holding a little grandchild," she mused. Her children were mostly on their own; her marriage had soured; she felt in the throes of "a mid-life phenomenon just like [what] Gail Sheehy" described. But in some strange way, she said, Olny seemed more like home than ever before.

Gilbert, dapper as he was donnish, had also returned to his station as the philosopher steeped in Saint Thomas, whose thought had prevailed in the church before Vatican II. Again this semester, both undergraduates and graduate students who shared Gilbert's classical predilections were eager to tap his erudition. He was enjoying himself, exuding an air of cool detachment, though as usual he was sorely vexed by threats he perceived against the authenticity of an ageless church. He was busy teaching and writing in defense of that church, visiting razor-edged criticisms on those who embraced a more modern vision of the church, the same opponents whose thinking he cavalierly dismissed in conversation. From the brief film segments of the papal visit that he had viewed, he was moved by both the messenger and the message. "I see what he's saying in continuity with what he is," Gilbert said. "He's got to be the most pro-life pontiff we've ever had. And then there's his apocalyptic note—that we're coming to a crunch unlike any other crunch, so we'd better think about what is really essential."

Anthony had heard rumors that his boss would move higher up in Celestron. In anticipation of such an eventuality, he entertained hopes of being asked to fill the vacancy. It was his last shot at promotion before retirement in less than five years. Either way, it would be okay, he told himself, but he also admitted that the old itch to keep achieving ran deep. At any rate, the possibility further confirmed his decision to forsake a foreign assignment in order to remain at company headquarters. The spoils usually belonged to those who kept close to home, he observed. His family, expanding by grandchildren, provided him more than enough reason in itself to justify his decision not to go far afield. That feeling was also bolstered by the impending World Series between the Cardinals and his team, the Twins. "The Twins are gonna do it," he said assuredly and, as it happened, presciently. While the pope traveled the United States, he had been paying calls at foreign affiliates of the company, but he had formed a distinct picture of what had happened. "The pope knew what he was going to say, and, sure enough, he said it," Anthony said. "But the Americans seemed to be saying very politely that he's got to start listening."

Bishop Sawicki had flown to Los Angeles to join his fellow bishops at their meeting with the pope. He thought his four colleagues chosen to speak had acquitted themselves very well and wished that John Paul had specifically addressed the points they had raised. "He flummoxed us in response," the bishop said. "What griped me and a lot of bishops in particular," he said, "was that the pope acted as if we had not been as engaged as we had been in writing our pastoral letters on nuclear arms and the economy. We had used an extensive process of collaboration we think can benefit the whole church. But that got no recognition." At the same time, he maintained, it would be mistaken to make too much of such an omission, because memories of such details of papal trips faded fast. He was back in his diocese tending to the myriad duties that resulted from too few hands attempting to handle the mounting desperation of that Rust Belt region.

Father Caron had celebrated the opening liturgy of the new semester at Saint Ambrose and was looking forward to a good year. Right about then, at the outset of his sixth year, he felt that he had come really to know the college well enough to assert leadership with some confidence that he had its needs and character in mind. New programs this fall in business and Japanese studies had added faculty and diversity, but Father Caron said he had his sights most fixed on steering Saint Ambrose in the direction of "a mainstream Catholic university." He hadn't worked out all the strategies for achieving that goal, he said, and he admitted that the goal itself was elusive, but he felt the call. He, too, had traveled to see the pope in New Orleans, where, in the company of other Catholic college presidents, he had listened to John Paul speak on higher education at the end of a long day through a steady rainfall. "I don't think it was chastening," he said of the pope's address. "Everything was said at a level of abstraction. I don't have a problem with that." He praised Father McNulty's forthright speech in Miami and the quartet of straight-talking bishops in Los Angeles. The question for him was whether the bishops would maintain the ground their spokesmen had staked out or retreat. "Will they continue to speak out that way?" as he hoped, he asked. "Or will they buckle under?"

Cindy and Caleb celebrated Paula's first birthday with members of their wider family, to the sheer, unknowing delight of the guest of honor. For the proud parents, such moments provided the sweet milestones in a journey marked by routines unceremoniously disrupted by the whims of two preschoolers. As the leaves turned yellow, orange, and red in the groves around their subdivision, they were as intensely focused as ever on that nucleus within that home comprising themselves and their offspring. Aside from Caleb's work, some Sunday church activity, and a few television shows, little else diverted their interest or energy from the dynamics of their own small organic unit and the many duties required to fill its needs. They had hardly noticed that the pope had been to America. They were too occupied in pursuing a much more private muse.

Acknowledgments

A LMOST FROM THE MOMENT THAT THE IDEA FOR THIS BOOK came to me, in the mists of one early morning in 1986, I had the cooperation and help of a wide variety of Catholic Americans. Some preferred to be anonymous; others are portrayed in these pages; still more lent assistance and moved on before I knew their identity.

Being afforded access to the personal thoughts and feelings of such a wonderfully diverse group has been a gift that itself deserves acknowledgment. I try never to take for granted the privilege of being allowed into a person's inner sanctum. Many granted me that privilege in the course of reporting and research and I am deeply grateful to them: lay people, priests, and bishops. Without them, of course, there would have been no story to tell.

While it would be impossible to thank each one of these contributors, I would like to single out for special mention those who agreed to be interviewed periodically over the course of the year. They make up the "gang of ten" whose testimonies are interspersed through the text. They gave unstintingly of their time and trust. My affection and admiration for each of them grew stronger with each talk or meeting. Their insights and honest struggles left a marked impression on me.

The three parishes—one each from the East coast, the Midwest, and the West coast—that hosted me for a week apiece also deserve heartfelt thanks. Living and immersing myself in a parish was made possible by the generosity of three extraordinary pastors and a cadre of lay people who steered me well and opened doors to revealing experiences. My esteem for those who effectively direct the course of something so complex as a parish only increased. I was especially struck by the multiple talents employed by the pastors.

Among others who extended generous welcomes were Brother Regis Fust of the Salvatorian Mission Warehouse, Charles Wilson of the St. Joseph Foundation, Dolores Leckey of the bishops' office on the laity, George Higgins of Catholic University, and Russ Shaw, then of the United States Catholic Conference, now director of public information for the Knights of Columbus. The cadre of religion newswriters with whom I have been happily associated also supplied me with many forms of help, not the least of which were much-needed critiques.

The Harper San Francisco staff has been a source of support from the outset. Publisher Clayton Carlson quickly and enthusiastically approved the proposal and remained its advocate. Tom Grady, who oversaw the editing of the manuscript, was always gracious and resourceful.

Friends enabled me to stay the course. The two who offered the most persistent incentives were Tom Fox and Bill Serrin. My son Matthew belongs in this rooting section too, as do Dan Cattau and Ari Goldman.

Charles Gray provided invaluable assistance by reviewing the manuscript in its initial form for glitches, gremlins, and gobbledygook. His sharp eye and yet sharper mind worked like a minesweeper, picking up the foreign objects submerged in those first pages. To this task, he devoted countless hours. For his gifts and for his example I am grateful. Thanks also to two members of the Trinity Episcopal Church staff, Dolores Wahlgren and Jan Charney.

Above all, I thank my wife, Mary Beckman, whose patience and encouragement enabled me to see this project through. She has been helpmate and soulmate; a source of both hope and editorial guidance. Though she can rightly detach herself from its contents, there is a solid sense in which this is as much her book as mine.

Index